Editorial Director
S P Dupuch

Senior Editor
Gordon Lomer

Contributing Editor
Suzanne Twiston-Davies

Publisher
Etienne Dupuch Jr

Etienne Dupuch Jr Publications Ltd
Oakes Field, PO Box N-7513
Nassau, The Bahamas
Tel (242) 323-5665, fax (242) 323-5728
e-mail: dupuch@bahamasnet.com
http://www.bahamasnet.com

Copyright © 1998 by Etienne Dupuch, Jr

ISBN 0-914755-67-6
ISSN 0067-2912

All rights reserved. Reproduction or transmission of the whole or any part of the contents without written permission is prohibited.
Printed in the United States of America

A Royal Bahamas Defence Force sentry stands guard at Government House, home and office of the Governor-General, Queen's representative in The Bahamas.

1999 Bahamas Handbook
and Businessman's Annual

Contents

FEATURES
- 58   **The Bahamas at the last centennial**
  Celebrations, squabbles and eyes on the future – welcome to 1900
- 72   **The Bahamas' silver jubilee**
  Nation on the move
- 80   **Atlantis at Bimini: fantasy or fact?**
  Two experts face-off

HISTORY
- 104   **High, mighty trod West Hill Street**
  Piety and wealth defined area
- 124   **New views on the Bahamian past**
  History rewritten about first inhabitants

FAMILY ISLANDS
- 138   **An Out Island wedding**
  "You give hogs away, not daughters!"
- 148   **Eco-resorts link nature, fun, luxury**
  Going green doesn't mean roughing it

13

BUSINESS & FINANCE
- 164   **Economy shifts into high gear**
  Economic engine keeps humming
- 186   **The Bahamas' stock market**
  More room for risk, more money for business
- 201   **Three Bahamian corporate entities**
  IBCs, regular companies and exempted limited partnerships
- 212   **The government's investment policy**
  Guidelines for would-be investors
- 218   **Confidence feeds construction boom**
  Employment sees all-time high
- 234   **Out Island projects keeping pace**
  Construction, infrastructure projects pump economy
- 241   **Property sampling**
  What's available, where, how much

BAHAMAS INFORMATION
265-456 Blue pages
    A-Z compendium of everything you need to know about living, working, vacationing and investing in The Bahamas

70

FREEPORT/LUCAYA
457	Shipping, hotels, real estate ... *Optimism prevails*
476	The West End's big comeback *Birth of a new era*
492	A big bunch of Roses *A family makes its mark on Freeport*
508	They spotted a winner in Miller *Bahamian key player*

FREEPORT INFORMATION
521-552 More blue pages
Handy facts and figures specific to Freeport/Lucaya

50

GOVERNMENT
554	Silver Jubilee anniversary honours
557	Governor-General
558	Cabinet ministers & portfolios
564	Ministers of state
565	Senators
569	House of Assembly
579	Parliamentarians' salaries; Parliamentary Secretaries
580	Permanent Secretaries; Commission chairpersons
581	Public service officials
584	Government offices
587	Bahamas diplomatic & consular representatives
591	Resident diplomatic & consular representatives
592	International organizations' representatives
592	Honorary consuls & representatives
594	Bahamas honorary consuls abroad

CLASSIFIED DIRECTORIES
255	Nassau
518	Freeport/Lucaya

YEAR IN REVIEW
595	Sept 1997 through Aug 1998
603	ADVERTISERS in this book
606	INDEX

109

SARA MOSS

marinas

Western light reflects on a New Providence marina. With 100,000 sq miles of ocean, marinas are an integral part of The Bahamas' infrastructure. Two new state-of-the-art marinas

were due onstream at press time: the Atlantis marina at Paradise Island, with cars tunnelling under the water, and the other at Old Bahama Bay at West End, Grand Bahama.

GARY SWEETING

GARRY PORTER

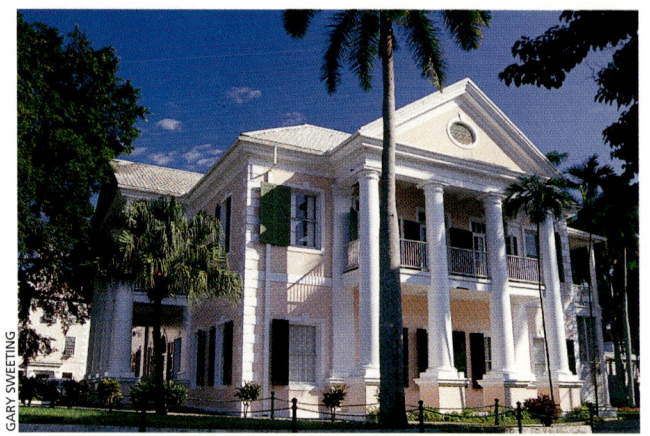

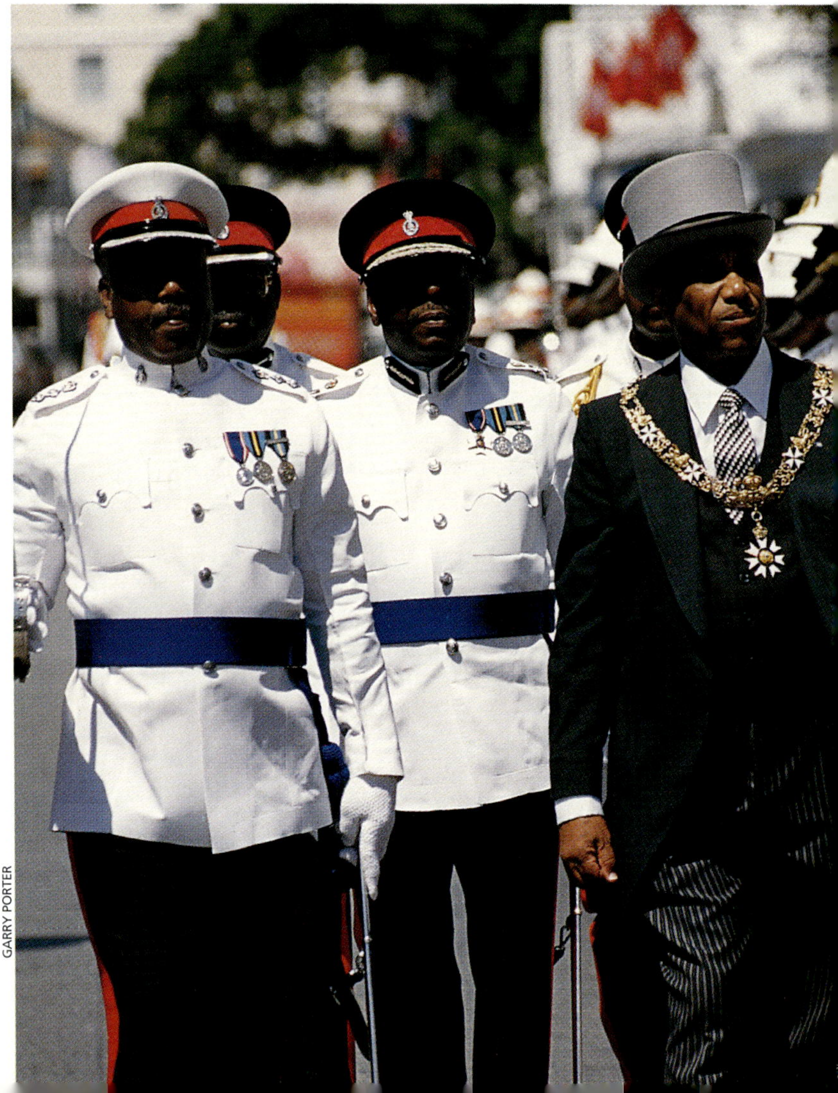

government

The stately Supreme Court Building on downtown's Bank Ln separates the Shirley St octagonal public library from the Bay St Senate. Sir Orville Turnquest, GCMG, QC, sixth Governor-General of The Bahamas, inspects an honour guard.

golf

There are 10 golf courses in The Bahamas, including Paradise Island Golf Club above. Two more are being completed on Grand Bahama and several others are on the drawing board for Nassau and the Out Islands. Better known as an award-winning actor, Sean Connery takes a pit stop on the Lyford Cay golf course where he is considered "most competitive, a fighter," with a handicap under 10.

SARA MOSS

disney

LONGER THAN THREE FOOTBALL FIELDS, THE 2,400-PASSENGER, NASSAU-REGISTERED *DISNEY MAGIC* DOCKS AT NASSAU, THE CAPITAL CITY, AND AT DISNEY-OWNED CASTAWAY CAY IN THE ABACOS. EVERYBODY JOINS THE BAND NEAR NASSAU HARBOUR.

Statues

SCULPTED IN GREECE PROBABLY IN THE LATE 12TH CENTURY, LIFE-SIZED HERCULES MEDITATES IN A VERSAILLES GARDENS LILY POND AT PARADISE ISLAND.

WHEN IT COMES TO INVESTING WORLDWIDE, TEMPLETON BELIEVES...

...SLOW AND STEADY WINS THE RACE.

- It is often said that the race doesn't necessarily go to the fleet of foot. It is often won by slow, steady persistence. Especially when applied to investing, choosing the path of persistence can have long-term advantages.

- Utilizing a global office network, Templeton managers search the world for promising investments for individuals, institutional and corporate clients worldwide. From start to finish, the Templeton organization's approach to investing supports the philosophy that there is value to be found all over the globe, not just in one country or on one continent. This global approach gives our funds diversity of investment opportunities.

- Templeton Worldwide provides professional management and a clear goal of long-term performance. To learn more about Templeton's global investment management, advisory and distribution services, call today.

        Nassau phone: 242-362-4600
        Nassau fax: 242-362-5281

TBH98

This is not an offer to provide services or sell securities in any jurisdiction where it may be prohibited.

Templeton Global Advisors Limited, P.O. Box N-7759, Nassau, Bahamas

tranquillity

A FRENCH ANGELFISH AND A YOUNG GIRL CAPTURE THE SERENITY OF THE OUT ISLANDS AND SURROUNDING WATERS, WHERE LIFE MOVES AT A GENTLER, KINDER PACE. ECO-RESORTS ARE PROVING YOU CAN RESPECT AND ENJOY THE ENVIRONMENT WITHOUT ROUGHING IT OR FOREGOING LUXURY.

Since 1795 our bank has had only one client...

...YOU!

Ferrier Lullin Bank & Trust (Bahamas) Ltd

Private bank of UBS

UBS House - East Bay Street
PO Box N-4890 - Nassau - Bahamas
Tel (242) 394 9100 - Telefax (242) 394 9140

Geneva - Luxembourg - Singapore

Ferrier Lullin & Cie

Krebs Communication SA

SARA MOSS

Compass

Paint factory colours and whimsical shapes make Island Records founder Chris Blackwell's Compass Point beckon for a visit or a meal. It is a magnet for photographers.

Unique And Individual Small Hotels Of Nassau Paradise Island

- Bay View Village
- Club Land'or
- Compass Point Beach Club
- Dillet's Guest House
- Graycliff
- Orange Hill Beach Inn
- Paradise Harbour Club & Marina
- Red Carpet Inn
- Sunrise Beach Club & Villas
- The Villas on Crystal Cay

HOTELS AS WARM AND INVITING AS THE PEOPLE WHO RUN THEM.

Introducing the Small Treasures of Nassau Paradise Island. An eclectic collection of guest houses, inns and small hotels offering a warm, gracious and most of all, genuine brand of Bahamian-style service. Discover one for yourself. Call 800-327-9019 ext 111 for a free directory.

For reservations call 800-523-3782. Visit our website www.vacmart.com.

THE ISLANDS OF THE BAHAMAS
It Just Keeps Getting Better®

Small Treasures
THE ISLANDS OF THE BAHAMAS
Experience our Bahamian Tradition and Hospitality

True craftsmen share the same passion:

The search for excellence.

BANQUE  ALLIANCE
(NASSAU) LTD

Private Banking and Trust Services

Alliance House, East Bay Street
P.O. Box N 1724
Nassau, The Bahamas

Switchboard: (242) 394-6161
Trust Dept: (242) 394-5874
Facsimile: (242) 394-6262

A wholly-owned subsidiary of Banque SCS Alliance S.A. Geneva, Switzerland

Surreys

TRAFFIC REVERSAL FROM MAY 31, 1998 SENDS SURREYS AND OTHER VEHICLES EAST ON BAY ST, MAIN ARTERY IN THE BAHAMAS' CAPITAL CITY, NASSAU.

ENJOYING SEPARATE VACATIONS. TOGETHER.

Abaco
She trails off. He sails off.

Eleuthera
He snoozes. She snorkels.

Grand Bahama Island
She bargains. He birdies.

Exuma
He dives. She tans.

Nassau/Paradise Island
They dance 'til dawn.

THE ISLANDS OF THE BAHAMAS
It Just Keeps Getting Better®
Call your travel agent • http://www.gobahamas.com

fish

ASK ANY BAHAMIAN AND HE'LL TELL YOU FISH LIKE THESE RED SNAPPERS AND JACKS BOUGHT FRESH AT THE DOCK OFFER GOOD VALUE AND THE BEST TASTE. BOIL' FISH AND GRITS ARE A BREAKFAST STAPLE.

Presenting infiniti.
The off-shore *global axxess*® card.

You've earned it. Now enjoy it.

You work hard to secure your off-shore funds. Don't you think it's time you started to enjoy them?

Now there's *infiniti*, the off-shore card that gives you the kind of access you've always wanted.

Only *infiniti* provides the benefits, convenience and acceptance of a Gold MasterCard® as well as our unique *global axxess*® program. Linking you to a worldwide network of electronic banking, cash transfers and tele-communication services.

All services are billed directly to your *infiniti* card. With all the protection, security and confidentiality of a Bahamian Trust Account.

AXXESS INTERNATIONAL Limited, 1 Norfolk House, Frederick Street,
P.O. Box CB-13663 Nassau BAHAMAS tel 242-356-9555 fax 242-356-9559
e-mail: axxess@bahamas.net.bs www.bahamas.net.bs/business/axxess

AXXESS INTERNATIONAL (UK) Limited, Southgate Chambers, 37-39 Southgate Street,
Winchester, ENGLAND, SO23 9EH tel +44(0)1962-849097 fax +44(0)1962-867367
e-mail: sales@axxess-international.com www.axxess-international.com

    issued by Leadenhall Trust Company Limited established 1976

Savour

"OUR LITTLE DARLINGS" IS THE PHRASE COINED BY CABINET MINISTER THE HON ALGERNON ALLEN FOR THE YOUTH OF THE NATION. THIS EXUMA LAD SAVOURS THE TASTE OF A MANGO.

boating

Cruise passengers to The Bahamas in 1997 numbered about 1.75 million and their island spending amounted to $105 million. Some cruise lines whisk passengers to their own private islands, like Holland America's Half Moon Cay and Disney's Castaway Cay. On the other hand, you decide where to go on the 115 ft megayacht *Ragazza,* which charters for $33,500 a week and sleeps eight comfortably.

COURTESY BOB SAXON ASSOCIATES

HURRICANE HOLE MARINA
Paradise Island, The Bahamas

Shell
Miles Ahead

- New docks for yachts of any size and draft
- Electricity — 110, 220, 440 volts
- Shell Gasolines, Diesel Oil and Marine Lubricants all day fuel service on Sundays and Holidays
- Fresh water and ice
- 24-hour security
- Laundry Facilities
- Modern showers and dressing rooms
- Swimming pool and poolside bar
- American Express, Visa and MasterCard accepted
- Near to restaurants, shopping, supermarkets, casinos and banks

Tel: (242) 363-3600
Fax: (242) 363-3604 • VHF Channel 16
P.O. Box SS-6317, Nassau, The Bahamas

PORTSIDE CONDOMINIUMS
Paradise Island, The Bahamas

Rent a piece of Paradise.

Located at Hurricane Hole Marina on beautiful Paradise Island, Portside Condominiums offers first class accommodations within hailing distance of shopping plazas, fine restaurants, a casino and Paradise Island's own international airport.

Units range from 1,400 to 2,900 sq ft, all with magnificent views of the harbour and township of Nassau. There is a beautiful, large, freshwater swimming pool and poolside bar also on the harbour, giving you elegant waterfront living on Paradise Island.

It's another world ... This is at last paradise found.

Tel (242) 363-3600
Fax (242) 363-3604
PO Box SS-6317, Nassau, The Bahamas

GRAHAM DUPUCH

GRAHAM DUPUCH

nature

Sea and sky are ubiquitous trade marks of the island, but flora and fauna are a close second. Bougainvillaea lavishes rich colours on garden walls while small lizards scamper about.

BANQUE PRIVÉE
EDMOND DE ROTHSCHILD LTD
NASSAU / BAHAMAS

𝒜 **name in banking**
Geneva, Lausanne,

𝒜 **tradition in portfolio management**
Lugano, Fribourg

𝒜 **passion, excellence**

Luxembourg, London,

Montevideo, Monaco,

Hong-Kong, Bahamas

51 FREDERICK STREET
PO BOX N-1136
NASSAU / BAHAMAS
TELEPHONE (1-242) 328 8121
FAX (1-242) 328 8115

churches

Known simply as The Kirk, St Andrew's Presbyterian Church dates back to 1810 with subsequent additions 1842-1864, according to Robert douglas in *Island Heritage,*

Architecture of The Bahamas. Interior marble wall plaques commemorating the deceased provide an intimate glimpse of Commonwealth history.

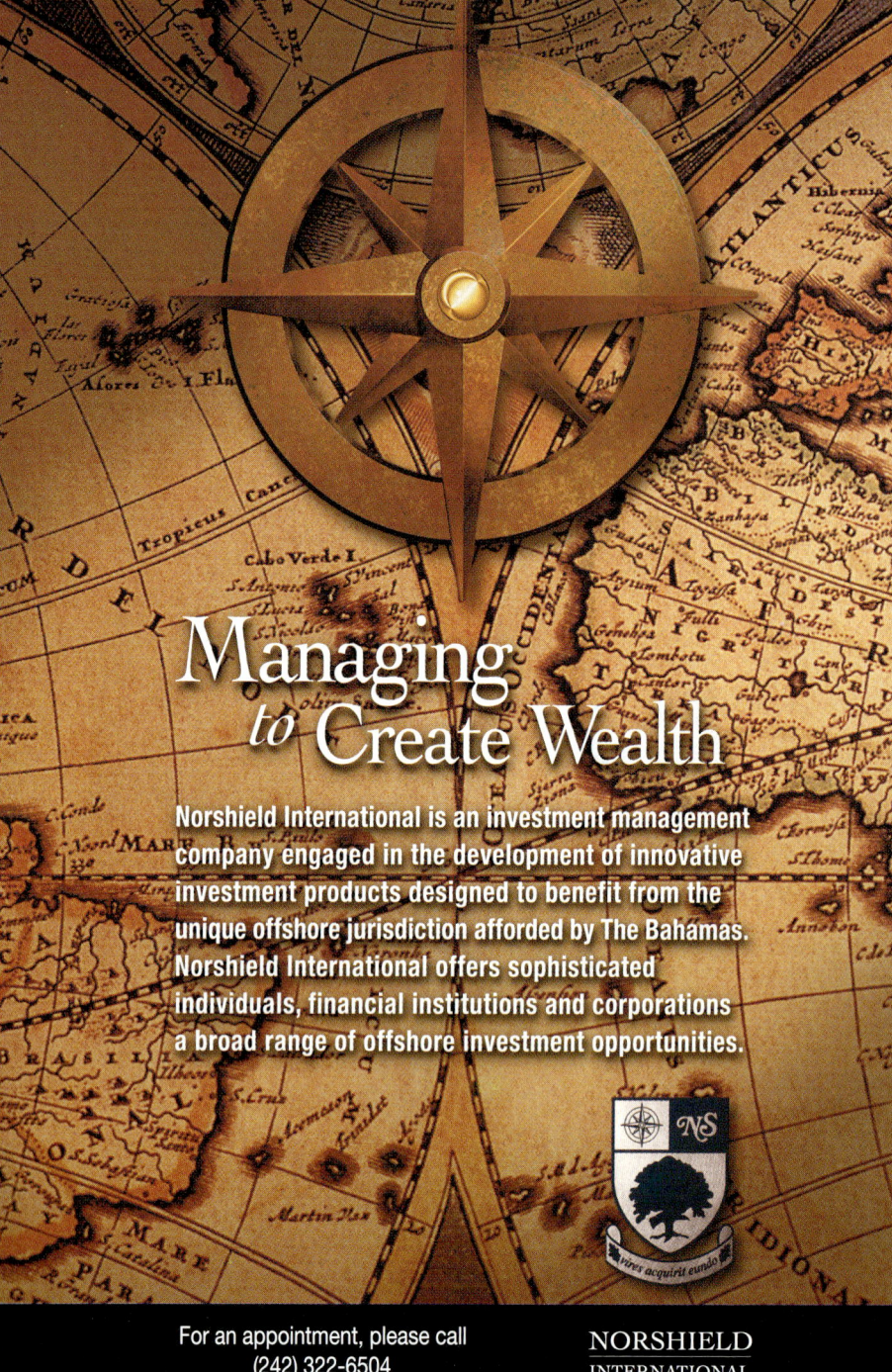

PAUL MOCKLER

dolphins

DOLPHINS PULL JACQUES MAYOL SKYWARD IN FREEPORT/LUCAYA WATERS. IN 1966, THE FRENCHMAN MADE A RECORD-BREAKING DIVE IN THE BAHAMAS. HERE HE IS ACCOMPANIED BY A PAIR OF UNDERWATER EXPLORERS SOCIETY DOLPHINS.

PRE-CONSTRUCTION PRICES

The Life of Nassau's Cable Beach

When you are looking for a luxurious oceanfront residence, an exciting second home for tropical vacations or an important investment opportunity, find out more about BAYROC, located on 7 acres of oceanfront property. Pre-construction priced from $560,000 to $1.6 million.

- Located on Nassau's famous Cable Beach with a secluded white sand beach
- Spacious 3 bedroom, 3 $1/2$ bathroom residences
- Lavishly landscaped grounds with waterfall entry and 24-hour security
- Two swimming pools, lighted tennis courts, fitness centre and sunset gazebo
- Within 10 minutes of International airport and Bay Street's duty-free shopping and financial district
- Management/maintenance services available
- There are no income, corporation, capital gains, inheritance or similar taxes in the Commonwealth of The Bahamas
- Ownership of a BAYROC home satisfies investment requirement for Bahamas residency
- Direct flights from many international airports

BAYROC
EXCLUSIVE BEACH RESIDENCES

For Further Information Call (242) 327-0112 • Fax (242) 327-0114
Visit our On-Site Sales Office on West Bay Street or website at www.bayroc.com

This is not an offer. The offering of the condominium interests will be made only by means of a prospectus.

SARA MOSS

banks

THIS OLD BAHAMIAN BUILDING JUST EAST OF THE KIRK HOUSES BANK HEADQUARTERS BEHIND A SHUTTERED FACADE AND A DOUBLE STAIRCASE.

GARRY PORTER

SARA MOSS

Silver

The Bahamas celebrated 25 years of independence from Great Britain in 1998 with public buildings like Senate Headquarters festooned in national colours. A marble statue of Queen

Victoria, who reigned and ruled over the colony of The Bahamas, remains centre stage in downtown Parliament Sq.

It's time . . . to cruise to
TREASURE CAY
HOTEL RESORT & MARINA, ABACO, THE BAHAMAS

Excellent Real Estate Opportunities

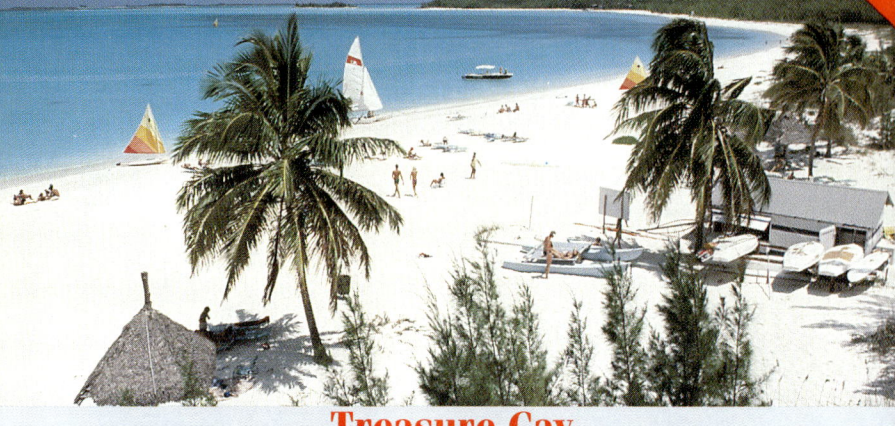

Treasure Cay
The Premier Out-Island Resort In The Bahamas

- Spectacular 3½-mile beach rated one of the top ten in the world
- 18-hole, 6,985-yard, par 72, Dick Wilson designed, championship golf course
- Accommodations include spacious rooms and suites alongside our marina, and luxurious two-bed, two-bath treasure villas on the beach
- Daily direct flights from Miami, Fort Lauderdale, West Palm Beach, Orlando and Nassau
- Pool, tennis, watersports and shopping
- Live entertainment on weekends
- Prime real estate including beach, canal and golf course lots available

Marina features:
- 150-slip full service marina
- Fuel station (diesel and gas)
- Marina and grocery store
- Laundry and shower facilities
- Boat rentals, charters and guides
- Excellent year-round fishing, highlighted by several fishing tournaments
- Fall/winter dockage specials
- Excellent diving and full service dive shop
- Marina-view restaurant and bar

Prime Hotel Sites Still Available

Hotel Reservations
US **1-800-327-1584** • Bahamas **(242) 365-8535** • Fax **(242) 365-8847**
Real Estate Office **(242) 365-8538**
Internet: http://www.treasurecay.com • e-mail: info@treasurecay.com
Treasure Cay, Abaco • The Bahamas

SARA MOSS

berries

THE PHOTOGENIC BUT PESKY BRAZILIAN PEPPER-TREE CROWDS OUT OTHER FORMS OF FLORA. IT PREFERS FULL SUN AND IS MOST VIBRANT AT CHRISTMAS.

Commonwealth Brewery Limited

At Commonwealth Brewery Limited we produce drinks made by Bahamians for Bahamians to the highest standards. So whether you enjoy Kalik, Heineken, Guinness or Vitamalt you can feel proud that you are enjoying the best of The Bahamas.

Support your local community and buy Bahamian. Help protect our environment by supporting our returnable bottle redemption program.

Commonwealth Brewery Limited
The Brewery of The Bahamas.

SARA MOSS

Smugglers

Local lore persists that this stairway called Smuggler's Steps was carved out of Clifton Pier limestone on Nassau's southwest shore in the early 1700s for pirate use.

GARRY PORTER

gazebo

A Greek gazebo once part of Swedish millionaire Axel Wenner-Gren's "Shangri-La" on Paradise Island, then named Hog, was moved to the harbour side of the island by its next owner, Huntington Hartford II. It is the wedding spot of choice for countless foreign and local brides and grooms.

GARRY PORTER

Foster & Dunhill
(Bahamas) Ltd

Compliant and efficient international investment, business, and tax strategies.

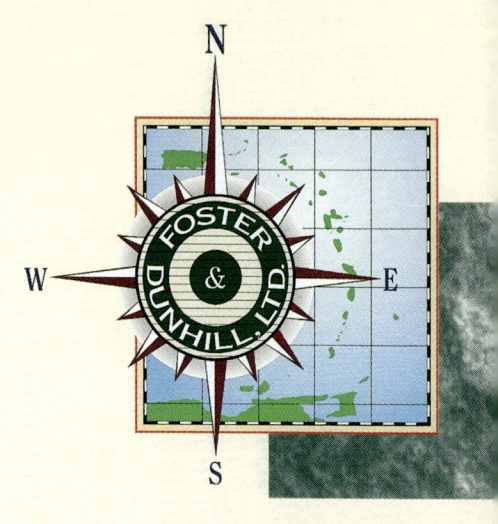

Foster & Dunhill is one of the most respected names in international financial circles with offices throughout the US and in key jurisdictions around the world including The Bahamas.

We can be relied upon to assist in the design, implementation and maintenance of a global strategy that is both legal and effective.

Foster & Dunhill (Bahamas) Ltd
International Financial Services
Tradewinds Bldg, 3rd Floor, Bay St
PO Box CB-13482
Nassau, The Bahamas
Tel 242-326-5210
Fax 242-326-5347
E-mail: gape@100jamz.com

US Headquarters
Two Urban Centre
4890 West Kennedy Blvd, Suite 140
Tampa, FL 33609
Tel 813-287-1515
Fax 813-287-0585
E-mail: ushq@foster-dunhill.com
URL: www.foster-dunhill.com

wildlife

FINE FEATHERS AND AN INTERIOR DESIGNER'S DREAM COLOURS EMBELLISH A MANDARIN DUCK (LEFT) AND A WOOD DUCK AT NASSAU'S ARDASTRA GARDENS AND CONSERVATION CENTRE.

LINDA M HUBER

JOCK HALL

JOCK HALL

investment

Freeport/Lucaya's vast state of flux in the last two years has been a direct result of multimillion dollar investments by subsidiaries of Hong Kong-based conglomerate Hutchison Whampoa Group of Companies Ltd. By the beginning of the new millennium, Grand Bahama is expected to be a showcase of resort, industrial, marine, commercial, aviation, and residential activity.

THE MOST PRESTIGIOUS ADDRESS IN THE CARIBBEAN IS ON GRAND BAHAMA ISLAND.

LUCAYAN MARINA VILLAGE, GRAND BAHAMA ISLAND

Come discover all the benefits of the French Riviera, Portofino and Monte Carlo in a tropical island setting. Here, internationally acclaimed Danish architects have created a luxury village of elegant one, two, three and four bedroom residences for vacation getaways or year-round living.

At Lucayan Marina Village, a merging of European design and craftsmanship and the tropics is evident at every turn, from large residential balconies to decades old shade trees and the brick and coral walkways along the 120 slip deep-water marina. The island is complete with international shoppes, fine restaurants, deserted beaches, watersports, golf, casinos, and endless summer.

A major center for offshore banking, residents enjoy both a tax-free environment and quality government services. Lucayan Marina Village is minutes from Freeport airport with daily flights to the U.S. and Europe. Visit Grand Bahama Island for a tour of Lucayan Marina Village, the most prestigious address on this side of the world.

LUCAYAN MARINA VILLAGE
GRAND BAHAMA ISLAND

Freeport, Grand Bahama Island, The Bahamas. Tel (242) 373-7616 • Fax (242) 373-7630

GRAHAM DUPUCH

SARA MOSS

beaches

Beaches encircling many Bahamian islands become uncrowded daytime playgrounds. Gold Rock, Grand Bahama beachgoers throw a ball around while an infant shovels sand in western Nassau.

53

DISCOVER THE NEW BAHAMAS AT WEST END

THE CUSTOMS HOUSE
Old Bahama Harbour
West End, Grand Bahama

Old Bahama Bay is the new Bahamas destination at West End. Out Island luxury is an easy cruise from the Florida coast.

Our new harbour will remain open through construction. Preview this great new resort & residential community now.

- Located 56 miles from Palm Beach • 150-slip deepwater harbour
- Dock space for yachts to 175 ft • New "Customs House" Restaurant
- Beachfront cottage resort • Spectacular new oceanfront homesites

DISCOVER THE NEW BAHAMAS

Old Bahama Bay
west end • grand bahama

For more information telephone (242) 346-6500

SARA MOSS

mangoes

The mangoes of summer turn from green to gold to red. Rich, ripe orange pulp is best eaten in the sea, Bahamians advise. Juice washes away there rather than trickling down chin or clothes. The trio above came from Sir Clement and Lady Maynard's orchard.

PETER RAMSAY

Choir

THE BAHAMAS NATIONAL YOUTH CHOIR performed in Moscow and St Petersburg, Russia, in May 1998 under attorney-musician-composer Cleophas Adderley, government's Director of Youth and Culture.

Features

NASSAU

A WINTER PARADISE

THE NEW YORK & CUBA MAIL STEAMSHIP CO.

WARD LINE

About 1,000 winter visitors cruised to Nassau from the US and Canada in 1900.

The Bahamas at the last centennial

BY DONN SELHORN

The Colony of the Bahama Islands entered the 20th century with celebrations, squabbles and eyes on the future.

Tourism on the rise, stray dogs, dynamiting of fish, low teachers' pay, rampant gambling, customs as top revenue source, treaty tizzy – sound familiar? Welcome to 1900.

The Colony of the Bahama Islands, as it was known at the time, had bounced back from the killer hurricane of the previous August that claimed 259 lives and caused great property damage. The talk along Nassau's Bay St was how the city had a good thing going with its influx of winter visitors.

After the colony's top three industries – sponge, fruit and sisal – greeting travellers was becoming a lucrative business. Lured by the weather and beaches, visitors were accounting for "a very large amount of money being put into circulation in Nassau," reported *The Nassau Guardian*. Two major hotels were available and Nassau's reputation as "a health and pleasure resort, will, it is hoped, be permanent."

The 1891 census listed the population of New Providence as 10,914, with no official count for Nassau. But in 1900, an estimated 1,000 winter visitors from the United States and Canada alone flocked to the colony's capital. Indicative of the tranquil summer and fall months, the Maypole Club announced it would host a dance on October 30 at Simms Hall on West Bay St "to break the dull monotony usually experienced just before the commencement of the winter season."

Tourism is born
The Royal Victoria was the "in place," although the newly-constructed Hotel Colonial was a worthy competitor. Both hotels were owned by H M Flagler, founder and so-called czar of Miami. The Colonial, which opened for the first time in February at a cost of £100,000,[1] could accommodate 700 guests and featured a giant ballroom with a dazzling array of electric lights. Visitors could also choose from several rental homes. For example, George Bosfield advertised his Villa Marlborough, located at the corner of Virginia and Nassau Sts, "expressly for the accommodation of Tourists preferring quiet home life to the bustle and excitement of hotel existence."

As part of Flagler's agreement with The Bahamas, he provided a regular steamship connection with the Florida coast. The port of Nassau was particularly active in winter, with Americans arriving almost daily from New York and Florida on such vessels as the *Antilla*, owned by the Bahamas Steamship Co Ltd, and the New York and Cuba mail steamer *Saratoga*. It was difficult to enter Nassau unnoticed, since names of ship passengers and hotel guests were usually published in the *Guardian*. First-class tickets between Nassau and New York ranged from $30 to $40 and Nassau-Miami sailings by the Florida East Coast Line were $12.50. For the benefit of Americans, Bahamas prices were often quoted in US currency.

Ready for action
The Boer War was into its second year in 1900. News of Great Britain's battles with the Dutch settlers in South Africa was cabled from England to the US and relayed to the colony, where patriotism among Bahamians was high. In addition to donating sponges to military hospitals, The Bahamas helped support families of English soldiers killed at the front with money raised at various benefits.

[1] *The average exchange rate for the pound in 1900 was US$4.87. A shilling was worth approximately 24 cents.*

H M Flagler, shown with his wife, Mary Lily, owned the Royal Victoria Hotel and the Hotel Colonial.

Tariff troubles

Responding to Mother England's call for colonial volunteers, The Bahamas formed contingents of would-be soldiers. Although they drilled religiously and were ready to report, none were called. If the colony considered this an affront, it was probably more peeved when Great Britain negotiated a five-year reciprocal treaty with the US.

The treaty, drafted in late 1899, allowed manufactured goods, fruits and vegetables from Jamaica, Barbados, Bermuda, British

Guiana and the Turks and Caicos Islands into the US duty free or at a reduced rate. For no apparent reason, The Bahamas was excluded. In January, with the treaty up for ratification, the colony was still complaining it had been "left out in the cold" when it should have occupied "a premier position in such a treaty."

The colony's sensitivity to tariff matters was understandable. In 1900, it exported over a million pounds of sponge, half of it to the US, plus 7.2 million dozen pineapples and about 400 tons of sisal to the US and other countries.

For sale

Nassau's shopkeepers conducted daily business with no shortage of merchandise for sale. At the corner of George and King Sts, the emporium owned by T H C Lofthouse held a grand opening to display two floors of men's and women's clothing. Well known manufacturers such as the Singer Sewing Machine Co advertised their wares at local outlets. Tennent's Lager Beer, brewed in Scotland, was the "Best Refresher in The Bahamas," while Eagle Brand condensed milk was "a carefully prepared and natural substitute for mother's milk."

The Colonial Cigar Factory, J C Coakley, proprietor, asked smokers to view "the best assortment of tobacco and Havana cigars in Nassau" at its store on Bay St, near Charlotte. The Delmonico Restaurant, opposite the Bank of Nassau on East Bay St, was serving dinners for 30 cents.

Royal Victoria Hotel

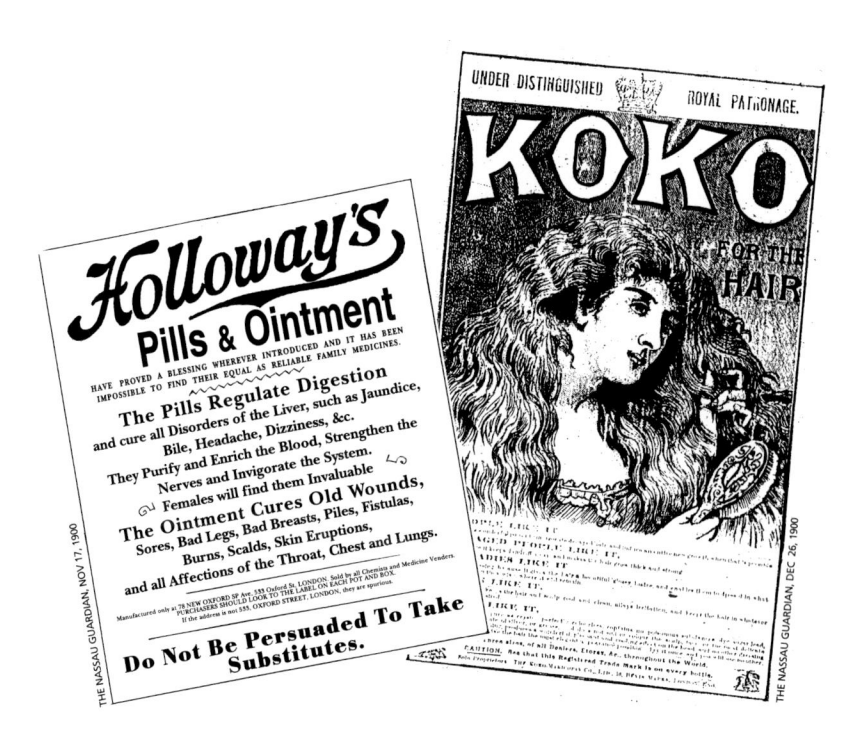

A balding woman swore she grew a mane 55 inches long after using Cuticura Soap. From London came Holloway's Pills & Ointment, said to cure "old wounds and all affections of the throat, chest and lungs" as well as "bad breasts and piles." A tonic called Phosferine, allegedly endorsed by "members of the British Royal Family," claimed to cure "lumbago, brain fag, nervous exhaustion, broken-down health and melancholia." If a person were beyond healing, there was always the Nassau Undertaking Co and Coffin Emporium, which boasted a "modern icebox" and metallic caskets "guaranteed" by William Lightbourn, president of the company. A competitor, the Johnson House, provided a "first-class hearse with plumes, nets, and two horses" for 50 shillings. A no-frills funeral, with only one horse sans plumes, cost only 24 shillings.

Advertisements by insurance companies appeared often after the 1899 hurricane and after a fire destroyed a dozen homes and buildings the next year. The October 2 fire at the corner of Marlborough and Dorchester Sts began at 2am in the home of J W Roberts, pastor of St John's Baptist Church. The flames spread to both sides of the street. A lone steam engine truck and volunteers passing buckets of water, plus a small steam pump from the nearby Hotel Colonial, helped fight the blaze. One eyewitness was quoted as saying if the winds had not been favourable, "two thirds of the town would have been laid in ashes." No deaths or injuries were reported.

Real estate sales were ongoing throughout the islands. Among them were 400 acres in Great Exuma known as "Hartwell." Offered by R Bowe in Nassau, the property contained land suitable for grapefruit, oranges or cattle grazing. Interested in a 12-room house on 50 acres about a mile from downtown Nassau? Contact H C Christie.[2] Over at Deep Creek, Andros, two houses and a coconut grove on 40 acres were put on the market by Mrs Leon E H Dupuch.[3]

Laws of the land

Nassau police and courts had a variety of mostly routine business. A Chinese seaman from the steamship *Antilla,* attempting to avoid

[2] *Father of Sir H G Christie*
[3] *Wife of the first* Tribune *publisher*

paying duty, was caught smuggling 20 pounds of coffee in a pillowcase. He was fined £10 and imprisoned two months. A youth convicted of larceny and accepting stolen property was sentenced to three months' hard labour and 20 strokes of a tamarind rod, "to be witnessed by the parents or guardian of the prisoner, if any."

A new law was passed to prohibit use of dynamite or other explosives to destroy fish. Charles Fraser, police commandant, offered a one pound reward to anyone reporting removal of coral or seafans from the Sea Gardens, in the waters between Hog[4] and Athol Islands. To stop a potential crime, a concerned father from Governor's Harbour published a notice stating "Clergy and Pastors are hereby forewarned from marrying my son, Alonzo A Bethel, he being not of age."

Increased gambling drew the ire of many.

Increased gambling drew the ire of many. The Rev F W Gotstick of Nassau's Trinity Church delivered a lengthy sermon on the subject. "Gambling is rife in Nassau," he exclaimed. Referring to a gambler who

[4] Now Paradise Island

The Hotel Colonial could accommodate 700 guests.

had been run out of Key West and introduced lottery games in Nassau, the minister noted "new germs have been brought from Key West and the disease has spread with great virulence. I beg you for God's sake, your children's sake, your city's sake and your church's sake to put away the accursed thing. Your very Christianity is at stake."

Maybe so, responded a man who identified himself only as "Bad Man," but he was making over five pounds a day selling lottery tickets, more than he could ever earn as a fisherman. As for the demoralizing influence, Bad Man said "our tourists and American cousins have done that already."

Fuelling debate

If Bahamas Governor G T Carter wanted to know the community's thoughts on issues, he could read the *Guardian's* letters to the editor. He was roundly criticized when he named Father Chrysostom Schreiner, a Roman Catholic priest and an American citizen, to the colony's Board of Education. The appointment became a *cause celebre* with letters flooding the *Guardian* derisively dubbing Fr Chrysostom an alien, an outsider and a foreigner. His decision-making would no doubt be influenced by the Roman Catholic Archbishop of New York.

Although a longtime Bahamas resident, the priest "is not of British birth, nor has he availed himself of the privileges of naturalization." Furthermore, the all-Protestant board was "English, distinctly English and not connected in any way with America." Adding fuel to the debate was an accusation Fr Chrysostom had uttered "anti-British and pro-Boer sentiments."

> **"The police permit the sidewalks to be blocked by loafers of both sexes ..."**

Augustus Adderley, a Bahamian living in London, wrote he hoped to rally the British press against the American-born priest. He chided Secretary of State for the Colonies Joseph Chamberlain, father of Neville Chamberlain, for not urging the Governor to be more selective in his appointments. For weeks Fr Chrysostom was so vilified by *Guardian* readers, the newspaper stopped publishing letters about him. At year's end, he was still on the board.

Nassau went into an uproar over the Board of Education appointment of a Roman Catholic priest, Father Chrysostom Schreiner.

Complaints against police were not uncommon. Some were accused of being drunk on duty; others refused to interfere in fistfights and similar violence because, they argued, they were unarmed and unable to protect themselves. Said one Bahamian, "The police permit the sidewalks to be blocked by loafers of both sexes, especially in the vicinity of grog shops. But the police have a 'hail fellow, well met' attitude. A gentleman told me he walked along Bay St and a woman deliberately threw her arms around his neck."

One street nuisance which drew the attention of the House of Assembly was the homeless, starving dogs travelling in packs, causing government to pass a bill to "ameliorate the condition."

When the Assembly reported the colony's third quarter financial statement, it showed a dip in income compared to the prior year – £16,160 vs £17,730. Not surprisingly, Customs was the big moneymaker, accounting for £14,976 of revenue.

A sampling of third quarter expenditures, which rose £8,847 compared to 1899:

Charges on account of Public Debt	£2,679
Public Works	4,235

Pensions Treasury	530
House of Assembly	535
Governor and Staff	311
Judicial Dept	1,477
Constabulary and Police	1,296
Education Dept	1,187
Post Office Dept	799
Medical Dept	187
Port and Marine Dept	326
Charitable Institutions	1,362
Prisons	338

The plight of Nassau's unfortunate did not go unnoticed. Rector J Hartman Fisher of St Agnes Church asked the public to donate old blankets he could distribute to the "many old, sick, and rheumatic persons who suffer much at night from the want of winter clothing." A citizen lamented the number of Bahamians who, required to remain in public schools only to age 13, could not read or write or sign their names – a situation blamed in part to teachers' "trifling salaries."

The night life

Anyone seeking relief from their daily grind had many choices. Entertainment ran the gamut from Florida minstrel shows to boat races. For example, an establishment called the Casino, built on the western part of Hog Island by J L Saunders, was primarily a family bath house that also booked a number of performers in its pavilion. One was the McGinley Circus Troupe from New York. Another show featured the Baums, James and Alfretta, in their "sensational double trapeze act; performing daring and muscular feats 45 feet in mid air." Ventriloquists were always popular as was Mademoiselle Florita who would conclude her act with "the most remarkable feats in contortion ever accomplished by any lady artist." To allay the public's fears, and perhaps to the disappointment of

> **Casino management assured them Mlle Florita's routine was "a strictly moral and first-class exhibition of artistic skill."**

some, the Casino management assured them Mlle Florita's routine was "a strictly moral and first-class exhibition of artistic skill."

"A Night With Robert Burns" was scheduled at St Andrew's Hall, with Rev R T Bailey reading Burns's humour and the Nassau Amateur Orchestra supplying music. The orchestra at the Hotel Colonial, led by a Mr Prouty, seemed to moonlight all over town. It would perform at bazaars, private parties, public concerts and other functions and played everything from popular dance numbers to *God Save the Queen*. Queen Victoria reigned and ruled over the colony as part of the British Empire. A new dance fad, the cakewalk, had just hit the colony and was catching on fast.

A typical boat race pitted the small yachts *Lurline* and *Britannia*, which were given a rousing sendoff by spectators at Rawson Square. After the yachts rounded a designated boat off Porgee Rocks and raced back to the square, the *Britannia*, owned by G W Armbrister and steered by Jerome Pyfrom of Governor's Harbour, outdistanced the *Lurline* piloted by owner Harold Adderley, by 10 minutes, 30 seconds.

On the scientific front, in July the colony's first x-ray machine, a contraption that appeared to be mostly wood and nails, arrived at the Nassau office of Dr T A Poole. "Its illuminating power is something

Nassau's Bay St around the turn of the century.

Marion "Joe" Carstairs, also born in 1900, built her own fiefdom on Whale Cay.

Born in 1900 on Watling's Island, Ida Butler remembers learning the ABCs.

marvellous," said a friend of the doctor. That same month, The Bahamas and Key West had a squabble when the colony, upon hearing stories of a smallpox epidemic on the Florida island, imposed a 14-day quarantine on all vessels from there. Key West officials called the stories "false rumours" and demanded the quarantine be lifted but the colony played it safe and the ban remained.

Celebrating victory

While celebrations large and small took place virtually every month in The Bahamas, few could have rivalled the spontaneous hoopla on May 31 when the colony received word that British troops had captured the Transvaal capital of Pretoria during the Boer War.

Loud cheers, brass bands and firecrackers erupted throughout Nassau. A 21-gun salute was fired in Rawson Square by a uniformed Naval Brigade. British ensigns and Union Jacks were put out at private homes and bunting was displayed on vessels in the harbour. The City Volunteer Fire Brigade led a torchlight procession to Government House, where a band played *God Save the Queen* and Governor Carter announced June 1 would be a national holiday.

The British clearly had the upper hand with the capture of Johannesburg and Pretoria. Stephanus Johannes Paulus Kruger, president of the independent South African Republic, fled from the capital to outlying areas of Transvaal. Months later, he sought aid in Europe but his pleas were rejected. The war would continue for another two years, but the battle was clearly in favour of the British. Kruger never returned to his homeland, dying in 1904.

In sharp contrast, one of The Bahamas' 243 churches, chapels and meeting-houses – St Matthew's in Nassau – quietly observed the centenary of the laying of the church's cornerstone. And the Nassau Women's Christian Temperance Union noted its 24th anniversary.

On May 24, Governor Carter gave a ball at Government House to celebrate Queen Victoria's 81st birthday and 63 years on the throne. Four months later, the Duke of Edinburgh, the Queen's second son, died of cancer at age 56.

Marion Barbara "Joe" Carstairs, granddaughter of one of the original trustees of Standard Oil, was born in England in February 1900. Racing speedboats for Britain, she became famous in the 1920s for being the fastest woman on water. Almost always dressed in men's clothing, this controversial figure would flee tax debts and a sour press in Britain to become owner of Whale Cay in The Bahamas. Carstairs developed the island, acting as ruler, judge and jury to the population – a role which eventually led to her downfall, disillusion and later abandonment of her island home. Carstairs died in December 1993, a few weeks short of her 94th birthday.

A Bahamian woman born Jan 14, 1900, on Watling's Island,[5] currently lives at the Sandilands Rehabilitation Centre in Nassau. Ida Butler, who had done a little farm work, came to Nassau when she was young and married Melvin Butler, a farmer from her home island. She vaguely recalls the early part of the century, but she emphasizes how she learned to read with no formal education. "Ain't had no learnin', but an old man taught me to spell," she said. "I learned the ABCs from him."

As 1900 drew to a close, Nassau treated Christmas and New Year's Eve in the traditional manner and speculated on a new era which was beginning to unfold.

Unsurpassed changes were to take place this next century. The Bahamas would boom in tourism and mega-resorts, earn a solid reputation as an offshore financial centre and become independent after more than 300 years of British rule.

[5] *Now San Salvador*

The Silver Jubilee year of 1998 celebrated 25 years of Bahamas independence.

The Bahamas' silver jubilee

BY DONN SELHORN

Great achievements, hard lessons round out 25 years of independence.

At 12:01am, July 10, 1973 in Nassau, The Bahamas flag was raised for the first time. Twenty-five years to the minute later, observers and participants were taken back in time to experience it again.

The Bahamas' Silver Jubilee echoed the original day, which was held before a crowd of 50,000 at historic Clifford Park. Parades, singing, fireworks – all were a part of the 1998 programme. Many of those present for the anniversary had witnessed the first celebrations, which started with quiet apprehension and turned to high-spirited festivities. The 24-year-old Prince Charles, who was representing the Queen, officially handed over the Instruments of Independence to then Prime Minister Lynden O Pindling, who was later knighted. More than 300 years of British colonial rule came to an end on that momentous day.

> **The Bahamas flag was raised for the first time.**

Prince Charles participated in 1973 Independence ceremonies with plume-hatted Sir John Paul, last Royal Governor and first Governor-General of The Bahamas, and Prime Minister Lynden O Pindling.

Global salutes

In the weeks following the Silver Jubilee anniversary, a series of balls and other gala observances were held, including a New York salute. From July 17-19, the top walls of Manhattan's Empire State Building were lit with The Bahamas' national colours.

In London, special guests at a Landmark Hotel reception were Rachel Rogers Hunter and her daughter, Christina, direct descendants of The Bahamas' first Royal Governor, Capt Woodes Rogers.

Other salutes took place in Miami and Toronto, with Prime Minister Hubert A Ingraham reminding audiences The Bahamas is a nation on the move. He used the occasions to promote the islands, peppering his remarks with a review of The Bahamas' progress.

> **The Bahamas is a nation on the move.**

"Leading economic indicators are all favourable; unemployment is at its lowest in 25 years; construction starts are at the highest level in over a decade; external reserves are at historic highs; the rate of increase in government borrowing has been reduced substantially and domestic interest rates for home owners and businesses remain low," said Prime Minister Ingraham, noting also the marked increase in direct foreign investment.

Business grows

Like any developing country, The Bahamas has experienced its share of struggles, but growing pains have been offset by continual progress. In 1973, the major industry in The Bahamas was tourism, accounting for two-thirds of the country's employment, with 1.5 million visitors. Tourism is still the No 1 industry, but the number of guests has more than doubled, with 3.4 million visitors in 1997. Latest available figures show the Gross Domestic Product has risen from 564.8 million in 1973 to 3.9 billion in 1997.

Recent changes to regulations in the financial services sector have enabled The Bahamas to maintain its top 10 ranking among the world's financial centres. Similarly, the commonwealth is now ranked third in the world in the shipping industry. In April 1995, a Hong Kong-based investor, Hutchison Port Holdings, joined the Grand Bahama Port Authority to become equal partners in one of the largest transshipment container ports in the world.

As well as business and tourism reforms, The Bahamas has experienced a host of changes on both the social and political fronts. In 1992 the Progressive Liberal Party's 25-year reign ended when the Free National Movement party won the general elections for the first time. The new government, under Prime Minister Ingraham, faced immediate challenges that included a debt in excess of $1 billion. If that weren't enough, Hurricane Andrew churned over the central and northern Bahamas the day before Ingraham officially assumed office. Despite setbacks, The FNM party moved in with promises to create jobs for Bahamians, as well as restore the image of The Bahamas as a major centre for both business and tourism.

"The red tape is being eliminated and is rapidly being replaced by a red carpet for investors," said Prime Minister Ingraham in March 1993 at a Palm Beach, FL business convention. "We (the government) strongly believe that foreign investment in The Bahamas is a win-win proposition for investors and Bahamians.

"We offer not only financial incentives to the investor, but an environment that is at the top of the wish list of the vast majority of those who live in North America," he added.

Tourism builds

The landscape has undergone a makeover, thanks largely to hotel construction and expansion. Sandals Royal Bahamian Hotel and SuperClubs® Breezes emerged on Nassau's world renowned Cable Beach. Sun International Hotels Ltd has invested nearly $450 million in its Phase II expansion on Paradise Island. The area is being transformed into a virtual theme park-beach resort featuring the lost continent of Atlantis. By the end of 1998, it was scheduled to double its hotel rooms to 2,400. The Canada RHK Group is restoring the fabled British Colonial Hotel in downtown Nassau. Freeport/Lucaya is experiencing hotel and resort industry changes, with exciting prospects for the future. The Lucayan Beach Hotel and its Casino were closed in 1997, the Atlantic Beach Hotel was imploded in 1998 and the Grand Bahama Beach Hotel was experiencing ongoing reconstruction in 1998 – all to rise phoenix-like in stages and renamed The Lucayan before the year 2000. (See *Shipping, hotels, real estate ...*, pg 457.)

> **For the first time in recorded history, snow fell on The Bahamas.**

While elaborate resorts were being created, two Nassau landmarks disappeared – the remnants of the 129-year-old Royal Victoria Hotel were gutted by fire in 1989 and the abandoned Montagu Beach Hotel was demolished four years later. Pan American Airlines, which introduced a regular United States-Bahamas flight in 1929, closed down its service in the mid-70s. Jan 19, 1977 is a day that will live in infamy. For the first time in recorded history, snow fell on parts of the northern Bahamas.

Expanding horizons

Adding to its international presence in the wake of United Nations membership in 1973, The Bahamas was admitted as an associate member of the European Economic Community in 1975, allowing export of manufactured goods to all EEC member countries duty-free. Three years later, The Bahamas Development Bank was created, paving the way for full membership in the Organization of American States in 1982.

By 1974 the government began paying out old-age pensions and

Two students and members of the Defence Force and Police Force re-enacted the flag ceremony in 1998.

other non-contributory social benefits. In October 1974, the National Insurance scheme was brought into operation for employed people, with the self-employed admitted more than a year later. Massive amounts were invested into overseas scholarships for Bahamian students. The College of the Bahamas was established in 1974 and then expanded. To safeguard its fishing industry and ecosystem, The Bahamas' exclusive economic water zone was extended to 200 miles, with a subzone of 12 miles within the area considered to be territorial waters. In 1993 legislation was passed to allow private broadcasting, resulting in radio licences being issued to The Tribune Ltd, Henry E Saunders Group and Jones Communications Ltd.

Local athletes began gaining recognition internationally, sparked by Elisha Obed winning the world junior middleweight boxing championship in Paris on Nov 13, 1975. Bahamian-born Rick Fox signed a $10 million contract with the Boston Celtics in 1994. In 1996, tennis professional Mark Knowles became the first Bahamian to rank in the top 10 in the world for tennis in both singles and doubles. Knowles competed at the US Open in 1994 and won the RCA Championships doubles title in 1995. In 1994 tennis pro Roger Smith was the only player at the US Open to take a set from the number one ranked player, Pete Sampras. Bahamian athletes have also captured Olympic Games track and field medals; bronze in 1992 and silver in 1996.

End of an era

Prominent government and business leaders died in the independence era. Among them were Sir Milo Butler, 72, first Bahamian Governor-General, who passed away Jan 22, 1979; Sir Roland Symonette, 81, first premier of The Bahamas (March 13, 1980); Hon Eugene A P Dupuch, 68, for whom The Bahamas' newly commissioned law school in Nassau was named (Sept 23, 1981); Dame Doris Johnson, 62, first female government minister (June 21, 1983); and American Wallace Groves, 86, one of the original developers of Freeport (Jan 30, 1988). Also Sir Cecil Wallace Whitfield, 60, who died (May 9, 1990) two years before his dream of an FNM victory at the polls became reality; Sir Etienne Dupuch, 92, long-time editor and publisher of *The Tribune* (Aug 23, 1991); and Sir Kendal Isaacs, 70, an elder statesman who was officially proclaimed "Hero of the Commonwealth of The Bahamas" upon his death May 25, 1996.

Since the first raising of the flag 25 years ago, The Bahamas has experienced many peaks and valleys. While approaching a new century, an independent Bahamas has learned there is much truth to the old saying, history balances the frustration of "how far we have to go" with the satisfaction of "how far we have come."

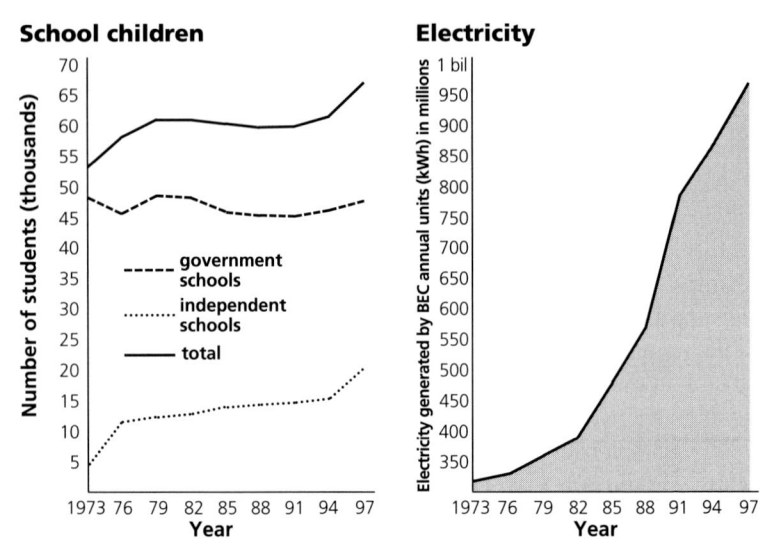

School children

Electricity

Construction

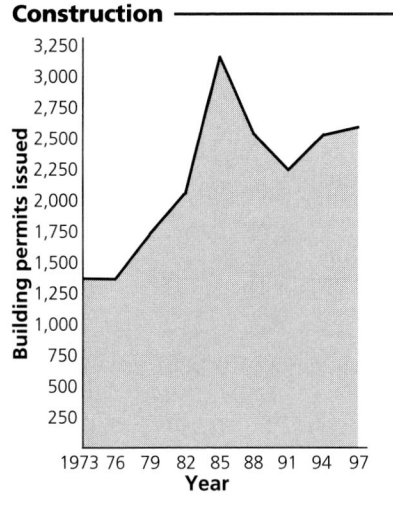

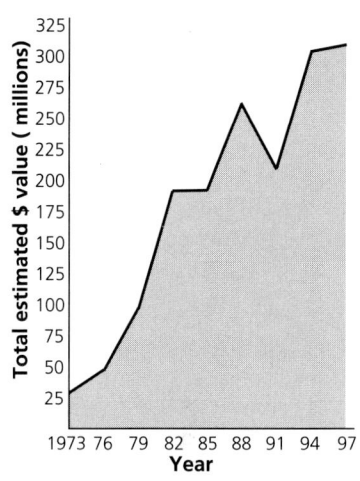

[Chart: Building permits issued vs Year, 1973–97]

[Chart: Total estimated $ value (millions) vs Year, 1973–97]

Vehicle information

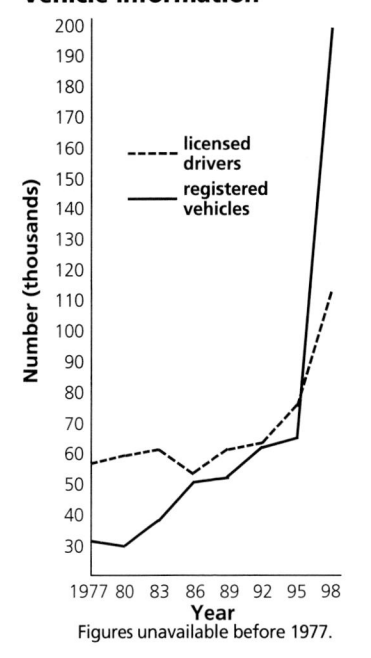

[Chart: Number (thousands) of licensed drivers and registered vehicles vs Year, 1977–98. Figures unavailable before 1977.]

Public Finance

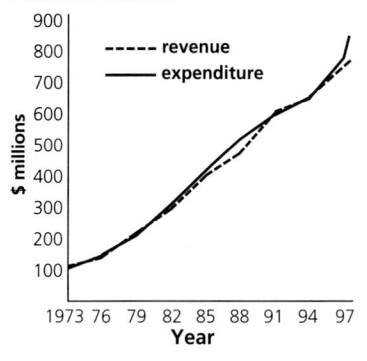

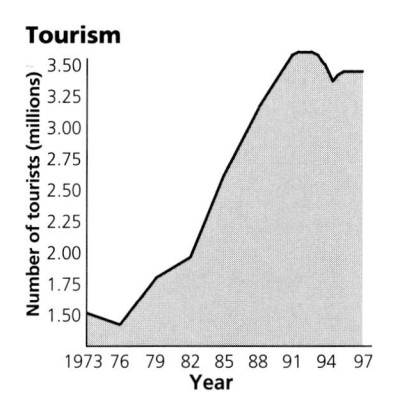

[Chart: $ millions (revenue and expenditure) vs Year, 1973–97]

Tourism

[Chart: Number of tourists (millions) vs Year, 1973–97]

Sampling of changes in Bahamas statistics since 1973. ⓘ

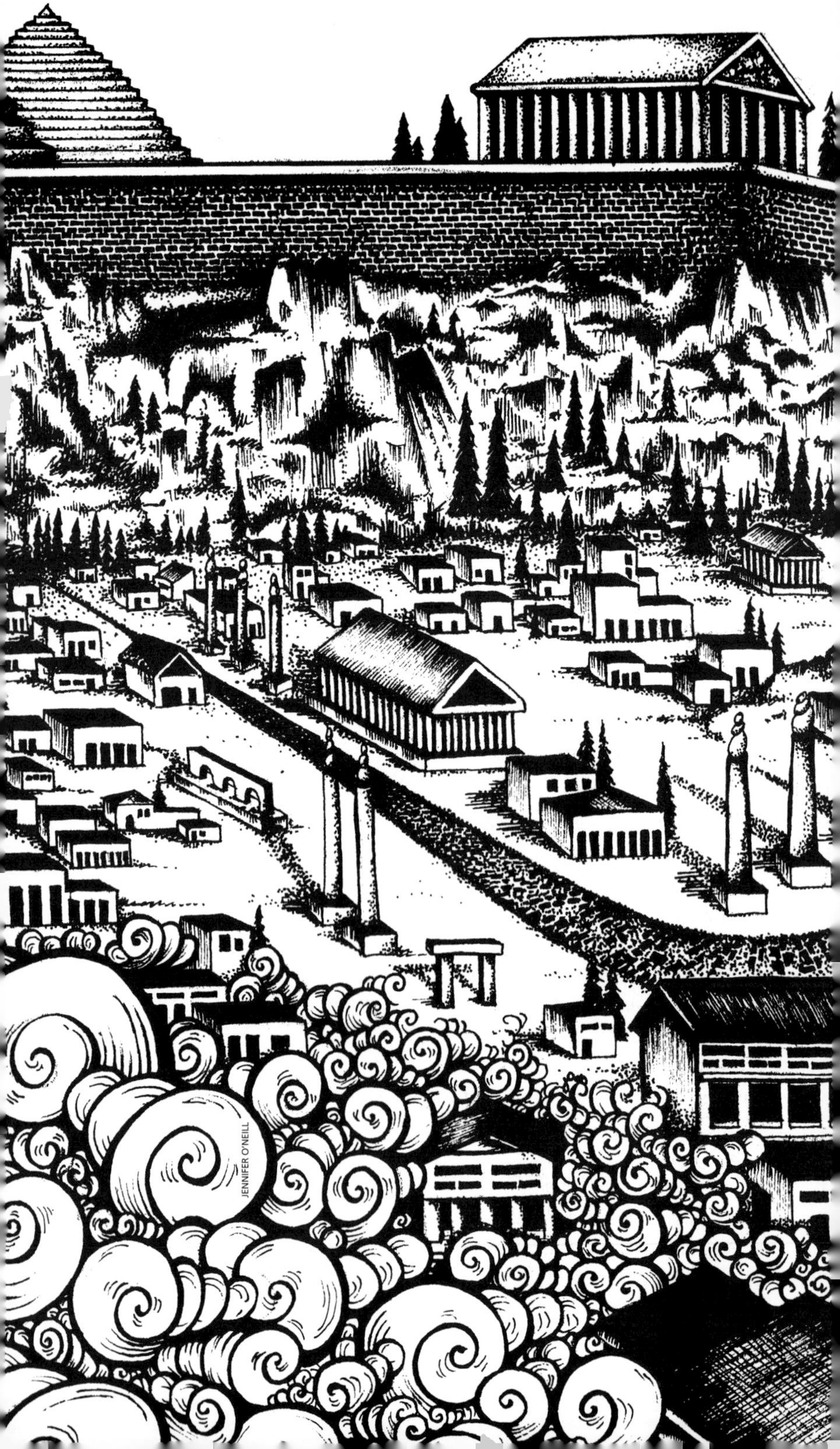
JENNIFER O'NEILL

Left: Artist's
depiction of the Lost
City of Atlantis.

Atlantis at Bimini: fantasy or fact?

BY PAUL J HEARTY, PhD, AND WILLIAM MICHAEL DONATO, MA

The **Bahamas Handbook** presents
two opposing viewpoints.

Nearly 24 centuries after Plato described the lost city of Atlantis in his works Timaeus and Critias, its location is still a source of discourse and dissension. Around 370 BC, the great Athenian philosopher described an island "larger than Lybia and Asia Minor" located beyond the Pillars of Hercules – probably the Straits of Gibraltar – in the "ocean stream." Plato spoke of "many temples built and dedicated to many gods, and gardens and places of exercise ..."

Around 10,000 to 12,000 years ago, the Atlanteans "became unseemly" and were defeated by the Athenians. "There occurred violent earthquakes and floods ... and Atlantis disappeared into the sea."

Although Plato's works were apparently unknown to psychic Edgar Cayce, he pinpointed Bimini as the lost city of Atlantis in his bedside "readings" of 1933. Cayce predicted Atlantis would rise again in 1968 or '69, along with temples "under the slime of ages of sea water" and an Atlantean healing well. Once dredging had begun, Cayce said, many artefacts would be found.

In 1968 Dr J Manson Valentine discovered "Bimini Road" in 15 to 20 ft of water a few hundred yards off the northwest coast of Bimini. He classified it as a megalithic site and claimed it to be the ruins of Atlantis.

A flurry of publications followed, some claiming the find "could alter our conceptions of prehistory and the origins of civilization," others dismissing it as a hoax. The **Bahamas Handbook** presents two opposing viewpoints.

Dr Paul J Hearty participates in a regional research programme on geological evolution of the Bahama Islands. His current studies include tropical island geology related to sea-level and global climate changes, and consulting in the areas of coastal hazards and groundwater pollution. He received his PhD on shoreline geology of the Mediterranean Sea from the University of Colorado (Boulder), and an Assistant Professorship from Duke University. Hearty has published more than 60 scientific articles and abstracts from his studies in the United States, the Canadian Arctic, Europe, Africa, Bermuda and The Bahamas.

Although Plato may have based the lost city of Atlantis on some credible oral history of his time, it is also possible he created it to convey a philosophical point, a position held by Richard Ellis in his book, *Imagining Atlantis*.

Even if Atlantis did exist, there are several excellent candidates among islands off the coast of Spain and Africa, including the Azores, Madeira and the Canary and Cape Verde Islands, which were well-known in Classical times and possibly in the earlier Phoenecian era. These islands lay beyond the Pillars of Hercules within the southerly flow of the Canary Current (Plato's "ocean stream"). They are volcanic islands subject to catastrophic eruptions, collapse and tidal waves which accommodate Plato's descriptions. Bimini fails to qualify in the majority of these characteristics.

> **Although Plato may have based Atlantis on some credible oral history ... it is also possible he created the lost city to convey a philosophical point.**

As a professional geologist with more than a decade's experience in studying the evolution and natural history of The Bahamas, I believe I can provide some insight on the subject.

Geological research has documented at least three catastrophic pulses of sea level rise around 14,000, 11,500, and 7,600 years ago, caused by breaking glacier-ice dams and disintegration of polar ice caps. These natural deluges are almost certainly the seed of countless convergent oral histories describing great floods in ancient times – including The Bible account.

After meeting pro-Bimini supporters William Donato, president of *The Atlantis Organization* newsletter (see Donato's viewpoint, following); Donnie Fields, Antiquarian; Joseph Frank, editor of *Ancient American* journal; and others during a visit to Bimini, I learned a great deal from the prodigious collection of data they had assembled over the years.

Their cornerstone hypothesis is that certain features of the Bimini phenomenon are human artefacts and structures, dating as much as 10,000 years before Plato's first description of Atlantis. But I feel there are alternative hypotheses to explain these artefacts employing the rigours of scientific method.

Atlantis-Bimini connection

The so-called Bimini Road is the most conspicuous and unique structure to give weight to the Atlantis-Bimini connection. It is composed of hundreds of large rectilinear limestone blocks extending nearly 1,600 ft with a J-shaped bend at the end. Atlantis believers maintain such a structure could only have been fabricated by humans.

This idea is defended by the very precise angles of the blocks, the Road's orientation to the existing shoreline, and its variable mineral composition of aragonite, calcite and other chemical elements. The stacking of the blocks and occurrence of various igneous and metamorphic rock types around the structure lend further support to the argument that it is man-made.

The Atlantis camp considers granite, volcanic rocks and some of the limestone rocks to be "sophisticated artefacts" which come from a foreign source. They contend the islands of The Bahamas may have undergone catastrophic vertical movements and may even have a volcanic core to account for the foreign stones.

They have also observed linear mounds in the bush of interior north Bimini during numerous fly-overs. Infra-red and true colour aerial photos reveal animal-like shapes in the limestone sands of the Bimini flats within a couple miles of Bimini Road. Fish, cat and seahorse forms light up under the infra-red film. Atlantis believers don't regard them as Atlantean in origin but they do interpret them as having "some sort of cultural connection (such as a daughter culture), since tendencies existed for one culture to build on the sacred sites of a previous culture."

The origin of these features has been attributed to the culture of Yuchi Indians, mound-builders of North America. The Atlantis

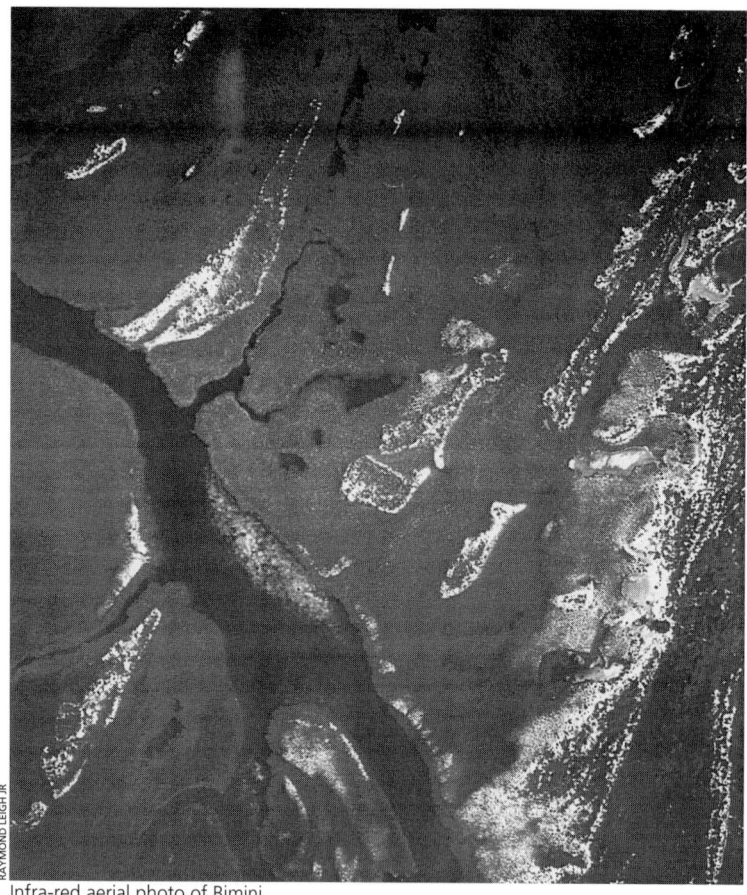

Infra-red aerial photo of Bimini
"zoomorphic mounds."

group claims a rectangular mound in the same area could have been the site of a sacrificial temple.

Unresolved questions

By presenting some insights into the geology of The Bahamas, I would like to propose testable alternative hypotheses to explain some of these occurrences in Bimini.

For over 100 million years the Bahama platform has been tectonically quiet, accumulating miles of horizontal strata of shallow-water limestone, experiencing little or no deformation and no known earthquakes. The earth's lithosphere beneath the platform evidently subsides to accommodate the load of new

Rectangular granite stone found at the Bimini site by Bill Keefe of Alice Town, Bimini.

limestone at the slow rate of about 10 inches every 10,000 years. There is no record of violent convulsions.

During the period Plato ascribed to the Atlantean culture, 10,000 to 12,000 years ago, The Bahamas was vastly different from the 700 islands and shallow turquoise seas we see today.

At that time, the melting of the great Ice Age glaciers was well under way. Sea level was rising, sometimes at catastrophic speeds. The best documented level of the sea at the time of Plato's Atlantis was somewhere between 150 to 200 ft below the present level. As a result, The Bahamas consisted of a few massive islands hundreds of miles across, perhaps as large as "Lybia and Asia Minor."

The sea level has changed, but the land has remained relatively stable. Great storms and hurricanes, along with changing sea levels, are responsible for creating much of the topography we now observe.

Geological studies around The Bahamas have documented two main phases of limestone formation: one around 5,000 years ago, and the other 2,000 to 3,000 years ago. To our knowledge, there are no deposits formed earlier within our present interglaciation (12,000 years ago to present).

Numerous peer-reviewed reports document the age of young bioclastic limestone throughout The Bahamas – like that composing Bimini Road – as being consistently 2,000 to 3,000 years old. Carbon-

Shifting beach sands along
the north coast of Bimini.

14 dates of rock cores in the Bimini Road come within this younger interval. Even though this indicates the sediments composing Bimini Road were in the process of forming 8,000 years after Atlantis and Bimini Road were supposedly built, Atlantis believers tend to disregard it. If these dates are invalid, they must be proven so and not simply ignored.

The next older interglacial rocks were formed 80,000 to 130,000 years ago. A hard crust or calcrete, iron-staining, and sometimes reddish soil in the older rocks also distinguish them from the 2,000-year-old rock type.

Given a well-established sea level and passive tectonic history, the interpretation of Bimini Road as a marine structure such as a wharf or harbour is immediately jeopardized, since the shoreline was miles away from the site and nearly 200 ft lower. The site was submerged by sea-level rise more than 5,000 to 8,000 years after the time of Plato's Atlantis.

Paving stones or beachrock?

Atlantis advocates cite the variable composition of aragonite and calcite in the limestone of Bimini Road as proof that the blocks are building stones rather than natural beachrock. But aragonite and calcite are both typical limestone minerals, and this variability is to be expected since organisms producing the bioclastic constituents of limestone form both minerals. When limestone ages, it tends to produce calcite.

They also claim the presence of parts-per-million of rare earth elements to be unusual, but many of these elements are common at such concentrations in seawater and in older eroded soils formed from atmospheric dust.

> **Tempests wield the power to neatly arrange or violently redistribute 100-ton stones.**

Brownish and reddish soil crusts are found on the older generation of limestone exposed along the beach near Bimini Road, and resistant flagstone of a variety of odd shapes can be shaped by rain, wave and biological erosion (bioerosion). Since the younger generation of limestone (formed 2,000 to 3,000 years ago) overlies the older one (80,000 to 130,000 years old), it is normal to find these hard soil crusts in the proximity of softer ones.

Physical, biological and chemical erosion attacks the edges of fractured blocks more aggressively than flat surfaces simply because the edges offer more surface to attack. A combination of limestone composition, polygonal fracture patterns and bioerosion of the edges of Bimini Road rocks account for their odd shapes.

Atlantis believers cite stacking of the stones, which they interpret as dolmen – a table-like archaeological structure – as evidence of human presence. Studying Pleistocene and recent hurricane deposits throughout The Bahamas, I have observed the natural stacking of rocks in submarine, intertidal and inland environments. Tempests wield the power to neatly arrange or violently redistribute 100-ton stones.

I have also found there are no "normal" characteristics of beachrock. Beachrock forms as a result of a number of processes, including sea-level position, extent of the fresh water lens, presence of dunes, and most of all, configuration of the land on which the rock is forming. This makes the orientation, thickness, layering and character of limestone formation highly variable.

As previously stated, the 2,000 to 3,000 year carbon-age of the Bimini Road rocks implies they did not exist when Atlantis might have. Most of north Bimini is overlaid with this very young formation, including that composing the animal-shaped mounds. The question of whether these zoomorphic mounds are man-made or natural could be easily resolved by carbon-14 dating, and by excavating a pit to determine if the sediments are beach stratified. If they are found to be stratified and less than 3,000 years old, they are natural beach ridges that acquired their form by wave action and storm washovers. If they are not stratified and much older than 3,000 years, then their potential human origin should be further investigated.

Nature loves lines

Nature loves lines and polygons and these are not at all uniquely human geometries. Rectilinear forms are found in a great variety of geological settings, and they include fault lines, fractures, ice-wedge polygons, mud cracks, basalt columns, and so on. Linear fractures tens of miles long, without displacement, are observed along nearly every deepwater margin in The Bahamas. Indeed, the rectangular geometry of the blocks composing Bimini Road are typical in many of the world's limestone coastlines.

A critical scientific point is that bioerosion rates in submerged limestone exceed several inches per 1,000 years. Bioerosion of limestone is caused by boring worms, clams, grazing fish and mollusks, echinoderms and a host of other organisms and processes.

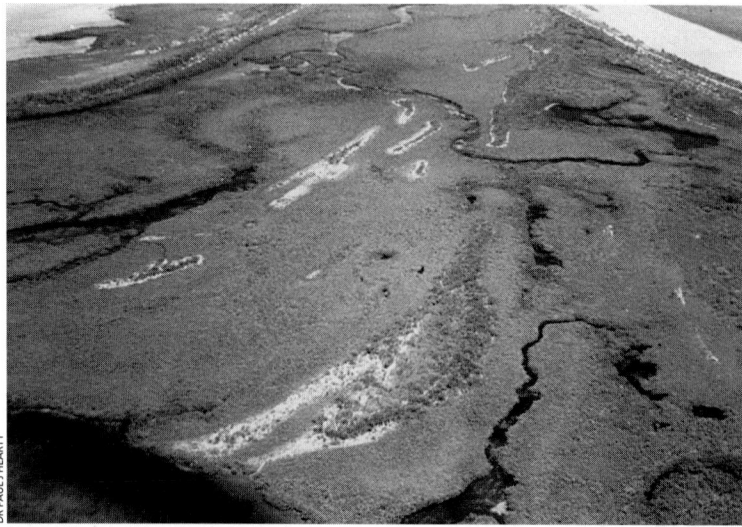

Natural beach ridges in North Bimini just inland from the modern beach. Bimini Road is interpreted by some geologists as a submerged form of this type of beach ridge.

Above: Polygonal stones in natural limestone 120,000 years old in Eleuthera, Bahamas.
Below: Rectilinear forms in natural beach rock in Inagua, Bahamas.

Linear fracture in 125,000 year old limestone at San Salvador.

The fastest rates of bioerosion are recorded in 2,000-year-old intertidal notches in natural limestone in The Bahamas, sometimes as much as 15 ft deep. Had effigies been carved in Atlantean limestone (or marble) by humans 10,000 to 12,000 years ago, that evidence would be long gone, replaced by nature's own sculptures.

If unequivocal human tooling of limestone or marble is discovered, it must be very young. The inscriptions on 20th century marble grave markers in the Bimini cemetery are already obscured by atmospheric processes, and these are not nearly as aggressive as their marine counterparts. It would be difficult to explain any original human tooling in limestone that has been submerged in seawater for even 500 years. The fact that blocks making up the Road have not been entirely digested by bioerosion proves their youth.

Volcanic and metamorphic stones

I suppose, although I cannot document, that the majority of several hundred ships that have run aground on Bimini shoals during storms over the past four or five centuries were using stones as ballast. The number of underwater salvage permits applied for in the Bimini area documents this ships' graveyard well enough. Since most of these wrecked ships departed from ports of advanced cultures (ie, the Mediterranean, Iberian Peninsula, British Isles, or even Havana or Caracas), it does not surprise me to learn of a great variety of rock types, some tooled, submerged in the area.

I can imagine a ship at port in Spain or Portugal preparing to sail to the New World, loading up with stone ballast near the large port cities of that era. Which stones would they use? I would guess stones near the beach, seawall or jetties, or perhaps stones from a defunct building near the port. They hoped to return to Europe loaded with New World riches and booty for ballast. If not, they would likely reuse the same ballast stones.

The presence of granite stones in Bimini only means ships using them for ballast ran aground in the frequent fury of the Florida Straits. It does not mean The Bahamas has a granite core or a volcanic history. Further, if an ancient city or glorious temple of Atlantean standards were to be built, would not the architect demand the stones be of similar colour, composition and sculpture rather than the random supply of odd stones found in Bimini?

Testing alternative hypotheses

Setting out to prove features observed in Bimini are man-made without considering and testing alternative hypotheses that they might be natural is unacceptable in science. It has probably lost the Atlantis-Bimini believers more credibility than their diverse methods and prodigious dataset have gained them. It is incumbent upon them to consider and test alternative hypotheses rather than dismiss the findings of other scientists as attempts to discredit their work.

In human history, there is a delicate intertwining of fantasy, folklore, fable and fact. Catastrophic events in earth history clearly

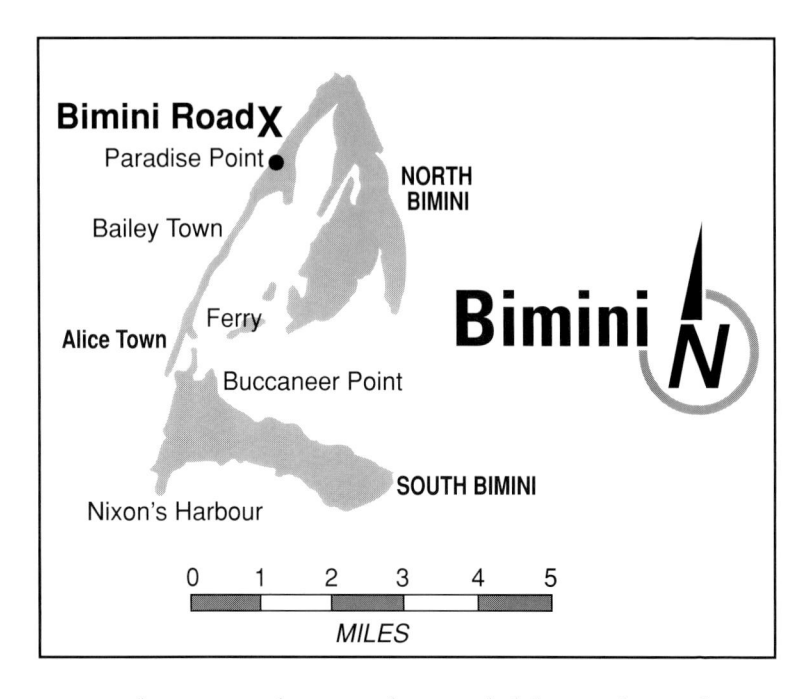

Bimini Road ✗
Paradise Point ●
Bailey Town
NORTH BIMINI
Ferry
Alice Town
Buccaneer Point
Bimini N
SOUTH BIMINI
Nixon's Harbour

0 1 2 3 4 5
MILES

impressed ancient civilizations who recorded them with awe, fear and fascination, and conveyed them to future generations by oral tradition. Globally and culturally convergent accounts of a "great flood" are almost certainly rooted in the occurrence of post-Ice Age sea level rise. Perhaps the legend of the lost city of Atlantis is based on the existence of a real city and culture at the dawn of civilization. But evidence of its occurrence at Bimini is doubtful unless proven by the diligent and rigorous standards required by scientific method.

Further reading

Ellis, Richard. *Imagining Atlantis*. Alfred A Knopf, New York, 1998.

Hearty, P J, and Kindler, P. *New perspectives on Bahamian geology: San Salvador Island, Bahamas,* Journal of Coastal Research, Vol 9 no 2, 1993a.

Hearty, P J, and Kindler, P. *An Illustrated Stratigraphy of the Bahama Islands: In Search of a Common Origin.* Bahamas Journal of Science, Vol 1 no 1, 1993b.

Hearty, P J. *On the Evolution of Bahamian Islands: An Excerpt from Nature's Anthology.* **Bahamas Handbook,** 1994.

Hearty, P J, and Kindler, P. *The Stratigraphy and Surficial Geology of New Providence and Surrounding Islands.* Journal of Coastal Research, vol 13, no 3, 1997.

Hearty, P J. *Enigmatic Boulders of Eleuthera.* **Bahamas Handbook,** 1998.

Shinn, E A. *Atlantis: Bimini Hoax.* Sea Frontiers, vol 24, no 3, 1978.

William Michael Donato, MA, is an anthropologist and archaeologist currently involved in several private archaeological projects. He is founder and editor of The Atlantis Organization, a research- and networking-oriented newsletter/organization.

According to Plato, the lost city of Atlantis was destroyed by a great cataclysm in 9600 BC. How likely was this? An analysis of marine organisms *(Foraminifera)* by Dr Cesare Emiliani found evidence of freshwater flooding around 11,600 years ago – 9600 BC – corresponding with the last major melting of the glaciers. This was accompanied by renewed volcanic activity, "super quakes," and a worldwide rise in sea levels of hundreds of feet.

In 1979 the Russians photographed the remains of walls and steps on the Ampere Seamount, currently 180 ft below the surface. It once stood 238 ft above sea level. In 1973, 25 miles off Gibraltar at a depth of 95 ft, Francisco Salazar and the Ancient Mediterranean Research Association investigated the remains of pillars, blocks, bowls and other artefacts. Off Morocco, Marc Valentin found a megalithic wall at a depth of 50 to 60 ft.

On the opposite side of the ocean are the Bahama islands, close to a major "subduction zone" where one tectonic plate slides under another. This perhaps explains The Bahamas' "tilt." Numerous other archaeological anomalies have been reported throughout the islands.

Duke University's discovery of granite in the Caribbean in the late 1960s was claimed by some geologists to be remnants of a former continent. They thought The Bahamas may have been part of this continent since, beneath the limestone capping, the northern banks present a continental component while the southeastern part appears more volcanic. Prior to the Pleistocene Meltdown, The Bahamas was a landmass of virtually thousands of square miles, providing ancient man with a pleasant and productive homeland as well as one of the largest and best protected harbours in the world, the Tongue of the Ocean. Was there a civilization here? The increasing tempo of the discovery of unique artefacts suggests this is the case, which is consistent with traditional histories of many of the hemisphere's indigenous peoples. Though artefacts have been found throughout The Bahamas, Bimini has the lion's share (with Andros a close second).

Bimini was known to the Indians as The Place of the Wreath (or Crown) and The Place of the Walls – the latter almost certainly referring to what is now called Bimini Road. Although early investigators thought the site was a road or wall, it is now thought to be some sort of foundation for another type of structure. It is at least 1,900 ft long at a depth of 20 ft, ³/₄ of a mile off Paradise Point in north Bimini. It is shaped like a reversed letter J with two smaller parallel lines inward of it known as Rebikoff's Pier.

Bimini Road

What is Bimini Road? To some of the first geologists who examined it, it was nothing more than beachrock broken into vaguely rectangular shapes, their contours smoothed by the action of sand and water on the ocean floor. They made certain critical assumptions that have since been proved false, including:

- Bimini Road has remained pretty much the same over the last few centuries.

A boat at the tip of the reverse J gives an indication of Bimini Road's length.

- The stones are of similar composition over the entire feature.
- They are randomly distributed.
- The rounded contours are due exclusively to erosive forces.
- All legitimate artefacts have been dropped by ships.

Methodological errors included taking too few samples in too limited an area; using hand-held coring devices rather than a tripod arrangement to assure a straight cut – essential for analyzing the rock bedding; and performing only a limited survey before taking samples. One geologist stated there was not a single stone set squarely atop another – yet three square stones sitting directly on top of one another were found in June 1998. I have personally photographed not only similar phenomena, but several dolmen-like objects and rocks stacked four layers high. Further, the scientists displayed an utter lack of knowledge of the history of the Road.

At the beginning of the century Bimini Road was listed as a "navigation hazard" on maps, and was said to stand eight to 10 layers high. There are still people living who remember it. For several years in the 1930s, barges came in and loaded large stones for shipping to Florida. Business records attest to this and a number of people witnessed it.

The stones composing Bimini Road have been found to contain several varieties of limestone, some of which have no obvious bedding. These components include calcarenite –a type of beachrock which takes longer to form – micrite and some rather unusual ones such as marble, igneous rock approximating syenite with three layers of algae, and metamorphic rock. New samples are awaiting identification. At least two of 11 samples submitted to a petrologist showed surface weathering – proving they were once on the surface.

Other factors mitigating against *in situ* formation of the stones include the fact that adjacent blocks have differing crystallization (aragonite and sparry calcite) as well as different constituents, structure and cementing.

Samples from Dr David Zink's Poseidia '77 expedition revealed significant differences in the trace element patterns of Bimini Road stones, beachrock and seafloor. The Road stones had significantly less trace elements than the seafloor, as might be expected in stones that had once been on the surface. If the stones had been underwater for great lengths of time, they would have absorbed these elements from the seawater itself.

The geologists' theory that the beachrock slid into alignment when the sand beneath it washed out fails to note the obvious: beachrock breaks into uneven sizes of different weights which move unequally. There are no perfect alignments of beachrock either above or below the surface in Bimini.

Definite patterns

Bimini Road stones comprise furrow spacing of only four to six inches, which is to be expected of intentionally placed stones, while the beachrock averages spaces of 27 to 31 inches. The Road stones feature dead straight alignments and definite patterns of five large stones next to five small ones, as well as an alternating pattern of five or six stones, recalling symbolic numbers in Plato's account. Bimini Road has a 90 degree arc in the curve of the J and possible

Aligned and fitted stones of Bimini Road are
among factors influencing pro-Bimini believers.

astronomical alignments. The most clearly artificial part of the Road is at its northern periphery – which the geologists did not examine – comprising 14 stones in a line next to rows of five, all in a grid pattern. The statistical probability of this occurring in nature is one in 43,359,500 followed by 51 zeroes!

The practice of using cleanly cut slabs with sharp right-angled configurations has been noted in Peru, and I have photographed a sharp-angled, wedge-shaped ramp under the rounded stones of Bimini Road. The Road as a whole is 14 degrees out of alignment with the ancient beach line and is all level; the beachrock is on a slant. In 1993 when a marine geologist removed a new coring, I asked him if it was beachrock. His answer was a short and to-the-point "no."

> **Bimini Road is the work of man. Even the seafloor appears to have been cemented over since its construction.**

Multiple lines of evidence point to the same inevitable conclusion: Bimini Road is the work of man. Even the seafloor appears to have been cemented over since its construction.

Uranium-Thorium dating of the seabed aged it at 14,992 years before present, with a margin of error of 585 years. An article which sought to discredit the Bimini finds omitted this older date while using more recent dates from the same report.

The Poseidia Expeditions discovered the first diagnosed artefacts in Bimini: an Indian grinding stone *(metate)* cemented into the ocean floor; a highly eroded piece of marble (among other pieces) described as a stylized head; the famous "tongue and groove" stone containing a mortise and tenon; a stone designated as the "keystone" with dimensions divisible by 10; and a worked stone containing two drill holes.

In 1991 Donnie Fields discovered a stone that was stylistically the exact counterpart of the keystone, complete with the same rounded corners and indentations, but differing in that it had a large projecting tenon while the other had a mortise.

My discoveries include a fallen truncated monolith – or large pillar of stone – broken into three sections, which would have stood

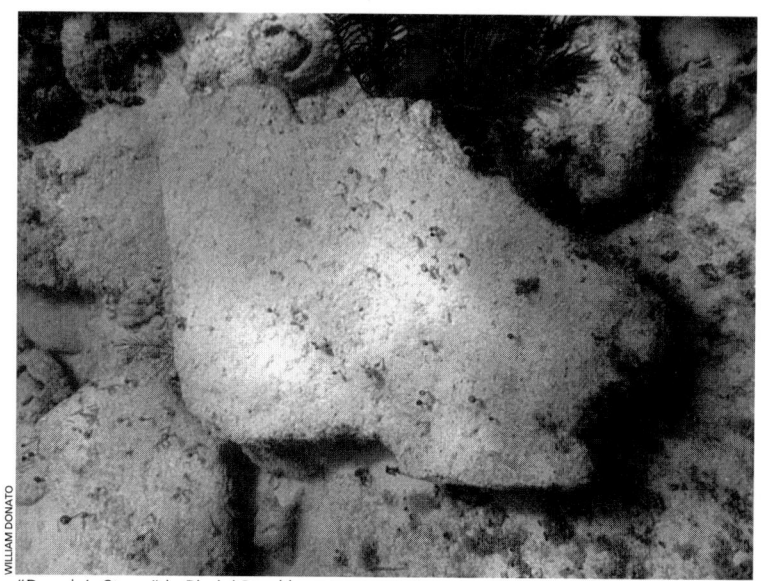

"Donnie's Stone" in Bimini Road has a tenon "plainly evident" at the bottom, says Donato.

around 17 ft 9 in; two flat equilateral hexagon stones and a third with extended ends; at least three *in situ* stones with mortises along their lengths; a tapered parallelogram-shaped building stone and the first indication that the large base stones were modified; and a stone with a straight cut along its width that looks as though it were meant to hold a slab.

In 1995 divemaster Bill Keefe removed a stone from the northern end of the longer parallel line. After it had been soaked in bleach for several days to remove encrustations, a rounded triangular mortise was discovered. The knowledge of stress revealed in its design is superior to that of both the Egyptians and Tiahuanacans. The University of Colorado has since verified Keefe's artefact.

One item, Bell's Column, was located in 1957 off the west coast of South Bimini, consisting of a tapering spire in a double-gear base with 10 to 12 ft long stone slabs nearby. It has never been found again.

Effigy mounds

The first zoomorphic effigy mound was discovered in east Bimini by Jim Richardson in the early 1970s, in the shape of a fish about 527 ft long. Dr Douglas Richards discovered its tail was oriented to 360 degrees (magnetic) north. Most of the mounds were discovered by

An aerial view of zoomorphic effigy mounds reveals a fish, a rectangle and a cat in east Bimini.

an aerial survey commissioned by Raymond Leigh Jr, including configurations resembling a cat, alligator, dolphin, frog, cobra, rectangle and triangle, as well as some undetermined ones. Some of these appear to have been modified sand ridges, such as the sea horse which I discovered. An archaeological seashell was found on the cobra. These mounds seem to have a common orientation and have been connected to the Yuchi Indians who claim two of their lineage groups, represented by the Fish and the Cat, originally came from Andros. The Yuchi make zoomorphic effigy mounds of white sand to be seen by "Those Above." All archaeologists that have seen photographs of these mounds regard them as legitimate, although they are not regarded as Atlantean.

A side-scan sonar revealed a clear image of a pyramid around 110 ft below the surface; a spire; and what appears to be the remnants of a city.

Cayce's prediction of healing sulphur waters in north Bimini might well refer to the Healing Hole, a spring-fed well in the swamp which

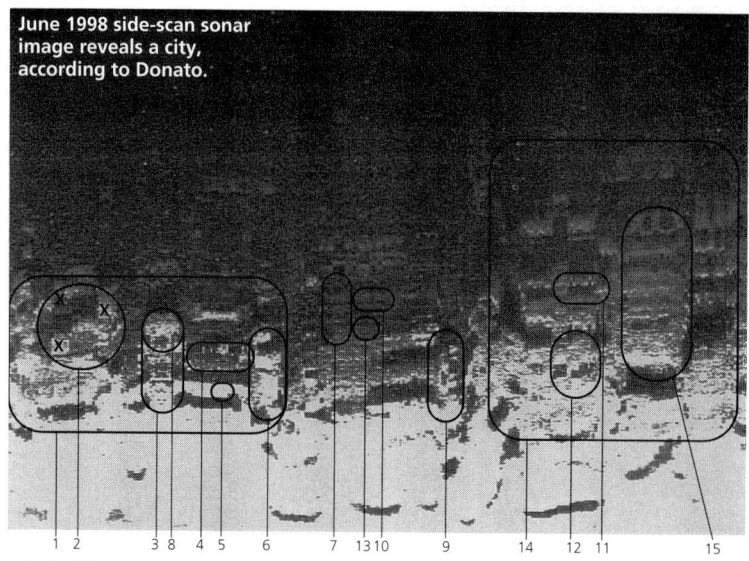

June 1998 side-scan sonar image reveals a city, according to Donato.

1. Multiple structures
2. Several rectangular structures (possible buildings)
3. Structure with stairway
4. Support elements (possible columns)
5. Small stairway
6. Possible street
7. Two post lintel systems
8. Roof
9. Possible street
10. Evenly spaced support elements (possible columns)
11. Doorway
12. Stairway
13. Broken wall section
14. Two multi-tiered structures
15. Doorways or windows

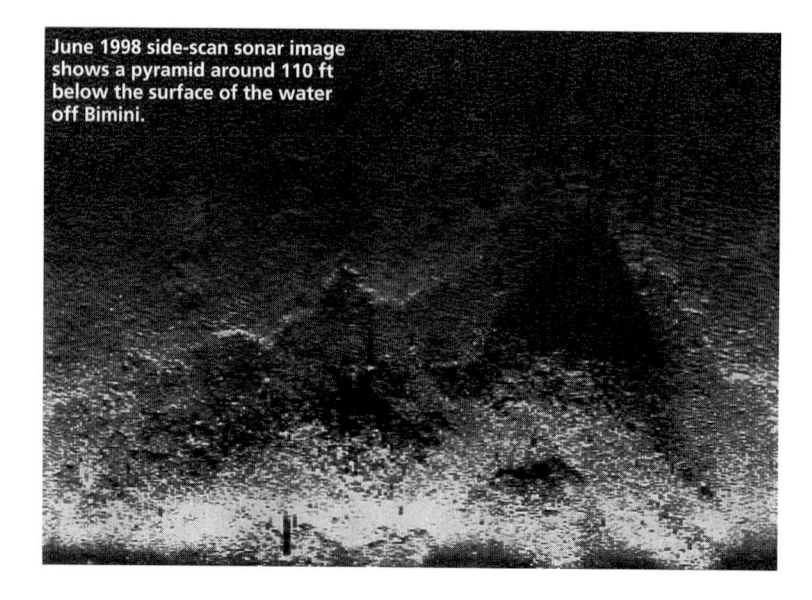

June 1998 side-scan sonar image shows a pyramid around 110 ft below the surface of the water off Bimini.

A tapered parallelogram building fragment at Bimini Road.

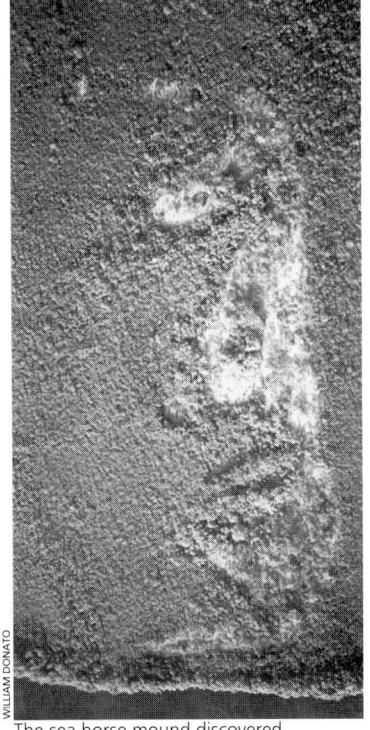

The sea horse mound discovered by Donato was believed to be a modified sand ridge.

has enough sulphur content to turn the metals silver and copper black after only a few minutes' exposure. The "sweet water" he predicted for the northern part of south Bimini has also been verified. Higher than normal amounts of lithium and magnesium have been found in the water, although the lithium content varies.

Side-scan sonar and aerial surveys have revealed numerous potential sites and the possibility of a city about 25 miles northeast of Bimini. In June 1998, a side-scan sonar revealed a clear image of a pyramid around 110 ft below the surface; a spire; and what appears to be the remnants of a city a couple of miles west of Bimini.

During Dr Joan Hanley's August 1998 expedition, further side-scan sonar work was done and "tech divers" using special equipment and gas mixtures discovered cave systems off Bimini. One was at the 300 ft level, on the former beach of 10,000 BC. Large rectangular stones appeared, as well as an ancient, sandy foot path with some stones on it. The dive leader said he would be willing to write a deposition stating he felt some of what they saw was the work of man.

Archaeological investigations begun in August were ongoing at press time. Only further research can determine if The Bahamas was once part of the lost city of Atlantis, but should this be verified, it will be the heritage of not just one nation, but of the entire human race.

Special thanks to Daniel Trifiletti, Donnie Fields, Dr David Zink, Dr Robert McKinney and Dr William Hutton.

Sources

William M Donato. *A Re-Examination of the Atlantis Theory* (master's thesis), 1979.
Dr David Zink, revised ed. *The Stones of Atlantis*, 1987.
Michael Craton. *A History of the Bahamas*, 1987.
Stephen K Boss. *Early Sequence Evolution On Carbonate Platforms: An Actualistic Model From Northern Great Bahama Bank* (doctoral dissertation, 1994).
Dr William Hutton. *Coming Earth Changes – The Latest Evidence*, 1996.
Hugh Lynn Cayce. *Earth Changes Update*, 1986.
J Manson Valentine. *Underwater Archeology In the Bahamas*, Dec 1976. Explorers Journal.
Robert A Adriance. *Atlantean Researches Off Bimini*, Nov 1957.
Charles Berlitz. *Atlantis – the Eighth Continent*, 1984.
E A Shinn. *Atlantis: Bimini Hoax.* Sea Frontiers, May-June 1978.
Mahlon M Ball. *Investigation of Submerged Beachrock Deposits off Bimini, Bahamas.* National Geographic Society Research Papers, vol 12, 1980.
Marshall McCusick and Eugene Shinn. *Bahamian Atlantis Reconsidered.* Nature, Sept 4, vol 287, 1980.
William M Donato. *The Atlantis Organization* (newsletter), 1990-present.
Edgar Evans Cayce, Gail Cayce Schwartzer and Douglas G Richards. *Mysteries Of Atlantis Revisited*, 1988.

History

A natty Triumph of the 1960s parks outside Lord and Lady Dudley's great house, Graycliff.

High, mighty trod West Hill Street

BY GORDON LOMER

Mountbatten was a house guest every year.

One of Nassau's quaintest streets nestles snugly between the home of the Queen's representative at one end and the House of The Lord at the other. West Hill St connects stately Government House with the serene, unassuming St Francis Xavier Cathedral.

Like its counterpart, East Hill St just east of Government House, West Hill sits on the ridge that once marked southern city limits. There the similarity ends, however, because East Hill was playful while West Hill was pious. Government House was and still is smack in the middle.

East Hill, where the Royal Victoria Hotel once stood, was a playground for blockade runners, rum runners and other assorted roustabouts. West Hill, on the other hand, reeked of religion.

The Bahamas' oldest church once graced West Hill's eastern end, a convent, a school and a rectory huddled in the middle and the Catholic cathedral still marks the street's western boundary.

West Hill was also a magnet for the great and near-greats as they visited with wealthy and titled foreigners who maintained lavish homes along the street. High society slept here. The street was reputedly frequented also by a ghost tapping a cane during excursions beneath lattice shuttered verandas.

Imported architectural styles

The nature of the terrain dictated architectural features of both West Hill and East Hill Sts. Because they were built on a slope in an effort to build as high as possible, houses on the north or downward side were built right to the street. Houses on the south or upward side of the street were set back with gardens between the street and houses.

Bahamian architecture employed imported styles, but adapted them to the demands of climate and availability of building materials. Coral limestone was widely used because it was easily sawed. Local woods included Madeira, pine, cedar, dogwood and horseflesh. Most of the homes along West Hill St had trellising and jalousies which encouraged cross-ventilation.

"Houses were functional. Many of them were wood, built by Northern Loyalists who had been shipbuilders. Houses were built the way they should be built today," according to Jackson Burnside III.

The southern ridge occupied by Government House slopes down to Nassau Harbour, shown here in the heady blockade running era of 1961-65.

Burnside, an architect and artist, was an active member of the Bahamas National Trust Historical Preservation Committee which identified historic buildings and sites it wanted to see preserved, including much of West Hill St.

Stroll along West Hill from Government House. The first building on your left is Graycliff, a fine example of Georgian colonial architecture. It was built originally in the 1720s by Capt John Howard Graysmith, a retired pirate whose ship, *Graywolf*, was scuttled off Nassau in 1726. The site contained some of the foundation of the oldest church, which was destroyed by the Spaniards in 1703. A plaque on the wall outside Graycliff commemorates the event.

French's Hotel

An advertisement for Graycliff, called Victoria House at the time, appeared in *The Nassau Guardian* in November 1844, six days after the paper started publishing. The proprietress, Mrs Nathaniel French, was offering board and lodging by the day, week or month. "This house," said the ad, "is located on one of the pleasantest and

Lord Dudley, third Earl of Staffordshire, and Lady Dudley owned Graycliff in the late 1960s.

Enrico Garzaroli transformed Graycliff into an upscale restaurant for the rich and famous.

most healthy situations of the town, and accommodations are adapted for families or for single persons."

The name Victoria House later changed to French's Hotel. An ad a few years later offered "strangers and invalids accommodations unsurpassed in the Bahamas. A carriage is kept, which will be hired to boarders at reduced rates. Breakfasts, luncheons, dinners or supper provided for any number on a short notice being given."

The building served as an officers' mess for the West India Regiment during the American Civil War. The Bahamas at the time was headquarters for blockade runners selling southern cotton to British mills in exchange for guns for the rebellious Confederacy. During the roaring '20s Graycliff again opened to the public under the ownership of Polly Leach, reputedly a close companion of Al Capone. The building was later bought by Canadians, Mr and Mrs I Walton Killam. They completely refurbished the mansion and added the large swimming pool surrounded by gardens next to the pool cottage. After Killam's death in 1955, his widow remained at Graycliff until she died in 1964.

Princess Alice

Lord Beaverbrook

The Duke and Duchess of Windsor resided at Government House during the 1940s when he was Royal Governor of the Colony of The Bahama Islands.

Lord and Lady Dudley

In 1966 the third Earl of Staffordshire, Lord Dudley, and Lady Dudley bought Graycliff. They were lifelong friends of the Duke of Windsor. Lady Dudley was the former wife of Prince Stanislaus Radziwill, who later married Lee Bouvier, younger sister of Jacqueline Kennedy. Visitors to Graycliff during the Dudley ownership included Lord Beaverbrook, Lord Mountbatten, the Duke and Duchess of Windsor, the Duke and Duchess of Kent and Princess Alice, among others.

The current owner, Enrico Garzaroli, purchased Graycliff in 1974 and transformed it into a five-star restaurant with one of the finest wine cellars in the Caribbean region. Nowadays, the rich and famous still dine here.

West Hill House, immediately west of Graycliff, was built about 1840 and at one time was occupied by Edward St George, co-chairman of the Grand Bahama Port Authority. The wooden house, also formerly owned by Sir Robert McAlpine, was purchased in 1995 by Garzaroli and is now his home.

Next door is Postern Gate, bought in 1997 by Garzaroli. This sprawling complex includes the main building right on the street and several buildings, originally staff quarters, at the back of the

1 Government House
2 Graycliff
3 West Hill House
4 Postern Gate
5 Former Hospital site
6 Villa Doyle
7 St Francis Xavier Cathedral
8 Sunningridge
9 Ranora House
10 Sisters of Charity Convent
11 O'Donnell House
12 Corner House

The Nassau Guardian
(1844) Ltd.

Audit Bureau of Circulations Member

- Best for display & classified ads
- Top quality printing of newspapers and other commercial jobs
- A well established tradition in The Bahamas.
- Best for objective news
- Best for news variety
- Biggest employer among private media operations in The Bahamas

Carter St, Oakes Field • PO Box N-3011
Administrative offices: (242) 323-5654 (to 6), 323-2365 or 328-5588 • Fax (242) 328-8943
E-mail: sfrancis@batelnet.bs
Advertising: (242) 325-4259 or 328-6884 • Fax (242) 328-6883 • E-mail: cubell@batelnet.bs
Classified advertising: (242) 328-6881 • Fax (242) 325-3379
Circulation: (242) 325-4316 • Fax (242) 325-3379 • E-mail: nasguard@batelnet.bs
Editorial: (242) 328-6868 or 328-6867 • Fax (242) 325-3379 • E-mail: devint@batelnet.bs
Commercial printing: (242) 356-6561 or 328-5311 • Fax (242) 328-5308

The Freeport News

Cedar St, Freeport, Grand Bahama • PO Box F-40007
Tel (242) 352-8321 • Fax (242) 352-8324

Villa Doyle, built by William Doyle, will be resurrected as the National Art Gallery of The Bahamas.

large property. The Graycliff Cigar Factory is currently located in two of the smaller staff buildings which have been restored. The factory produces about 1,500 hand-rolled cigars a day.

Postern Gate means back door or side entrance, but nobody seems to know to what. Initially built about 1840, Postern Gate was at one time owned by Canadian Richard Todd, who wintered here. The main building facing West Hill St is being transformed into a factory, exclusive membership cigar-friendly restaurant to be called The Humidor, another public dining room and several large suites.

Further along the south side of West Hill is the site of a former hospital which stood immediately west of Hospital Ln opposite steps down to Queen St. Believed to have been built about 1780, the hospital site is shown on the 1788 plot plan of the city. Some parts of the foundation remain.

Sweeping statement

Villa Doyle, at the corner of West and West Hill Sts, stands today as a yellow shell awaiting reincarnation as the National Art Gallery of The Bahamas. The two-storey building was "the finest building in Nassau," according to architect/artist Robert Douglas, who has sketched many of The Bahamas' finest old buildings. The style was

In computing, networks and communications, you're known by the company you keep ...

For today's organizations, use of technology and effective communications are the lifeblood of the business. At *The Systems Resource Group*, we've been helping leading Bahamian companies maximize their benefit from technology since 1990. Whether you need Professional Services, Business Solutions or Value Added Internet Services, you're in the right company.

Business Solutions

Lotus *Microsoft* NOVELL COMPAQ micros digital

Professional Services

Disaster Recovery • Strategic Planning • Network Support
Security Threat and Vulnerability • Project Management
Groupware • Intranets/Extranets

INTERNET

Leased-Line & Dial-Up Connectivity • Wide Area Communications
International Fax Services • Internet Commerce
Web Site Development • Offshore Hosting

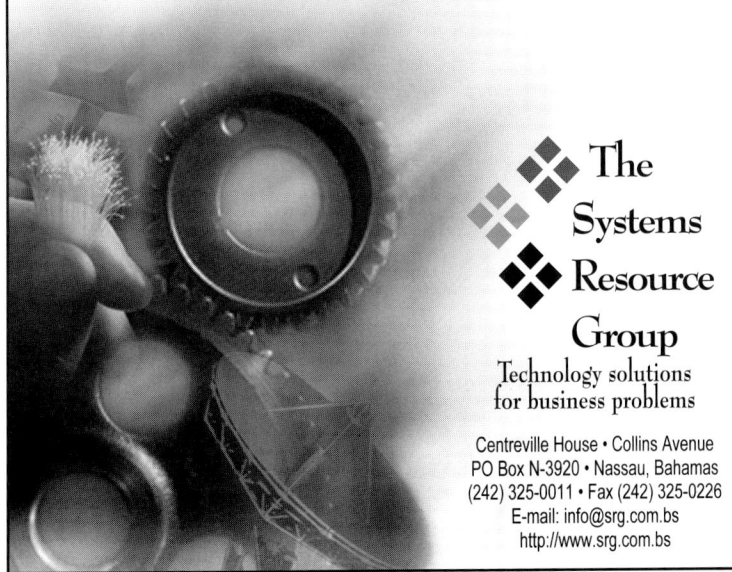

The Systems Resource Group

Technology solutions for business problems

Centreville House • Collins Avenue
PO Box N-3920 • Nassau, Bahamas
(242) 325-0011 • Fax (242) 325-0226
E-mail: info@srg.com.bs
http://www.srg.com.bs

not typical of Nassau but rather along the lines of Mississippi or Louisiana manors. It was built about 1865 by William Doyle, a former education department employee and attorney. Later knighted, he became Chief Justice and president of the Legislative Council (now the Senate).

Sir William was appointed Chief Justice of the Leeward Islands in 1875 and later Chief Justice of Gibraltar. He died in England in 1879 during his Gibraltar term. His widow sold the house four years later to William Robert Pyfrom for £1,000. A few months later Pyfrom also bought the cottage on the property for £157.5.0.

After Pyfrom's death, one of his daughters occupied Villa Doyle until about 1924, when it was sold to Walter Kingsbury Moore (later Sir Walter Moore), president of the Legislative Council, for £6,000. At his death, Sir Walter left the property to the trustees of Trinity Methodist Church and it was later sold to Baroness Von Hoyningen Huene, the former Nancy Oakes.

It was subsequently sold to Keith Aranha in 1978 for $150,000. His plans to convert the building to apartments were aborted and government acquired the building in 1994 with plans to turn it into the Bahamas National Art Gallery. Restoration was to begin in late 1998.

St Francis Xavier Cathedral anchors the western end of West Hill St.

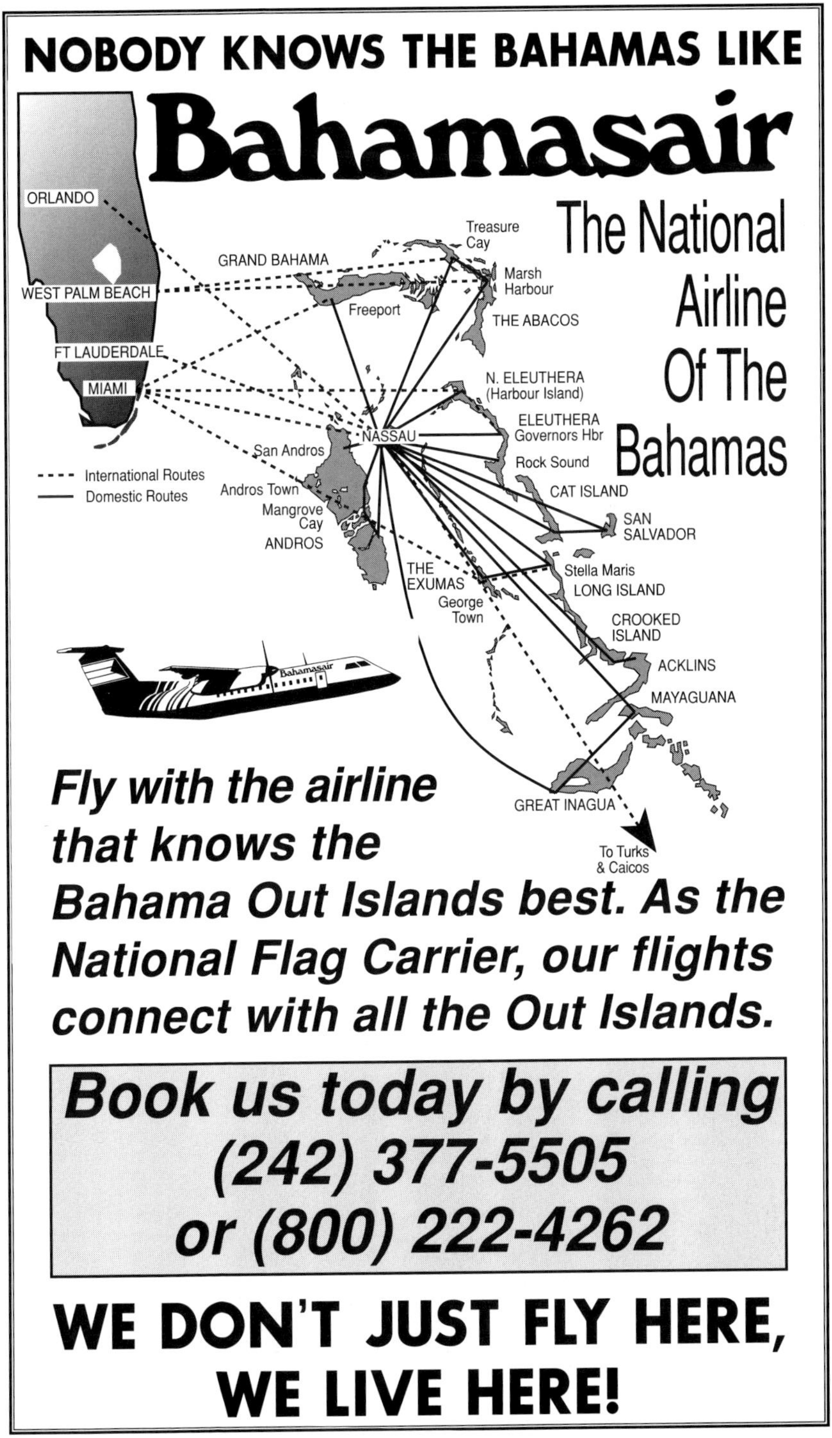
NOBODY KNOWS THE BAHAMAS LIKE
Bahamasair
The National Airline Of The Bahamas
ORLANDO
WEST PALM BEACH
FT LAUDERDALE
MIAMI
GRAND BAHAMA
Freeport
Treasure Cay
Marsh Harbour
THE ABACOS
N. ELEUTHERA (Harbour Island)
ELEUTHERA Governors Hbr
Rock Sound
NASSAU
San Andros
Andros Town
Mangrove Cay
ANDROS
CAT ISLAND
SAN SALVADOR
THE EXUMAS
George Town
Stella Maris
LONG ISLAND
CROOKED ISLAND
ACKLINS
MAYAGUANA
GREAT INAGUA
To Turks & Caicos
International Routes
Domestic Routes
Bahamasair
Fly with the airline that knows the Bahama Out Islands best. As the National Flag Carrier, our flights connect with all the Out Islands.
Book us today by calling (242) 377-5505 or (800) 222-4262
WE DON'T JUST FLY HERE, WE LIVE HERE!

Father Cornelius George O'Keeffe was first resident priest of the new St Francis Church.

Archbishop Michael Corrigan recruited Sisters of Charity and Benedictines to serve Catholics in Nassau.

St Francis Xavier Cathedral across the street had its beginning as St Francis Xavier Church. The cornerstone was laid August 25, 1885, on land bought from a Presbyterian minister. Ceremonies included placing a bottle containing items that would identify the place and period in an excavation under the cornerstone. Items encapsulated included an Agnus Dei – a figure of a lamb with a cross and banner symbolizing Christ, the most recent issue of *The Nassau Guardian*, some coins and a scroll which read:

"The Apostolic Catholics, commonly known as the Roman Catholics, assembled to lay the foundation of this little Church dedicated to St Francis Xavier. Although the Cross of Christianity was first planted on one of these Bahama Islands on its discovery by Christopher Columbus in AD 1492, this is the first Catholic church ever built in these islands.

"The members are few compared with other countries of the Globe. This edifice is being built by voluntary subscription, the Rev Father Charles[1] O'Keeffe being the principal donor."

Lightning strikes

During construction the following year, a furious lightning storm hit,

[1] *Correct name Cornelius, not Charles*

killing one workman and damaging the roof, walls and door. The church opened nine weeks later and the first mass was celebrated Nov 7, 1886, by Rev J A Ryan of New York. Father O'Keeffe, the resident priest, apparently migrated back and forth between Nassau and New York seasonally.

The church was officially dedicated in February 1887 when New York Archbishop Michael Corrigan celebrated high mass and named the church. Two years later Father O'Keeffe, citing overt prejudice against Catholics and lack of assistants and financial support, returned to New York for good and the doors of little St Francis Xavier Church were locked.

That same year Archbishop Corrigan attempted to secure some of the world's best missionaries for the small band of disappointed Catholics in Nassau. He recruited Sisters of Charity from Mount St Vincent-on-the-Hudson, NY, and Benedictine priests from St John's Abbey, MN. St Francis has flourished ever since and in 1960 was elevated to the status of Cathedral.

Coming back along the north side of West Hill you pass Sunningridge, on the western side of the steps leading down to Queen St. This was a magnificent old home with several roofs and a tower. Like most homes on that side of the street, it had three storeys on the street side and four storeys on the downhill northern side. The 1788 plot plan of Nassau indicates there was a building on the site currently occupied by Sunningridge.

Sunningridge, with its mahogany staircase and enclosed second and third floor verandas facing north, was one of the most attractive buildings along the historic street. From the top northern windows, a panoramic view of the harbour and ocean spreads out impressively.

In the late 1920s and early into the '30s, the house was occupied by the late Sir Harold Christie. It was later believed to have been owned or occupied by Swedish industrialist Axel Wenner-Gren. The American embassy used Sunningridge as a residence for a few years and it was more recently owned by the late attorney Julian Maynard.

Sunningridge and much of the rest of the north side of the street, including the convent and O'Donnell House, have since been acquired by Canadian developer Jeffrey Waterous. Sunningridge has been gutted and Waterous plans to restore it. The terraced courtyard contained a covered well, swimming pool and cottage, all of which have been lost to time.

Sir Harold Christie

Axel Wenner-Gren

House within a house

Next door is Ranora House, which is really a house within a house. The original three-storey edifice was built as the rectory for St Mary the Virgin (Anglican) Church on nearby Virginia St in the late 1860s. It was called St Mary's Villa. A cottage and guest house at the bottom of the garden served as a children's day school. The bishop held Sunday school and religious classes in the garden. When Rev William Lowndes became rector at the turn of the century, the rectory was considered too large so the church purchased a smaller one on Delancy St. It maintained the original villa and for many years it was rented out. Among the tenants was Capt Frederick Lobb of the Imperial Lighthouse Service. His daughter, Evelyn, started the Boy Scout movement in Nassau about 1912.

After World War I, the Anglican Church sold the house to Sir George and Lady Johnson. The church requested it retain some connection with the diocese, so the name St Mary's Villa remained until 1939, when Lady Johnson sold it to Mrs Cora Munson of the Munson Shipping Lines. Mrs Munson renamed it Ranora House, incorporating three letters of her husband's name and three of hers. Architect Frederic Soldwedel redesigned the home for Mrs Munson, adding the east and west wings and moving the main entrance from West Hill St to the eastern courtyard.

NASSAU UNDERWRITERS AGENCY LTD

NUA is the leading Bahamian insurance agency providing a complete range of expert professional services.

NUA has offices in Nassau and Freeport and representatives throughout the Family Islands.

THE PLAZA, MACKEY ST PO BOX N-4870	RIIBO PLAZA, McKENZIE ST PO BOX F-42211
(242) 393-3403	**(242) 352-2018**
(242) 393-3633 OR **393-3413** FAX (242) 393-8025 CABLES: BROKER	**(242) 352-2117** FAX (242) 352-5254

NUA FOR ALL YOUR INSURANCE NEEDS

REPRESENTING:

BAHAMAS FIRST
General Insurance Company Limited
A Bahamian-owned General Insurance Company

NASSAU SURVEY AGENCY LIMITED

LLOYD'S AGENCY

NASSAU, THE BAHAMAS

CLAIMS SETTLING AGENTS
MOTOR LOSS ADJUSTERS

PO BOX N-4870
Tel (242) 393-3403
Cables: "LLOYDS AGENT" Nassau

Eric Cottell owns and resides at Ranora House.

The house was later sold to Bethlehem Steel Corp, and it served as the temporary home in 1965 of the Royal Governor, Sir Ralph Grey, while Government House just half a block away was being renovated.

The current owners, Eric and Betty Cottell, who love the street, purchased the house in the early 1970s. The Cottells found an English granite tombstone in the garden with the name Bethel inscribed but have no idea whom it commemorates. They added their own elegant touches to an already highly elegant dwelling, retaining much of the grandeur of the original dwelling.

Among additions are four-foot long binoculars that came off a WWII German warship. Cottell mounted them on an upper balcony facing the harbour and looking through the lenses, he can clearly see people on a cruise boat entering Nassau Harbour a mile away. He also proudly displays an immense Austrian oven in one of the house's many parlours.

Sisters of Charity

East of Ranora House was the Sisters of Charity Academy and Convent. A month after the consecration of St Francis Xavier

ORBITEX® GROUP OF FUNDS

Invest In The Revolution℠

Today, the world is re-calibrating itself. Bringing about changes that make the future a bright and promising place.

As open information continues to tear down barriers Orbitex is there, looking throughout this new world for forward-thinking companies.

It's a classic opportunity. Right now.

Orbitex Strategic Natural Resources Fund

Orbitex Info-Tech and Communications Fund

Orbitex Asian High Yield Fund

Orbitex Asian Select Advisors Fund

Orbitex Growth Fund

Please enquire about our other funds.

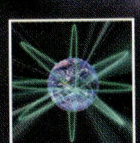

Why your clients should invest with Orbitex now:

- **Timely:** Deregulation is creating new competition, and the Internet is generating tremendous new growth opportunities.
- **Vision:** We call our technology view FutureNet℠. It's our belief that telecommunications, and especially networking, will drive global change.
- **Outstanding performance**

**Maritime House • Frederick St
PO Box N-9932 • Nassau, The Bahamas
Tel 242.356.6456/7 • Fax 242.356.5875**
For access to specialized investment opportunities, call 1.888.ORBITEX (1.888.672.4839) • http://orbitexusa.com

Please call for more information on the Orbitex Group of Funds, including a prospectus which details charges and expenses. There are special risks associated with international investing including currency fluctuations, economic conditions, and different government regulations and accounting standards, so please read the prospectus carefully before you invest or send money. There are additional risks to investing in funds that lack industry diversification. High-yield securities are generally subject to greater market fluctuation, and loss of income and principal, than investments in lower-yielding, higher-quality securities. Distributor: Funds Distributor Inc.

Make The Bahamas Your First Resort

A stable democracy. Laws that guarantee confidentiality in banking while preserving the integrity of the offshore sector. Proximity to the United States. A tax free environment. An educated, trained and capable work force. Excellent modern infrastructure.

These are only some of the ingredients which have created an appealing climate for over 400 banks and trust companies.

It's smart, safe and simple to do business here...and the climate continues to improve. Both the government and the private sector are committed to ensuring that regulations are simplified to accommodate today's investors.

For decades investors have placed us at the top of their list of hospitable business climates and we intend to stay there!

Democracy, stability and confidentiality are words you can bank on in The Bahamas.

For more information about The Bahamas call (242) 322-2193 or fax your business card or letterhead to (242) 322-4321.

The Bahamas
Stability and Integrity

THE CENTRAL BANK OF THE BAHAMAS

INTERNATIONAL FINANCIAL SERVICES... DESTINATION OF CHOICE...

THE BAHAMAS

A progressive business environment...
An established international business community...
The Bahamas is committed to being one of the world's most competitive international financial services centres.

The Bahamas provides an ideal climate for offshore investment. It is home to more than 400 banks and financial institutions from 36 countries. The country has adopted appropriate legislation and business friendly policies. And it provides excellent services including accounting, legal and a highly skilled workforce.

Bahamas Financial Services Board (BFSB) is a joint initiative of the Financial Services Sector and the Government of The Bahamas. An organisation of multiple financial service disciplines, we pool the resources and expertise of the enterprises and professionals of our country's financial services sector to promote and serve the industry.

BFSB's programs are supported by a strong relationship with the Government of The Bahamas, noted for its commitment to maintaining a policy and economic environment required for continued strong growth of the financial services industry.

For more information or a copy of our brochure, please contact:

Barry J. Malcolm, Executive Director
Bahamas Financial Services Board
P.O. Box N-1764
Nassau, Bahamas
TEL: 242-393-8777

BAHAMAS
FINANCIAL SERVICES BOARD

TO OUR OFFSHORE SPECIALISTS, NASSAU ISN'T JUST AN ISLAND.

IT'S INTERNATIONAL.

If you need help and advice on offshore Private Banking, Trust and Company Management Services, you don't need to go to the ends of the earth. Dedicated specialists in all these areas are based in Nassau. Being international means we bring an understanding of your specific requirements, and can apply our expertise quickly and efficiently. Call us now and you'll find all your international needs can be met in The Bahamas.

THE ROYAL BANK OF SCOTLAND
INTERNATIONAL

For further information call Matt McNeilly on (242) 322 4643.

THE ROYAL BANK OF SCOTLAND INTERNATIONAL IS REGISTERED AS A TRADING NAME OF THE ROYAL BANK OF SCOTLAND (NASSAU) LIMITED WITH THE REGISTRAR GENERAL'S DEPARTMENT, NASSAU, BAHAMAS. REGISTERED OFFICE: PO BOX N-3045, 3rd FLOOR, BAHAMAS FINANCIAL CENTRE, SHIRLEY & CHARLOTTE STREETS, NASSAU, BAHAMAS.

Church, the Hon Jacob Webb deeded a large piece of property on the north side of West Hill St to Archbishop Corrigan. Ten years later, in August 1897, the Archbishop handed over the property, which included the building immediately east of Ranora House, to the Sisters of Charity. The Sisters of Charity Convent was built for a paltry £300, according to the building contract in the original deeds. When the first five Sisters of Charity came, they taught school for about 150 pupils, only half a dozen of whom were Catholic. Into the early 1970s, some 21 nuns lived at the convent and taught in the Nassau Catholic school system. The western part of the convent was where the academy began.

The academy was the forerunner of Xavier's College on West Bay St. Today, the chapel remains. Reconstruction is underway on the whole complex, to be called West Hill Place. Plans include workshops for student artists and a small art gallery, some retail space, a restaurant with two dining rooms in what used to be the school, and an executive business centre in the old convent building.

Buried gold?

The O'Donnell House next to the convent was originally constructed around 1805, according to Sibilla O'Donnell-Clark, who lived there more than 30 years and has fond memories of the property.

"We knew it was old when we bought the house in 1959. It was probably built before the street even existed. We found an old Canadian newspaper dated 1810 in a wall. We peeled the paper off the wall but it fell apart. It used to be a pirate's house, so legend goes. It would have been ideal because from the upper floors you can see the lighthouse and the harbour entrance. The pirates could see a ship in trouble coming into the harbour. They would hurry down and plunder it. There was supposed to be gold buried in the gardens but we didn't find any of it. We did find a huge cannon ball that must weigh 100 lbs. I still have that."

She came to Nassau in 1959 with her husband, Columbus, and they stayed with her husband's mother, who owned Balcony House on nearby Market St. They bought the house on West Hill St and moved in the following year.

"The house had been owned since about 1910 by a Canadian named Dalley, as far as I know," says O'Donnell-Clark. "Apparently Paul Meeres, the legendary Bahamian dancer, used to perform there in the large drawing room."

Columbus O'Donnell and his wife, Sibilla, now O'Donnell-Clark, owned the West Hill premises where longtime friend Lord Mountbatten was a yearly house guest.

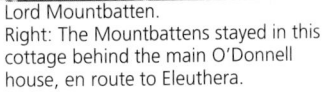

Lord Mountbatten.
Right: The Mountbattens stayed in this cottage behind the main O'Donnell house, en route to Eleuthera.

The latticed main house was built of horseflesh wood. It retains much of its early splendour, and there is an elegant guest house to the east and behind O'Donnell House. The O'Donnells were longtime friends of the Earl of Mountbatten and his family and the Mountbattens spent some time in the guest house every year for three decades on their way to Eleuthera, where they wintered at Windermere Island. Mountbatten's daughter, Countess Mountbatten of Burma, still visits O'Donnell-Clark. The property is currently leased by Waterous and serves as headquarters for his Nassau-based Mercantile Petroleum company. Waterous uses the guest house as his office and has renamed the property Mountbatten House.

The Fold, believed to have been built around 1840, and Corner House (1880) at Cumberland St across from Graycliff, are now one property and are undergoing extensive renovations. Corner House, with its broad wooden siding, steep shingled roof and thick coral walls, was once owned by a British Army captain named Meade.

Much of the north side of the street is currently covered with boarding and scaffolding. If the developer succeeds in his professed plan to restore authentically, West Hill St could ultimately return to its former grandeur, albeit without its former piety.

Early cave drawings believed to be Lucayan in origin.

New views on the Bahamian past

BY JULIAN GRANBERRY, PhD

Archaeologists have learned more about The Bahamas' first inhabitants in two decades than they did in two centuries.

Who says you can't change the past? In just two decades, new avenues into long-gone eras have been forged and the results for Bahamian archaeology have been little less than revolutionary. The years before 1492 – long a two-paragraph stopgap in history books – have begun to come alive. We have learned more in 20 years than we did in two centuries.

The instruments of this information renaissance have been the local citizenry – assisted by the Department of Archives, Bahamas Historical Society, Bahamas National Trust (BNT) and a number of other organizations – and at least a dozen professional and avocational archaeologists. With the help of training programmes, informational workshops and coverage by the local press, public perception of the Bahamian pre-Columbus past has gone from a matter of no concern to one of great interest.

Dr Julian Granberry at Lucayan Caverns, Grand Bahama.

It was, for instance, traditionally assumed The Bahamas' first inhabitants were Lucayan Indians who came to the islands rather late – some time between 1000 and 1200 AD – and that their point of origin was Hispaniola, the closest land mass to the south. They were thought to be an offshoot of the Taïno people of that island.

In 1982, however, a unique aboriginal site – probably a small shell-fishing and tool-making camp – was discovered on Paradise Island by participants in the Programme on Bahamian Prehistory and Archaeology, a series of workshops jointly sponsored by the Bahamas Historical Society, Department of Archives, College of The Bahamas (COB) and San Salvador field station. The site yielded copious quantities of an S-shaped shell tool, but pottery – a distinctive Lucayan material – was not present. Although the Lucayans did use shell to manufacture different kinds of tools, other

These finds place first settlement of the archipelago 700-900 years earlier than previously thought.

sites have not yielded the kind found in such great numbers on Paradise Island. These implements were identical to Cayo Redondo culture shell tools recovered from sites along the northeastern coast of Cuba, the latest of which have been dated to 300-400 AD.

Later in 1982, a similar site was found in Grand Bahama on a reef-protected beach cove like the one on Paradise Island. The Lucayans did not settle in this type of locale. As agriculturists, they preferred better land behind protective beach dunes.

Great implications

A tentative conclusion to be drawn from this small constellation of distinctive non-pottery sites with their unique shell implements is that they represent people who came to the islands before the Lucayans – a population that originated in northeast Cuba and arrived in The Bahamas well before 300-400 AD.

The implications are great, for these finds place first settlement of the archipelago 700-900 years earlier than previously thought. It also implies the presence of a pre- and non-Arawak people who did not practise farming as a way of life, but who relied on the sea as their major source of food.

Three duhos, Lucayan ceremonial stools, were found in a Long Island cave.

Erika Moultrie works Deadman's Reef, the Grand Bahama archaeological site.

In 1984 archaeologists Dr Mary Jane Berman and Dr Perry Gnivecki started excavation of a site in San Salvador known as Three Dog, where they found not only the usual Lucayan pottery – Palmetto ware – but two other largely unrelated pottery types. One of these at least has close affinities with the northeast coastal Cuban Arawak ware, Arroyo del Palo. The Arroyo del Palo site dates to 600-700 AD.

When Berman and Gnivecki sent materials from Three Dog for radiocarbon-dating, results gave a date of approximately 685 AD, 300-500 years earlier than any other known Lucayan site. Here, as in the case of Paradise Island, the most probable source of origin was not Hispaniola to the immediate south, but Cuba.

In 1992 William F Keegan, an archaeologist specializing in the Antilles and Lucayan archipelago, discovered the Coralie site on Grand Turk in the neighbouring Turks and Caicos Islands. The site yielded pottery of a very early style called Ostiones ware. Materials from Coralie have been radiocarbon-dated to 705-1170 AD, again significantly earlier than previously thought. Unlike the pottery at Three Dog, which most resembles Cuban ware, the Coralie Ostiones has its closest affinities with pottery from northern Hispaniola, south of Turks and Caicos.

Such pottery artefacts, which 20 years ago were lumped together as Palmetto ware, have now been separated into three major varieties: Crooked Island ware, of definite Hispaniolan origin; Abaco

Red ware, of likely Cuban origin; and Palmetto ware, a local creation combining characteristics of the other two. It became clear the Lucayan people had dual origins, and it is now believed The Bahamas and Turks and Caicos were initially settled either by non-Arawak people from Cuba some time around 300-400 AD – a hypothesis which demands more investigation – or by migrants from both Hispaniola and Cuba during the late 600s and early 700s AD.

Using a number of chemical techniques, careful examination of pottery pieces found on every Bahamian island indicates that although most were produced locally with native clay, some were trade ware brought from Cuba or Hispaniola. This is as true of the northern Bahamas as it is of the central and southern islands, indicating the presence of an ongoing trade network of considerable proportions – not only between the settlements on individual islands but also between The Bahamas and Cuba and Hispaniola. There have even been isolated finds of Florida-like trade goods in the Abacos. This reinforces Columbus's statement the Lucayans knew where Cuba was and led him there with ease.

After correlating the original Lucayan names for every island in The Bahamas and Turks and Caicos, I found these, too, indicate

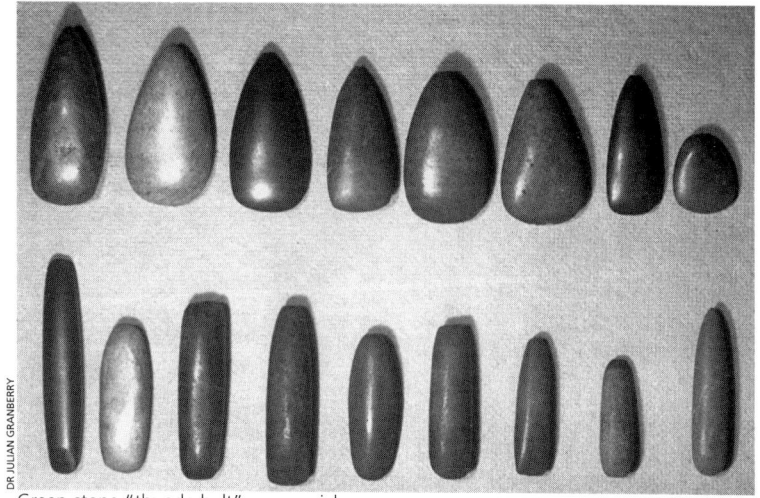

Green-stone "thunderbolt" ceremonial celts (axes) from Lucayan sites.

there were at least two migrations of Arawak-speaking people into The Bahamas: one from Cuba and the other from Hispaniola. Their fusion gave rise to the Lucayan people.

Major advancement

The second major advancement in our knowledge of the Lucayans is that we now know much more about their settlements. In 1960 only 61 sites had been found in the entire archipelago. In 1996 the Department of Archives listed a total of 501. The majority were discovered within the past 20 years, most in the 1980s by Keegan of the Florida Museum of Natural History and Stephen Mitchell of California State University.

Some islands, such as Grand Bahama, were said to be without any sites in 1960, yet today we know much of its southern coast was populated by a series of extremely large, linear villages spread along the coast behind the dunes.

It was previously thought Lucayans were mainly cave-dwellers, but we now know their villages were located in the open. Of the 501 sites found, only 111 are cave sites and they have been shown to be ceremonial in nature. So far they have yielded only evidence of formal burials and ceremonial paraphernalia, such as three spectacular duhos – stools of the ruling class – found in a cave site at Long Island. Grand Bahama boasts one of the archipelago's largest and most important ceremonial sites at the Lucayan Caverns in Lucayan National Park, where a combined burial and ceremonial function of considerable complexity is clearly evident.

The Lucayans' open-air villages were located on lands with coppice vegetation behind high dunes of leeward bays, with beaches a short distance across the dunes. The dune between the village and the sea is usually quite steep, and the village tends to spread lengthways for some distance – in some cases as much as $3/4$ of a mile – on prime land between the dune and marshy inland mangroves.

Since the early 1980s, many of these sites have been excavated by professional archaeologists under permit from the Department of Archives. In addition to Three Dog at San Salvador and Coralie at Grand Turk, among the more important sites are the huge Pigeon Creek site at San Salvador – perhaps the largest village site in The Bahamas – and the Deadman's Reef site on the south coast of Grand Bahama, where some 17,000 artefacts had been unearthed by the end of 1997. Extremely large village sites have been found on San Salvador, with a total of 45 known sites; the Abacos, also with a total of 45; Cat Island, with 32; Acklins Island, with 31, and on

---

DOCTORS HOSPITAL
1 9 8 6 ♥ L I M I T E D

HOSPITAL SERVICES
- ♥ INTENSIVE CARE UNIT
- ♥ OPERATING SUITE
- ♥ DELIVERY SUITE
- ♥ NEWBORN NURSERY
- ♥ RADIOLOGY
  - GENERAL X-RAY
  - ULTRASOUND
  - CAT SCAN
  - MRI
  - MAMMOGRAPHY
  - NUCLEAR MEDICINE
- ♥ RESPIRATORY THERAPY
- ♥ CARDIAC CATHETERIZATION
- ♥ PHYSICAL THERAPY (REHABILITATION)
- ♥ OUT PATIENT PHARMACY
- ♥ NUTRITIONAL COUNSELLING
- ♥ CLINICAL LABORATORY
- ♥ ELECTROENCEPHALOGRAPH (EEG)
- ♥ ELECTROCARDIOGRAM (ECG)
- ♥ CHILDBIRTH CLASSES
- ♥ CHAPEL
- ♥ 24-HOUR EMERGENCY SERVICES

DOCTORS HOSPITAL
PO BOX N-3018
COLLINS AVE & SHIRLEY ST
NASSAU, THE BAHAMAS
TEL (242) 322-8411 • TELEFAX (242) 322-3284

DOCTORS HOSPITAL
HEALING HANDS ♥ WE CARE

ALL THAT A HOSPITAL SHOULD BE

We bring the world

BaTelCo's range of products and services puts the world at your fingertips.

Leased Line Services/ International Business Services

For point-to-point communications from your business to The Bahamas, or from The Bahamas to your office, with speeds of 9.6 kbps up to 128 kbps.

Toll Free 1-242-300

Install a toll-free line at your business in Nassau or Freeport and make it convenient for your Family Island customers to reach you.

Paid 1-800

Available to subscribers in The Bahamas. Just dial 1-880 or 1-881 for easy access.

• Sales – Mall at Marathon (242) 394-5000 • JFK (242) 323-4911

to your business

Mobile Trunking
Motorola's newest generation of two-way trunked radios.

Cellular Services
Local and International

Bahamas Direct Prepaid Card
Saves you time and money at home and abroad

Phone Cards
Use in The Bahamas to make local and international calls.
Available in denominations of $5, $10 and $20.

The most modern phone system for your business
Let our friendly sales staff advise you on your requirements.

Get your feet wet with Batelnet
Batelco's internet service provider

Batelpage
Batelco's Domestic Flex Paging System

Gift Certificates
A great gift for someone special so that they may choose from a variety of our products.

Customer local area signaling service
Class from BaTelCo featuring Caller ID.

Coming soon
Frame Relay

BATELCO

We keep you in touch with the world

• Marketing (242) 328-0990 • Fax (242) 328-0966 • e-mail: bmrkt@batelnet.bs

Abaco Red ware found at Grand Bahama.

most of the larger Bahamian islands. The greatest concentration of village sites so far has been found on Long Island, which has 59 sites.

Ruling class

Information gathered from these sites points to a religiously, politically and socially sophisticated people whose customs – although related to the lands of their origin – were distinctly Bahamian. They indicate local customs developed in The Bahamas rather than being replicated from their Taïno cousins or other peoples further south in the Caribbean.

We know sites were clustered in groups, indicating a close political relationship between them and the likelihood of an accompanying elite or ruling class. One leader from this class is known from the records of Columbus and Fr Bartolomé de Las Casas to be Caonabó, or The Golden One. Though a Bahamian native, Caonabó became the cacique (king) of the Maguana Kingdom in neighbouring Hispaniola. On the basis of this information and the known distribution of Lucayan sites, it is probable the islands were politically divided into rulerships, perhaps akin to provinces.

Although we have considerable documentary information on the social, political and religious life of the people of Hispaniola, there is nothing for The Bahamas and Lucayans. It is consequently

These tools made from shells were found at Deadman's Reef, Grand Bahama.

dangerous to extrapolate from those Taíno sources and assume the same was true for the Lucayans. Undoubtedly there were wide similarities, but we must await further archaeological corroboration before a final, full-scale picture of Lucayan life can be painted.

Suffice it to say the Bahamian past has been extended by at least 500-700 years as a result of archaeological research of the past two decades. Where we previously thought The Bahamas had been settled in approximately 1200 AD, we now have a date no later than 700 AD, and if indications of an earlier non-Lucayan, non-agricultural, non-pottery-making population from Cuba are correct, perhaps as early as 300-400 AD – maybe even earlier.

Information gathered from these sites points to a religiously, politically and socially sophisticated people whose customs ... were distinctly Bahamian.

Lucayan origins have also become clearer. Our assumptions of a single, monolithic origin in Hispaniola have been replaced by the theory of a multiple origin in at least Hispaniola and Cuba, and there are intriguing hints of possible Puerto Rican and Virgin Island connections as well.

Even though our view of the Lucayan past has become much clearer, it is still partly clouded. There is much to be done before we can pinpoint exactly who the Lucayans were, how they worshipped and how their societies were organized. There is every indication, however, that the wheels of the archaeological time machine are whirring efficiently, and with new legislation in the pipeline toward protection, preservation and elucidation of the Lucayan past, that far horizon continues to be increasingly illuminated.

Dr Julian Granberry is a professional archaeologist and linguist specializing in Antillean and Lucayan archaeology and native American linguistics. He has degrees from Yale (BA), the University of Florida (MA), and the University of Buffalo (PhD). He is a Fellow of the Royal Geographical Society and has spent more than 50 years working on Bahamian prehistory. Granberry is currently a research archaeologist with R Christopher Goodwin & Associates, Inc, of Frederick, MD, as well as language coordinator for Native American Language Services, a firm specializing in preparation of practical language materials for native American tribal governments.

Family Islands

Newlyweds Charles and Doris Rahming pose with his mother, Rosemary Clarke.

An Out Island wedding

BY SUZANNE TWISTON-DAVIES

Take a step back in time to Moore's Island, Abaco.

"Mr and Mrs Neville Stuart and Mistress Rosemary Clarke request the honour of your presence as their children, Doris Stuart and Charles Rahming, are united in Holy Matrimony, Saturday, 25th of January at 1 o'clock at the Zion Baptist Church, Moore's Island, Abaco."

There was a time when getting married in the Abacos was a culturally unique experience. In Hope Town, for instance, "turning out" was a traditional part of the ceremony. This involved the groom calling on his bride at her home so they could walk to the church together. When the honeymoon was over, they would attend the first Sunday Service in their full wedding attire.

Now that the western world's white wedding has been adopted on a universal scale, even ceremonies in the smallest of Abaco settlements follow the tradition – albeit with a cultural twist.

Moore's Island (formerly More's Island) is one of the smallest inhabited isles in The Bahamas, its population 494 at the last census. This is where our bride, Doris Stuart, hails from. The tiny settlement is located near Castaway Cay (Gorda Cay) off the west coast of Abaco, which means First Island in the Lucayan Arawak language.

No one seems to know how the name Moore's came about, but there was a magistrate of this name in Abaco in the late 1700s. It is

Abaco

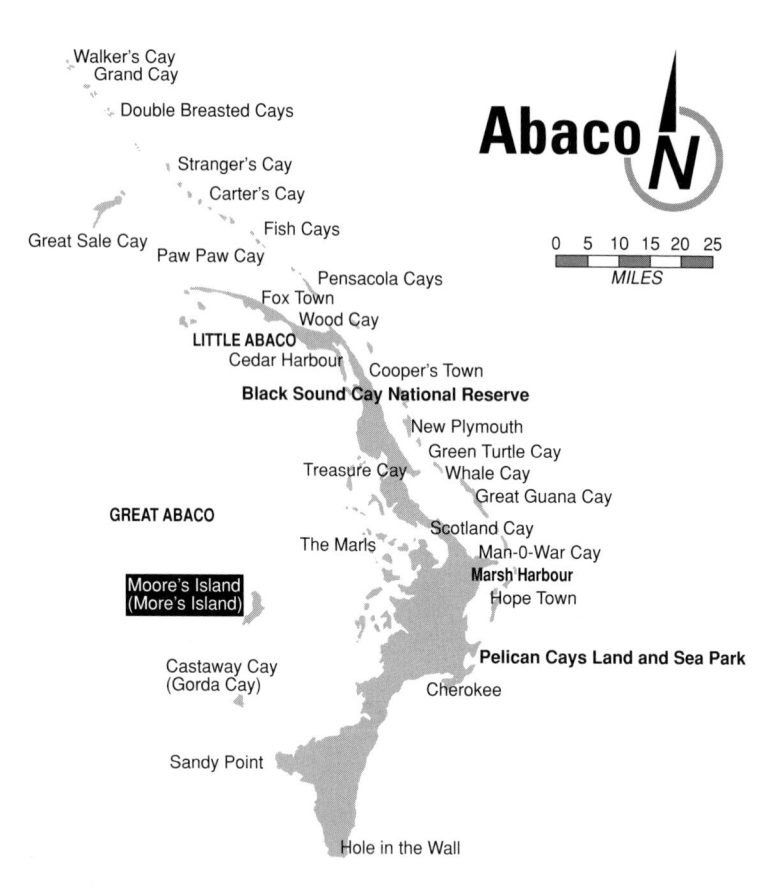

Walker's Cay
Grand Cay
Double Breasted Cays
Stranger's Cay
Carter's Cay
Great Sale Cay
Fish Cays
Paw Paw Cay
Pensacola Cays
Fox Town
Wood Cay
LITTLE ABACO
Cedar Harbour
Cooper's Town
Black Sound Cay National Reserve
New Plymouth
Green Turtle Cay
Treasure Cay
Whale Cay
Great Guana Cay
GREAT ABACO
Scotland Cay
The Marls
Man-O-War Cay
Marsh Harbour
Moore's Island (More's Island)
Hope Town
Castaway Cay (Gorda Cay)
Pelican Cays Land and Sea Park
Cherokee
Sandy Point
Hole in the Wall

0 5 10 15 20 25 MILES

thought his family or its freed slaves moved there. Exploring it now is like going back half a century.

The main source of income is fishing, although many young people are leaving for Freeport and Nassau to seek other forms of income. The water comes from wells with pumps that have to be turned on and off for showers and toilet-flushing. There are only a few small shops, and electricity and television came only recently. The houses are mostly bright and colourful – blue, yellow and pink-painted wood – some comprising just two or three rooms.

Meet the bride and groom

Doris is one of four daughters and five sons born to Neville and Loretta Stuart. Neville is a lobster fisherman, with some of his sons as crew, and Loretta runs a dry goods store. Doris left Moore's Island to study cosmetology at Grand Bahama's Industrial Training Centre,

If This Is Your Idea Of A Great Get-Away...

Have We Got News For You.

Call Us Today

Nassau Intl Airport
377-9000

Paradise Isl Airport
363-3095

Complimentary Pick-up Service

Budget®

All The Difference In The World.℠

An Independent Budget System Licensee

Purple and white balloons embellish the stark church as the couple exchanges vows.

and stayed on when she was offered a job as hairdresser at La Belle Beauty Salon, Xanadu Beach Resort and Marina.

The bridegroom, Charles Rahming, whose father died when he was young, lives with his mother in Hawksbill outside Freeport, Grand Bahama. Rosemary Clarke, his mother, is an attractive lady in her 40s who is sole breadwinner for her four children. She has been a housekeeper to the same family for 24 years. Rosemary is a devoted churchgoer and usher at a small church in Lewis Yard. Both her daughters are regular churchgoers, and one is married to a gospel singer.

> **"I took all my children to church every single Sunday. A child will not depart from it."**

"I took all my children to church every single Sunday. A child will not depart from it," she avers.

Charles, a nice-looking man of 25, is a security guard at the Rand Memorial Hospital. He is also a devout Christian, soft-spoken and polite. His ambition is to become a pastor, and he often stands up in church to preach the gospel from a chosen text, say a prayer or "minister" to the congregation. Apart from religion, one of his more absorbing interests is football.

On Friday nights after football practice, Charles would attend the youth meeting at his church. One evening, sitting in front of him,

Palm fronds form a backdrop for the bridal party.
The bridegroom's mother stands beside the bride.

was an unknown, petite young lady he thought he would like to know better. He shyly introduced himself, they talked and he found out her name was Doris. He asked if he could take her out.

The romance developed quickly and on Doris's 24th birthday, Charles proposed.

The excitement mounts

Their personal world filled with excitement, and Charles was to meet his future in-laws. He and Doris drove to McLean's Town, a coastal village at the east end of Grand Bahama, then her father, Neville, transported the couple to Moore's Island on his lobster boat. On the way, Charles lost face at fishing when he couldn't catch a single one, while his fiancée hauled them in hand over fist!

When they got there, Charles stayed in a neighbouring house. All discussions centred on who would be best man, bridesmaids, groomsmen ... and there were many to choose from in a society

The bride's parents, Mr and Mrs Neville Stuart, appear with the newylweds. Mr Stuart wears a blue suit. Mrs Stuart's hat, jacket, dress and shoes are pink.

overflowing with brothers and sisters, nephews and nieces.

Asked if he would give the bride away, her father made the memorable statement: "No, you give hogs away, not daughters!" So one of the bride's brothers was deputed in his place.

As the day drew closer, it was time for Charles's mother and her family and friends to make the trip to Abaco. When they reached the bride's home at 8pm, they received a great welcome. Doris's mother, used to feeding large numbers, produced a huge dinner of boil' fish and grits, home-made bread and johnny cake.

The day is here

Suddenly the day is here, and even more guests fly in from Freeport on Zig Zag Airlines. Despite its ominous name, the flight goes smoothly and the passengers get a good view of the island. Its highest point is 110 ft at the northern end, far higher than anywhere on Grand Bahama.

The Moore's Island airstrip, its surface somewhat resembling pockmarks on the face of the moon, is not any pilot's favourite place – though it is due for lengthening and re-surfacing. The passengers are slightly aghast to see there is no airport building. Even the Airport Inn is a long walk away. How are they to get to the wedding without a taxi? But small-island living is such that if a plane is seen to fly over, someone will catch a ride to the airstrip in hopes of securing a seat on the plane on its way back. Indeed here is Eustace

McBride dropping off a would-be passenger. With a huge grin and a truck, he offers to give the new arrivals a ride.

Eustace drops off a couple of guests for quick refreshments at his cousin's café in the village of Hard Bargain, so called, he thinks, because the first settlers found the water hard. Or more likely, hard to find! The Department of Archives in Nassau suggests it is because this was where early settlers met to bargain for produce.

The café is just up the road from the tiny harbour, and a few men are gathered on the quay to help a young fisherman unload his catch. He has been out since 8am, equipped only with bathing trunks and spear, and has returned with 40 large grouper that slither and glitter on the quayside. Not a bad catch for $4\frac{1}{2}$ hours' work.

Time to be seated

People collect outside the church, the women wearing huge hats and bright clothes with gold or silver accessories. Then it is time to be seated. Everyone knows the service must start promptly, since the pastor has another engagement and will not brook any feminine whims. Bahamian brides have been known to be up to $1\frac{1}{2}$ hours late.

The bridegroom seated in the front pew looks calm, though claims in a whisper to be a bundle of nerves. He is wearing a white dinner jacket. The best man and five groomsmen are wearing black dinner jackets, and look self-conscious holding large purple and white bouquets on their laps.

The only discordant note is that most of the groomsmen are chewing gum.

The silk flowers were arranged by Charles's sister, Yvonne, a professional florist. Real flowers would have suffered if flown in a small, hot plane.

The bouquets match the purple and white balloons festooned around the church to brighten its normally severe interior. The organist, Lavern Williams, plays *Oh, My Love*, and a brilliant blue sea glitters outside the church window.

Excited whispers give way to an expectant hush as the bridesmaids appear at the door in purple satin, off-the-shoulder dresses and long gloves. The groomsmen proceed slowly down the aisle, one by one, to meet their partners. The man bows, hands the young lady a bouquet, turns and escorts her to the chancel step, her hand

Charles smooches his bride at the schoolhouse reception.

gracefully perched on top of his. Their carefully rehearsed walk – left foot sliding forward, feet together, right foot forward, feet together – has become a traditional Bahamian wedding march, although it is not of historical significance.

The only discordant note is that most of the groomsmen are chewing gum, which somewhat takes away from the dignity of the occasion. "It's because they were frightened!" explains a bridesmaid later on. The ring-bearer is Charles's small nephew, Sean Meadows. Dressed in white satin tails, he walks solemnly up the aisle holding the ring cushion. Now the white carpet is rolled down, and the flower girl, Kerstella Simms – with an important frown – scatters purple petals ahead of her aunt, the bride, who appears in a stunning outfit on the arm of her brother. She looks serene and beautiful.

Pastor Knowles looks intently at the congregation over the top of his spectacles. "Charles, wilt thou take this woman to be thy lawful wedded wife ..." "Yes!" interrupts Charles. "Speak out, Charles," says the pastor mildly, "but not yet." He continues, "To have and to hold from this day forward, for better or for worse?" "I do," says Charles firmly. The congregation cheers and claps.

Towards the end of the ceremony, the pastor says, "Charles, you may kiss the bride, but don't take too long as I have a plane to catch!"

During the signing of the register, Opal Dawkins sings *There's A Place In My Heart For You Evermore*. "That's right, girl, hit that note, darlin'!" calls an approving voice from the back of the church.

Before the newlyweds make their way down the aisle, the pastor gives them a brief talk about marital duties. "Charles, you have promised to take Doris 'for better or for worse.' She might have a disaster. Do you realize you will have to be there and cherish her?" "Quite right! Quite right!" cries the congregation. They want to be sure this Freeporter won't let their girl down.

First walk together

Now Mr and Mrs Charles Rahming embark on their first walk together, proudly leading the bridal group to the church door. The cars are waiting and the newly-weds are driven to the island's other settlement, The Bight, for official photographs.

They are to be gone an hour, so the congregation winds its way slowly down the long road to the schoolhouse, where trestle tables are set up with white cloths, huge purple bows and purple sequins. Purple and white balloons bob jauntily in the breeze from the open door, and a huge white, tiered cake is admired by all the island's small boys who have suddenly appeared on the run. A dozen lady guests arrive carrying enormous hot dishes. Everybody pitches in to help at a Bahamian celebration.

As soon as the bridal party arrives, crawfish, steak, baked macaroni, peas 'n rice and more are produced to be consumed with many bottles of *Asti Spumante*. The guests fall to with alacrity, eating steadily through many speeches and toasts. These are variously grateful, moving, religious, reminiscent and amusing.

Then the bouquet is thrown, "arrested" in mid-air by a policewoman, Charles's cousin Coral Taylor. The garter is caught by Hubert Stuart, Charles's neighbour in Freeport. Traditionally, they should be the next people to find "a better half." Finally, the bride and groom stand up for their first dance together as man and wife.

The music is all quick-steps and fox-trots, as befits a gathering of people with old-fashioned values and a quaint attitude to life.

As they dance together, the newly-weds look lovingly into each other's eyes and all who watch feel like intruders on an intimate moment. Given their religious devotion and love for each other, it seems they are truly embarking on a happy and rewarding future together.

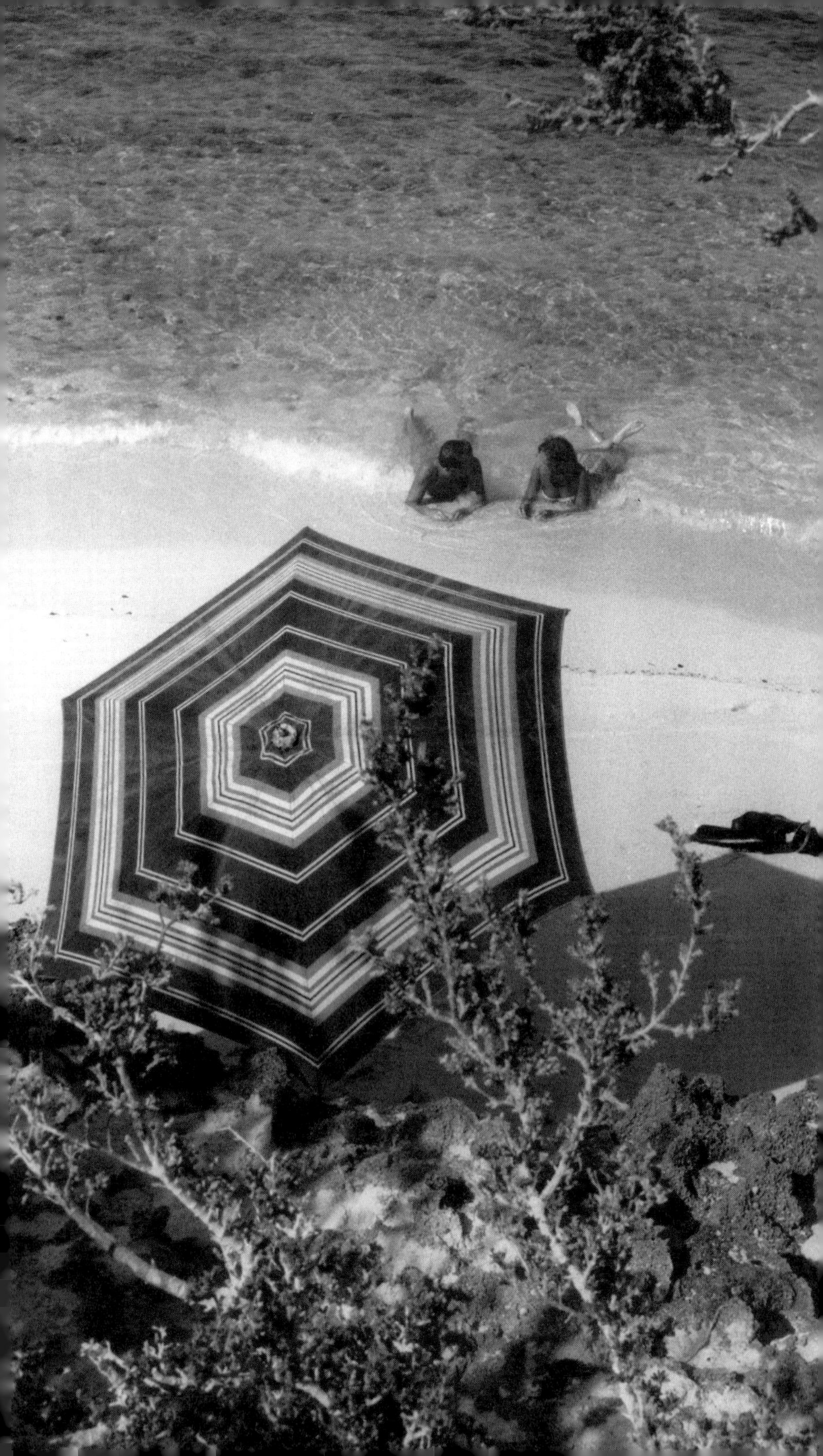

Eco-resorts link nature, fun, luxury

BY DIANE PHILLIPS

You don't have to rough it or forego the frills.

Strolling down the sands of Stocking Island with waves lapping gently at the shore of a pristine beach, it's hard to believe what lies before you is a resort classified as the premier ecotourism model in The Bahamas.

Where are the tents, poles and mosquitoes? Where are the sleeping bags and kerosene lanterns? What happened to roughing it?

Tropically classic one-storey cottages rise on the hillside. Large wooden verandas with crisply-painted white railings overlook a dazzling, aquamarine sea. A green and white striped awning that would not look out of place at the Ritz or Claridge's shields the main building's generous breakfast patio from the scorching sun. Brilliantly coloured flowers line winding stone paths.

Hotel Higgins Landing in the southeast Bahamas is a labour of love that pays heed and homage to its surroundings while proving eco-resorts are not about giving up luxury. You don't have to rough it to protect it.

Experts vary on their definition of an eco-resort, but certain principles are universally accepted. Among them: is the resort of a sustainable design with minimal if any external power supply? Does it use gray (laundry) water and recycle? Is it low-rise, low impact, environmentally friendly? Is the construction of natural materials? Are the cleaning agents biodegradable? Does it convert garbage into compost? Most importantly does it add more to the environmental and to the cultural experience than it takes away?

These are among the features *Islands* magazine staff looked for when they named Hotel Higgins Landing the best ecotourism resort in The Bahamas and one of the five best in the Caribbean.

"In six years of giving awards we have looked at hundreds of properties," said *Islands*, which in 1997 reviewed 39 entries from 23 islands. "The properties that stood out ... were the ones that made a difference on their island. They preserved an island's cultural or natural environment and they promoted tourism."

When Higgins Landing became the first Bahamas recipient of the award, the accompanying feature said, "On Stocking Island, a miniscule Bahamian Out Island with no roads or power and a population of just seven, Americans David and Carol Higgins have fashioned a small eco-resort that is a marvelous example of low-impact land and resource use."

The private, five-cottage mini-resort proves sensitivity to the environment can co-exist with visitor pleasure, blending love and preservation of surroundings with a vacation experience that is gentle, fulfilling and unforgettable – from its ambience to its gourmet food.

Islands magazine named Higgins Landing the best ecotourism resort in The Bahamas and one of the five best in the Caribbean.

David Higgins calls Stocking Island, where Higgins Landing is situated, a natural treasure.

Search for magic

The Higginses are in their mid-40s, retired engineers from the northwestern United States who worked for large companies: David as a civil engineer with nuclear power plants and Carol, among other projects, on the US SuperFund for the Environmental Protection Agency, where she saw "what horrors a simple municipal landfill could turn into."

When they set foot on Stocking Island, across picturesque Elizabeth Harbour from George Town, they knew they had found what they wanted.

"It was love at first sight," says Carol, using the only cliché she would utter all day. Trying to make their way up the hillside, she says, "the bush was so thick you couldn't see through it," so overgrown, they couldn't measure the elevation. But Carol was determined to pinpoint the exact spot for their future home. The year was 1992.

In the years since they visited the Caribbean and dreamed of returning, their sensitivity to the environment had sharpened. No longer did they just want to "find a place." They wanted to build a place that would respect its surroundings and resources. "We didn't come here as hard core environmentalists," confesses Carol, "but as we got more familiar with it, we began to understand and appreciate how fragile and special it is." Adds David, "Stocking Island is a natural treasure. It's pretty unique."

Absolutely crazy

The couple built their dream resort one step at a time using a single radial saw and one small concrete mixer "barged" across the harbour on two Boston Whalers rafted together. With their own hands – and the help of a few local workers – they fashioned the resort's five cottages, main hall and kitchen, utility buildings, dive shop, library and beach bar. They cleared the land by hand, carefully preserving indigenous trees and shrubs. They forged a narrow trail and refused to let anyone cut down a single tree. As they began to build, they hand-cracked stone.

"It took us three months to crack the stone and get the sand, carrying it up from the beach bucket by bucket," says Carol. "We

Thatched shade "umbrellas" dot Higgins Landing beach.

Greening efforts

According to Bahamas land planner and eco-buff Glenn Franklin, whose company Land Design of Nassau has been responsible for landscape design in many common areas, "When you build a resort, you shouldn't damage that land at all. You shouldn't even use a bulldozer," she says.

Franklin points to international award-winners like the eco-tents of St John at Maho Bay Camps, US Virgin Islands. The *Geo-Lite* eco-lodges generate their own electricity, recycle their own waste and store and pump their own water.

The Bahamas, she says, has a way to go, but greater sensitivity to the need for protecting the environment – the basis for attracting tourists – is leading to positive efforts.

Access to international markets, investor protection, integrity and efficiency are the hallmarks of any properly regulated and fully functional securities market.

SECURITIES COMMISSION OF THE BAHAMAS

Amid the increasing cost of capital formation and the challenges to traditional corporate relationships, businesses and investors are continually seeking new and innovative ways to lower costs and increase profitability.

By responding to the needs of investors, The Bahamas will enhance its position as one of the world's premier financial centres by providing new securities legislation, an independent regulator and a competitive full service international and domestic Securities Exchange.

The Bahamas is committed to enhancing its long-term competitiveness and growth in this global market.

To obtain more information about all aspects of securities and mutual funds in The Bahamas, contact:

Securities Commission of The Bahamas
PO Box N-8347 • Nassau, The Bahamas
Tel (242) 356-6291/2 • Fax (242) 356-7530
e-mail: secbd@batelnet.bs

MeesPierson's global trust network.

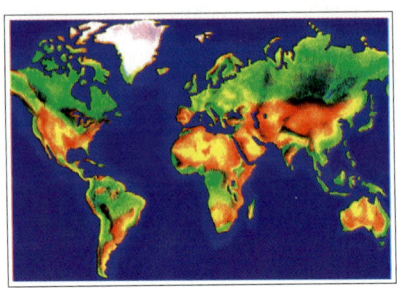

MeesPierson Trust, since 1720, offers a highly personalized level of service together with a long-standing experience and a dedicated commitment to its clients and professional advisors. It does so through a network of offices controlled through MeesPierson International AG, located in Zug, Switzerland, in both common and civil law offshore jurisdictions and financial centres.

In addition to a complete range of private banking, trustee and corporate management services (including protection, enhancement and management of assets), MeesPierson Trust provides highly specialized services to the owners of intellectual property, sportsmen and performing artists. To the international mutual funds and unit trust industry it provides comprehensive administration and trustee services. The MeesPierson global network services fund sponsors and managers by combining professional expertise with advanced administration and investment trading systems technology.

Through its parent company, MeesPierson, a leading continental European merchant bank with its main offices in the Netherlands, MeesPierson Trust is part of the Fortis Group, a substantial Dutch and Belgian international financial services group operating in the fields of banking, investment and insurance. **MeesPierson Trust**

Windermere House, 404 East Bay Street, P.O. Box SS-55-39 Nassau, Bahamas,
Tel: (242) 393-87 77, Fax: (242) 393-05 82.
Amsterdam, Antwerp, Aruba, Bahamas, Bermuda, British Virgin Islands, Budapest, Cayman Islands, Channel Islands, Curaçao, Dublin, Geneva, Hamburg, Hong Kong, Isle of Man, Liechtenstein, London, Luxembourg, New Brunswick, New York, Panama, Rotterdam, Singapore, St. Maarten, The Hague, Tokyo, Zug, Zurich.

THE ROAD TO THE NEW MARKET

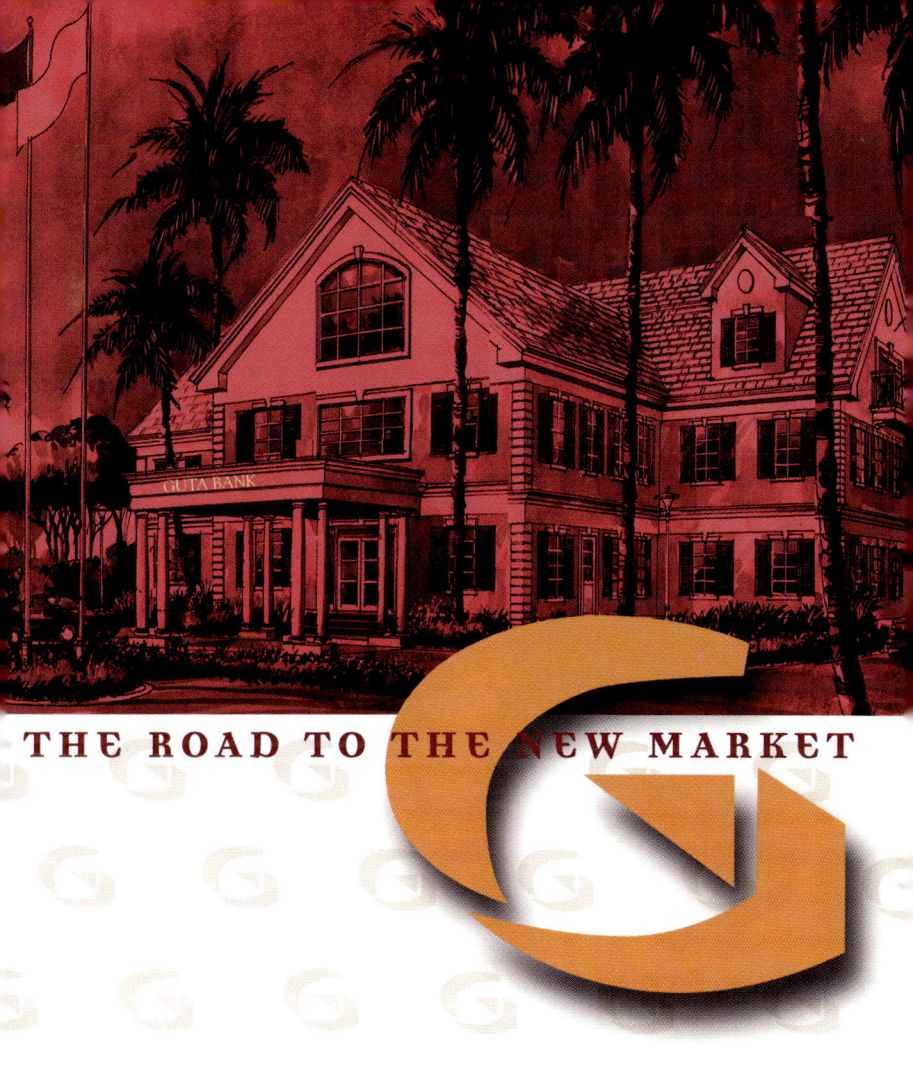

GUTA BANK
& TRUST LIMITED

PO Box N-7543, Centreville House
Collins Avenue, Nassau, NP, Bahamas
Tel (242) 356-7772 or 356-7773
Fax (242) 356-3914
e-mail: gbtl@bahamas.net.bs

The Bahamas
A Picture Perfect Opportunity

The Commonwealth of The Bahamas offers the perfect climate in which to conduct a wide range of business activities. One of the most stable political democracies in the western hemisphere, this strategically located archipelago – a mere 50 miles off the coast of the United States of America – provides excellent opportunities for the discerning investor and offers a safe harbour for corporate and personal assets.

A vibrant and mature international financial centre linked to every major market in the world, The Bahamas boasts over 400 banks and trust companies and handles an estimated $200 billion of Eurocurrency business. The full range of modern financial services thrive here, including private banking, company registration, captive insurance, ships registry, estate, portfolio and trust management and asset protection.

In addition to financial services, opportunities abound in The Bahamas in areas such as hotel and resort development, agro industry, fisheries, manufacturing, information and data processing services, and pharmaceutical.

Supported by the finest professional management, legal and accountancy infrastructure, The Bahamas government continues to enact legislation designed to simplify and streamline the processing of investment proposals and business registration. Freedom from taxes, proximity and access to major world markets, a trained workforce, political stability, security and economic opportunity are all realities of business in The Bahamas.

The Bahamas offers you a business environment in which doing business is easier and more profitable.

For more information about doing business in The Bahamas, please contact:

BAHAMAS INVESTMENT AUTHORITY
FINANCIAL SERVICES SECRETARIAT

CECIL WALLACE-WHITFIELD CENTRE
P.O. BOX CB-10980 • NASSAU, THE BAHAMAS
TELEPHONE: (242) 327-5970. TELEFAX: (242) 327-5907

didn't take any sand from above the high water mark. We were so picky the crew thought we were absolutely crazy."

During construction, David built a fabrication table using the top of an abandoned houseboat, placing in the middle of it the one sophisticated piece of equipment to be used on the job – a $300 radial arm saw from Sears. All the construction is post and beam, strong enough so that when Hurricane Lily swept through Exuma, the hotel withstood winds of over 120 miles an hour without damage. Leftover wood from the main buildings was used to build the beach bar. Rather than disturb the environment during construction, lumber that arrived on a 40 ft flatbed across the harbour was brought over by boat and walked up the hill. No vehicle was allowed to transgress the natural terrain and the Higginses have been in Exuma for six years without dreaming of owning a car. Transportation for them and their guests is by boat.

Almost everything becomes compost or is recycled. Biodegradable kitchen scraps like potato peels, coffee grounds and egg shells go into a bio-bin, considerably reducing garbage to put into a landfill. Everything is solar-powered. State-of-the-art compost toilets operate with a cup of water. Several cisterns collect 25,000 gallons of rainwater and the overflow is routed to a Kolaps-A-Tank under a deck, for watering the garden. Bright yellow allamandas creep up

Ecotourism and The Bahamas government

The Bahamas Ministry of Tourism takes ecotourism seriously, and has created a separate section within its Business Development Department devoted exclusively to eco- and sustainable tourism.

Angela Cleare, Director of Business Development, says the government views ecotourism as a vehicle to create employment and foreign exchange, while enhancing and maintaining the natural and cultural resources and heritage of the islands. Initiatives include Green Management Workshops and solar energy seminars for hoteliers and others involved in the hospitality industry.

The World Trade Organization (WTO) points out ecotourism is the fastest growing segment of the tourism industry. Mainstream tourism is increasing by four to five per cent annually, while eco-travel has been experiencing a 30 per cent annual growth.

"And within that framework," says Cleare, "birding (bird watching and identification) is overtaking golf as a tourism draw." (See *Birding in The Bahamas,* **Welcome Bahamas,** 1998.)

the wall of the building that houses a solar-powered laundry, the blooms fed by recycled water from the washing machine. The same water nurtures a vegetable garden where vines of fresh cherry tomatoes, greens, spices and peppers are harvested for guests. "From one inch of rain we can collect 3,000 gallons of water," says David. The mini-resort can survive up to six months without rain.

Despite its dedication to low environmental impact, there is a feeling of superb luxury and unmistakable quality about Hotel Higgins Landing, from the freshly-squeezed orange juice on the patio in the morning to the five-course meal in a dining room outfitted with oak antiques.

"Ecotourism doesn't exactly mean a campground with mosquitoes and no luxury," says David. "Sometimes the connotation is that eco means rustic, going without, but that doesn't have to be the case."

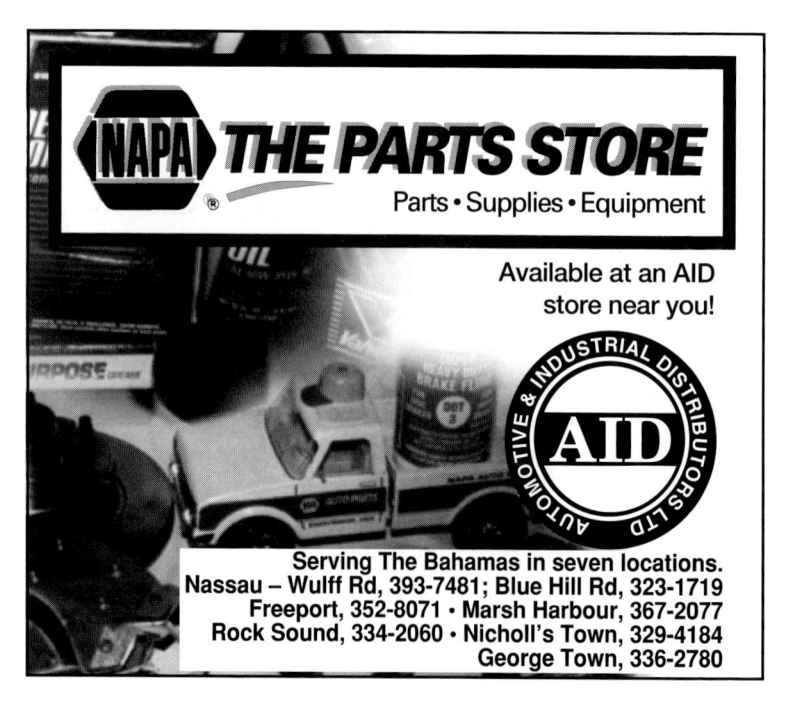

What the Higginses created is a model world of Family Island hospitality, where guests are treated to gourmet meals in a dining room furnished with Pennsylvania Dutch antiques and Oriental rugs, where often home-grown food is served by candle-light. In cottages with shutters and screens but no windows, natural breezes cool the air. Hot showers await. Hand-sewn quilts and pillow covers made by the Amish adorn traditional oak furniture.

Celebrities have stayed, so have members of royalty. Guests come from as far afield as Australia. By day they dive, swim, snorkel, sail, windsurf or just unwind. They go kayaking, take a pedal boat, wander well-marked nature trails or sunbathe on Sand Dollar Beach. At sundown, hors d'oeuvres are served in the casual beach bar. With no more than 10 guests at a time, there is never a feeling of being crowded and always an opportunity to make friends.

Netica's different

Former Bahamas National Trust (BNT) president Pericles Maillis says ecotourism is "not a mysterious thing." He describes it as "purposeful travel for exploring another place's historical, cultural and natural features."

This is what Netica's Different of Abaco tries to offer some 18 miles from Marsh Harbour. Created on a swampy area once considered so worthless it was used as the community dump, the nature resort has been called an environmental showcase.

TROPICAL BROKERAGE SERVICES LTD.

IMPORTS • EXPORTS

- Customs clearing
- Air & sea shipments
- International or domestic shipments
- Packing & crating
- Warehouse storages 40,000 sq ft

* OFFICE & HOUSEHOLD MOVING JOBS *

TEL **(242) 393-3524**, 393-0150,
393-6210 or 393-6218
AIRPORT (242) 377-8995
FAX (242) 393-0440 or 393-6342
PO BOX N-8294, SOLDIER RD

Netica Symonette's Different of Abaco consists of a bonefishing lodge, bird sanctuary, cultural village and beach club. Feathered friends appear to heed her voice.

Rich in foliage, mangroves and indigenous trees that make a natural habitat for birds and wildlife, the eco-resort is especially popular among birdwatchers. Telescopes on balconies have helped identify some 57 species of wild birds – including herons, coots, great hairy woodpeckers, bobtail quails and more. Donkeys, iguana, wild boar, geese, ducks, peacocks and flamingos roam the acreage.

Veteran hotelier Netica Symonette built the resort in three phases: the first an eight-room bonefishing lodge and bird sanctuary, the second a Bahamian cultural village, and the third, a beach club with 20 suites on a long stretch of pristine beach near Cherokee Sound, an area renowned for excellent bonefishing. A nature trail joins the Bahamian Heritage Village with the Seashell Beach Club.

Fourteen Lucayan huts complete with twin beds, hammocks and canoes replicate the way the first settlers lived in The Bahamas.

Sheer dedication

If protecting the environment satisfies part of the definition of an eco-resort, Small Hope Bay Lodge in Andros can be classified as such not so much because of its construction as its sheer dedication to education and preservation of the reefs.

satellite bahamas
We bring you the world on a dish!

HOME ALONE WITH YOUR FAVOURITE STARS!

Call us today for Home Entertainment Systems, quality Surround Sound Systems, including sales, service and installation. We also have 18" DSS systems and subscription packages.

393-4200

Top of the hill, Mackey St • e-mail satellite@bahamas.net.bs

POISED FOR THE 21ST CENTURY
BAHAMAS TECHNICAL & VOCATIONAL INSTITUTE
BTVI
BUILD • STRIVE • STRENGTHEN
...... AND BEYOND

The Bahamas technical and vocational institute

At BTVI we're building a skilled labour force

We offer a number of short courses, one year and two year programmes for which certificates are awarded.

Programmes
- Automotive trades
- Business equipment technician
- Barbering • Carpentry • Horticulture
- Computer troubleshooting & servicing
- Conch shell jewellery/souvenir manufacturing
- Office technology • Upholstery
- Drafting & blueprint reading • Welding
- Masonry • Plumbing • Electronics
- Painting & decorating • Tailoring
- Arts & crafts • Air conditioning & refrigeration
- Electrical installation, TV, radio & VCR repair

Mission ◄ ◄ ◄ ◄ ◄ ◄
To produce skilled individuals by providing quality technical and vocational training that will enable them to participate in national development.

Nassau Campus
Old Trail Rd
PO Box N-4934
Tel (242) 393-2804/5
Fax (242) 393-4005

Freeport Campus
Settlers Way & Peach Tree St
PO Box F-40477
Tel (242) 352-2190
Fax (242) 351-4028

Small Hope Bay Lodge at Andros caters primarily to divers.

Located near the world's third largest barrier reef, Small Hope Bay is primarily a dive resort, though bonefishing is available. Assistant manager Edison "Moose" Blackwell calls the resort that won the 1997 Bahamas Cacique Award for ecotourism "eco-sensitive."

While it isn't completely self-sufficient and doesn't supply its own power by solar energy, it does pay tribute to its heritage. Sitting on two acres of beachfront, the 17-cabin resort is decorated in locally produced Androsia cloth and straw work. Natural vegetation has been preserved. Bottles and cans are sent to Nassau for recycling. Only biodegradable cleaning agents are used.

The main thrust is protecting and teaching others to protect the reefs and marine life. Every Monday night a marine biologist shows slides to guests. Dive instructors like Harrington "Skeebo" Frasier inject humour into dive trips but add sensitivity. No spearing is allowed. Even the compressor for dive tanks uses food grade oil that would not adversely affect marine life if it were to spill.

Environmental conscience

In Nassau, the 150-room Comfort Suites is proof that larger, mass market resorts can operate with an environmental conscience.

While it cannot strictly be classified as an eco-resort, the hotel on Paradise Island is leading the way in energy management and recycling of resources. An energy management system operates throughout the property. A motion sensor in every guest room sends a message to turn off lights and air-conditioning if the room has

Glenn Franklin

Angela Cleare

been unoccupied 30 minutes. It saves wasted electricity and saves the hotel thousands of dollars a month.

"Forty-nine solar panels provide the bulk of hot water," says Comfort Suites general manager Jeremy MacVean, whose attention to the environment has earned him chairmanship of the Ministry of Tourism's Ecotourism Committee. "A 90,000-gallon rainwater system collects rainwater off the roof." The collected water, heated by solar power, is used in the hotel laundry. Low energy fluorescent bulbs are used in place of higher energy incandescent bulbs throughout the property.

"We're doing all forms of recycling," says MacVean. "We never throw away sheets or towels. We dye them a different colour and use them as rags. Sometimes we use them as drop cloths or if we have

Greening efforts

Among other resorts whose efforts at "greening" have been lauded by the Bahamas Ministry of Tourism are the Club Peace and Plenty, George Town, Exuma; Nassau's Orange Hill Beach Inn, Orange Hill; Dillet's Guest House, Chippingham; SuperClubs® Breezes Bahamas, Cable Beach; and Bay View Village, Paradise Island.

In a world full of changes, it's important to have things you can count on.

Harbour Bay Shopping Centre
Oakes Field Shopping Centre
Rosetta Street
Lyford Cay
Independence Shopping Centre
Market Street
Village Road
Cable Beach Shopping Centre
Seagrape Shopping Centre/Winton
South Beach Shopping Centre

Freeport/Downtown Shopping Centre
Lucaya/Seahorse Plaza
Eight Mile Rock

Administrative Headquarters:
East-West Highway, Nassau, The Bahamas
Tel (242) 393-2830 • Fax (242) 393-1232

CITY MARKETS
WHERE SHOPPING IS A PLEASURE
THE MEAT PEOPLE

WINN DIXIE
FREEPORT

**Food Stores
The Low Price Leaders.**

Jeremy MacVean, shown with solar heating panels at Comfort Suites, says a lot of what he does makes pure economic sense.

Environmental sensitivity can be good business. Profit and preservation are not enemies.

enough on hand for what we need at the moment, we donate them to a charity like the St Matthew's Church Home for the Aged."

The hotel was one of the first to replace individually wrapped soap bars in guest rooms with a refillable liquid soap dispenser that doubles as shampoo. Before that, they donated leftover soap pieces to the Salvation Army. "Now we have no wastage of soap and shampoo at all and no waste. It saves all those little plastic bottles going into the garbage." Clippings, garden cuttings and trash go into a compost heap and eventually into the ground to build up soil.

The hotel's efforts won it a 1997 Caribbean Hotel Association Infrastructure Award. "A lot of the stuff I'm doing," says MacVean, "makes pure economic sense in terms of minimizing use of energy with no adverse effect on our guests."

Like resorts in the Family Islands, Comfort Suites is learning that environmental sensitivity can be very good business. Profit and preservation are not enemies.

Business

Top: *Disney Magic* docks at Disney-owned Castaway Cay, formerly Gorda Cay, in the Abacos. The cruise liner also visits Nassau.
Bottom: Waterfields Company produces pure drinking water from seawater.

Economy shifts into high gear

BY GORDON LOMER

Broad range of proposals, plans and projects keep economic engine humming.

Foreign investment and confidence feeding on one another have sprung the Bahamian economic coil. Investment has bred confidence that stimulated more investment, creating an upward economic spiral.

Buoyed by a host of real estate, construction and government projects, the Bahamian economy has shifted into high gear. Infrastructure upgrading and major buildings, as well as corporate construction and residential developments, have fuelled the engine. (See *Confidence feeds construction boom*, pg 218, and *Out Island projects keeping pace*, pg 234.)

Moderate dips in tourism numbers caused by hotel room closures to make way for more tempered the boom, but confidence still permeates the business sector.

The impending establishment of the Bahamas Securities Exchange and accompanying domestic capital market and international and domestic stock exchange prompted several locally based companies to go public by offering common shares. Most were oversubscribed, and at press time some of the stocks had risen by more than 40 per cent in less than nine months.

The financial sector continues to thrive as evidenced by the increasing number of corporate office buildings mushrooming as headquarters for banks, trusts, securities brokerages and other financial institutions.

In a proactive joint venture between the private sector and government, the Bahamas Financial Services Board (BFSB) was formed in April and launched in July 1998. Its aim was to promote and create "a sense of excitement for The Bahamas' financial services sector globally," according to executive director Barry Malcolm. The board's diverse and growing membership includes representatives of government organizations, firms in banking, trusts, financial management, insurance, mutual funds, accountancy, law and investment consultants. Promotional tours involving private meetings with leading international legal, accounting and investment management firms have taken board members to Miami, Washington, New York, London and Geneva in 1998. Further global promotional trips are planned.

> "A sense of excitement for The Bahamas' financial services sector globally."

Broad financial sector

There are 418 licensed banks and trust companies from nearly 40 countries operating in The Bahamas. The Central Bank of The Bahamas supervises all banks and trust companies and is responsible for licensing and compliance.

Other elements in the offshore financial sector include captive insurance, international business companies and partnerships and mutual funds. In the four years to 1998, growth in the mutual fund sector has been nearly 25 per cent. There are now about 50 licensed administrators managing some 600 funds with assets of approximately $85 billion located principally outside The Bahamas.

The majority of offshore funds are denominated in United States dollars, but some funds trade in other foreign currencies including Swiss francs, German Deutschmarks and Euros.

The Bahamas has pioneered the fine tuning of the International Business Company (IBC), a confidential corporate flexible business structure that provides limited liability and a host of offshore advantages. There were 44,000 registered IBCs in The Bahamas in 1995. As of August 1, 1998, more than 80,000 IBCs had been created. Among the advantages of IBCs are that companies and their shareholders have a 20-year exemption from taxes, duties, licence fees and exchange control regulations.

The Bahamas has already earned a world-wide reputation as one of the globe's premier financial centres and tax havens. Tax advantages are the big drawing card for many foreign investors, including complete absence of income tax, inheritance and capital gains taxes, estate tax, succession tax and gift tax.

As a tax haven, The Bahamas offers many advantages including first grade legal and accounting services, flexibility, quality banking and financial services, proximity to world trade routes and markets, and an investor-friendly government.

At 25.532 million gross tons ... The Bahamas passed Greece for the first time.

The Bahamian shipping industry continues on an upswing and The Bahamas now stands in third place in terms of tonnage of registered vessels – behind Panama and Liberia. At 25.532 million gross tons, an increase of 4.6 per cent over 1996 figures, The Bahamas passed Greece for the first time.

The Bahamas Maritime Authority has opened an office in New York, and maintains a world-wide panel of nautical inspectors.

Major shipping firms which fly the Bahamian flag include Exxon International, Carnival Cruises, Teekay Shipping, Maersk Line, Holland-America Cruises, Disney Cruise Line and Chevron. One of the most active shipping companies in The Bahamas and a leader in cargo ship design, Dockendale Shipping, was to move into new headquarters in early 1999. Dockendale Shipping and Manx Ltd will share the five-storey Dockendale House & Manx Corporate Centre, on the site of the old Bahamian Club overlooking the entrance to Nasssau Harbour. Dockendale operates a fleet of 16 general purpose cargo ships around the world.

No 1 in cruise ships

A recently formed Bahamas Shipowners Association (BSA) boasts a membership of more than 300 companies representing about 800

Barry Malcolm

Livingstone Coakley

ships. Of more than 1,400 ships under Bahamian registry, about 50 per cent are tankers, general cargo vessels and cruise liners. The Bahamas, with some 50 passenger ships in the registry, ranks first in the world in that category.

New cruise ships which started stopovers in The Bahamas during the past year include Royal Caribbean's *Enchantment of the Seas* and Disney Cruise Line's *Disney Magic*. In 1999 Royal Caribbean will launch the world's largest liner, the 3,110-passenger *Voyager of the Seas*. Another Disney liner, *Disney Wonder*, is entering service in 1999. Cruise lines now own or lease at least five islands in The Bahamas, most of which have been converted to stopover playgrounds, including Little San Salvador and Gorda Cay, renamed Half Moon Cay and Castaway Cay respectively.

New water supply

Steady foreign investment in vacation or second homes, tourism and light industrial development signalled a positive growth in the Bahamian economy in 1997 and fuelled the boom in construction. On John F Kennedy Drive west of Nassau International Airport, a $12 million seawater reverse osmosis plant was opened early in 1998. The Waterfields Company plant can process and supply daily to the Water & Sewerage Corporation of The Bahamas some 2.5 million gallons of pure drinking water from seawater.

Growth was significant also in public sector investment, in airports, roads, schools, health clinics and the redevelopment of

CORPORATE BANKING WITH BARCLAYS

BUSINESSMASTER ... ELECTRONIC BANKING AT YOUR FINGERTIPS!

WITH **YOUR** PC AND **OUR** BUSINESSMASTER SOFTWARE YOU CAN NOW ACCESS BARCLAYS COMPUTER AND YOUR ACCOUNT ANYTIME, ANYWHERE!

- *Manage your business accounts via direct link with Barclays.*
- *Receive up-to-date balance and transaction reports.*
- *Order payments to any bank, anywhere in the world.*
- *Move funds between accounts even when the bank is closed.*
- *Secure, easy to use, easy to install and cheap to run.*
- *Electronic mail link with Barclays.*
- *Adaptable for large and small businesses.*

TO ARRANGE A PERSONAL DEMONSTRATION CALL KEN DONATHAN ON (242) 356-6163 TODAY!

BARCLAYS
WE SPEAK BUSINESS

Barclays Bank PLC
PO Box N-8350
Nassau, Bahamas

Predictions by Norman Solomon almost 20 years ago came to pass.

Nassau's Prince George Dock. Unemployment dipped below double digit figures for the first time in a decade, with the total labour force reaching almost 150,000, up from 143,000 in 1992.

> **Unemployment dipped below double digit figures.**

The Inter-American Development Bank (IDB) estimated the real Gross Domestic Product (GDP) grew by 3.5 per cent in 1997. At market prices GDP was estimated at $3.9 billion in 1997, up from $3.8 billion in '96. The per capita GDP grew marginally in 1997 to $13,891 from $13,429 in '96.

As one famous broadcaster used to say as he closed his nightly TV newscast: "And that's the way it was." But what of the future?

Back to the future

Nearly 20 years ago the **Bahamas Handbook** asked several prominent Bahamians and Bahamas residents their predictions for The Bahamas for the year 2000. The prognostications were dead on in some cases. In other cases, a little further into the future, perhaps.

Norman Solomon, for instance, predicted in 1982 that the Progressive Liberal Party "will have fallen long since. Its successor will have produced a superior performance, as a result of which the economy of the country will have taken a leap forward." The Free

Private Banking just keeps getting better in The Bahamas - because Private Banking is UBS

Accounts in our bank can be opened with a minimum of USD 200,000 - or equivalent in other assets. Please contact Marco Gallus or Gian F. Pinösch

UBS

UBS (Bahamas) Ltd.
UBS House, East Bay Street, PO Box N-7757, Nassau, The Bahamas
Phone (242) 394-9300, Fax (242) 394-9333

> "Never will there be the colossal dominance of one party over the other again."

National Movement (FNM) swept into power in the 1992 election and repeated with a larger majority in 1997.

Livingstone Coakley, former Minister of Education and Minister of Tourism, on the other hand, forecast a population of 400,000 (the official government estimate is 303,069) welcoming four million visitors annually. He also envisioned "a promising oil strike in the seabed between Bimini and Grand Bahama, with geologists forecasting recovery of 150,000 barrels a day for 25 years." He may have been a little ahead of his time. However, 16 years later Coakley says "oil is still a possibility."

By 2000, Coakley feels, the FNM will still be in power, although there will be considerable wrangling for leadership.

MB&H

McKINNEY, BANCROFT & HUGHES
COUNSEL AND ATTORNEYS-AT-LAW

Commercial litigation including tortious liability
• Corporate law including local companies and International Business Companies (IBCs) • Trusts • Admiralty law
• Personal injury • Banking • Real property • Conveyancing
• Divorce and matrimonial law • Labour law • Insurance • Probate
• Liquidation and bankruptcy • Trademarks, patents and copyrights

MEMBER OF LEX MUNDI, A GLOBAL ASSOCIATION OF 125 INDEPENDENT LAW FIRMS

Mavera House • 4 George St, PO Box N-3947 • Nassau, The Bahamas
Tel (242) 322-4195 (to 9) or 322-4214/5, Fax (242) 328-2520
Freeport office: PO Box F-40437, Freeport, Grand Bahama
Tel (242) 352-7425 (to 7) or 352-7434, Fax (242) 352-7214
e-mail: mcbanhu@bahamas.net.bs

Deltec Panamerica Trust Company Limited

(A subsidiary of Deltec International SA)

In today's complex world, discriminating investors require a personal and sophisticated service from their investment advisor.

For this reason, Deltec provides high quality financial services and will structure an investment portfolio to reflect the special needs of each client, from the most conservative, to the seasoned risk taker and always supported by detailed research and careful monitoring.

Deltec offers a wide range of investment management advice, trustee services, mutual fund management and administration, private banking and corporate services. Through its affiliated company in New York, Deltec Asset Management Corporation, it is able to closely monitor the major stock markets of the world and can seek out, for its clients, unique investment opportunities.

With fifty years of successful portfolio management and investment services, Deltec has experienced trust managers on hand to ensure that each client is guided from the very early stages, right through to the regular provision of prompt and efficient personal banking and trust service.

The New Accounts Officer
Deltec Panamerica Trust Company Limited
Deltec House, Lyford Cay
PO Box N-3229, Nassau, The Bahamas
Tel (242) 302-4100
Telex 20 101 • Cable: Pandeltec
Telefax (242) 362-4623

"Over the next 10 years you will see the PLP coming back. Never will there be the colossal dominance of one party over the other again.

"The next 25 years? I can't go that far. Tourism will still be the backbone of the economy and I can see increasing tourist traffic from South America and the Pacific Rim," predicts the former tourism minister.

Other views

In late 1998, the **Bahamas Handbook** again asked several prominent leaders and thinkers to envisage what the country would be like at the turn of the century, 12 years down the line (2010) and 25 years hence. Following is a sampling of what might be in store.

James Smith, Ambassador for Investment and Trade, sees The Bahamas 25 years from now with an ethnically diverse population of more than a million, among other things.

"Over the past 25 years since independence, The Bahamas has grown in national self-confidence; its major institutions in the public sector (health, education, welfare, defence) are controlled and operated by nationals. Many of the major private operations (retail,

---

PINDLING & CO
Attorneys at Law

Professional team of Bahamian lawyers specializing in a variety of legal and administrative services.

Our services include:
Incorporations and management of Bahamian and International Business Companies (IBCs)
Immigration (including Permanent Residence & Citizenship)
Real Estate Purchase and Development • Mortgages
Wills, Probate and Administration of Estates
Intellectual Property Registration and Protection
Commercial Litigation and Commercial Insolvency
Full Legal and Administrative Support
Entertainment Law

For further information please contact us at:

Nassau	Freeport
Wavecrest House, West Bay St	International Bldg
PO Box N-8174	West Mall & McKenzie St, PO Box F-44356
Nassau, NP, The Bahamas	Freeport, GB, The Bahamas
Tel (242) 325-3443	Tel (242) 351-2600
Fax (242) 325-2109	Fax (242) 352-5670

e-mail: pindling@bahamas.net.bs

DARIER HENTSCH
PRIVATE BANK & TRUST LTD

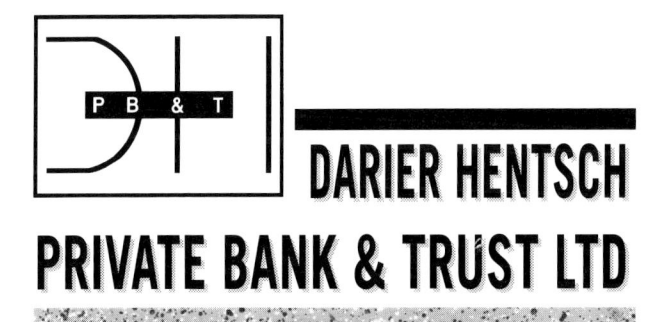

Affiliated with
- **Darier Hentsch & Cie, Geneva (Switzerland)**
  Private Banking since 1796

Offering a full range of international banking services.

Management and advisory services for international investments of individuals and institutions.

Darier Hentsch Private Bank & Trust Ltd
Charlotte House, Charlotte St
PO Box N-4938
Nassau, The Bahamas

Tel (242) 322-2721
Telefax (242) 326-6983
Telex NS20 382 Cable: DHPBT, NAS BAH

James Smith, Ambassador for Investment and Trade.

wholesale, financial services and parts of tourism) are owned and operated by Bahamians solely or in collaboration with foreign equity-partners.

"The Bahamas has demonstrated its ability to compete efficiently on many levels, particularly in services (managerial, accounting, marketing, information systems) and is now ready to expose those talents on regional and international stages.

> "One can expect the small and medium size businesses to branch outwards in the Caribbean."

"Over the next two to five years, one can expect the small and medium size businesses to branch outwards in the Caribbean seeking new opportunities and strategic business alliances (John Bull is already operating in Cuba) and a number of service providers in the financial industry are providing back office operations for Latin American and Caribbean based companies. Bahamian workers, via exchange programmes and short-term foreign attachments, are likely to become more cosmopolitan in outlook and consequently, more adaptive to the globalization processes now in vogue in virtually every developed country in the world.

"The long-term political stability of The Bahamas will continue to be attractive to inward direct investment. However, the rate of investment inflows will rise and fall in accordance with the country's cost of living index as compared with other competing nations in the hemisphere.

"In the longer term (25 years or more), The Bahamas, with a population of over a million people, will have joined the ranks of modern states as a small developed country. Its associations with hemispheric and global trading partners (WTO, NAFTA, FTAA) would have deepened to the extent that Bahamian nationals will be employed throughout the world. The country is likely to be multi-lingual (Spanish, French, because of the Haitian legacy, and English).

"Religious and cultural institutions will be faced with difficult challenges, having to compete with the increased secularization on the one hand, and an enlarged and ethnically diversified population on the other. In a word, The Bahamas, in 25 years, will take its place among the developed states of the world," predicts Smith.

Continuity, consistency, commitment

Ian D Fair, chairman of MeesPierson (Bahamas) Ltd and chairman

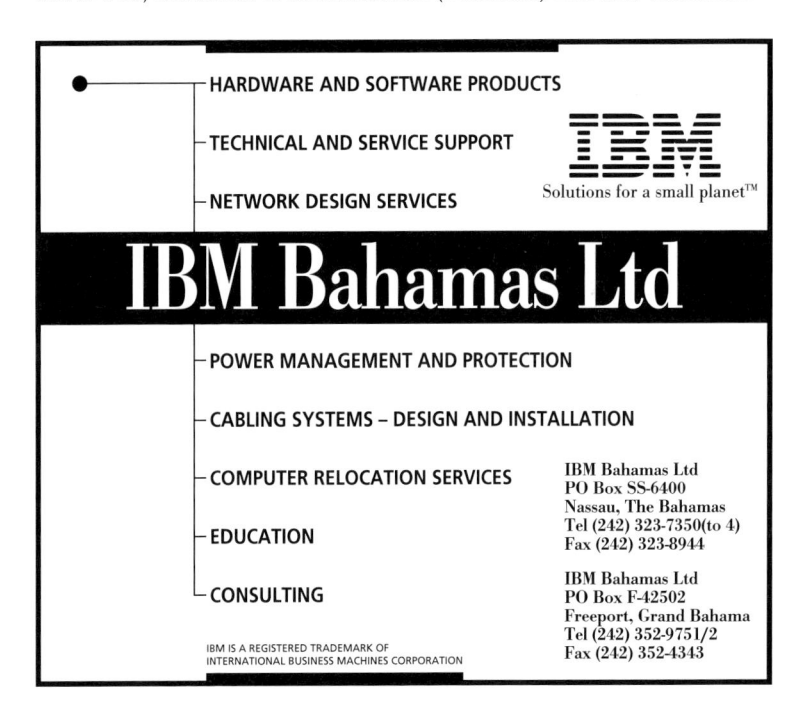

IBM Bahamas Ltd

- HARDWARE AND SOFTWARE PRODUCTS
- TECHNICAL AND SERVICE SUPPORT
- NETWORK DESIGN SERVICES

IBM — Solutions for a small planet™

- POWER MANAGEMENT AND PROTECTION
- CABLING SYSTEMS – DESIGN AND INSTALLATION
- COMPUTER RELOCATION SERVICES
- EDUCATION
- CONSULTING

IBM Bahamas Ltd
PO Box SS-6400
Nassau, The Bahamas
Tel (242) 323-7350(to 4)
Fax (242) 323-8944

IBM Bahamas Ltd
PO Box F-42502
Freeport, Grand Bahama
Tel (242) 352-9751/2
Fax (242) 352-4343

IBM IS A REGISTERED TRADEMARK OF INTERNATIONAL BUSINESS MACHINES CORPORATION

of the Bahamas Financial Services Board, was "very encouraged and optimistic for the future of The Bahamas. In the past six years we have re-established ourselves as a reputable and responsible member of the world community. Many investors, tourists and second home owners are attracted to our shores. We have a high level of educated and intelligent Bahamians who to a great extent want to return home after their studies and initial work experience; this differs sharply from many Caribbean and offshore locations. As compared to these other locations we need far fewer numbers of expatriate labour; this gives us a much higher level of continuity, consistency and commitment to our two major industries, tourism and financial services.

> **"For the first time in our history we have a focused and bipartisan approach."**

"In the financial services arena, for the first time in our history we have a focused and bipartisan (private and public sector) approach as a result of the newly formed Bahamas Financial Services Board.

OCEANIC
Bank and Trust Limited

- Private banking
- Investments
- Trust administration
- Corporate services
- Mutual fund administration

Established in The Bahamas in 1969 as Rawson Trust, Oceanic is the combined entity of Rawson Trust, New World Trustees and Oceanic Bank.

PO Box N-8220
Nassau, Bahamas

Tel 242-322-8822
Fax 242-328-7330

Ian D Fair

We are the only truly independent nation in the world providing these services. This gives us a huge advantage in the future provided we play our cards effectively and responsibly.

"The biggest challenges we face are finding effective long term solutions to the number of children born out of wedlock, the re-establishment of the family structure and values (which was a key foundation of our early development), education (continued and focused attention is needed), crime and unemployment. All these elements are inextricably linked – solve one or two and you go a long way to solving them all.

Crystal ball gazing
"Over the next two years I see a culmination of the early plans of the FNM Government as regards the repositioning of tourism, the development on Grand Bahama and financial services which will have a very positive effect on the pool of available employment.

"If we are less likely to be tempted to tinker or experiment with our jewels in the crown, we will treat them with the utmost care."

"Clearly 12 and 25 years are harder to predict and require a degree of crystal ball gazing. We do need to broaden our economic base, but not at the cost of doing anything to jeopardize our existing two major industries. There is really nothing wrong with a focused economic base. If we are less likely to be tempted to tinker or experiment with our jewels in the crown, we will treat them with the utmost care.

"Provided we face up to the challenges mentioned previously and develop lasting and effective solutions, I remain optimistic for our future," says Fair.

Mike Power, General Manager, Hutchison Whampoa, Container Port & Airport, likens Grand Bahama to a ship, and what is going on as her voyage. At the start of the next millennium, "my vision of

Surety Bank & Trust Co Ltd
The only private bank on Paradise Island

Offering:
asset protection trusts, international investments, custodial services and more ...

Suite 6
Hurricane Hole Plaza
Paradise Island, The Bahamas
PO Box SS-5857
Nassau, The Bahamas

Tel (242) 363-4276 • Fax (242) 363-4344 • e-mail: surety@batelnet.bs what we might see includes the Container Port about double its present size and handling the equivalent of nearly a million 20 ft containers a year.

"I believe you will also see a thriving cruise port with perhaps several thousand passengers moving between the airport and cruise port as they start and finish their cruise in Freeport from their homeported cruise ship.

"Perhaps you might also see the start of a large duty-free shopping complex, with factory outlet type shopping that is such a fast growing market in the region, with thousands of shoppers being fed from cruise ships, ferries, aircraft and perhaps even day trippers fed by 60 knot high speed ferry services we are working to attract to Grand Bahama.

"To one side of the harbour, you might be amazed to see a large cruise liner – lifted completely out of the water – with hundreds of people carrying out repairs and refurbishment.

"You will find the renewed Lucayan strip bustling with new visitors. And at the airport you could expect to see a much larger number of jet aircraft than we are used to, with many happy tourists moving through new and greatly improved facilities.

PRICEWATERHOUSECOOPERS

PricewaterhouseCoopers, Bahamas is one of the leading firms of accountants and management consultants in The Bahamas. The firm has expertise in the delivery of a wide range of services, including the following:
- Auditing
- Accounting
- Corporate Services, including the Formation and Maintenance of Companies
- Management and IT Consultancy
- Insolvency Services
- Business Advisory Services

Offices in Nassau and Freeport:

PO Box N-596 or N-3910
Providence House
East Hill St
Nassau, The Bahamas
Tel (242) 322-1061 or 322-8543
Fax (242) 326-7668 or 326-7308

PO Box F-42682
Suite A
Regent Centre East
Freeport, The Bahamas
Tel (242) 352-8471
Fax (242) 352-4810

"I envision many more Bahamian business ventures in operation, a whole new generation of Bahamian entrepreneurs having their first chance in business, and, just as important, real opportunities for Bahamian graduates in engineering, computer sciences and other technology related disciplines – outside just the hospitality and finance sectors of industry – to find themselves challenging, sustainable and rewarding long-term job opportunities within their own homeland, and without having to take their very real talent overseas.

"For me though, like all voyages in the past, I get my kick out of the fervent hope and belief that in future years, when people talk of the amazing voyage of Grand Bahama, I will be able to say with great pride: 'You know something, I was part of the crew.'"

John J Issa, chairman, SuperClubs® SuperInclusive® resorts, has always had an affection for the people of The Bahamas, "and my confidence in the people and their future has been such that all my investments in The Bahamas over the years have been long term investments.

"Should the people of The Commonwealth continue to live their lives as decent God-fearing people, the nation and its economy have nowhere to go but up."

KPMG

Chartered Accountants
- Audit & Related Services
- Corporate Finance Advisory Services
- Corporate Recovery & Insolvency
- Management Consulting
- Information Technology Services

Centreville House
Collins Avenue
PO Box N-123
Nassau, NP, The Bahamas
Tel 242 322 8551
Fax 242 326 5622

International Building
PO Box F-40025
Freeport, Grand Bahama
The Bahamas
Tel 242 352 9384
Fax 242 352 6862

Optimistic view

Nancy Kelly, who, with her husband, David, owns Kelly's Home Centre, one of Nassau's longest established retail businesses, was positive about the future of the country. "Of course, I'm an optimist. The future depends on a lot of things. We will have to be more on our toes and continue to provide better service because of increasing competition from Cuba.

"We've got to get crime under control, and maybe should consider bringing in foreign police. Our judicial system must be revamped, and the educational standards in the public school system improved.

"The family unit must be restored, and some way we must find a method of providing for the teaching of values. Education is the crux in establishing values and I would like to see Bahamians become much more community-minded.

"I would like to see more segments of the community represented in government. Not just lawyers, but a broad cross-section of Bahamian life.

"I think it will be a wonderful thing when BaTelCo and BEC go public. The government should not be in business, just as it shouldn't have been in the hotel business."

AN OFFSHORE OPPORTUNITY FOR THE HIGH NET WORTH INVESTOR

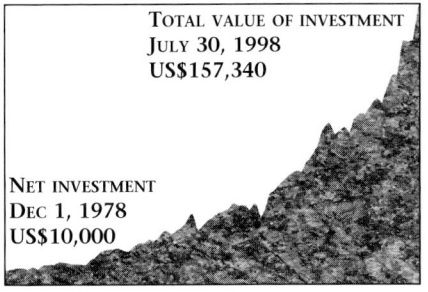

TOTAL VALUE OF INVESTMENT
JULY 30, 1998
US$157,340

NET INVESTMENT
DEC 1, 1978
US$10,000

Past performance is not necessarily a guide to future performance. Share value can go down as well as up.

For more current information, a copy of the explanatory memorandum and our brochure, contact your offshore financial advisor or Robert Lotmore at Best Funds Distributors Inc.

Best Funds Distributors Inc
PO Box N-3242, Nassau, Bahamas
Tel (242) 393-8622 or 394-0522
Fax (242) 393-3772 or 394-0523
E-mail: bestfund@batelnet.bs • Website: www.bestint.com

BEST

John Issa

"The duty structure should be re-examined. A revamped duty structure would encourage more Bahamians to be in the retail sector. I worry about the business of getting into Caribbean and other free trade organizations. We just can't do it and remain income tax free.

"I'm also concerned about the advantages the government allows the hotels. They are taking care of the hotels. They can't let foreigners get their way completely. We need the foreigners, there's no question about that, but the government is giving them a lot of freeway.

"I'm very optimistic about the future. I think The Bahamas is in a good position to go anywhere it wants, and it can go great places," says Kelly.

Cuba watch

Fred A Hazlewood, president, John Bull Ltd, warns of the emergence of Cuba: "Tourism is the clock that makes us tick, and although there are circumstances beyond our control, we must be

> *In asset management your interests, along with ours, have always been parallel.*
>
> *The results honor us both.*

For portfolio management and other banking services to the international investor:

NORDFINANZ BANK ZURICH
NASSAU BRANCH

The Valuable Relationship

Norfolk House, Frederick Street, P.O. Box N-7529, Nassau, Bahamas
Telephone (242) 32-33347, Telex 20-277 nfzn, Telefax (242) 32-82177
Head Office: Zurich, Switzerland
Subsidiary of the Swiss Private Banking Group
UNION BANCAIRE PRIVÉE, Geneva

HANDELSFINANZ-CCF BANK INTERNATIONAL LTD

Member of group **CCF**

WHERE YOU WILL RECEIVE A HIGH DEGREE OF SERVICE AND CAREFUL ATTENTION

**Maritime House • Frederick Street
Post Office Box N-10441
Telephone (242) 328-8644/328-1737
Telefax (242) 328-8600
Telex 20623 HANFIN
NASSAU, THE BAHAMAS**

A wholly owned subsidiary of
CREDIT COMMERCIAL DE FRANCE–PARIS

Henry Ansbacher

Ansbacher in the Bahamas

The Henry Ansbacher Group is a well established merchant and offshore banking organisation with a proud tradition of providing quality financial services tailored to meet the needs of its corporate and personal clients around the world.

Ansbacher (Bahamas) Limited specialises in the provision of trustee and executorship services, corporate and investment management, offshore banking, pension services, mutual funds and registrar and transfer services. For further information please contact:

The Managing Director
Ansbacher (Bahamas) Limited
PO Box N-7768
Ansbacher House
Bank Lane
Nassau
Bahamas
Telephone +1 242 322 1161
Facsimile +1 242 326 5020
E-mail ansbbah@batelnet.bs

Ansbacher (Bahamas) Limited

A member of the First National Bank of Southern Africa Group

In The Bahamas since 1805 and as one of the world's largest and strongest Insurance Groups, we can take care of your personal and commercial insurance needs.

Call us and we will put you in touch with one of our agents

Nassau
328-7888

Freeport
352-4564

ROYAL & SUNALLIANCE

Nancy Kelly

extremely aware that when the US drops its embargo against Cuba, this one monumental decision will be severely felt in The Bahamas.

"It does not take much for a cruise ship to change its compass reading when it is leaving Florida! It does not take much for private yachtsmen to alter their itineraries. Travel agents will be positioned to be able to offer a new destination in the Caribbean which combines the qualities of mountains, rivers, lakes, beaches, sun and excellent hotel facilities, plus being extremely inexpensive.

"It will be like pulling a plug in a sink of water as visitors flock to see the old/new Cuba. As I once read, Havana is now a Latinized Paris by the sea! Uncle Sam's going to very soon reconcile with Cuba as he has done with China and this decision will affect The Bahamas dramatically. It will also be felt, in varied degrees of less significance, from Disney World to Trinidad."

The Bahamas' stock market

BY ERICA WELLS

Skeptics wonder, 'Are we ready?' But the success of recent initial public offerings speaks for itself.

The Bahamas is joining First World markets with a stock exchange which could be the key financial engine for economic growth and income distribution.

Expected to be in place by 1999, The Bahamas Stock Exchange will be equipped with state-of-the-art technology, strict regulations and a nine-member Securities Commission of The Bahamas, formerly known as the Securities Board, to monitor the industry.

In 1969 Bahamas Supermarkets became the first company in The Bahamas to make an equity public offering. At press time, 13 companies were trading shares with a market capital of around $1.6 billion – and each of them was oversubscribed in the initial offering. The fact that other companies are now formulating initial public offerings, with at least one public utility company in the process of being privatized, means the figure could jump to $5 billion within the next five years.

Without the stock market, investors have limited investment options, which means trading practically stops once shares are bought.

"If you have a surplus of funds or savings, you are limited in terms of what you can do with it," said Larry Gibson, market analyst and

Sandra Knowles and T Baswell Donaldson of the Securities Commission of The Bahamas discuss ongoing developments of the stock exchange.

former head of the Securities Task Force. The only options available to Bahamians without the exchange include real estate, where most Bahamians are already overdiversified; bank deposits, which can yield low returns; and government bonds, he added.

"With the lack of investment alternatives, people tend to buy stock and put it under a mattress, or just hold it," said Gibson.

Why a stock market now?

According to experts, a securities market is particularly attractive to The Bahamas in the current economic climate for its potential to:
- Provide a means for efficient movement of domestic savings.
- Provide savers with an alternative investment option.
- Make prices of financial services drop.

Compelling reasons to establish the exchange now, Minister of Finance William Allen pointed out, include the vibrancy of the offshore sector, its growing mutual funds industry and the potential for market-makers among The Bahamas' large number of highly respected financial institutions.

They can take advantage of offshore benefits of tax planning.

Julian Francis, Governor of the Central Bank of The Bahamas, says the existence of the stock exchange provides more opportunities for new businesses to be created. Investments provide businesses with money for start up and development – money which may not be available otherwise. Often, banks are unwilling to offer start up loans for new businesses because of the uncertainty involved. The stock market provides more room for risk and more money for business. Ultimately, the stock market produces a faster movement of currency which results in a faster moving economy.

"It creates an environment in which business is able to grow and develop more readily ... " Francis said. "The more business that develops, the more jobs that are created ... The fundamental issue here is the extent to which money moves around in the economy."

International Portfolio Analytics Ltd

Mutual Funds

Brokerage Services

Banking & Trust Services

Financial Advisory Service

Pension Fund Management

Norfolk House • Suite 300 • Frederick St
PO Box CB-12407 • Nassau, The Bahamas
Tel (242) 356-7371 • Fax (242) 356-7375
URL: http://www.ipa. • E-mail: ipa@offshore.bs

International Trade & Investments Limited

Comprehensive Offshore Services

Since 1990 we have been providing discreet and personal offshore financial management services to discerning clients, large and small.

For individual attention to your special needs come and talk to us or visit our website at: **www.itiltd.com**

Marlborough House, Third floor,
Cumberland St, PO Box N-1201,
Nassau, The Bahamas.
Tel (242) 356-2036 • Fax (242) 356-2037
Toll-free from the US or Canada:
1 (800) 370-8921
e-mail: itiltd@itiltd.com

IBC formations • Tax-free investments
Asset Protection

"Nobody does it better"

Global links

A unique feature of The Bahamas Stock Exchange is its separate listing and trading of domestic and international issues. The Bahamas' domestic exchange promises to have a healthy listing of approximately 25 companies within its first two years of operation. At least initially, foreigners will not be allowed to trade on the domestic exchange. Sandra Knowles, executive director for the Securities Commission of The Bahamas, says locking out foreign investors from the domestic exchange protects local businesses and investors from an imbalance in foreign ownership. This regulation protects against the money being withdrawn by foreign investors – a move which can be damaging to the economy, said Francis.

"When you open up the economy to the influx of foreign currency, you really have to know what you're doing," said Francis, adding that a smaller economy is much more vulnerable when dealing with large pools of money.

While local markets will remain attractive to Bahamas residents, foreign markets may not. Residents would have to apply for investment dollars at a 25 per cent premium, hindering them from

---

Dupuch & Turnquest & Co
founded in 1948

Counsel & Attorneys-at-Law, Notaries Public

Full range of legal services including:
- Company incorporation
- Maintenance & management
- Banking law
- Bank formation & services
- Conveyancing matters • Trusts
- Probate & administration of estates
- Civil litigation • Labour law
- Admiralty matters
- Licences & permits • Contracts
- Immigration matters • Family law
- Misc services, eg notarizations & authentications

Bank America House, 308 East Bay St
PO Box N-8181 • Nassau, NP, The Bahamas
Tel (242) 393-3226/9 • Fax (242) 393-6807

Chancery House, The Mall
PO Box F-42578 • Freeport, GB, The Bahamas
Tel (242) 352-8134/5 • Fax (242) 352-5687

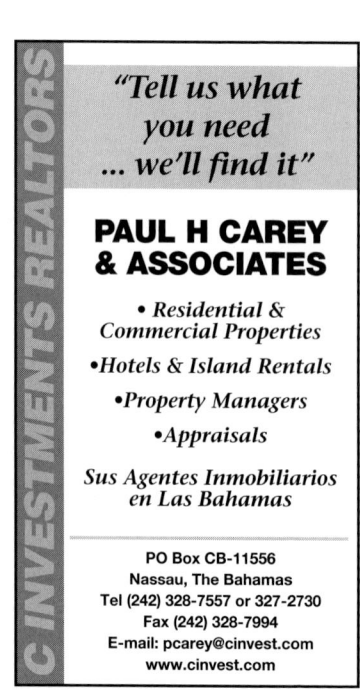

"Tell us what you need ... we'll find it"

PAUL H CAREY & ASSOCIATES

- Residential & Commercial Properties
- Hotels & Island Rentals
- Property Managers
- Appraisals

Sus Agentes Inmobiliarios en Las Bahamas

PO Box CB-11556
Nassau, The Bahamas
Tel (242) 328-7557 or 327-2730
Fax (242) 328-7994
E-mail: pcarey@cinvest.com
www.cinvest.com

UEB
UNITED EUROPEAN BANK
Subsidiary of Banque Nationale de Paris and Dresdner Bank Groups

International Private Banking and Corporate Services with the highest level of expertise and in the best Swiss tradition.

- Offshore company formation and management
- Trust services
- Investment management
- Custodian services
- Estate planning

**UNITED EUROPEAN BANK & TRUST (NASSAU) LIMITED
NASSAU**

Subsidiary of United European Bank Geneva, Switzerland
Apsley House, 75 Frederick St, PO Box N-4915, Nassau, The Bahamas
Tel (242) 322-4456, Fax (242) 326-2280

GENEVA • LUGANO • ZURICH • MONTEVIDEO • NICOSIA • SAO PAULO • LUXEMBURG • MONACO • NASSAU

CHRISTIE, DAVIS & CO.
established 1973

(Incorporating the former partnership of Christie, Ingraham & Co.)
COUNSEL AND ATTORNEYS-AT-LAW • NOTARIES PUBLIC
Perry G Christie; Philip E Davis
Nassau chambers associates: Philip McKenzie, LL B (Hons);
Simone Fitzcharles, BA, LL B (Hons); Ian D Cargill, BA, BA Law (Hons);
Jewel G L Major, BA
Freeport chambers associate: R Wallace Allen

Specializing in:
- Companies, including formation of companies
- Banking and trusts • Land/property transactions
- Industrial relations • Personal injuries
- Criminal and civil litigation

Over 40 years' experience

NASSAU CHAMBERS	FREEPORT CHAMBERS
Del-Bern House, 11 Victoria Ave,	Bank of The Bahamas Bldg,
PO Box N-7940	Woodstock St & Bank Ln, PO Box F-2343
Nassau, The Bahamas	Freeport, Grand Bahama, The Bahamas
Tel (242) 322-2715 (to 8) • Fax (242) 326-7360	Tel (242) 352-8311 • Fax (242) 352-4458

investing in foreign markets. The premium applies to all foreign capital investments for Bahamas residents.

Foreign investors will be attracted to the Bahamas Stock Exchange because they can take advantage of offshore benefits of tax-planning and receive confidentiality and privacy. The Bahamas' reputation as a tax haven with a thriving offshore sector is expected to attract listings for large numbers of international companies – at press time, numerous applications had been received from companies in North and South America.

"The Bahamas provides easier access to those investors whose offshore industry normally could not be tapped by their domestic market," said Owen Bethel, president of Montaque Securities International.

In order to stay internationally competitive, it is expected The Bahamas' investment rate will be kept lower than New York's. Combined with other positives, European and Asian investors are expected to show interest because of the time zone – the same as New York's. When markets are closed in Europe and Asia, the stock exchange is still open for trading in The Bahamas.

If The Bahamas follows the advice of financial analyst Reece Chipman, the exchange will list blue chip companies – large companies with high market attraction – to establish credibility and attract major players from around the globe. Knowles confirms this is the plan, saying medium to large companies will increase confidence in the stock exchange, especially when growth becomes apparent.

Regulatory structure

Steps have been taken to establish strategic links with major international depositories such as CEDEL and EUROCLEAR, which provide global custody clearing and settlement systems. In September 1996, The Bahamas was admitted as a full member of the International Organization of Securities Commission (IOSCO), the umbrella organization for securities market regulators worldwide.

On the domestic level, the exchange is regulated by the Securities Commission in accordance with the Securities Industry Act. It is incorporated as a limited liability company and has the status of a self-regulatory organization with necessary powers to fulfil its role.

According to Knowles, the Securities Commission provides a balance between protecting investors and bolstering their confidence in the market to foster capital growth.

Island Business Centre

...serving all of your offshore business and financial needs.

PREMIER BUSINESS CENTRE
IBC Express Package
Re-invoicing
Bahamas Bank Account
Equipped office for client use

CORPORATE ACCOUNTS OFFICE
Bill Paying
Accounting
Bookkeeping

24hr LIVE ANSWERING & FAX SERVICE
Direct lines
Message centres
24hr fax (send or receive)
live operators
7 days a week, 24hrs a day

POSTAL SERVICES
Bahamas Business Address
Receive and send mail
Priority/UPS/FEDEX
Mail forwarding (anywhere)
Mail report (call us or we'll call you!)

Island Business Centre offers you the opportunity to operate in or relocate your corporate headquarters to the ISLANDS OF THE BAHAMAS. Allow us to incorporate your company in an International Premier Financial Destination.

Euro Canadian Centre, 2nd fl, Marlborough St & Navy Lion Rd
PO Box SS-19197 ste 1001 • Nassau, Bahamas
Tel (242) 356-9301/2, fax (242) 328-8187
E-mail: RDCL@batelnet.bs or chipman@ibcinvestments.com
www.ibcinvestments.com • www.investbahamas.com

It also further enhances The Bahamas' reputation as a major offshore financial jurisdiction by providing registration of the securities exchanges. Clearing and settlement departments, custody services, member firms, stockbrokers, dealers and traders will be registered and tracked.

"The registration serves a number of important functions. First, it tells everyone in the world who is allowed to operate in the market. Second, it reassures investors, that the company or individual they are dealing with meets the industry's fit and proper standards," said Knowles. She added the stock exchange allows for a "price discovery," which lets the investor know what the company is actually doing. Member companies must submit reports quarterly, making all information open for public scrutiny.

Other functions include:
- Maintaining surveillance over the securities market to ensure fair and equitable dealings.
- Formulating principles to regulate and govern the mutual funds industry.
- Creating and promoting conditions to foster orderly growth and development of capital markets.
- Meeting requirements of the Securities Industry Act and other written laws.

Objectives of the Securities Industry Act include:
- Providing, regulating and maintaining facilities for conducting business.
- Upholding rules and regulations governing member companies, stockholders and trading.
- Promoting orderly development and interests of the securities market.
- Developing rules governing listing/delisting of securities.

Vaughn L. Culmer & Associates
INSURANCE AGENTS & BROKERS LTD.
Providing All Classes Of Insurance

- Automobile
- Marine
- Homeowners
- Commercial
- Group & Individual Major
- Medical
- Life
- Pension
- Wellness Programmes
- Third Party Administrators

#7 Rosetta St (four doors east of Hawkins Hill) • PO Box N-4456, Nassau, The Bahamas
Tel (242) 356-0159 • Fax (242) 356-0169

AMEE International was general project consultant/manager for recent renovations of the entire premises of Coutts (Bahamas) Ltd on Cable Beach.

Design Projects
From Concept Through Completion

- *Planning*
- *Interior Design*
- *Architecture*
- *Engineering*
- *Construction Management*
- *Product Supply & Installation*

- *Office & Residential*
- *Hospitals*
- *Shopping Centres*
- *Hotels & Motels*
- *Education Facilities*
- *Industrial Structures*

AMEE INTERNATIONAL

3 Village Rd
PO Box N-8688
Nassau, The Bahamas
Tel (242) 393-1605
Fax (242) 393-2963

The Britannia Consulting Group

"Legitimate, compliant offshore investment structures for prudent onshore investors"

Tax and wealth planning structures using

- annuities
- life insurance
- captive insurance
- limited partnerships
- limited liability companies

"Invest offshore & sleep at night!"

Hywel L Jones
President and Managing Director

Trade Winds Bldg, 3rd floor
Bay St, PO Box CB-12724
Nassau, The Bahamas
tel (242) 326-5205
fax (242) 326-5349
e-mail: britannia@batelnet.bs
www.bahamasnet.com/britannia

- Regulating conduct of investors transacting business.
- Ensuring compliance with rules of the exchange.
- Monitoring activities of member firms.

Caribbean links

In March 1996, The Bahamas and four Caribbean countries signed an agreement with the National Association of Securities Dealers Automated Quotation System (NASDAQ), providing for a Central Securities Depository (CSD) in each country that will automate, clear, settle and guarantee trades.

> "The debate will not be whether or not we were ready for it, but what took us so long."

An electronic trading system, common to all five members, will eventually link the exchanges to act as one unit. This sets the stage for The Bahamas' entry into a regional exchange. The electronic system means brokers would log onto a main computer, enter, buy and sell lists and execute orders as they come in, rather than buy and sell on the shop floor.

Compared to other exchanges in the region, such as the Cayman Islands, Jamaica, Trinidad and Tobago – The Bahamas' exchange will be smaller, but not for long, said Francis.

"Our exchange may be smaller than our regional partners' initially, but I think we will become bigger very quickly because our economy is larger ... per capita," he said.

Is The Bahamas ready?

While skeptics ask if The Bahamas is ready for a stock exchange, the success of initial public offerings suggests it is. There have been more offerings in the last two years than in the previous 10, each enjoying phenomenal victory.

An example is Abaco Markets, primarily engaged in the wholesale and retail sale of groceries, which set a record for The Bahamas in October 1997 when its offering was oversubscribed by more than 100 per cent.

"We are very excited at the opportunities presented by entering this new era, not only as Abaco Markets, but as the country, itself, gears up towards the future stock exchange," Reginald Sands, Abaco

Markets' director, said at the company's initial offering. In April 1998, the company paid out its first dividends at 8.5 cents a share to nearly 1,000 shareholders.

However, the point has been raised that levels of expertise and service required in a stock exchange system are incompatible with The Bahamas' experience in offshore financial services.

"The skills and culture of professional participants in a stock market are quite different from the financial industry culture that has prospered in The Bahamas to date," said Allan D Grody, president of New York-based Financial InterGroup and advisor to a Bahamian-based company dealing with offshore investors.

"The current Bahamian financial community performs a relatively passive activity, obtaining clients and generating fees for administering accounts … The securities market professional, on the other hand, performs a proactive activity, risking one's capital to provide both the product (securities) and the liquidity for those securities in the secondary market," he said.

Efforts to foster a deeper understanding of securities and securities markets have been made since plans for a stock exchange were first announced in 1995, both by the Securities Commission and by private companies. Companies offering intensive courses in securities training have begun to spring up, and Fidelity Bank and Trust (Bahamas) Ltd has launched FINDEX, a stock market barometer, to measure the exchange's performance for investors, potential investors and other interested parties.

Grody said, "Preparing a country for a stock exchange, especially in The Bahamas where a securities market culture does not yet exist, is a formidable undertaking. Doing it right is more critical to creating an enduring marketplace than doing it quickly."

The last word, though must go to Gibson. "We should have had a stock exchange five to 10 years ago … Within two years of having the exchange the debate will not be whether or not we were ready for it, but what took us so long."

GOMEZ & NAIRN   RSM
International

Chartered Accountants and Consultants

We offer:

Consulting • Corporate services
General accounting • Auditing

Worldwide services through
RSM International

90 Sumerset House
Thompson Boulevard
PO Box SS-5212
Nassau, The Bahamas
Tel (242) 356-4114
Fax (242) 356-4125
E-mail: gomezassociates@batelnet.bs

CHASE

The Chase Manhattan Private Bank
and Trust Company (Bahamas) Limited
PO Box N-3708
Nassau, The Bahamas
Tel (242) 356-1300
Fax (242) 325-1706 or 326-5513

A true private bank is one that makes you wonder if you're the only client

To us, each client is unique and each portfolio is different. At Pictet, Switzerland's leading private bankers, you will find a privileged and stable partner in your portfolio manager. Your relations are based on trust. You share decisions in a climate of confidentiality. To the extent that you might ask us whether you're our only client. Nothing could please us more.

Pictet Bank and Trust Limited
Twenty years of private banking in Nassau

PICTET
1805

Geneva • London • Luxembourg • Montreal • Nassau • Singapore • Tokyo • Zurich

For further information, please contact Yves Lourdin, Pictet Bank and Trust Limited,
Charlotte House, PO Box N-4837, Nassau, The Bahamas
Tel (242) 322-3938/9 or 323-7172 • Fax (242) 323-7986 • Telex 20 308 • www.pictet.com

Three Bahamian corporate entities

BY PETER G FLETCHER, ATTORNEY-AT-LAW, JEROME E PYFROM & CO

IBCs, regular companies and exempted limited partnerships.

According to the *Offshore Financial Centres* handbook, the test of a good offshore jurisdiction incorporates several factors – including political, social and economic stability, adequate economic opportunities and ease of communication.

In The Bahamas, there is all this and more. Consider the following:
- Strong legislation which keeps pace with the ever-changing needs of the marketplace.
- The continued absence of taxes and exchange controls for non-residents.
- Banking secrecy in an era where it is being eroded in such traditional jurisdictions as Switzerland and Liechtenstein.
- Sophisticated banking and trust services.
- A competent, experienced infrastructure of well-known service providers in accountancy, law, consultancy, computers and translation.
- An abundance of investment incentive programmes and tax concessions.

It's no wonder more and more of the world's investors are choosing to do business in The Bahamas.

The first step in any transaction is usually to set up a vehicle for conducting business. In The Bahamas, there are three main entities to choose from: international business companies (IBC), "regular" companies formed under the Companies Act 1992, and exempted limited partnerships (ELP).

International business companies

The IBC is a corporate vehicle designed with the offshore investor in mind. Incorporated under the International Business Companies Act, 1989, it has become one of the mainstays of The Bahamas' offshore financial industry. More than 80,000 IBCs had been registered as of August 1998 and continue to be incorporated at a rate of 15,000 every year. Key characteristics of the IBC include:

Flexibility
The IBC can be used for any number of different purposes:
- As anonymous vehicles to hold bank accounts or brokerage accounts in The Bahamas and elsewhere.
- To own real estate in jurisdictions other than The Bahamas.

Delivering the Caribbean to the World

DHL delivers documents, packages and cargo to more than 225 countries and territories.

Fast, reliable, safe and secure.

Our air express network is the world's most extensive, backed by a team that treats your business as if it were their own.

DHL WORLDWIDE EXPRESS®

Your Name In Good Hands.

157 Nassau St, PO Box 3735, Nassau, Bahamas • Ph (242) 325-8266 • Fax (242) 325-7814
6D Kipling Bldg, PO Box F-42513, Freeport, Bahamas • Ph (242) 352-6415 • Fax (242) 352-6413

- To collect royalties and commissions arising from international transactions.
- As vehicles in The Bahamas' multi-billion dollar offshore mutual fund business.

If there is an international transaction, no matter how simple or complex, the chances are a Bahamian IBC is ideal for the job.

Privacy

IBCs are not required by law to publicly file details of the identities of officers, directors or shareholders, or to file any financial statements. If a member of the public knows the name of a particular IBC and visits the Registrar of Companies, only standard documentation will be found. No information about ownership or control of the company is available unless the company voluntarily files it.

> The IBC ... has become one of the mainstays of The Bahamas' offshore financial industry.

Cardinal International was formed in 1994 as an international financial services company offering responsive, accurate, technically strong and cost competitive services to the financial community. It has expanded to a full service financial group offering Banking, Custody, Trust, Private Banking, Fund Administration and Brokerage Services. Assets under administration exceed $2 billion.

Cardinal
INTERNATIONAL

The Cardinal International Group

Cardinal International Bank & Trust Company Ltd.
- regulated by the Central Bank of the Bahamas and carries an unrestricted bank and trust license.

Cardinal International Corporation Limited
- regulated by The Securities Board and holds an unrestricted license under the Mutual Fund Act 1995.

Cardinal International (Dublin)
- serving European clients in their own time zone.

Cardinal International Securities Limited
- seeking membership of the Bahamas Stock Exchange.

Nassau Office:
Stephen Hancock
Wendy Warren
Norfolk House, 3rd Floor
Frederick Street
P. O. Box N 3935, Nassau, Bahamas
Telephone: (242)356 6326
Faxes: (242) 356 6328/6630
E-mail: Cardinal@offshore.bs

Dublin Office:
Angus Stewart
Graham Margot
Glendenning House
6/8 Wicklow Street, Dublin 2
Telephone: (3531) 6798199
Faxes: (3531) 678455
E-mail: eire@cardinal-int.demon.co.uk

Shares
Shares in IBCs can be "registered," ie, issued to a named person or company, or issued to "bearer," which means the person who holds the shares is entitled to exercise the privileges of a shareholder.

No taxes/exchange control
The Bahamas has no income, inheritance, wealth or capital gains tax, which means IBCs are also tax free. Even if taxes are introduced in The Bahamas at a later date, the IBC remains tax free for 20 years from its creation. IBCs are also exempt from exchange controls, with no approvals required for them to establish and operate Bahamian bank accounts.

Local management
Every Bahamian company must have a registered agent in The Bahamas, usually attorneys, accountants or a financial institution. There is considerable range in the cost of such services, so the offshore investor is well advised to shop around.

Costs
Bahamian IBCs with minimal authorized capital can usually be established for less than $1,500. In these cases, ongoing maintenance fees on a calendar year basis are usually in the range of $750 – which includes an annual government registration fee of $250.

Prohibitions
As IBCs are specifically prohibited from conducting business with Bahamas residents, they are not appropriate vehicles for setting up operating companies in The Bahamas or purchasing real property here. The Act expressly permits an IBC to engage local attorneys and accountants to represent the company and to establish bank and brokerage accounts in The Bahamas.

Regular companies
Another type of Bahamian company incorporated under the Companies Act, 1992, is commonly referred to as a regular company. In April 1998, 44,500 were in existence.

BAHAMAS FIRST

General Insurance Company Limited

Third Terrace & Collins Avenue

PO Box N-1216

Nassau, The Bahamas

Telephone (242) 326-5439

Fax (242) 326-5472

A BAHAMIAN-OWNED GENERAL INSURANCE COMPANY

"INSURING A BETTER BAHAMAS"

Nature of business
Regular companies are used to conduct everyday business in The Bahamas, renting premises and hiring local employees. They are often used to take title to real estate here – which explains why so many have names such as Beach Properties Ltd, Seaview Holdings Ltd and Sunset Ltd.

Reporting requirements
Although companies incorporated under the Companies Act face greater reporting requirements than IBCs, such requirements are still not as demanding as those for companies incorporated onshore. Regular companies must file annual returns that disclose the identity of officers, directors and shareholders. While they cannot issue shares to bearer, they can issue shares to a nominee in trust for the real beneficial owner – with approval from the Exchange Control Department – which prevents members of the public from obtaining information on ownership.

DOMINION INVESTMENTS LTD

- Full service investment dealer • Investment management
- Offshore mutual funds • Asset protection
- International tax planning
- Company management

CONTACT
M MARTIN TREMBLAY, CA
TEL (242) 326-4528
FAX (242) 326-4721

BAHAMAS FINANCIAL CENTRE
SHIRLEY & CHARLOTTE STS
PO BOX SS-6827
NASSAU, THE BAHAMAS

Officers and directors
Regular Bahamian companies must have a minimum of two shareholders and two directors.

Costs
Regular companies are more expensive to establish and operate than IBCs. The cost to incorporate a regular company with minimum authorized capital is usually in the range of $1,900. Ongoing maintenance costs are also higher – usually in the range of $1,500 per year – principally because the government licence fee for such companies owned by non-Bahamians is $1,000 per year.

Exchange control
Bahamas exchange control regulations control the flow of foreign currency in and out of the country, which helps maintain the Bahamian dollar on par with the United States dollar. Regular companies must obtain permission from the Exchange Control Department to invest in The Bahamas and issue shares to non-residents. In circumstances where a regular company is used to take title to real property in The Bahamas, the Exchange

---

LENNOX PATON
Counsel and Attorneys-at-Law
Notaries Public
Nassau, The Bahamas • Established 1971

Banking	**Litigation**
Commercial	**Private Clients**
Corporate	**Real Estate**
Insurance	**Shipping**
Investment Funds	**Trusts**

Legal services in The Bahamas for financial institutions, private clients and their advisors.
For further information, please contact
Michael L. Paton, PO Box N-4875,
Devonshire House, Queen St, Nassau, The Bahamas
Tel (242) 328-0563 • Fax (242) 328-0566
e-mail: lexpaton@bahamas.net.bs

Control Department will designate the company as "resident" and authorize issue of shares to beneficial owners or their nominees; although any proposed changes in shareholding must be approved by them.

Exempted limited partnerships

ELPs are specialized entities created in The Bahamas under the Exempted Limited Partnerships Act, 1995.

> Bahamian ELPs ... are flexible vehicles which can be used for any number of transactions ...

The general rule under Common Law is that all partners are jointly and severally responsible for any liabilities incurred in the partnership. An ELP, which exists by virtue of the statute, allows for the general partner to be solely responsible for all liabilities of the partnership, with limited partners liable only to the extent of their investment in the partnership. The result is that while exempted partners enjoy the profits of the partnership, their liability is limited solely to funds they have contributed.

Flexibility
Bahamian ELPs, like IBCs, are flexible vehicles which can be used for any number of transactions – from securities investment to real estate ownership in other countries.

Tax implications
Bahamian ELPs are free of any taxes in The Bahamas for (at least) 50 years. They allow US taxpayers the substantial advantage of treating partnership income as part of their personal income, as opposed to corporate income which is taxed at a higher rate.

Asset protection
A properly structured ELP can provide limited partners with asset protection against law suits by giving the general partner discretion as to whether to make a distribution to the limited partners. In this sense, an ELP can be set up to function in the manner of an asset protection trust to ward off potential creditors.

Bahamas Incorporation Services Limited

Charlotte House • Box N-3230 • Nassau, The Bahamas

Over 35 years' experience in the offshore industry

- Company Incorporations
- Assistance in Opening Bank Accounts and Brokerage Accounts
- Referrals to Corporate Trustees, Attorneys and Real Estate Brokers
- Hold Mail or Mail Forwarding
- Shelf Companies Available
- Registered Offices

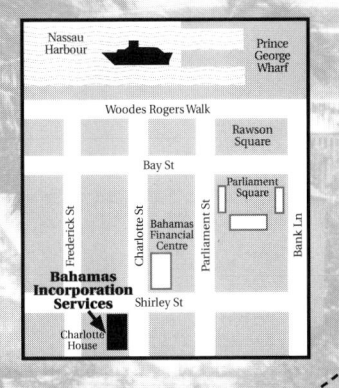

Bahamas Incorporation Services Limited
Tel (242) 322-2965
Fax (242) 322-2874
e-mail: jpyfrom@bahamas.net.bs
http://www.ibcoffshore.com

Cost

The cost of establishing an ELP depends on the scope and complexity of the partnership agreement, although some practitioners may have precedents which can be adapted to fit specific requirements. Government fees are $850 to form the partnership and a licence fee of $475 for each subsequent calendar year.

Reporting requirements

Upon creation of an ELP, the general partner files a one-page statement with the Registrar which includes the company name, general nature of business, the name of the general partner and the registered office. The identity of limited partners and details of the partnership agreement do not have to be disclosed.

Prohibitions

ELPs are prohibited from doing business with residents of The Bahamas for exchange control purposes. The Act requires the general partner to file a statement every year to the effect that the company has not done business with Bahamian residents.

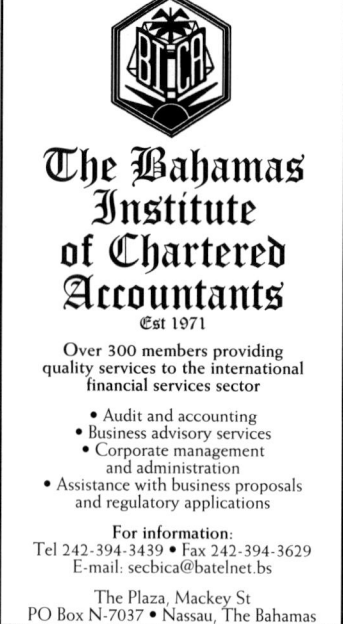

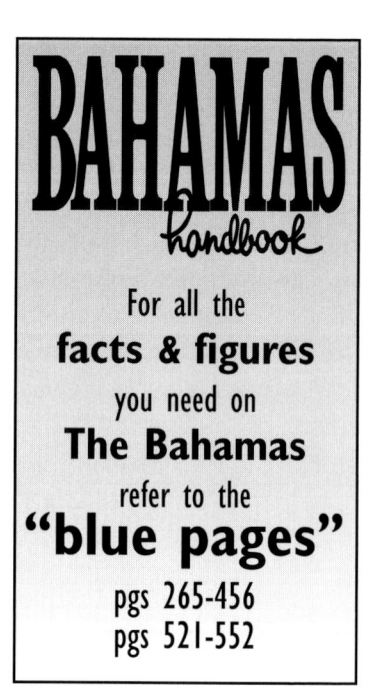

The Bahamas Institute of Chartered Accountants
Est 1971

Over 300 members providing quality services to the international financial services sector

- Audit and accounting
- Business advisory services
- Corporate management and administration
- Assistance with business proposals and regulatory applications

For information:
Tel 242-394-3439 • Fax 242-394-3629
E-mail: secbica@batelnet.bs

The Plaza, Mackey St
PO Box N-7037 • Nassau, The Bahamas

BAHAMAS handbook

For all the **facts & figures** you need on **The Bahamas** refer to the **"blue pages"**

pgs 265-456
pgs 521-552

Financial Planning With Trust & Confidentiality

Investment & Financial Advisors
International Offshore Securities Trading
Fund Administration
Offshore Corporate Formation & Management
Estate & International Tax Planning
Portfolio & Asset Management

**Originator of the successful
MSI – Preferred Investment Fund, Ltd,
the only Bahamian Dollar Mutual Fund in The Bahamas**

Montaque Securities International

Saffrey Square, Bay St, PO Box N-8303, Nassau, NP, The Bahamas
Tel (242) 356-6133 • Fax (242) 356-6144
e-mail: montaque@batelnet.bs • website: www.montaquesecurities.com

---

Scotiatrust

Trust services
Company administration services
Administrative services for investors
Cubicle banking and cubicle trust services
Custody services
Discretionary investment management services
Mutual fund services
The Scotia offshore mutual funds
Pension plan services
Services for Canadian immigrants

The Bank of Nova Scotia Trust Company (Bahamas) Limited
PO Box N-3016, Nassau, The Bahamas
Tel (242) 356-1500 • Fax (242) 326-0991
e-mail: scotiatr@bahamas.net.bs

BAHAMAS • CAYMAN • JERSEY, CHANNEL ISLANDS • HONG KONG

The government's investment policy

BY PETER G FLETCHER, ATTORNEY-AT-LAW, JEROME E PYFROM & CO

Guidelines for would-be investors

Many people who visit The Bahamas and enjoy the agreeable weather and lifestyle ponder buying a home here and becoming a resident. Or maybe they see business opportunities and think about setting up a business. It's an attractive thought, and for investors from some jurisdictions, there could be favourable tax considerations in living or working abroad. But what is involved?

How does a person become a resident? Would a non-Bahamian be allowed to set up and operate a business? How much would a person have to invest? What sorts of approvals would be needed? Where should the investor start?

Answers to basic questions about investment in The Bahamas are now readily at hand in the form of a 1998 statement of the government's Investment Policy. Copies of the policy statement are available from the Office of the Prime Minister, PO Box CB-10980, Nassau, The Bahamas, tel (242) 327-5826, and on the internet at www.interknowledge.com/bahamas/investment.

The policy statement confirms essentials of government's investment policy mapped out in 1992 under which The Bahamas

Ptc
PRIVATE TRUST

A licensed bank, trust company and mutual fund administrator, providing a range of international offshore financial services including:
- Asset protection and discretionary trusts
- Company formation and administration
- Mutual fund administration
- Estate planning and executorships
- Nominee, fiduciary and escrow services
- Managed bank and trust company services

The Private Trust Corporation Limited
Charlotte House, Charlotte St, PO Box N-65, Nassau, The Bahamas
Tel (242) 323-8574 • Fax (242) 326-8388
e-mail: privatetrust@batelnet.bs

M&M
MORGAN & MORGAN GROUP

MORYMOR TRUST CORPORATION LIMITED

Company Formation and Administration
Worldwide Ship Registration

50 Shirley St
PO Box CB-13937
NASSAU, THE BAHAMAS
Tel (242) 326-5859
Tel (242) 323-2321
Fax (242) 322-5567

• PANAMA • LONDON • GENEVA • ZURICH • LUGANO • MADRID • LISBON • PIRAEUS •
• TORTOLA (B.V.I.) • BELIZE • NASSAU • TOKYO • HONG KONG • SINGAPORE •

has seen significant investment inflows in resort and infrastructure development. It highlights government commitment to creating an "investor-friendly" atmosphere in The Bahamas while ensuring that investments which do proceed are a benefit to Bahamians.

Most initial questions potential investors have can be answered by the policy statement. For example:

What if a non-Bahamian wants to buy a house in The Bahamas and retire here? Could he or she become a resident of The Bahamas?

The policy statement answers this question. Accelerated consideration for annual or permanent residence without the right to work is given to persons who purchase a residence valued in excess of $500,000.

Government welcomes such investors provided they are of sound character and able to prove they can support themselves without the need to work in The Bahamas. However, investors in major operating businesses may be granted permanent residence with the right to work in their own business.

Banco Santander
Trust & Banking Corporation (Bahamas) Ltd.

PO Box N-1682 • Nassau, Bahamas
Bahamas Financial Centre, 3rd Floor
Tel (242) 322-3588 or 326-1500
Fax (242) 322-3585

A member of Santander Group - Spain

Would a non-Bahamian be permitted to set up a business like a small, tourist oriented 20 room hotel or a high-end condominium development?

The Bahamas encourages non-Bahamian participation in business activities such as development of tourist resorts, development of upscale residential town houses and condominium complexes and banking and financial services. But government generally reserves other activities such as retail and wholesale operations, real estate agencies, public transportation services, newspapers and magazines for Bahamians. Some project proposals fall into grey areas and there are certain exceptions, so consultation with a local attorney or chartered accountant may be helpful for the investor.

Are there government incentive programmes which could reduce a project's start-up costs?

There are a number of incentive programmes such as those available under the Hotels Encouragement Act, the Industries Encouragement Act and the Export Manufacturing Industries Act. These programmes, under which import duties on raw materials and

❖ **Charleston**
Private Management Limited

"Your Global Partner for Wealth Enhancement and Asset Protection"

Management Services:
**Limited Duration Companies • Limited Partnership
International Business Companies**

Corporate Services:
**Registered Office • Registered Agent
Corporate Management • Fund Administration**

FOR FURTHER INFORMATION, PLEASE CONTACT:
Charleston Private Management Limited
1st Floor, Kings Court, Bay St, PO Box EE-17213,
Nassau, The Bahamas
Tel (242) 325-6841. Fax (242) 325-6864
E-mail: cpmgnt@batelnet.bs

equipment and other charges can be reduced or waived altogether, are quite often critical to viability of a project.

What if an investor must bring in technical people to develop the project?

Investors generally request work permits for themselves and key personnel, particularly during start-up phases of a project. Government adopts a flexible and reasonable immigration policy intended to accommodate investors' needs while protecting its citizens' interests. The fundamental policy is that necessary work permits for key personnel will be granted, though investors are recommended to make these requirements known to government at an early stage in discussions.

Does it make sense for an investor to get in touch with officials early on in the planning stages of a project?

Potential investors should always begin by thoroughly reviewing government's policy statement and discussing their plans with a local attorney or chartered accountant. The investor will also profit by early dialogue with the Bahamas Investment Authority (BIA), a government agency established in government's own words as "a one-stop-shop" for investors. BIA does not make the ultimate decision to approve or disapprove projects. This is determined by a cabinet-level committee chaired by the Prime Minister. BIA is there to assist the investor and its guidance is important to the investor.

Where to shop, dine, stay, play, invest

what-to-do

Nassau • Cable Beach • Paradise Island   Freeport/Lucaya

In Nassau & Freeport/Lucaya, pick up our free What-to-do magazine for the most complete guide available.

Available at hotels, shops, restaurants, Ministry of Tourism booths, airport, dock, tour desks, car rental agencies.

FIDELITY
BANK & TRUST INTERNATIONAL LIMITED

Innovative Financial Solutions for **NOW** and the future

- **BANKING**
- **CORPORATE FINANCE**
- **PENSION ADMINISTRATION**
- **ASSET MANAGEMENT**
- **BROKERAGE SERVICES**

Capitalize on your future prospects, open an investment account in The Bahamas.

Fidelity Bank & Trust
International Limited
51 Frederick Street,
P.O. Box CB-12337,
Nassau, The Bahamas
Telephone (242) 356-7764
Telefax (242) 326-3000

Subsidiaries:
British American Bank
(1993) Limited
Nassau, The Bahamas

British American Bank
Georgetown, Grand Cayman

THE HIGHEST QUALITY PETROLEUM PRODUCTS THROUGHOUT THE BAHAMAS

FAMILY ISLAND DISTRIBUTORS & MARINAS

SAM GRAY
Exuma Docking Services
George Town, Exuma
Tel (242) 336-2101 or 336-2620
Fax (242) 336-2023

FARMER'S CAY MARINA
Farmer's Cay, Exuma
Tel (242) 355-4060
Fax (242) 355-4063

STANIEL CAY YACHT CLUB
Staniel Cay, Exuma
Tel (242) 355-2024
Fax (242) 355-2044

CARTER ENTERPRISES
Riding Rock Marina, San Salvador
Tel (242) 332-2631
Fax (242) 331-2020

ROY HARDING
Long Island Petroleum Distributors Ltd
Salt Pond, Long Island

SPANISH WELLS YACHT HAVEN
Spanish Wells, Eleuthera
Tel (242) 333-4255 or 333-4328
Fax (242) 333-4649

E LORAINE STURRUP
Tropical Petroleum Distributors
Marsh Harbour, Abaco
Tel (242) 367-2282 or 367-2170
Fax (242) 367-4442

PATRICK ROMER
Morgan's Bluff, Andros
Tel (242) 329-2519 or 329-3044
Fax (242) 329-3367

TRIPLE J MARINE
Abaco
Tel (242) 367-2163
Fax (242) 367-3388

STELLA MARIS RESORT & MARINA
Stella Maris, Long Island
Tel (242) 338-2051
Fax (242) 338-2052

PINNACLE FUEL SUPPLIERS LTD
South Caicos, Turks & Caicos
Tel (649) 946-3417
Fax (649) 946-3377

KNOWLES, CAT ISLAND
Tel (242) 377-6509 or 377-6512 (HQ, Nassau)
Fax (242) 377-6541 (HQ, Nassau)

ESSO STANDARD OIL SA LTD HEADQUARTERS
PO Box CB-10998, Nassau, The Bahamas
Tel (242) 377-6509 or 377-6512 • Fax (242) 377-6514 • Customer Service (242) 377-6541

Only the sun covers The Bahamas ... better

ZNS NETWORK

ESTABLISHED SINCE 1936
ZNS still stands for **quality.**
With state-of-the-art equipment, highly trained and qualified staff, we are proud to be the **national voice**, the **eyes** and **ears** of The Bahamas.

First in broadcasting. First in quality.

ZNS 1 1540 AM 107.1 FM 107.9 FM	Adult contemporary/ Talk shows
ZNS II FM 104.5 FM	Top 40/pop contemporary
ZNS II AM 1240 AM	Religious & educational, drama, documentaries & talk shows
ZNS III AM 810 AM	Freeport, Grand Bahama Adult contemporary/top 40
ZNS TV 13	Nassau, Abaco, Freeport, Parts of Exuma & North Eleuthera

THE BROADCASTING CORPORATION OF THE BAHAMAS
Tel (242) 322-4623. Fax (242) 322-3924. E-mail: bcbcorp@batelnet.bs
PO Box N-1347, Nassau, The Bahamas.
Tel (242) 352-9713. Fax (242) 352-2152.
PO Box F-42403, Freeport, Grand Bahama.

SERVING THE ENTIRE BAHAMAS

The first name in real estate in The Bahamas ...

ESTATES CLUB
THE ART OF MARKETING PROPERTY

Our listings offer unrivaled Waterfront, Beachfront and Hilltop properties

- Lyford Cay
- Cable Beach
- Paradise Island
- Port New Providence
- Family Islands

- Islands
- Estates
- Lots
- Houses
- Condominiums
- Commercial Properties

75 Shirley St
PO Box N-732, Nassau, Bahamas

Telephone (242) 322-2305
Facsimile (242) 322-2033

Website: www.damianos.com
E-mail: damianos@bahamas.net.bs

DAMIANOS
REALTY CO. LTD.
SINCE 1945

Investment project guidelines

To assist potential investors, BIA has developed a set of project proposal guidelines which must be submitted to the BIA along with appropriate supporting documents. Basic categories of information which should be included in an investment proposal are:

Name and address of applicant	Names and addresses of project principals
Description of project (executive summary)	Proposed location of project
Capital requirements (total capital involved; breakdown of start-up costs)	Land requirement
Financial arrangements (letters of credit, commitment letters from financial institutions)	Employment projection
Potential environmental impact	Proposed start-up date
Concessions requested (legislative incentives sought)	Management/personnel requirements (work permits required)

As any attorney or chartered accountant will tell you, even though investment by non-Bahamians is encouraged, government takes the task of evaluating investment programmes seriously. Proposals which involve areas of activity reserved for Bahamians or which are inadequately financed or poorly organized or which have potentially negative environmental impact will not be accepted. For this reason, homework, planning and early consultation with local professionals and BIA are the key to a successful start to an investment project. See also **Bahamas information section, Investing,** National investment policy.

Peter G Fletcher is a partner in Jerome E Pyfrom and Co, counsel and attorneys-at-law. He is a member of the Bar of England and Wales (Lincoln's Inn) and The Bahamas Bar Association. His areas of practice include offshore companies, trusts and international commercial transactions.

SARA MOSS

Confidence feeds construction boom

BY GORDON LOMER

Residential, corporate, tourist and public projects abound.

Construction at an unprecedented pace in the residential, commercial, government and tourism sectors has generated momentum in the Bahamian economy that is threatening to strain the work force. Employment is at an all-time high.

Government projects include infrastructure upgrading, roads and water works, schools and major buildings. Tourism facilities on a grand scale are in full swing in Nassau, Paradise Island, Grand Bahama and several of the Out Islands. (See *Out Island projects keeping pace*, pg 234.)

According to the Central Bank of The Bahamas' quarterly review for Jan-March of 1998, estimates of building activity registered "significant strengthening" propelled by "steady foreign investments within tourism and strong expenditures on housing."

"In particular, the sharp upturn in the value of residential investments (31.5 per cent) underpinned a 21.3 per cent appreciation in building starts to an estimated $48.3 million.

"Future investments, as indicated by building permits granted, advanced by 50.5 per cent to $99.8 million from a fairly stable

Left: A $450 million expansion programme at Atlantis, Paradise Island reshapes the skyline with Royal Towers and its 1,208 rooms and suites.

position last year due to a pickup in both the residential and commercial components," according to the Central Bank.

Commercial development continues in Freeport with the Freeport Container Port expanding and spawning additional construction projects including corporate office, retail, storage and ecotourism developments. A $10.6 million redevelopment of Freeport Harbour's passenger terminals and development of a 20,000 sq ft retail complex were to be completed by the middle of 1999.

Lucayan strip

Reconstruction of the 52-acre Lucayan hotel strip area to be called The Lucayan will signal a rebirth of tourism on Grand Bahama.

Phase one of the project, the re-opening of the 540-room Grand Bahama Beach Hotel,* was to be completed by February 1999. Phase two, scheduled for September 1999, includes the opening of the central check-in building for all hotels, the 244-room Lucayan Beach Hotel* and the new 2,000-seat convention centre. Phase three, to be finished by December 1999, includes the new 800-room hotel and casino. The whole complex will be woven together with a

David Pantin

Senior vice president and general manager of The Lucayan, David Pantin is responsible for the pre-opening and management of the 1,600-room luxury resort. He brings 20 years of industry experience to the task.

Born in Trinidad in 1959, Pantin received his early education at Wimbledon College in the UK and spent four years in management training with Trusthouse Forte. Prior to his Freeport appointment Pantin was vice president of operations and member of the board of Hilton, UK, responsible for 14 hotels. He spent two years as vice president of the Caribbean and Western Atlantic for Forte Hotels. Based in Nassau, he held full divisional responsibility for five luxury Forte hotels.

His significant experience in the establishment of world class resort hotels included management and marketing of two of Europe's prestigious resort hotels, the Old Course Hotel at St Andrews, Scotland, and Dromoland Castle, Ireland. He has held senior management posts at the Hyde Park Hotel and historic Café Royal, London, and at Plaza Athénée Hotel, New York.

His professional qualifications include Certified Hotel Administrator and the UK's Hotel and Catering International Management Association diploma.

being renamed

HG C
Since 1922

The Bahamas' Oldest and Most Extensive Real Estate Service

• Paradise Island • Private Islands • Lyford Cay
• Condominiums • Prime Beachfront • Family Islands
• Residential/Commercial • Rentals/Property Management

Exclusive homes, waterfront condominiums, beautiful beaches or your own private island!

The Bahamas' widest selection of prime property. We have over 75 years' experience as The Bahamas' leading real estate company.

HG C
Since 1922

H. G. CHRISTIE LTD
Real Estate

Millar's Court • PO Box N-8164 • Nassau • Bahamas
Telephone (242) 322-1041 • Fax (242) 326-5642
www.hgchristie.com • e-mail: sales@hgchristie.com
Eleuthera (242) 332-2503   Abaco (242) 367-4608

The exclusive Bahamas affiliate for

CHRISTIE'S GREAT ESTATES

Multiple Listing Service
MLS

RECOGNIZED BY WHO'S WHO IN LUXURY REAL ESTATE

REALTOR

BAHAMAS CHAMBER OF COMMERCE

BAHAMAS REAL ESTATE ASSOCIATION MEMBER

series of open air and covered walkways, streams, water falls and tropical landscaping. Shuttle service will carry visitors from the check-in area to their respective hotels within The Lucayan.

Atlantis, Paradise Island's **Royal Towers,** a massive $450 million expansion programme, has already transformed the once quietly secluded Hog Island into a fantasy world. It includes 1,208 new rooms and suites, a 50,000 sq ft casino spanning a shark-infested lagoon, new 25,000 sq ft ballroom and convention space. Atlantis construction has spawned infrastructure projects including the second Paradise Island Bridge, a tunnel beneath the new 100-ft channel from Nassau Harbour into a $78 million marina, improved roadways on the island and a multi-storey parking garage.

The new $19.8 million three-lane one-way span onto Paradise Island ties in with the new eastward traffic flow on Bay St. The traffic pattern changed May 31, 1998 and the bridge was to open by the end of 1998. The old bridge was slated to be one way off the island, feeding downtown or Cable Beach traffic west via Shirley St.

The **British Colonial Hotel's** $100 million redevelopment of its 13-acre downtown waterfront property is in full swing and on schedule. The first phase, the $30 million restoration of the historic

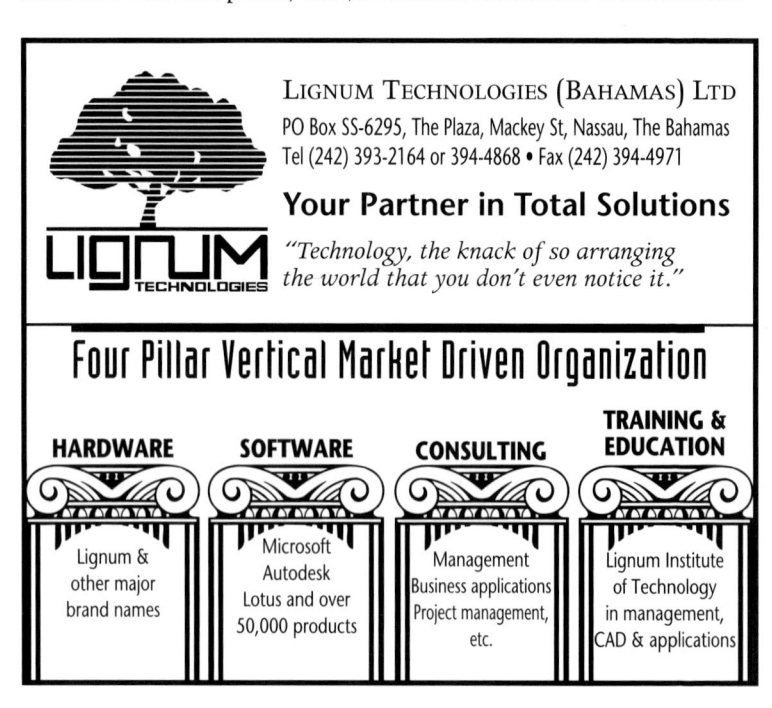

LIGNUM TECHNOLOGIES (BAHAMAS) LTD
PO Box SS-6295, The Plaza, Mackey St, Nassau, The Bahamas
Tel (242) 393-2164 or 394-4868 • Fax (242) 394-4971

Your Partner in Total Solutions

"Technology, the knack of so arranging the world that you don't even notice it."

Four Pillar Vertical Market Driven Organization

HARDWARE	SOFTWARE	CONSULTING	TRAINING & EDUCATION
Lignum & other major brand names	Microsoft Autodesk Lotus and over 50,000 products	Management Business applications Project management, etc.	Lignum Institute of Technology in management, CAD & applications

Paradise FOUND

it's that simple.

Sales
•
Rentals
•
Appraisals
•
Property Management
•
Residential, Commercial and Private Island
Properties throughout The Bahamas

GRAHAM REAL ESTATE

Phone (242) 356-5030 or (242) 356-3702 • Fax (242) 326-5005
PO Box CB-13443 • 107 Shirley Street • Nassau, Bahamas
e-mail: grahamre@batelnet.bs

main building, was to be completed by March 1999. Phases two and three involve creation of office suites, possible space for the Bahamas Securities Exchange, 150 oceanfront condos, 300 apartments and a marina and retail space. The hotel portion will be managed by Hilton International.

Dockendale House & Manx Corporate Centre, new executive office complex rising on the site of the old Bahamian Club beside Xavier's College, will offer some 50,000 sq ft of space when completed.

Global Life Assurance is developing **Goodman's Bay Corporate Centre** on Sea View Dr. It will include 80,000 sq ft of upscale office space, indoor and outdoor parking and a swimming pool.

Cable Beach

The construction boom is reverberating along the Cable Beach hotel strip. **Superclubs® Breezes Bahamas** plans a $20 million expansion adding 150 suites to the existing 400 rooms, as well as another pool, beach bar and three theme restaurants.

A $12 million refurbishment will redo in Bahamian motif all 411 rooms and suites at the **Nassau Beach Hotel.** The lobby, dining and banquet areas have been upgraded and a second pool has been added. Work on the rooms was expected to be completed by May 1999.

BAYROC's planned ultra luxurious 74-unit residential development on seven acres of Cable Beach will include a cascading 18-ft waterfall feeding two swimming pools via a fresh water stream, 68 three-bedroom units and six penthouses. Priced from $560,000 to $1.6 million, they average 2,000 sq ft with large balconies. Covered parking for owners, tennis courts and a fitness centre will complete the gated complex.

A $65 million improvement and expansion programme has been completed at **Sandals Royal Bahamian Resort & Spa** with the addition of about 200 new suites, new restaurants, a huge solar heated pool and convention and meeting space. The project brought the all-inclusive resort's room count to 406.

The Mediterranean-type village of **Sandyport** west of Cable Beach, a sprawling multi-use resort and residential gated community, currently contains about 170 completed town houses and homes. They range from $235,000 for a one-bedroom unit to $595,000 and $695,000 for three- and four-bedroom town houses. A stand alone house is priced at $795,000, while two newer ones are in

BDO

BDO Mann Judd
Chartered Accountants

- Audit & Accountancy
- Company Management & Formation
- Insolvency Services
- Management Consulting
- Business Advisory Services

Ansbacher House, East Street
PO Box N-10144
Nassau, NP, The Bahamas
Tel (242) 325-6591 • Fax (242) 325-6592

Jerome E. Pyfrom & Co.

Counsel and Attorneys-at-Law
Notaries Public

Services

- Real Estate Transactions
- Company Incorporation & Management
- Trust and Estate Planning
- International, Commercial & Financial Transactions

Partners: Jerome E. Pyfrom & Peter G. Fletcher
Associate: Kenneth A. Toppin

Charlotte House, Charlotte Street
PO Box N-3950, Nassau, The Bahamas
Tel (242) 322-2871•Fax (242) 322-2874
e-mail: jpyfrom@bahamas.net.bs

the $1.5 million range. Single family canal front building lots are available from $180,000.

Plans include about 800 homes in Sandyport, offices, village square with church, cafes, shops and an upscale fitness facility.

West Bay St

Caves Point, West Bay St, at Blake Rd, is 90 per cent sold. Only eight three-bedroom units starting at $495,000 and one $1.25 million penthouse remained in the summer of 1998. The whole project was to be completed by April 1999.

Across West Bay St, Caves Point is beginning a second residential development to include 35 three-bed, three-bath apartments and the same number of town houses, all with a spectacular ocean view. This gated community will include tennis courts and pools. Phase two of the project will involve development of a shopping village called Caves Village, with cafeterias, restaurants and upscale boutiques. Phase three will be a business centre with executive offices to the west.

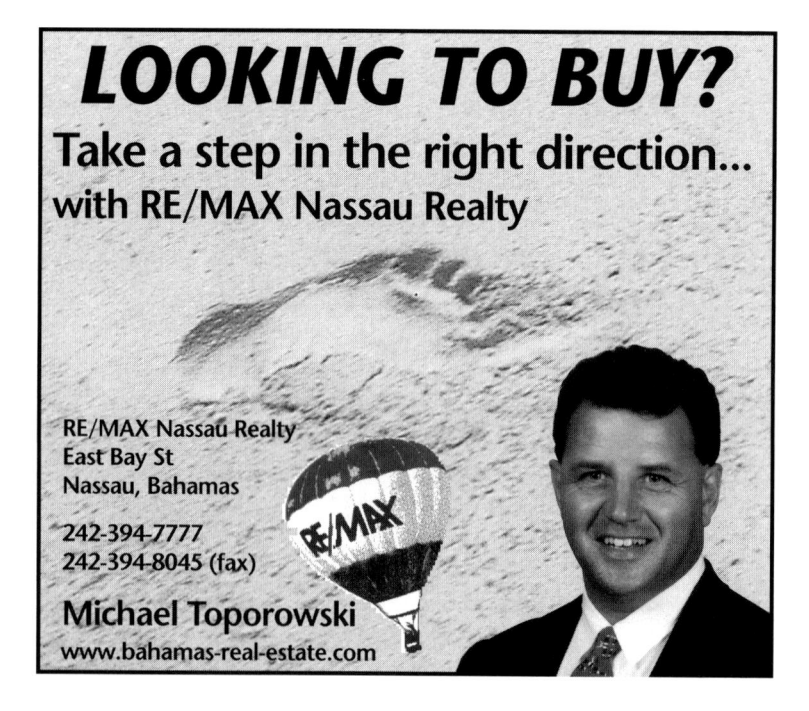

LOOKING TO BUY?
Take a step in the right direction...
with RE/MAX Nassau Realty

RE/MAX Nassau Realty
East Bay St
Nassau, Bahamas

242-394-7777
242-394-8045 (fax)

Michael Toporowski
www.bahamas-real-estate.com

Providing years of invaluable **experience** while helping you establish your **future**

Sales
Executive rentals
Development

Nassau & throughout
The Bahama Islands

Durrant-Harding
Real Estate Company Ltd

Saffrey Sq, Bank Ln • PO Box SS-5277
Tel (242) 326 2461 • Fax (242) 326 4509
E-mail: sales@durrantharding.com
www.durrantharding.com

Bayside Development has broken ground on a 12-acre tract at West Bay St and Blake Rd, where **Oceanic Bank** and **Pictet Bank** are developing a 100,000 sq ft four-building complex to include executive office space, luxury condos and both banks' headquarters. The offices, on about six acres, are to be completed by late 1999.

Islands of Old Fort sets a new standard in upscale elegance.

The residential units are slated for completion about six months later.

South along Blake Rd, **Doctors Hospital (West)** will include an emergency clinic, ambulance service, a walk-in clinic, medical fitness centre, lab and pharmacy, 10 in-patient beds and administrative offices.

Islands of Old Fort sets a new standard in upscale elegance with 45 canal front homes in the $1.8 to $2.3 million range. All eight houses in the development's first phase at Old Fort Bay, immediately east of Lyford Cay, are under construction. Bahamian architecture features deep verandas, high ceilings, hurricane shutters and shade louvres, complemented by clay tile roofs and ceramic tile flooring.

Lyford Cay Real Estate Co Ltd

Our area of expertise is Lyford Cay

Sales

Rentals

Appraisals

PO Box N-7776
Harbour Green, Lyford Cay
Tel (242) 362-4703/4
Fax (242) 362-4513
Nassau, Bahamas

EDEN FOR SALE

bahamasnet

www.bahamasnet.com/realestate

PO Box N-7513, Nassau, The Bahamas
Tel (242) 323 5665 Fax (242) 323 5728
email info@bahamasnet.com

Lyford Cay area

Cavalier Construction, the firm that built the 200-room addition to Sandals and the Caves Point project, is building at least four homes in the $2 million to $12 million range inside the exclusive confines of **Lyford Cay.**

Just outside Lyford Cay, **Lyford Enterprises** has erected a $6 million, six-storey building with 66,000 sq ft of executive office space.

Also on the edge of Lyford Cay is **Guaranty Trust Bank's Lyford Manor,** an office complex of three buildings with nearly 30,000 sq ft of office space slated for completion in September 1999.

Clifton Cay on the other side of Lyford Cay proposes development of some 637 dwelling sites, including 28 oceanfront lots, 84 canal lots, 85 golf lots, 61 elevated ridge lots and 381 cluster development units. The project would also include a marina, tennis courts and an 18-hole golf course.

South Ocean Beach Hotel and Golf Club, recently acquired by the same Canadian group that purchased the British Colonial Hotel, is undergoing a facelift and renovation, while the golf course is being completely rejuvenated.

JEANNE I THOMPSON

COUNSEL & ATTORNEY-AT-LAW
NOTARY PUBLIC

GENERAL LAW SPECIALIZING IN LITIGATION, FAMILY LAW AND PROPERTY MATTERS.

CHAMBERS
42 QUEEN ST
PO BOX N-4375
NASSAU, THE BAHAMAS

TEL (242) 322-2605 or 326-5037
FAX (242) 325-6667
E-MAIL: JAYTEE@BAHAMAS.NET.BS

Sandals Royal Bahamian Resort & Spa has undertaken a $65 million improvement and expansion project.

Royall Beach Estates in the south east, on the ocean side of the South Ocean golf course, features 44 luxury condominiums. Prices range from $275,000 for a two-bedroom unit to $425,000 for a three-bedroom penthouse. Phase one, with five two-bedroom units, one single bedroom apartment and two three-bedroom units, was to be ready early in 1999.

Venice Bay, a planned canal-laced community at Millar's Pond on the south side of New Providence, will include 532 home sites, marina and a 30-room hotel on 10 acres. It will have a swimming pool, ¾-acre park, and the preserved historic site of old slave quarters.

Treasure Cove, one block east of St Andrew's School on Yamacraw Rd, is a 282-lot gated project of homes for middle income buyers, in the $140,000 to $206,000 range.

BEEPERS

(((*B E L Communications Ltd*)))
Tel/fax (242) 328-4503 (Town Centre Mall, Nassau)

Bahamas Electronic Lab Co
We specialize in:
- AIRCRAFT COMMUNICATIONS SYSTEMS
- RADAR EQUIPMENT • ELECTRONIC EQUIPMENT, SUPPLIES & REPAIRS • RADIO PAGING • BEEPERS

30 Yellow Pine St, PO Box F-43219, Freeport, GB
Tel (242) 352-2286 • Fax (242) 352-9529

Investing in real estate
is one of the most important
decisions you will ever make.
You deserve the best guidance possible.
And in The Bahamas,
that means Bahamas Realty,
appointed by Sotheby's as its exclusive affiliate.
Five principals with more than
120 years experience,
three offices and a reputation
that is international.
Choose with confidence,
Bahamas Realty.
The most comprehensive and largest real estate
and property management company
in The Bahamas.

BAHAMAS REALTY

Exclusive Affiliate
SOTHEBY'S
International Realty

SALES, RENTALS, APPRAISALS, PROPERTY MANAGEMENT

PO BOX N-1132, Nassau, Bahamas
Tel (242) 393-8618, Fax (242) 393-0326

PO BOX AB-20856, Marsh Harbour, Abaco, Bahamas
Tel (242) 367-3262/3, Fax (242) 367-3260

e-mail: brealty@bahamasrealty.bs   http://www.bahamasrealty.bs

Seapointe, on a beach in the gated community of **Port New Providence** in the southeast corner of New Providence, offers waterfront town houses with docking facilities, tennis courts, clubhouse and 24-hour security. Luxury three-bedroom, $3^1/_2$ bath town houses start at $495,000.

Montague Sterling Centre on part of the old Montagu Beach Hotel property is a 23,000 sq ft five-storey executive office development overlooking Montagu Bay. Rising to the east is the new regional office of the Russian **Guta Bank and Trust.**

The old Pilot House hotel on Bay St across from Nassau Yacht Haven is now **Gold Circle House** after a $6 million refurbishment converted the aging 120-room inn into a condo complex of 37 one- and two-bedroom units. Executive offices and retail space occupy the original front building on the property.

Several other gated communities are on the drawing-boards of various developers.

Public projects

Major Public Works projects and infrastructure tied in with real estate/construction development in recent months include the $19.8 million Paradise Island Bridge, mentioned earlier; and a new $5.88 million Customs headquarters building on Thompson Blvd.

The downtown area is also undergoing a public sector rejuvenation with the $13.8 million development on a tract of land at Poinciana Hill between Meeting and Delancy streets. This three-storey building is to be headquarters for some of government's social departments, including health, housing and social development.

The Post Office on East Hill St, which houses several government departments, has undergone a $3.38 million refurbishment. The $8.5 million project for redevelopment of Prince George Dock, including the Junkanoo Museum, was to be completed in 1998.

Transportation corridor projects in the works to improve east-west and north-south traffic movement in New Providence will cost an estimated $20 million. The traffic reversal project was put into effect at a cost of $1.2 million.

For more information on Bahamas real estate, visit Bahamasnet at www.bahamasnet.com/realestate or www.bahamasnet.com/business/realestate

Bring The World To Your Shore

ShipRight
FEDERAL EXPRESS

Shipping Services Expressly For The Caribbean.
At Federal Express, we know shipping is a way of life here, as much as the sand and the sea. That's why we've created a group of special services just for the Caribbean.

Ship Right To Save Time And Money. Our new, lower-ed FedEx Letter® and FedEx Pak for documents, or International Priority® shipping for er boxes and freight, give you *next-day delivery* to *most locations* in the Caribbean he continental US! And our new rate schedule means your fees per pound *decline* on vier shipments, even up to 1000 lbs or more.

p Right To The Rest Of The World. With our Caribbean air network, you're connected n the world's most comprehensive delivery services. When you **Ship Right,** Federal Express gs the world to your shore!

Nassau pick ups call 322-1791.

AU (Main Office)
de Plaza, Thompson Blvd
#3
322-5656 (to 8)

NASSAU (Business Service Center)
Norfolk House, Frederick St
Ground Floor
Call 323-7611

FREEPORT
Seventeen Plaza
Call 352-3402/3

FedEx
Federal Express

COURTESY OLD BAHAMA BAY

Out Island projects keeping pace

BY GORDON LOMER

Construction, infrastructure projects pump economy.

The Bahamas Out Islands are enjoying a construction boom akin to those of New Providence and Grand Bahama. Projects range from residential developments to airport and roadways work throughout the islands.

On the largest of the Bahamian islands, Andros, a planned 346-site development for a gated residential project of single family homes is under way near San Andros in North Andros. **Port Atlantic Shores** will include an 18-hole golf course and marina, facilities for diving, deep sea fishing, bonefishing and hunting, plus ample parkland and a small business area.

In South Andros, the **Emerald Palms Resort** between Congo Town and Driggs Hill, if bought from the government's Hotel Corporation of The Bahamas, is to be refurbished into a first class dive resort. It would be part of a worldwide network of dive operations.

"Andros is a sleeper," says Larry Roberts of Bahamas Realty Ltd.

Abaco continues to show signs of real estate and construction activity with the opening of permanent offices in Marsh Harbour for Bahamas Realty and H G Christie.

Left: Old Bahama Bay at West End, Grand Bahama has a $20 million development programme in progress.

The Lucayan at Freeport/Lucaya brings three resorts into one complex including children's facilities, a convention centre and casino.

About 100 second homes are under various stages of construction, according to Robert Sweeting, Member of Parliament for South Abaco. "In Guana Cay alone there must be 25 being built," says Sweeting, "and there's lots of second home construction going on at Scotland Cay and Hope Town as well. Mostly Europeans, Canadians and Americans are building."

The development at the north end of North Bimini, $350 million **Bimini Bay Hotel Marina and Casino,** will include 500 single family homes, a 1,500-unit condominium, 500-room American style hotel, 250-room all-inclusive European type facility, 200-room ecotourism resort, 18-hole golf course, casino and 300-slip marina.

Old Bahama Bay, a $20 million redevelopment of the old Jack Tar Hotel site at West End, Grand Bahama was started in July 1997.

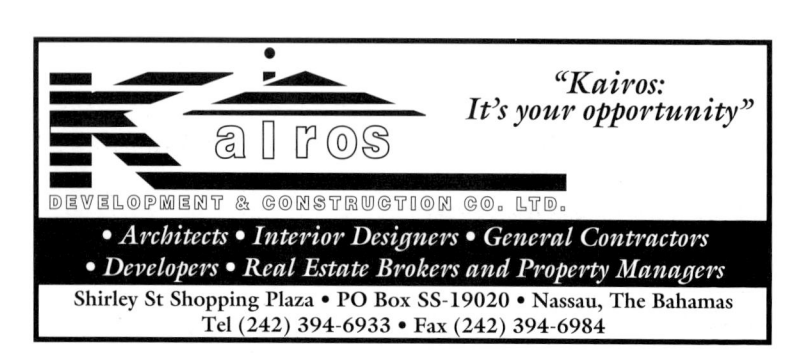

Kairos

"Kairos: It's your opportunity"

DEVELOPMENT & CONSTRUCTION CO. LTD.

• *Architects* • *Interior Designers* • *General Contractors*
• *Developers* • *Real Estate Brokers and Property Managers*

Shirley St Shopping Plaza • PO Box SS-19020 • Nassau, The Bahamas
Tel (242) 394-6933 • Fax (242) 394-6984

"The island is coming to life on a scale that is up market and done with style." It includes a 150-slip marina at the site of the former hotel's old marina. "The island is coming to life on a scale that is up market and done with style," says developer Bill Criswell, whose plans include a gated residential community, beachfront cottage-style resort, pools, restaurants and private docks for canal front home sites.

Exuma projects

In Exuma, a new $70 million development is about to blossom at Ocean Bight. **Emerald Bay Resort,** on 346 acres sold recently by the Hotel Corporation, and on adjacent acreage, will eventually include three hotels, 10,000 sq ft casino, 18-hole Greg Norman-designed golf course and 100-slip marina. Developers estimate phase one of the project, which includes a 200-room hotel, 100 residential lots, 120 condominiums and the marina, could be completed by spring of 2000, with overall completion by 2003.

FRANK HANNA
CLEANING CO LTD
Cleaning and Janitorial Services

For home, shop, furniture, & upholstery cleaning.

Prompt dependable service.

We sell industrial floor polishers, "Wet Vacs" and all your cleaning supplies

Free Estimates

Serving New Providence & the Family Islands.

Tel 323 4531 • 325 3306
Fax 325 3305
9th Terrace & Collins Ave
PO Box N-8321

RESAR

Islands • Residential & commercial properties
• Management & rental agents

Real Estate Sales and Rentals (Bahamas) Ltd.

Harris Bldg, 58 Shirley St
PO Box N-1110, Nassau, The Bahamas

Tel (242) 322-2680
M Barbara Brown
Fax (242) 325-6353

Purchase of Emerald Palms in South Andros was being negotiated at press time.

Oceania Heights Development Ltd is a 50-acre spread of ocean-view lots in a gated resort community that will include private clubhouse, tennis courts and other leisure facilities. Quarter- and half-acre lots range from $80,000 to $200,000, and work is already under way for the resort's $500,000 clubhouse.

February Point, an 80-acre peninsula in Flamingo Bay, south of George Town, Exuma, commenced early in 1998 with a 48-unit town house complex. A full range of recreational facilities will be added as well as a clubhouse, marina, tennis courts, pools and a restaurant.

JBR BUILDING SUPPLIES LTD
ESTABLISHED 1959

7AM–5PM MON TO FRI, 7AM–4PM SAT
WULFF RD OPP MACKEY ST • PO BOX SS-5664 NASSAU, THE BAHAMAS
TEL (242) 393-0512/3, 393-8006 or 393-8225 • FAX (242) 393-8013

TOPS LUMBER & PLUMBING SUPPLIES

7AM–5PM MON TO FRI, 7AM–4PM SAT
WILTON ST NEXT TO D W DAVIS • PO BOX SS-5664 NASSAU, THE BAHAMAS
TEL (242) 325-3507, 328-0478 or 394-0641 • FAX (242) 394-0642

EVERYTHING FOR THE BUILDER. TOP QUALITY, FAIR PRICES & DELIVERY

Cruise lines are buying, developing and renaming Bahamian islands and including them as stopovers in their cruise schedules. The 2,400-acre island of Little San Salvador, between the southern tip of Eleuthera and the northern point of Cat Island, was acquired in 1997 as a stopover by Holland America Line. About five miles long, it has been renamed **Half Moon Cay.** Disney Cruise Line bought Gorda Cay in southern Abaco and renamed it **Castaway Cay.** The island is a regular port of call for the 1998-launched *Disney Magic*, which carries 2,400 passengers.

Infrastructure

Meanwhile Public Works projects in the Out Islands have kept pace with private development. Nearly 700 miles of roads have been completed at a cost of more than $60 million. Water and road works valued at $6.38 million have been undertaken recently in Exuma.

At South Eleuthera a $2.3 million upgrade of the Rock Sound airport opened that facility for direct, big jet flights from Milan, Italy to service Club Fortuna. In Abaco $6.5 million has been earmarked for roadwork at Marsh Harbour and Sandy Point and another $3.5 million for a new dock facility at Marsh Harbour.

LAND DESIGN
OF
NASSAU
LIMITED

EXPERTISE:

LANDSCAPE ARCHITECTS
COASTAL PLANNERS
HORTICULTURALISTS

SPECIALISTS IN:

ISLAND STYLE DESIGN
BIDS AND CONTRACTS
PROJECT MANAGEMENT

PO BOX CB-12662, NASSAU, THE BAHAMAS
TEL (242) 356-3489 • FAX (242) 356-4448

Gold Circle
Company Ltd.

REAL ESTATE SALES & DEVELOPMENT

ISLANDS   HOTELS   HOUSES   CONDOS

Gold Circle House

"We make prime property affordable."

BROKERS
DEVELOPERS
PROPERTY MANAGERS

APPRAISERS
ARCHITECTS
BUILDING CONTRACTORS

GOLD CIRCLE HOUSE, EAST BAY ST
THE GOLDEN INN BUILDING, SOLDIER RD
TEL (242) 393-8477 OR 393-8823 • FAX (242) 393-4508

REAL ESTATE

Following is a sampling of properties available in The Bahamas at press time.

NEW PROVIDENCE & PARADISE ISLAND

CABLE BEACH: La Playa. A private estate on 1½ acres of lushly landscaped beachfront property. This 10,000 sq ft eight bdrm, six bath home has a stately formal living room and dining room, marble fireplace, mahogany framed picture windows and staircase, wine cellar, cedar closets, whirlpool tub, pool, chef's kitchen, guest cottage and staff quarters. $4.5 million. Contact John Christie at H G Christie Ltd, PO Box N-8164, Nassau, tel (242) 322-1041, fax (242) 326-5642, e-mail: christie@bahamas.net.bs, www.hgchristie.com

CABLE BEACH: Sulgrave Manor. Elegant old world charm. Fourth floor beach front condominium with superb ocean view. Three bdrm, three bath, living room, dining room, two balconies. Tastefully furnished with antique furniture and Persian rugs. 24 hr security. $750,000. Contact Gregory Graham, Graham Real Estate, tel (242) 356-5030, fax (242) 326-5005, e-mail: grahamre@batelnet.bs

CABLE BEACH: Newly renovated home on the beach in the heart of Cable Beach within walking distance of hotels and golf course. Three bdrm, three bath, furnished, wet bar, 24 hr security, covered parking, heated pool. $720,000. Contact C Investments Realtors, PO Box CB-11556, Nassau, tel (242) 328-7557, fax (242) 328-7994, e-mail: pcarey@cinvest.com, www.cinvest.com

CAVES POINT: Oceanfront deluxe residential community offering three bdrm and penthouse apartments. Facilities include an oversized "edgeless" pool with sunbathing decks, two additional pools, a fitness centre with state-of-the-art equipment, two gazebos, pier with diving platform and steps to a beautiful sandy beach. Contact Caves Development Corporation Ltd, PO Box CB-13647, Nassau, tel (242) 327-1575, fax (242) 327-1569.

EAST BAY ST: Waterfront estate consisting of four bdrm, 6½ bath house on 300 ft of waterfront. The 8,000 sq ft living area has a large formal dining room, family room, den, breakfast room, study, his/her master baths, two-car garage, large pool and patio, guest house, central air, and enclosed grounds. Partly furnished. $1,750,000. Contact Damianos Realty Co Ltd, PO Box N-732, Nassau, tel (242) 322-2305, fax (242) 322-2033, e-mail: damianos@bahamas.net.bs, www.damianos.com

EAST BAY ST: Hilltop estate on 5½ acres of fully enclosed landscaped grounds. Main house is 5,000 sq ft with three bdrm, 3½ baths, family room, two-car garage, pool, patio, tennis court, central air, standby generator. Three bdrm staff house. $2.1 million. Contact Damianos Realty Co Ltd, PO Box N-732, Nassau, tel (242) 322-2305, fax (242) 322-2033, e-mail: damianos@bahamas.net.bs, www.damianos.com

LAKE CUNNINGHAM: Dale House. Built on 11½ acres of lush resort land this newly renovated estate features a four bdrm, 4½ bath main residence with views of the lake from the second floor, white marble floors, crown mouldings, bay windows, French doors, handpainted wall decor, cottage with private terrace, pool, custom kitchen, antique furnishings, electric security gates, and abundant privacy. Fit for royalty. $5,250,000. Contact John Christie, H G Christie Ltd, PO Box N-8164, Nassau, tel (242) 322-1041, fax (242) 326-5642, e-mail: christie@bahamas.net.bs, www.hgchristie.com

LYFORD CAY: La Rochefort. Situated hilltop on more than an acre of beautifully terraced and landscaped land. Designed with meticulous attention to detail, this 10,000 sq ft home has five bdrm, eight bath, large reception area, marble floors, gourmet kitchen, breakfast room, library, staff apartment, three-car garage, elevator, pool and patio. $12 million. Contact Damianos Realty Co Ltd, PO Box N-732, Nassau, tel (242) 322-2305, fax (242) 322-2033, e-mail: damianos@bahamas.net.bs, www.damianos.com

LYFORD CAY: Six bdrm, six bath cottage with tennis court, pool and three-car garage. $5.5 million. Contact Powell's Marketing & Management Services Ltd, tel (242) 328-7238 or 356-0801; fax (242) 326-2491, e-mail: cpowell@bahamas.net.bs, www.bahamasnet.com/powells.html

LYFORD CAY: Three bdrm, 2½ bath house with pool, pool house, garage, security, satellite, central air. $1.8 million. Contact Powell's Marketing &

Knoll
"Good design is good business"

InterDesign Ltd
PO Box SS-6223, Nassau, Bahamas
Tel 242-393-7252
Fax 242-393-5028

POWELL'S MARKETING AND MANAGEMENT SERVICES
Real Estate Sales, Rentals & Management

**Modern and traditional houses.
Waterfront and inland properties.
Residential and commercial.**

Mrs Edith R Powell *(Manager)*
**Tel (242) 328-7238 or 356-0801
Fax (242) 326-2491**
No 30 Ludlow St • PO Box N-4225
Nassau, The Bahamas

Management Services Ltd, tel (242) 328-7238 or 356-0801; fax (242) 326-2491, e-mail: cpowell@bahamas.net.bs, www.bahamasnet.com/powells.html

LYFORD CAY: Superb ocean front property with beautiful beach. Four bdrm with *en suite* baths and two bdrm staff quarters. Contact Lyford Cay Real Estate Co Ltd, PO Box N-7776, Nassau, tel (242) 362-4703, fax (242) 362-4513.

LYFORD CAY: Canal front home with three bdrm and *en suite* baths. Staff bdrm and bath. Contact Lyford Cay Real Estate Co Ltd, PO Box N-7776, Nassau, tel (242) 362-4703, fax (242) 362-4513.

LYFORD CAY: Immaculate house on golf course. Three bdrm with *en suite* baths. Contact Lyford Cay Real Estate Co Ltd, PO Box N-7776, Nassau, tel (242) 362-4703, fax (242) 362-4513.

LYFORD CAY: Single story residence on ½-acre lot. Three bdrm, three bath, sunken living room, dining room, kitchen and breakfast room, family room, covered porch/patio, pool, one-car garage with large storage room and bath. Landscaped. Approx $1,200,000 gross. Contact Gregory Graham, Graham Real Estate, tel (242) 356-5030, fax (242) 326-5005, e-mail: grahamre@batelnet.bs

LYFORD CAY: Two-storey 6,448 sq ft residence on a tranquil canal front property in this exclusive gated community. Elegant formality with playful island charm. Three bdrm, three bath, great room, dining room, family room, kitchen, guest house, 2½

HOLOWESKO & COMPANY
COUNSEL & ATTORNEYS-AT-LAW

REPLY TO:
PARLIAMENT ST
PO BOX N-4911
TEL (242) 322 2315
    OR 322 1055
FAX (242) 322 5419

BRANCH OFFICE:
WEST BAY ST
PO BOX N7776-111
NASSAU, THE BAHAMAS
TEL (242) 362 6251/2
FAX (242) 362 5871
E-MAIL: LHOLOWESKO@BAHAMAS.NET.BS

Traditional Bahamian architecture features shutters, quoins, balconies and detailed railings.

car garage, and maid's quarters. $4 million. Contact C Investments Realtors, PO Box CB-11556, Nassau, tel (242) 328-7557, fax (242) 328-7994, e-mail: pcarey@cinvest.com, www.cinvest.com

MONTAGU BAY: Windwhistle. Located on the crest of the ridge overlooking Montagu Bay, this grand waterfront estate with 4,582 sq ft of air conditioned space boasts a five bdrm, four bath residence with natural pine floors, cypress ceilings, a screened-in furnished veranda, fruit orchard, two bdrm guest cottage and efficiency apartment. $3,750,000. Contact John Christie, H G Christie Ltd, PO Box N-8164, Nassau, tel (242) 322-1041, fax (242) 326-5642, e-mail: christie@bahamas.net.bs, www.hgchristie.com

OLD FORT BAY: Gated waterfront community next to Lyford Cay. Four bdrm, 4½ bath 5,775 sq ft home has travertine floors, tray ceilings throughout, breakfast room overlooking heated pool, separate dining room, living room with covered patio and fireplace, two-car garage, dock and dock house, one bdrm guest cottage. $9,300,000. Contact Damianos Realty Co, PO Box N-732, Nassau, tel (242) 322-2305, fax (242) 322-2033, e-mail: damianos@bahamas.net.bs, www.damianos.com

PALMDALE: Investment property not far from Paradise Island Bridge. Three buildings each with eight one-bed apartments. $650,000. Contact Barbara Brown, Real Estate Sales & Rentals Bahamas Ltd, PO Box N-1110, Nassau, tel (242) 322-2680, fax (242) 325-6353.

PARADISE ISLAND: Two bdrm, two bath harbourside condominiums. Dock space available. Contact Barbara Brown, Real Estate Sales & Rentals, PO Box N-1110, Nassau, tel (242) 322-2680, fax (242) 325-6353.

PARADISE ISLAND: Portside. Ten prestigious condominiums surrounding Hurricane Hole Marina. 1,457-2,800 sq ft. Renting fully furnished from $4,000 per month for two bdrm, 2½ bath units. Every residence has central air, marble floors and baths. Top-of-the-line modern appliances and breathtaking views of the sea with patios overlooking marina. 24 hr security. Rentals include real estate commission. Contact Damianos Realty Co, PO Box N-732, Nassau, tel (242) 322-2305, fax (242) 322-2033, e-mail: damianos@bahamas.net.bs, www.damianos.com

PARADISE ISLAND: Large harbour front three bdrm, 3½ bath furnished town house with large private patio off living room and covered patio off master bdrm, both overlooking the sea; security gated, rolldown shutters, two docks. $1.1 million. Contact Damianos Realty Co, PO Box N-732, Nassau, tel (242) 322-2305, fax (242) 322-2033, e-mail: damianos@bahamas.net.bs, www.damianos.com

PARADISE ISLAND: Three bdrm, 2½ bath 1,800 sq ft apartments on the harbour. Pre-construction prices $750,000. Contact C A Christie Realtors, PO Box N-8245, Nassau, tel (242) 326-4800, fax (242) 326-5684, e-mail: cacreest@batelnet.bs, www.bahamasnet.com/cac.html

PARADISE ISLAND: Four three bdrm, 2½ bath two-storey villas each with a separate pool. Optional loft can be used as a bdrm, bath or study. $995,000. Contact C A Christie Realtors, PO Box N-8245, Nassau, tel (242) 326-4800, fax (242) 326-5684, e-mail: cacreest@batelnet.bs, www.bahamasnet.com/cac.html

YOUR WINDOW OF
(real estate) OPPORTUNITY.

MORLEY REALTY
LIMITED

East Shirley St, PO Box SS-19085
Nassau, Bahamas
E-mail: morleyrealty@morleyrealty.com
Web: www.morleyrealty.com

Tel 242-394-7070
Fax 242-394-7069

**Prudential
Referral Services** *Plus*
INTERNATIONAL NETWORK

Sandyport west of Cable Beach combines town houses, individual homes, timeshare in a gated community.

PARADISE ISLAND: Three bdrm 2,700 sq ft beachfront town house. 24 hr security. Partial view of beach. Excellent rental opportunities. $689,000. Contact Michael Toporowski, RE/MAX Nassau Realty, tel (242) 394-7777, fax (242) 394-8045, www.bahamas-real-estate.com

PARADISE ISLAND: Lakefront three bdrm, three bath villa 60 yds from the beach. Private pool. Attached studio apartment with separate entrance. $600,000. Contact Gregory Graham, Graham Real Estate, tel (242) 356-5030, fax (242) 326-5005, e-mail: grahamre@batelnet.bs

SANDYPORT: Waterfront five bdrm, 4½ bath semi-furnished penthouse condo. 24 hr security, private beach club. $599,000. List #2840. Contact Bahamas Realty Ltd, PO Box N-1132, Nassau, tel (242) 393-8618, fax (242) 393-0326, www.bahamasrealty.bs

WEST BAY ST: Mediterranean style five bdrm, 5½ bath home overlooking Old Fort Bay. Fully furnished and equipped, sweeping verandas, outdoor patio, pool, covered pool bar & barbecue, guest cottage/office, three-car garage, standby generator, 80 ft dock. $3,975,000. List #3007. Contact Bahamas Realty Ltd, PO Box N-1132, Nassau, tel (242) 393-8618, fax (242) 393-0326, www.bahamasrealty.bs

WESTERN NEW PROVIDENCE: Overlooking Old Fort Bay on 100 ft of waterfront. Main house, two-car garage, pool, bayside gazebo, guest cottage.

THE EXPONENTIAL ELECTRICAL INDUSTRY

"Work that's Autographed with Quality"

LICENSED 3-Ø CONTRACTORS
Electrical Sales & Service
Installations: Residential, Commercial & Industrial
RISER DIAGRAMS • PANEL SCHEDULES
#39 FINLAYSON ST, PO BOX N-4362, NASSAU, THE BAHAMAS
TEL (242) 325-6079 or 324-8512 • FAX (242) 322-1193

C A CHRISTIE REAL ESTATE

REFLECTING THE QUALITY OF THE BAHAMAS

SPECIALIZING IN RESIDENTIAL AND COMMERCIAL PROPERTIES AND PRIVATE ISLANDS, LAND DEVELOPERS • BAHAMAS GOVERNMENT ASSESSORS

Reginald Court, #5 George St, PO BOX N-8245, NASSAU, THE BAHAMAS
TEL (242) 325-7960, 325-3957 or 322-8093 or 322-6311 • FAX (242) 326-5684
www.bahamasnet.com/cachristie

$3,975,000. Contact The Real Estate Exchange, PO Box F-43393, Freeport, tel (242) 351-4731, fax (242) 351-4736, e-mail: realestatex@batelnet.bs

YAMACRAW: New homes in a gated community. 1,580 sq ft and up. Financing available. Development is 60% sold out. Starting at $149,000. Contact Michael Toporowski, RE/MAX Nassau Realty, tel (242) 394-7777, fax (242) 394-8045, www.bahamas-real-estate.com

ABACO
Private 25 plus acre island. Four bdrm, three bath main house with commanding views from covered verandas and outdoor patios. Fully furnished and equipped. Solar electricity with two standby diesel generators, 80,000 gal capacity rain water tank. Other amenities include a two bdrm caretaker's cottage, one bdrm gardener's cottage, boat house, beach cabana, protected anchorage and dock. $3 million. Contact Bahamas Realty Ltd, PO Box N-1132, Nassau, tel (242) 393-8618, fax (242) 393-0326, www.bahamasrealty.bs

CLOVE CAY: Three bdrm, three bath 3,000 sq ft residence on one of the best equipped and developed private islands. Three stage water purification system, 15,000 watt solar six (six-day energy reserve); solid concrete dock, covered boat house with concrete ramp, winch, independent power system and fresh water shower; two separate storage facilities; concrete walkways; 1,100 cu ft walk-in cold storage; new 19 ft Boston Whaler Outrage with 200 hp Yamaha engine; small portable generator; extensive landscaping. $3,600,000 gross. Contact Gregory Graham, Graham Real Estate, tel (242) 356-5030, fax (242) 326-5005, e-mail: grahamre@batelnet.bs

MAN-O-WAR CAY: Cave Hill. Breathtaking waterfront estate lushly landscaped with tropical foliage. Main residence, guest cottage, boat house and well protected harbour with docks. $1,550,000. Contact John Christie, H G Christie Ltd, PO Box N-8164, Nassau, tel (242) 322-1041, fax (242) 326-5642, e-mail: christie@bahamas.net.bs, www.hgchristie.com

SCOTLAND CAY: Fly onto a private airstrip and walk to your three bdrm home with a view of the Atlantic Ocean. $350,000. No cars allowed, only boats, planes and golf carts. Private moorage included. Contact Michael Toporowski, RE/MAX Nassau Realty, tel (242) 394-7777, fax (242) 394-8045, www.bahamas-real-estate.com

SPANISH CAY: This 185-acre private island has impressive features including $7\frac{1}{2}$ miles of waterfront, 5,000 ft jet runway, 70-slip full service marina, 95 unsold home sites, underground utilities, four tennis courts, paved streets, two restaurants, five hotel suites, and much more. Perfect for development opportunities or as an idyllic private island. $9 million. Contact Damianos Realty Co, PO Box N-732, Nassau, tel (242) 322-2305, fax (242) 322-2033, e-mail: damianos@bahamas.net.bs, www.bahamas.net.bs/design/damianos

ATLANTIC FINANCIAL NETWORK

... offering a wide range of financial services and investment opportunities. Headquarted in a rapidly expanding, investor friendly tax haven and stable financial centre ... The Bahamas. One goal ... your success.

Enjoy your dream!

Investment Masters

Investment brokers and managers offering a wide array of corporate services and opportunities.

Achieve your dream!

tel (242) 323-TIME

Insurance Governors

Insurance brokers and managers offering protection against every risk under the sun.

Secure your dream!

tel (242) 394-8700
fax (242) 394-6694

Atlantic First
Insurance Company

The company that puts you first.

tel (242) 32-FIRST

Royal Caribbean Estates

Real estate brokers, managers and developers (Inc Castle Construction Co). Offering the best of The Bahamas and the Caribbean

Experience your dream!

tel (242) 39-DREAM
(242) 394-6688

Atlantic Accounting

Accounting services for emerging investors, businesses and professionals.

Advance your dream!

tel (242) 394-6845

Beaumont House, Bay St • PO Box SS-6236 • Nassau, The Bahamas
tel (242) 328-2000 • fax (242) 328-4642

BROKERS INVITED AND PROTECTED

OCEANIA PROPERTIES LTD
AND BAY PROPERTIES LTD

Specializing in Leisure Resort Land Development
George Town, Great Exuma
Yachting Capital of The Bahamas

Oceania

If the prospect of the world's clearest ocean, balmy breezes and pristine beaches aren't enough to excite you, let's talk money. TAX FREE MONEY.

Oceania Properties offers stunning ocean-view lots for sale with enormous investment potential. Vacation at our luxurious resort on Exuma and see for yourself. For more information, drop the coupon in the mail.
If you prefer, call us at (242) 356-4880/1 or fax us at (242) 356-4628.

I am interested in:
- purchasing an Oceania Properties Lot
- building a vacation home with income earning potential
- hotel/condominium joint-venture investment
- purchasing a luxury condominium/townhouse

Name:
Address:
State/Province: Country:
ZIP/Postal Code: Home Telephone:
Occupation: Work Telephone:

Have you ever visited The Bahamas before?   yes   no
Best time to reach you: morning   afternoon   evening
To: Oceania Properties Ltd • PO Box CB-12067 • Nassau, The Bahamas

We've got it!

The Most Comprehensive Website in The Bahamas

- Business
- Investment
- Real Estate
- Government
- Shopping
- Dining
- Entertainment
- Activities

OVER 300 PAGES OF INFORMATION!

As an information provider affiliated with The Bahamas' most prominent publisher, Bahamasnet offers the latest, most up-to-date information. Access current vacation and business information with the click of a mouse.

Join our select list of prestigious clients – including government agencies, international corporations, prominent local businesses and institutions.

DESIGN · HOSTING · DEVELOPMENT

Catch the Wave

bahamasnet
www.bahamasnet.com

PO Box N-7513, Nassau, The Bahamas
Tel (242) 323 5665 Fax (242) 323 5728
email info@bahamasnet.com

Mosko's
Group of Building Companies

Mosko's United Construction
The premier building & civil engineering contractor in The Bahamas with over 40 years' experience.

Bahamas Marine Construction
Leading marine construction company in the Islands. Projects include pilings, bulkheads, bridges and salvage operations.

N.P. Building Supplies
Producing and supplying up to 500 cubic yards of quality-controlled ready mixed concrete per day.

Mosko's Furniture
Manufacture and installation of the finest furniture, cabinetwork and millwork since 1925.

For all your building needs

PO Box N-641 • Nassau, The Bahamas
Tel (242) 322-2571 • Fax (242) 325-2571

TREASURE CAY: Home sites are available at this 1,400-acre self-contained resort with a 3½-mile beach rated by *National Geographic* as one of the top 10 in the world. Amenities include par 72 Dick Wilson designed championship golf course, 150-slip marina, dive shop and hotel with villas on the beach. Jet airport nearby with daily flights from Florida. Over seven miles of seawall provide home sites on the canal/marina, golf course and beach front. Over 700 homeowners to date. Hotel sites available. Contact Anne Albury or Marcellus Roberts at Treasure Cay Ltd, Real Estate Division, tel (242) 365-8538, fax (242) 365-8587.

TREASURE CAY: 12-acre hotel site on one of the most beautiful beaches in the world. All utilities and infrastructure in place. Jet airport (can land B-727s) only seven miles away, 150-slip marina and championship golf course within walking distance. Contact Anne Albury or Marcellus Roberts, Treasure Cay Ltd, Real Estate Division, tel (242) 365-8538, fax (242) 365-8587.

ELEUTHERA

GOVERNOR'S HARBOUR: Unicorn Cay. 415-acre estate overlooking 3,700 ft of magnificent beach. Includes 6,000 sq ft Spanish colonial home with caretaker's cottage, central air, sauna, alarm, jacuzzi, tennis courts and pool. Ideal for a resort hotel or private estate. $5,250,000. Contact John Christie, H G Christie Ltd, PO Box N-8164, Nassau, tel (242) 322-1041, fax (242) 326-5642, e-mail: christie@bahamas.net.bs, www.hgchristie.com

NORTH ELEUTHERA: 100 acres of prime real estate on some of the finest beaches in The Bahamas. Perfect for hotel, condominium, or time-share resort development. 15 minutes from Nassau. Easy access to all utilities. Contact First Atlantic Realty, tel (242) 352-7071, fax (242) 351-2505, e-mail: firstatlantic@batelnet.bs

WINDING BAY: Eden. Three bdrm, four bath home on five-plus acres with 412 ft beach front. Extensive landscaping. Guest suite with kitchenette, bath and dressing area, maid's area and bath, garage, two cisterns. $786,375 gross. Contact Gregory Graham, Graham Real Estate, tel (242) 356-5030, fax (242) 326-5005, grahamre@batelnet.bs

WINDERMERE ISLAND: Shell Sea. Spectacular ocean view three bdrm, three bath home on 1½ beautifully landscaped lots with 225 ft of prime beach frontage, pool, French doors, powder room, pickled pine ceilings and his and her closets. $1,250,000. Contact John Christie, H G Christie Ltd, PO Box N-8164, Nassau, tel (242) 322-1041, fax (242) 326-5642, e-mail: christie@bahamas.net.bs, www.hgchristie.com

EXUMA

CRAB CAY: Lush tropical acreage containing 30-60 ft hills with rich soil and good vegetation. Can easily be connected to Great Exuma near George Town. Crab Cay, 200 acres, is surrounded by 8-10 ft deep water and is a perfect location for resort development. $5,300,000. Contact C A Christie Real Estate, PO Box N-8245,

Nassau, tel (242) 326-4800, fax (242) 326-5684, e-mail: cacreest@batelnet.bs, www.bahamasnet.com/cac.html

LITTLE EXUMA: Brand new 2,100 sq ft Mediterranean style home on the beach, 15 miles south of George Town. $515,000. Contact Michael Toporowski, RE/MAX Nassau Realty, tel, (242) 394-7777, fax (242) 394-8045, www.bahamas-real-estate.com

OCEANIA HEIGHTS: Approx 15 miles from George Town, Exuma and 130 miles from Nassau, near Moss Town Intl Airport. 42½ acres of stunning ocean view lots with enormous investment potential. This gated community will offer a private club house, tennis courts, croquet lawns, shuffle board courts and a putting green. Contact Phillip Minnis, PO Box CB-12067, Nassau, tel (242) 356-4880/1, fax (242)356-4628.

GRAND BAHAMA

BELL CHANNEL CLUB & MARINA: An exclusive beach front community of luxuriously furnished two bdrm, two bath suites and three bdrm, 3½ bath town houses. Private patios, ocean and channel views, central air, designer interiors, cable TV, whirlpool tubs, bidets, security gate, 25-slip marina, private pool and beach, social bar, tennis court. Prices on application. Contact Megeve Investments Ltd, PO Box F-44053, Freeport, tel (242) 373-2673 or 373-3801; fax (242) 373-3802.

EASTERN GRAND BAHAMA: Ocean front cottage on 4.929 acres. One bdrm, one bath. Addition of 500 sq ft. Fully equipped with washer and dryer. $300,000. Contact RE/MAX Freeport Northern Bahamas, PO BOX F-42480, tel (242) 352-7305, fax (242) 352-3560, e-mail: remaxfpo@concentric.net

FREEPORT: Single storey home on golf course. Six bdrm, five bath, office, formal living room, dining room, kitchen, utility room, pool and sauna. $595,000. Contact RE/MAX Freeport Northern Bahamas, PO BOX F-42480, Freeport, tel (242) 352-7305, fax (242) 352-3560, e-mail: remaxfpo@concentric.net

FREEPORT: Exclusive ocean front and canal front lots in a gated community. Lush natural landscaping and privacy for individual land owners. Prices start at $180,000 for canal front lots and $390,000 for ocean front lots. Contact RE/MAX Freeport Northern Bahamas, PO BOX F-42480, Freeport, tel (242) 352-7305, fax (242) 352-3560, e-mail: remaxfpo@concentric.net

FREEPORT: Waterfront lots from $75,000, beachfront lots from $200,000 per acre, golf course lots from $25,000 and several choice lots for hotel and condominium development. Contact Century 21 Harry Dann & Co Ltd, PO Box F-42431, Freeport, tel (242) 352-7492, fax (242) 352-7493, e-mail: century21@harrydann.com, www.century21harrydann.com

FREEPORT: Executive waterfront home minutes from beach, $185,000. Beach front home at $500,000. Contact The Real Estate Exchange Ltd, PO Box F-43393, Freeport, tel (242) 351-4731, fax (242) 351-4736, e-mail: realestatex@batelnet.bs

FREEPORT: Eightplex (one bdrm) apartment building producing income of $46,800 per year. $340,000. Fifty unit (studio) apartment building fully rented, $1,600,000. Contact The Real Estate Exchange Ltd, PO Box F-43393, Freeport, tel (242) 351-4731, fax (242) 351-4736, e-mail: realestatex@batelnet.bs

FREEPORT: Industrial/commercial park with office/manufacturing/medical and storage facilities for lease. Units from 25-17,000 sq ft, 60,000 sq ft total. Innotec, tel (242) 352-7511, fax (242) 352-3748.

FREEPORT: New executive style four bdrm, three bath home on the waterfront in a quiet neighbourhood. Walking distance to beach. Two minutes from Intl Bazaar $450,000. Contact First Atlantic Realty, tel (242) 352-7071, fax (242) 351-2505, e-mail: firstatlantic@batelnet.bs

LUCAYAN MARINA VILLAGE: Midshipman Rd, 10 mins from Freeport Intl Airport. Private waterfront residential community of luxury homes with unobstructed views of marina and Bell Channel. Amenities include a pool, 125-slip full service marina, restaurants and 24 hr security. Private shuttle ferries residents and guests to Port Lucaya Marketplace. Prices start at $450,000. Contact New Hope Holding Co Ltd, PO Box F-43234, Freeport, tel (242) 373-7616, fax (242) 373-7630.

OLD BAHAMA BAY: Private residential community and resort being developed with 24 private estates, 150-slip marina, beachfront cottage-style resort, pool,

---

Waste Disposal A Problem?

Bahamas Waste Management Systems Ltd specializes in offering solutions to your waste disposal problems. We offer prompt, reliable collection of garbage from your residential or commercial site. We can also provide any size compactor or container for the healthy storage of waste material.

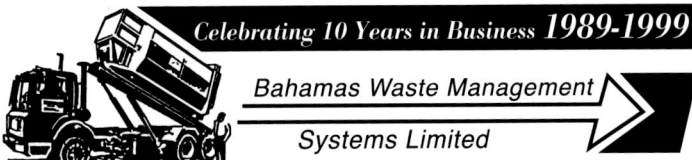

Celebrating 10 Years in Business **1989-1999**

Bahamas Waste Management Systems Limited

NEAR THE JUNCTION OF JOHN F KENNEDY DR & FARRINGTON RD • PO BOX N-44, NASSAU, THE BAHAMAS
TEL (242) 328-7671, 328-2383 OR 328-2393
FAX (242) 322-7049 • CELLULAR 357-9730
Family Island service available in: • North Andros • Harbour Island, Eleuthera

Stocking Island overlooks the western side of Elizabeth Harbour in the Exumas.

tropical landscaping, full security with gated entry and private dockage. Contact John Christie, H G Christie Ltd, PO Box N-8164, Nassau, tel (242) 322-1041, fax (242) 326-5642, e-mail: christie@bahamas.net.bs, www.hgchristie.com

PRINCESS ISLE: An ultra luxurious, private, residential gated community comprising 53 waterfront estate home sites on a 60-acre peninsula. Each estate is approx one acre with 150 ft waterfront as well as canal dockage. $390,000-$2.7 million. Contact Gene E Bruey, Princess Realty, PO Box F-40685, Freeport, tel (242) 352-7411, fax (242) 352-7966.

WATERS EDGE: Luxurious waterfront individual one- and two-storey family homes. Secure gated community. Protective harbour and docking facilities. Beautiful landscaping. Leases from $2,350-$5,000 per month. Sales from $295,000-$545,000. Financing available. Contact Wendy Johnson, property manager, Waters Edge Development Ltd, tel (242) 352-7511, fax (242) 352-3748.

**Contractors count on
Commonwealth – so can you!**

**Storefronts
Windows
Steel doors
Wood doors
Aluminum doors
Hurricane protection
Acoustical ceilings
Architectural building supplies**

Tel (242) 325-2505/7 or 325-1292/4 • Fax (242) 325-1204
e-mail: cbs@batelnet.bs • PO Box SS-6268
Robinson Rd (opp Podoleo St)
Open Mon–Fri • 7am–5pm

executive printers of the bahamas, ltd

ep

The best choice for all your printing needs.

Continuous computer forms

Snap apart carbon & NCR forms

Full colour scenic bank cheques

Register forms

Full colour printing

Duplicating

Letterheads, envelopes, business card

Tel (242) 393-5011

Fax (242) 393-6425

PO Box N-4555

Nassau, The Bahamas

BAHAMAS CLASSIFIED DIRECTORY

See also **Freeport/Lucaya Classified Directory**, pgs 518-520

ACCOUNTANTS/ACCOUNTING FIRMS
Alan E H Bates & Co 258
Atlantic Accounting .... opp 248
Bahamas Institute of
   Chartered Accountants 210
BDO Mann Judd 225
Gomez & Nairn 199
KPMG 182
PricewaterhouseCoopers 181

AIR CARGO
DHL Worldwide Express 202
Federal Express (FedEx) 233
Tropical Brokerage Services Ltd 155

AIR-CONDITIONING & REFRIGERATION EQUIPMENT & SERVICING
Islandwide Airconditioning Co Ltd 258
Taylor Industries Ltd 261

AIRLIFT/AIR AMBULANCE & AMBULANCE SERVICES
LifeFlight 136
See also **Hospitals** and
Medical/Emergency Services.

AIRLINE
Bahamasair 115

ANSWERING SERVICE
Island Business Centre 193

APPLIANCES – SALES, SERVICE & REPAIR
Islandwide Airconditioning Co Ltd 258
Taylor Industries Ltd 261

ARCHITECTS
AMEE International 195
Gold Circle Co Ltd 240
Kairos Development &
   Construction Co Ltd 236
Land Design of Nassau Ltd 239

ATTORNEYS/NOTARIES PUBLIC
See **Law Firms.**

AUDIO/VIDEO SYSTEMS
Satellite Bahamas 157

AUDIT & RELATED SERVICES
See **Accountants/Accounting Firms.**

AUTOMOBILE ACCESSORIES, PARTS & REPAIRS
Automotive and Industrial
   Distributors Ltd (AID) 154

BANKS, FINANCIAL HOUSES & TRUST COMPANIES
Ansbacher (Bahamas) Ltd .... bet 184-185
Axxess International Ltd 26
Banco Santander Trust & Banking Corp
   (Bahamas) Ltd 214
Bank of Nova Scotia Trust
   Co (Bahamas) Ltd, The 211
Banque Privée Edmond
   de Rothschild Ltd 33
Banque SCS Alliance (Nassau) Ltd 22
Barclays Bank PLC 169
Best Funds Distributors Inc 183
Cardinal International Group, The 203
Central Bank of
   The Bahamas, The .... bet 120-121
Charleston Private Management Ltd 215
Chase Manhattan Private Bank
   & Trust Co (Bahamas) Ltd, The 199
Darier Hentsch Private Bank
   & Trust Ltd 175
Deltec Panamerica Trust Co Ltd 173
Dominion Investments Ltd 206
Ferrier Lullin Bank & Trust
   (Bahamas) Ltd 19
Fidelity Bank & Trust
   International Ltd .... opp 216
Foster & Dunhill (Bahamas) Ltd 48
Guta Bank & Trust Ltd .... bet 152-153
Handelsfinanz-CCF Bank
   International Ltd .... bet 184-185
International Portfolio Analytics Ltd 188
International Trade & Investments Ltd .. 189
MeesPierson Trust .... bet 152-153
Montaque Securities International 211
Morymor Trust Corp Ltd 213
Nordfinanz Bank Zurich .... opp 184
Norshield International 36
Oceanic Bank & Trust Ltd 178
Orbitex Group of Funds .... opp 120
Pictet Bank & Trust Ltd 200
The Private Trust Corp Ltd 213
RBC Dominion Securities
   (Global) Ltd .... Back cover
Royal Bank of Canada .... Back cover
Royal Bank of Scotland
   International, The .... opp 121
Scotiatrust 211
Surety Bank & Trust Co Ltd 180
Templeton Global Advisors Ltd 17
UBS (Bahamas) Ltd 171
United European Bank & Trust
   (Nassau) Ltd 191

BATTERIES – AUTOMOTIVE, HEAVY EQUIPMENT & MARINE
Automotive & Industrial
   Distributors Ltd (AID) 154
Nassau Bicycle Co Ltd 257
Harbourside Marine 102

BEEPERS/CELLULAR/PAGERS
Bahamas Telecommunications Corp
   (BaTelCo) 132-133
BEL Communications Ltd 230

Set sail with us ...

Visitors' best source of information on The Bahamas

Dupuch
PUBLICATIONS
Etienne Dupuch Jr Publications Ltd

PO Box N-7513, Nassau, The Bahamas, Tel 242-323-5665 • Fax 242-323-5728

BICYCLES, MOTOR CYCLES & SCOOTERS
Nassau Bicycle Co Ltd 257

BOATS – MANUFACTURE & SALES
Harbourside Marine 102
Nassau Bicycle Co Ltd 257

BREWERY/LIQUOR MANUFACTURE LOCAL & EXPORT
Commonwealth Brewery Ltd 44

BROADCASTING
See **Communications & Broadcasting**; **Radio Station**; and **Television Station**.

BUILDING CONTRACTORS
Bahamas Marine
    Construction Co Ltd .... opp 249
Gold Circle Co Ltd 240
Kairos Development &
    Construction Co Ltd 236
Mosko's Group of
    Building Cos .... opp 249
Mosko's United
    Construction Co Ltd .... opp 249

BUILDING SUPPLIES
Automotive & Industrial
    Distributors Ltd (AID) 154
Commonwealth Building
    Supplies Ltd 253
JBR Building Supplies Ltd 238
NP Building Supplies .... opp 249
Tops Hardware & Plumbing Supplies 238

BUSINESS SYSTEMS CONSULTING, MANAGEMENT, TROUBLE-SHOOTING
IBM Bahamas Ltd 177
Lignum Technologies (Bahamas) Ltd 222
Systems Resource Group, The 113

CABINETRY
Mosko's Furniture .... opp 249

CAPTIVE INSURANCE
Britannia Consulting Group, The 196
Guta Bank & Trust Ltd .... bet 152-153
See also **Insurance**.

CAR RENTALS
Avis 323
Budget 141

CHARTERED ACCOUNTANTS
See **Accountants/Accounting Firms**

CLAIMS SETTLING
McKinney, Bancroft & Hughes 172
Nassau Survey Agency Ltd 119

CLEANING/JANITORIAL SERVICES
Frank Hanna Cleaning Co Ltd 237

CLEANING PRODUCTS/EQUIPMENT
Frank Hanna Cleaning Co Ltd 237

COASTAL PLANNERS
Land Design of Nassau Ltd 239

COMMUNICATIONS & BROADCASTING
BEL Communications Ltd 230
Bahamas Telecommunications Corp
    (BaTelCo) 132-133
Bahamasnet .... 228, bet 248-249, 263, 505
BaTelNet 132-133
Broadcasting Corp
    of The Bahamas, The .... bet 216-217
Satellite Bahamas 157
ZNS Network .... bet 216-217

COMPUTERS – SALES, SERVICE & SUPPLIES
IBM Bahamas Ltd 177
Lignum Technologies (Bahamas) Ltd 222
Systems Resource Group, The 113

CONDOMINIUMS
BAYROC Exclusive Beach Residences 38
Portside Condominiums 31
See also **Real Estate**.

CORPORATE FINANCE, MANAGEMENT & ADVISORY SERVICES
Alan E H Bates & Co 258
Ansbacher (Bahamas) Ltd .... bet 184-185
Atlantic Financial Network .... opp 248
Axxess International Ltd 26
Bahamas Incorporation Services Ltd 209
Bahamas Institute of
    Chartered Accountants 210
Banco Santander Trust & Banking Corp
    (Bahamas) Ltd 214
Bank of Nova Scotia Trust
    Co (Bahamas) Ltd, The 211
Banque Privée Edmond
    de Rothschild Ltd 33

Nassau Bicycle Co., Ltd.
distributors for Yamaha Outboard Motors

YAMAHA

Factory Trained Technicians
Full line of parts & accessories
Centreville Shopping Plaza
5th Terrace, off Collins Ave
Tel (242) 322-8511 • Fax (242) 323-7583

257

Banque SCS Alliance (Nassau) Ltd 22
Barclays Bank PLC 169
BDO Mann Judd 225
Best Funds Distributors Inc 183
Britannia Consulting Group, The 196
Cardinal International Group, The 203
Charleston Private Management Ltd 215
Chase Manhattan Private Bank
  & Trust Co (Bahamas) Ltd, The 199
Darier Hentsch Private Bank
  & Trust Ltd 175
Deltec Panamerica Trust Co Ltd 173
Dominion Investments Ltd 206
Ferrier Lullin Bank &
  Trust (Bahamas) Ltd 19
Fidelity Bank & Trust
  International Ltd .... opp 216
Foster & Dunhill (Bahamas) Ltd 48
Gomez & Nairn 199
Guta Bank & Trust Ltd .... bet 152-153
Handelsfinanz-CCF Bank
  International Ltd .... bet 184-185
International Portfolio Analytics Ltd 188
International Trade & Investments Ltd .. 189
Investment Masters .... opp 248
KPMG 182
MeesPierson Trust .... bet 152-153
Montaque Securities International 211
Morymor Trust Corp Ltd 213
Nordfinanz Bank Zurich .... opp 184
Norshield International 36
Oceanic Bank & Trust Ltd 178
Orbitex Group of Funds .... opp 120
Pictet Bank & Trust Ltd 200
PricewaterhouseCoopers 181
Private Trust Corp Ltd, The 213
RBC Dominion Securities
  (Global) Ltd .... Back cover

Royal Bank of Canada .... Back cover
Royal Bank of Scotland
  International, The .... opp 121
Scotiatrust 211
Surety Bank & Trust Co Ltd 180
Templeton Global Advisors Ltd 17
UBS (Bahamas) Ltd 171
United European Bank & Trust
  (Nassau) Ltd 191

COURIER SERVICE
DHL Worldwide Express 202
Federal Express (FedEx) 233

CREDIT CARD
Axxess International Ltd 26
Infiniti Global Axxess............................... 26
MasterCard 26

CUSTOMS BROKERS
Tropical Brokerage Services Ltd 155

DRY CLEANING & LAUNDRY SERVICE
New Oriental Cleaners 259

**ELECTRICAL CONTRACTORS,
SUPPLIES & MAINTENANCE**
Automotive & Industrial
  Distributors Ltd (AID) 154
Exponential Electrical Industry, The 247
Taylor Industries Ltd 261
Western Electric 262

**ELECTRONIC/ELECTRICAL EQUIPMENT –
SUPPLIES & REPAIRS**
BEL Communications Ltd 230

ENGINEERS
Mosko's Group of Building Cos ...... opp 249
Mosko's United Construction
  Co Ltd .... opp 249

ALAN E H BATES & CO
CHARTERED ACCOUNTANTS

AUDIT & ACCOUNTING • CORPORATE SERVICES • BUSINESS ADVISORY SERVICE

3RD FLOOR, KINGS COURT, BAY ST • PO BOX N-63, NASSAU, THE BAHAMAS
TEL (242) 322-8464 • FAX (242) 328-6772 OR 327-1636
MEMBER FIRM OF MACINTYRE STRÄTER INTERNATIONAL LIMITED

ISLANDWIDE AIRCONDITIONING CO LTD
SPECIALIZING IN
TEMPSTAR brand • Sales, service & parts • Commercial • Residential
• Industrial • Central air • Package units • Installations • Repairs

FREE ESTIMATES. CALL 326-3934 OR 326-3935
East St, south of Malcolm Rd, PO Box CB 11896, Nassau, The Bahamas

FAX SERVICES
Island Business Centre 193

FINANCIAL SERVICES
Bahamas Financial
    Services Board ....bet 120-121
Bahamas Investment Authority Financial
    Services Secretariat (BIA) .... opp 153
Central Bank of
    The Bahamas, The .... bet 120-121
Securities Commission of
    The Bahamas .... opp 152
See also **Banks, Financial Houses & Trust Companies; Corporate Finance, Management & Advisory Services;** and **Investment Advisory/Asset Management Services.**

FOOD PRODUCTS – WHOLESALE & RETAIL
Asa H Pritchard Ltd 129
City Markets Food Stores 161
Island Seafoods Ltd 262

FUEL
See **Gasoline and Petroleum Products**

FURNITURE (incl CUSTOM DESIGNED & HANDMADE)
InterDesign 242
Mosko's Furniture .... opp 249

GARBAGE DISPOSAL – COMMERCIAL & RESIDENTIAL
Bahamas Waste Management
    Systems Ltd 251

GASOLINE – BULK/STATIONS
Esso Standard Oil SA Ltd .... bet 216-217

GENEALOGY/FAMILY TREE RESEARCH
Holowesko & Co 243

HARDWARE – TOOLS & GARDENING SUPPLIES
Automotive & Industrial
    Distributors Ltd (AID) 154
Commonwealth Building Supplies Ltd .. 253
JBR Building Supplies Ltd 238
Tops Hardware & Plumbing Supplies 238

HORTICULTURALIST
Land Design of Nassau Ltd 239

HOSPITALS
Doctors Hospital (1986) Ltd 131
Miami Children's Hospital 136
Mount Sinai Medical Center 136
See also **Airlift/Air Ambulance & Ambulance Services** and **Medical/Emergency Services.**

HOTEL & RESTAURANT SUPPLIES
Asa H Pritchard Ltd 129
City Markets Food Stores 161
Island Seafoods Ltd 262

Keep them looking good!

INTERNATIONAL FABRICARE INSTITUTE

If Sun Sea San, New Oriental man, can't keep your clothes looking good, he'll say so.
Even well-made garments have their problems. So, for regular beauty treatments, bring your clothes to us.
We'll give them the special care they need!

Need alterations or repairs?
We have a full time seamstress at Cable Beach
Tell Sun Sea San what you think of him!
Call our Quality Hotline 322-4407

New Oriental Cleaners

Shirley St at Mount Royal Ave 322-4406, Nassau St, Super Wash Bldg 323-7249,
Cable Beach Shpg Ctr 327-6882, Wullf Rd at Montrose Ave 323-4343,
Mackey & Madeira St 322-2352, Shirley St opp Okra Hill 393-2908,
Prince Charles Shpg Ctr 393-7177, Golden Gates Shpg Ctr 361-3382,
East St south of Wullf Rd 326-7649,
Do Drop In, Ross Corner 322-3733

HOTELS
Small Treasures 21
  Bay View Village, Club Land'or,
  Compass Point Beach Club, Dillet's Guest
  House, Graycliff, Orange Hill Beach Inn,
  Paradise Harbour Club & Marina, Red
  Carpet Inn, Sunrise Beach Club & Villas,
  The Villas on Crystal Cay.
Treasure Cay Hotel Resort
  & Marina (Abaco) 42

HOUSEHOLD SUPPLIES
Automotive & Industrial
  Distributors Ltd (AID) 154

IMPORT & EXPORT SERVICES
DHL Worldwide Express 202
Federal Express (FedEx) 233
Tropical Brokerage Services Ltd 155

INCORPORATION SERVICES
Alan E H Bates & Co 258
Bahamas Incorporation Services Ltd 209
BDO Mann Judd 225
Britannia Consulting Group, The 196
Christie, Davis & Co 191
Dupuch & Turnquest & Co 190
Island Business Centre 193
Jerome E Pyfrom & Co 225
Lennox Paton 207
McKinney, Bancroft & Hughes 172
Pindling & Co 174
PricewaterhouseCoopers 181
See also **Accountants/Accounting Firms;**
Banks, Financial Houses & Trust
Companies; Corporate Finance,
Management & Advisory Services;
Investment Advisory/Asset Management
Services; and **Law Firms.**

INDUSTRIAL/LAWN EQUIPMENT
MANUFACTURE & SALES
Automotive & Industrial
  Distributors Ltd (AID) 154
Commonwealth Building
  Supplies Ltd 253

INFORMATION TECHNOLOGY SERVICES
IBM Bahamas Ltd 177
KPMG 182
Lignum Technologies (Bahamas) Ltd 222
Systems Resource Group, The 113

INSURANCE
Atlantic First Insurance Co .... opp 248
Bahamas First General
  Insurance Co Ltd 119, 205
Insurance Governors .... opp 248
Nassau Underwriters Agency Ltd 119
Royal & Sun Alliance .... opp 185
Vaughn L Culmer & Assocs Insurance
  Agents & Brokers Ltd 194
See also **Captive Insurance** and **Title**
Insurance.

INTERIOR DESIGN & DECORATING –
COMMERCIAL & RESIDENTIAL
AMEE International 195
InterDesign 242
Kairos Development &
  Construction Co Ltd 236

INTERNET SERVICES
Bahamas Telecommunications Corp
  (BaTelCo) 132-133
Bahamasnet .... 228, bet 248-249, 263, 505
BaTelNet 132-133
Systems Resource Group, The 113

INVESTMENT ADVISORY/ASSET
MANAGEMENT SERVICES
Alan E H Bates & Co 258
Ansbacher (Bahamas) Ltd .... bet 184-185
Atlantic Financial Network .... opp 248
Axxess International Ltd 26
Bahamas Incorporation Services Ltd 209
Bahamas Institute of
  Chartered Accountants 210
Banco Santander Trust & Banking Corp
  (Bahamas) Ltd 214
Bank of Nova Scotia Trust
  Co (Bahamas) Ltd, The 211
Banque Privée Edmond
  de Rothschild Ltd 33
Banque SCS Alliance (Nassau) Ltd 22
Barclays Bank PLC 169
BDO Mann Judd 225
Best Funds Distributors Inc 183
Britannia Consulting Group, The 196
Cardinal International Group, The 203
Chase Manhattan Private Bank
  and Trust Co (Bahamas) Ltd, The 199
Charleston Private Management Ltd 215
Darier Hentsch Private Bank
  & Trust Ltd 175
Deltec Panamerica Trust Co Ltd 173
Dominion Investments Ltd 206
Ferrier Lullin Bank & Trust
  (Bahamas) Ltd 19
Fidelity Bank & Trust
  International Ltd .... opp 216
Foster & Dunhill (Bahamas) Ltd 48
Guta Bank & Trust Ltd .... bet 152-153
Handelsfinanz-CCF Bank
  International Ltd .... bet 184-185
International Portfolio Analytics Ltd 188
International Trade & Investments Ltd .. 189
Investment Masters .... opp 248
KPMG 182
MeesPierson Trust .... bet 152-153
Montague Securities International 211
Morymor Trust Corp Ltd 213
Nordfinanz Bank Zurich .... opp 184
Norshield International 36
Oceanic Bank & Trust Ltd 178
Orbitex Group of Funds .... opp 120
Pictet Bank & Trust Ltd 200
PricewaterhouseCoopers 181
Private Trust Corp Ltd, The 213

RBC Dominion Securities
  (Global) Ltd .... Back cover
Royal Bank of Canada .... Back cover
Royal Bank of Scotland
  International, The .... opp 121
Scotiatrust 211
Surety Bank & Trust Co Ltd 180
Templeton Global Advisors Ltd 17
UBS (Bahamas) Ltd 171
United European Bank & Trust
  (Nassau) Ltd 191

INVESTMENT OPPORTUNITIES
See **Investment Advisory Services**
and **Real Estate.**

LANDSCAPE ARCHITECTS
Land Design of Nassau Ltd 239

LAW FIRMS
Christie, Davis & Co 191
Dupuch & Turnquest & Co 190
Holowesko & Co 243
Jeanne I Thompson 229
Jerome E Pyfrom & Co 225
Lennox Paton 207
McKinney, Bancroft & Hughes 172
Pindling & Co 174

LOSS ADJUSTERS
Nassau Survey Agency Ltd 119

MAILBOX SERVICE
Island Business Centre 193

MANAGEMENT CONSULTING
BDO Mann Judd 225
KPMG 182
PricewaterhouseCoopers 181

MARINAS/MARINE FUEL
Esso Standard Oil SA Ltd .... bet 216-217
Hurricane Hole Marina 30
Treasure Cay Hotel Resort
  & Marina (Abaco) 42

MARINE SUPPLIES
Harbourside Marine 102
Nassau Bicycle Co Ltd 257

MEDIA
See **Communications & Broadcasting,
Newspaper, Radio Station** and **Television
Station.**

MEDICAL/EMERGENCY SERVICES
Doctors Hospital (1986) Ltd 131
LifeFlight 136

Miami Children's Hospital 136
Mount Sinai Medical Center 136
See also **Airlift/Air Ambulance &
Ambulance Services** and **Hospitals.**

NETWORK PLANNING
IBM Bahamas Ltd 177
Lignum Technologies (Bahamas) Ltd 222
Systems Resource Group, The 113

NEWSPAPER
Nassau Guardian, The 111

OFFICE/MEETING ROOM FACILITIES
Island Business Centre 193

**OFFICE SUPPLIES, MACHINERY,
EQUIPMENT – SALES, INSTALLATION &
SERVICE**
Bahamas Telecommunications Corp
  (BaTelCo) 132-133
IBM Bahamas Ltd 177
Lignum Technologies (Bahamas) Ltd 222
Systems Resource Group, The 113
Taylor Industries Ltd 261
See also **Furniture.**

PETROLEUM PRODUCTS & LUBRICANTS
Automotive & Industrial
  Distributors Ltd (AID) 154
Esso Standard Oil SA Ltd .... bet 216-217

PLUMBING SUPPLIES
Automotive & Industrial
  Distributors Ltd (AID) 154
Commonwealth Building
  Supplies Ltd 253
JBR Building Supplies Ltd 238
Tops Hardware & Plumbing Supplies 238

PRINTING
Executive Printers
  of The Bahamas, Ltd 254
Nassau Guardian, The 111

**PROFESSIONAL MOVERS –
PACKING & CRATING**
Tropical Brokerage Services Ltd 155

PROPERTY/LAND DEVELOPMENT
Bay Properties Ltd .... bet 248-249
C A Christie Real Estate 247
Durrant-Harding Real Estate Co Ltd 227
Gold Circle Co Ltd 240
H G Christie Real Estate 221
Oceania Properties Ltd .... bet 248-249
Royal Caribbean Estates .... opp 248

TAYLOR INDUSTRIES LTD Since 1945
Window & Wall Air Conditioners
Amana • **6,500-18,000 BTU** • *Emerson* **15,000-32,000 BTU**
Home • Office • Shop • Apartment
111 Shirley St, PO Box N-4806 • Nassau, The Bahamas
tel (242) 322-8941 (to 6) • fax (242) 328-0453 • Closed 12:30-1:30pm

PROPERTY MANAGEMENT
Bahamas Realty 231
C A Christie Real Estate 247
C Investments Realtors (Century 21) 190
Gold Circle Co Ltd 240
Graham Real Estate 223
H G Christie Real Estate 221
Kairos Development &
   Construction Co Ltd 236
Lyford Cay Real Estate Co Ltd 228
Morley Realty Ltd 245
Paul H Carey & Assoc (Century 21) 190
Powell's Marketing &
   Management Services 242
Real Estate Sales & Rentals
   (Bahamas) Ltd 237
Royal Caribbean Estates .... opp 248

RADIO STATION
Broadcasting Corp
   of The Bahamas, The .... bet 216-217
ZNS Network .... bet 216-217

READY MIXED CONCRETE
NP Building Supplies Ltd .... opp 249

REAL ESTATE – APPRAISALS, RENTALS & SALES
Bahamas Realty 231
Bay Properties Ltd .... bet 248-249
BAYROC Exclusive Beach Residences 38
C A Christie Real Estate 247
C Investments Realtors (Century 21) 190

Damianos Realty Co Ltd .... opp 217
Durrant-Harding Real Estate Co Ltd 227
Gold Circle Co Ltd 240
Graham Real Estate 223
H G Christie Real Estate Ltd 221
Kairos Development &
   Construction Co Ltd 236
Lyford Cay Real Estate Co Ltd 228
Morley Realty Ltd 245
Oceania Properties Ltd.............. bet 248-249
Paul H Carey & Assoc (Century 21) 190
Portside Condominiums 31
Powell's Marketing &
   Management Services 242
Real Estate Sales & Rentals
   (Bahamas) Ltd 237
Re/Max Nassau Realty 226
Royal Caribbean Estates .... opp 248
Treasure Cay Hotel Resort
   & Marina (Abaco) 42

SATELLITE SERVICES
Satellite Bahamas 157

SCHOOL – TECHNICAL/VOCATIONAL
Bahamas Technical & Vocational
   Institute (BTVI) 158

SEAFOOD – WHOLESALE & RETAIL, EXPORT & IMPORT
Island Seafoods Ltd 262

ISF ISLAND SEAFOODS, LTD.
PO Box N4401
Nassau, The Bahamas

Exporters of:
Lobster Tails

Importers of:
Seafood,
Fresh Fruit & Vegetables,
Fresh US Beef,
Frozen Pork, Lamb,
Veal & Poultry

Tel (242) 393-6132 or
393-3878
Fax (242) 393-7043

CERTIFIED ANGUS BEEF

WESTERN ELECTRIC
"We satisfy your current needs"

Three phase electrical contractors
specializing in
**Electrical Maintenance
and Construction**

Wilton St opp DW Davis
PO Box SS-5085,
Nassau, The Bahamas

Tel (242) 323-4132
Fax (242) 325-8254

SHIP REGISTRATION
Lennox Paton 207
Morymor Trust Corp Ltd 213

SHIPPING COMPANIES
DHL Worldwide Express 202
Federal Express (FedEx) 233
Tropical Brokerage Services Ltd 155

STOREFRONT SYSTEMS
Commonwealth Building
    Supplies Ltd 253

TELEVISION STATION
Broadcasting Corp
    of The Bahamas, The .... bet 216-217
ZNS Network .... bet 216-217

TELEVISIONS – SALES & SERVICE
Taylor Industries Ltd 261

TILES – SUPPLIES/CLEANING AGENTS
Automotive & Industrial
    Distributors Ltd (AID) 154
Frank Hanna Cleaning Co Ltd 237

TITLE RESEARCH & INSURANCE
Holowesko & Co 243

TOURISM INFORMATION
Bahamas Ministry of Tourism 24

TRAVEL/TRAVEL AGENTS
Bahamas Ministry of Tourism 24
Bahamasair 115

TRUCKING
Tropical Brokerage Services Ltd 155

WAREHOUSE STORAGE
Tropical Brokerage Services Ltd 155

**WASTE DISPOSAL – COMMERCIAL
& RESIDENTIAL**
Bahamas Waste Management
    Systems Ltd 251

WORLD-WIDE WEB
See **Internet Services.**

The Most Complete Website in The Bahamas

OVER 300 PAGES OF INFORMATION

- Shopping
- Dining
- Entertainment
- Activities
- Business
- Investment
- Real Estate
- Government

DESIGN · HOSTING · DEVELOPMENT

bahamasnet
www.bahamasnet.com

PO Box N-7513, Nassau, The Bahamas
Tel (242) 323 5665 Fax (242) 323 5728
email info@bahamasnet.com

New Providence

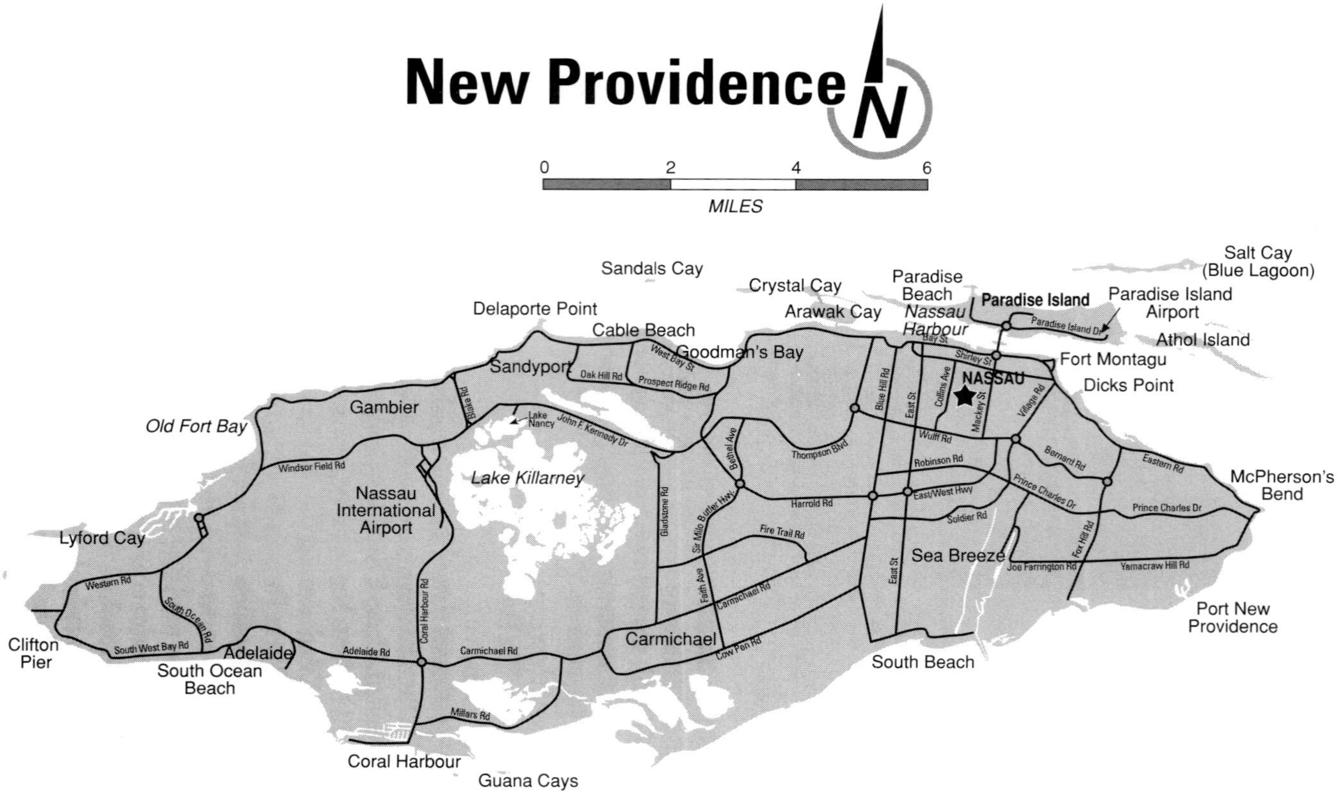

Bahamas Information

Blue page index, this section

Accommodations
Accounting firms
Agriculture
AIDS/HIV
Air service
Airports
Ambulance/air ambulance services
Animals
Arawak Cay
Architectural firms
Archives
Art galleries & museums
Asset Protection Trusts
Atlantic Undersea Testing
   & Evaluation Centre (AUTEC)
Awards
Bahamahost
Bahamas Agricultural
   & Industrial Corp (BAIC)
Bahamas Air Sea Rescue Assoc (BASRA)
Bahamas Development Bank (BDB)
Bahamas Family Planning Assoc (BFPA)
Bahamas Financial Services Board (BFSB)
Bahamas Historical Society
Bahamas Humane Society (BHS)
Bahamas Investment Authority (BIA)
Bahamas National Trust (BNT)
Bahamas Red Cross Society
Balance of payments
Banking
Banks
Birds
Boating
Broadcasting
Budget
Building contractors
Building costs
Building permits
Business licence fee
Business name registration
Cable television
Camping
Captive Insurance
Car rental companies
Caribbean Basin Initiative (CBI)
Caribbean Community &
   Common Market (CARICOM)
CARIBCAN
Casinos
Censorship
   (films, plays & printed material)
Chamber of Commerce
Churches
Cinemas
Citizenship
Climate
Community organizations
   & service clubs
Company formation
Constitution
Consumer protection
Copyright laws
Cost of living
Courier services
Crime
Cruise ship incentives
Cruising facilities
Culture & cultural activities
Currency
Customs
Defence Force
Dentists
Departure tax
Divorce
Doctors
Driver's licence & vehicle information
Drugs
Economy
Education
Electricity
Emergency numbers
Employers' organizations
Engineering companies
Entertainment
Exchange Control
Export
Export entry
Extradition
Fire services
Fishing
Fitness
Flora & fauna
Forts
Free Trade Area of the Americas (FTAA)
Freight services
Gambling
Geography
Golf courses
Government
Governors
Gross Domestic
   & Gross National Product
Gun permits
Harbour control
Health/medical services
History
Holidays

Hospitals & clinics
Hotels
Hotels encouragement
Hunting
Hurricanes
Immigration
Immovable Property Act
Import & export statistics
Import entry
Industrial relations
Industrial Tribunal
Industries encouragement
Industry
Inflation
Insurance
International Business Company (IBC)
International Persons Landholding Act
Internet
Investing
Judicial system
Junkanoo
Law firms
Libraries
Liquor Laws
Lomé IV Convention
Lotteries
Mail-boats
Manufacturing
Marinas & cruising facilities
Marine parks & exhibits
Marine research
Marriage licences
Motor vehicle insurance
Museums
Mutual funds
National Anthem
National Insurance
National parks & reserves,
  & protected areas
National symbols
Nature centres
Newspapers
North American Free
  Trade Agreement (NAFTA)
Organization of American States (OAS)
Paradise Island
Passports
People-to-People
Pharmacies
Police force
Population
Ports of entry
Postal information
Potter's Cay
Property tax
Property transactions

Public finance
Public health
Radio stations
Real estate companies & developments
Religion
Royal Bahamas Defence Force
Royal Bahamas Police Force
Schools
Ship registration
Shipping
Shopping
Social services
Sports
Statistics
Stock market
Straw markets
Tax benefits for Canadians
  by H Heward Stikeman
  & Paul J Setlakwe
Tax benefits for Europeans
  by Howard M Liebman
Tax benefits for US citizens & companies
  by P Bruce Wright
  & Arthur J Lynch
Telecommunications
Television
Theatre & performing arts
Time
Tourism
Trade agreements
Trade unions
Transportation
Trusts
Vaccination requirements
Veterinarians
Visas for Bahamians
Voting
Wages
Water rates
Water skiing
Weather
Weights & measures
Wildlife Preserves
World Trade Organization (WTO)
Yachts
YWCA
ZNS
Zoo

ACCOMMODATIONS

Accommodations in New Providence, Paradise Island, Grand Bahama and the Family, or Out, Islands include something for everyone and every budget. In Nassau and Paradise Island, 66 hotels (6,810 rooms) include opulent suites, guest houses and cottages with ocean views available throughout the year. According to the Hotel Licensing Unit of the Ministry of Tourism, as of May 1998, Grand Bahama offered 27 hotels with 3,185 rooms; the Family Islands,122 hotels with 2,526 rooms.

Most resorts and hotels are either on or near the ocean. Larger facilities offer access to world-class golf courses, tennis courts, spectacular beaches, watersports, snorkelling, skin-diving and scuba equipment and instruction, swimming pools (some with water slides), parasailing and nightclubs. Contact the concierge to make further arrangements at nearby facilities.

During high season,* a furnished three-room suite (two bedrooms and lounge), rents from about $400-$995 per day on Paradise Island. Similar accommodations rent from about $350-$1,000 per day in Nassau. Double room rates average $150 per day in Nassau and $200 on Paradise Island.

Special package rates offered by tour operators in North America and Europe include air fare, accommodations, sightseeing and transfers. A typical package advertised in *The Miami Herald* in June 1998 offered three days/two nights in some Nassau and Paradise Island hotels from $209. In the same month, *The New York Times* carried advertisements offering four-day packages from $369.

Modified American Plan (room, breakfast and dinner) or European Plan (room only) are available at most hotels. Guest houses in downtown Nassau are often less expensive. While many are room only, restaurants in the area are plentiful and conveniently located.

Guests in the Family Islands enjoy a relaxed, casual atmosphere in many small hotels. During high season, double room rates average $75 per day. Larger resorts, comparable to those in Nassau, are found on several of the islands with double room rates averaging $140 per day. Dining facilities outside Family Island hotels are often limited. Modified American Plan (room, breakfast and dinner) or European Plan (room only) are available at most hotels.

* *High season rates are applicable Dec 20, 1998- April 17, 1999. Summer rates, April 18, 1999- Dec 23, 1999, are slightly lower. There is a room occupancy tax which includes 4% government tax and a 4% tax added by member hotels of the Nassau/Paradise Island Promotion Board and Paradise Island/Cable Beach Tourism Development Assoc to fund joint promotional and advertising budgets. Most major hotels add another 2% tax, and a maid tax of $3 per person per night. Some hotels also add an energy tax of $3 per person per night.*

See also **Hotels** and **Freeport/Lucaya information, Accommodations.**

ACCOUNTING FIRMS

Atkinson, Ronald, & Co
BDO Mann Judd
Bates, Alan E H, & Co
Beneby & Co
Butler & Taylor
Cooper, Graham M, & Co
* Deloitte & Touche
Demeritte, Richard C, & Co
Ernst & Young
Galanis, Philip, & Co
Gibson-Saunders, R, & Co
Gomez & Gomez
 (Grant Thornton Intl)
Gomez & Nairn (RSM Intl)
Hepburn, F A, & Co
* Hepburn, Michael, & Co
* KPMG
Lockhart, ME, & Assoc
* Pannell Kerr Forster
* PricewaterhouseCoopers
Rankin Elias & McDonald

* *Freeport office also.*

AGRICULTURE

Approx 90% of agricultural land available in The Bahamas is owned by the government. Under the Ministry of Agriculture (Incorporation) Act, 1993, the Prime Minister has leased 64,087 acres of prime agricultural land to the Minister of Agriculture for 50 years, enabling him to hold and lease the land to Bahamian farmers for a max of two consecutive 21-year terms.

Lands made available were 13,869 acres in Andros, 39,676 acres in Abaco and 10,542 acres in Grand Bahama.

In 1997, the value of the agricultural sector was estimated at approx $56.44 million, a 6.8% increase over '96 estimates of $52.85 million.

A Plant and Animal Health Unit monitors the importation of fruit, vegetables and ornamentals into The Bahamas. All commercial importers of fresh produce, ornamentals, meat, milk, eggs and poultry must obtain permission from the Dept of Agriculture prior to importation.

Subsidies are available for Bahamian farmers in the form of interest-free credit on purchase of supplies from the Ministry's Fish & Farm Store on Potter's Cay Dock.

In 1994, a census of agriculture was conducted for the first time since '78, providing important baseline data on the agricultural sector. The report on findings is available from the Ministry of Agriculture at a price of $10 per copy.

Agricultural Manufactories Act
The Agricultural Manufactories Act, 1965, offers exemptions from Customs duty on all machinery, fixtures, supplies, farm trucks and a wide range of production, building and processing material imported for the construction or alteration of an agricultural factory.

Crops
Crop production for export is presently concentrated on four islands: Abaco, Andros, Grand Bahama and Eleuthera. Agricultural exports for 1996 amounted to an estimated 24,079 short tons compared to 26,008 short tons in '95. Exports consisted mainly of citrus fruits (grapefruit, lemons, limes and oranges), but also included cucumbers, okra, avocados, papaya, squash, tomatoes and zucchini.

Projected citrus exports will include an expanded acreage of lemons and the introduction of tropical crops such as passion fruit and melons. About 95% of export crops are exported to the US. The government is engaged in trade negotiations to allow Bahamian grapefruit into Japan.

Packing house produce purchases for 1996 amounted to 2,168.26 short tons* valued at $1.2 million. The comparable figures for 1995 were 2,266.08 short tons valued at $1.42 million.

The marketing of domestic crops is facilitated by packing houses in Andros, Cat Island, Exuma, Long Island and Eleuthera. There is also a government managed wholesale marketing facility in New Providence, at Potter's Cay Dock.

To reduce the occurrence of gluts of any produce item during the Aug-May production period, and to allow farmers a more stable input (labour and capital) and income pattern, the Dept of Agriculture has encouraged farmers to expand sweet potato, banana, onion, Irish potato and pigeon pea acreage. These crops have a more inelastic demand pattern. Additionally, farmers in Abaco, Andros, New Providence and Grand Bahama are encouraged to establish orchards to capitalize on the large export market for Persian limes, grapefruits and exotic tropical fruits.

* Does not include produce purchases at the Produce Exchange.

Poultry
Broiler statistics revealed production had increased from $21 million in 1996 to $22.4 million in '97.

Bahamas Poultry Ltd, the largest poultry producer in The Bahamas, is part of Bahamas Poultry Group of Companies in Grand Bahama, and has 18 broiler growing houses with 25,000 chickens in each.

Egg production decreased from an estimated 4.45 million dozen in 1996 to 4.23 million dozen in '97. Based on consumption levels of about 4.6 million dozen eggs in 1990, self-sufficiency has been estimated at 96%.

Livestock
One of the areas of emphasis in the new agricultural policy is livestock production, and the aim is to make each island self-sufficient in poultry and pork production. Establishment of a modern meat processing plant is a top priority. The Dept of Agriculture is developing a national mutton production programme, targeted at small farmers in the central and southern Bahamas. The Island Specific Programme aims to improve incomes of livestock and crop farmers throughout the country.

AIDS/HIV

As of Dec 31, 1997, a total of 2,868 AIDS cases had been reported in The Bahamas. A further 4,099 individuals were reported to be HIV positive, without symptoms of the disease.

By the end of 1997, a total of 6,967 persons were known to be infected with HIV/AIDS. Between 1985 and '97, 1,874 persons with AIDS had died. In 1996 and '97, a slight decline in the number of new reported HIV infections had been noted.

The disease occurs in The Bahamas primarily among heterosexuals, with a male to female ratio of 1.1:1.

Worldwide statistics revealed that as of Dec 1996, 22.6 million people were living with HIV/AIDS – approx 12.6 million males, 9.2 million females and 830,000 children.

Although the number of AIDS and HIV cases in The Bahamas seems comparatively high, this has been attributed to stringent reporting procedures. The National HIV/AIDS Programme enforces a vigilant follow-up of new HIV/AIDS cases, advising them to adopt safer sex practices. This voluntary, confidential contact tracing programme is effective in controlling the spread of HIV, a policy not adopted in other countries.

The Samaritan Ministry
This programme of caring ministry was established in 1988 to help people suffering in any way as a result of AIDS – the afflicted, their families and friends.

Trained volunteers are known as Samaritans. Training involves 2½-hour sessions once a week for 10 weeks, with presentations on the art of listening effectively and compassionately, dealing with feelings; and ministering to people experiencing sickness, depression and hospitalization, as well as people dying of AIDS. The programme has trained 250 people, of whom about 50 remain active.

The Ministry is also active in educational programmes for youth and church groups and service organizations. It operates a drop-in centre giving support and guidance to the AIDS afflicted.

Contact Sister Clare Rolle, OSB, Prioress, St Martin's Monastery, PO Box N-940, Nassau, tel 323-5517, fax 325-1377.

AIDS Foundation of The Bahamas
This non-profit, non-governmental organization was founded on World AIDS Day, Dec 1, 1992, to promote the fight against AIDS and HIV infection.

Although not involved with direct care of individuals, the Foundation persuades and stimulates other agencies to take on new projects wherever possible. Main objectives are
1. Helping to house the terminally ill, with emphasis on people with AIDS, and aiding the establishment and funding of such housing facilities throughout The Bahamas.
2. Informing and educating the public about all aspects of HIV/AIDS, including prevention.
3. Cooperating with organizations which have similar objectives.
4. Raising and distributing funds in line with stated objectives.

This work includes care and support of

persons with AIDS and HIV infections and their families. The Foundation also aims to promote and sustain continuing research on the local AIDS and HIV problem. It is maintained by donations and annual subscriptions. Membership applications are available from the AIDS Foundation of The Bahamas, PO Box CB-12003, Nassau, The Bahamas, tel 325-5120/1, fax 325-5113.

The AIDS Secretariat
The AIDS Secretariat was founded in 1989. It is the central organizing body in the Ministry of Health to coordinate and implement strategies and projects in the national programme on HIV/AIDS.

The Secretariat is responsible for long-term prevention programmes for all segments of the community, as well as organizing training for groups such as health care workers, teachers, students and volunteers.

The Secretariat also addresses psychological and social issues of persons with HIV/AIDS and their families.

Contact the AIDS Secretariat, Ministry of Health, PO Box N-3720, tel 325-5120/1, 325-5113.

See also **Public health services.**

AIR SERVICE

The following services were in effect in June 1998. They are subject to change. Connections to other North American cities are available via the major cities listed below.

Between Nassau and
Atlanta ....Delta
Charlotte.....................USAir
Chicago ....American Airlines,[1] Delta[1]
Cincinnati ....Delta[1]
Dallas ....American Airlines,[1] Delta[1]
Ft Lauderdale ....American Eagle, Bahamasair, Gulfstream Intl
Los Angeles ....American Airlines,[1] Delta[1]
Miami ......American Eagle, Bahamasair, Gulfstream Intl
Montreal ....Air Canada,[1] Delta,[1] American Airlines[1]
Nashville ......American Airlines,[1] Delta[1]
New York ....American Airlines,[1] Delta[2]
Orlando ....American Eagle, Bahamasair, Comair
Philadelphia ....American Airlines,[1] Delta,[1] USAir[1]
Pittsburgh ....USAir[1]
Raleigh/Durham....American Airlines,[1] Delta,[1] USAir[1]
Tampa........American Airlines,[1] Comair
Toronto ....Air Canada,[3] American Airlines,[1] Delta[1]

Between Freeport and
Baltimore ....LB Ltd (formerly Laker Airways)
Chicago ....LB Ltd (seasonal)
Cincinnati..................LB Ltd (seasonal)
Cleveland ....LB Ltd (seasonal)
Ft Lauderdale ....Gulfstream Intl, LB Ltd
Greenville/Spartanburg ....LB Ltd
Hartford ....LB Ltd (seasonal)
Memphis ....LB Ltd (seasonal)
Miami ....American Eagle, Bahamasair, Gulfstream Intl
Raleigh/Durham ......LB Ltd (seasonal)
Richmond..................LB Ltd (seasonal)

Between Paradise Island and
Ft Lauderdale ....PanAm Air Bridge,[1] Continental Connection
Miami ....PanAm Air Bridge,[1] Continental Connection
West Palm Beach ....Continental Connection

Between Nassau and
Amsterdam..........................British Air
London ....British Airways
Paris..AOM
Frankfurt ....Condor Air

Between Eleuthera and
Milan, Italy ....Air Europe

[1] One stop-over and/or possible change of plane en route. [2] Non-stop Sat, Sun only. [3] Sun only.

Family (Out) Island flights
Bahamasair, the national airline, has scheduled flights linking Nassau, Grand Bahama and various Family Island settlements with Miami. PanAm Air

Bridge operates daily Miami-Bimini, Paradise Island-Bimini and Ft Lauderdale-Walker's Cay services.

American Eagle travels to Miami from Governor's Harbour, Marsh Harbour and George Town. Gulfstream Intl flies to Miami from Marsh Harbour and Treasure Cay. It also flies to Ft Lauderdale from Marsh Harbour and North Eleuthera. There is further service (Sat, Sun) to West Palm Beach from Marsh Harbour.

USAir travels from Marsh Harbour and Treasure Cay, as well as North Eleuthera, to Ft Lauderdale.

Services are also provided between Marsh Harbour and Toronto; Treasure Cay and New York, and Miami and Governor's Harbour. Charters are available in Nassau through Bahamasair, Cleare Air, Congo Air, Le-Air, Reliable, Sandpiper Air/4 Way Charter, and Sky Unlimited.

Some charter operations are based in Grand Bahama and Family Islands such as Andros and Abaco.

AIRPORT PARKING
Parking lots at Nassau Intl and Paradise Island airports are operated by the Dept of Civil Aviation.

Nassau Intl
Long and short term parking is available at Nassau Intl Airport. Park in the long term area if you will be away from your vehicle more than four hours. The fee for short term parking is $2.25 for each hour or less. Long term parking is $2 for the first hour or part thereof and $1 for each additional hour up to four hours. Cost for a full day, exceeding four hours, is $5 for the first day and $2 for each additional day or part thereof.

Parking permits for government officers are $75 per year and $125 for others employed at the airport.

Parking meters are available for a max period of 20 mins of continuous parking. The first 10 mins cost 50¢ and each additional period of 10 mins or less costs 50¢. Bahamian or US 25¢ coins may be used.

Vehicles parked in no-parking zones may be towed to the Civil Aviation holding compound. A fine of $50 must be paid to have the vehicle released.

Paradise Island
The parking lot offers 24-hour security, good lighting and a pay phone.

Vehicles parked in no-parking areas may be towed away at the expense and risk of the owner, as well as incurring a possible fine.

Car park rates are $2 for the first hour or any part thereof; each additional hour or part thereof is $1.50, not exceeding a total of $6 the first full day. Each additional day, or part thereof, incurs a $2.50 charge.

Airline offices in Nassau
Air Canada
  Reservations 1-800-776-3000
Air Jamaica
  Nassau Flight Services 325-4692
  Reservations 1-800-523-5585
American Airlines/American Eagle
  Reservations 1-800-433-7300
Bahamasair
  Nassau Intl Airport ....377-7377 or
           377-8222
  Reservations 377-5505
           or 1-880-222-4262
Carnival Airline
  Reservations 377-6449
Continental Connection
  Paradise Island Airport 363-3169
  Reservations 363-2845
           or 1-800-786-7202
Delta/Comair
  Reservations 1-800-221-1212
Gulfstream Intl
  Reservations 377-4314
           or 1-800-231-0856
PanAm Air Bridge
  Paradise Island Airport 363-1687,
  (305) 371-8628 or 1-800-424-2557
USAir
  Nassau Intl Airport 377-8886
  Reservations 1-800-622-1015

AIRPORTS

Fig 1.0 is a Civil Aviation Dept list of civil airports and airstrips with runway specifications. Also included is basic information on the location and size of the facilities and whether they are designated as ports of entry for international flights.

Heliports

There are two heliports in the vicinity of New Providence, with emergency airlift/air ambulance service provided by Paradise Island Helicopters on Paradise Island. The heliports are privately owned and leased to the operators. They are not ports of entry.

The Paradise Island Heliport, owned by Sun Intl, is on the south side of the island west of Paradise Island Bridge. Approx dimensions are 173.2 x 173.2, 30,000 sq ft at coordinates 250489N, 771951W. The heliport is leased to Paradise Island Helicopters, which operates a Bell Jet Ranger 206B four-passenger aircraft.

A second heliport on Blue Lagoon Island (Salt Cay) measures 60 x 60, 3,600 sq ft at coordinates 250580N, 771647W.

The frequency 130.75 MHz CTAF* is monitored. Nassau Harbour Traffic monitors frequency 128.82 MHz CTAF. Call ahead for clearance.

* *CTAF: Common Traffic Advisory Frequency.*

AMBULANCE/AIR AMBULANCE SERVICES

Able Aviation & Air Ambulance Inc
1-880-ABLE JET (225-3538)
Collect (561) 465-0893
Advanced Air Ambulance (AAA)
1-800-633-3590
Collect (305) 232-7700
Aero Ambulance Intl
1-800-443-8042
Collect (954) 776-2600
Air Ambulance Network Inc (AANI)
1-800-522-3467
Collect (813) 934-3999
Air Ambulance Professionals Inc (AAPI)
1-800-752-4195
Collect (305) 491-0555
Air-Evac Intl
(954) 772-0003
Amelia Airways – Air Ambulance
1-800-546-4648
Associates Air Ambulance Inc (AAA)
1-800-546-4648
Collect (954) 771-3151
Commercial Airline Escort Services
(Emergency & non-emergency)
1-800-752-4195
Collect (954) 491-0555
Global Med-Tec*
(242) 394-3388 or 394-2582
Med-Evac Air Ambulance Service*
(242) 322-2881 or 323-8919

* *Ground ambulance service also provided.*

See also **Doctors**.

ANIMALS

A valid import permit ($10) is required to import any animal into The Bahamas. Animals must be six months or older. Persons wishing to apply for an import permit may phone in their request to 325-7502/9, or write to the Director of Agriculture, Dept of Agriculture, PO Box N-3028, Nassau, The Bahamas, stating their name and address, the type, age and number of animals they wish to import, the country of export and origin, the purpose for importing the animal(s) as well as anticipated date of arrival, and destination in The Bahamas.

For the US, Canada and the UK, main provisions of the import permit as it applies to dogs and cats are:
1. Dogs and cats over the age of six months arriving from the US and Canada must be accompanied by a veterinary health certificate issued within 48 hours of embarkation, and a valid certificate of rabies vaccination for either the one-year- or three-year-duration vaccine.
2. The one-year-duration vaccine must have been administered within not more than 10 months

FIG 1.0
CIVIL AVIATION DEPT LIST OF CIVIL AIRPORTS

ISLAND/AIRPORT LOCATION ON ISLAND	CO-ORDINATES	PORT OF ENTRY	DIMENSIONS
Abaco			
Gorda Cay SW (Pvt)	2605N 7731W	x	2,400 x 60
Marsh Harbour C (Gov)	2631N 7704W	√	5,000 x 100
Mores Island S (Gov)	2619N 7733W	x	2,640 x 140
Sandy Point[1] S (Gov)	2600N 7723W	√	4,500 x 100
Scotland Cay CE (Pvt)	2638N 7703W	x	3,300 x 100
Spanish Cay NE (Pvt)	2657N 7731W	√	5,000 x 80
Treasure Cay NC (Gov)	2645N 7723W	√	7,000 x 150
Walker's Cay[1] N (Pvt)	2716N 7823W	√	2,800 x 60
Acklins			
Spring Point C (Gov)	2227N 7357W	x	5,000 x 150
Andros			
Andros Town C (Gov)	2442N 7747W	√	4,000 x 100
Congo Town SE (Gov)	2409N 7734W	√	5,300 x 100
CA Bain Airport SE (Gov)	2417N 7740W	√	5,000 x 75
San Andros N (Gov)	2503N 7802W	√	5,000 x 100
Berry Islands			
Big Whale Cay S (Pvt)	2524N 7746W	x	2,600 x 60
Chub Cay SE (Pvt)	2525N 7752W	√	5,000 x 100
Great Harbour Cay N (Pvt)	2545N 7750W	√	4,536 x 80
Great Stirrup Cay[2] N	2549 33N 7753 45W	x	6,000 x 300
Little Stirrup Cay[2] N	2549 38N 7755 35W	x	6,000 x 300
Little Whale Cay S (Pvt)	2527N 7745W	x	2,000 x 50
Bimini			
Ocean Cay S (Pvt)	2530N 7909W	x	1,650 x 80 1,600 x 60
South Bimini S (Gov)	2542N 7915W	√	5,000 x 100
Cat Island			
Arthur's Town NW (Gov)	2438N 7539W	x	7,000 x 150
Cutlass Bay SW (Pvt)	2409N 7523W	x	2,450 x 60
Hawks Nest CW (Pvt)	2409N 7530W	x	3,000 x 100
New Bight W (Gov)	2419N 7526W	√	3,970 x 100
Cay Sal			
Cay Sal (Pvt)	2342N 8024W	x	2,000 x 100
Crooked Island			
Colonel Hill C (Gov)	2245N 7408W	x	3,500 x 60
Pitts Town N (Pvt)	2250N 7420W	x	2,240 x 60
Eleuthera			
Governor's Harbour C (Gov)	2517N 7619W	√	7,950 x 150
North Eleuthera N (Gov)	2529N 7640W	√	4,500 x 100
Rock Sound S (Gov)	2454N 7609W	√	7,200 x 150
Exuma			
Black Point NW (Gov)	2403N[3] 7623W[3]	x	2,683 x 80[3]
Darby Island C (Pvt)	2351N 7613W	x	1,500 x 100
Exuma Intl (Moss Town) S (Gov)	2333N 7552W	√	7,000 x 150
Farmer's Cay NW (Gov)	2356N 7618W	x	2,000 x 50
Hog Cay SE (Pvt)	2324N 7627W	x	2,500 x 100

ISLAND/AIRPORT LOCATION ON ISLAND	CO-ORDINATES	PORT OF ENTRY	DIMENSIONS
Exuma (cont)			
Lee Stocking Isl S (Pvt)	2347N 7605W	x	3,000 x 75
Little Darby Isl C (Pvt)	2352N 7612W	x	2,000 x 50
Norman's Cay N (Gov)	2436N 7648W	x	3,000 x 70
Rudder Cut Cay C (Pvt)	2353N 7614W	x	2,700 x 100
Sampson Cay C (Pvt)	2413N 7628W	x	2,300 x 60
Staniel Cay C (Pvt)	2410N 7628W	x	3,030 x 75
Grand Bahama			
Deep Water Cay E (Pvt)	2638N 7756W	x	2,000 x 100
Freeport Intl W (Pvt)	2633N 7841W	√	11,000 x 150
Inagua			
Matthew Town W (Gov)	2057N 7339W	√	7,000 x 100
Long Island			
Deadman's Cay C (Gov)	2315N 7507W	x	4,000 x 100

ISLAND/AIRPORT LOCATION ON ISLAND	CO-ORDINATES	PORT OF ENTRY	DIMENSIONS
Long Island (cont)			
Hog Cay N (Pvt)	2336N 7519W	x	1,800 x 50
Stella Maris N (Pvt)	2323N 7515W	√	3,700 x 60
Mayaguana			
Mayaguana C (Gov)	2223N 7301W	√	7,700 x 150
New Providence			
Nassau Intl W (Gov)	2502N 7727W	√	8,240 x 150 11,000 x 150
Paradise Island E (Pvt)	250443N 771750W	√	3,100 x 100
Ragged Island			
Duncan Town S (Gov)	2211N 7543W	x	3,800 x 75
Rum Cay			
Port Nelson C (Pvt)	2339N 7450W	x	2,400 x 100
San Salvador			
Cockburn Town NW (Gov)	2404N 7430W	√	4,100 x 150 scheduled for extension to 8,000 ft

[1] Sufferance port – Customs by request.   [2] Water aerodromes, domestic use only. Physical, not splashdown, coordinates.   [3] Unconfirmed.

and not less than one month prior to arrival in The Bahamas.

3. The three-year-duration vaccine must have been administered within not more than 34 months and not less than one month prior to arrival in The Bahamas.

Dogs and cats under six months old are prohibited importation from the US and Canada and all countries that are rabies endemic. Dogs and cats from the UK or any rabies-free country may enter without a rabies vaccination if accompanied by a veterinary health certificate and certificate stating there have been no cases of rabies in that country of origin for the previous year.

Animals not meeting these conditions are not allowed to enter the Commonwealth.

A duty for permanent entry of all animals into The Bahamas is levied, based on the cif value of the animal plus 2% stamp duty.

Entry duties
Dogs & cats 10%
Horses 15%
Sheep & goats 10%
Cattle 15%
Pigs 10%

Fees for dog licences
Male or spayed female $2
Female $6

Fee schedule for services provided by Dept of Agriculture
Import permits for cattle, sheep, goats, pigs, horses, dogs, cats & other large animals $10
Inspection of horses & other large animals for export $40
Duty-free permits $5
Import permits for plants, fruit & vegetables ....$2 per pg
Import permits for tropical fish, bees & other invertebrates $10
Where possible, permits should be paid via international or postal money orders.

The Bahamas is a party to the Convention on International Trade in Endangered Species (CITES). Import or export of any specimen listed must comply with the requirements of CITES.

For general information on animals, see **Bahamas Humane Society; Flora & fauna; Veterinarians;** and **Wildlife preserves.**

ARAWAK CAY

Heritage Village at Arawak Cay, off West Bay St, across from Fort Charlotte's Clifford Park, is part of the Ministry of Tourism's vision to develop an authentic out-island village atmosphere for Bahamians and visitors.

A lively fish and conch vendor's area features a colourful mix of stalls offering fresh Bahamian seafood prepared to order. Fried fish, conch salad, conch fritters, crack' conch and crack' lobster are popular Bahamian specialities.

Recent additions include a police station, a story-telling porch and an extensive "village green" where festivals, cultural events and concerts are held. At press time, plans had been announced to build a rock oven on the site.

ARCHITECTURAL FIRMS

Following is a sampling of architectural firms staffed by architects licensed with the Professional Architects Board in accordance with the Professional Architects Act, 1994.

AB Architects; tel 393-2207
Adderley, Jonathan A, & Assoc; tel 393-8893
Albury Assoc Ltd; tel 325-8932
Alexiou & Assoc Ltd; tel 325-7363
Architects Ken Lam & Assoc; tel 326-2114
Architectural Design Assoc Ltd; tel 327-1874
Architecture +; tel 356-9080
Arcop Ltd; tel 394-2600
Armbrister, Reginald, & Assoc; tel 364-4651
Behagg, Neil, & Assoc; tel 327-8109
Brad's Design Build; tel 327-3220
Braynen, Rodney, & Assoc; tel 393-1874
Burnside, Jackson, Ltd; tel 394-1886
Chisholm, Lawrence, & Assoc; tel 324-1454
Dean, Thomas; tel 324-1170
Ferguson, Amos Jr, & Assoc; tel 393-6732
Forbes, Larry G B, Architects; tel 356-4062
Higgs, Gerard, & Assoc; tel 356-2740
Jervis, Anthony, & Assoc, Architects Ltd; tel 326-6217
Jones, Winston G, & Assoc Architects Ltd; tel 325-1520
Lafleur, Bruce, & Assoc Ltd; tel 323-8421
Matthews, Sean, & Assoc; tel 356-4538
Miller, Roston H, & Assoc Ltd; tel 323-4543
Minns Architecture & Assoc Ltd; tel 394-4736
Moss, Michael; tel 356-5913
Robertson Ward Assoc Ltd; tel 322-2945
Rolle, Alvan K, & Assoc; tel 326-8141
Sawyer, Garth, & Assoc; tel 356-7814
Space Intl; tel 356-7723
Stewart, Bruce, Architect Ltd; tel 324-1196
Sweeting, Kevin, & Assoc; tel 328-8916
White, David; tel 324-1547
Woods, Wellington, & Assoc; tel 325-3883

ARCHIVES

The Dept of Archives, Mackey St, Nassau, serves as the repository for records and archives of the government as well as private deposits, including archives of the Anglican Church.

Until completion of the new national museum, the Dept serves as official caretaker of the material culture, artefacts, monuments and antiquities of the nation, and supervises Bahamian forts, the Pompey Museum at Vendue House on Bay St, and the Balcony House Museum on Market St.
See **Art galleries & museums.**

The Dept of Archives has a microfilm collection of historical documents dating back as far as 1700, a photograph collection, oral history collection and a number of maps, plans and prints. Artefacts include ceremonial duhos (carved wooden stools) used by chiefs or religious leaders of the Lucayans. Hand-paper repair of documents and book-binding are carried out in a repair-bindery room. A small photographic laboratory has been established, as well as a records management programme for centralization and disposal of non-current government records.

Publications available at the Dept of Archives are the *Guide to the Records of The Bahamas, Supplement to the Guide to the Records of The Bahamas* and 29 booklets on past exhibitions, as follows:
  The Lucayans
  Columbus and the Encounter 1492
  Highlights in Bahamian History 1492-1983
  The Exploration and Settlement of The Bahamas 1500-1700
  The Bahamas in the Early and Mid-Eighteenth Century 1700-1775
  The Bahamas in the Age of Revolution 1775-1848
  The Loyalist Bi-Centennial
  Aspects of Slavery
  Aspects of Slavery II
  The Bahamas in the Mid-Nineteenth Century
  The Bahamas in the Late Nineteenth Century
  The Bahamas in the Early Twentieth Century
  The Historical Development of the Southern Bahama Islands up to 1900
  The Early History of the Church up to 1910
  The Bahamas During the World Wars 1914-1918 and 1939-1945
  The Bahamas 10 Years After Independence 1973-1983
  The Bahamian-American Connection
  The Boat-Building Industry of The Bahamas
  Constitutional Development in The Bahamas
  A Selection of Historical Buildings of The Bahamas
  Junkanoo
  The Pineapple Industry of The Bahamas
  The Salt Industry of The Bahamas
  Settlements in New Providence
  The Peoples of The Bahamas
  The Sponging Industry
  The Tricentenary of Nassau: The Development of the Metropolis of The Bahamas up to the Early Twentieth Century
  The Central Bahama Islands 1492-1920
  Highlights in the History of Communication in The Bahamas 1784-1956

Booklets containing transcripts from St Matthew's Cemetery and Christ Church Cathedral Cemetery have been printed, as well as:
  The Life and Times of The Lucayans, The First Bahamians
  A Guide to African Villages in New Providence
  A Guide to Selected Sources for the History of the Seminole Settlements at Red Bays, Andros 1817-1980
  Loyalists, Slavery, Emancipation and Junkanoo
  Important Facts About The Bahamas
  Bahamian History Through Archaeology
  Some Personalities in Bahamian Education
  A User's Guide to the Records Centre

Looking Back: A Guide to Geneological Research in the Dept of Archives
Preservum: The Journal of the National Archives, Vol 1, #1, Sept 1996
Published annual reports for 1977-'96 are available, along with the booklet *The First Ten Years 1969-1979 – A History of the Bahamian Archives.*

The Dept of Archives is open 10am-4:45pm weekdays except holidays. Contact Dr Gail Saunders, Director of Archives, Dept of Archives, PO Box SS-6341, Nassau, The Bahamas, tel 393-2175 or 393-2855, fax 393-2855.

ART GALLERIES & MUSEUMS

Andrew Aitken Frame Art Gallery: Madeira St, Palmdale. Wide selection of Bahamian artists in a variety of styles. Lithographs and prints are the most popular items. Mon-Sat 8:30am-5:30pm. Tel 328-7065.

The Bahamas Historical Society Museum: corner of Shirley St and Elizabeth Ave, offers a detailed look at Bahamian history. Displays include an Amerindian-style dugout canoe and various artefacts of the Loyalist era, late 19th century and early 20th century. Mon-Fri 10am-4pm, Sat 10am-12 noon. Tel 322-4231.

Balcony House Museum: Market St. This 18th century landmark is perhaps the oldest wooden house of its kind in The Bahamas. The Central Bank of The Bahamas purchased the building in 1985 and restored it to its original state with the assistance of the Ministry of Works, The Dept of Archives and The Antique Warehouse. The museum is open Mon, Wed and Fri 10am-4pm (closed for lunch 1-2pm). Tel 322-2193 ext 2278.

Caripelago: West Bay St opp Sandals Resort, features the artwork of Bahamian artists and products of the Caribbean. Sun-Thurs 7:30am-10pm, Sat 7:30am-11pm. Tel 327-4749.

The Central Bank of The Bahamas: Market St, hosts frequent local cultural art exhibitions featuring established and upcoming Bahamian artists. Mon-Fri 9:30am-4:30pm. Tel 322-2193.

Chan Pratt's Art Gallery: Bonney Way, off Johnson Rd. Commission your own paintings in oils or water colours. Renowned Bahamian artist Pratt specializes in Bahamian landscapes and old Bahamian homes. Mon-Sat 9am-9pm. Tel 364-4047.

Charlotte's Gallery: Charlotte St, displays a variety of artists and styles, featuring Bahamian paintings, pottery, prints and creative gifts. Mon-Sat 10am-5pm. Tel 322-6310.

Dept of Archives: Mackey St, off Shirley St. See **Archives.**

Doongalik Studios: 18 Village Rd, offers artwork and designer products in frequently changing exhibits. Specializing in the arts of Junkanoo, its mission is to celebrate Bahamian culture. Items available include paintings, sculpture, furniture, posters, note cards, postcards and Junkanoo masks. Mon-Fri 9am-5pm, Sat by appt. Tel 394-1886.

Island T'ings: Bay St, selling indigenous arts and crafts, casual wear and souvenirs, 14 kt gold jewellery – anything and everything Bahamian, including local jams, chutneys, olive oils and herbs and spices. Mon-Sat 9am-6pm. Tel 326-1024.

Junkanoo Expo: Prince George Wharf, displaying a colourful collection of costumes worn in the twice-yearly Junkanoo parade in Nassau (Boxing Day, Dec 26, and New Year's Day). A gift shop sells Junkanoo souvenirs, including artwork, posters and music. Daily 9am-5pm. Tel 356-2731. See also **Junkanoo.**

The Kennedy Gallery: Parliament St, in the Baypark Bldg, features a wide variety of water colours, oils, acrylics and pencil drawings including originals and limited edition prints, photographs, sculptures, bronzes, glasswork and more. Mon-Sat 9am-5pm. Tel 325-7662.

Lyford Cay Gallery: Lyford Cay Shopping Centre, carries a wide selection of oils, watercolours, prints and sculptures by international artists. Mon-Fri 9am-5:30pm (Sat 9am-5pm Nov-April). Tel 362-4034.

Marlborough Antiques: Marlborough St, offers antiques, including furniture, silver, glass, brass, as well as books and artwork by a selection of Bahamian artists, including co-owner Brent Malone. Mon-Sat 9:30am-5:30pm. Tel 328-0502.

Museum of Art Ltd: East Bay St, includes a permanent art gallery of mainly 18th and 19th century European paintings and a newer collection of paintings and art from the western world. Exhibitions of local and international art, as well as cultural events and local productions, and a souvenir shop of art-related items. Mon-Sat 10am-1pm or by appointment. Tel 393-4711.

Nassau Art Gallery: East Bay Shopping Centre, near the Paradise Island Bridge, features the work of Elyse Wasile, including handpainted, limited edition porcelain collector's plates. Mon-Fri 9am-4pm. Tel 393-1482.

Nassau Glass Company: Mackey St, has a large selection of Bahamian art, including oils, watercolours, acrylics, prints, posters and batiks. Mon-Fri 8am-4:30pm, Sat 8am-1pm. Tel 393-8165.

The Nassau Public Library & Museum: Shirley St, a former 18th century jail, now documents The Bahamas' colourful past in books and a small selection of artefacts and historical documents. Mon-Thurs 10am-8pm, Fri 10am-5pm, Sat 10am-4pm. Tel 322-4907.

National Art Gallery: West Hill St. The stately 1880s Villa Doyle is being restored as the National Art Gallery of The Bahamas. A National Art Gallery Foundation – chaired by archivist and historian Dr Gail Saunders – is overseeing its restoration and operation. The gallery will be part of the national museum system. Tel 328-5801.

Paradise Tees: Hurricane Hole Plaza, Paradise Island, highlights original oils and watercolours and the work of such Bahamian artists as Chan Pratt and Eddie Minnis. Mon-Sat 9am-9pm, Sun 9am-6pm. Tel 363-2609.

The Pompey Museum of Slavery & Emancipation at Vendue House: Bay St, a former 18th century slave auction site, houses the history of slavery and emancipation in The Bahamas in photographs, artefacts and replicas. The distinctive and colourful artwork of Amos Ferguson is displayed on the second level. Mon-Fri 10am-4:30pm, Sat 10am-1pm. Tel 326-2566/8.

ASSET PROTECTION TRUSTS
See **Investing**.

ATLANTIC UNDERSEA TESTING & EVALUATION CENTRE (AUTEC)

The US Navy's Atlantic Undersea Testing and Evaluation Centre – AUTEC – is based at Andros, largest Bahama island and site of the mile-deep Tongue of the Ocean. The four-station centre was formally dedicated in 1966 as part of the Naval Undersea Warfare Centre to research submarine and anti-submarine warfare.

Andros was chosen because the immense ocean drop-off to some 6,000 ft was so close to shore that the US Navy could use relatively short cables to connect underwater detectors to "read-out" facilities at the base.

The base, the world's largest laboratory of its kind, is run by a maintenance and operations contractor employing approx 425 US personnel and 130 Bahamians. The US Navy, headed by an officer-in-charge, employs 50 military personnel.

AWARDS

A number of awards have been established to give Bahamian achievers due recognition. They include the

Order of Merit, Cacique Awards, Marlin Awards and the Dundas Annual National Seasons Awards (DANSA).

Order of Merit

This award was established in 1996 to recognize Bahamian "heroes" who achieve excellence in five specific nation-building categories: religion, public service, industry and commerce, sports and youth development and music/entertainment/creative arts.

Nominees must show evidence of advancement in the goals of their particular category, and exhibit excellence and achievement, provide consistent and significant contributions, and have a positive impact on national development. Order of Merit recipients are recognized during Independence celebrations (July 10) at Government House each year.

In 1998 Order of Merit awards were deferred in favour of Silver Jubilee Awards recognizing 100 individuals and institutions that made outstanding contributions to growth and development of The Bahamas during the first 25 years of independence. Silver Jubilee Award recipients were presented with specially minted gold coins and certificates. See **pgs 554-556.**

Cacique Awards

The Cacique Awards were created by the Ministry of Tourism in 1995 to recognize individuals who have made valuable contributions to the growth and development of the tourism industry. Categories include lifetime achievement, hotelier of the year, employee of the year, photography, writing, ecotourism, retail, music & entertainment and arts & crafts.

Governor-General's Youth Award

The Governor-General's Youth Award, formerly known as the Bahamas Duke of Edinburgh's Award, provides a programme of extracurricular activities to promote self confidence and character development for young Bahamians 14-25 years. Participants work toward gold, silver or bronze medals by completing activities over 1-3 years in four categories: skills, physical recreation, expeditions and community service.

Marlin Awards

The Marlin Awards were introduced in 1996 to recognize Bahamian gospel music. The 14 categories include outstanding duo/group, outstanding new artist, outstanding album of the year and outstanding song of the year.

Dundas Annual National Seasons Awards (DANSA)

The DANSA awards give credit to the talented contributions of Bahamians and residents to plays, musicals and revues at the Dundas Centre for the Performing Arts. Categories include production, choreography, special effects, costume and make-up, sound, set design, best actor/actress and best director.

See also **Theatre & performing arts.**

BAHAMAHOST

Bahamahost is a lecture series and self improvement training programme designed in 1978 by the Ministry of Tourism to upgrade quality of service in the hospitality industry. The programme's goal is to help individuals develop personal growth, self esteem and confidence. Participants are familiarized with the country's history, geography, civics, economics and places of interest. In addition, they receive attitude and motivation training.

More than 18,000 people are qualified Bahamahosts, including public service drivers, hotel and restaurant employees, salespersons, government employees and straw vendors.

The Bahamahost programme is coordinated by the Industry Training Tourism Awareness Unit, the education and training arm of the Ministry of Tourism for The Bahamas' hospitality industry. The Unit also offers a variety of other programmes to the Bahamian community.

Contact the Ministry of Tourism, Industry Training/Tourism Awareness Unit, Bahamas Tourism Training Centre, Thompson Blvd, PO Box N-3701, tel 326-5179 or 326-6183, fax 325-3412.

BAHAMAS AGRICULTURAL & INDUSTRIAL CORP (BAIC)

The Bahamas Agricultural and Industrial Corp (BAIC) promotes, encourages and facilitates business development in The Bahamas. Its main area of concern is small manufacturing operations and cottage industries, as well as administering the properties vested in it by the government. It provides technical assistance, advice and guidance to small businesses and entrepreneurs.

BAIC is structured to meet the government's goal of economic diversification and job creation through the development of small and medium-sized enterprises in The Bahamas. BAIC performs its function through a number of specialized areas which fall under four major depts: administrative services; project development; marketing, research and public relations; and business advisory services.

Services offered by BAIC include:
1. Identifying investment/business opportunities and developing project profiles.
2. Advising and assisting potential local entrepreneurs with regard to establishing a new business or managing and improving an existing one.
3. Providing factory space for processing and manufacturing activities in the Industrial Park at subsidized rates.
4. Conducting entrepreneurial seminars and workshops for local businesses and entrepreneurs.
5. Coordinating and liaising with other government agencies for receipt, processing and implementation of business inquiries.
6. Providing for market testing of Bahamian-made products at local and international trade shows.

BAIC also offers technical assistance through its relationship with local organizations such as the Caribbean Technological Consultancy Services (CTCS) of the Caribbean Development Bank; the Caribbean Export Development Project (CEDP) of the CARICOM Secretariat; the Centre for the Development of Industry (CDI); and the Centre for the Promotion of Imports (CPI). BAIC works closely with the Bahamas Development Bank for financing viable projects that would contribute to the economic development of The Bahamas.

Contact the general manager, BAIC, PO Box N-4940, tel 322-3740/3, fax 322-2123.

See also **Bahamas Development Bank.**

BAHAMAS AIR SEA RESCUE ASSOC (BASRA)

BASRA, a volunteer organization supported by donations from the public, is the official search and rescue organization of The Bahamas.

Its headquarters are manned by one full-time employee during the day and volunteers after hours with assistance from the police answering service. VHF, SSB and aircraft radios are monitored seven days a week.

BASRA owns two vessels, a self-righting 38 ft Lochin and a 25 ft Boston Whaler, both of which are specially designed and equipped for rescue work. Nassau Flying Club aircraft are also utilized. The US Coast Guard is called upon for emergency night searches.

Contact BASRA, East Bay St, PO Box SS-6247, tel 325-8864, fax 325-2737.

BAHAMAS DEVELOPMENT BANK (BDB)

The Bahamas Development Bank (BDB) was established by an Act of Parliament on Oct 8, 1974, and opened its doors to the public on July 21, '78.

The BDB finances self-employed individuals, cooperatives and small businesses for development enterprises which contribute to the economic growth and well-being of the country.

These enterprises should create new employment opportunities; utilize local materials and resources; reduce imports or increase exports; introduce new technology and skills; and place new wealth into new hands, particularly in the Family Islands. The BDB finances short term loans (six months to one year), medium term loans (one year to five years) and long term loans (five years to 10 years).

The major sectors financed by the BDB include tourism and ancillary services; industrial enterprises; agro-based industrial enterprises; farming; fishing; marine and land transportation and small businesses.

During its years of business, the BDB has approved loans at $79.3 million, affecting 22 Bahamian islands and cays. Total assets of the BDB at Dec 31, 1997 were $25.8 million.

BDB headquarters are in Cable Beach, Nassau. Banking hours are Mon-Fri 9:30am-4:30pm. Contact the Bahamas Development Bank, PO Box N-3034, tel 327-5780 (to 6), fax 327-5047.

See also **Bahamas Agricultural & Industrial Corp (BAIC); Industries encouragement;** and **Manufacturing.**

BAHAMAS FAMILY PLANNING ASSOC (BFPA)

This private, non-profit organization is approved and supported by the Ministry of Health, although it is not government funded.

The BFPA is an affiliate of the Intl Planned Parenthood Federation (IPPF) and Caribbean Family Planning Affiliation Ltd. It has operated a clinic on East Ave, Centreville, since 1988, and is staffed by a qualified nurse with family planning experience.

Obstetricians and gynaecologists hold regular visiting hours at the clinic five days per week. All visits are confidential.

The clinic is currently the only one of its kind in The Bahamas. Plans are under way to expand services to Freeport and the Family Islands.

The BFPA is governed by an executive committee and its officers. Daily activities are supervised by a full-time, salaried executive director. Funding is provided by four sources: the IPPF; modest, fixed charges for client services and medication (except in cases of proven hardship); members' annual dues; public contributions and fund-raising events.

Contact Elizabeth Grant, executive director, Bahamas Family Planning Assoc, PO Box N-9071, tel 325-1663.

BAHAMAS FINANCIAL SERVICES BOARD (BFSB)

The Bahamas Financial Services Board (BFSB) was launched on July 1, 1998 to proactively market the country's financial services sector. BFSB is a joint venture between the private sector and The Bahamas government.

BFSB is a multi-disciplinary organization, drawing on expertise and contacts in every field involved in the country's financial services industry. Membership includes government organizations and companies involved in banking, trust, financial services, insurance, mutual fund administration, public accountancy, legal firms and investment advisors. Others who have an interest in the financial services industry can join BFSB as associate members.

With appropriate legislation and business friendly policies in place as well as excellent support, including accounting and legal services and a highly skilled workforce, The Bahamas provides an ideal climate for offshore investment. Upcoming legislation to create a stock exchange is intended to further position The Bahamas as one of the world's most reputable, secure and well-regulated offshore centres.

Contact Barry Malcolm, Executive Director, Bahamas Financial Services Board, PO Box N-1764, Nassau, tel (242) 326-7001, fax (242) 326-7007.

BAHAMAS HISTORICAL SOCIETY

The Bahamas Historical Society, Shirley St and Elizabeth Ave, Nassau, is a non-profit cultural and educational organization dedicated to stimulating interest in Bahamian history and to collecting and preserving related material. The society operates a small museum at its headquarters with historical, anthropological and archaeological artefacts spanning more than 500 years of Bahamian history.

The museum is open Mon-Fri 10am-4pm and Sat 10am-12 noon, although these hours are subject to change. The society holds monthly talks and publishes an annual journal.

Contact the president, PO Box SS-6833, tel 322-4231.

See also **Archives; Art galleries and museums;** and **History.**

BAHAMAS HUMANE SOCIETY (BHS)

The Bahamas Humane Society (BHS) is the oldest charity in The Bahamas. It was founded in 1924 by the wife of a former colonial secretary and was originally called the "Dumb Friends League."

BHS is affiliated with numerous international organizations including World Society for the Protection of Animals (WSPA). Since 1989, BHS has been given membership in the Standards of Excellence Programme sponsored by The American Humane Assoc. BHS is the only humane organization in the Caribbean to qualify for membership.

BHS employs two full-time veterinarians and maintains an animal hospital and shelter. It offers 24-hour emergency ambulance service and provides care for sick, injured and abandoned animals. BHS also conducts an education programme for schools and youth groups and provides tours of the animal shelter. Cruelty to animals investigations are carried out by trained BHS inspectors.

New modern facilities, officially opened in 1998, include grooming services and a new treatment centre.

BHS employs a staff of 14 as well as a number of volunteers. The board of directors consists of 12 people. While the clinic generates some funds, it depends mainly on donations and fund-raising events.

BHS is not responsible for collection of stray or dead animals. This falls under jurisdiction of the Ministry of Agriculture and Fisheries and the Dept of Environmental Health Services, respectively.

Application forms are required for adopting dogs and puppies. Approval usually takes two to three days. The fee is $40 for dogs and $30 for puppies. Adoption of cats and kittens may be approved immediately upon completion of a successful interview. The fee is $20 for cats and $15 for kittens. Adoptive owners must agree to bring puppies and kittens back to BHS to be spayed or neutered (included in the fee). No mature animal is allowed to be adopted from the shelter unless it has been spayed or neutered.

Tel 323-5138 or 325-6742.

See also **Animals.**

BAHAMAS INVESTMENT AUTHORITY (BIA)

The Bahamas Investment Authority (BIA), developed in early 1993, is a one-stop investment facilitator under the umbrella of the Office of the Prime Minister. It is the government agency responsible for investment policy formulation, international and domestic promotion of investment opportunities in The Bahamas as well as review and evaluation of investment proposals. The role of the BIA includes:
1. Administering the National Investment Policy of The Bahamas.

2. Assisting international investors during implementation of approved investment projects.
3. Arranging international investment promotions for investors interested in business opportunities in The Bahamas.
4. Coordinating investment matters with other government agencies.
5. Ensuring effective administration of the range of incentives available under all investment and business encouragement legislation.
6. Keeping legislation and regulations in the financial services sector competitive internationally.

The National Economic Council (NEC) is the approval body for investments in The Bahamas. It coordinates investment matters with all agencies of the government, thus simplifying the process for the investor. The NEC meets regularly to consider investment proposals.

Investors should be guided by the National Investment Policy.

Contact the Bahamas Investment Authority (BIA), Office of the Prime Minister, PO Box CB-10980, Nassau, The Bahamas, tel (242) 327-5970, fax (242) 327-5907.

See also **Investing, National Investment Policy.**

BAHAMAS NATIONAL TRUST (BNT)

The Bahamas National Trust (BNT) celebrates its 40th anniversary in 1999. Since its creation in 1959, the BNT has been dedicated to conservation of the natural and historic resources of The Bahamas, and has won national and international recognition for its achievements.

One of the most celebrated of BNT accomplishments is the saving of the nearly extinct West Indian flamingo, national bird of The Bahamas. As a result of the BNT's conservation efforts, there are 60,000 flamingos in Great Inagua. Equally important are BNT programmes to prevent extinction of the green turtle, white-crowned pigeon, Bahama parrot and the hutia.

The BNT administers the country's entire national park system comprising more than 320,000 acres in 12 parks and protected areas.

The Exuma Land and Sea Park was the first of its kind in the world in that it was the first placed under a single management authority. The first marine fishery reserve in the wider Caribbean has been set aside within the Park.

BNT maintains close ties with major scientific organizations in the US, including the US National Park Service, New York Zoological Society, Smithsonian Institution, National Audubon Society, American Museum of Natural History and Rosenstiel School of Marine Sciences at the Univ of Miami, all of which are represented on the BNT Council.

BNT headquarters are at The Retreat, an 11-acre Nassau property with one of the finest private collections of palms in the western hemisphere. Guided tours are conducted by volunteers at 12 noon on Tues, Wed, and Thurs. Additional tours may be arranged by appointment and cost $2 per person. Group costs are by arrangement.

BNT is maintained by annual subscriptions of BNT members, donations, a small annual grant from the government and an endowment fund. Dues and fees paid by US citizens are tax deductible when paid in US dollars to the Environmental Systems Protection Fund. Membership in this non-profit, non-governmental organization is an annual subscription of $15. Presently, there are more than 4,000 members. Membership applications are available from the Bahamas National Trust, PO Box N-4105, tel 393-1317, fax 393-4978, e-mail: bnt@bahamas.net.bs

See also **Marine parks & exhibits; Nature centres;** and **Wildlife preserves.**

THE BAHAMAS RED CROSS SOCIETY

Established in 1939, The Bahamas branch of the Intl Red Cross is a non-profit "emergency relief" organization with approx 1,000 members – 300 youth and 700 adults.

The society provides a number of programmes and services throughout The Bahamas, including social welfare to the aged and housebound; youth development; training; rehabilitation clubs; hospital transport; education of the deaf; Family Island development and disaster and emergency relief.

It has an annual operational budget of approx $390,000 financed by fund-raising, donations, membership subscriptions and a government grant.

Contact the Bahamas Red Cross Society, PO Box N-8331, tel 323-7370, fax 323-7404.

BALANCE OF PAYMENTS

See **Fig 1.1**.

BANKING

On Dec 31, 1997, there were 418 institutions licensed to carry on banking and/or trust business under The Banks and Trust Companies Regulation Act, either within or from the Commonwealth of The Bahamas. Of these, 291 were permitted to deal with the public, 109 had licences restricting their activities to specific areas, and 18 had non-active licences.

Of the 291 public institutions, 21 were designated by the Exchange Control Dept to deal in Bahamian and foreign currencies and gold. Of these 21, 11 trust companies were designated authorized agents to deal in foreign securities, eight were authorized dealers in gold, foreign currency and Bahamian dollars, and two were authorized agents/dealers operating in Bahamian and foreign currency and securities and in gold and foreign currencies. Of the remaining 270 public institutions, there were 77 Eurocurrency branches of banks based in the US, UK, South America, Asia and Europe. Of the remaining 193, 120 were subsidiaries of banks or other institutions based outside The Bahamas and the remaining 73 were Bahamian-based banks and/or trust companies.

Interest rates

The average interest rates on deposits, as of Dec 31, 1997, were 3.35% for savings deposits, and 5.30% (lower maturity) to 5.28% (higher maturity) for fixed deposits.

Average rate charged for consumer loans was 14.71%, other local loans 9.30%, 10.06% for residential, and 10.55% for commercial mortgages.*

* *In April 1980, legislation was enacted to exempt banks and trust companies from the provision of the Rate of Interest Act which prohibits interest rates in excess of 20% per annum. This amendment facilitated the worldwide dealings of licensed financial institutions in The Bahamas in case of changing international monetary conditions. The 20% ceiling still applies to non-licensed lending institutions and individuals.*

Banking hours

Banks are open Mon-Thurs, 9:30am-3pm and Fri, 9:30am-5pm. Commonwealth Bank opens at 8:30am.

Central Bank

The central financial institution in The Bahamas is the Central Bank of The Bahamas. It was established in June 1974 by an Act of Parliament as successor to The Bahamas Monetary Authority. Its responsibilities include:

1. Safeguarding the value of the Bahamian dollar.
2. Credit regulation, note issue.
3. Administration of Exchange Control regulations.
4. Administration of banks and trusts legislation.
5. Compilation of financial statistics.

The Central Bank of The Bahamas, like most other central banks, does not accept deposits from, nor make loans to, the public but acts as a banker to banks and to the government.

For queries on banking in The Bahamas, contact the Central Bank of The Bahamas' Bank Supervision Dept,

FIG 1.1
BALANCE OF PAYMENTS

	B$ millions			
	1996 (revised)		1997 (provisional)	
	Credit	Debit	Credit	Debit
Current Account	**1,981.7**	**2,218.9**	**2,040.8**	**2,445.3**
Goods & services	1,851.4	1,976.8	1,889.5	2,170.5
Goods	273.2	1,263.1	295.2	1,278.1
Merchandise	201.7	1,261.6	230.4	1,276.5
Oil trade (local consumption)	–	194.4	–	192.2
Non-oil merchandise	201.7	1,067.2	230.4	1,084.3
Goods procured in port by carrier	71.5	1.5	64.8	1.5
Services	1,578.1	713.6	1,594.3	892.5
Transportation	41.2	154.7	49.6	182.3
Travel	1,397.9	234.6	1,424.7	249.8
Insurance services	–	72.0	–	64.7
Construction services	–	20.4	–	125.7
Royalty and license fees	–	6.5	–	9.5
Offshore companies' local expenses	110.0	–	91.0	–
Other services	9.2	178.8	9.2	214.9
Government services	19.8	46.7	19.8	45.7
Income	84.5	233.5	101.3	264.0
Compensation of employees	–	29.1	–	31.1
Investment income	84.5	204.4	101.3	232.9
Direct investment	–	–	–	–
Official transactions	10.6	16.5	8.6	12.8
Other private interest & dividends	73.9	187.9	92.7	220.1
Current transfers	45.8	8.6	50.0	10.7
Capital and Financial Account	**317.5**	**161.5**	**543.3**	**173.8**
Capital account	–	24.4	–	13.0
Financial account	317.5	137.1	543.3	160.7
Direct investment	112.9	25.4	260.2	64.2
Equity	88.6	10.7	222.6	41.3
Land purchases/sales	24.3	14.7	37.6	22.9
Other investments	204.6	111.7	283.1	96.6
Public sector long term loans	7.8	26.0	54.5	37.5
Other public sector capital	20.8	27.7	35.4	36.0
Domestic banks	60.4	37.4	63.7	2.5
Other private	115.7	20.4	129.5	20.5
Net errors & omissions	**73.6**	**–**	**91.4**	**–**
Overall Balance	**–**	**7.6**	**56.5**	**–**
Change in external foreign assets (increase = debit)	**7.6**	**–**	**–**	**56.5**

Figures are supplied by the Central Bank of The Bahamas and are subject to subsequent updating.

Frederick St, PO Box N-4868, Nassau, The Bahamas, tel (242) 322-2193.

See also **Investing** and **Exchange control**.

Private banking

Offshore banking and finance, the No 2 industry in The Bahamas behind tourism, accounts for approx 15% of the country's Gross Domestic Product (GDP). Nassau, the capital, ranks highly in the top 10 offshore jurisdictions worldwide and is arguably the leading offshore banking centre in North and South America.

The 418 banks and trust companies licensed to do business in The Bahamas represent premier institutions of the global financial industry. Most banks are engaged in private banking – personalized management of assets for high net worth individuals. This includes investment counselling and financial analysis, stock trading in currencies and precious metals, and management of trusts, mutual funds and pension fund assets.

One of the greatest advantages of private banking is that a host of services is offered under one roof. Personal attention factor is also crucial.

The political stability of the Bahamian government and absence of taxes are factors in The Bahamas' attractiveness as an offshore jurisdiction. Sound fiscal and economic policies have ensured the Bahamian dollar remains on par with the US dollar (since 1966) and there is an experienced combination of both local and international staff officers.

The hallmark of Bahamian private banking is confidentiality, protected by government legislation and vigilance within the industry. Laws against money laundering do not affect bank secrecy although "suspicious transactions" must be reported to Bahamian authorities. Banks do not file tax or information returns with the IRS, and the bank secrecy provision in the Banks Act forbids bank executives from divulging information on a customer's account to tax collectors, attorneys or foreign courts.

Money laundering

The Bahamas has enacted strict legislation as part of continuing efforts against money laundering. The Money Laundering (Proceeds of Crime) Act, 1996 was the first and only one of its kind among offshore jurisdictions to make money laundering a criminal matter.

The legislation, which calls for sentences of up to 10 years for anyone convicted of laundering money, permits bankers to inform The Bahamas' Supervisory Authority or Attorney General of suspicious transactions and provides for confiscation of proceeds of drug trafficking. A procedure for relief by aggrieved parties is laid out in the legislation, including right of appeal to The Bahamas' Court of Appeal. A banker who is aware of a suspicious transaction but fails to report it to the authorities is liable for prosecution.

The Money Laundering (Proceeds of Crime) Act, 1996, and Money Laundering Regulations, 1996, amended the former Act and Regulations:

1. To cover the proceeds of all criminal conduct in addition to drug-related activities.
2. To make it a criminal offence for a bank not to have in place procedures to combat money laundering.
3. To recognize guidance notes issued by the Central Bank of The Bahamas.

The Tracing and Forfeiture of the Proceeds of Drug Trafficking Act, 1987, calls for reporting of cash deposits over $5,000. It followed the "know your customer" programme, which made it mandatory for banks to do background checks on investors.

The Bahamas has signed mutual legal assistance treaties on criminal matters with the US, Canada and the UK, and was the first country to ratify the 1988 US Convention on the Illicit Traffic in Narcotics, Drugs and Psychotropic Substances.

BANKS

Banking and financial services offered in The Bahamas include asset protection; private and commercial banking; captive insurance; portfolio management; foreign exchange transactions; administration and establishment of trusts; company formation; securities transactions and mutual funds.

Definition of terms

Authorized dealer: A bank authorized by the Central Bank to deal in gold and all foreign currencies. It may open and maintain accounts in such currencies within limits issued in Exchange Control notices by the Central Bank. Under authority delegated by the Central Bank, an authorized dealer may approve certain applications for foreign currency within specified currencies and specified limits.

Authorized agent: A bank or trust company authorized by the Central Bank to deal in Bahamian and foreign currency securities and to receive securities into deposits (ie, to act as custodians) in accordance with terms of the Exchange Control Regulations Act and Exchange Control notices issued by the Central Bank.

Public licensee: One who is permitted to carry on banking and/or trust business with the public. The institutions' Exchange Control designation determines whether the licensee is resident or non-resident.

Resident: Resident status allows a bank or trust company to deal only in Bahamian dollars; operations in foreign currencies require Exchange Control authorization. Trust companies with resident status are allowed to deal in foreign currency securities on behalf of non-resident customers.

Non-resident: A non-resident designation permits a bank and/or trust company to operate freely in foreign currencies. Exchange Control approval is necessary to operate a Bahamian dollar account to pay local expenses.

Restricted: A restricted bank and/or trust company is one allowed to carry on business for certain specified persons usually named in the licence (not included in the list following).

Non-active: A non-active company is either in voluntary liquidation or wishes to keep the word bank or trust in the company's name even though it is not carrying on banking or trust business (not included in the list following).

Nominee: A nominee company is one which holds securities and other assets in its name on behalf of clients of its parent bank or trust company (not included in the list following).

These public banking (B) and trust (T) companies were licensed in The Bahamas as of June 30, 1998. Current information can be obtained from the Central Bank, tel 322-2193.

Authorized dealers & agents
Barclays Bank, plc ....B & T
Royal Bank of Canada ....B

Authorized dealers
Bank of The Bahamas Ltd ....B & T
British American Bank (1993) Ltd ......B
CIBC Bahamas Ltd ....B & T
Citibank, NA ....B
Commonwealth Bank Ltd ....B
Finance Corp of Bahamas Ltd ......B & T
Scotiabank (Bah) Ltd ....B

Authorized agents
Ansbacher (Bah) Ltd ....B & T
Bank of Nova Scotia
   Trust Co (Bah) Ltd ....B & T
CIBC Trust Co (Bah) Ltd ....B & T
Chase Manhattan Private Bank
   & Trust Corp (Bah) Ltd ....B & T
Cititrust (Bah) Ltd ....B & T
Coutts (Bah) Ltd
   (resident branch).....................B & T
ITK Trust Co Ltd ....B & T
Lloyds Bank Intl (Bah) Ltd ....B & T
Morgan Trust Co of
   The Bahamas Ltd ....B & T
Pictet Overseas Trust Corp Ltd ....T
UBS Trustees (Bah) Ltd ....T

Other public licensees

ABC – Roma Banking Ltd ....B
Ahlia Banking Ltd ....B
Alliance Bank & Trust Ltd ....B & T
Amazonas Intl Bank Ltd ....B & T
American Bank & Trust Co Ltd ....B & T
Americas Intl Bank Corp Ltd ....B
Apache Intl Finance Ltd ....B
Apax Bank & Trust Co Ltd ....B & T
Arner Bank & Trust (Bah) Ltd ....B & T
Aserval Intl Private
  Bank & Trust Ltd ....B & T
Austrobank (Overseas) Ltd ....B & T
BAC Intl Bank Ltd ....B & T
BBA – Creditanstalt Bank Ltd........B & T
BBM Bank Ltd ....B & T
BNC (Nass) Ltd ....B
BNP Private Bank
  & Trust (Bah) Ltd ....B & T
BSI – Banca della Svizzera Italiana ......B
BSI Overseas (Bah) Ltd..................B & T
BSI Trust Corp (Bah) Ltd.......................T
BSJ Intl Bank & Trust Co Ltd ....B & T
Banca del Gottardo.......................B & T
Banca Serfin, SA ....B
Bancafe (Nass) Ltd ....B & T
Banco Andino (Nass) Ltd ....B & T
Banco BBA Creditanstalt, SA ....B
Banco BBM Investimentos SA ....B
Banco Barclays e Galicia (Bah) Ltd ......B
Banco Bilbao Vizcaya, SA ....B
Banco Boavista, SA ....B
Banco CCF Brazil, SA...........................B
Banco Cacique SA ....B
Banco de Bogota (Nass) Ltd ....B
Banco de Comercio e Industria, SA ....B
Banco de Credito del Peru..................B
Banco de Credito (Overseas) Ltd ....B
Banco de Santander ....B
Banco del Istmo (Bah) Ltd ....B & T
Banco del Pichincha Ltd ....B & T
Banco do Brasil, SA ....B
Banco Espirito Santo e
  Comercial de Lisboa ....B
Banco Excel Economico SA ....B
Banco Fibra SA ....B
Banco Internacional de
  Costa Rica Ltd...........................B & T
Banco Nacional de Mexico, SA ....B & T
Banco Popular Intl Ltd ....B & T
Banco Privado (Bah) Ltd ....B & T
Banco Prosper SA ....B
Banco Real, SA ....B & T
Banco Safra (Bah) Ltd ....B
Banco Santander Brasil Intl Ltd ....B
Banco Santander Trust & Banking
  Corp (Bah) Ltd ....B & T
Banco Sociedad General de Credito
  (Bah) Ltd ....B
Bank Al Taqwa Ltd ....B
Bank Fuer Handel und Effekten
  (Overseas) Ltd ....B
Bank Leu Ltd ....B
Bank of Baroda ....B
Bank of Hawaii ....B
The Bank of Nova Scotia ....B
Bank of Nova Scotia Intl Ltd ....B
The Bank of Tokyo-Mitsubishi
  Trust Co ....B & T
BankAmerica Trust & Banking Corp
  (Bah) Ltd ....B & T
BankBoston NA ....B
BankBoston Trust Co Ltd..............B & T
Bankers Trust Co..........................B & T
Bankinvest Bank & Trust Ltd ....B
Banque Privee
  Edmond de Rothschild Ltd ......B & T
Banque SCS Alliance
  (Nass) Ltd ....B & T
Barclays Finance Corp (Bah) Ltd..........B
Base Bank Ltd ....B
Boavista Banking Ltd ....B
Brascan Intl Bank Ltd..........................B
Brasilinvest Transcontinental
  Bank Ltd ....B & T
Bridge Bank Ltd..................................B
British Bank of Latin America Ltd ....B
CBI-TDB Intl Trust Ltd ....T
California Canton Intl Bank Ltd ....B & T
Cambridge Bank Ltd ....B
Capital Securities
  Bank & Trust Ltd ....B & T
Cardinal Intl Bank & Trust Co Ltd ....B & T
Chase Bank of Texas, NA ....B
The Chase Manhattan Bank ....B & T
Citco Bank & Trust Co (Bah) Ltd ...B & T
Citibank-Colombia (Nass) Ltd ....B & T
Citicorp Banking Corp.......................B
Cofivalle Finance (Bah) Ltd ....B
Cogeba Bank & Trust (Bah) Ltd ....B & T
Colombian Santander Bank
  (Nass) Ltd ....B
The Commercial Bank of Kuwait,
  SAK ....B
Commercial Intl Bank &
  Trust Co Ltd ....B & T

CoreStates Bank NA ....B & T
Corner Bank (Overseas) Ltd ....B & T
Corpobank & Trust Ltd ....B & T
Coutts (Bah) Ltd ....B & T
Credit Lyonnais ....B
Credit Suisse (Bah) Ltd ....B & T
Credit Suisse First Boston ....B
Credito Italiano Finance Corp Ltd ....B
Dah Sing Bank Ltd...............................B
Darier, Hentsch Private
  Bank & Trust Ltd ....B & T
Dartley Bank & Trust Ltd ....B & T
The Deltec Banking Corp Ltd..............B
Deltec Panamerica Trust Co Ltd ....T
Dominion Charter Bank Ltd................B
Emirates Merchant Bank Ltd ....B & T
Eni Intl Bank Ltd ....B & T
Equator Bank Ltd ....B & T
Euro Canadian Bank
  & Trust Co Ltd ....B & T
Euroasia Bank Ltd ....B
Eurobanco Bank Ltd ....B & T
European American Bank ....B & T
Experta Trust Co (Bah) Ltd ....T
FTB Bank Ltd ....B
Federal Bank Ltd ....B
Fenicia Intl Bank Ltd ....B
Ferrier Lullin Bank &
  Trust (Bah) Ltd ....B & T
Finagro Intl Bank & Trust Co Ltd ..B & T
Finec Intl Bank Ltd...............................B
Finter Bank & Trust (Bah) Ltd ....B & T
First American Bank of New York ......B
First Fidelity Bank, NA,
  Pennsylvania ....B
First Imexco Bank Ltd ....B
First Investment Bank (Bah) Ltd ....B
The First Newland Bank Ltd ....B
First Overseas Bank Ltd ....B
First Union National Bank ....B
First United Bank Ltd ....B
Fleet Bank, NA ....B
FonteCindam (Bah) Bank Ltd ....B & T
Garantia Banking Ltd ....B & T
Geneva Private Bank &
  Trust (Bah) Ltd ....B & T
Gonet Bank & Trust Ltd.......................B
Gottardo Trust Co Ltd ....B & T
Graphus Bank Intl Ltd ....B
Guaranty Trust Bank Ltd ....B & T
Guta Bank & Trust Ltd ....B & T
HSBC Asset Management
  Bahamas Ltd ....T

HSBC Investment Bank Asia Ltd..........B
Habib Banking Corp Ltd ....B & T
Hampton Bank Intl (Bah) Ltd ....B & T
Handelsfinanz-CCF Bank Intl Ltd ......B & T
Hang Seng Bank (Bah) Ltd ....B
Hang Seng Bank Trustee (Bah) Ltd ....T
Harris Trust & Savings Bank ....B
Heritage Bank Ltd ....B
The HongKong & Shanghai
  Banking Corp Ltd ....B
HongKong Bank (Bah) Ltd ....B
Hottinger Bank (Bah) Ltd ....B
Iberatlantico Bank & Trust Ltd ......B & T
Inarco Intl Bank, NV ....B & T
Incobank & Trust Ltd....................B & T
The Industrial Bank of Japan Ltd ....B
The Industrial Bank of
  Japan Trust Co Ltd ....B & T
Indusval Intl Bank Ltd ....B & T
Inter Pacific Trust Co Ltd ....T
Interbank Overseas Ltd ....B & T
Intercredit Bank & Trust Ltd..........B & T
Intl Financial
  Bank & Trust Co Ltd ....B & T
The Intl Finverbank (Bah) Ltd ....B
Interpro Bank & Trust Co Ltd ......B & T
InterTrust Bank Ltd ....B & T
Isthmus Intl Bank (Bah) Ltd ....B & T
Istituto Bancario San Paolo di Torino,
  SPA ....B & T
The Jersey Private Bank & Trust
  (Nass) Ltd ....B & T
Latin American Investment
  Bank (Bah) Ltd ....B
Leadenhall Trust Co Ltd ....T
Leopold Joseph (Bah) Ltd....................T
Leu Trust & Banking (Bah) Ltd ......B & T
Liberal Banking Corp Ltd..............B & T
Liberty Bank & Trust Co of Tulsa ....B
Manufacturers & Traders Trust Co
  (M & T Bank).................................B
Marine Midland Bank, NA ....B
Marka Bank Ltd ....B
Mayflower Intl Bank Ltd ....B
MeesPierson (Bah) Ltd..................B & T
Mega Securities Bank &
  Trust Co Ltd ....B & T
Metropolitan Bank (Bah) Ltd ....B
Monteverdi Intl Bank &
  Trust Co Ltd ....B & T
Morgan Guaranty Trust Co
  of New York ....B
Morymor Bank Ltd ....B

NBD Bank ....B
National Bank of Canada ....B
National Bank of Canada
 (Intl) Ltd ....B & T
National Westminster Bank, plc ....B
NationsBank of Texas, NA ....B
New Hemisphere
 Capital Bank Ltd ....B & T
The New Millennium Bank Ltd.......B & T
New World Trust Corp.........................T
New World Trustees (Bah) Ltd ....B & T
Nordfinanz-Bank Zurich,
 Nassau Branch ....B & T
Novo Bank & Trust Ltd ....B & T
Occidental Bank & Trust Intl Ltd ....B & T
Oceanic Bank & Trust Ltd ....B & T
Overseas Caribbean Bank Corp Ltd ....B
Overseas Union Bank &
 Trust (Bah) Ltd ....B & T
PNC Bank, NA ....B
PT Bank Central Asia ....B
Pactual Overseas
 Bank & Trust Ltd ....B & T
Pan American Bank Ltd ....B & T
Pasche Bank & Trust Ltd ....B & T
Pictet Bank & Trust Ltd ....B & T
Prime Bank & Trust (Bah) Ltd ....B & T
The Private Trust Corp Ltd ....B & T
Providence Trust Ltd ....T
Republic National Bank
 of New York (Intl) Ltd ....B & T
Riggs Bank & Trust Co (Bah) Ltd ....B & T
Riggs National Bank of
 Washington, DC ....B
Royal Bank of Canada Trust Co
 (Bah) Ltd ....B & T
The Royal Bank of Scotland
 (Nass) Ltd ....B & T
Rural Intl Bank Ltd ....B
SRL Bank Intl Ltd ....B & T
Santander Investment Bank Ltd ....B
Santander Merchant Bank Ltd ....B
Sanwa Bank California ....B
Signet Bank (Bah) Ltd ....B & T
Signet Bank/Virginia ....B
Sofisa Intl Bank Ltd ....B
Southern Cone Investment Bank &
 Trust Ltd ....B & T
Southern Union Bank
 & Trust (Bah) Ltd ....B & T
Standard Chartered Bank ....B
Standard Chartered Bank
 (Bah) Ltd ....B

State Bank of India ....B
Sud Bank & Trust Co Ltd ....B & T
Suisse Security Bank
 & Trust Ltd ....B & T
The Sumitomo Bank of California ......B
Sumitomo Trust & Banking
 Co Ltd...B & T
Summit Bank & Trust Co Ltd ....B
Surety Bank & Trust Co Ltd ....B & T
Target Bank Ltd ....B & T
Thorand Trust & Management Ltd ....T
Towerbank (Bah) Ltd ....B & T
Trade Finance Bank & Trust Ltd ....B & T
Transamerica Bank &
 Trust Co Ltd ....B & T
UBS (Bah) Ltd ....B & T
UP Bank and Trust Ltd..................B & T
Unibanco-União de Bancos
 Brasileiros, SA ....B & T
Union Trust Co ....B
United European
 Bank & Trust (Nass) Ltd ....B & T
United Overseas Bank & Trust Co
 (Bah) Ltd ....B & T
Universal Capital Bank Ltd ....B
The Valley National Bank of Arizona ......B
Vencred Bank & Trust Co (Bah) Ltd ....B
Votorantim Bank Ltd ....B
W & P Bank & Trust Co Ltd ....B & T
Wall Street Intl Bank
 & Trust Ltd ....B & T
Wells Fargo Bank, NA ....B
Westrust Bank (Intl) Ltd................B & T
Winslow Bank & Trust Co Ltd ....B & T
The Winterbotham Trust Co Ltd ....B & T
Workers Bank Ltd ....B

BIRDS

The birds of The Bahamas are from the US, Cuba, and the Caribbean. The majority of birds in the northern Bahamas are of North American origin, while more Caribbean species are found in the south. Although there are more than 200 species of birds in The Bahamas, only a few are endemic to The Bahamas. These include the Bahama woodstar hummingbird, the Bahama swallow and Bahama yellowthroat. The Bahama parrot is an endemic sub-species closely related to the Cuban parrot and Cayman parrot.

Other birds seen in The Bahamas of interest to birdwatchers are the West Indian woodpecker, Bahama mockingbird, red-legged thrush, great lizard cuckoo, loggerhead kingbird, black-cowled oriole and Greater Antillean bullfinch.

Inagua is ornithologically the richest island, with a rookery of approx 60,000 flamingos, roseate spoonbills and a large proportion of the world population of reddish egrets. The Bahama parrot is also found in Inagua. These birds are under the protection of the Bahamas National Trust (BNT), which administers the 287 sq mile Inagua National Park.

The lagoons and mangrove swamps of The Bahamas attract a variety of herons and egrets. Sea birds and waders abound on the coasts and hummingbirds are common. At the other extreme of size is the Magnificent frigatebird, which pilots have encountered at 8,000 ft. There are many North American migrants.

The Wild Birds Protection Act is designed to ensure the survival of all bird species throughout The Bahamas. Hunters should obtain a copy of the Act from Government Publications, the Old Lighthouse Bldg, Bay St, Nassau.

*1. **Closed season April 1-Sept 15 on the following birds:** Eurasian-collared (red-necked) dove, zenaida (wood) dove and mourning (Florida) dove.

*2. **Closed season Mar 31-Sept 28:** All wild ducks and geese (except whistling, Bahama, white jaw and ruddy ducks), bobwhite quail, chukar partridge, Wilson's or Jack snipe and coot, ring-necked pheasant, guinea fowl, black-crowned night heron.

*3. **Closed season Mar 1-Sept 28:** White-crowned pigeon.

4. **Totally protected species:** All other birds except those listed in (1), (2) and (3) may not be shot, killed or caught at any time.

5. **Status of hunters:** Only Bahamian citizens, permanent residents and licensed foreigners or those who have resided in The Bahamas for a continuous 90-day period may hunt here.

6. **Bag limits:** At present, 50 wild birds may be taken by one person per day. The possession limit is 200 birds at any one time.

7. **Wild bird reserves:** It is an offence to hunt, kill or capture any wild bird in certain areas. A list of these places, condensed below, may be obtained from the Ministry of Agriculture and Fisheries, Nassau.

New Providence area: Paradise Island, Lake Cunningham, Waterloo, Adelaide Creek, Goulding Cay, Prospect Ridge Waterworks, Skyline Heights and The Retreat (BNT).

The Abacos: Pelican Cays Land & Sea Park and Black Sound Cay Reserve.

Andros: High Cay, Grassy Creek Cays and Rocks, North Rocks and Small Rocks, Washerwoman's Cut Cays including Dolly Cay, Sister Rocks, Pigeon Cay and Joulter Cays, Big Green Cay and Little Green Cay.

Berry Islands: Crab Cay and Mammy Rhoda Cay.

Eleuthera: Wood Cay, Water Cay and Schooner Cays, Bottle Cay, Cedar Cay and Finley Cay.

Exuma: Big Galliot Cay, Channel Cays, Flat Cay, Big Darby Island, Little Darby Island, Guana Cay, Goat Cay, Betty Cay, Pigeon Cay, Cistern Cay, Harvey Cay and Rocks in vicinity of Leaf Cay, Exuma Cays Land and Sea Park area.

Grand Bahama: Peterson Cay and Lucayan National Park.

Inagua: BNT areas have by-laws which are in force.

Little San Salvador: Little Island or Little San Salvador and Goat Cay.

---

* *During closed season on these birds, it is an offence to kill, capture or have in possession any such bird unless it can be proved the bird was taken in season.*

8. Penalties: Any person who commits an offence against the Act is liable to a fine of up to $500 or one month imprisonment. The gun, ammunition, car, boat or plane and all equipment used on the hunting expedition are liable to be forfeited and auctioned. If the car, boat or plane is used by another person who commits an offence, the owner could still lose his property by forfeiture unless he proves he did not commit an offence and had reported the incident to police or game wardens.

9. The Act provides a reward of $500 or one-half the proceeds of the sale of forfeited articles, whichever is the greater, to persons who give information leading to conviction of the offender.

See also **Flora & fauna** and **Wildlife preserves.**

BOATING

The Bahamas is a boater's paradise with some 700 islands, inlets and cays stretching over 100,000 miles of virtually pollution-free ocean. Chartering a yacht, bareboating, deep-sea fishing or day or dinner cruises are aqua-adventure possibilities. Family Islands such as the Abacos and Exumas are considered among the finest boating destinations in the world.

Motor boating

It is forbidden to drive a motor boat in the 200 ft zone of water directly offshore any Bahama island – unless the boat is approaching or leaving a marina, jetty, dock, etc, at a speed not exceeding three knots.

It is illegal to drive a boat in a reckless manner, or while under the influence of drugs or alcohol. It is illegal for anyone under 16 years of age to drive a motor boat with an engine of more than 10 hp, unless aged 14 or 15 and supervised by someone 16 or over.

Water skiing

Water skiing within the 200 ft zone is prohibited, unless the skier is being towed within a lane clearly marked with buoys or ropes. Water skiers are required to wear an efficient flotation device. In the towing boat there must be a look-out (in addition to the driver) aged 16 or over. Skiing is forbidden in hours of darkness.

Boat registration

The Water Skiing and Motor Boat Control (Amendment) Act, 1980, requires annual registration of Bahamian motor boats with an engine rated over 10 hp. Any person wishing to use such boats in Bahamian waters must apply to the port controller in Nassau or administrator in the Family Islands. Initial registration fees are:

Motor boats less than:
15 ft in length $10
15 ft or over, but less than 30 ft $20
30 ft or over,
　but less than 50 ft $100
50 ft or over,
　but less than 100 ft $200
100 ft or over $400
Fishing boats primarily designed to
　navigate under sail, with an auxiliary
　engine of less than 10 hp .... nil

The port controller or administrator where the boat is registered must be notified of any change of ownership or the fitting of a new engine to the registered boat. The registration number must clearly show on both sides of the boat's bow. Failure to comply may result in a fine up to $75.

Any person using an unregistered motor boat to which the Act applies is liable to a fine up to $75 plus an additional fine equal to twice the appropriate registration fee.

Duty on boats

Customs and stamp duty are not payable on foreign-registered/foreign-owned pleasure boats that remain in The Bahamas up to one year after having been imported initially under their own power and subject to specified conditions. Thereafter, written application for an extension of a cruising permit must be made to the Comptroller of Customs and once approved, a $500 fee (for one year) is applicable. The vessel may then remain in The Bahamas provided it is not used for commercial purposes or hire. The max period a vessel may remain in The Bahamas under this provision is three years, thereafter full Customs duties must be paid. Vessels temporarily imported, otherwise than under their own power, must be re-exported within 12 months of arrival, or full Customs duties must be paid.

Bahamians or others employed here more than six months pay Customs duty and stamp duty on importation of pleasure craft. Customs duty depends on length of craft and gross tonnage (Customs duty for a pleasure craft over 30 ft is 5%. Stamp duty is 7%).

Customs and stamp duty are not payable on foreign-registered/foreign owned pleasure boats 23 ft or more in length imported as cargo for temporary use and entered at a designated port of entry. See **Ports of entry.** The Comptroller of Customs must be satisfied the vessels are to be shipped out of The Bahamas.

Temporary permits cost $50. Proof of export must be supplied to Customs within a reasonable time of actual exportation.

See also **Marinas & cruising facilities.**

BROADCASTING
Radio stations (government-owned)
The Broadcasting Corp of The Bahamas is a government-owned corporation operating on its own revenue out of studios at Third Terrace (East), Centreville, Nassau and at the Kipling Bldg, Pioneer's Way, Freeport, Grand Bahama.

ZNS-1: Radio Bahamas (ZNS-1) transmits on 50,000 watts and is received throughout The Bahamas 24 hours a day. Programming is adult contemporary/talk shows.

ZNS-2: ZNS-2 is powered by 1,000 watts. Programming which is religious is simulcast on FM at 107.1 MHz, and 107.9 MHz in the southeastern Bahamas. ZNS-2 operates 6am-12 midnight at 1240 AM on the dial.

ZNS-FM: The ZNS-FM stereo station went on the air in Nassau July 10, 1988, at frequency 104.5 MHz. It operates 24 hours with a contemporary music format and has a transmitting power of 5,000 watts.

ZNS-3: Radio Bahamas Northern Service was established in May 1973, and transmits on a frequency of 810 kHz with 10,000 watts. It broadcasts from Freeport, Grand Bahama, throughout the northern Bahamas and to a small section of South Florida. Its programming parallels that of ZNS-1.

Radio stations (private)
In 1993, legislation was passed to allow private broadcasting in the region. Thus far, Nassau radio licences have been issued to The Tribune Ltd, Henry E Saunders Group and Jones Communications Ltd.

100 JAMZ: The first private radio station in The Bahamas, established Oct 10, 1993, transmitting on a frequency of 100.3 FM with 5,000 watts. The station, on Shirley and Deveaux Sts, Nassau, is owned by The Tribune Radio Ltd and operates 24 hours. 100 JAMZ is received in New Providence and Grand Bahama. Format is island and urban music. At press time, 100 JAMZ was preparing to negotiate an agreement with Cable Bahamas which would allow family islands as far south as Mayaguana to receive the station.

MORE FM: This station on Carmichael Rd officially aired in Dec 1995. It covers New Providence on a frequency of 94.9 FM with an effected radiated power (ERP) of 5,000 watts. MORE FM operates 24 hours with an "eclectic" format. It is owned by the Henry E Saunders Group.

LOVE 97: Operational since Sept 24, '94. Frequency is 97.5 FM with 5,000 watts, operating 24 hours with an adult/contemporary format. Owned by Jones Communications Ltd, the station is on East St North.

Radio licences

The Bahamas Telecommunications Corp (BaTelCo), John F Kennedy Dr, Nassau, provides free application forms for licences which are renewable annually. Licence fees per year are:
Fixed private stations $75
Amateur (ham) operators $6
Mobile stations (eg, in trucks) $15
Marine radios: pleasure boats $15
    ocean-going work vessels $30

Citizens band equipment, which requires no licence, is limited to five watts and 23 channels max.
    Contact BaTelCo, PO Box N-3048, tel 323-4911.
    See also **Cable television** and **Television**.

BUDGET
See **Public finance**.

BUILDING CONTRACTORS
Sampling only:

Cavalier Construction Co Ltd
    Tel 323-5171, fax 325-5244
Gilles Deal
    Tel 324-3596
Mosko's United Construction Co Ltd
    Tel 322-2825, fax 325-2571
Osprey Developers Building Contractors
    Tel 322-2429, fax 325-9127
Sunco Builders & Developers Ltd
    Tel 323-4966, fax 323-7656
Treco, Carl G, Contractors Ltd
    Tel 393-8725, fax 393-0732

BUILDING COSTS
See **Cost of living** and **Building permits**.

BUILDING PERMITS
Bahamas building permits issued by the Ministry of Public Works

Year	Permits issued	Estimated value (B$)
1993	2,480	227,075,127
1994	2,525	306,541,123
1995	2,333	259,321,639
1996	2,483	653,929,369
1997	2,607 *	311,496,582*

Provisional

Rates for commercial and residential properties

Floor area	Cost of permit
Up to 500 sq ft	$10
501-1,000 sq ft	$8/100 sq ft
1,001-1,500 sq ft	$10/100 sq ft
1,501-5,000 sq ft	$15/100 sq ft
5,001-10,000 sq ft	$20/100 sq ft
Over 10,000 sq ft	$25/100 sq ft

Other charges
To build a wall, fence or any boundary
    structure .... $8/100 linear ft
Removal of sheds,
    garages & other structures
    (non-demolition) .... $25 minimum
Reclamation of land .... $5/100 sq ft
Building of small private docks
    & any size swimming pool ...... $5/sq ft

Renewals
Where gross area of floor space is:
Up to 1,000 sq ft $10
1,001-1,500 sq ft $25
1,501-5,000 sq ft $45
5,001-10,000 sq ft $60
Over 10,000 sq ft $100

Deposits
Up to 500 sq ft $5
501–1,000 sq ft $10
1,001–1,500 sq ft $25
Over 1,500 sq ft .... 10% of total fee

Other projects
Approval from the Dept of Physical Planning is required for land excavations and removal of protected trees.
    Approval from the Docks Committee, Port Dept, is required for the building of docks and marinas.

BUSINESS LICENCE FEE

The Business Licence Act, 1980, made it mandatory for anyone operating a business aimed at obtaining a turnover to apply for and obtain a license.

Annual licence renewal applications and payments are due every Jan-April. Fees are based, in the case of most businesses, on their annual gross receipts less the "cost incurred in producing that turnover." They range from nothing for a petty business to 1½% of turnover or $500,000 (whichever is greater) for "a very large business with a very high profit," per year. See **Fig 1.2**.

Companies designated non-resident under the Exchange Control Regulations Act pay an annual fee of $100.

Companies licensed under The Banks and Trust Companies Regulation Act, 1965 (which imposes separate fees), are not required to pay for a business licence. Gas stations pay a fixed fee of ⅕ of 1% of turnover (a business with a turnover of $250,000 per year or more).

The Act's definition of "business" includes all types of manufacturing and commercial undertakings, and covers professions such as law, accounting and medicine. Where a business consists of separate and distinct undertakings, a separate licence must be obtained for each.

A Bahamian or Bahamian company (ie, one with 100% Bahamian ownership) wishing to start a new business may commence operations as soon as the application for a licence is submitted, and prior to determination of the application, provided the company has complied with requirements of all other government agencies. A non-Bahamian or a company not 100% Bahamian-owned must wait for the licence application to be approved.

The Act provides for automatic annual renewal for Bahamian businesses (if other statutory requirements have been met). Renewal of a non-Bahamian business licence is at the discretion of the Minister of Finance and Planning, whose decision "shall not be called into question by any court."

Business licence fee schedule
See **Fig 1.2**.

Highlights of amendments to Business Licence Act

Businesses with a turnover less than $50,000 (based on the gross income derived from the selling of goods or services) are not required to pay a fee. They are, however, required to register under the Act.

A rebate of 5% of the fee for medium and 3% for large and very large businesses is offered for each Bahamian employee (not permanent resident) added to the workforce on a full-time basis (up to a max of 10 employees). These employees would have to have been employed for a period not less than eight months.

Rebates for employee increases are good for one year only. The figure used is the net Bahamian employee increase in the previous calendar year (ie, the change from Jan 1, 1997 to Dec 31, '97).

Earning a rebate in subsequent years requires more Bahamians to be added to the workforce. National Insurance will be consulted to verify employment figures included with the application.

Following are further amendments to the Business Licence Act:
1. "Gross profit" is defined as turnover less allowable cost, which is defined in the Act.
2. Business licences may be suspended if fees are not paid.
3. Where a business operates out of the owner's premises, no business licence will be granted unless real property taxes are up-to-date.
4. Medium, large and very large businesses require a certificate from a qualified, professional accountant verifying accuracy of the amount of turnover and gross profits.
5. The Ministry of Finance's secretary of the revenue has power to have the books of a licensee audited at

FIG 1.2
BUSINESS LICENCE FEE SCHEDULE

Profit (gross)	Petty under 50,000	V small 50,000-100,000	Small 100,000-250,000	Medium 250,000-1,000,000	Large 1,000,000-28,000,000	V large 28,000,000 plus
Low (under 25%)	–	$250	$500	0.5% of turnover	0.5% of turnover	½ of 1% of turnover or $140,000 (the greater)
Medium (25-50%)	–	$500	$750	1.00%	1.00%	1% of turnover or $280,000 (the greater)
High (50-75%)	–	$700	$1,000	1.50%	1.50%	1½% of turnover or $420,000 (the greater)
Very high (over 75%)	–	$800	$1,250	1.50%	1.50%	1½% of turnover or $500,000 (the greater)

least once a year. Books are to be maintained for at least two years.

6. Businesses importing goods must provide a current business licence for Customs inspection when requested.

See also **Company formation; Investing;** and **National Insurance.**

BUSINESS NAME REGISTRATION

Before a company is incorporated, its proposed name must be approved – by phone if one wishes – by the Registrar General as meeting requirements laid down in the Companies Act, 1992, International Business Companies Act, 1989, The Business Names Act, The Banks and Trust Companies Regulation Act, and The Insurance Act.

The Business Names Act is not administered by the Companies Section but by a separate section of the Registrar General's Dept.

See also **Company formation.**

CABLE TELEVISION

In 1994, The Bahamas government issued a 15-year exclusive licence for installation and operation of cable television throughout The Bahamas to a company comprised of Cable 2000 Inc, a Canadian company, and Bahamian interests. Non-Bahamian ownership, which began at 49%, has been reduced to 43.5% as a result of the agreement to gradually increase Bahamian ownership to 60%.

Two of the public utility corporations, The Bahamas Electricity Corp (BEC) and The Bahamas Telecommunications Corp (BaTelCo), each hold 10% of the shares. The remaining 29% were made available to the Bahamian public.

In Aug 1995, the company's share offering generated over 3,000 Bahamian shareholders. Cable Bahamas also purchased CATV in Grand Bahama, giving the company a monopoly for cable TV services in The Bahamas.

The first subscribers in New Providence came on stream in Mar 1995.

Cable television service has been provided to New Providence, Grand Bahama, Paradise Island, Bimini and Abaco. Eleuthera, Inagua, Long Island, Exuma and the Berry Islands were slated to receive cable TV before 1999.

Cable Bahamas installs, free of charge, cable service in government-operated and church-operated schools, charitable organizations and government ministries. A parliamentary channel permits live broadcasts of parliamentary proceedings.

In Jan 1997, Cable Bahamas introduced SelectVISION service which delivers 20 channels of first-run movies to hotel rooms and homes in New Providence. This service represents a $1.5 million investment by Cable Bahamas.

See also **Television.**

CAMPING

While camping is not illegal in The Bahamas, it is not recommended. If you want to camp on government property, you must obtain a permit from the Ministry of Public Works. The application form will provide you with regulations and restrictions. If you are camping in a remote area, it would be wise to advise someone of your whereabouts. Before lighting a camp fire, obtain permission from the Fire Dept on the island in question.

CAPTIVE INSURANCE
See **Insurance.**

CAR RENTAL COMPANIES

Avis, downtown.....................326-6380
or 322-2889
Nassau Intl Airport.............377-7121
Paradise Island...................363-2061
Budget Rent A Car
Nassau Intl Airport.............377-9000
or 377-7405
Paradise Isl Airport.............363-3095
Davis Car Rental....................324-2165
or 364-5042

Dollar Rent A Car
Nassau Intl Airport............377-7231
or 377-8300
Downtown 325-3716
Hertz 377-8684
Kemco Importers
Car Rentals & Sales 323-2178
Teglo Car Rentals..................362-4361
Wallace's U-Drive-It Cars 393-8559
See also **Driver's licence & vehicle information; Insurance; Motor vehicle insurance;** and **Transportation.**

CARIBBEAN BASIN INITIATIVE (CBI)

The Caribbean Basin Initiative (CBI) was established by the US in 1982 to promote growth in the Caribbean region, including The Bahamas, by stimulating investment in non-traditional industries producing goods for the US market. CBI permits duty-free import of most products shipped from the Caribbean.

The duty-free provisions were made permanent in 1990 and other enhancements to CBI were added. If a product is not entirely grown, produced or manufactured in one or more CBI countries, certain minimum value-added and substantial transformation requirements are imposed.

Products eligible for duty-free importation into the US include:
- Electronic and electro-mechanical assembly.
- Ethnic and regional foods (eg, spices, jams, liqueurs and confectioneries).
- Fresh and frozen seafood.
- Handicrafts, giftware and decorative accessories.
- Medical and surgical supplies.
- Ornamental horticulture.
- Recreational items, such as sporting goods and toys.
- Tropical fruit products.
- Winter vegetables.
- Wood products, including furniture and building materials.

However, the CBI law excludes the following articles from duty-free entry status:
- Canned tuna.
- Certain leather, rubber and plastic gloves.
- Certain leather apparel.
- Footwear (except disposable items and footwear parts such as uppers).
- Luggage, handbags and flat goods.
- Most textiles and apparel.
- Petroleum and petroleum products.
- Watches and watch parts, if any components originated in a Communist country.

Bahamian exports currently benefiting from CBI regulations include chemicals, seafood and pharmaceuticals. In 1996, the US imported from The Bahamas a total of $165.4 million worth of products, representing an increase of $9.4 million over 1995 trade figures.

CARIBBEAN COMMUNITY & COMMON MARKET (CARICOM)

The Caribbean Community and Common Market (CARICOM) emerged from the spirit of the British West Indies Federation of 1958-62. The present organization was immediately preceded by the Caribbean Free Trade Assoc (CARIFTA). CARICOM, with a common market as an integral part, was established in 1973. The Caribbean community has three primary objectives: integration of the economies of member states; functional cooperation in areas to include education, health, air transportation, meteorology and labour relations; and coordination of foreign policies, including the sharing of foreign embassy and foreign representative facilities.

The CARICOM treaty is currently being amended by a series of protocols aimed at deepening the integration process.

CARICOM heads of government meet twice yearly. The 1999 meetings will be held in Suriname and Trinidad. The Bahamas became the 13th member state of CARICOM on July 4, 1983, but is not a member of the common market. The other CARICOM members include Antigua and Barbuda, Barbados, Belize, Dominica, Grenada, Guyana, Jamaica, Montserrat, St Kitts and Nevis, St Lucia, St Vincent and the Grenadines, and Trinidad and Tobago. The British Virgin Islands are an associate member of the Caribbean community.

The CARICOM Secretariat is headquartered at The Bank of Guyana Building, PO Box 10827, Georgetown, Guyana. Tel (011) 592-2-52961/2, fax (011) 592-2-57341.

CARIBCAN

In 1986, the Canadian government established CARIBCAN, a programme to encourage trade, investment and industrial cooperation with the Commonwealth Caribbean region.

There are 18 countries or dependent territories eligible to receive benefits of the duty-free provisions of CARIBCAN. These are: Anguilla, Antigua and Barbuda, The Bahamas, Barbados, Belize, Bermuda, the British Virgin Islands, the Cayman Islands, Dominica, Grenada, Guyana, Jamaica, Montserrat, St Kitts and Nevis, St Lucia, St Vincent and the Grenadines, Trinidad and Tobago, and the Turks and Caicos Islands.

The programme's basic objectives are to expand Canadian and Commonwealth Caribbean trade and promote new investment opportunities in the region.

CARIBCAN's main feature is duty-free access to the Canadian market for most exports from the Commonwealth Caribbean countries. There are some notable exclusions, such as textiles and clothing, footwear, leather garments, refined petroleum oils and methanol, which continue to be subject to the General Preferential Tariff.

Goods may qualify for CARIBCAN treatment if at least 60% of the ex-factory price to Canada is made up of materials, parts or produce of CARIBCAN countries. A certificate of origin issued by the Customs Dept or designated certifying agency of the exporting country is required for the goods to enter Canada duty free.

Canadian imports from CARIBCAN countries are fairly diversified. The most important are bauxite from Jamaica, iron and steel from Trinidad and Tobago, organic chemicals from The Bahamas and food and beverages from other Caribbean territories. CARIBCAN also permits the in-bond bottling of Caribbean rum in Canada. In the three years from 1995-97, goods imported into Canada from The Bahamas averaged CDN$16,075,000 (US$11,720,000) per year. Average Canadian exports to The Bahamas over the same period were CDN$20,925,000 (US$15,220,000). These figures do not reflect the growing bilateral trade in services.

The CARIBCAN programme contains measures to encourage Canadian investment and industrial cooperation with the region, such as providing access to the federal government's international trade centres to assist Caribbean trade commissioners in their trade promotion efforts in Canada.

Another Canadian organization which can assist Caribbean exporters with the CARIBCAN programme is The Trade Facilitation Office (TFO), which provides practical assistance for promotion of Caribbean exports to Canada by helping producers in trade fair participation, bringing business visitors to Canada, preparing practical market information papers and maintaining a database matching importers and exporters.

Contact the Trade Commissioner, Canadian High Commission, 30-36 Knutsford Blvd, Kingston 5, Jamaica, WI, tel (876) 926-1500 (to 7), fax (876) 960-3861.

CASINOS
See **Entertainment** and **Gambling**.

CENSORSHIP (FILMS, PLAYS & PRINTED MATERIAL)

The Bahamas Plays and Films Control Board reviews films, synopses of films and stage plays intended for public showing, classifying the material as:

A: Suitable for universal exhibition or performance (US: **G**).

B: Suitable for adults and persons under 18 when accompanied by a parent or other responsible adult (US: **PG 13** and **PG**).

T: Suitable for any person over 15 (US: **PG 13**).

C: For adults only, with persons under 18 not admitted whether accompanied by an adult or not (US: **R**).

D: Unapproved films or plays, although the board may change the classification if portions of the work it deems "undesirable in the public interest" are excised.

The board is appointed for a two-year period, along with other government boards.

A max fine of $2,000 and/or imprisonment for a term not exceeding six months is the penalty for any public performance or exhibition given without authorization by The Bahamas Plays and Films Control Board. Any persons concerned in the organization or management of that performance or exhibition; and any other person who, knowing or having reasonable cause to suspect the contravention, allows premises to be used or made available for the performance or exhibition, will be held liable.

If an obscene play or film is exhibited in public or private, any person responsible for presenting or directing that showing (whether for gain or not) will be liable, on summary conviction, to a fine not exceeding $2,000 or to imprisonment for a term not exceeding six months; or, on conviction on information, to a fine not exceeding $5,000 and/or to imprisonment for a term not exceeding three years.

In addition, if the Governor-General considers a publication to be contrary to the public interest, he may prohibit its importation, including future issues. Any person who imports, publishes, sells, offers for sale, distributes, reproduces, or possesses any publication which has been prohibited is subject to imprisonment for one year or a fine of $500 or both for a first offence. A person is liable to two years' imprisonment if he or she publishes, sells, or offers for sale any blasphemous or obscene book, writing, or representation.

CHAMBER OF COMMERCE

The Bahamas Chamber of Commerce is a non-profit, non-political corporate body of businesses and professionals. Its primary interest is promoting, fostering and protecting Bahamian commerce and industry. It also provides government with a responsible vehicle for dialogue with the private sector.

Since the Chamber is concerned with all phases of the Bahamian economy, it maintains active standing committees which parallel the areas of responsibility of most government ministries. These committees meet at least monthly. Much of their routine business concerns recommendations to government and requests from government for private sector cooperation on various projects such as Free Trade Area of the Americas (FTAA).

Membership of the Bahamas Chamber of Commerce comprises representatives from every business sector. Offices are located on the corner of Shirley St and Collins Ave, PO Box N-665, Nassau, The Bahamas, tel (242) 322-2145, 322-3320 or 326-5443/4; fax (242) 322-4649.

CHURCHES
See **Religion**.

CINEMAS

Nassau has two spacious cinemas offering first-run movies, concession stands and adequate parking.

The Shirley St Theatre is a single-screen theatre featuring a Surround Sound system, two shows daily and a total of 824 seats (490 downstairs; 334 balcony). Seats for the matinee cost $4 downstairs and $5 balcony for adults and $1 for children (under 12). Evening seats cost $5 downstairs and $6 balcony for adults, $1.50 for children. Tel 393-2884.

RND Cinemas is a six-screen multiplex theatre in the Prince Charles Shopping Centre, Prince Charles Dr. Each auditorium seats approx 200 people and has the latest projection equipment and DTS Surround Sound. Each movie is shown four times daily in addition to late-night shows on Fri and Sat. Matinee seats cost $5 for adults and $1.50 for children (under 12). Evening seats (after 5pm) cost $6 for adults and $2.50 for children. Call 394-6956 or 394-FILM (3456) for a recording of movies and show times. A new six-screen RND West, on John F Kennedy Dr, was scheduled to open June 1999.

At press time, construction had begun on the seven-screen Galleria Cinemas, at Marathon Mall, scheduled to open Nov 1998.

CITIZENSHIP

The Constitution of The Bahamas contains detailed provisions of who is, or who can become, a citizen. Other provisions affecting the acquisition or loss of citizenship are contained in The Bahamas Nationality Act, 1973.

1. Under the Constitution, those who became or were eligible to become citizens on the date of independence – July 10, 1973 – include:
   a. A person born in The Bahamas who was, on July 9, 1973, a citizen of the UK and colonies.
   b. A person born outside The Bahamas if his father did, or

would have before his death, become a citizen of The Bahamas, provided this person is or was a citizen of the UK and colonies on July 9, 1973.
   c. A person who was registered as a citizen of the UK and colonies under the British Nationality Act, 1948, by virtue of having been registered in the former colony of the Bahama Islands under that Act. Excepted from this provision are those persons registered under the British Nationality Act, 1948, and who were not resident in The Bahamas on Dec 31, '72; or who were registered on or after Jan 1, '73, or who on July 9, '73, possessed the nationality of some other country.
2. Other sections of the Constitution relate to those persons born after July 9, 1973. They provide that:
   a. A person born in The Bahamas after that date shall be a citizen if either of his parents was a citizen of The Bahamas.
   b. A person born in The Bahamas, neither of whose parents is a citizen, shall be entitled to be registered as a citizen of The Bahamas, subject to exceptions or qualifications prescribed in the interests of national security or public policy, by making application within 12 months after his 18th birthday. Such persons, if they are citizens of another country, will be required to renounce that citizenship, take an oath of allegiance, and make a declaration of intent concerning residence.
   c. A person born outside The Bahamas after July 9, 1973, whose father is Bahamian by birth and the parents are married, regardless of the mother's nationality. If the child is illegitimate and the mother is not Bahamian, or if legitimate and the father was also born outside The Bahamas, though of Bahamian parents, he is not Bahamian.
   d. A person born legitimately outside The Bahamas after July 9, 1973, if his mother is a citizen of The Bahamas, is entitled to make application between the ages of 18 and 21 years to be registered as a citizen, subject to national security and public policy considerations. He is required to renounce any other citizenship, take an oath of allegiance and make a declaration of intent concerning residence. If his mother registers him as a minor prior to his 18th birthday and it is approved, renunciation would not be necessary and dual nationality would result.
   e. If a child is born illegitimately abroad and the mother is Bahamian, he is a Bahamian citizen by birth.
   f. Any woman who, after July 9, 1973, is married to a person who is or becomes a citizen of The Bahamas is entitled upon making application to be registered as a citizen, provided she is still married to that person and subject to national security and public policy considerations. Once approved, she does not have to renounce her previous nationality.

In all cases (with the exception of 1a, 1b and 1c), registration as a citizen is subject to exceptions or qualifications prescribed in the interests of national security or public policy.

Prior to independence, the designation "Bahamian status" was given to some British subjects who met certain qualifications, including at least five years' residence in The Bahamas, and to others who automatically acquired Bahamian status by marriage. Bahamian status conferred on them equal rights with Bahamians with regard to employment and business.

Foreigners who were not British subjects qualified for Bahamian status by becoming British subjects naturalized in The Bahamas.

Aliens who are not entitled to be registered or naturalized by virtue of an existing status are nevertheless able to apply for citizenship in The Bahamas under the Nationality Act. Qualifications include:
1. Seven years' lawful residence of the 10 years immediately preceding, and inclusive of, date of application, ie, work permit, residency permit or permanent residence certificate.
2. Knowledge of the English language.
3. Intent to continue residing in and making The Bahamas their permanent home.

See also **Immigration.**

CLIMATE

Having a tropical maritime climate with winter incursions of modified polar air, generally The Bahamas experiences neither frost, snow, sleet, hail nor extreme temperatures. A unique exception occurred on Jan 19, 1977, when parts of the northern Bahamas experienced a brief flurry of light snow. The lowest recorded temperature was 41.4°F on Jan 20, '81. See **Fig 1.3.**

In centrally-situated New Providence, winter temperatures seldom fall much below 60°F and usually reach about 75°F in the afternoon. In summer, temperatures usually fall to 78°F or less at night and seldom rise above 90°F during the day. Winter temperatures are somewhat lower in the more northerly islands than in New Providence, and some 5° higher in the southern islands. In summer, temperatures tend to be similar all over The Bahamas. Sea surface temperatures normally vary between 74°F in Feb and 83°F in Aug.

Humidity

Humidity is fairly high, especially in summer months. Winds are predominantly easterly throughout the year but have a tendency to become northeasterly from Oct-April and southeasterly from May-Sept. Wind speeds are, on average, below 10 knots; in winter months, periods of a day or two of north and northeast winds of about 25 knots may occur.

There are more than seven hours of bright sunshine per day in Nassau on average, though periods of a day or two of cloudy weather can occur at any time of year. Daylight hours vary from 10 hours, 35 mins in late Dec to 13 hours, 41 mins in late June.

Rain showers occur any time of year, but the rainy months are May-Oct; for example, in Nassau, rainfall averages 2 ins a month from Nov-April and 6 ins a month from May-Oct. In the northern islands, it is up to 20% more. The southern islands normally receive only half the Nassau total. Rainfall is mainly in the form of heavy showers or thundershowers, which clear quickly.

Hurricane season

Nassau can be affected by hurricanes or tropical storms between June and Nov, the greatest risk being in Aug, Sept and Oct.

Hurricane Andrew of Aug 23-24, 1992, affected mainly North Eleuthera, Harbour Island, Spanish Wells, Bimini, Chub Cay, Cat Cay and the Berry Islands. Hurricane Erin passed through The Bahamas in Aug 1995, causing damage (although minimal) in eight islands. The category one hurricane packed max winds of up to 103 miles per hour.

Based on figures compiled for the past 90-year period, Nassau may expect to experience hurricane conditions an average of once every nine years. An efficient warning system gives ample notice for necessary precautions to be taken.

See also **Hurricanes.**

FIG 1.3
CLIMATOLOGICAL MEANS FOR 1961-90*

	JAN	FEB	MAR	APR	MAY	JUN	JUL	AUG	SEP	OCT	NOV	DEC
TEMPERATURE (°F)												
Highest temperatures	86.4	88.7	87.8	91.2	92.3	93.2	93.4	95.0	93.2	91.8	90.0	86.7
Mean of daily max temperatures	77.3	77.5	79.7	81.8	84.6	87.3	89.1	89.3	88.4	85.4	81.8	78.7
Mean daily temperatures	69.9	70.0	72.0	74.2	77.5	80.4	82.3	82.2	81.1	78.7	74.9	71.4
Mean of daily minimum temperatures	62.1	62.5	63.8	66.2	69.8	73.3	74.7	74.8	74.4	71.9	68.0	63.8
Lowest temperatures	41.4	45.8	44.6	48.6	55.5	59.0	64.2	64.4	59.5	59.9	52.0	41.5
HUMIDITY												
Mean relative humidity (%)	78	78	76	74	77	79	77	79	81	80	78	78
Mean dew point (°F)	62.6	62.6	63.5	64.9	69.5	73.5	74.6	75.0	74.7	71.8	67.6	64.0
WIND												
Mean wind speed in knots	8.0	8.6	8.9	8.3	7.9	7.2	7.1	6.9	6.2	7.4	8.1	7.8
SUNSHINE												
Mean hours of bright sunshine	7.1	7.6	8.3	9.2	8.7	7.7	8.8	8.6	7.1	7.2	7.4	6.9
Mean length of day – hours	10.3	11.3	12.0	12.7	13.3	13.7	13.5	13.0	12.3	11.6	11.0	10.6
RAINFALL												
Mean rainfall in inches	1.86	1.59	1.57	2.12	4.58	9.17	6.21	8.50	6.75	6.91	2.23	2.04

*The Dept of Meteorology updates these tables every 10 years and the next review will be in 2000.

COMMUNITY ORGANIZATIONS & SERVICE CLUBS

There are organizations and clubs in The Bahamas which provide a range of services, advice, companionship and more. These include:

Abilities Unlimited 325-2150
AIDS Foundation 325-5120/1
L'Alliance Française 356-0961
American Men's Club
  of The Bahamas................322-8663
American Women's Club 327-5639
Bahamas Air Sea Rescue Assoc
  (BASRA)........325-8864 or 322-3877
Bahamas Assoc for the
  Mentally Retarded 356-9777
Bahamas Assoc for the
  Physically Disabled 322-2393
Bahamas Assoc for Social Health
  (BASH)..........356-2274 or 323-6117
Bahamas Council on
  Alcoholism 322-1685
Bahamas Council for
  the Handicapped 322-4260
Bahamas Family Planning
  Assoc 325-1663

Bahamas Girl Guides
  Assoc 322-4342
Bahamas Heart Assoc 327-0806
Bahamas Historical Society 322-4231
Bahamas Humane Society
  (BHS) 323-5138
Bahamas National Pride
  Assoc 326-3330
Bahamas National Trust
  (BNT) 393-1317
Business & Professional
  Women's Club of NP 392-1538
Bahamas Red Cross 323-7370
Bahamas Sickle Cell Assoc 328-8085
Canadian Men's Club 327-3485
Canadian Women's Club 323-3117
Cancer Society of
  The Bahamas 324-2429/324-1063
Crippled Children's
  Committee 328-6147
The Crisis Centre 328-0922
Drug Action Service 322-2308/9
Drug Free Achievers 322-2308/9
Hispanic Women's Club 327-7447
Innerwheel Club of
  East Nassau 324-3013
Innerwheel Club of Nassau 356-7243
Jugs Inc 393-5784
Kidney Foundation of
  The Bahamas 322-4381
Kiwanis Club of
  Fort Montagu 327-7038
Kiwanis Club of Nassau, AM 362-1412
Kiwanis Club of NP 394-6901
Kiwanis Club of CB 326-7833
Kiwanis Club of Nassau 364-2597
Kiwanis Club of Over-the-hill .. 393-6393
  or 326-5677
Lions Club 323-6900
Nassau Amateur Operatic
  Society 364-0677
Nassau Chapter of
  Links Inc 328-7238
Nassau Jaycees 322-1161
Nassau Music Society 322-8306
National Drug Council 325-4633/4
National Pan-Hellenic
  Council, Inc 364-4340
Pilot Club of Nassau 328-0990
Rotary Clubs of:
  East Nassau, Nassau,
  Southeast Nassau, West Nassau
  Rotary recorded info line 325-5906

Royal Life Saving Society 325-2104
Samaritan Ministry 323-5517
Scout Assoc of The Bahamas
  (President) 325-2757
Teen Challenge 325-2149
Toastmasters Intl 324-7770
  or 364-6793
Training Centre for
  the Disabled 322-2272
Women's Corona Society
  in The Bahamas 327-5053
Young Women's Christian
  Assoc (YWCA) 323-5526
Zonta Club of Nassau 322-8100
  or 302-2011

Many of these phone numbers are office numbers of volunteer individuals, and are subject to change.

COMPANY FORMATION

In order to incorporate a company in The Bahamas, a copy of the memorandum of association must be filed with the Registrar General.

The memorandum should be signed by a minimum of two subscribers and witnessed by an additional person. The witness will have to sign and swear to an affidavit stating that the two subscribers signed the memorandum in his presence.

A subscriber who is not a resident of The Bahamas, or his nominee, must get permission from the Controller of Exchange. Such permission is usually not difficult to obtain.

There is a filing fee of $300 for each memorandum of association. The memorandum gives the company name and its authorized capital (if limited by shares). It must also state the part of the Commonwealth of The Bahamas in which the registered office is proposed to be situated.

Articles of association may be filed with the memorandum of the company at the time of incorporation, or within six months thereof, for a fee of $30. The incorporators may adopt the "ready-made" articles embodied in the first schedule of the Companies Act. If no articles are submitted within the six-month period, those listed in the first schedule are adopted. The articles should be signed by a minimum of two subscribers and witnessed by an additional person.

Before a company is incorporated, its proposed name must be approved – by phone if one wishes – by the Registrar General as meeting requirements laid down in the Companies Act, 1992, The Business Names Act, The Banks and Trust Companies Regulation Act, and The Insurance Act.

Stamp duty is payable on authorized capital and any further increases. For every memorandum of association of a company where the capital is up to and including $5,000, duty is $60. For every additional $1,000, or fraction thereof, the duty is $3.

If the authorized capital is increased after incorporation, additional fees are payable to the Treasury on filing the resolutions. An increase of $6 is payable for every $1,000 increase or fraction thereof.

An annual licence fee of $350 is payable for a registered company in which Bahamians beneficially own 60% or more of the shares. If Bahamians beneficially own less than 60% of the shares, the company must pay an annual fee of $1,000. The fee should be paid by Jan 1 of each year but payment may be up to 30 days later in some cases.

Non-profit companies under the provisions of section 14 of the Companies Act, 1992, do not have to pay an annual fee and their stamp duty is reduced to $5.

Foreign or overseas companies

To be registered under the provisions of the Companies Act, 1992, a company must have been incorporated outside The Bahamas and must deposit with the Registrar General particulars about the company and a copy of documents of incorporation certified and authenticated under public seal of the country under whose laws it has been incorporated.

Stamp duty for a foreign company is $600 and the registration fee is $50. All foreign companies registered under this section must pay an annual fee of $1,000.

Requirements for all companies

All companies must file with the Registrar General copies of the names of all company officers, directors and managers and a registered office address. In the case of banks, proper records must be kept and annual statements showing the bank's true financial position must be published in *The Gazette*.

Every company which has its capital divided into shares must file an annual return at the Registry, containing the following information:
1. A list of company members stating the names, addresses and occupations of all members mentioned and the number of shares held by each.
2. Amount of the company's capital and number of shares into which it is divided.
3. Number of shares taken from the formation of the company up to the date of summary.
4. Amount of calls made on shares.
5. Amount of calls received.
6. Amount of calls unpaid.
7. Amount of shares forfeited.
8. Names, addresses and occupations of persons who have ceased to be members since the last list was compiled and number of shares held by each.
9. The registered number of the company.

Companies except those registered under section 14 of the Companies Act, 1992 (non-profit companies), must send the Registrar General a copy of the register containing the names, addresses and occupations of its directors or managers and must give any subsequent changes which take place in such officers and directors.

Every company registered under the Companies Act, 1992, must forward to the Registrar General, before Jan 1 in each year after the year in which the company first commenced business, a return declaring whether or not 60% of its shares are beneficially owned by Bahamians.

Companies may be public or private. Public companies are those in which shares are to be offered to the general public. Such companies must submit a prospectus or statement containing specific information as required by the Act in relation to the company's operations. All other companies are private. Companies must hold a statutory meeting every year, and one must be held within three months from the date the company is incorporated. Meetings may be held outside The Bahamas.

The Central Bank may allow a company to be incorporated with its capital expressed in a foreign currency and to conduct its affairs in that currency. Application for such approval should be submitted to the Central Bank, PO Box N-4868, Nassau, The Bahamas. Tel (242) 322-2193, fax (242) 322-4321.

International Business Company (IBC)

An IBC may be incorporated in The Bahamas within 24 hours from the time the proper documents arrive at the Registrar General's Dept. In urgent cases, it may be incorporated within 20 mins while waiting.

Register an IBC name by:
1. Visiting the Registry of Companies, Mon-Fri 9:30am-4:30pm.
2. Telephoning the 24-hour company name reservation service. Tel (242) 322-7147 or 322-7160; fax (242) 322-5553.
3. Writing to Registrar General's Dept, PO Box N-532, Nassau, The Bahamas.

Approval will be given immediately. Confirmation within New Providence is faxed and confirmed by mail; confirmation overseas and in Freeport is by mail. Documents of incorporation should then be submitted for registration with the incorporation fee. IBC fees are $250 where the authorized capital is less than $50,000, and $1,000 when authorized capital exceeds $50,000. Incorporation documents must include the memorandum of association and the articles of association. If the articles are not provided with the memorandum, they must be submitted within 30 days from the date of incorporation.

Documents of incorporation are then inspected. If approved, a certificate of incorporation will be issued within 24 hours from the time the documents arrive at the Registry. If urgent, it may be issued within 20 mins.

Where an IBC is registered by Dec 31 of any year, an annual licence fee must be paid to the Registrar General by July 31 of the following year. A merger or consolidation of an IBC may be established within 24 hours from the time the Registrar receives documents and payment.

A company incorporated under the Companies Act, 1992, or incorporated outside of The Bahamas may apply to continue in The Bahamas as a company incorporated under the IBC Act if it meets the Act's provisions. Contact the Registrar General's Dept, Registry of Companies, PO Box N-532, Nassau, The Bahamas, tel (242) 322-8038, fax (242) 322-5553.

An IBC is exempt from all Bahamian taxes and stamp duties, including income or other taxes for 20 years. IBCs also are exempt from Exchange Control regulations in The Bahamas. Other advantages are:
1. No minimum capital required.
2. Only two shareholders.
3. Shares may be issued with and without par value.
4. Shares may be issued in registered form or issued to bearer.
5. Only one director or registered agent.
6. Director or directors or registered agent may be individuals or corporations, banks or trust companies. The registered agent must be based in The Bahamas.

7. IBCs need not file annual reports and the names of directors, officers and shareholders are not registered.
8. An IBC may transfer assets in trust for the benefit of its creditors, shareholders or other persons having an interest.
9. IBCs may be limited by shares or guarantee, or "unlimited."

Limited Duration Company (LDC)
The most significant aspect of the 1994 amendment to the IBC Act was the introduction of the Limited Duration Company (LDC), a hybrid of the IBC. The LDC is basically structured like the IBC except that the "life" of the company is limited to 30 years or less. The company name must also state its LDC status. The transfer of a share or interest of a member requires the unanimous resolution of all other members if stipulated in the articles of the company. The articles may also provide for certain members to manage the company based on their share or other ownership interest. Properly structured, the LDC can have the characteristics of a partnership and be treated as such for tax purposes in the US.

Exempted Limited Partnership (ELP)
The ELP allows the character of a normal partnership to be structured to provide more flexibility in transacting business. Like the IBC, the ELP is free to carry on every lawful business anywhere in the world except that it cannot transact business with the public in The Bahamas. However, this does not specifically preclude doing business with IBCs or foreign companies registered in The Bahamas under the Companies Act, 1992.

An ELP must have one or more general partners who assume responsibility for all debts and obligations of the partnership in the event the assets of the partnership are inadequate, and at least one limited partner. A general partner may also have an interest as a limited partner. Partners may be from anywhere, although at least one general partner must be a Bahamas resident or incorporated under the IBC Act, 1989, or Companies Act, 1992, of The Bahamas. Under the Exempted Limited Partnership Act, 1995, every ELP must have a registered office in The Bahamas and must be registered with the Registrar of Companies.

Certain disclosures must be made as to the general nature of business of the ELP (eg, investments) and the names and addresses of general partners. Certain subsequent changes in the nature of the partnership must be filed with the Registrar.

An ELP is exempt for 50 years from the issuance of the certificate of registration from any business licence fee, stamp duty, income tax, capital gains tax or any other tax on income or distributions. It is also exempt from provisions of the Exchange Control Regulations Act, except where a partner is a resident of The Bahamas for Exchange Control purposes. Partners, their executors or administrators, are also exempt from any estate, inheritance, succession or gift tax on any interest in the partnership.

Copies of the legislation referred to in this article may be obtained for a small fee from Government Publications, PO Box N-7147, Nassau, The Bahamas, tel (242) 322-2410.

See also **Business licence fee; Business name registration; Exchange control;** and **Investing.**

CONSTITUTION
When independence from the UK was achieved on July 10, 1973, a new Constitution representing the supreme law of the land went into effect for the Commonwealth of The Bahamas.

The Constitution proclaims The Bahamas as a sovereign democratic state, establishes requirements for citizenship and guarantees fundamental human rights such as freedom of conscience, expression and assembly. It also protects the privacy of the home and prohibits deprivation of property without compensation and/or due process of law.

The Bahamas retains its ties with the Commonwealth of Nations and also retains the British monarch as its head of state. The Queen is represented in The Bahamas by a Governor-General who is appointed and serves at Her Majesty's pleasure.

There is a bicameral parliament consisting of a Senate and a House of Assembly. The Senate has 16 members, nine appointed by the Governor-General on the advice of the Prime Minister, four on the advice of the Leader of the Opposition and three on the advice of the Prime Minister after consultation with the Leader of the Opposition. This arrangement provides for the Opposition to have no less than four members in the Senate and to claim up to three more based on its numerical strength in the House of Assembly.

The House of Assembly must have at least 38 elected members. This number may be increased on the recommendation of the Constituencies Commission, which is charged with reviewing electoral boundaries at least every five years. Present membership is 40.

The executive branch consists of a Cabinet of at least nine members, including the Prime Minister and the Attorney-General. All Ministers must be Members of Parliament and the Prime Minister and the Minister of Finance must be members of the House of Assembly. Up to three Ministers can be appointed from among the Senators.

An independent judiciary, including a Supreme Court and a Court of Appeal is provided for, along with the right of appeal to Her Majesty's Privy Council.

Also provided under the Constitution are a Public Service Commission, Public Service Board of Appeal, a Judicial and Legal Service Commission and a Police Service Commission.

The Constitution can be amended by an Act of Parliament but there are two categories of provisions – entrenched and specially entrenched – which can be amended only by a prescribed voting formula and with approval by the electorate in a referendum.

The entrenched provisions include those relating to establishment of the public service and qualifications for Members of Parliament. These provisions can be amended only by a two-thirds majority vote in both houses of parliament and by referendum.

The specially entrenched provisions relate to citizenship, fundamental rights, establishment and powers of parliament, the Cabinet and the judiciary. These can be amended only by a three-quarters majority vote in parliament and by referendum.

CONSUMER PROTECTION

The Ministry of Consumer Welfare is committed to protecting consumers from exploitation and ensuring controls and standards are enforced.

The three main areas for consumer protection are availability, price and quality, with the government responsible for providing the legislative and environmental framework under which adequate and effective competition is encouraged.

Government efforts to ensure a wide range of choice for goods and services are considered more effective than legislative price control, as the consumer becomes the regulator.

The government has initiated consumer protection programmes with the main thrust on competition and consumer choice and awareness. However, as long as price control remains in force as a mechanism of consumer protection, it will be enforced and any infractions prosecuted. Deliberate overpricing of goods may result in:

1. A fine not exceeding $5,000; or
2. Imprisonment for a term not exceeding 12 months.

A significant aspect of consumer protection is the development of a national system of standards, quality control and quality assurance involving relevant government agencies.

The Consumer Action Line deals with complaints involving all aspects of consumer rights – eg, price control, faulty goods, problems with rents and with utility corporations. Mediation and moral persuasion are used to reach a mutually acceptable solution.

The Consumer Advocacy Group publishes *Consumerism Today*, a monthly consumer education booklet. Speaker's Corner is a programme administered by the Consumer Protection Division through schools, service clubs and church groups to educate the public on their rights as consumers.

COPYRIGHT LAWS

A new Copyright Act was expected to come into force by the end of 1998. When it becomes law, it will repeal the Copyright Act, 1956, on which it is based. The new Act introduces a Copyright Royalty Tribunal which will advise on royalty rates and receive and disburse payments. A Copyright Registry, overseen by a Registrar of Copyrights, will receive applications, register claims and issue certificates of registration.

Although current copyright laws in The Bahamas contain the ingredients for general copyright protection, they do not cover modern concerns such as computer-generated work and digital transmissions. The new Act is expected to bring The Bahamas to world standards and is an important concern in the signing of future international agreements.

COST OF LIVING

Food, autos and some items of clothing are comparatively expensive in Nassau because of freight and Customs duties.

Residents are billed monthly for electricity charges and quarterly for water charges. Telephone rental is on a monthly basis. The average deposit for electrical service varies with home size and location, ranging from $150 to more than $1,000, with about $200 as average. Telephone deposits range from $50-$500 for landlords, and $150-$500 for tenants. A $55 water deposit is required for buildings with one water closet or bathroom and $115 for those with two or more.

Virtually all homes and apartments for rent or sale are basically furnished. Rents vary according to location and season. Summer is the best time for apartment hunting.

In general, an efficiency apartment rents monthly on a one-year lease for $300-$500; one bedroom, $450 and up; two bedrooms, $700-$6,000. A two-bed detached house can rent for $1,200-$4,000. A three-bed detached house or condo rents for $2,200-$5,000 per month depending upon location. Short-term leases usually include utilities. Rent is higher for short-term leases.

Building costs for an average three-bed house – living room, dining room, kitchen, bath and patio – is a minimum of $70 per sq ft, which comes to $105,000 for a 1,500 sq ft home. The price varies according to materials used, building standards and area. According to a Nassau builder, Lyford Cay building costs range from $150-$250 and higher per sq ft.

Medical care and dentistry can be less costly than in the US. An out-patients clinic at Princess Margaret Hospital in Nassau is available at $10 per visit – but you may wait several hours for treatment. Specialists' office calls average $60-$100. At Princess Margaret Hospital a bed on the public ward is $30, plus additional expenses. Semi-private and private rooms are $275-$290 per day, including nursing services. Hospital room rates at Lyford Cay Hospital are $450 per day for a semi-private room; and at Doctors Hospital $450 private and $390 semi-private, per day. Round-the-clock nurses are included in the cost at Doctors Hospital.

New Providence has well-stocked supermarkets carrying US brands as well as a range of name brands from other countries.

New Providence prices (July 1998)
Food

½ gal Superbrand milk $2.35
1 doz extra large eggs $1.35
6 oz Starkist chunk light tuna
  in spring water.......................$0.98
2kg (4.4 lbs) Caribbean sugar $1.68
5 lbs Robin Hood
  all purpose flour......................$2.48
5 oz bar Dial bath soap $1.08
16 oz Hickory sweet
  sliced bacon...........................$2.98
1 lb ground beef $2.59
32 oz Mueller's spaghetti $2.68
8 oz Nescafé classic $6.48
8 oz Nescafé decaf....................$11.08
100 Lipton Yellow Label
  tea bags.................................$8.18
32 oz Kraft mayonnaise $3.38
5 lbs potatoes $2.99
1 head iceberg lettuce $1.19
1 lb Bahamian-grown
  tomatoes $1.99
½ gal Superbrand ice cream $3.28
1 lb Country Crock
  soft margarine $1.48
8 oz Superbrand
  plain lowfat yogurt..................$0.78
1 loaf Roman Meal
  wholewheat bread..................$2.49
1 gal Aquapure water $1.25
1 case Coca-Cola sodas $11.81
5 lbs Uncle Ben's rice $3.88
98 oz Ultra Tide unscented........$10.89
8 oz Kraft salad dressing $2.08
64 oz Tropicana orange juice
  not from concentrate..............$5.58
14½ oz Carnation
  evaporated milk $0.78
½ lb President butter $0.78
3 lbs onions $2.49
18 oz Kellogg's Corn Flakes $3.78
8 oz Kraft cheddar cheese (sharp)....$2.88

Other items & services
1 pack filter cigarettes* $3.80
New York Times (Sun edition)......$6.25

1 litre (33.8 oz)
  Tanqueray gin $11.95
1 litre Bacardi rum $9.35
1 litre Drambuie $25.95
1 litre Absolut vodka $10.95
1 case beer (Kalik) $31.50
1 case beer
  (Coors & Coors light) $29.75
1 case premium beer
  (Heineken) $35.85
Shampoo and set*..................$16-$25
Manicure* ....$12-$20
Men's haircut*.........................$15-$20
Women's haircut* ....$15-$35
1 US gal Esso Optima IV gasoline
  (premium unleaded)................$2.29
1 US gal Esso Optima IV gasoline
  (super premium unleaded) $2.38
Dry cleaning:
  1 dress*..................................$7.20
  1 men's suit* $7.45
* Prices vary.

COURIER SERVICES
Three major international courier companies and several smaller ones serve New Providence and the Family Islands.

DHL World Express.................325-8266
Federal Express.......................322-1791
UPS/GWS 322-8907

It costs $10-$13 to send a package under 2 lbs to Freeport, $17-$27.50 to Miami, $18-$27.50 to New York, and $25.50-$39 to London, England.
See also **Postal information.**

CRIME
The Royal Bahamas Police Force is employed throughout The Bahamas for maintenance of law and order, preservation of peace, prevention and detection of crime, apprehension of offenders and enforcement of all laws with which it is charged. The government has undertaken to improve police performance with a number of measures which include increasing the vehicle fleet, improving communications and boosting

numbers in the ranks by implementing ongoing recruitment programmes. The strength of the Royal Bahamas Police Force stands at about 2,200.

In the 1995/96 budget, government provided the funds to fully integrate the criminal justice system, provide secure police communications, and computerize the police control room and patrol cars to help in the fight against crime. The government has entered into an agreement with CDR Intl of London to establish a permanent detective training school as part of the existing police college to better train and equip detectives and the Police Force on the whole.

In 1996, The Bahamas witnessed its first hanging in 12 years. Since then, there has been no execution of capital punishment in The Bahamas. There are 24 people on death row.

The latter part of 1996 witnessed a gradual resurgence of dangerous drugs trafficking activities in the entire Caribbean region. Cocaine seizure in The Bahamas was up in 1996 by 30% over '95 but marijuana seizure continued to drop by 35% in '96, compared to the same period in '95. Marijuana and cocaine seizures for 1997 are higher than in '96.

While dangerous drugs transiting The Bahamas are not reflected on the streets of the nation, hard core users of cocaine, crack and marijuana are responsible for a disproportionate number of crimes, particularly robberies, burglaries, thefts and house and shop break-ins. As of March 1998, crimes against the person, such as murder, attempted murder, manslaughter, rape and armed robbery were on the decline.

The Bahamas enjoys diplomatic relationships with many countries and the Royal Bahamas Police Force cooperates with law enforcement agencies of these countries and is a member of INTERPOL. The Bahamas also has extradition treaties with many countries in the international community.

See also **Drugs; Extradition; Judicial system;** and **Royal Bahamas Police Force.**

CRUISE SHIP INCENTIVES

In 1995, Parliament passed the Cruise Ship (Overnighting Incentives) Act, granting concessions to encourage tourism in The Bahamas. The Act allows cruise ships docked at Prince George Dock for at least 18 hours, or travelling to or from Bahamian designated ports, to operate casinos, shops and sell liquor, 7pm-3am.

The Act also provides discounts on port tax. Cruise ship lines transporting up to 400,000 passengers per year to The Bahamas are charged the regular fee of $15 per person. For every passenger over this 400,000 limit, not exceeding 500,000, the cruise line pays $10 per person. For every passenger exceeding 500,000 in the course of a year, the cruise line pays $5 per person.

See also **Customs; Departure tax; Gambling; Hotels encouragement;** and **Shopping.**

CRUISING FACILITIES

See **Marinas & cruising facilities;** and **Freeport/Lucaya information, Marinas.**

CULTURE & CULTURAL ACTIVITIES

See **Art galleries & museums; Entertainment; Junkanoo; National anthem; National symbols;** and **Theatre and performing arts.**

CURRENCY

Legal currency of The Bahamas is the Bahamian dollar, although the US dollar is normally accepted throughout the islands. The Bahamian dollar is on par with the US dollar.

The Canadian dollar was worth approx B$0.6745 and the pound sterling approx B$1.6972 on Sept 15, 1998.

CUSTOMS

Generally, the *ad valorem* (of the value) tariff for imported goods is 35%, clothing 25%.

Some items have a higher tariff, such as fine cut tobacco 160%, pool tables 100%, automobiles 45-65%, car parts and accessories 50%, video tapes 65%, cigarettes containing tobacco 210%. A 7% stamp duty is also payable on these goods.

Some staple food items have a low duty tariff, including cheese 10%, pasta 10% and potatoes nil. In addition to duty, there is a 2% stamp duty on food.

There are no Customs duties on the most popular tourist items: china, crystal, fine jewellery, leather, crocheted linens and tablecloths, liquor, perfume and cologne, photographic equipment and accessories, sweaters and watches. However, variable Customs stamp duty is applicable to those duty-free products imported to The Bahamas, as follows:

Duty-free goods stamp duty (% of value)

China, crystal, cameras, sweaters (wool, cashmere or Angora) & photographic accessories 8%
Wristwatches & clocks with watch movements 10%
Fine jewellery & fine jewellery incorporating pearls, precious & semi-precious stones 10%
Crocheted table linens & table linens..........................10%
Leather goods 20%
Perfume, cologne & toilet waters 20%
Still & sparkling wines 50%
* Brandy, gin, rum, vodka, whiskey, cordials, liqueurs & other spirits....$10 per Imperial gal

* *If goods being imported are for processes carried on at any Bahamas distillery or brewery, then 7% (stamp duty) of the value of the goods is paid.*

Customs duty on vehicles varies – according to value and intended use – from 45-65% of the cif (cost/insurance/freight) value of the vehicle. For example, a new or used car not for public service of cif value exceeding $20,000 is 65%. Motor vehicles for the transport of 10 or more persons, including the driver, carry a 45% rate of duty and golf carts, 50%.

Customary stamp duty

There is usually a 7% stamp duty of the cif value of imported goods requiring an entry (with the exception of those items indicated above).

For Customs purposes the value includes the cost of the goods, ocean or air freight and all other charges incidental to their importation. There is also a $10 stamp duty on exports.

Duty exemptions

Certain items may be imported exempt from Customs duty, including:
1. All goods imported with the prior approval of the Minister of Finance and Planning by a charitable organization to be used exclusively for charitable purposes;
2. Models, teaching aids, sound recordings, scientific apparatus and materials to be used exclusively for the purpose of scientific or cultural institutions, if approved by the Minister of Finance and Planning.

Additional information on Customs duty and exemptions may be found in the Tariff Act, 1996. Copies may be obtained from Government Publications, Old Lighthouse Bldg, Bay St, PO Box N-7147, Nassau, The Bahamas, tel (242) 322-2410.

Duty-free importation

Certain items are basically duty free, but a 7% stamp duty is charged on the cif value. These include:
1. Orthopaedic appliances, surgical belts, trusses etc; splints and other fracture appliances; artificial limbs, eyes, teeth and other artificial body parts; hearing aids and other

appliances worn, carried or implanted to compensate for a defect or disability.
2. Paintings, drawings and pastels executed entirely by hand other than industrial drawings or hand-printed manufactured articles.
3. Antiques over 100 years. Proof of age from a recognized antique assoc required.

Contact Bahamas Customs for further information.

Temporary importation
Certain goods may be imported on a temporary basis against a security bond or deposit in addition to payment of the prescribed fees, which is refundable on their re-exportation. They include:
1. Any fine jewellery, approved as such by the Comptroller of Customs, imported on consignment, and upon executing a security bond, if satisfactory proof can be given:
   a. For the exportation thereof to the exporter and country from whom and from where it was imported within a period of six months, and
   b. For the payment of duty on any such jewellery not exported from The Bahamas within the six-month period.
2. Goods for business meetings or conventions for a period up to one month after the meeting or convention is over.
3. Travelling salesman's samples. Goods must not be for sale, they must be approved by the Comptroller of Customs and the sales person must have a valid immigration permit. A deposit is required equal to the prescribed duty on the goods, and is refunded upon re-exportation of the goods within three months of arrival.
4. Automobiles or motorcycles brought into the country by a *bona fide* visitor for not more than six months. A deposit equal to the prescribed duties is required and is refunded upon re-exportation provided the vehicle has not been used for commercial purposes while in The Bahamas. Only one such permit per family may be issued during any calendar year.
5. Photographic and cinematographic equipment belonging to members of the foreign press, radio, TV or motion picture services, as well as clothes and props belonging to actors and actresses accompanying these services, are allowed temporary importation for up to 90 days upon approval of the Ministry of Tourism and Ministry of Finance and Planning. Application for an extension of temporary importation may be made to the Minister of Finance and Planning.
6. Any goods such as special tools for repair work or testing equipment may be imported on the payment of 7% Customs and stamp duties of the cif value. Also, a refundable deposit equal to what the prescribed duty would be on a regular import is required. Prior approval for this must be obtained from the Ministry of Finance and Planning, for which an application should be made to the Comptroller of Customs, PO Box N-155, Nassau, The Bahamas, tel (242) 326-4401.

Import & export entry requirements
For clearance of commercial imports via air and sea cargo/freight, a completed entry (four copies) is required. Imports by sea are released to the importer on presentation of forms processed at Customs House, Thompson Blvd. For goods by air, entry forms are presented to the Customs officer in the Air Express building at Nassau Intl Airport. Similar facilities also exist at Family Island ports of entry. Entries are required for goods sent via parcel post, by sea or air, if the goods are of a commercial nature or of

a value in excess of $100. Commercial goods imported by parcel post with a value of less than $500 require no entry.

Goods may be cleared through Customs without proper invoices by provisional entry. The importer leaves a deposit sufficient to cover duty (usually double the estimated duty of the imports), with the understanding that when the invoices arrive, the provisional entry must be adjusted. The residue of the deposit made is refunded after payment of the proper duty amount. Payment in a foreign currency for goods imported to The Bahamas may be arranged by a Bahamas bank after presentation of Exchange Control approval.

There is a 7% stamp duty on the value of imported goods, except inexpensive gifts (up to $100) arriving by post. See **Export entry**.

Importing possessions
A person settling in The Bahamas as a resident pays duty on household effects, eg, furniture, china and appliances. Most personal effects such as clothing and articles of personal adornment already in use and possession are not dutiable if imported as accompanied passenger baggage.

Duty-free quotas for *bona fide* visitors to The Bahamas
In the case of *bona fide* visitors arriving in The Bahamas, certain items may be brought in free of Customs and stamp duty. They include:
1. Apparel, toilet articles and similar personal effects.
2. One qt of alcoholic beverage; one qt of wine; 1 lb in weight of tobacco or 200 cigarettes or 50 cigars (adults only).
3. Any other articles up to the value of $100.

Duty-free quotas for returning Bahamians and residents
A Bahamian through birth or naturalization, or a person granted permission by the Immigration Dept to reside in The Bahamas and who has been in residence for over one year, may return from two trips abroad annually with duty-free goods worth up to $300 (does not apply to children under 12 years). A resident who has been abroad for over one year may bring in $500 worth of goods duty free. No stamp duty is payable in either situation.

Duty-free quotas for Bahamas residents going abroad
US: Bahamians and Bahamas residents visiting the US may take with them duty-free gifts worth up to US$100. These gifts may not include alcoholic beverages or cigarettes. To take advantage of this $100 gift exemption, the visitor must remain in the US at least 72 hours. He may use this exemption once every six months.

Visitors to the US (over the age of 21) may also bring in duty- and tax-free, one litre of alcoholic beverages for their own use. Also allowed duty- and tax-free, besides personal effects, are 200 cigarettes for personal use.

If the individual is not entitled to or does not qualify for the $100 gift exemption, he may take with him duty-free articles up to $25 in value for personal or household use. Neither the $100 gift exemption nor the $25 exemption may be grouped together for members of a family.

Canada: Bahamians or Bahamas residents may take with them on a visit to Canada duty free, apart from personal effects, any number of gifts valued up to CDN$40 provided these gifts are not advertising matter. For personal use, persons 16 years of age or older may take in 200 cigarettes, 50 cigars and 2 lbs of tobacco. Forty ounces of liquor may be brought in for personal use provided the individual meets the age requirement of the province or territory through which he enters Canada.

UK: Those visiting the UK from The Bahamas (or from outside the EU) may

take in, free of duty and tax, 200 cigarettes or 100 cigarillos or 50 cigars or 250g of tobacco. Alcohol and alcoholic beverage allowance:
Still table wine............................2 litres
and
Spirits or strong liqueurs over 22%
    alcohol by volume.....................1 litre
or
Fortified or sparkling wine,
    & other liqueurs ....2 litres
or
An additional still table
    wine allowance ....2 litres

These allowances are not for persons under the age of 17. The allowance for perfume is 50g (2 fl oz), 8 fl oz toilet water and £145 sterling worth of other goods including gifts, souvenirs, cider and beer. All goods must be obtained outside the EU.

All other goods
Goods brought into the UK worth more than £145 sterling will have duty charged on the full value, not just on the value over £145 sterling.

Rates of duty and tax are complicated and change from time to time so it is advisable to check with your airline or travel agent for current regulations when making reservations.

Duty-free quotas for visitors leaving The Bahamas
US residents: Each US resident (including a minor) may take home duty-free purchases up to US$600 in retail value if he has been outside the US more than 48 hours and has not taken the exemption in 30 days. The exemption may include up to two litres (67.6 oz) of liquor per person over 21, provided one litre is manufactured in The Bahamas or another CBI (Caribbean Basin Initiative) country; 200 cigarettes; and 100 cigars (Cuban cigars not allowed) per person regardless of age. A single household family travelling together may pool exemptions, ie, a family of four may take home US$2,400 worth of goods.

Articles up to US$1,000 value accompanying the traveller, in excess of the US$600 duty-free allowance, are assessed at a flat rate of 10%. For example, a family of four would prepare a joint declaration for goods purchased, say, for US$4,500. Each family member would be eligible for a US$600 exemption, for a total of US$2,400. The remaining US$2,100 would be assessed at a duty rate of 10%. Thus, total duty for the purchases from this trip would be US$210. You may not apply the flat rate more than once every 30 days.

If the returning US resident is not entitled to the US$600 duty exemption due to the 30-day or 48-hour minimum limitations, he may still import, duty free, US$200 worth of personal or household items. This exemption may not be pooled.

Articles purchased in US duty-free shops and brought back into the US may not be included in your exemption and are dutiable.

One person, on one day, may receive a shipment of goods purchased in The Bahamas and sent to an address in the US so long as the value does not exceed US$200. The shipment will be passed free of duty by US Customs, unless there is reason to believe the shipment is one of several lots of a single order. Supporting documents are required.

Antiques, food, trade marks, US money
Antiques are admitted to the US duty free provided they are over 100 years old. The Bahamas store selling an antique should provide the buyer with a form indicating the value and age of the object. The buyer must present this form to US Customs.

Importation of fruit, plants, meat, poultry and dairy products is generally prohibited. There are, however, exceptions. Contact the US Dept of Agriculture, tel 377-7127.

More than $10,000 in US or foreign coin, currency, travellers' cheques, money orders and negotiable instruments or investment securities in bearer form must be reported to Customs. It is not illegal to transport or cause to be transported any amount into or out of the US, but over $10,000 must be reported on Customs Form 4790 available at all US ports of entry.

Certain items carrying a trade mark or trade name may be brought into the US in specified amounts only, or not at all. Importation of Bahamian tortoise or turtle shell goods is prohibited. Many medicines sold over the counter in The Bahamas are not allowed entry.

For a copy of *Know Before You Go,* contact US Customs at Nassau Intl Airport, tel (242) 377-7126. Or contact the US Customs Service, Washington, DC, 20229.

Canadian residents: A Canadian may take advantage of one of three categories of duty-free exemptions. If he has been out of Canada for 24 hours, he may make a verbal declaration to claim a CDN$50 duty-free allowance any number of times per year, which would not include alcohol or tobacco. If he has been out of the country for 48 hours any number of times per year, a written declaration must be made; he may claim a CDN$200 allowance which could include up to 200 cigarettes, 50 cigars and 2 lbs tobacco, and 1.1 litres (40 oz) alcohol.

Anyone who has been out of Canada seven days or more, any number of times per year, may make a written declaration and claim the CDN$500 exemption, including the amounts of alcohol and tobacco indicated for the CDN$200 allowance.

In general, the goods brought in under personal exemption must be for personal or household use, as souvenirs of the trip or as gifts for friends or relatives. Goods brought in for commercial use, or on behalf of another person, do not qualify and will be subject to full duties. Goods declared in a child's name must be for his or her use only.

For the importation of tobacco, the claimant must be over 16 years of age. In case of liquor, wine or beer, the person must have attained the age prescribed by the provincial or territorial authority at the point of entry.

Goods acquired in The Bahamas or elsewhere outside continental North America, may be shipped or mailed separately if declared at the first port of entry.

UK residents: Same allowances as Bahamian residents visiting the UK. See **Duty-free quotas for Bahamas residents going abroad, UK.**

Sending gifts from The Bahamas
To the US: Any number of gifts may be sent to the US from The Bahamas. The recipient pays no US duty if the gift he receives is worth US$100 or less. If the gift is worth more than US$100, he pays duty on the full value. According to US regulations, the duty-free status applies under the following conditions:
1. Only US$100 worth of gifts may be received by the US addressee in one day.
2. Value of the gifts must be clearly written on the package, as well as the words "unsolicited gift."
3. No cigars, cigarettes or liquor may be sent as gifts. Perfumes valued at more than US$5 may not be sent.
4. Persons in the US are not permitted to send money to The Bahamas for gifts to be shipped to them duty free. Gifts must be unsolicited.
5. Shops and commercial firms may wrap and mail the duty-free gifts for customers who pay for them personally in The Bahamas.
6. Persons may not mail a gift addressed to themselves.

To Canada: *Bona fide* unsolicited gifts may be sent to Canada duty free as long as they are valued under CDN$40 and do not contain any alcoholic beverages, tobacco products or advertising matter. If the gift is valued at more than CDN$40, the receiver will have to pay regular duty and tax on the excess amount.

To the UK: *Bona fide* gifts sent to the UK are subject to duty and VAT unless they comply with the following rules:
1. The value of the goods must not exceed £145 sterling.
2. They must be private gifts; this means they must be addressed to a private person in the UK and sent by a private person abroad.
3. The gifts must not be for commercial or trade use, but only for personal or family use.
4. They must not be paid for by the recipient, either directly or indirectly.
5. Any tobacco products, alcoholic beverages, perfumes or toilet waters sent at one time must be within the allowances mentioned. Anything over these allowances is liable to charges.
6. They must be of an occasional nature only.

DEFENCE FORCE
See **Royal Bahamas Defence Force.**

DENTISTS[1]
Nassau
Dr Robert E W Bailey
Dr Kay Sweeting Bain
Dr S Cambridge
Dr Antoine Clark
Dr Desiree Clarke
Dr Vaughan Conliffe
Dr Norman Cove
Dr A Coverley
Dr Ricardo Crawford
Dr Mark Davies
Dr A P Davis
Dr C W Eneas Jr
Dr Sparkman Ferguson
Dr Charles Forbes
Dr Emmanuel Francis
Dr Gill I Gibson
Dr John A Godet
Dr Melanie G Halkitis
Dr Ronald Levanthal
Dr Kirk Lewis
Dr Nigel Lewis
Dr H Mitchell Lockhart
Dr John H Louis Jr
Dr John V Louis (periodontist)
Dr Kareem McIver
Dr Veronica McIver
Dr C McMillan
Dr Michelle Mackey
Dr Kendal Major (periodontist)
Dr M Major
Dr Anyia Moss
Dr Derwin Munroe
Dr R Peet-Iferenta
Dr Joyous Pickstock
Dr Munir Rashad (oral surgeon)
Dr Kimberley Richardson (child and adolescent dentistry)
Dr Osmond W A Richardson (oral surgeon)
Dr Cheryl Rolle
Dr L Barry Russell (orthodontist)
Dr Marlene Sawyer
Dr Rosemund Smith
Dr E Strachan-Moxey
Dr W Stuart
Dr Sidney Sweeting
Dr W Thompson (orthodontist)
Dr Therese Thompson-Bonamy
Dr C O Vanderpool
Dr Annette Warren
Dr Adra Gibson Washington
Dr James Washington Jr
Dr David Weech
Dr Marsha Williams-Bethel
Dr Cynthia Wood

Family Islands
Abaco, Dr Jacolin Archer, Dr V McWeeney, Dr James Newman,[2] Dr Howard Spencer,[2] Dr Therese Thompson-Bonamy[2]
Berry Islands, Dr Michael Ryan
Eleuthera, Dr Camille Arcidi, Dr Mark Davies,[2] Dr Hadassah Knowles, Dr Roy Schatzley
Exuma, Dr William Lee

[1] *Some of these dentists are members of the Intl Dental Federation and/or the Bahamas Dental Assoc (BDA).*
[2] *Visiting dentists.*

See also **Freeport/Lucaya information, Dentists.**

DEPARTURE TAX
Air
A $15 government departure tax must be paid in cash by every traveller six yrs

and over upon departure from The Bahamas. It is collected at departure by airline personnel at check-in ticket counters.

There is an additional $3 security fee for international passengers departing Freeport, Grand Bahama.

Sea
Departure tax for passengers travelling by cruise ship, known as port tax, is payable by the cruise ship line and is usually included in the price of the ticket. Children under six yrs are exempt. See **Cruise ship incentives.** There is a $7 international ticket tax on the price of each airline or cruise ship ticket purchased in The Bahamas. This is included in the price of the ticket and should not be confused with the departure tax.

DIVORCE

In The Bahamas, a husband or wife may petition for divorce on grounds of adultery, cruelty, sodomy, desertion, separation, homosexuality, bestiality, and, in the case of a wife, if her husband has been found guilty of rape during the course of the marriage. A petition for divorce may be filed after two years from the date of the celebration of the marriage, unless permission is gained from the Court to petition earlier.

Three months after a *decree nisi* is granted, the divorce may become final and a *decree absolute* issued provided that, where appropriate, a judge is satisfied with arrangements made for the welfare of children. In special cases, this period may be reduced to six weeks. Marriages not consummated may be annulled.

A couple of any nationality may obtain a divorce in The Bahamas if it can be established that the husband is domiciled here. Otherwise, the wife may petition if she can establish that:
1. She and her husband have lived three years of their married life here and that these years directly preceded commencement of the suit and
2. Her husband had deserted her and has gone abroad.

In 1997, 435 divorces were granted in The Bahamas compared with 410 in 1996.

A divorce obtained abroad will be recognized in The Bahamas if the court is satisfied the party obtaining the divorce had a real, substantial connection with the country in which the divorce was obtained.

DOCTORS
New Providence
Some doctors listed have a general practice in addition to specialization:

Anaesthesia
Dr S Bascom
Dr Glen Beneby
Dr A C Hamilton-Rappel
Dr B McCartney
Dr R Neymour
Dr G Pennerman
Dr Sy Pierre
Dr P de Souza
Dr M Weech

Cardiology
Dr C Brown
Dr J Lightbourne (paediatric cardiologist)
Dr D Sands (cardiac thoracic surgery)
Dr C Dean Tseretopoulos

Dept of Public Health
Dr E McPhee
Dr P Whitfield

Dermatology
Dr C Gooding
Dr H Orlander
Dr Q M S Richmond
Dr B E Sears

Gastroenterology
Dr H Munnings
Dr L Nembhard

General practitioners
Dr Gloria Ageeb
Dr T Bartlett

Dr C Basden
Dr C Chaney
Dr R E Crawford
Dr K R Culmer
Dr L W Culmer
Dr E L Donaldson
Dr Agreta Eneas
Dr N Fox
Dr E Fung Chung
Dr N R Gay
Dr M Gerassimos
Dr R Gorospe
Dr E Gray
Dr M I Hale
Dr M Ingraham
Dr R Ingraham
Dr T P Jupp
Dr I Kelly
Dr L J McCarroll
Dr M Moxey
Dr M Ritchie
Dr B E A Rolle
Dr H Simmons
Dr C Strachan
Dr Ada D Thompson
Dr J Wavell Thompson
Dr B Tynes
Dr R Van Tooren
Dr F W Walkine
Dr G White
Dr P Whitfield
Dr A Zervos

Internal medicine
Dr T R Allen
Dr C W M Bethel
Dr C Chin
Dr James A Constantakis
Dr J Eneas
Dr P Gomez
Dr J A Johnson
Dr J A Lunn
Dr V Nwosa (Rheumatology)
Dr A Sawyer
Dr A M Thompson-Hepburn
Dr C Dean Tseretopoulos

Nephrology
Dr J Eneas
Dr I Grant-Taylor
Dr J Johnson
Dr R Knowles
Dr A Sawyer

Neurosurgery/neurology
Dr M Ekedede
Dr C Munnings
Dr E Newry

Obstetrics & gynaecology
Dr E M Achara
Dr A Carey
Dr B Carey
Dr R Carey
Dr A Donaldson
Dr M Hall
Dr J Johnson
Dr Lyons
Dr F Mackay
Dr H Minnis
Dr B Nottage
Dr R Patterson
Dr M Sawyer
Dr G Sherman
Dr H Simmons
Dr J Stewart

Oncology & haematology
Dr J Lunn
Dr C Sin Quee (paediatrics)

Ophthalmology
Dr K W Knowles
Dr R McKinney
Dr K J A Rodgers
Dr J Sweeting

Orthopaedics
Dr David Barnett
Dr R L Gibson
Dr W Thompson

Paediatrics
Dr G Bethel
Dr J Colaco
Dr J Davis-Dorsett
Dr P Forte
Dr J Lightbourne
Dr S Lochan
Dr P McNeil
Dr Patrick D Roberts
Dr Paul B Roberts
Dr D Sands
Dr G Sands
Dr Y Skeffrey
Dr J Wilson

Pathology
Dr A Anees
Dr M Blanco

Dr G Bruney
Dr D Grammatico
Dr A Hanna
Dr K Subramanyam

Plastic surgery
Dr E Jacobs

Physiatry
Dr K de Souza

Psychiatry
Dr D Allen
Dr T Barrett
Dr N Clarke
Dr B Humblestone
Dr M Neville
Dr H Podlewski

Radiology
Dr L Carroll
Dr E Darville
Dr A Pandya
Dr S Payne

Surgery
Dr W Campbell (ENT)
Dr W Chea
Dr C Diggiss
Dr I E Farrington
Dr W Gibson (ENT)
Dr N Hepburn
Dr C Johnson (ENT)
Dr J McCartney
Dr L Munroe
Dr R Ramsingh (ENT)
Dr M Rashad (oral)
Dr P Thompson

Urology
Dr J Evans
Dr R Roberts

Private practitioners, Family Islands
ABACO
Marsh Harbour: Dr F Boyce, Dr J S Fifer, Dr M Gerassimos (weekends), Dr E Lundy, Dr B Rolle
Treasure Cay: Dr R Wilson

ELEUTHERA
Governor's Harbour: Dr David Sands (available every two weeks)

Medical officers, Family Islands (government)
ABACO
Cooper's Town: Dr F Biney
Marsh Harbour: Dr H Ameeral

ACKLINS & CROOKED ISLAND
Spring Point: Dr A Ajibade

ANDROS
Fresh Creek: Dr A Lambo
Kemp's Bay: Dr J Duruaku
Mangrove Cay: Dr J Duruaku
Nicholl's Town: Dr M Consulta

BERRY ISLANDS
Bullock's Harbour: Dr P Duncombe

BIMINI
Alice Town: Dr P Duncombe

CAT ISLAND
Smith's Bay: Dr In Pa Kim

ELEUTHERA
Governor's Harbour: Dr N Bacchus
Harbour Island: Dr J Carter
Rock Sound: Dr R Guina

EXUMA
George Town: Dr S Appiah
Steventon: Dr A Swamy

GRAND BAHAMA
See **Freeport information, Doctors.**

INAGUA
Matthew Town: Dr D Mukerjee

LONG ISLAND
Deadman's Cay: Dr F Lincoln
Simms: Dr R Sirra

SAN SALVADOR
Cockburn Town: Dr P Gunabe

Penal/prison service
Dr M Sunduram, Dr J Pedroche

See also **Ambulance/air ambulance services** and **Hospitals & clinics.**

DRIVER'S LICENCE & VEHICLE INFORMATION

The Bahamas follows the British system of driving on the left-hand side of the road. As most cars are generally imported from the US, they have the steering wheel on the left.

The speed limit downtown and in congested areas is 25 mph. Everywhere else in The Bahamas, it is 30 mph. Cars travelling west of the Ministry of Works building on John F Kennedy Dr (towards the airport), on Independence Dr and Harrold Rd, may travel at 45 mph.

There are three types of driver's licences in The Bahamas, which cover the following vehicles:
1. Motor vehicles with standard shift or automatic transmission.
2. Two-wheel vehicles (motor cycles, scooters, etc).
3. Commercial and public service vehicles.

The Road Traffic Dept and Driving Test Centre are in the Clarence A Bain Bldg, Thompson Blvd and Moss Rd. All applications for driving permits and licences are processed there.

At press time, it had been announced that new driver's licences were to carry the bearer's photograph and personal information such as date of birth, gender and address, with a valid passport or voter's card being presented at the time of application. Drivers are required by law to have licences in their possession at all times.

See **Fig 1.4** for information on the number of drivers licensed and vehicles registered in New Providence and Grand Bahama.

Driver's licence requirements

Applicants must be at least 17 yrs to qualify to drive a motor car, motor cycle or motor-assisted cycle equipped with pedals. First-time applicants must secure a learner's permit for $10 and then take a combined oral and driving test when they are ready to drive unaccompanied.

The oral test concerns highway code (traffic regulations). Appointments are made for tests at the Road Traffic Dept (Clarence A Bain Bldg, Thompson Blvd) and must be kept promptly. A fee of $10 is charged. If an applicant finds that after making an appointment for a test he is unable to attend, he should inform the Road Traffic Dept at least 24 hours beforehand. Failure to do so will result in forfeiture of the $10 fee.

A period of 45 mins is allowed for each applicant's test. Latecomers are rescheduled for a later date – possibly as much as three months later. A driver's licence costs $15 and is renewable by the end of the driver's month of birth on an annual basis for $15, or for three years at a cost of $45.

Drivers holding a valid licence issued outside The Bahamas may apply to the Road Traffic Dept for a Bahamian licence. The licence is issued upon presentation of the driver's current valid licence at a fee of $15 per annum, renewable by the end of the driver's month of birth.

A separate application for a separate permit must be made to receive a public service (chauffeur's) licence. There is an additional fee of $50 to drive a tour car, $40 to drive a taxi and $75 to drive an omnibus. The applicant must present current criminal and traffic records and three passport-sized photos, and must successfully complete a road test and written examination.

Visitors or persons staying, but not working, in The Bahamas may drive on their foreign licence for up to three months. Expatriates must have a valid Bahamian driver's licence once they start work. Periods of settling in are not considered. The licence is necessary only when employment actually begins.

Motor cyclists (drivers and passengers) are required by law to wear a protective helmet. Laws on use of seat-belts and child restraint seats are expected to be introduced. The Road Traffic Dept advises the public to wear seat-belts through its road safety programmes, and reports seat-belt use is increasing.

Competitive prices. Priceless service.

When you need transportation in The Bahamas, call Avis and take advantage of great rates and service. Whether it's a sporty subcompact or a larger, roomier car like the Ford Taurus, you'll find Avis offers a wide selection of dependable cars at rates that make it easy and economical to get around.

What's more, you can count on Avis for friendly and efficient service from people who really care about pleasing you. Competitive prices. Priceless service. That's what we mean when we say "We try harder" at Avis.
For Avis reservations, stop in or call:

Daily Rental
Nassau (242) 326-6380
Freeport (242) 352-7666

Monthly/Mini Lease
Contact Mrs S Hanna
VP Administration
(242) 322-4062

Intl Reservations
Call toll free
1-800-228-0668

AVIS®
We try harder.®

Licencee: Airport Rent A Car Ltd.

FIG 1.4
1998 LICENSED DRIVERS & VEHICLES REGISTERED

Licensed drivers	New Providence	Grand Bahama
Private	97,399	24,967
Provisional	9,088	2,517
Public service	3,929	1,034
International	3,285	116
Total	113,701[†]	28,634*

Vehicles registered	New Providence	Grand Bahama
Private cars	175,477	37,247
Government-owned cars	869	74
Private trucks	15,780	5,842
Government-owned trucks	256	18
Private motor cycles	716	213
Government-owned motor cycles	750	27
Government-owned miscellaneous vehicles	65	1
Private miscellaneous vehicles	598	135
Taxi-cabs	1,135	1,042
Self-drive cars	970	818
Self-drive scooters	1,040	159
Tour cars	220	–
Buses	65	288
Government-owned buses	70	7
Public service buses	312	153
Livery cars	92	–
Total	198,415*	46,024*

[†] As of Aug 1998. * As of June 1998.

Vehicle inspection

All vehicles must be taken to the Road Traffic Dept for inspection before being licensed to operate on the streets. The fee is $20. The Controller of Road Traffic and the police are empowered to demand a further examination of any vehicle they consider to be of questionable roadworthiness.

Privately-owned vehicles are inspected annually by the end of the owner's month of birth. Public service vehicles are inspected twice annually, usually in May and Oct. Company and government-owned vehicles are inspected in Mar.

When a vehicle is inspected for the first time, the owner must produce a certificate of insurance. Owners of newly imported vehicles must present a certificate of ownership issued by the Dept of Customs. Owners of omnibuses and self-drive cars must present a receipt of payment for all outstanding fees owed to the Road Traffic Dept.

Inspectors examine hand and foot brakes; tyres; headlights; parking lights; signal lights; stop lights and dip switch; windshield; muffler; bodywork and mirrors. In public service vehicles further inspections are made of seats, floors, other interior, body, trunk, tyres, windows and doors.

Vehicle ownership (licensing)
A vehicle ownership fee is paid annually by the end of the owner's month of birth. The fee is $75-$360, depending on size of the vehicle. There is a fee of $10 for transfer of a vehicle already licensed. The new owner must also present a bill of sale, the registration card with his name entered in the space provided, and proof that the vehicle is covered by minimum Road Act Insurance.

Licence plates
There are different colour plates for private cars, public service vehicles, trucks and motor cycles. Private car, truck and motor cycle licence plates have a blue background with yellow numbers and/or letters. Bonded vehicles have orange backgrounds with black numbers and the words "bonded vehicle" embossed at the top. Trade or OT plates are orange with orange letters preceded by OT.

Public Service vehicles have either a yellow, white, black, green or orange background, as follows:
1. **Taxi cabs:** Yellow background with black letters and numbers.
2. **Tour cars:** White background with red letters preceded by TC.
3. **Self-drive cars & scooters:** White background with green numbers preceded by SD.
4. **Livery plates:** Black background with yellow numbers and letters.
5. **Public schedule buses:** Green background with yellow numbers and letters.
6. **Private schedule buses:** Green background with white letters and numbers.
7. **Privately chartered buses:** Green background with black letters and numbers.
8. **Miscellaneous:** Orange background with white letters and numbers.

Licence plate numbers are now issued for life, in an attempt to reduce problems in trying to trace car ownership information. It also helps the Road Traffic Dept to better manage its vehicular database. A duplicate plate (ie, to replace one that was lost) costs $5, or $10 for the pair.

Importing an automobile
Cars imported to The Bahamas should be insured before leaving the dock. All cars from right-hand drive countries must have their headlights adjusted to dip left. The car should be driven directly to the Road Traffic Dept for inspection and registration.

For import duty on motor cars and public service vehicles, see **Customs**.

See also **Motor vehicle insurance** and **Insurance**.

DRUGS

The Dangerous Drugs Act, chapter 213, makes it an offence for an unauthorized person to import, export or be in possession of Indian hemp (marijuana), cocaine, morphine, opium, or lysergic acid (LSD) in The Bahamas. The only exception is for a qualified person (registered medical practitioner, registered dentist, licensed veterinary surgeon or licensed pharmacist) to whom special permission is granted for medical or scientific purposes.

The provisions of the Act are stringently enforced and visitors from countries where drug laws are less strict should be aware of Bahamian law in this respect. The Act, amended in 1988, provides the following penalties for contravention of its provisions:
1. On conviction on an indictable charge of possession with intent to supply, a fine of up to $200,000 or imprisonment for two years to life or to both such fine and imprisonment, and
2. On summary conviction, a fine of up to $100,000 or to imprisonment for 1-5 years, or both such fine and imprisonment.

The Tracing and Forfeiture of Proceeds of Drug Trafficking Act, 1987, created new offences for drug trafficking and the ancillary offence of facilitation of a drug trafficking offence, and provided that any person convicted of such offences or who could be shown after conviction of such an offence to have "benefited from drug trafficking," should be liable to the increased fine and the additional penalty of confiscation of the proceeds of drug trafficking without compensation.

The Act also empowered investigating authorities to commence an investigation of such offences, or to trace the proceeds of such offences, on the basis of either knowledge or suspicion that a person had trafficked, facilitated and/or benefited from a drug trafficking offence.

The confiscation may take the form of a monetary fine on the assessed value of the proceeds of drug trafficking and, for this purpose, a receiver may be appointed to take possession of such proceeds and to sell them to qualified people, for medical or scientific purposes, to realize the fine.

See also **Crime**.

ECONOMY

The Bahamas is a stable, upper-middle income developing nation, according to a US Dept of Commerce report prepared by the US Embassy in Nassau.

The Bahamian economy continued to record positive growth in 1997, supported by steady foreign investments in tourism, vacation homes and industrial developments, which sustained a boom in construction activity. Significant growth was also evident in public sector investments, the financial services sector and in agriculture and fisheries production due to increased exports of lobster. In the tourism sector, estimated industry earnings stabilized marginally above $1.41 billion, following an increase of 4.8% in 1996.

Gross Domestic Product (GDP)

The Gross Domestic Product (GDP) is the sum of the remuneration of Bahamian labour, capital and land employed in the creation of The Bahamas economy. When indirect taxes are included in the total, it is known as GDP at market prices. When they are not included, it is known as GDP at factor cost.

Based on estimates made by the Inter-American Development Bank (IDB), real GDP in The Bahamas grew by 3.5% in 1997 compared to 4.2% in 1996. GDP at market prices was estimated at $3.9 billion in 1997 compared to $3.8 billion in 1996. Using these figures, the 1997 GDP per capita was $13,891 compared to $13,429 in 1996.

The Bahamian economy is based mostly on tourism and offshore banking. The agricultural and industrial sectors are comparatively small.

The Bahamas is the leading Caribbean region tourist destination, and the tourism sector has long been the engine of the Bahamian economy. Tourism generates about 50% of the total GDP and directly or indirectly employs about 50,000 people, roughly half the total workforce.

According to the Ministry of Tourism, more than 3.4 million vacationers arrived in The Bahamas in 1997 (down 0.7% since '96). This was due mainly to fewer stopover visitors from the US resulting in a lower growth rate for New Providence (4.1%). Also, arrivals to Grand Bahama contracted by 9.7%, because of reduced demand for package tours as well as limited room capacity due to temporary closures of some hotels. Air arrivals were relatively stable at 1.368 million, while sea visitors recorded a smaller increase of 1.1% to 2.071 million. Total tourism expenditure increased from $631.1 million in 1981 to $1.410 billion in '97.

The banking and finance sector is the second pillar of the Bahamian economy, accounting for roughly 15% of GDP. According to the Central Bank of The Bahamas' 1997 survey, the sector employs 3,860 persons, 95.7% of whom are Bahamians; total salaries and wages paid are estimated to be in the region of $132 million per year.

The majority of banks and trust companies are engaged in the management of assets for wealthy individuals. They are generally non-resident or offshore companies that generate no Bahamian dollar earnings and cover all their expenses for administrative cost, utilities, maintenance and other local overhead by bringing in foreign exchange. Including salaries, total expenditure for these items by the banks is in the region of $288 million per year.

Commercial fishing is reserved exclusively for Bahamians. However, several foreign investors are involved in aquaculture projects.

The Bahamas Electricity Corp (BEC) and Bahamas Telecommunications Corp (BaTelCo) are government owned, as is the national airline Bahamasair, although the Free National Movement (FNM) administration has expressed plans to invite private investment.

Foreign investors enjoy complete freedom of repatriation on their investments and profits. Among major foreign investments in The Bahamas are the Grand Bahama container port by Hong Kong's Hutchison Port Holdings (HPH); the Atlantis, Paradise Island mega-resort by Sun Intl Hotels Ltd; the Nassau Marriott Resort and Crystal Palace Casino and Convention Centre, Cable Beach, by the Ruffin Hotel Group, which has also acquired Coral Island off Arawak Cay and the Nassau Beach Hotel; the multi-million-dollar fantasy island Castaway Cay, Abaco, by Disney Cruise Line; Sandals Royal Bahamian Resort & Spa, Cable Beach, by Sandals Resorts; and SuperClubs® Breezes Bahamas, Cable Beach, by SuperClubs® SuperInclusive® Resorts.

Gross National Product (GNP)

The Gross National Product (GNP) either at market prices or factor cost differs from GDP by including the income of Bahamian capital earned abroad, and by excluding the contribution of foreign capital to the Bahamian economy. Such contributions are represented by interest, dividend receipts and payments from and to abroad.

According to the Dept of Statistics, the current GNP had been calculated but was not approved for release to the public at press time. However, in 1995, the net property and entrepreneurial income received from abroad totalled $97 million, which put the GNP at market prices at an estimated $2,972 million.

National debt

According to the Central Bank of The Bahamas' *Quarterly Economic Review*, Dec, 1997, The Bahamas had accrued a debt of $1.679 billion, an increase of $135 million (8.7%) over '96. Of this amount, direct liabilities of the government grew by $137 million (11.1%) to $1.372 billion, while government guaranteed debt of the public corporations fell by $2.1 million (0.7%) to $307 million.

In the first quarter of 1997, The Bahamas registered a national debt of $1.558 billion; this increased to $1.632 billion in the second quarter, $1.651 billion in the third quarter of the year.

Inflation

Consumer price inflation, measured as the average variation in the retail price index, declined to 0.5% in 1997 from 1.4% in '96, partly reflecting lower inflation in the US, due to the fixed parity between the Bahamian and US dollars.

Smaller increases were measured for most cost components of the index including food and beverages (1.6%), housing (0.2%) and medical and health care (1.2%). In addition, education costs registered a larger decrease of 3.5%, amid lower tuition for computer training.

Unemployment was 9.8% as of Dec 1997, a significant decrease from 11.5% in '96.

EDUCATION

Bahamian education comes under the jurisdiction of the Ministry of Education.

There are currently 223 schools in The Bahamas. Of these, 172 (77.1%) are fully maintained by the government and 51 (22.9%) independent. In New Providence, 45 are government-owned and 29 independent. In the Family Islands, 127 are government-owned and 22 independent.

See **Fig 1.5** for a breakdown of the school population.

Schools in The Bahamas are categorized as follows:

	Age
Preschool	2-5
Primary	5-11
Secondary	11-16+
All-age	5-16+
Special education	all ages
(for students with severe learning disabilities)	

Free education is available in Ministry schools throughout The Bahamas.

The Ministry of Education, in consultation with the University of Cambridge Local Examinations Syndicate, introduced The Bahamas General Certificate of Secondary Education (BGCSE) in 1993. A wide range of subjects covering academic, technical and vocational areas is offered. Grades are on a seven point scale, A-G. It is based on the UK General Certificate of Secondary Education (GCSE), and is targeted to a wider range of abilities than the former GCE O levels.

Independent schools provide primary and secondary education. The term "college" connotes a fee-paying school rather than a university.

Several private schools of continuing education offer secretarial and academic courses. The government-operated Princess Margaret Hospital offers a nursing course through the School of Nursing, at the College of The Bahamas' Oakes Field Campus.

Literacy

Eighty-five per cent of Bahamians are literate; 15% cannot read or write, according to the Let's Read Bahamas Secretariat. Literacy is based on the number of students completing sixth grade. While more than 95% of Bahamians complete sixth grade, they are not all functionally literate. The National Literacy Project – Let's Read Bahamas – was established by the Ministry of Education in 1994. To become a Let's Read Bahamas volunteer, contact project director, Let's Read Bahamas, Ministry of Education, PO Box N-3913, tel 356-7643, fax 356-7644.

Higher education

Four government-operated institutions in The Bahamas offer higher education:
- The College of The Bahamas.
- The University of The West Indies (regional).
- The Bahamas Hotel Training College, sponsored by the Ministry of Education and hotel industry.
- The Bahamas Technical and Vocational Institute, formerly the Industrial Training Centre (ITC).

There has been a marked increase in private institutions offering tertiary level education and degrees. Every school must be registered with the ministry, although prospective students should check each one to determine accreditation.

In addition, some US schools offer higher education in The Bahamas. Examples are Univ of Miami and Nova Southeastern Univ, which offer degree programmes with weekend and/or night classes held in Nassau.

NEW PROVIDENCE SCHOOLS

A sampling of schools in New Providence follows. For a complete list, including the Family Islands, contact the Ministry of Education, PO Box N-3913, Nassau, The Bahamas, tel (242) 322-8140.

Nursery schools & kindergarten

Infant Education Centre Ltd: East Court, Centreville. For children 2-5 yrs. Four terms, $300 per term. 7:30am-3:30pm. After school care until 6pm (extra). Tel 325-8567. **Nursery division,** 9th Terrace, Centreville. For children

FIG 1.5
SCHOOL POPULATION 1996-97

	Government	Independent	Total
Primary			
New Providence	16,317	6,193	22,510
Family Islands	7,136	1,759	8,895
All-age			
New Providence	–	2,421	2,421
Family Islands	3,367	1,220	4,587
Secondary			
New Providence	12,593	4,080	16,673
Family Islands	7,192	1,852	9,044
Special schools			
New Providence	354	–	354
Family Islands	88	–	88
Preschools/Nursery			
New Providence	387	2,146	2,533
Family Islands	185	523	708
Totals	47,619	20,194	67,813

Figures are supplied by the Ministry of Education.

---

6 wks-2 yrs. 7:30am-6pm. $30 weekly. PO Box N-10576, tel 326-5855.

Kids Montessori School: Montrose Ave. For children 2½-5 yrs. Three terms, $520 per term. 9am-12 noon. Montessori method of teaching prepares children for all other schools. Renée Roth, headmistress, PO Box N-953, tel/fax 323-8508 or tel 324-3182.

Munro School: William Ct off William St (behind the Shirley St Theatre). For children 2-5 yrs. Four terms, $540 per term. 8:30am-1pm. Nursery and kindergarten classes, including grade one preparation. "Art is our speciality." Ministry of Education approved curriculum. Qualified teachers. Sylvia Munro, PO Box N-134, tel 393-2957, fax 393-1847.

Wee Wisdom School: Collins Ave, Centreville. For children 2½-5 yrs. Three terms. K2-K3 (2-3 yrs) $450 per term, $1,450 per year; K3-K5 (3-5 yrs) $500 per term, $1,500 per year. 9am-2:30pm. A division of Nassau Christian Schools. Baptist Intl Missions Inc, PO Box N-3923, tel 322-1586 or 393-2641.

Private primary schools
Lyford Cay School: Lyford Cay. For children 3-13 yrs. Three terms: nursery (3 yrs by Sept 1) $1,800 per term; reception (4 yrs by Sept 1) $1,800 per term; grades 1-6 (5-11 yrs) $1,925 per term; grades 7-9 (11-13 yrs) $2,000 per term; 9am-3pm. An application and testing fee of $70 (non-refundable) and development fund fee of $500 per student (non-refundable) required upon acceptance. Principal, PO Box N-7776, tel 362-4774 or 362-4269; fax 362-4128.

Xavier's Lower School: West Bay St. Roman Catholic. Students 4-11 yrs. Three terms, $1,613 per year plus $80-$85 book fee, $5 PTA and $12 insurance fee, all for first term only. Kindergarten-grade 6. Approx 450 pupils and 29 lay teachers, one priest, one sister, one nurse and one guidance counsellor. Diane Cepero, headmistress, Xavier's Lower School, PO Box N-7076, tel 322-3077, fax 325-1571.

Private primary-secondary schools

Jordan-Prince Williams School: Cowpen Rd. Baptist. For students 4-18 yrs. Three terms: primary section $450 per term; senior section $550 per term. Incidentals: uniforms and text books. Senior section students may take BGCSE and Pitman exams. Commercial subjects, computer courses and physics also offered. Approx 1,120 students. Principal, Jordan-Prince Williams School, PO Box GT-2198, tel 361-4046 or 361-4847; fax 361-1193.

Kingsway Academy: Bernard Rd. Inter-denominational, Christian school. Kindergarten-grade 12. Three terms, $800-$885 per term depending on grade level; $65 book fee for kindergarten-grade 6; $200-$300 for grades 7-12. Classes: kindergarten-grade 6, 8:30am-2:45pm (2pm on Fri); grades 7-12, 8:30am-2:55pm (2pm on Fri). Curriculum for all grades includes computer and Spanish. Senior students take BGCSE, PSAT and SAT exams. Approx 850 pupils. Carol Harrison, administrator, PO Box N-4378, tel 324-6269 or 324-6889; fax 393-6917, e-mail: kingsway@bahamas.net.bs

Queen's College: Village Rd. Methodist. For students 3-11 yrs (primary school) and 11-18 yrs (high school). Three terms: early learning centre, $595; grades 1-6, $781; grades 7-12, $891; college prep, $950; 6th form, $1,050 per term. Incidental fees include equipment deposit, $300; uniforms, annual magazine, materials for practical subjects and selected workbooks. Students may sit PSAT, SAT, Pitman and BGCSE exams. A-level studies in selected subjects are offered at the Centre for Further Education, subject to demand. Approx 1,200 pupils, 80 teachers. Principal, Queen's College, PO Box N-7127, tel 393-2153, 393-1666 or 393-2646; fax 393-3248.

Respect Academy: Dean's Lane, Ft Charlotte, on the campus of The Medical Arts Institute. International student body, grades 7-12. Three terms, $449 per term. Rolling admissions. College and career prep with strong entrepreneurial emphasis. Students take BJC, BGCSE, PSAT, SAT and Pitman exams. Approx 180 students and 12 full-time teachers. Executive director, PO Box SS-5630, tel 323-2767 or 328-3948; fax 323-2764.

St Andrew's School: Yamacraw Rd. Independent, non-denominational. Students $3^{1}/_{2}$-18 yrs. Three terms, $1,200-$2,450 per term depending on class. Incidental fees: uniforms. Students take BGCSE, SSAT, PSAT and SAT exams. Approx 720 students and 60 teachers. Principal, St Andrew's School, PO Box EE-17340, tel 324-2621, fax 324-0816, e-mail: principal@batelnet.bs

St Anne's School: Fox Hill. Anglican. Students 5-18 yrs. Three terms: primary, $660 per term plus $50 books first term only; secondary, $715 per term. Incidental fees: uniforms, books and equipment. Students take BJC, BGCSE, Pitman, PSAT and SAT exams. Admission by exam. Approx 700 students with 38 teachers in the secondary dept and 19 primary dept. Cynthia Wells, principal; Sammy Bethell, vice principal of the secondary dept, Sonia Johnson, vice principal of the primary dept, St Anne's School, PO Box SS-6256, tel 324-1203 or 324-1226 (secondary dept); 324-1481 (primary dept); fax 324-0805.

St John's College: Bethel Ave. Anglican. Established in 1947. Students 4-17 yrs. Three terms: preparatory dept, $660 per term, plus $50 books first term only; senior dept $715 per term. Incidental fees: uniforms, books and equipment. BJC, BGCSE, PSAT and SAT exams. Admission to senior dept is by examination. Approx 1,040 students, 48 full-time teachers in secondary dept and 28 full-time in preparatory dept. Principal, St John's College, PO Box N-4858. Tel 323-3030 or 322-3249.

Tambearly School: Sandyport, Cable Beach. International student body, 4-15 yrs. Prepares students for integration into schools abroad. All students utilize the computer and take French or Spanish, music and sports. Three terms, $1,725 per term, kindergarten-grade 6; $1,850 per term, grades 7-9. Accommodates up to 16 students per class. Approx 160 pupils, and 11 full-time and 4 part-time teachers. Alice Langford, principal, PO Box N-4284, tel 327-5965, fax 327-5963, e-mail: tambearly@bahamas.net.bs

Private secondary schools
Aquinas College: Madeira St. Roman Catholic. Six years. Three terms. Grades 7-12. Prepares candidates for BJC, BGCSE and American College Board exams. Tuition: $1,470 per year. Registration: $30 (non-refundable). Uniforms. Approx 500 students, 36 teachers. Elizabeth Miller, principal, PO Box N-7540, tel 322-8933/4, fax 323-1612.

St Augustine's College: Bernard Rd. Roman Catholic. Grades 7-12. Students 11-18 yrs. Education equivalent to British comprehensive schools, incorporating elements of American junior and senior prep school along with computer science. Three terms, $2,220 per year plus a $50 seat fee. Students sit BGCSE, PSAT, SAT, and 75% of graduating students receive a minimum of five subject passes with grade C or better. Entrance exams are held in Jan of each year. Approx 1,010 students and 77 teachers. PO Box N-3940, tel 324-1511.

Special service schools
Blairwood Academy: Village Rd, south of Queen's College. Kindergarten-grade 12. Three terms. Blairwood Academy is an alternative school, dedicated to average to bright students who benefit from a small structured environment. Special programmes for students with learning disabilities, language deficits or attention deficits. There is a full-day school programme, after-school tutoring and summer school. Testing and evaluations can be done to diagnose learning strengths and weaknesses. The school maintains contact with an extensive network of related professionals and can provide referrals to other services as needed. PO Box N-524, tel 393-1303 or 394-3329; fax 393-6952, e-mail: bwa1@batelnet.bs

Hopedale Centre: Highbury Park, immediately west of Holy Cross Church off Soldier Rd. For students 5-21 yrs who have not been successful in traditional classroom settings. Approx 35 pupils with eight to a class, or one-on-one if necessary. Eight teachers. Structured, supportive classroom environment and basic skills curriculum. Ungraded programme allows students to work at their own pace. An individual education plan (IEP) for each student is based on special learning needs. All students utilize the computer. Life skills, vocational and career training are part of the curriculum. Arlene Davis, director, PO Box N-8883, tel 393-8924, fax 394-4792.

Tertiary education
The Bahamas Hotel Training College: This school was established to satisfy demands of the developing tourism industry in The Bahamas, Caribbean and other Commonwealth countries. It is a tripartite body consisting of the government, hotel industry and Bahamas Hotel Catering and Allied Workers' Union. The college is financed by the government through the Ministry of Labour, Immigration and Training; by the hotel industry through The Bahamas Hotel Assoc, Nassau/Paradise Island/Cable Beach Promotion Board and Grand Bahama Island Tourism Board; and by the Bahamas Hotel Catering and Allied Workers' Union.

The mission of the college is to develop human resources for national and international tourism, hospitality and allied industries by providing quality vocational technical training and applied academic education. Programmes include the national diploma in hospitality and catering operations; the national diploma in culinary arts; the national apprentice chef programme; the national apprentice pastry chef programme; bookkeeping and front office skills programme; culinary skills programme; housekeeping skills programme and numerous freestanding special interest, food, language and diploma accredited courses.

The two-campus facility is accredited by the Commission of Occupational Education (COE), with the main campus in New Providence and support campus in Grand Bahama. The college also provides educational & training opportunities for Family Island industry personnel. PO Box N-4896, Nassau, The Bahamas, tel (242) 323-5804.

Bahamas Technical & Vocational Institute (BTVI): Old Trail Rd. The mission of BTVI is to produce skilled individuals by providing quality technical and vocational training to enable them to participate in national development.

Programmes have an integrated design, combining three 12-week centre-based periods of instruction and one four-week work experience period. Programmes offered include construction, mechanical, electrical and service trades, including crafts and souvenir manufacturing. The crafts programme is designed to develop and produce native craft items for the tourist trade in Nassau. There are approx 1,200 trainees at the campus on Old Trail Rd and 300 in Grand Bahama. PO Box N-4934, tel 393-2804, fax 393-4005.

College of The Bahamas (COB): Established in 1974, the College has three campuses: Oakes Field and Grosvenor Close on New Providence, and Freeport, Grand Bahama. Associate degree courses are also offered in Exuma, Andros, Abaco and Eleuthera. The college offers a wide range of programmes leading to the Bachelor's and Associate's degree and diplomas and certificates in seven major disciplines – business and administrative studies, teacher education, humanities, nursing and health sciences, social sciences, natural sciences and technology. Bachelor's degrees can be obtained in accounting, banking and finance, computer information services, management, nursing and teacher education (primary and secondary levels).

The Centre for Continuing Education and Extension Services offers general interest courses, professional development seminars, short certificate courses and upgrading courses for adult learners. The college is associated with two field stations in Andros and San Salvador where various research projects are conducted.

The Centre for Entrepreneurship was launched in October 1997 to encourage entrepreneurship in The Bahamas by providing assistance and services to emerging businesses. Modelled after the Dingman Centre for Entrepreneurship at the University of Maryland, the Centre is housed in the Base Road Business Centre on Nassau St.

COB operates on a semester system, Sept-Dec and Jan-April, with a summer session, May-June. Tuition fees as of Sept 1997 were $25 per credit hour, for Bahamians on courses up to Associate's degree level, and $50 for non-Bahamians. Fee structure for upper level programmes varies and may be obtained from the admissions office at the address below. Approx 3,000 students. Enquiries and applications should be sent to Admissions Office, College of The Bahamas, PO Box N-4912, Nassau, The Bahamas, tel 323-8550/2.

Eugene Dupuch Law School: This new law school operated by the Council of Legal Education is conducting classes from temporary quarters at the Bahamas Hotel Training College for the 1998-99 school year. The school is named in honour of the late Eugene A P Dupuch, QC. The law library is temporarily located immediately east of the Clarence A

Bain Building on Thompson Blvd. Construction of the Law School building, which will be immediately south of the Bahamas Hotel Training College, was to begin in Nov 1998 and end Sept '99.

Graduates of Eugene Dupuch Law School will receive a Certificate of Legal Education, a professional qualification enabling the holder to be called to the bars in West Indian countries. The two-year programme includes civil procedure and practice I; civil procedure and practice II; conveyancing and registration of title; criminal practice and procedure; evidence and forensic medicine; landlord and tenant; legal drafting and interpretation; office management and accounting; remedies; status, rights and obligations of the legal profession; and succession.

A six-month programme will be offered for common law professionally trained persons. Graduates will be eligible to be called to the bars of West Indian countries. Coordinator, Eugene Dupuch Law School, PO Box SS-6394, Nassau, The Bahamas, tel 322-1141 (to 4), fax 356-4179.

Grosvenor Academy: A division of International Language Resources (ILR), Grosvenor Close, 64 Shirley St. Variety of courses for all age groups, preschool to adult. Language courses predominate, but general interest courses are also offered, along with enrichment/remedial courses for children. A full-time English as a Foreign Language (EFL) programme started in June 1998.

ILR also serves The Bahamas business community with translation and interpreting, as well as on-site language courses tailored to the needs of a particular business or industry. Dr John Knowles, PO Box SS-19823, tel 323-2078; fax 394-3562.

Success Training College: Bernard Rd. The nation's first private college was established in 1982. The college believes that no person should be denied education because of limited economic means or academic achievement. The college's admission policy is designed to accommodate aspiring individuals from all levels of society who want to improve their skills and expand their knowledge. Students can pursue Associate degrees and diplomas in 29 majors. Certificate courses are also available in an array of disciplines. Office of Admissions, PO Box FH-14161, tel 324-7770 or 324-7555; fax 324-0119.

University of The West Indies: The Bahamas has been affiliated with the University of the West Indies since the early 1960s. It is regional, serving most of the English-speaking Caribbean, and has three campuses on the islands of Jamaica, Trinidad and Barbados. It maintains an administrative office and full-time representative in Nassau through whom Bahamian students may seek admission to any of the campuses. The UWI representative's office also coordinates distance education programmes of the University in areas such as agriculture, agribusiness management, construction management, education, accounting, economics and management studies.

The Centre for Hotel and Tourism Management, a dept of the Faculty of Social Sciences of the University, was established in The Bahamas in response to the growing economic importance of tourism in the region.

The final two years of the three-year degree programmes in hotel or tourism management are completed in Nassau under the instruction of specialized teachers from several countries. In a 12-week, full-time internship, students gain practical industry-related experience between the fall and spring semesters (Dec-Mar) of years two and three. Internships are arranged in The Bahamas and supporting countries.

Students with a College of The Bahamas Associate's degree in areas such as business, banking, finance and marketing may transfer directly to the programme in Nassau, otherwise they would have to complete one year in the Faculty of Social Sciences at any of the University's three campuses before transferring to Nassau. Representative's office, PO Box N-1184, Nassau, The Bahamas, tel 323-6593, fax 328-0622.

Schools for the handicapped
Bahamas Red Cross Centre for Deaf Children: Horseshoe Dr. Government-assisted. Preschool-18 yrs, with some students integrated in special classes in government primary and high schools. Help is also given to hearing-impaired children in ordinary classes. No tuition fees. General studies with the help of modern hearing-aid equipment. Classes 9am-3pm. Approx 60 students, 13 specialist teachers. Also parental guidance, comprehensive audiological testing facilities, and counselling for deaf people of all ages. Audrey Thomas-Barnett, Bahamas Red Cross Centre for Deaf Children, PO Box N-91, Nassau, The Bahamas, tel 323-6767.

The Salvation Army Erin Harrison Gilmour School for the Blind & Visually Handicapped Children and May & Stanley Smith Resource Centre: 33 Mackey St. Co-ed for school-aged blind and partially-sighted students. Although the school follows curriculum guidelines of the Ministry of Education, adaptations are made for individual students in motor development, mobility training and daily living skills. The cane is used for mobility training. Special media are used to teach blind and partially-sighted students, including Braille machines, large print material, writing guides, talking calculators and abacus equipment. Adult blind can take computer classes with talking computers. A library is available to visually impaired people with books in Braille, talking books and giant print books. Blind and partially-sighted students are encouraged to study for and sit the BGCSE. Divisional Commander, PO Box N-205, Nassau, The Bahamas, tel 394-3197 or 393-2745.

Stapledon School: Dolphin Dr. Government-owned. For the educable and trainable mentally and physically handicapped. The curriculum includes ceramics, crafts and a programme that teaches basic farming skills. Speech therapy, physiotherapy and counselling are provided. Approx 120 students, 18 teachers. Tuition free. Classes 9am-3pm. Apply to headmistress, Stapledon School, or Special Services Division, PO Box N-3913, Nassau, The Bahamas, tel 323-4669 or 323-6000.

ELECTRICITY

In New Providence, electricity is generated by the Bahamas Electricity Corp (BEC) at Clifton Pier and Blue Hills Power Stations. Seven diesel-driven alternators are used at Clifton Pier, and one combined cycle unit (comprising a steam and a gas turbine) and six simple cycle gas turbines at Blue Hills.

In the Family Islands, BEC generates and distributes electricity in Bimini; north, central and south Andros; Cooper's Town, Green Turtle Cay, Marsh Harbour, Mores Island and north Abaco; Black Point, Exuma Cays; Exuma; San Salvador; Great Harbour Cay; Eleuthera; Cat Island; Long Island; Ragged Island; Mayaguana; and Rum Cay. Total electricity consumers connected by BEC in New Providence, Paradise Island and the Family Islands as of Sept 30, 1995, amounted to 65,141.

For principal rates in New Providence, Paradise Island and designated Family Islands, see **Fig 1.6**.

New Providence, Paradise & Family Islands
Total annual units* (kWh) generated by BEC
1992-93 873,756,248
1993-94 930,252,300
1994-95 949,179,122
1995-96 976,541,000
1996-97 1,031,370,000

* Each year's figure refers to the 12-month period ending Sept 30, ie, the 1992-93 figure reflects Oct 1, '92-Sept 30, '93.

Total installed capacity ....224.0 MW
max demand 1997 ....154.0 MW
(New Providence only)

FIG 1.6
PRINCIPAL ELECTRICITY RATES IN NEW PROVIDENCE/PARADISE ISLAND & DESIGNATED FAMILY ISLANDS

	Oct 1, 1997 B$
Tariff A – residential	
For electricity supplied to premises used as private residence:	
1. For each unit up to 800 units per month	0.1679
2. For each unit in excess of 800 units per month	0.1937
3. Min charge per month	3.36
Tariff B – commercial	
1. Electricity supplied to commercial installations, max demand of which does not exceed 10 kVA:	
a. Each unit of electricity	0.1924
b. Min charge per month	6.78
2. Electricity supplied to commercial installations, max demand of which exceeds 10 kVA:	
a. Max demand charges per kVA per annum	123.96
b. Unit charges – for each unit of electricity	0.1382
c. Min charge per month kVA demand	10.33
Tariff C – churches, open-air cinemas, floodlit sports arenas with max demand of 10 kVA or more	
1. Max demand charges per kVA per annum	46.56
2. Each unit of electricity	0.1421
3. Min charge per month kVA demand	3.88
Tariff D – temporary service*	
1. Each unit of electricity consumed	0.2118
2. Connection fee	10.00
3. Meter rental per month	7.00
4. Cost of installing connection	–
Special tariff – street lighting	
Electricity supplied per unit consumed	0.1421

* Service will be disconnected if used to supply any part of a permanent electrical installation not inspected and passed by a BEC Inspector, or if the premises are being used for residential or commercial purposes.

Supply voltages & frequency
3 phase, 4 wire, 208/120 volts, 60 cycles.
1 phase, 3 wire, 240/120 volts, 60 cycles.

Fuel surcharge provisions
Basic rates and charges shall be increased by a surcharge of $0.0001 for each unit of electricity consumed.
The surcharge of $0.0001 is increased or decreased as follows:
1. By $0.001557 per unit for every $1 per barrel increase/decrease in the price of automotive diesel oil above or below $30 per barrel.
2. By $0.000807 per unit for every $1 per barrel increase/decrease in the price of Bunker "C" fuel oil above or below $20 per barrel.

A "true up" adjustment to yearly fuel surcharge begins with bills rendered on Nov 1 of each year, by adding or subtracting an amount equal to the difference between actual fuel cost and fuel cost recovered during the

12 months from Oct 1, divided by the estimated number of units to be sold during the ensuing year from Nov 1.

Other charges
1. Special reading, check reading, fuse replacement.....................$ 5
2. Meter test minimum $10
3. Visit with intent to disconnect:
   residential $10
   commercial $15
4. Reconnection fees $20

EMERGENCY NUMBERS
Police..919
Fire..........919, 322-1225 or 326-7056
Ambulances
   Princess Margaret Hosp 322-2221
   Med-Evac (ambulance/emergency airlift services) 322-2881
   Global Med-Tec (ambulance/emergency airlift services) 394-2582
                                    or 394-3388
Hospitals
   Doctors 322-8411
   Princess Margaret 322-2861
   Lyford Cay 362-4025
Aircraft Crash & Rescue 377-7077
Bahamas Air Sea Rescue Assoc (BASRA)......325-8864 or 322-3877
Bahamas Electricity Corp (BEC) ....323-5561 (to 4)
Crime Tips...................328-TIPS (8477)
The Crisis Centre 328-0922
Stat Care Medical & Emergency Centre ....328-5596 (to 8)

EMPLOYERS' ORGANIZATIONS
Locations of the following organizations are in Nassau:

Assoc of Tertiary Institutions in The Bahamas (ATIB), PO Box N-4912.
Bahamas Assoc of Land Surveyors, PO Box N-7782.
Bahamas Assoc of Social Workers, PO Box GT-2699.
Bahamas Boatmen's Assoc, PO Box N-552.
Bahamas Chemical Manufacturing Assoc, PO Box N-1534.
Bahamas Contractors' Assoc, PO Box N-4632.
Bahamas Employers' Confederation, PO Box N-166.
Bahamas Glass Bottom Boat Assoc, PO Box N-552.
Bahamas Hotel Employers' Assoc, PO Box N-7799.
Bahamas Inst of Professional Engineers, PO Box N-7869.
Bahamas Manufacturers Agents & Wholesalers' Assoc, PO Box N-272.
Bahamas Mechanical Contractors' Assoc, PO Box FH-14316.
Bahamas Motor Dealers' Assoc, PO Box N-4177.
Bahamas Professional Photographers' Assoc, PO Box N-586.
Bahamas Real Estate Dealers' Assoc, PO Box N-4051.
Bahamas Soft Drink Bottlers' Assoc, PO Box N-272.
Bahamas Supermarket Operators' Assoc, PO Box N-4206.
Bahamas Used Tyres & Commodities Assoc, PO Box N-3308 or N-1979.
Bahamas Welding Contractors' Assoc, PO Box N-1283.
Corp of Accountants & Auditors, PO Box N-1669.
Nassau Assoc of Shipping Agents, PO Box N-1451.
Natl Consumer Assoc, PO Box CB-11671.
Professional Photographers' Assoc, PO Box N-7458.
Restaurant Owners Assoc of The Bahamas, PO Box N-7799.

ENGINEERING COMPANIES
Sampling only:
Abadean Engineering Ltd
American Middle East Engineers Intl
Bahamas Industrial Enterprises Ltd
Bahamas Institution of Professional Engineers

Brown & Assoc Engineering
  & Consultants
Cavalier Construction Co Ltd
Chee-A-Tow, G Ray
Cox, George V, & Co Ltd
Hanna, Paul E, & Assoc
Lockhart, Hiram, & Assoc
Island Mechanical Ltd
LTD Surveying & Engineering Ltd
McAce Technical Services
Mosko's United Construction Co Ltd
Proton Engineering
Quantum Technologies Ltd
Rowlands Engineering Ltd
The Engineering Group Ltd
Treco, Larry A, Consulting Engineer

ENTERTAINMENT

A number of native shows, bands and cabaret acts are staged at hotels, clubs and restaurants throughout the Bahama Islands. In New Providence, veteran performers King Eric and his Knights appear at the Nassau Beach Hotel on Cable Beach. The show includes Bahamian and Caribbean songs, dance, limbo and fire-eating displays. The hotel's Café Johnny Canoe is host to a Fri night Junkanoo rush-out, where visitors experience the colour, rhythm and excitement of Bahamian culture-in-action. See **Junkanoo**.

Atlantis, Paradise Island's entertainment complex, which was to open in Dec 1998, was to provide entertainment for the whole family, including music, shows and more. The Jokers Wild Comedy Club at Atlantis features top comics from the US and Canada.

A high energy Caribbean revue is staged nightly except Mon at the Rainforest Theatre in the Nassau Marriott Resort and Crystal Palace Casino. *Caribe* features musical revues, dance numbers, elaborate costumes and more.

Baha Men, Ambasah, Visage, Nita, Eugene Davis and Funky D are popular Bahamian performers.

Gaming
New Providence offers two internationally renowned casinos – the 35,000 sq ft Crystal Palace Casino in the Nassau Marriott Resort and the 50,000 sq ft casino in Atlantis, Paradise Island's entertainment complex, slated to open in 1998. Both casinos feature craps, roulette, blackjack, baccarat and Caribbean stud poker 10am-4am. The Crystal Palace Casino also offers big six wheels and the casino at Atlantis is to feature let-it-ride poker, casino war and Vegas shoot-out. Slot machines are open 24 hours. On Sat and Sun, tables at Crystal Palace Casino are open 24 hours.

Nightclubs
There is a thriving night life in New Providence with many clubs open until 4am or later. These include the Zoo, West Bay St; Waterloo, East Bay St; the Culture Club, Nassau St (closed at press time); 601, Bay St; the Drop Off, Bay St; Club DV8, West Bay St; and Le Paon, Radisson Grand Resort, Paradise Island.

See also **Cinemas; Gambling;** and **Theatre & performing arts.**

EXCHANGE CONTROL

Exchange control is the imposition of rules and regulations on transactions whereby a country conserves its foreign currency resources. In The Bahamas, exchange control is administered by the Central Bank of The Bahamas. The Central Bank is, therefore, responsible for the control and regulation of gold and foreign currency under the Exchange Control Act, 1952, and the Exchange Control Regulations, 1956.

Legal tender: The Bahamian dollar is legal tender in the Commonwealth of The Bahamas; all other currencies are foreign, although the US$ is accepted and is on par with the B$.

Residential status: For exchange control purposes, the world has been divided into two categories: The Bahamas and the rest of the world. The Central Bank has the authority to determine residential status of all persons (including legal entities). Resident individuals are either citizens of The Bahamas or citizens of other countries who have been so designated by the Central Bank. Residents are subject to many, although liberal, exchange control regulations. Residents in The Bahamas may not purchase foreign currency, maintain foreign currency accounts or remit foreign currency abroad without the prior permission of the Central Bank.

Non-resident individuals are citizens of a country outside The Bahamas who may reside in but are not gainfully employed in The Bahamas. These persons are subject to minimal currency regulations. Foreign currency deposits held by non-residents are exempt from exchange control regulations.

Foreign citizens who are gainfully employed within The Bahamas for one year or longer are regarded as "temporary residents." Such persons may be eligible for certain exemptions which permit them to retain all existing non-Bahamian assets, to operate foreign currency accounts and to repatriate Bahamian assets on leaving The Bahamas.

Investment currency: This is a pool of foreign currency available for capital investment abroad by residents. Central Bank permission is required for its acquisition and disposition. Investment currency changes hands at a premium determined by the demand and supply for the foreign currency.

Authorized agents/dealers: The Central Bank appoints authorized agents for the purpose of dealing in Bahamian and foreign currency securities and receiving securities into deposit. Authorized dealers are banks permitted to deal in all foreign currencies, and are also appointed by the Central Bank to approve certain exchange control applications under delegated authority as laid out in exchange control Notices. Presently, there are 11 authorized agents, eight authorized dealers and two authorized agents/dealers.

Direct investment: This works two ways – by non-residents inward and residents outward.

1. The prior permission of the Investments Board is required for a non-Bahamian to invest in property in The Bahamas in excess of five acres or property which is acquired for commercial use. If the non-resident investment in The Bahamas is made with foreign currency which is converted to Bahamian dollars, it is accorded "approved status," facilitating the investor's repatriation of income and capital gains accruing from his investment.

2. Permission for resident companies in The Bahamas to extend their business outside The Bahamas depends largely on the probability of a good return to The Bahamas via increased income of foreign currency and/or increased exports. Direct investment outside The Bahamas must be an extension of an existing business within The Bahamas. Foreign currency to finance direct outward investments is normally purchased through the investment currency market.

Purchase of property outside The Bahamas: Residents of The Bahamas are permitted to purchase one piece of property outside The Bahamas for use by the family. If the application is approved by the Central Bank, the foreign currency necessary to acquire the property must be purchased through the investment currency market.

Loans: Resident companies wholly owned by residents require Exchange Control permission to borrow foreign currency.

Personal allowance cards (dollar cards): Residents may submit application to the Central Bank for a dollar card, which permits the resident to purchase foreign currency drafts of up to $10,000 per card. It is renewable on presentation of the used dollar card, but a new one must be picked up for each calendar year. The card is used to pay credit card bills only.

Payment for imports: Prior permission from exchange control is required to purchase foreign currency for payment of non-oil imports in excess of $100,000. This requirement applies in New Providence and Grand Bahama. Authorized dealers in the Family Islands (excluding Grand Bahama) can sell foreign currency for imports without prior Central Bank permission. Application for purchase of foreign currency to pay for imports must be accompanied by a relevant invoice.

Allowances: Residents of The Bahamas are normally permitted to convert $1,000 into foreign cash/travellers' cheques per person per trip and $500 for individuals up to the age of 18 yrs per person per trip for personal and holiday travel purposes. Commercial banks (authorized dealers) may issue and approve payments without exchange control permission. Supporting documents (ie, passport and airline ticket) and completion of Delegated Authority Exchange Form (E1) are required.

Business travel limit: $10,000 in cash or travellers' cheques per resident per annum.

Medical: Authorized dealers may sell up to $1,000 per person per trip in cash/travellers' cheques. There are no limits on amounts being paid directly to hospitals/clinics abroad by way of draft or wire transfer, where supported by appropriate invoices.

Educational: Authorized dealers may sell up to $3,000 cash/travellers' cheques per person per trip. There are no limits on amounts being paid directly to schools abroad by way of draft or wire transfer, where supported by appropriate invoices.

Emigration: A resident leaving The Bahamas must apply to the Central Bank to convert his Bahamian assets. Currently, he is permitted to convert up to B$25,000 to foreign currency at the official rate of exchange. His remaining assets are blocked for a period of four years. If he wishes to convert his blocked assets within the four-year period, he has to go through the investment currency market, which involves paying a premium on all foreign currency purchased. However, immediately after leaving, the emigrant is permitted to convert all income accruing from his Bahamian assets at the official rate of exchange. Temporary residents are permitted to repatriate all of their Bahamian dollar balances.

Eliminating Exchange Control: There has been significant business interest in eliminating exchange control in The Bahamas. Financial experts argue that exchange control discourages foreign investment and that eliminating it will boost investor confidence. Some feel eliminating exchange control could cause a massive outflow of currency, which would deplete the country's reserves and devalue the Bahamian dollar. Others argue strongly that exchange control is incompatible with The Bahamas' position as a leading financial centre, and that capital account controls could be relaxed without significant risk of a destabilizing export of local funds by enforcing control measures such as regulating pension funds' and insurance companies' investments outside The Bahamas. At press time, there were no official plans to eliminate exchange control.

See also **Banking, Central Bank; Import entry; Property transactions, Intl Persons Landholding Act;** and **Investing.**

EXPORT

See **Bahamas Investment Authority; Import & export statistics; Industries encouragement;** and **Manufacturing.**

EXPORT ENTRY

An export entry form is required for goods being exported from The Bahamas. The goods normally are subject to $10 stamp duty. Forms are available at several Nassau book shops and office supply stores. Completed forms should be taken to Bahamas Customs, Thompson Blvd, Oakes Field, Nassau.

Ordinary parcels, clothing, gifts, tourist items, etc, to be sent through post offices or parcel post do not incur the $10 stamp duty as they do not require an export entry form.

See also **Customs**.

EXTRADITION

In 1990, an Extradition Treaty was signed between The Bahamas and US in response to drug trafficking and other crimes. The agreement established more effective cooperation between the two countries and allowed for extradition of persons accused or convicted of extraditable crimes.

The Extradition Act, 1994, allows for persons accused or convicted of certain offences to be extradited to and from Commonwealth countries and foreign states. Extradition requests must be made through diplomatic channels. Persons against whom extradition is sought must have their case heard in a Bahamian court, which must find that there is a case to answer. Before the order may be issued, the treaty state must satisfy the Bahamian court that they are in possession of information against the accused which would constitute a crime in The Bahamas. The Bahamian court is not concerned with the guilt or innocence of the fugitive.

FIRE SERVICES

Royal Bahamas Police Force Fire Services operates under provisions of the Fire Services Act, which gives the Director of Fire Services overall responsibility for fire defence policies, as well as the Commissioner of Police as the Fire Authority. Presently, Deputy Superintendent of Police, Hosea Douglas, is the Fire Services CEO.

New Providence

Fire Services consists of 108 trained fire suppression/extrication technicians, including managers, supervisors and line staff. Officers are stationed in New Providence and deployed between six stations strategically positioned throughout the island. The administration section consists of a fire prevention unit, arson investigation unit, mechanical repair workshop, and a general maintenance unit. The operations division is responsible for all supression and extrication efforts, and is divided into three dutied guards – blue, green and red. The fire control room within each guard receives fire reports, as well as the police control room.

Family Islands

Grand Bahama Fire Services is structured similar to New Providence's but with 31 officers.

There are four trained professionals in Eleuthera, strategically placed throughout the island. They receive assistance from police officers and volunteers.

One trained driver/pump operator, fire suppression/extrication officer is stationed in Arthur's Town, Cat Island. Police officers and volunteers assist in the event of fire.

Training

Enlistees in Fire Services undergo a six-month training programme on policing (law, evidence, Road Traffic, social studies, history and company policies) at the Police Training College. Additionally, there is comprehensive training in fire suppression techniques, aircraft crash and rescue, cruise ship and yacht fires, physics, chemistry and principles of effective extrication. At the completion of entry level training, officers are posted at operational duty shifts for further hands-on experience. Local training may be supplemented with studies in the US and UK.

Volunteer training targets small communities which may not have fire engines. Islands with a complement of volunteers include Abaco, Bimini, Eleuthera and Cat Island.

The brigade responds to approx 1,650 structural, vehicle, vessel and bush fires per year in New Providence. During 1997, there were 1,891 calls.

Fire Services is equipped with modern firefighting equipment.

New Providence:
- One KME aerial ladder truck
  Water capacity .... 150 gals
  Gals per minute (GPM) 1,500
- Two Mack MS200 pumper trucks
  Water capacity .... 1,000 gals
  GPM 750
- Two Mack MS300 pumper trucks
  Water capacity .... 1,000 gals
  GPM 1,000

Abaco: Cherokee Sound, Green Turtle Cay and Sandy Point each have a Hale portable pump.

Andros: Kemp's Bay has one Mack MS200 pumper truck. Nicholl's Town has one 1965 Mack truck.

Berry Islands: Bullocks Harbour has one Hale portable pump.

Cat Island: Arthur's Town has one 1976 Howe Intl fire truck.

Crooked Island: Colonel Hill has one Hale portable pump.

Eleuthera: Spanish Wells has one Hale portable pump. Harbour Island has one 1976 Dodge Intl fire truck. Governor's Harbour has one 1965 GMC fire truck. Rock Sound has one 1969 Ford fire truck.

In the event of a fire dial 919 or the district police or fire station.

FISHING

Bahamian waters produce a variety of game- and food-fish. Anglers from all parts of the world come to test their skill. World record (line) game fish caught in The Bahamas include: amberjack, one; bonefish, six (three line; three fly rod); dolphin, three; wahoo, six. Modern facilities to accommodate sportsfishermen are available throughout The Bahamas.

Following is a list of some of the game species found in Bahamian waters, with a guide to seasons and locations where they can be caught.

Allison tuna: On and off throughout the year but best months are June, July and Aug. All deepwater areas.

Amberjack: Nov-May. Near all reef areas and around old wrecks.

Barracuda: Year-round. Found throughout The Bahamas, especially near reefs. Also in shallow water and occasionally offshore.

Blackfin tuna: May-Sept. Plentiful in vicinity of Nassau.

Bluefin (giant) tuna: May 7-June 15. Bimini, Cat Cay and West End, Grand Bahama.

Blue marlin: Off and on throughout the year but best months are June and July. Found all along the western side of The Bahamas, from Bimini and Cat Cay to Walker's Cay; off Andros, at the Berry Islands near Chub Cay; both sides of Exuma Sound and in the Atlantic Ocean from North Eleuthera to Green Turtle Cay, Abaco.

Bonefish: Year-round. This king of the shallow waters can be found in quantity throughout the islands.

Dolphin (Mahi-Mahi): Winter and spring. All deepwater areas.

Grouper: Year-round. All reefs throughout The Bahamas.

Kingfish: May-July. Good fishing all over, but Berry Islands and western Abaco among the best spots.

Sailfish: Summer and fall. Berry Islands, Chub Cay, Bimini, Cat Cay, West End, Walker's Cay and Exuma Sound.

Tarpon: Year-round. Best bets are Andros and Bimini.

Wahoo: Nov-April, best months Jan and Feb. Most plentiful in Exuma Sound around the cays and at the lower end of Eleuthera. Other good areas: Northeast Providence Channel from Nassau to Spanish Wells and in the Northwest Providence Channel around the Berry Islands and off Sandy Point, Abaco.

White marlin: Winter and spring. Bimini east to Eleuthera, and Walker's Cay south to Exuma Sound in the ocean, or nearby deep channels.

Following is a summary of the Fisheries Resources (Jurisdiction and Conservation) Regulations, 1986:

Underwater fishing (spearfishing)
It is illegal:
1. To use underwater breathing apparatus to capture any fish or marine product. Exceptions are a snorkel or air compressor (hookah). A permit to use an air compressor must be issued by the Dept of Fisheries, Ministry of Agriculture and Fisheries. Permits are issued to Bahamians only, for the months of Aug-Mar. Applicants must provide proof of dive competency. Divers are limited to a depth between 30-60 ft. Visitors to the Bahamas may use an air compressor for observation purposes only and may not harvest any resources while using it. See **Licences** following.
2. To use any device other than a Hawaiian sling for the discharge of a missile underwater. (The Hawaiian sling is a device – usually made of wood or plastic – for discharging a missile by the force of a rubber spring.)

Licences: Foreign vessels intending to engage in sportfishing must have a permit. Several rules apply under this permit:
1. Fishing gear is restricted to hook and line unless otherwise authorized. Only six lines are allowed in the water at one time, unless otherwise authorized. Cost of the permit is $20 per trip or $150 annually. (Note: If more than six reels are allowed on a party fishing boat, for instance, the permit is $10,000 annually.)
2. The bag limit for kingfish, dolphin and wahoo is a max combined total of six fish per person on the vessel, comprising any combination of these species.
3. Vessel bag limits for other marine products are 20 lbs of scalefish, 10 conch and six crawfish per person at any time. The possession of turtle is prohibited. The above amounts may be exported by the vessel upon leaving The Bahamas.

A $50 permit is required to conduct foreign fishing for scientific or research purposes. A licence is required to engage in foreign fishing – fishing by a non-Bahamian vessel – for commercial purposes. Such permission can only be issued to foreign states which have a fishery treaty with The Bahamas.

Bahamian commercial fishing vessels 20 ft in length or greater must get a valid fishing permit. "Bahamian" in relation to a fishing vessel is one *bona fide* owned by a citizen of The Bahamas resident in The Bahamas; or a company registered in The Bahamas under the Companies Act in which all the shares are beneficially owned by citizens of The Bahamas resident in The Bahamas.

It is illegal to export any marine product for commercial purposes unless:
1. The person involved has an export licence for the product he wishes to export.
2. The product is inspected by a fisheries inspector at the time of export.
3. The export duty on the product, if any, is paid.

A $10 permit is required for the use of an air compressor (hookah) in fishing. Its use is restricted to Aug 1-Mar 31, and to a water depth range of 30-60 ft.

Prohibitions
It is illegal to:
1. Use bleach or other noxious or poisonous substances for fishing or have such substances on a fishing vessel without written approval from the Minister.
2. Use firearms or explosives for fishing.
3. Spearfish within one mile off the coast of New Providence; one mile off the southern coast of Freeport, Grand Bahama; 200 yds off the coast of all other Family Islands.
4. Use fishing nets with a minimum mesh gauge of less than two ins.

Exceptions are nets used for catching goggle-eyes and pilchards.
5. Use a scalefish trap which does not have a self-destruct panel and minimum mesh sizes less than 1 in x 2 ins for rectangular wire mesh traps and 1½ ins (greatest length of mesh) for hexagonal wire mesh traps.
6. Take corals.
7. Build artificial reefs without permission from the Minister.
8. Sell fish in New Providence without a permit from the Minister. Exceptions are those with a peddler's permit or shop licence.

Crawfish (spiny lobster): Closed season for crawfish is April 1-July 31.

The minimum size limit for crawfish is a carapace length of 3¼ ins from the base of the horns to the end of the jacket, or 5½ ins tail length. A $10 permit is required to trap crawfish.

Crawfish traps, unless otherwise approved, should be wooden slat traps not more than 3 ft in length, 2 ft in width and 2 ft in height with slats not less than 1 in apart. It is illegal to possess an egg-bearing crawfish or to remove eggs from a female crawfish.
Conch: It is illegal to catch or possess conch with a shell which does not have a well-formed lip.
Turtles: Closed season for turtles is April 1-July 31. It is illegal to capture or possess a hawksbill turtle. Minimum size limit for a green turtle is 24 ins back length and for a loggerhead turtle, 30 ins back length. All turtles captured must be landed whole. Taking or possessing turtle eggs is prohibited.
Scalefish: It is illegal to:
1. Capture bonefish by nets.
2. Buy or sell bonefish.
3. Catch grouper and rockfish weighing less than 3 lbs.
4. Export live rock or small reef fish for commercial purposes.
5. Export hermit crabs.

Stone crab: Closed season is June 1-Oct 15. Minimum harvestable claw length is 4 ins. It is illegal to catch female stone crabs.
Marine mammals: It is illegal to capture, export or molest marine mammals. People who wish to capture such mammals for scientific, educational or exhibitional purposes must apply to the Minister for permission.
Sponge: The minimum size limit is 5½ ins for wool and grass sponge and 1 in for hard-head and reef sponge.

Long-line fishing
Long-line fishing is defined by the Fisheries Resources (Jurisdiction and Conservation) Act, 1993, as the use of 10 or more baited fish hooks connected to a main line or cable capable of extending beyond 20 yds from the point where it is cast.

Under the Act (Amendment) (No 2), long-line fishing is illegal without a permit. It stipulates that no person shall:
1. Have in his possession on a fishing vessel any apparatus intended for use in long-line fishing.*
2. Use for fishing within the exclusive economic zone (as defined by the Act) any apparatus for long-line fishing.*

*Unless written permission is provided by the Governor-General. This is given only where it would not endanger elements essential to sustainable fishery development or prejudice the development and expansion of ecotourism.

Any person who contravenes the Act is guilty of an offence and liable on summary conviction, subject to provisions of the Act, to a fine of not less than $50,000 or to imprisonment for a term of one year, or to both such fine and imprisonment.

Applications for permits and licences may be obtained from the Dept of Fisheries, East Bay St, PO Box N-3028, tel 393-1014/5.

FITNESS
Opportunities for fitness maintenance and improvement abound in New Providence. Two major fitness centres, Gold's Gym, tel 394-4653, at the corner of Mackey and East Bay Sts, and

the Palace Spa, tel 327-6200, at the Nassau Marriott Resort, Cable Beach, serve residents and tourists, with state-of-the-art equipment and a variety of aerobics classes. Both centres offer daily and weekly rates in addition to long-term memberships. Smaller fitness facilities are scattered throughout the island. Some hotels also offer fitness facilities for guests. Another Gold's Gym was planned at Sandyport, just west of the Cable Beach strip.

The Sivananda Yoga Retreat on Paradise Island offers an alternative look at fitness and relaxation. Asana (or posture) classes are held at 8am and 4pm daily. Non-guests participate in classes for a nominal fee.

See also **Sports**.

FLORA & FAUNA

The mandate of the Wildlife Conservation Unit of the Dept of Agriculture is to conserve present Bahamian biodiversity and prevent further extinction of indigenous species. Several species have been lost over the last hundred years or so.

Local fauna comprises an abundance of invertebrates, including many species of ants and spiders, paper wasps, honey bees, land crabs, the chalice sponge, conch, crawfish, some 90 species of butterflies, and the giant bat moth. It is believed 13 species of mammals are endemic to The Bahamas, of which 12 are bats. The other is the hutia, a rodent-like creature once nearly extinct. It was rediscovered on East Plana Cay, where it is now thriving, and has been translocated to two cays in the Exuma Cays Land & Sea Park. There are also established populations of wild pigs, donkeys, racoons and the Abaco wild horse. Several species of whales and dolphins, including humpback and blue whales and the spotted dolphin, are found in seas around the Bahama islands.

Reefs & marine life

There are some 900 sq miles of reefs in The Bahamas, including the third longest barrier reef in the world off the east coast of Andros. The reefs are rich with a diversity of marine life including green moray eels, cinnamon clownfish, queen angelfish, barracudas, the Nassau grouper, the placid nurse shark and inflatable porcupine fish. Reefs, like rain forests, are important as they help to reduce atmospheric carbon dioxide levels implicated in global warming.

Birds

About 230 species of birds either migrate to or live in the Bahama islands. Some of these are rare or endangered. They include the Bahama parrot, now found only in Abaco and Great Inagua, Bahama woodstar hummingbird, Bahama swallow, osprey, Kirtland's warbler, golden-winged warbler, red-bellied woodpecker, West Indian flamingo and West Indian tree duck. Other interesting birds include the great blue heron, barn owl, peregrine falcon and Bahama duck.

Reptiles

Some 44 species of reptiles are found in The Bahamas. These include the Cat Island freshwater turtle, Inagua freshwater turtle, green sea turtle, loggerhead sea turtle and hawksbill sea turtle. Several turtle species are now endangered. There are also 10 species of snake, including the Bahamian boa constrictor, pygmy boa and blind worm snake. There are no poisonous snakes in The Bahamas. There are 29 species of lizard, including iguanas and curly-tailed lizards. Several iguana species are now rare.

Poisonous species

There are a few poisonous flora and fauna in The Bahamas. Some are:

Poison ivy and **Poisonwood** are both members of the sumac family, which also includes mango, cashew and pistachio. Poisonwood and poison ivy contain the poison urushiol, which causes a rash, and in cases of smoke inhalation, lung damage. Most people don't have a reaction to urushiol on first exposure, but three-quarters do on further contact.

Manchineel is a highly poisonous tree because of its poisonous green fruit and toxic latex. Rain water or dew from these trees can cause a violent skin rash, and can cause temporary blindness if brought into contact with the eyes.

The **black widow spider** or bottle spider is possibly the most venomous species in The Bahamas. Its small, jet-black body is characterized by a red hourglass-shaped marking on its underside. The venom of the black widow is a powerful neurotoxin, capable of killing a human but more likely to cause severe pain followed by weakness, tremors, cramps and aches.

The **centipede,** a caterpillar-like creature which can grow to eight inches long, injects a potent venom into its victim.

The **Cuban treefrog** is covered with an irritating mucus which causes local inflammation and itching when rubbed into a cut or abrasion, and can cause excruciating pain, swelling and temporary blindness when brought into contact with the eyes.

Three species of stingray live in Bahamian waters, the **eagle ray, southern stingray** and **yellow stingray.** Some stingrays have tail barbs with venom glands. The most common injury results from stepping on barbs of a stingray half-buried in the sand.

The **Portugese man-of-war** is a coelenterate that appears as a translucent blue float on the ocean surface with hanging tentacles as long as 80 ft. Poisons discharged by the tentacles can be lethal to humans.

Extinct species
Extinct species include the New Providence iguana, monk seal, paleoprovidence tortoise, chickcharnie owl and Bahamian population of American crocodiles. Several plant species are now endangered, including some native hardwood trees and a number of orchid and agave species.

A few introduced or exotic species have become pests in The Bahamas. The ring-necked dove, introduced in 1975, has displaced some native birds. Three plant species – the casuarina or Australian pine, Brazilian pepper and bottlebrush trees – have become established in certain areas, replacing local vegetation.

The Bahamas is a signatory to the Convention on Trade in Endangered Species (CITES) and the Biodiversity Convention. Several acts directly or indirectly protect native species. These include:
- Agriculture and Fisheries Act.
- Wild Bird Protection Act.
- Wild Animal Protection Act.
- Fisheries Resources (Jurisdiction and Conservation) Act.
- Plant Protection Act.
- Bahamas National Trust Act.

An extensive network of protected areas has been designated. This includes wild bird reserves managed by the Dept of Agriculture and national parks managed by the Bahamas National Trust (BNT).

BNT plays an integral role in protecting Bahamian plants and animals primarily through its involvement in protecting threatened habitats. Its major national park is in Inagua, where it maintains the largest breeding colony of West Indian flamingos in the western hemisphere. This colourful and unusual bird is the Bahamian national bird.

Plants, trees & mangroves
The Bahamas has over 1,370 species of plants, and 121 of these are not found anywhere else in the world. Common plants include the Bahamian pine, mahogany, lignum vitae, sea grapes, orchids, guinep, pigeon plum, guana berry, bay geranium and the night-blooming cereus, a large cactus. There are also three mangrove species – black, white and red. The most northerly islands of The Bahamas are dominated by the Caribbean pine, whereas the southeast islands are

dominated by hardwood coppice and have distinctly xerophytic vegetation in places.

Trees: African tulip *(Spathodea campanulata)*, Australian pine *(Casuarina)*, bead tree *(Adenanthera pavonina)*, black mangrove *(Avicennia germinans)*, bottle brush *(Callistemon)*, buttercup tree *(Cochlospermum vitifolii)*, butterfly flower *(Bauhinia)*, buttonwood *(Conocarpus erectus)*, calabash *(Crescentia cujete)*, cancer tree *(Jacaranda coerulea)*, cedar *(Cedrela odorata)*, cork tree *(Thespesia populnea)*, dogwood *(Piscidia piscipula)*, Dutchman's pipe *(Ilex cassine)*, rubber tree *(Ficus elastica)*, five fingers (poui) *(Tabebouia bahamensis)*, frangipani *(Plumeria)*, golden shower *(Cassia fistula)*, gumelemi (gumbo-limbo) *(Bursera simaruba)*, horseflesh *(Caesalpinia vesicaria)*, horse radish *(Moringa oleifera)*, hummingbird trumpet *(Tabebuia)*, Jerusalem thorn *(Parkinsonia aculeata)*, jumbie bean (jumbey) *(Leucaena glauca)*, lignum vitae (national tree) *(Guaiacum sanctum)*, manchineel *(Iley cassine)*, mangrove *(Rhyzophora mangle)*, milkberry (wild saffron) *(Bumelia americana)*, monkey fiddle *(Araucaria)*, shaving brush tree *(Pachira insignis)*, palms: coconut, date, fan, fishtail, pond top, royal, silver thatch *(Palmae)*, pain in back *(Trema lamarckiana)*, pine: Norfolk, island, yellow *(Pinus caribea)*, poisonwood *(Metopium toxiferum)*, poor man's orchid *(Bauhinia)*, pride of India *(Lagerstroemia speciosa)*, quicksilver *(Thouinia discolor)*, rose of Venezuela *(Brownea grandiceps)*, Royal poinciana *(Delonix regia)*, sandbox *(Hura crepitans)*, satin leaf *(Chrysophyllum oliviforme)*, sea hibiscus *(Mahoe thespesia)*, wild mammee *(Clusia rosea)*, woman's tongue *(Albizzia lebbek)*, yellow elder (national flower of The Bahamas) *(Stenolobium stans)*.

Shrubs: Angel's trumpet *(Datura arborea)*, aralia *(Polyscias balfouriana)*, Bahamas blue pea *(Clitorea ternata)*, crepe myrtle *(Lagerstroemia indica)*, croton *(Codiaeum)*, four o'clock *(Mirabilis jalapa)*, gardenia *(Gardenia augusta)*, governor bailey *(Clerodendrum splendens)*, hibiscus *(Hibiscus)*, jasmine (Madagascar) *(Stephanotis floribunda)*, Joe bush *(Jacquinia)*, lucky seed *(Thevetiana peruviana)*, match-me-if-you-can *(Acalypha)*, natal plum *(Carissa grandiflora)*, oleander *(Nerium oleander)*, pearl necklace *(Sophora tomentosa)*, pigeon berry *(Duranta excelsa)*, plumbago *(Plumbago capensis)*, poinsettia *(Euphorbia pulcherrima)*, pride of Barbados *(Caesalpinia pulcherrima)*, sage *(Lantana)*, snowberry *(Chiococca alba)*, sea lavender *(Statice latifolia)*, shell ginger *(Alpinia speciosa)*, strong back *(Bourreria ovata)*, snakeroot (bitter bush) *(Picrodendron baccatum)*, sweet Margaret (guanaberry) *(Drypetes diversifolia)*, Turk's cap *(Malvaviscus arboreus)*, wild guava *(Catesbaea spinosa)*.

Climbers & vines: Allamanda *(Allamanda cathartica)*, bleeding heart *(Clerodendrum thomsonae)*, cereus (night blooming) *(Hylocereus undatus)*, chalice flower *(Solandra guttata)*, Christmas flower *(Turbina corymbosa)*, dipladenia *(Dipladenia amoena)*, honeysuckle *(Tecomaria capensis)*, love vine *(Cuscuta)*, Mexican flame vine *(Senecio confusus)*, moon flower *(Calonyction aculeatum)*, Pandora vine *(Podranea ricasoliana)*, paper flower *(Bougainvillaea)*, passion flower *(Passiflora)*, potato vine *(Solanum jasminum)*, queen's wreath *(Petrea)*, rangoon creeper *(Quis qualis indica)*, sky blue flower *(Thunbergia)*, stephanotis *(Stephanotis floribunda)*, Virginia creeper *(Parthenosissus quinquefolia)*, coral vine *(Antigonon leptopus)*, Easter lily vine *(Beaumontia grandiflora)*.

Grasses: Bamboo *(Bambusa)*, guinea grass *(Panicum maximum)*, sugar cane *(Saccharum officinarum)*.

Lilies: Aloe *(Aloe vera)*, century plant *(Agave americana)*, Spanish bayonet *(Yucca aloifolia)*.

Tuberous plants: Elephant's ear *(Caladium)*.

Succulents: Hummingbird cactus *(Pedilanthus tithymaloides)*, life-leaf *(Bryophyllum)*.

Cactus: Queen of the night *(Selenicereus grandiflorus)*.

Fruit trees: Avocado pear *(Persea americana)*, banana *(Musa spp)*, Barbados cherry *(Malpighia glabra)*, beach almond *(Terminalia catappa)*, breadfruit *(Artocarpus communis)*, cashew *(Anacardium occidentale)*, coconut *(Cocos nucifera)*, date *(Phoenix dactylifera)*, fig *(Ficus carica)*, governor's plum *(Flacourtia indica)*, grapes *(Vitis spp)*, grapefruit, tangerine, sour orange, lime, lemon, shaddock, calamondin *(Citrus spp)*, guava *(Psidium guajava)*, guinep *(Melicocca bijuga)*, kumquat *(Fortunella spp)*, longan *(Euphoria longan)*, loquat *(Eriobotrya japonica)*, lychee *(Litchi chinensis)*, mamey *(Mammea spp)*, mango *(Mangifera indica)*, natal plum *(Carissa grandiflora)*, papaya *(Carica papaya)*, passion fruit, granadilla *(Passiflora spp)*, peach *(Prunus persica)*, pineapple *(Ananas comosus)*, plantain *(Musa paradisiaca)*, sapodilla *(Achras zapota)*, sea grape *(Coccoloba uvifera)*, strawberry *(Fragaria spp)*, Suriname cherry *(Eugenia uniflora)*, soursop, custard apple, sugar apple *(Annona spp)*, tamarind *(Tamarindus indica)*, tung oil *(Aleurities fordii)*, pomegranate *(Punica granatum)*.

Fruit vines: Cantaloup, cucumber, musk melon, watermelon *(Cucumis)*.

Vegetables: Beans: red, lima, white *(Legumes)*, beetroot *(Beta vulgaris)*, breadfruit *(Artocarpus incisus)*, broccoli, Brussels sprout, cabbage *(Brassica olerace)*, carrot *(Daucus carota)*, cauliflower *(Brassica olerace botrytis)*, celery *(Apium graveiens)*, cho-cho *(Sechium edule)*, corn *(Zea mays)*, eddoe *(Colocasia esculenta)*, eggplant *(Solanum melongena)*, lettuce *(Lactuca sativa)*, okra *(Hibiscus esculentus)*, onion *(Allium cepa)*, peas: pigeon *(Cajanus indicus)*, sweet *(Pisum sativum)*, peppers: sweet, hot *(Capsicum)*, potato: Irish *(Solanum tuberosum)*, sweet *(Ipomoea batatas)*, pumpkin *(Amaranthus caudatus)*, squash *(Cucurbita pepo)*, Swiss chard *(Lactuca)*, tomato *(Lycopersicon esculentum)*, turnip *(Brassica rapa)*, watercress *(Lepidium sativum)*, yam *(Dioscorea)*.

Herbs: Basil *(Ocimum basilicum)*, chives *(Allium schoenoprasum)*, dill *(Peucedanum graveolens)*, parsley *(Petroselinum crispum)*, sage *(Salvia officinalis)*, thyme *(Thymus vulgaris)*.

See also **Animals; Bahamas Humane Society; Birds; Fishing;** and **Wildlife preserves.**

FORTS

Fort Charlotte, West Bay St, overlooking Clifford Park. Completed in 1789, this fort was built to guard the western entrance to Nassau Harbour. Visitors may tour the fort, which features the original dungeons.

Fort Fincastle, off East St, south of downtown Nassau. Completed in 1793, this ship-shaped structure is near the 126 ft water tower built in 1928 as a water supply reservoir. The water tower provides a superb view of the harbour and Nassau.

Fort Montagu, East Bay St. Completed in 1742 on the western point of Montagu foreshore, this fort was built to guard the eastern entrance to the harbour.

Fort Nassau. Built 1697 on the site now occupied by the British Colonial Hotel, Fort Nassau was destroyed within six years by a Spanish-French invasion. It was reconditioned in 1744, and finally razed in 1837 to make way for military barracks.

Remains of fortifications can be seen at Winton, Blue Hills, South West Bay, Old Fort, Potter's Cay and Paradise Island.

FREE TRADE AREA OF THE AMERICAS (FTAA)

At the Summit of The Americas in Dec 1994, Prime Minister the Rt Hon Hubert Ingraham, along with 33 other democratically-elected heads of state, signed a Declaration of Principles affirming the commitment of The Bahamas to negotiate a proposed Free Trade Area of the Americas (FTAA) by the year 2005. The free trade zone would stretch from Alaska to Argentina.

Principle objectives are promotion of prosperity through economic integration and establishment of a free trade area in which barriers to trade in goods and services and investment will be progressively eliminated by 2005. The Prime Minister has stated that efforts would be made to maintain the existing Bahamas tariff regime. Recently, The Bahamas reduced the number of tariff items from over 100 to less than 30, to simplify the process and further encourage investment. More than 50% of government revenues are derived from import duties.

The two major economic sectors in The Bahamas are services – tourism and finance – although there are exports of rum, pharmaceuticals, salt, aragonite and crawfish. However, the government has pledged to negotiate an agreement based on the individual interests of The Bahamas, and seeks to secure other benefits and concessions for these two sectors.

See also **Trade agreements**.

FREIGHT SERVICES

Goods to be sent as air freight from New Providence should be taken to Nassau Intl Airport for handling by the airline which will transport them or to a forwarding agent. Intl goods being exported require an export entry form.

Goods to be sent via ship should be taken to the shipping company or the dock, depending on company policy, or handled by a forwarding agent.

See **Export Entry** and **Shipping, Cargo shipping** and **Shipping agencies**.

Incoming freight

Freight not claimed at the dock or air cargo section within five working days is sent to a government warehouse. Storage rates are based on size. There is a charge for transporting goods to the warehouse. Goods not claimed within three months may be put up for auction.

GAMBLING

Casino gambling is legal in The Bahamas for non-residents 18 yrs and older. Bahamas residents are prohibited from gambling in the casinos under a max penalty of a $500 fine or six months' imprisonment. There are casinos at Cable Beach and Paradise Island, and in Freeport/Lucaya, Grand Bahama. All are owned by the government and leased to the present operators.

The Crystal Palace Casino is operated by Ruffin Leisure Industries. The Paradise Island casino is operated by Sun Intl Ltd. The Princess Casino in Freeport is operated by Princess Casinos Ltd, a subsidiary of Princess Properties Intl. The Lucayan Beach Casino located in Lucaya, is presently closed for renovations, and will re-open as part of The Lucayan resort development before the new millennium.

Games include roulette, blackjack, poker, baccarat, craps, slot machines, the wheel of fortune, the 'big six' and Caribbean stud poker.

A licence to operate a 1,000 sq ft casino at the Columbus Isle Club Med, San Salvador, has been approved but opening date has not yet been announced.

Sports betting

An Act to make provision for sports betting in The Bahamas was passed by Parliament in Oct 1995. The Act, amending the Lotteries and Gaming Act, allows for placing bets on any athletic game or sport other than horse racing that takes place within or outside The Bahamas.

Sports betting cannot, however, be conducted by telephone or other telecommunicative device, nor on behalf of another person.

The Bahamas offers two full service Las Vegas-style sports books at the Nassau Marriott Resort & Crystal Palace Casino in Cable Beach, New Providence, tel 327-6200 ext 6882, and Bahamas Princess Casino in Grand Bahama, tel (242) 352-7811.

Cruise ship gaming
The Cruise Ships (Overnighting Incentives) Act, 1995, allows cruise ships docked at the Prince George Dock for at least 18 hours, or travelling to or from Bahamian designated ports, to operate casinos 7pm-3am. The ship must have made no less than 20 voyages a year from outside the country to one of the designated ports – Great Harbour Cay, Rock Sound or Nassau – and must arrive at the Prince George Dock no later than 11am and depart no earlier than 3am the following day.

Eleven lines are licensed to operate casinos at the Bahamian designated ports: Carnival, Celebrity Cruises, Costa, Cunard Line/Seabourn, Dolphin/Majesty, Holland America, Norwegian, Premier, Princess Cruises, Royal Caribbean and Royal Majesty.

Bahamian residents or anyone gainfully employed in The Bahamas may not participate in cruise ship gaming unless employed by the licensee or operator of the casino, and gaming is within the course of their employment.

Ships failing to comply with the guidelines and regulations set out in the Act may be fined $1,000-$20,000.

See also **Entertainment** and **Lotteries**.

GEOGRAPHY
The Bahamas comprises a 100,000 sq mile archipelago that extends over 500 miles between southeast Florida and northern Hispaniola; between longitudes 72°35'W and 80°30'W and latitudes 20°50'N and 27°30'N.

The waters surrounding The Bahamas are virtually free of pollution and silt, making them among the clearest and most colourful in the world. Bordered on the west by the great "ocean river" known as the Gulf Stream, the islands have a near-perfect climate. Highest land elevation is 206 ft.

Some of the deepest water in the world is in the Tongue of the Ocean (TOTO) east of Andros and flanked by the world's third longest barrier reef. More than one mile deep, these waters are utilized for oceanographic research by scientists of the Atlantic Undersea Testing and Evaluation Centre (AUTEC), a multi million dollar joint US-UK research base. See **Atlantic Undersea Testing & Evaluation Centre (AUTEC)**.

The estimated land area of The Bahamas has been listed as 5,382 sq miles by the Dept of Lands and Surveys. Grand total for all land, including small uninhabited rocks and islets, is approx 5,400 sq miles. Figures are subject to change as more accurate surveys and maps are completed.

Modern mapping techniques are allowing advances in re-measuring the islands, some of which have suffered considerable loss of coastline due to erosion and man-made features, while there is some accretion to others. See **Fig 1.7** for land area of islands and their highest point.

GOLF COURSES
See **Sports** and **Freeport/Lucaya information, Golf courses**.

GOVERNMENT
See **Government section**.

GOVERNORS
Proprietary Governors
1670	Hugh Wentworth
1671	John Wentworth
1676	Charles Chillingsworth
1677	Capt Robert Clarke
1682	Robert Lilburne
1687	Thomas Bridges
1688	Lieut Governor Stede
1689	Cadwallader Jones
1693	Nicholas Trott
1696	Nicholas Webb
1699	Read Elding
1700	Elias Hasket

FIG 1.7
LAND AREA OF ISLANDS & THEIR HIGHEST POINT

Island	Highest point (ft)	Area (sq miles)	Island	Highest point (ft)	Area (sq miles)
Abaco	120	649	Inagua (Lt)	99	49
Acklins	142	150	Little San Salvador	93	8
Andros	102	2,300	Long Cay	108	9
Berry Isl	80	12	Long Isl	178	173
Bimini	20	9	Mayaguana	131	110
Cat Isl	206	150	New Providence	123	80
Cay Sal Bank	10	2	Plana Cays	63	6
Conception Isl	66	4	Ragged Isl	116	9
Crooked Isl	155	92	Rum Cay	130	30
Eleuthera	168	200	San Salvador	123	63
Exuma (Gt & Lt)	125	72	Samana Cay	80	15
Exuma Cays	130	40	Other cays	–	24
Grand Bahama	68	530			
Inagua (Gt)	120	596	**Total (sq miles):**		**5,382**

1701	Ellis Lightfoot		1882	Sir C C Lees, KCMG
1703	Edward Birch		1884	Sir H A Blake, KCMG
1716	Roger Mosteyn		1887	Sir Ambrose Shea, KCMG
			1895	Sir William F Haynes-Smith, KCMG

Royal Governors

1717	Woodes Rogers		1898	Sir G T Carter, KCMG
1721	George Phenny		1904	Sir William Grey-Wilson, KCMG
1728	Woodes Rogers		1912	Sir George Haddon-Smith, KCMG
1733	Richard Fitzwilliam			
1738	John Tinker		1914	Sir William L Allardyce, KCMG
1759	Maj-Gen William Shirley		1920	Maj Sir Harry Cordeaux, KCMG, CB
1767	Gen Sir Thomas Shirley, Bt			
1774	Montfort Browne		1926	Sir C W J Orr, KCMG
1779	John Maxwell		1932	The Hon Sir Bede Clifford, KCMG, CB, MVO
1787	Earl of Dunmore			
1797	William Dowdeswell		1936	The Hon Sir Charles Dundas, KCMG, OBE
1801	John Halkett			
1804	Charles Cameron		1940	HRH The Duke of Windsor, KG, Kt, KP, GCB, GCSI, GCMG, GCIE, GCVO, GBE, ISO, MC
1820	Gen Sir Lewis Grant			
1829	Sir J C Smyth			
1835	Lieut Col W M G Colebrook			
1837	Sir F Cockburn		1945	Sir William L Murphy, KCMG
1844	George B Matthew		1950	Sir George Sandford, KBE, CMG
1849	John Gregory		1951	Maj-Gen Sir Robert A R Neville, KCMG, CBE, RM
1854	Sir A Bannerman			
1857	Charles John Bayley, CB		1953	Rt Hon Earl of Ranfurly, KCMG
1864	Sir Rawson W Rawson, CB		1957	Sir Raynor Arthur, KCMG, CVO
1869	Sir James Walker, KCMG, CB		1960	Sir Robert de Stapeldon Stapledon, KCMG, CBE
1871	Sir G C Strachan, RA, KCMG			
1873	Sir John Pope-Hennessy, KCMG		1964	Sir Ralph Grey (later Lord Grey of Naunton), GCMG, KCVO, OBE
1874	Sir W Robinson, KCMG			
1880	T F Callaghan, CMG			

1968   Sir Francis Cumming-Bruce
        (later Lord Thurlow), KCMG
1972   Sir John Warburton Paul,
        GCMG, OBE, MC
        (to July 9, 1973)

Governor-Generals from independence – July 10, 1973
See **Government section**.

Honours & Decorations

Bt	Baronet
CB	Companion of the Bath
CBE	Commander of the British Empire
CMG	Companion of St Michael and St George
CVO	Commander of the Royal Victorian Order
GBE	Knight (or Dame) Grand Cross of the British Empire
GCB	Knight Grand Cross of the Bath
GCIE	Knight Grand Commander of the Indian Empire
GCMG	Knight Grand Cross of St Michael and St George
GCSI	Knight Grand Commander of the Star of India
GCVO	Knight Grand Cross of the (Royal) Victorian Order
ISO	Imperial Service Order
JP	Justice of the Peace
KBE	Knight Commander of the British Empire
KCMG	Knight Commander of St Michael and St George
KCVO	Knight Commander of the Royal Victorian Order
KG	Knight of the Garter
KP	Knight of St Patrick
Kt	Knight
MC	Military Cross
MVO	Member of the Royal Victorian Order
OBE	Officer of the British Empire
QC	Queen's Counsel
RA	Royal Army
RM	Royal Marine

GROSS DOMESTIC & GROSS NATIONAL PRODUCTS (GDP/GNP)
See **Economy**.

GUN PERMITS

The Firearms Act, 1969 (amended '74, '89 and '94), sets out government policy on firearms, establishes comprehensive procedures for controlling their possession by private individuals, and states fees payable.

Under the Act, there are three licence categories: revolvers, rifles and guns. Revolvers include all handguns including magazine-fed selfloaders, commonly called automatics, and cylinder-fed revolvers. Rifles apply to rimfire and centrefire shoulder arms. Guns mean smooth bore guns such as shotguns with barrels not less than 20 ins in length. Air guns and air rifles are prohibited weapons.

Completely forbidden are tear-gas pens, military arms such as artillery, flame-throwers, machine guns and automatic carbines. Exempt from any licensing requirements are toy guns, dummy firearms and spear guns designed for underwater use.

Licensing procedures for each of the three legal firearms categories are:

Revolvers
A special licence, granted sparingly, is issued by the Commissioner of Police. A person wishing to import or possess a revolver must fill out an application form. A reason considered acceptable by police must be given for possession of a handgun and must be verified by police investigation before the special licence is issued. The licence is then carried to Customs or parcel post if the revolver is being imported, or to the dealer if it is being purchased locally. Revolvers or pistols being imported are subject to a Customs charge of $50 plus 50% of their value.

Rifles, other firearms & ammunition

An application form for the issue of a firearm certificate must be completed and submitted to the Commissioner of Police. A separate application must be made for each firearm and each quantity of ammunition. Presentation of the certificate and payment of duty, if an import, will bring the rifle, firearm or ammunition into possession.

Guns

An application for a gun licence is made to the Commissioner of Police in New Providence, or to the administrator of a Family Island district. A separate application must be made for each gun. Presentation of the gun licence and payment of duty, if an import, will bring the gun into possession.

Fees

Gun licences issued under the Act cost $50. Rifle licences cost $100. A revolver requires a special licence costing $250. All must be renewed annually. A dealer's licence costs $250, and the licence expires on the yearly anniversary of the date of issue. Replacement of a lost certificate, special licence or licence costs $5.

Temporary importation

Temporary importation of guns (excluding handguns) must be authorized by the Police Commissioner.

Exemption

Non-residents of The Bahamas visiting aboard a foreign vessel are not required to obtain permits or pay any fees or duty on firearms during the visit. This exemption is limited to three months following the arrival of the vessel at her first port of call. Conditions are:
1. Possession of firearms aboard the vessel must be declared to a Customs officer or an administrator within 48 hours of arrival.
2. The firearms are not used in the territorial waters of The Bahamas.
3. They are not brought ashore.

A note of caution

Any person introducing a revolver into The Bahamas or found in possession of a revolver in contravention of the Act is liable to a $10,000 fine and:
1. On conviction on information to imprisonment for a term of not less than three years.
2. On summary conviction before a Stipendiary and Circuit Magistrate to imprisonment for a term of not less than two years.

Similarly strict measures are applied to persons found with any other firearms or ammunition without a licence as detailed under the Act.

Although not a provision of the law, the police recommend that all applicants for the possession of firearms ensure there is a safe place to deposit firearms and ammunition. Stolen firearms may be used to perpetrate crime.

HARBOUR CONTROL

Nassau Harbour Control regulates and gives clearance to all ships entering and leaving Nassau Harbour. Permission must be obtained from Harbour Control for the movement from one berth to another while in the harbour. The office operates 24 hours.

Small fishing boat or small pleasure craft users should telephone Harbour Control at 322-1596 before leaving the harbour so the whereabouts of these vessels can be ascertained if late or overdue.

The VHF radio frequencies of Harbour Control are: Channels 06, 09, 12, 14, 16, 20, 65, 66, 68, 73, 74 and 79. The Bahamas Telecommunications Corp (BaTelCo) maintains a constant watch on VHF Channel 16, the emergency frequency. For commercial traffic, VHF Channel 27 should be used through the Nassau marine operator.

AM radio ship-to-ship frequencies are 2182, 2638 and 2738 kHz, however, 2638 and 2738 have been phased out, and cannot be re-licensed. They should be used only in emergencies. The international emergency frequency, 2182 kHz, is controlled by BaTelCo. For commercial traffic, AM frequency 2198 should be used. Single sideband frequencies are 3300.0, 4139.5, 5057.0, 8100.0.

HEALTH/MEDICAL SERVICES
See **AIDS/HIV; Ambulance/air ambulance services; Bahamas Family Planning Assoc; Dentists; Doctors; Hospitals & clinics; Public health;** and **Vaccination requirements.**

HISTORY
Before recorded history, what was to become The Bahamas was inhabited by Aborigines of Mongol descent. Their roots dated to the first great migration from the Old World to the New.

During the last Ice Age up to 100,000 years ago, ancestors of the original Bahamians came to the Americas by way of a land bridge that once linked Alaska with Siberia.

Lucayans, the Amerindians here when Columbus arrived on Oct 12, 1492, were part of what is called the Neolithic Revolution. The word *Lucayan* comes from *Lukku-Cairi*, or *Island People*. They were excellent farmers, good potters, weavers of cotton fibres, expert divers and skilled navigators in dugout canoes of their own invention. Only recently have their community sites been excavated and their artefacts retrieved from caves sometimes used as sacred burial vaults.

In April 1995, late Blue Holes Foundation director Rob Palmer discovered a 500-year-old ceremonial Lucayan canoe in an Andros blue hole, the oldest artefact found in the region at that time.

At press time, the age was being verified of thousands of artefacts, bones and fossils unearthed in July 1997 at the site of a former Lucayan Indian settlement near Deadman's Reef, Grand Bahama.

Important dates in the past 506 years of Bahamian history are:

1492: New World discoverer Christopher Columbus landed first at a Bahamian island called Guanahani. He renamed it San Salvador, Castilian for Holy Saviour.

1625: French settlers made an unsuccessful effort to colonize what was created as a Barony of the Bahamas. When a supply ship arrived from France, no trace of the first colony could be found.

1628: A treasure-laden Spanish galleon believed to have been captured by Dutch freebooter Piet Heyn sank just off Lucaya, Grand Bahama. In 1964, an estimated $2.8 million in treasure was recovered from the ancient wreck.

1647: The Company of Eleutherian Adventurers, a Pilgrim group, founded the first republic in the New World. Its purpose was to colonize the depopulated Bahama Islands and claim them for Great Britain. The colonists arrived in 1648 and took over an island the Amerindians called Cigatoo. It was renamed Eleuthera, after the Greek word for freedom.

1656: A Spanish galleon with treasure estimated to be worth more than $2 billion sank in the Little Bahama Bank. Captain Herbert Humphreys began salvaging the *Nuestra Señora de las Maravillas* in the late 1980s and announced his most recent find in '91.

1670: Six Lords Proprietors of South Carolina were granted the Bahama Islands by King Charles II of England.

1695: Lords Proprietors authorized construction of a fort and city on the island of New Providence. The city, called Charles Towne in honour of King Charles II, was renamed Nassau. The new name honoured King William III, formerly Prince of Orange-Nassau.

1697: Fort Nassau was completed on the site now occupied by the British Colonial Beach Resort. Artefacts are on display at the resort.

1717: Captain Woodes Rogers was named first Royal Governor of the Bahama Islands. He restored order by ending the rule of pirates and paved the way for a representative Assembly.

1729: The Bahamas House of Assembly first officially convened. The House has met in the west building of Parliament on Bay St since 1805.

1741: Construction of Fort Montagu began at the eastern entrance to Nassau Harbour. Completed in 1742, it still stands as a tourist site.

1776: Eight American Colonial warships captured Fort Montagu and Fort Nassau for a short period. This is believed to be the first foreign occupation by the US. In 1778, Americans again invaded.

1782: Spaniards, irked by pirate and privateer raids on their shipping, re-captured the Bahama Islands.

1783: The Bahama Islands were restored to Great Britain by treaty. Andrew Deveaux, a Loyalist from South Carolina who was unaware of the agreement, seized the islands in the name of the crown.

The immigration of American Loyalists began. Many brought their slaves and set up a plantation economy. A cotton blight was later to wipe out this lifestyle. Ruins of old plantation homes dot the Bahama Islands to this day.

1789: Completion of the main portion of Fort Charlotte overlooking the western entrance to Nassau Harbour. This major tourist attraction was restored in 1993 at a cost of $1 million.

1793: Fort Fincastle, shaped like a paddle-wheel steamer, was built at one of New Providence Island's highest points. Today, a water tower nearby serves as a favourite lookout for visitors and residents.

1838: Slavery was fully abolished. Agriculture declined. Wrecking, controlled by licences, flourished until the Imperial Board of Trade dotted the islands with lighthouses. Some are still in operation, with Abaco's candy-striped Hope Town lighthouse the most revered and photographed.

1861-65: The American Civil War brought great wealth to Nassau, a major supply base for the Confederacy. Nassau's first resort hotel, the Royal Victoria, was built.

1892: The first Florida to Nassau telegraph submarine cable was laid and began operations. It came ashore at what is now called Cable Beach.

1898: Nassau was officially developed as a fashionable winter season resort with the Hotel and Steam Ship Service Act.

1914: John Ernest Williamson shot the first undersea motion picture in history. Since then, many films have used Bahamian locations, including the James Bond classic, *Thunderball*. In 1996, *Zeus and Roxanne* was filmed in Grand Bahama starring Steve Guttenberg and dolphins from the Underwater Explorers Society (UNEXSO).

1920: US prohibition of alcoholic beverages brought a boom to the Bahama Islands, where liquor was legal and plentiful.

1930s: Famous writers came to live and work in The Bahamas, among them Ernest Hemingway, Zane Grey and John Steinbeck.

1940: A destroyers-for-bases agreement between the US and UK led to establishment of bases at Grand Bahama, Eleuthera, San Salvador and Mayaguana. They were to play a major role in the early days of the Space Age when missile tracking stations were set up on Bahama bases.

1942-45: Nassau became a Royal Air Force Training Base and western bastion of an "air bridge" which ferried aircraft to World War II war zones.

1950: Nassau, aided and abetted by the 1940s governorship of the fashionable Duke of Windsor, joined front ranks as a year-round resort.

1955: Signing of the Hawksbill Creek Agreement, which paved the way to establish Freeport/Lucaya as the second-largest city in the country.

1962: Universal suffrage granted; Bahamian women voted for the first time.

1964: The Colony gained internal self-government. The late Sir Roland Symonette was named Premier. Leader of the Opposition was Lynden O

Pindling, head of the Progressive Liberal Party (PLP).

1966: The first bridge connecting New Providence to Paradise Island was built. Another was due to be completed in Dec 1998.

1967: The PLP won the majority of House of Assembly seats and Pindling became the new Premier.

1969: Constitution revised. The Colony of the Bahama Islands became a Commonwealth; Pindling became Prime Minister.

1973: The Bahama Islands became the free and sovereign Commonwealth of The Bahamas on July 10, ending 325 years of British rule.

1990: The $300-million Crystal Palace Resort and Casino, Cable Beach, formally opened, launching a new era of mega-resorts in The Bahamas.

The International Business Companies (IBC) Act became law, crystallizing The Bahamas' reputation as a top offshore financial centre.

1991: Multi-million-dollar expansion programme effected major seaport and airport improvements in Nassau, Freeport and the Family Islands.

1992: The opposition Free National Movement (FNM) was voted in as the new government Aug 19, ending the Progressive Liberal Party (PLP)'s 25-year rule. The Rt Hon Hubert A Ingraham became Prime Minister.

The Bahamas celebrated the 500th anniversary of the landing of Columbus at Guanahani/San Salvador.

1994: Official fifth Bahamas tour of Her Majesty, Queen Elizabeth II, constitutional Bahamas head of state represented by the Governor-General. While in The Bahamas, the Queen officially opened the Bahamas Tourism Training Centre, Nassau, and the Garnet Levarity Justice Centre, Freeport.

1995: Tricentennial of the city of Nassau, which was officially named on April 12, 1695.

Sun Intl Hotels Ltd, of South Africa, opened the Atlantis, Paradise Island resort and casino, complete with a legendary waterscape featuring the world's largest outdoor aquarium and shark collection.

Large scale improvements to Prince George Wharf, Bay St and downtown Nassau included a makeover of the historic Parliament buildings and Government House.

1996: At the Atlanta Centennial Olympics, The Bahamas track and field team won the silver medal in the women's 4x100m relay.

Security officer Alfred Rolle became the first Bahamian inducted into the World Martial Arts Hall of Fame. Mark Knowles became the first Bahamian to reach the top 10 rankings in tennis, and teamed with Canadian Daniel Nestor to rank fourth in the world in doubles.

The Bahamas' first execution in 12 years took place with the hanging of Thomas Reckley, 44.

1997: The Free National Movement (FNM) was voted in for a second term on Mar 14.

The first female Speaker of the House, The Hon Rome Italia Johnson, was appointed.

The $78 million Freeport Container Port was officially opened, transforming Freeport into a major world transshipment centre.

1998: Construction on Royal Towers at Atlantis, including 1,208 new rooms, a 50,000 sq ft casino, additional water features and convention space was scheduled for completion by the end of the year. The Marina at Atlantis and the new bridge linking Nassau and Paradise Island were also to be completed in 1998.

Implosion of the Atlantic Beach Hotel in Lucaya, GB, kicked off construction on The Lucayan, a Harbour Plaza Resort, scheduled to open by the new millennium.

The Bahamas celebrated its 25th anniversary of independence on July 10.

The direction of traffic flow on Bay and Shirley Sts was reversed to reduce congestion and streamline traffic routes.

See also **Archives** and **Bahamas Historical Society.**

HOLIDAYS
The following public holidays are observed in The Bahamas:
- New Year's Day
- Good Friday
- Easter Monday
- Whit Monday
  (seven weeks after Easter)
- Labour Day (first Fri in June)
- Independence Day (July 10)
- Emancipation Day
  (first Mon in Aug)
- Discovery Day (Oct 12)
- Christmas Day (Dec 25)
- Boxing Day (Dec 26)

Holidays which fall on Sat or Sun are usually observed on the previous Fri or following Mon. Stores in New Providence and most Family Islands are closed on holidays.

HOSPITALS & CLINICS
Princess Margaret Hospital: Shirley St, Nassau, 436 beds. Acute care hospital. Government operated with private wards accommodating all major specialities. Specialist services include: medical, surgical, paediatrics, obstetrics and gynaecology, oncology, cardiovascular, neurology, urology, nephrology, opthamology, dental, radiology and psychiatry. Ambulatory care facilities include: intensive care unit, neonatal intensive care unit, accident and emergency, general practice, speciality clinics, dialysis unit, burns unit, physiotherapy, occupational therapy and speech therapy.

Diagnostics and other allied health services include: stat lab, general laboratory with blood bank, radiology with mammography, diagnostic imaging, EKG and pharmacy services. Chief medical officer: Dr Merceline Dahl-Regis, Ministry of Health Headquarters, tel 322-7425. Hospital administrator Andil LaRoda, tel 325-0048.

Doctors Hospital: Corner of Shirley St and Collins Ave. Acute care, privately-operated hospital with 72 patient beds. Medical specialities are emergency medicine; ear, nose and throat; general surgery; orthopaedic surgery; obstetrics and gynaecology; ophthalmology; internal medicine; family medicine; gastroenterology; urology; cardiology; cardiovascular surgery and paediatrics. There are three operating rooms, one with laminar flow; intensive care unit with eight beds; maternity suite with 14 beds, nuclear medicine, electroencephalography. Emergency doctors are on the premises 24 hours a day, seven days a week. All staff in the ER are ACLS (Advanced Cardiac Life Support) certified. Ancillary depts: clinical laboratory, blood bank, radiology (x-ray, ultrasound, mammography, MRI and CT scans), pharmacy, ECG, diet and nutrition counselling, physical therapy, cardiac catheterization and comprehensive rehabilitation. The medical staff comprises most physicians in private practice. Chief executive officer Barry Rassin, FACHE, tel 322-8411.

Sandilands Rehabilitation Centre: Fox Hill Rd. Government owned. Comprises the 130-bed **Geriatric Hospital** and the 352-bed **Sandilands Psychiatric Hospital**.

Sandilands Psychiatric Hospital: Built in 1956 to accommodate, treat and rehabilitate patients with mental illnesses and substance abuse related problems so they may return to their respective communities. The hospital includes a max security unit, Timothy O McCartney child and adolescent unit, lignum vitae (drug) unit, detox and evaluation unit, Brian Humblestone alcoholic unit and day hospital facilities. Services for rehabilitation include special education, recreational therapy, occupational therapy, psychological evaluation and social services.

The hospital also provides a child guidance day care programme, a half-way house for long stay patients and psychiatric out-patient care at Princess Margaret Hospital.

The Geriatric Hospital: Established in 1965 to provide comprehensive medical and nursing care to elderly patients who are chronically ill and unable to be cared for at home or in any other community facility. The hospital is staffed by a consultant, medical officer, podiatrist, qualified dentists and team of nurses.

Other depts include physical therapy, occupational therapy, food services, pharmaceutical services, small laboratory services and social services. An out-patient gerontology clinic is located at the Ann's Town clinic. Hospital administrator: Herbert Brown, tel 324-6881 or 324-1553.

The Lyford Cay Hospital/ Bahamas Heart Institute: Lyford Cay, 12 in-hospital beds, including three-bed coronary care unit and four-bed telemetry unit. There is also an operating theatre, x-ray and laboratory as well as an emergency room with a doctor on call 24 hours. Specialist treatment is offered in cardiology, internal medicine and family practice. Echocardiography, stress echocardiography, transtelephonic ECG, peripheral vascular ultrasound, holter monitoring, exercise stress testing, enhanced extracorporeal counter pulsation (EECP), recompression chamber/hyperbaric oxygen therapy, colposcopy and cryosurgery, are also available. The hospital is also the home of the Bahamas Hyperbaric Centre, the only recompression facility for dive-related injuries in New Providence. The full-time cardiologist is also on the staff of the Cleveland Clinic, Ft Lauderdale, FL; Duke Medical Center, Durham, NC and the Miami Heart Institute, Miami Beach, FL. The hospital is affiliated with all three institutions. Tel 362-4025.

Stat Care Medical & Emergency Centre: Nassau and Delancy Sts. The first free-standing health care facility designed exclusively to provide comprehensive emergency services in The Bahamas. The centre offers on-site consultation with board-certified speciality physicians. If requested, the patient can be admitted directly to the tertiary care facility as an in-patient. Specialists are on call in obstetrics, gynaecology, urology, cardiology, nephrology, rheumatology, general surgery, orthopaedic surgery, paediatrics, family medicine, general medicine, internal medicine and neurosurgery.

The facility is open daily 8am-11pm, including weekends and holidays, tel 328-5596/8.

Family Island clinics
The Ministry of Health operates 116 clinics of varying size, complexity and scope of services. In cases where more medical assistance is needed, patients are flown to Princess Margaret Hospital in Nassau. Visitors needing medical assistance in the northern Bahamas may receive coverage from the Rand Memorial Hopital, Grand Bahama.

Other services
Community and environmental health services are offered throughout The Bahamas. A bachelor's and an associate degree programme in nursing are offered through the College of The Bahamas. There is also a basic course in clinical or practical nursing and six post-basic courses. A nursing cadet programme was implemented by the Ministry of Health in 1996.

HOTELS

See **Fig 1.8** for hotel listings. Only hotels with 20 rooms or more are listed for New Providence, Paradise Island and Grand Bahama, although smaller hotels and guest houses are available. Generally, Family Island hotels listed here have 15 rooms or more. Hotels with fewer rooms are available at:
Abaco: Elbow Cay, Green Turtle Cay, Man-O-War Cay, Marsh Harbour, Sandy Point, Spanish Cay and Wood Cay.
Acklins: Spring Point.
Andros: Blanket Sound, Cargill Creek, Fresh Creek, Kemps Bay, Mangrove Cay, Nicholl's Town, North Andros, Staniard Creek.
Berry Islands: Great Harbour Cay.
Bimini: Alice Town, Bailey Town, South Bimini.

Cat Island: Fernandez Bay, New Bight, Orange Creek, Port Howe.
Crooked Island: Cabbage Hill, Colonel Hill, Landrail Point.
Eleuthera: Dunmore Town, Governor's Harbour, Gregory Town, Harbour Island, Rock Sound, Spanish Wells, Tarpum Bay, Upper Bogue.
Exuma: George Town, Staniel Cay.
Grand Bahama: Deep Water Cay, West End.
Inagua: Matthew Town.
Long Island: Stella Maris, Thompson Bay.
Mayaguana: Abraham's Bay.

Contact the Ministry of Tourism, Nassau, tel 322-7500.

See also **Accommodations.**

HOTELS ENCOURAGEMENT

The Bahamas, with tourism as its No 1 industry, gives special encouragement to private capital for building hotels and resorts throughout the country.

The Hotels Encouragement Act provides Customs duty exemptions on materials imported to construct and equip hotels, as well as tax guarantees and concessions for improvement of guest facilities.

Investors must apply in writing to the Office of the Prime Minister, citing details of the proposed hotel or residential club, amenities, estimated cost and proposed plans for location and building(s). A project application form must be filed with the Ministry of Finance and Planning and plans submitted to the Dept of Physical Planning for land use approval. Plans must also be approved by the Dept of Public Health and Ministry of Public Works.

The government then may enter into an agreement with the investor to be exempt from Customs duties on materials imported to construct, extend, equip, furnish or complete the hotel.

Upon approval, the investor may also import duty free the construction plant to construct, extend, equip, furnish and complete the new facility.

The exemption active dates are decided upon by government.

The new facility is exempt from real property taxes and any other taxes hereafter imposed on real property for 10 years from the date the new hotel opens. There is further exemption from real property taxes in excess of $20 for every bedroom in the hotel for the second 10 years of operation.

Hotel earnings, or rental paid for lease or sub-lease, are exempt from direct taxation for 20 years from the opening date. If the investor or operator is a company, there is an exemption from direct tax "on or against dividends declared in respect of its indebtedness" for the same 20-year period.

Existing hotels and new hotels may be rehabilitated, remodelled, air-conditioned or extended, and exemption from payment of Customs duty may be obtained on materials imported for such alterations by applying in writing to the Permanent Secretary, Office of the Prime Minister, stating nature, extent, and estimated cost of the alterations in order to obtain approval in principle from government. This approval in principle must be obtained prior to purchases if the investor wishes to receive exemption from payment of Customs duty.

To obtain these concessions, a new hotel in New Providence must have at least 20 bedrooms and suitable public rooms for the accommodation and entertainment of guests. A new hotel on the other islands must have at least five bedrooms.

These concessions apply to all amenities offered in conjunction with the hotel: golf courses, marinas, harbours, roads, airfields, etc.

Contact the Office of the Prime Minister, PO Box N-7147, Nassau, The Bahamas, tel (242) 327-5826, fax (242) 327-5806.

See also **Customs** and **Investing.**

HUNTING
See **Birds.**

FIG 1.8
HOTELS

Hotel/location	No of rooms	Beach/water-front	Pool	Tennis	Golf[1]	Diving[1]	Tel (242)	Fax (242)
New Providence								
Astoria Hotel, Nassau & West Bay Sts	70	√	√	x	x	√	322-8666	322-8660
British Colonial Beach Resort, No 1 Bay St	174	√	√	√	x	√	322-3301	322-2286
Casuarinas of Cable Beach	78	√	√	√	x	√	327-7921	327-8152
City Lodge, Okra Hill	42	x	√	x	x	x	394-2591	394-3636
Colony Club Resort, St Albans Dr	96	x	√	x	x	x	325-4824	325-1240
The Corner Hotel, Carmichael Rd & Faith Ave	25	x	x	x	x	x	361-7445	361-7448
El Greco Hotel, Augusta & West Bay Sts	27	√	√	x	x	√	325-1121	325-1124
Grand Central Hotel, Charlotte St	35	x	x	x	x	x	322-8356	325-2018
Guanahani Village,[2] Cable Beach	35	√	√	√	x	√	327-7568	327-8311
Harbour Moon Hotel, Bay & Deveaux Sts	30	x	x	x	x	x	323-7330	328-0374
Island Outpost (cottages), Compass Point, Love Beach	19	√	√	√	x	√	327-4500	327-3299
Lyford Cay Club, Lyford Cay	clubhouses 47 cottages 20	√	√	√	√	√	362-4271	362-5277
The Montagu Beach Inn Hotel, Village Rd & Shirley St	33	x	√	x	x	x	393-0475	393-6061
Nassau Beach Hotel, Cable Beach	411	√	√	√	x	√	327-7711	327-8829
Nassau Harbour Club, East Bay St	50	√	√	x	x	x	393-0771	393-5393

Hotel/Location	No of rooms	Beach/water-front	Pool	Tennis	Golf[1]	Diving[1]	Tel (242)	Fax (242)
Nassau Marriott Resort & Crystal Palace Casino, Cable Beach	850	√	√	√	√	√	327-6200	327-6459
Ocean Spray Hotel, West Bay St	29	x	x	√	x	√	322-8032	325-5731
Orange Hill Beach Inn, West Bay St	32	√	√	x	x	√	327-7157	327-5186
The Orchard Hotel, Village Rd	28	x	√	x	x	√	393-1297	394-3562
Poinciana Inn, Bernard Rd	38	x	√	x	x	√	393-1897	394-1039
Radisson Cable Beach Golf Resort, Cable Beach	700	√	√	√	√	√	327-6000	327-6987
Red Carpet Inn, East Bay St	36	x	√	x	x	√	393-7981	393-9055
Sandals Royal Bahamian Hotel, Cable Beach	306	√	√	√	√	√	327-6400	327-6961
South Ocean Golf, Beach & Dive Resort,[2] Adelaide Rd	250	√	√	√	√	√	362-4391	362-4810
SuperClubs® Breezes, Cable Beach	391	√	√	√	√	√	327-5356	327-5155
Towne Hotel, George St	46	x	√	x	x	√	322-8450	328-1512
West Bay Beach Hotel	40	x	x	√	√	√	323-1000	326-5251

New Providence timeshare (no of villas not rooms)

Hotel/Location	No of rooms	Beach/water-front	Pool	Tennis	Golf[1]	Diving[1]	Tel (242)	Fax (242)
Guanahani Village, Cable Beach	35	√	√	√	x	√	327-5236	327-5059
South Ocean Golf, Beach & Dive Resort, Adelaide Rd	30	√	√	√	√	√	362-4391	362-4728
Westwind I Club, Cable Beach	21	√	√	√	√	√	327-7680	327-7251
Westwind II Club, Cable Beach	54	√	√	√	√	√	327-7211	327-7529

Hotel/Location	No of rooms	Beach/water-front	Pool	Tennis	Golf[1]	Diving[1]	Tel (242)	Fax (242)
Paradise Island								
Atlantis, Paradise Island Resort & Casino, Casino Dr	2,413	√	√	√	√	√	363-3000	363-3524
The Beach Tower, Casino Dr	455	√	√	√	√	√	363-3000	363-3724
Coral Towers, Casino Dr	692	√	√	√	√	√	363-3000	363-3524
The Ocean Club, Paradise Island Dr	58	√	√	√	√	√	363-3000	363-2424
Royal Towers	1,208	√	√	√	√	√	363-3000	–
Bay View Village, Bay View Dr	30	x	√	√	√	√	363-2555	363-2370
Club Land'or,[2] Paradise Beach Dr	72	√	√	√	√	√	363-2400	363-1198
Club Med, Casuarina Dr	300	√	√	√	√	√	363-2640	363-3496
Comfort Suites, Paradise Island Dr	150	x	√	√	√	√	363-3680	363-2588
Paradise Island Fun Club, Harbour Rd	250	√	√	√	√	√	363-2561	363-3803
Radisson Grand Resort Paradise Island, Casino Dr	360	√	√	√	√	√	363-2011	363-3900
Sunrise Beach Club & Villas,[2] Casino Dr	33	√	√	x	x	√	363-2234	363-2308
Yoga Retreat (by ferry)	54	√	x	√	x	x	363-2902	363-3783
Paradise Island timeshare (no of villas not rooms)								
Club Land'or, Paradise Beach Dr	72	√	√	√	√	√	363-2400	363-3403
Marriott's Paradise Island Beach Club, Ocean Ridge Dr	44	√	√	√	√	√	363-2814	363-2130
Paradise Harbour Club & Marina, Paradise Island Dr	22	√	√	x	√	√	363-2992	363-2840

Hotel/Location	No of rooms	Beach/waterfront	Pool	Tennis	Golf[1]	Diving[1]	Tel (242)	Fax (242)
Sunrise Beach Club & Villas, Casino Dr	33	√	√	x	x	√	363-2234	363-2308
Freeport, Grand Bahama								
Island Palm Resort, The Mall	150	x	√	x	√	√	352-6648	352-6640
Bahamas Princess Resort & Casino:								
Princess Country Club[2], The Mall & W Sunrise Hwy	565	x	√	√	√	√	352-6721	352-6842
Princess Towers, W Sunrise Hwy	400	x	√	√	√	√	352-9661	352-7142
Princess Vacation Club, Sunrise Hwy	98	x	√	√	√	√	352-6721 (ext 4541)	352-6842
Castaways Resort, The Mall & Intl Bazaar	130	x	√	x	√	√	352-6682	352-5087
Freeport Resort & Club,[2] Rum Cay Dr	49	x	√	√	√	√	352-5371	352-8425
Royal Islander, The Mall	100	x	√	x	√	√	351-6000	351-3546
The Running Mon Marina & Resort, 208 Kelly Ct & Knotts Blvd	32	√	√	x	x	√	352-6833	352-6835
Sun Club Resort, East Mall & Settlers Way	46	x	√	√	√	√	352-3462	352-5759
Xanadu Beach & Marina Resort,[2] Sunken Treasure Dr	179	√	√	√	x	√	352-6782	352-5799
Lucaya, Grand Bahama								
Bell Channel Inn, King's Rd	32	√	√	x	√	√	373-1053	373-2886
Club Fortuna Beach,[2] Doubloon Rd & Churchill Dr	204	√	√	√	√	√	373-4000	373-5594
The Lucayan, Royal Palm Way	1,600	under construction (Reef Village, The Breakers Cay, Lighthouse Point)					373-1333	373-2396
Reef Village		scheduled to open Feb 1999						

Hotel/Location	No of rooms	Beach/waterfront	Pool	Tennis	Golf[1]	Diving[1]	Tel (242)	Fax (242)
New Victoria Inn, Midshipman Rd & Victoria Pl	40	x	√	x	x	x	373-3040	373-3874
Pelican Bay at Lucaya, Royal Palm Way	48	√	√	x	x	√	373-9550	373-9551
Port Lucaya Resort & Yacht Club, Bell Channel Bay Rd	160	√	√	x	x	√	373-6618	373-6652
Redwood Motel, Bell Channel Rd & Royal Palm Way	28	x	√	x	√	√	373-7881	373-6154
Silver Sands Hotel, Royal Palm Way	80	x	√	√	x	x	373-5700	373-1039
Taino Beach Hotel & Yacht Club,[2] Jolly Roger Dr	67	√	√	√	√	√	373-5640	373-4421

Grand Bahama timeshare (no of villas not rooms)

Hotel/Location	No of rooms	Beach/waterfront	Pool	Tennis	Golf[1]	Diving[1]	Tel (242)	Fax (242)
Princess Vacation Club Intl, Princess Country Club, The Mall & W Sunrise Hwy, Freeport	96	x	√	√	√	x	352-6721 (ext 4541)	351-8042
Freeport Resort & Club, Rum Cay Dr, Freeport	49	x	√	√	√	√	352-5371	352-8425
Royal Holiday Club, Xanadu Beach & Marina Resort, Sunken Treasure Dr, Freeport	34	√	√	√	√	√	352-5843	352-5867
Taino Beach Resort Vacation Club, Jolly Roger Dr	42	√	√	√	√	√	373-4677	373-4421
Viva Vacation Club Club Fortuna Beach, Doubloon Rd & Churchill Dr	18	√	√	√	√	√	373-4000	373-8591

Abaco

Hotel/Location	No of rooms	Beach/waterfront	Pool	Tennis	Golf[1]	Diving[1]	Tel (242)	Fax (242)
Abaco Beach Resort & Boat Harbour, Queen Elizabeth Dr, Marsh Harbour	58	√	√	√	√	√	367-2158	367-2819
Abaco Inn, Hope Town	16	√	√	x	x	√	366-0133	366-0113

Hotel/Location	No of rooms	Beach/water-front	Pool	Tennis	Golf[1]	Diving[1]	Tel (242)	Fax (242)
Banyan Beach Club, Treasure Cay	23	√	√	x	√	√	365-8111	365-8112
Bluff House Beach Hotel, Green Turtle Cay	25	√	√	√	x	√	365-4247	365-4248
Different of Abaco/ Great Abaco Bonefish Lodge, Casuarina Point	18	√	√	x	x	x	366-2150	327-8152
Green Turtle Club & Marina, Green Turtle Cay	42	√	√	x	x	√	365-4271	365-4272
Guana Beach Resort, Great Guana Cay	15	√	√	x	x	√	365-5133	365-5134
Hope Town Harbour Lodge, Hope Town	19	√	√	x	x	√	366-0095	366-0286
Treasure Cay Hotel Resort & Marina, Treasure Cay	80	√	√	√	√	√	365-8535	365-8362
Walker's Cay Hotel & Marina, Walker's Cay	68	√	√	√	x	√	353-1252	353-1339
Abaco timeshare Abaco Towns-by-the-sea, Bay St, Marsh Harbour	64	√	√	√	x	√	367-2227	367-3927
Andros Andros Lighthouse Yacht Club, Fresh Creek	20	√	√	√	√	√	368-2305	368-2300
Emerald Palms-by-the-sea, Driggs Hill	20	√	√	√	x	√	369-2661	369-2667
Mangrove Beach Hotel & Resort, Mangrove Cay	20	Closed for renovations at press time.						
Small Hope Bay Lodge, Small Hope Bay	21	√	x	x	x	√	368-2013	368-2015
White Sand Beach Hotel, Mangrove Cay	13	√	x	x	x	x	369-0159	–
Berry Islands Great Harbour Cay/ Tropical Diversions (villas)	18	√	√	√	√	x	367-8838	367-8115

Hotel/Location	No of rooms	Beach/water-front	Pool	Tennis	Golf[1]	Diving[1]	Tel (242)	Fax (242)
Bimini								
Bimini Big Game Club & Hotel, Alice Town	49	√	√	√	x	√	347-3391	347-3392
Cat Island								
Cutlass Bay Club, Cutlass Bay	13	√	√	√	x	√	342-3085	342-5048
Fernandez Bay Village, Fernandez Bay, New Bight	12	√	x	√	x	√	342-3043	342-3051
Greenwood Beach Resort, Port Howe	20	√	√	x	x	√	342-3053	342-3053
Orange Creek Inn, Orange Creek	16	√	x	x	x	√	354-4110	354-4042
Sea Spray Hotel, Orange Creek	15	√	x	x	x	√	354-4116	354-4161
Eleuthera								
Cambridge Villas, Gregory Town	16	x	√	x	x	√	335-5080	335-5308
Club Eleuthera, Rock Sound	108	√	√	√	x	√	334-4055	334-4057
Club Med, Governor's Harbour	288	√	√	√	√	√	332-2270	332-2855
Coral Sands Hotel, Harbour Island	33	√	x	√	x	√	333-2350	333-2368
The Cove Eleuthera Hotel, Rock Sound	26	√	√	√	x	√	335-5142	335-5338
Ethel's Cottages, Tarpum Bay	18	√	x	x	√	√	334-4233	–
Palmetto Shores Vacation Villas, Palmetto Point	10	√	x	x	x	√	332-1305	332-1305
Pink Sands, Harbour Island	20	√	√	√	x	√	333-2030	333-2060
Romora Bay Club, Harbour Island	30	√	x	√	x	√	333-2325	333-2500

Hotel/Location	No of rooms	Beach/ water- front	Pool	Tennis	Golf[1]	Diving[1]	Tel (242)	Fax (242)
Valentine's Yacht Club & Inn, Harbour Island	21	x	√	√	x	√	333-2080	333-2135
Ventaclub Eleuthera, Winding Bay	138	√	√	√	√	√	334-4054	334-4057
Exuma								
Club Peace & Plenty, George Town	35	√	√	x	x	√	336-2551	336-2093
The Palms at Three Sisters, Mount Thompson	12	√	x	√	x	√	358-4040	358-4043
Peace & Plenty Beach Inn, George Town	16	√	√	√	x	√	336-2250	336-2253
Two Turtles Inn, George Town	12	√	x	x	x	√	336-2545	336-2528
Long Island								
Cape Santa Maria Beach Resort, Seymours	20	√	x	√	x	√	338-5273	338-6013
Stella Maris Resort, Stella Maris	42	√	√	√	x	√	338-2051	338-2052
San Salvador								
Club Med, Columbus Isle	286	√	√	√	x	√	331-2000	331-2458
Riding Rock Inn	42	√	√	√	x	√	331-2631	331-2020

[1] Facilities on premises or by arrangement. [2] Hotels also offering timeshare.

HURRICANES

The Bahamas receives improved weather forecasting from the US National Hurricane Center in Coral Gables, FL.

The Center's warning time increased to 24 hours in advance of a storm. A five-day coastal weather forecast is available to boaters. This is doubly welcome in the Family Islands where materials for surviving severe storms are less readily available.

According to the National Hurricane Service, the doppler radar network will cover all of the US by the end of the decade. The network already covers portions of The Bahamas, as do satellites positioned in geosynchronous orbit above North America.

Improved satellite reporting, a new generation of doppler radar, better reports from hurricane-hunting aircraft and greater understanding of expanded information from inside a storm will lead to upgraded predictions of storm track and future direction as well as greater knowledge of a storm's internal dynamics.

The GOES-8 satellite gives forecasters more information about wind speed and storm direction, as well as forces within the storm and location of the precise centre of cyclone winds. Rain bands, wind shear factors and other elements – even severe thunderstorms – are tracked with the same accuracy.

Hurricane hunter aircraft will fly higher and faster so scientists can sample greater areas and provide more data from tropical ocean environments.

Weather forecasting is a relatively new science. Techniques and results are being steadily upgraded. Hurricane specialist Dr Edward Rappaport, of the National Hurricane Service, estimates the 12- to 72-hour forecast of a storm's track and intensity has improved by about 0.5% per year – representing an improvement of 10% over the past 20 years. The Hurricane Research Division predicts skill levels will improve by 20% by the year 2000.

Only in 1994 did aircraft begin to regularly penetrate hurricanes and report findings. But hurricanes are unpredictable. They have swept full circle, reversed course, even dissipated, only to reconstitute themselves and deliver a devastating punch at unsuspecting areas.

See also **Climate**.

IMMIGRATION

Renowned as one of the most politically stable countries in the western hemisphere, The Bahamas has enjoyed uninterrupted parliamentary democracy for 269 years since its introduction in 1729.

A former British colony, The Bahamas gained its independence on July 10, 1973. It is located just 60 miles from Miami at its nearest island, Bimini, and around 480 miles from Haiti in the south. At some points, Cuba, which borders the southwest perimeters, is less than 25 miles from Bahamian cays. As a result, The Bahamas contends with a serious immigration situation.

The government is committed to an amicable solution, and as such, its immigration policy is aimed at ensuring the reasonable security, well-being and economic progress of The Bahamas and its people.

The government gives consideration to citizenship, permanent residency and work permits for non-Bahamians provided there is compliance with the immigration laws of The Bahamas and policies of the government. Accelerated consideration is given to applications for annual or permanent residence by major international investors and to fit and proper owners of residences valued in excess of $500,000.

As The Bahamas is a major tourist resort, every effort is made to keep visitors' immigration formalities to a minimum. Non-commonwealth citizens should inquire at the nearest British Consulate or Bahamian Embassy for entry requirements, as they vary from country to country.

Each person entering The Bahamas must fill out, upon entry, an embarkation-disembarkation card. In the case of non-residents, the designated portion is retained and must be surrendered upon departure from the country.

All visitors are required to have a return or onward ticket and a document permitting them to enter another country. They may also be asked to produce evidence of sufficient funds to allow them to sustain themselves while in The Bahamas.

Visitors may reside in The Bahamas for a max of eight months, provided they can indicate means of financial support for this period. They may be asked to indicate a friend or relative with whom they will be staying. Visitors are not allowed to engage in any form of gainful occupation while in The Bahamas.

Anyone found guilty of smuggling or assisting in the smuggling of illegal immigrants may be fined $5,000 and sentenced to a max of two years in prison and confiscation of any aircraft or boat used in the act.

Passports
Passports are required by all persons except:
1. Citizens of the UK and colonies, and Canadian citizens on temporary visits not exceeding a stay of three weeks. However, passports are required for re-entry into the UK. British visitors' passports are accepted.
2. Citizens of the US entering The Bahamas as *bona fide* visitors for a period not exceeding eight months who are in possession of proof of nationality, ie, birth certificate, naturalization certificate etc.

Visas
Visas are required by all persons entering The Bahamas except:
1. British Commonwealth citizens and landed immigrants of Canada, for visits not exceeding 30 days if in possession of Form 100.
2. US citizens entering as *bona fide* visitors for a stay not exceeding eight months.
3. Alien residents of the US who, upon arrival, are in possession of US alien registration cards for visits not exceeding 30 days.
4. Nationals of the following countries for visits not exceeding 14 days: Argentina, Bolivia, Brazil, Chile, Costa Rica, Ecuador, El Salvador, Guatemala, Honduras, Nicaragua, Panama, Paraguay, Peru, Suriname, Uruguay and Venezuela.
5. Nationals of the following countries for visits not exceeding three months: Austria, Denmark, Finland, France, Germany, Israel, Japan, Mexico, Republic of Ireland, South Africa and Sweden.
6. Nationals of the following countries: Belgium, Greece, Iceland, Italy, Liechtenstein, Luxembourg, Netherlands, Norway, San Marino, Spain, Switzerland and Turkey.
7. Persons in possession of a valid residence or work permit issued by the Director of Immigration.
8. Persons in transit, including stateless persons in possession of a valid refugee or stateless person's travel document, provided they are in possession of valid passports and tickets to some destination outside The Bahamas and that their stay, while awaiting onward passage on the first available ship or aircraft, does not exceed three days. This exemption does not apply to nationals of Haiti and Dominican Republic who must always possess visas even in direct transit by air.

Applications for visas from persons in the following categories must be referred to the nearest Bahamian Consular Office:
1. Nationals of the Dominican Republic.
2. Nationals of Haiti.
3. Nationals of Colombia.
4. Nationals of Asian countries, ie nationals of China, including nationals resident in Hong Kong; North and South Korea, Vietnam, Thailand, Myanmar (formerly Burma).

Visas for persons in the following categories may be granted without prior reference:
1. Nationals of countries not mentioned in the previous paragraph provided that a *bona fide* visit is only intended for a period not exceeding three months.
2. Stateless persons who must be in possession of a document permitting re-entry into their country of residence and whose *bona fide* visit is only intended for a period not to exceed three months.

There are a number of ports of entry at which one may lawfully enter The Bahamas from foreign countries. See **Ports of entry** and **Airports.**

Procedure for obtaining an annual residence permit
Persons wishing to reside in The Bahamas on an annual basis may qualify under one of four categories:
1. Spouse or dependent of a citizen of The Bahamas.

2. Spouse or dependent of a permit holder.
3. Independent economic resident.
4. Resident home owner, or seasonal resident home owner.

The following documentation is required for:

Category 1
a. Immigration Form 1, Section B, completed and notarized with $4 in Bahamian postage stamps affixed thereon.
b. A covering letter from the supporting applicant stating relationship and accepting financial responsibility for the subject of the application.
c. Birth, marriage and/or any certificate evidencing dependence of the subject of the application.
d. The applicant's birth certificate.
e. Medical certificate dated not more than 30 days prior to submission.
f. Police certificate issued less than six months earlier.
g. Two passport-size photographs
h. A processing fee of $25.

For an annual residence permit, a head-of-household pays $1,000 and each dependent, $25. However, if an applicant is married to a Bahamian citizen, a resident spouse permit may be issued, provided the marriage has existed for less than five years. The resident spouse permit is issued for a max period of five years. A one-time fee of $250 is charged to cover the permit, regardless of the amount of time remaining in the five-year period. An application is made for permanent residence or citizenship after five years or more of marriage. See **Permanent residence,** this heading.

Category 2
a. Items (a) through (h) of category (1).
b. A copy of the sponsor's work permit, permit to reside, certificate of permanent residence or other lawful authority to reside in The Bahamas.

Category 3
a. Items (a) through (h) of category (1), except item (c).
b. Financial reference from a reputable bank verifying economic worth, ie, citing a figure range.
c. Two written character references.

Category 4
Under this category, non-Bahamians who own second homes in The Bahamas may apply to the Director of Immigration for an annual home owner's residence card. This card is renewable annually and entitles the owner, spouse and any minor child/children endorsed on the owner's card when travelling with the owner, to enter and remain in The Bahamas for the validity of the card. The fee is $500 per year, and is intended to facilitate entry into The Bahamas with minimal formalities by:
1. Obviating the need for return tickets.
2. Obviating provision of proof of maintenance ability upon entering the country.
3. Entitling the holder to visit for a stay of up to one year.

Requirements for qualifying under this category are:
1. Letter of request.
2. Two passport-size photographs of applicant.
3. Application form.
4. Proof of property ownership in The Bahamas.
5. Processing fee of $25.

Successful applicants in any of these categories are not permitted to engage in employment.

Procedures for obtaining a work permit

An inflexible principle of The Bahamas government is that no expatriate may be offered a position that a suitably qualified Bahamian is available to fill.

Employers with vacant posts are required to advertise locally and consult The Bahamas Employment

Exchange. If unsuccessful in fulfilling their requirements by these methods, they may apply to the Dept of Immigration for permission to recruit outside The Bahamas.

The following documentation will then need to be submitted:

1. Application Form 1, Section A, completed and notarized with $4 in Bahamian postage stamps affixed.
2. A covering letter from the prospective employer stating reasons for the application, the position, and the period of time needed.
3. Two passport-size photographs with signature on reverse of prints.
4. Police certificate covering a period of five years' residence immediately preceding the application or a sworn affidavit in lieu of same.
5. Medical certificate dated not more than 30 days prior to submission.
6. Written references from previous employer(s).
7. Copies of exam certificates referred to in the application.
8. Copies of local newspaper advertisements with replies thereto and results of interviews, if held.
9. Certificate from the Dept of Labour (Employment Exchange) indicating that a Bahamian is not available to fill the position.
10. A processing fee of $25.

Normally an application will not be processed if the prospective employee is already in The Bahamas, having entered as a visitor.

Work permit fees range from $250 to $7,500 per year depending on the category. The Bahamas Immigration Bahamianization Policy, which is critical to the granting of work permits, provides that:

1. Whenever there is a position which a Bahamian is qualified to fill, he should be given the position in preference to anyone else.
2. The Bahamian must be given that job on the same terms and conditions as his expatriate counterpart.
3. Where the company has a career structure, whether here or abroad, the Bahamian employee must be given the same opportunities for advancement as would be afforded other employees.
4. The Bahamian must be helped whenever possible to broaden his skills in his chosen field of endeavour by constant exposure to further training at home and abroad.

Where work permits have been granted, each employer will be required to identify a suitable Bahamian to understudy the expatriate so that the Bahamian trainee will fill the expatriate's position within a reasonable time frame.

Bona fide and genuine investors usually have little difficulty in complying with these requirements.

Employers may obtain permits for longer periods than the standard one-year period in respect to certain key personnel on contract. Such contracts should indicate their renewal would be subject to obtaining the necessary immigration permission, and they may be endorsed to the effect that the employee is expected to train or be replaced by a suitable Bahamian within a stipulated period.

Each permit issued by the Immigration Board relates to a specific post. Permits are not altered by the Director of Immigration to reflect change of employment or residence. However, a person holding a work permit may make application for a new one (his new employer having been unsuccessful in recruiting a qualified Bahamian to fill the post) without having to leave the islands.

The renewal of a permit on expiration is not automatic. Generally, no expatriate may be continually employed in the country in any capacity for more than five years. However, there are likely to be cases where hardship will be caused by rigid implementation of this policy; according to government, this factor will be kept in mind in applying the regulations.

An employer must inform the Dept of Immigration within 30 days that a non-Bahamian employee is no longer employed or be liable to a fine not exceeding $150.

A non-Bahamian who ceases to be employed must take his permit to the Dept of Immigration for cancellation within seven days of ceasing to be employed. The permit shall be deemed cancelled with effect from expiration of that seven-day period. An employee failing to comply with this regulation is liable to prosecution and may, if convicted, be liable to a fine not exceeding $100.

Bonding
A bond is required for each person granted a work permit, if necessary, to repatriate the employee and his dependents and to pay any public charges, including medical expenses, incurred by the employee.

Travelling salesman's permit
Travelling salesmen planning to do business in The Bahamas must obtain work permits from the Dept of Immigration, and a licence from the Licensing Authority. The requirements for such a permit are:
1. Completed Immigration Dept Form I (notarized, with $4 in stamps), with two passport-size photographs signed on the reverse, and a police certificate.
2. Two letters of character reference.
3. Passport or other travel document.
4. A letter from salesman's company stating he is travelling to The Bahamas to sell on its behalf. Letter should be addressed to: Director of Immigration, PO Box N-831, Nassau, The Bahamas.
5. Two letters sponsoring him as a salesman from two sponsors in The Bahamas in the type of business on which he plans to call.
6. A complete list of accounts on which he will call.
7. Payment of an annual fee of $3,000 (a permit may be obtained for any period up to six months at a prorated fee).

The licence is issued when the approved work permit is presented at the Licensing Authority office.

Permanent residence
Applicants for this status of residency must be of good character and prepared to show evidence of financial support. Such an applicant must also state that he intends to reside permanently in The Bahamas.

Persons may apply for permanent residence in any of the following categories provided they satisfy statutory requirements of The Bahamas:
1. As the spouse of a citizen of The Bahamas, and in the case of a male, he must have been married for not less than five years.
2. As an economic applicant; that is, one who seeks to permanently reside in The Bahamas because of:
    a. Investment – business or home.
    b. Established roots through family ties.

Persons who held valid certificates of permanent residence prior to the Immigration Act, 1975, continue to hold such status automatically.

To initiate an application in either of the above categories, the requisite application form should be completed in duplicate, notarized and submitted along with the following documents to the Ministry of Labour, Immigration and Training:

Category 1
(Application Form IV A)
   a. Two passport photographs.
   b. A police certificate of not more than six months' issue, covering five years' residence immediately prior to the date of application, or where these are not issued, a sworn affidavit in lieu of same.
   c. Birth certificate.
   d. Spouse's birth certificate.
   e. Marriage certificate.
   f. Proof of immigration status in The Bahamas.
   g. Processing fee of $25.

Spouses of Bahamians may be issued a certificate of permanent residence with the right to engage in gainful employment. In the case of males, such application may only be made after five years of marriage to the Bahamian wife. Females married to Bahamians may apply at any time after marriage.

**Category 2
(Application Form IV)**
a. Items (a) through (g) in category (1).
b. A financial reference from a reputable bank verifying economic worth.
c. Two written character references.
d. A medical certificate dated not more than 30 days prior to submission of the application.
e. Proof of ownership of property and/or investment in The Bahamas in the form of copies of conveyances, deeds or mortgage contracts, etc.

A person holding a certificate of permanent residence who wishes to include his wife, or dependent child under the age of 18 and ordinarily resident in his household, may have them endorsed on the certificate at the time of his original application or at a subsequent date, subject to such conditions as might be laid down by the Immigration Board.

Cost of a permanent residence certificate varies according to status. A person who has resided in The Bahamas at least 10 years and less than 20 years and who holds a work permit may pay anything from $1,000-$5,000.

A person who has resided in the country at least 20 years and who holds a work permit may pay anything from $500-$2,500. The spouse of a Bahamian citizen pays $250. A person without a work permit, or holding a work permit in one of the top professional categories, and who has resided in The Bahamas for less than 10 years, not married to a Bahamian citizen, pays up to $10,000.

Persons who held valid certificates of permanent residence prior to the Immigration Act, 1975, continue to hold such status automatically.

Persons who formerly possessed Bahamian status (belongers) whose applications for citizenship were not determined by Aug 1, 1976, should have also applied for permanent residence. Belongers who failed to make such application prior to Aug 1, 1976, ceased to have immigration status. Persons in this category, on acquiring a permanent residence certificate, would continue to enjoy the same rights and privileges they had known under the old Bahamian status, with the exception of the right to vote in a parliamentary election.

Permanent residents who were formerly belongers enjoy the new status for life. The certificate is free and contains no restriction regarding the right of the holder to engage in gainful employment.

A certificate of permanent residence may be revoked if the person holding the certificate:
1. Has been ordinarily resident outside The Bahamas continuously for a period of three years.
2. Is or was imprisoned for a criminal offence for one year or more.
3. Has so conducted himself that in the opinion of the Immigration Board it is not in the public interest that he should continue to enjoy the privileges conferred by the certificate.
4. Being the wife of a holder of a permanent residence certificate, she becomes legally separated from her husband or the marriage is dissolved or annulled.

**Temporary annual
residence permit**
A person attending an institution of higher education in The Bahamas on a full-time basis or as a trainee pays $25 a year.

Business investors
Non-Bahamian investments are facilitated by a business-sensitive legal framework and investor-friendly climate supported by the Bahamas Investment Authority (BIA), Office of the Prime Minister, PO Box CB-10980, Nassau,

The Bahamas, tel (242) 327-5970 (to 4), fax (242) 327-5907.

Although an investor is granted a licence by the Licensing Authority, he must still apply for a work permit if he is to be resident and an employee of/or operating the business himself.

Contact the Director of Immigration, Ministry of Labour, Immigration and Training, PO Box N-831, Nassau, The Bahamas, tel (242) 322-7530.

See also **Citizenship** and **Investing**.

IMMOVABLE PROPERTY ACT

See **Property Transactions, Intl Persons Landholding Act**.

IMPORT & EXPORT STATISTICS

Commodity classifications, from the Dept of Statistics, are based on the Standard Intl Trade Classifications (SITC). See **Fig 1.9** for the latest available information.

IMPORT ENTRY

Commercial banks may approve and issue payment for goods imported into The Bahamas, on behalf of the Exchange Control Dept of the Central Bank of The Bahamas, Frederick and Market Sts, Nassau.

The Import Entry Form (1) must be completed in quadruplicate and taken to the bank with supporting invoice(s) and payment. However, the form must first be approved by Exchange Control if value of the goods (non-oil imports only) is more than $100,000.

Commercial banks may also issue and approve payment for travel, medical and educational purposes without Exchange Control permission upon completion of Delegated Authority Exchange Form (E1) and supporting documents. The bank supplies the form to be completed at time of payment.

See also **Exchange control**.

INDUSTRIAL RELATIONS

Industrial Relations Chapter 296 Statute Laws of The Bahamas, as amended 1996, makes it unlawful for a trade union to operate in The Bahamas – or for any person to take part in its activities – unless the union is registered.

Applications to register a trade union should be made to the Registrar of Trade Unions at the Labour Dept.

The Registrar shall refuse to register a trade union if the union's principal objects are unlawful or contrary to statutory objects, or if its name is misleading or so similar to an existing name as to deceive the public, or if there is failure to comply to specified balloting procedures.

Upon registration, the trade union is issued a certificate as evidence of that registration. Every trade union is required to have a registered office. Unions may own or lease land, but all real and personal property is vested in the trustees of the union.

No person under the age of 16 may be a member of a trade union. A union may not have foreign connections without a proper licence in writing from the Minister responsible for Labour.

An employer is required to recognize a union as bargaining agent if more than 50% of his employees are members. An employer has 14 days to accept or reject a union claim for recognition. No employee can be dismissed or adversely treated as a result of his union involvement.

All industrial agreements between employer and union must be sent in writing to both the Industrial Tribunal and the Minister responsible for Labour. The Minister has 14 days to make comments to the tribunal. After taking these comments into consideration, the tribunal may register the agreement if found to contain no illegalities. Properly registered industrial agreements are considered binding.

Any strike is illegal that has a purpose other than the furtherance of a trade dispute, or if designed to coerce the government. The same applies to a lockout. A picket must be

FIG 1.9
IMPORT & EXPORT STATISTICS

Value of 1996 domestic exports & re-exports

Section (totals rounded off)	B$ 000 (provisional)
0 Food & live animals	74,782
1 Beverages & tobacco	4,949
2 Crude materials, inedible, except fuel	32,166
3 Mineral fuels, lubricants & related materials	6
4 Animal & vegetable oils, fats & waxes	6
5 Chemicals & related products	17,278
6 Manufactured goods classified chiefly by materials	7,793
7 Machinery & transport equipment	33,412
8 Miscellaneous manufactured articles	7,435
9 Commodities & transactions not classified according to kind	399
	$178,226[1]

Exports of commodities to principal trading areas (domestic & re-export)

Trading areas	B$ 000 (provisional)
UK	2,917
Canada	4,114
US	132,703
CCC [2]	2,835
EU [3]	25,760
Other countries	12,435
OPEC [4]	376
	$181,142[5]

[1] Excludes bullion and specie. [2] Caribbean Commonwealth Countries. [3] European Union. [4] Organization of Petroleum Exporting Countries. [5] Total exports by principal trading areas ($181,142,000) differs from combined total ($178,226,000) of domestic exports and re-exports as the UK total ($2,917,000) is also included in EU total.

Value of 1996 imports

Section (totals rounded off)	B$ 000 (provisional)
0 Food & live animals	224,270
1 Beverages & tobacco	20,629
2 Crude materials, inedible, except fuel	27,272
3 Mineral fuels, lubricants & related materials	192,921
4 Animal & vegetable oils, fats & waxes	3,915
5 Chemicals & related products	124,782
6 Manufactured goods classified chiefly by materials	207,109
7 Machinery & transport equipment	339,415
8 Miscellaneous manufactured articles	206,288
9 Commodities & transactions not classified according to kind	17,561
	$1,364,163[1]

Imports of commodities from principal trading areas	
Trading areas	B$ 000 (provisional)
UK	8,925
Canada	6,496
US	1,188,309
CCC [2]	3,554
EU [3]	30,903
Other countries	102,923
OPEC [4]	31,977
	$1,373,087 [5]

[1] Excludes bullion and specie, includes goods entered conditionally free at Freeport, Grand Bahama.
[2] Caribbean Commonwealth Countries. [3] European Union. [4] Organization of Petroleum Exporting Countries.
[5] Total imports by principal trading areas ($1,373,087,000) differs from imports by section ($1,364,163,000) as the UK total ($8,925,000) is also included in the EU total.

able to produce on his person written authorization by a trade union official, and he must picket peacefully near a place or building where a party to the dispute works, with no more than 14 other pickets.

Contact the Registrar of Trade Unions, Labour Dept, PO Box N-1586, Nassau, tel 326-6987.

See also **Industrial Tribunal** and **Trade unions**.

INDUSTRIAL TRIBUNAL

The Bahamas Industrial Tribunal was appointed by the government in April 1997, with wide powers to resolve conflict in the workplace, including power to order reinstatement and levy damages. The Tribunal hears disputes in both essential and non-essential services. Hearings are held in public, at the Nassau headquarters on Thompson Blvd, and at the regional office in Freeport.

The Tribunal consists of a president at the Nassau headquarters, and two vice-presidents, one in Nassau, and one at the regional office in Freeport. The Tribunal is assisted by two panels, of six persons each, representing workers and employers. Panelists are recommended by their union or employer association and appointed by the Director of Labour for a three-year term.

Tribunal hearings are informal and follow normal court practice, with evidence followed by cross-examination. The service is free, and parties may represent themselves.

Industrial Tribunal, Monument Bldg, Nassau, tel 325-6923, 325-6954 or 325-6942; fax 325-7614. Regional Office, Freeport tel (242) 352-3797.

See also **Industrial relations** and **Trade Unions**.

INDUSTRIES ENCOURAGEMENT

To broaden the base of the Bahamian economy, the government has a policy of diversification which means encouragement of industries other than tourism. In 1970, the Industries Encouragement Act was passed to provide incentives for manufacturers of approved products. These incentives include duty-free importation of machinery and raw materials as well as tax exemptions.

The Office of the Prime Minister is responsible for administration of the Act. The Minister, designated by the Act, may declare a manufactured product an approved product if it is in the public interest and the product would benefit The Bahamas, "both economic and social considerations being taken into account." Every approved manufacturer can import into The Bahamas duty free:

1. Machinery and raw material necessary to manufacture the approved product.
2. Any scheduled article for the purpose of constructing,

reconstructing, altering or extending, but not repairing, the factory premises. Scheduled articles include all building materials, tools, plant equipment, pipes, pumps, conveyor belts or other materials or appliances necessary. In New Providence, this excludes equipment used to manufacture wooden door frames, moulding, cement tiles or cement blocks.
The manufacturer is guaranteed no export taxes on the approved product, no income tax in respect of any profits or gains from the product's manufacture, and no real property tax on factory premises – for the statutory period. If the manufacturer's date of production was prior to Jan 1, 1976, the statutory period extended through Dec 31, '89. Otherwise, it lasts 15 years from the date agreed to be production date.

An amendment to the Industries Encouragement Act requires payment of a 7% stamp duty by persons registered thereunder.

Application for registration considerations under the Industries Encouragement Act, 1970, must be addressed to the Permanent Secretary, Office of the Prime Minister, PO Box CB-10980, Nassau, The Bahamas, tel (242) 327-5826, fax (242) 327-5806.

The Tariff Act
The fourth schedule of the Tariff Act provides for duty exemptions on certain goods. In addition to specified agricultural, floricultural, horticultural and fisheries industry goods, the following items may be imported duty free as a result of a 1993 amendment to the Act's schedule:
1. Bottles, cans, labels and other packing materials.
2. Processing equipment.
3. Printing equipment.
4. Garment and other manufacturing equipment.

These relate to goods being imported for use in the manufacture of handicraft items or in cottage industry or light industry, as approved by the Minister responsible for the Act. The Minister establishes conditions under which such duty-free importation may be allowed.

The amendment to this Act is intended to further encourage development of The Bahamas' domestic manufacturing sector.

Application for concessions under the Act is made on prescribed forms to Financial Secretary, Ministry of Finance and Planning, PO Box N-3017, Nassau, The Bahamas, tel (242) 327-1530 (to 7), fax (242) 322-1474.

See also **Bahamas Agricultural Industrial Corp (BAIC); Bahamas Development Bank (BDB); Caribbean Basin Initiative (CBI); Caribbean Community & Common Market (CARICOM); CARIBCAN; Exchange control; Export;** and **Manufacturing.**

INDUSTRY
Tourism, which annually attracts more than three million visitors to The Bahamas, continues to be the linchpin of the Bahamian economy, representing 50% of the Gross Domestic Product (GDP). In 1997 visitors to The Bahamas spent $1.4 billion. See also **Tourism.**

Banking/finance is the No 2 industry, representing 15% of the GDP. There are 418 licensed banks and trust companies in The Bahamas. At the end of 1997, the banking industry employed 3,860 persons. See also **Banking** and **Economy.**

The government is the largest employer with a staff of 50,000, approx half of the national workforce.

The construction boom continues to play a major role in the economy. In 1997, 2,607 construction permits were issued at a value of $311.5 million.

Domestic exports include crawfish, other seafood, fruit and vegetables, rum and crude salt.

Provisional totals from the Dept of Statistics for 1996 showed exports of rum valued at $4,465,200.

During 1996, The Bahamas exported $17,802,775 worth of crude salt to the US, Canada, Jamaica, Iceland, Colombia and Venezuela.

The lobster industry exported $54,137,580 worth of spiny lobster.

The Bahamas Maritime Authority's ship registry is a burgeoning industry. At 1,400 vessels, The Bahamas had the world's third largest fleet in 1997, with a gross tonnage of 25.5 million GT. This represented a 4.6% increase over 1996.

Industries in Freeport include manufacturing of chemicals, polystyrene and fragrances, as well as agriculture, limestone processing and oil-related industries.

Oil is not refined in The Bahamas. The Bahamas Oil Refining Company (BORCO), in Grand Bahama, operates as a terminal which transships, stores and blends oil. South Riding Point Holding also transships and stores oil.

See also **Freeport/Lucaya Information, Agriculture** and **Industry.**

Petroleum

Under the Petroleum Act, 1971, and the Petroleum Regulations, 1978 (as amended), foreign enterprises may apply for a permit, licence or lease for petroleum exploration in The Bahamas. A permit gives the non-exclusive right to carry out geophysical or geological studies but does not guarantee the granting of a lease or licence.

A licence gives the sole right to enter the licensed area and search for hydrocarbons. According to Petroleum Regulations, companies holding petroleum exploration licences are entitled to a renewal after expiry of the initial licence term, but must drill an exploratory well in the first year of the renewal period.

There is currently one petroleum exploration licensee in the Bahamas – Ferguson GDM/Offshore Resources, Ltd. Another applicant has been approved but the licence had not been executed at press time.

Contact the Permanent Secretary, Office of the Prime Minister, PO Box CB-10980, Nassau, tel (242) 327-5826, fax (242) 327-5806.

See **Agriculture, Manufacturing** and **Freeport/ Lucaya information, Industry.**

INFLATION
See **Economy.**

INSURANCE

Responsibility for the prudential regulation of all insurance activity in or through The Bahamas rests with the Registrar of Insurance Companies, Parliament St, a dept of the Ministry of Finance and Planning. It is concerned with the ongoing prudential monitoring and control of insurers, agents, brokers, salesmen, and, on the international scene, underwriting managers and non-resident insurers. Registered insurers writing local business pay a premium tax of 2% of gross premiums collected each quarter.

All local insurance operations (as distinct from offshore, or captive, insurance) are covered by the Insurance Act, 1969. At press time, the Insurance Act was being revised. A new Insurance Bill was expected to be presented to Parliament before the end of 1998.

As of July 31, 1998, 72 insurers were licensed to write local business; 10 indigenous companies and 62 foreign companies writing through local offices. In support of this activity, there are 19 agents, 28 brokers who are also agents, and four brokers.

In addition to legislation concerning insurance companies, there is a Road Traffic Act making insurance on all motor vehicles mandatory. Sections of the Act apply to public service vehicles and private passenger cars, commercial vehicles and motorcycles. Under the terms of the Act, it is compulsory to carry insurance against bodily injury or death to any person arising out of the use of a vehicle; this applies to passengers in certain vehicles such as buses, taxis, tour cars and jitneys. The Act lays out penalties for operating a vehicle without valid insurance.

The Act requires that insurance be carried only to provide indemnity against claims for bodily injury or death and not against property damage. This results in two types of insurance policies being available for what is commonly known as third party insurance. The minimum requirement by law is provided under what is defined as an "act" policy* whereas the third party policy extends to include damage to property arising from the use of a vehicle, such as damage caused to another car.

Marine insurance is written with respect to cargo and hull policies. Also available are protection and indemnity covers, which can be extended to include oil pollution liabilities imposed under the Merchant Shipping (Oil Pollution) Act.

Insurance companies, agents and brokers dealing with general insurance business are members of The Bahamas General Insurance Assoc. Those insurers handling life and health business belong to The Bahamas Assoc of Life and Health Insurers.

*At press time, plans had been announced to eliminate "act" insurance but legislation was not yet in place.

Offshore insurance

An offshore insurer is an insurance company which is either incorporated in The Bahamas under the Companies Act, 1992, or incorporated elsewhere but registered under The Bahamas Foreign Companies Act and:
1. Is registered under the Insurance Laws of The Bahamas.
2. Insures only risks located outside The Bahamas.
3. Manages its business from within The Bahamas.

The Bahamas offers a convenient and professionally administered location for such operations. There is a well equipped and capable regulatory office (the office of the Registrar of Insurance Companies) and an adequate professional infrastructure to support such business as may materialize. In addition to the government's own efforts to promote The Bahamas, The Bahamas Assoc for Intl Insurance, comprised of some 26 members drawn from the management, legal, banking and accounting professions, also works actively in developing the offshore insurance business.

The activity of offshore insurance companies is regulated by the original Insurance Act, 1969, or the External Insurance Act, 1983. To qualify for registration as an external insurer under the External Insurance Act, it is necessary to demonstrate (inter-alia) that the offshore or captive insurer would be accepting not less than $500,000 in insurance premiums from an affiliated company (related business). All other applicants would be accommodated under the Insurance Act, as non-resident insurers.

Whichever legislation is considered appropriate, the application process and subsequent ongoing statutory requirements are similar, but once registered, the offshore insurer may only carry on the particular business described in the business plan and submitted at the time of application.

Registrar's requirements

Before an offshore company may be registered, the Registrar of Insurance Companies must be satisfied with:
1. Fitness of key parties to engage in the proposed operation.
2. Business ethics involved.
3. Feasibility of the planned business.
4. Security of outwards reinsurance.

This process may be facilitated by introductory meetings between the applicant and the Registrar.

Both insurance laws lay down the minimum capital and surplus requirements with requirements for external insurers based on the nature and scope of business presented. The Registrar would not expect to see an initial capitalization of less than US$250,000, which would normally be in cash and adequate to support the proposed volume of business.

Once licensed, the insurer is subject to minimal but important ongoing reporting requirements consisting basically of filing an annual audited financial statement. In addition, the External Insurance Act calls for submission of certain statutory statements indicating compliance with the terms of registration.

All offshore insurers incorporated in The Bahamas are expected to operate through one of the registered underwriting managers. There are currently five such management companies registered, all of which operate out of Nassau.

As of July 31, 1998, 15 companies were registered under the External Insurance Act, 1983. This Act was amended on Dec 24, 1996.

Contact the Office of The Registrar of Insurance Companies, Ministry of Finance and Planning, PO Box N-3017, Nassau, The Bahamas, tel (242) 328-1068, fax (242) 328-1070.

For copies of insurance laws and regulations, contact Government Publications, PO Box N-7147, Nassau, The Bahamas, tel (242) 322-2410.

Captive insurance
The captive insurance industry is governed in The Bahamas by the External Insurance Act, 1983. The Act allows companies to underwrite business from outside The Bahamas, confers advantageous solvency margins and allows captives to trade in any currency (except Bahamian).

Other provisions of the Act include a confidentiality clause to protect the policyholder, and tax exemptions for a period of 15 years from the date of first registration.

Captive insurance companies – alternative providers of protection against the risk of damage or loss and third party liabilities – differ from traditional firms in the nature of risks they underwrite or reinsure. They minimize the cost of risk management and may substantially reduce, or even avoid, other expenses such as administration and settlement of claims, loss control expenses, brokerage commissions and other acquisition costs and consulting fees.

Captives also allow self-insurance of a company with a better loss history than its industry average, plus centralization and tailoring of a company's risk management programmes to improve loss control efficiency. They offer cash flow benefits; access to the reinsurance market; wider cover than the conventional market – such as providing coverage for a new or potentially hazardous product – and the chance to diversify into open market insurance services and generate profits from outside or unrelated business.

Annual fees payable by captive insurance companies in The Bahamas:
External insurer........................$2,500*
Underwriting manager................$650*

* *The fees may be reduced by the amount of the annual company registration fee which, at present, is $1,000 per year.*

See also **Investing**.

INTERNATIONAL BUSINESS COMPANY (IBC)
See **Company formation** and **Investing**.

INTERNATIONAL PERSONS LANDHOLDING ACT
See **Property transactions**.

INTERNET
There are three Internet access providers in The Bahamas: Bahamas On-Line, BaTelNet and Tribune Radio Ltd/100 Jamz.

Bahamas On-Line is the Internet arm of The Systems Resource Group (SRG), and offers a full range of both dial up and high-speed dedicated access. The latter is available through unlicensed wireless spread spectrum radio, or leased line services from either telephone or cable companies. Connection to the Internet is via private international satellite to UUNET's backbone in the US. The Professional Services division provides comprehensive value added Internet services to the business community, including Virtual Private Networks, remote application access, Internet enabled applications, offshore hosting, domain name registration, web site development and international fax services. Tel 325-0011, fax 325-0226, e-mail info@srg.com.bs (http://www.srg.com.bs)

BaTelNet is owned and operated by Bahamas Telecommunications Corp (BaTelCo) and offers dial-up accounts, business accounts and educational student packages for users in New Providence, Grand Bahama, Abaco and Eleuthera. Tel 394-7NET or (242) 300-2638 (http://www.batelnet.bs)

Tribune Radio Ltd (TRL)/100 Jamz was the first Internet service provider in The Bahamas. TRL's Internet service commenced operations in Sept 1995, incorporating satellite technology used by 100 Jamz Radio Network. TRL provides a full range of Internet services from regular dial-up accounts to dedicated Internet circuits. Tel 328-4771.

The most comprehensive website on the Bahamas, Bahamasnet (http://www.bahamasnet.com), is produced by Bahamas Multi Media Ltd, an affiliate of Etienne Dupuch Jr Publications Ltd. The Bahamas Ministry of Tourism's website (http://www.gobahamas.com), also provides information on The Bahamas.

INVESTING

The Bahamas is a tax-free financial centre with close proximity to the US, good communications and infrastructure and sound investment-oriented legislation. There are 418 banks and trust companies, reputable, well-known law and accounting firms, and an established, experienced and highly qualified financial community.

Non-Bahamians wishing to open a business or local branch are assured of an investor-friendly climate with a business sensitive legal framework and government committed to building free enterprise with minimal red tape. To this end, the government has established an investor's "one-stop-shop" for which The Bahamas Investment Authority (BIA) has operational responsibility.

The prospective investor should submit to the BIA a project proposal with supporting documents. See **National Investment Policy,** this section.

See also **Bahamas Investment Authority (BIA); Immigration, Business investors.**

Asset Protection Trusts (APTs)

In an increasingly litigious society, professionals, companies and high net worth individuals are seeking legitimate ways to protect their assets against possible future creditors.

The Fraudulent Dispositions Act, introduced as law in The Bahamas on April 15, 1991, protects assets from all litigation started more than two years after the assets were placed in the trust. Under the Act, foreign judgements are not recognized. The creditor must institute independent proceedings in the Bahamian courts and must prove intent to defraud.

An APT offers a high degree of safety and confidentiality. It involves the settlor giving legal title to property to a trustee to hold and use for the benefit of a beneficiary. It is most often used as part of a traditional estate plan and typically formed along with an International Business Company (IBC). Because the assets legally belong to the trustee rather than the settlor, they cannot be seized by creditors.

The highest degree of asset protection is afforded those assets which can be physically located offshore. As long as physical assets remain outside The Bahamas, a judge may assert jurisdiction over them on behalf of a successful plaintiff.

Basically, the objective of the APT is to avoid litigation altogether by using a package involving prudent use of professional advice and foreign legislation. It is not intended to protect crooked or incompetent individuals against possible creditors.

International Business Company (IBC)
See **Company formation**, Intl Business Company (IBC).

Mutual funds
According to KPMG, assets of The Bahamas' mutual funds industry are estimated at approx $40 billion, comprising some 400 funds.

Mutual funds enable individual investors with mutual investment objectives to pool their resources, thus minimizing risk, and are generally organized as limited companies or trusts. Most Bahamas-operated funds are open-ended, in which investors may invest or withdraw on demand.

The collective assets are typically managed by professional investment advisers. Fund promoters are responsible for issuing a prospectus, also called an offering or information memorandum, which contains the investment objectives and risks, redemption and dividend policies, and administration details, including fees.

The objectives and administrative structure of unincorporated mutual funds are governed by a trust deed and trust law. Incorporated funds are registered companies governed by companies' legislation and articles of assoc.

The Mutual Funds Act, 1995, established reporting, disclosure and monitoring requirements on mutual funds operating in or from The Bahamas. It provides that funds must be licensed by either the Securities Commission or a mutual fund administrator with an unrestricted licence.

An authorized mutual fund has a minimum equity interest purchase of $50,000, and its equity interests are listed on a recognized stock exchange. However, it must still file with the Securities Commission a current offering document, register with the Commission and pay the annual registration fee.

An exempt mutual fund is one where the equity interests are held by not more than 15 investors, and which is licensed in a prescribed jurisdiction.

Mutual funds in The Bahamas tend to be established by financial institutions with a local banking presence and marketed to their own clients, or established by small groups as private funds.

Although Bahamian mutual funds are free from taxation, individual investors in the fund must comply with their own country's tax laws. However, onshore tax liabilities can legally be minimized if "mind and management" of the fund is established offshore.

While fund management and administrative functions should be conducted offshore, investment advisers and management may be located in the major financial centres.

Trusts
A trust is created when a settlor confers control of assets, ie, the trust fund, to a trustee for management and eventual distribution to beneficiaries under the terms and conditions contained in a trust deed and memorandum of wishes. The memorandum of wishes may be changed at any time, and although it is not legally binding, responsible trustees will follow the settlor's wishes as closely as possible without abrogating their responsibility as trustees for the beneficiaries.

Trustees may be individuals or a trust corporation. If a Bahamian company acts as trustee, it must have a trust licence issued by the Central Bank of The Bahamas under the Banks and Trust Companies Regulation Act. Individual trustees do not need to be licensed. To establish a Bahamian trust under the Trusts (Choice of Governing Law) Act, at least one of the trustees must be resident in The Bahamas, and the trust must be governed by the laws of The Bahamas although none of the assets, nor the settlor nor beneficiaries need be resident or located here.

Bahamas banking secrecy ensures absolute privacy and confidentiality, provided assets are not derived from actions or activities which are illegal in The Bahamas. A Bahamian trust need not be registered here, although the Central Bank may need to know identity of the beneficiaries if an application is made to have the trust designated non-resident for exchange control purposes. If the trustee is designated an authorized agent, the Central Bank will not need to know identity of the beneficiaries and will accept the authorized agent's assurance that beneficiaries are non-residents of The Bahamas.

Many trusts are established by settlors in "forced heirship" jurisdictions such as the countries of Latin and Central America, Continental Europe and the Islamic countries of the Middle and Far East. The Trusts (Choice of Governing Law) Act, 1990, protects a Bahamian trust from any "forced heirship" claims or the enforcement of other foreign law rules adverse to the trust concept.

Trusts in The Bahamas benefit from complete tax immunity, including income tax, withholding tax, capital gains tax, inheritance tax, gift tax and death duty. Perpetuities are at present not permitted. The settlor may be named as a beneficiary.

A trust ensures the settlor is able to arrange confidentially for an orderly succession to his estate. It may also be used as a commercial vehicle to carry out trading transactions. Special tax provisions which apply exclusively to companies may thus be avoided. They may also be established to hold and manage pension funds, charitable donations and employee profit-sharing schemes as well as being used as family holding units to hold shares on companies trading throughout the world. A trust may be the controlling unit of a multinational trading concern or a partner in a partnership. Properties can also be held and preserved for those who cannot hold them for themselves, such as minors or bankrupts. The trust agreement has validity under law beyond the life of the client.

Clients are given standardized ready-made trust agreements or especially tailored trust agreements. All trust deeds should be drafted in The Bahamas by reputable Bahamian lawyers. Administration charges vary according to the company and type of trust set up. One major Bahamas-based company charges a minimum $4,000 acceptance fee for a custom-tailored trust, with an annual fee starting at 1.25% of the total and a minimum termination fee of 1%. For a standard or discretionary trust, the acceptance fee starts at $3,000, the annual fee at $3,600 – around 1.25% – and the termination fee at around 1%.

Trustees Act, 1998
A Trustees Act, passed by Parliament in 1998, replaces the Trustee Act, 1893 and several other pieces of trust legislation. Some provisions of the Act are:
1. Recognizing the existence of "protectors" of trusts.
2. Giving legislative weight to trusts designed to protect beneficiaries from creditors, under certain circumstances.
3. Providing a legal basis to create a trust for a purpose that is not charitable, under certain circumstances.
4. Eliminating payment of income tax, capital gains tax, estate tax, inheritance tax, succession tax, gift tax, and other charges and duties by a beneficiary who is treated as a non-resident for exchange control purposes.
Note: These provisions would not affect a situation where the asset in question is real property located in The Bahamas, even if the beneficiaries are non-resident

for exchange control purposes. Stamp duty is payable if the trust owns property in The Bahamas conveyed to a beneficiary or third party.
5. Clarifying the law on what beneficiaries are and are not entitled to know about the existence and details of a trust and trustee's deliberations.

The Act provides the flexibility necessary to sustain The Bahamas as a top-level offshore trust jurisdiction.

Securities market/ stock exchange

The Securities Board Act, 1994, establishes the structure and functions of the Securities Commission on matters dealing with securities and capital markets, including mutual funds. The Securities Commission plans to establish a stock exchange in The Bahamas. At press time, the Bahamas Stock Exchange was expected to be operational in 1999.

NATIONAL INVESTMENT POLICY

In 1994, the government introduced a National Investment Policy to support an investment friendly climate and foster economic growth and development of The Bahamas. An edited version of the policy document follows:

The investment environment

To undergird the National Investment Policy the government will provide:
1. A politically stable environment conducive to private investment.
2. An atmosphere where investments are safe and the expropriation of investment capital is not a considered option.
3. A legal environment based on a long tradition of parliamentary democracy, the rule of constitutional and statute laws and where security of life and personal property are guaranteed.
4. A stable macro-economic environment bolstered by a prudent fiscal policy, a stable exchange rate, flexible exchange control rules and free trade.
5. An environment in which freedom from capital gains, inheritance, withholding, profit remittance, corporate, royalties, sales, personal income, dividends, payroll and interest taxes is ensured.
6. Essential public services, a well-equipped police constabulary, modern health and education facilities and other social services.
7. Dependable public utilities.

The government is also committed to enhancing the image of The Bahamas as an international financial centre. To this end the government will:
1. Maintain The Bahamas as a leading financial services centre.
2. Monitor all developments in the international financial markets and amend any rules, regulations or legislation that would preserve and enhance the competitiveness of the financial services sector of the Bahamian economy.
3. Ensure the operation of a clean financial centre with specific rules and regulations to prevent laundering of criminally derived assets.
4. Support the Central Bank of The Bahamas in its commitment to bank supervision and promoting high standards of conduct and sound banking practices.
5. Support the self regulatory measures of the Assoc of International Bank and Trust Companies (AIBT), particularly the established code of conduct for banks and trust companies.
6. Continue enforcement of bank secrecy laws.

Investment incentives

Investment incentives under the following Acts include exemption from the payment of Customs duties* on building materials, equipment and approved raw materials and real property taxes for periods up to 20 years.

- Export Manufacturing Industries Encouragement Act.
- Industries Encouragement Act.
- Agricultural Manufactories Act.
- Tariff Act.
- Free Trade Zone Act.
- Hotels Encouragement Act.
- Spirits and Beer Manufacture Act.

* Customs duty exemptions do not apply to personal consumables.

The following preferential trade arrangements are also in effect:
- Lomé Convention.
- General System of Preference (GSP).
- CARIBCAN.
- Caribbean Basin Initiative (CBI).

Other incentives include:
1. Investors may acquire publicly owned lands for approved developments on concessionary terms and acquire low cost space for lease for industrial enterprises.
2. Government will provide special training and retraining for Bahamian workers to ensure the continuing availability of a highly skilled labour force.

Administration of policy

The National Economic Council (NEC), headed by the Prime Minister, is responsible for executive management of the investment policy. Operational activities are the responsibility of the Bahamas Investment Authority (BIA).

Project proposal

An international investor seeking to do business in The Bahamas should submit to BIA a project proposal containing the following:
1. Name and address, including telephone/fax.
2. Executive summary of project.
3. Type of business – whether share company, partnership, individual or joint venture.
4. Principals – investors, major beneficial shareholders, including their dates and places of birth, as well as passport or social security numbers.
5. Proposed location.
6. Land requirements.
7. Start-up date.
8. Employment projections – number of Bahamian and non-Bahamian employees.
9. Management/personnel requirement – years of experience, training and work permits* for key personnel.
10. Financial arrangements for project, including bank reference.
11. Environmental impact – toxic waste, disposal procedures, toxic input.
12. Total capital investment in project with a breakdown of items and start-up cost. Minimum investment is $250,000.

* Necessary work permits for key personnel will be granted. Businesses requiring permits for persons other than key personnel are encouraged to consult BIA in advance.

Areas targeted for overseas investors

Following is a list of certain investment areas especially targeted for international investors. However, the list is not exhaustive, and investors interested in areas not included should consult BIA. Joint ventures with Bahamian partners are encouraged, with the choice of partner being at the discretion of the investor.
1. Touristic resorts.
2. Upscale condominium, timeshare and second home development.
3. International business centres.
4. Marinas.
5. Information/data processing.
6. Assembly industries.
7. Hi-tech services.
8. Ship registration, repair and other ship services.
9. Light manufacturing for export.
10. Agro-industries.
11. Food processing.
12. Mariculture.
13. Banking and other financial services.
14. Captive insurance.
15. Aircraft services.
16. Pharmaceutical manufacture.
17. Offshore medical centres.

Areas reserved for Bahamians
1. Wholesale and retail operations.*
2. Commission agencies engaged in the import/export trade.
3. Real estate and domestic property management agencies.
4. Domestic newspaper and magazine publications.
5. Domestic advertising and public relations firms.
6. Nightclubs and restaurants, except speciality, gourmet and ethnic restaurants, and restaurants operating in a hotel, resort complex or tourist attraction.
7. Security services.
8. Domestic distribution of building supplies.
9. Construction companies, except for special structures for which international expertise is required.
10. Personal cosmetic/beauty establishment.
11. Shallow water scalefish, crustacea, mollusks and sponge-fishing operations.
12. Auto and appliance service operations.
13. Public transportation.

* *International investors may engage in the wholesale distribution of any product they produce locally.*

Access to credit facilities
The Bahamas Development Bank (BDB) was created to help Bahamians establish new businesses or expand existing concerns through the provision of concessionary funding and technical assistance, for projects which generate jobs and which contribute to the economic growth and development of The Bahamas.

Joint ventures between international investors and Bahamians may access funding from BDB, although the equity of the overseas investor may not be borrowed from the BDB or domestic capital market. Bahamians may, however, borrow a percentage of their contribution from the BDB or domestic capital market.

Contact the BIA, Office of the Prime Minister, Sir Cecil V Wallace Whitfield Centre, Cable Beach, PO Box CB-10980, Nassau, The Bahamas, tel (242) 327-5970 (to 4); fax (242) 327-5907.

See also **Bahamas Financial Services Board (BFSB); Bahamas Investment Authority (BIA); Banks; Business licence fee; Company formation; Hotels encouragement; Industries encouragement; Property transactions;** and **Trade agreements.**

JUDICIAL SYSTEM
English Common Law is the basis of the Bahamian judicial system, although there is a large volume of Bahamian Statute Law. The highest tribunal in the country is the Court of Appeal, which sits on a full-time basis throughout the year. Five judges are appointed by the Governor-General, including the resident president, two resident judges and two non-resident judges. Generally, three judges sit to conduct hearings. In practice, they are usually leading judges of the Commonwealth HQ, and they need have no former ties with The Bahamas.

The Chief Justice or one of the other eight Justices who are appointed by the Governor-General preside in the Supreme Court, which has general, civil and criminal jurisdiction. In addition there is a Supreme Court and two resident Justices in Freeport, Grand Bahama, dealing with the northern region of The Bahamas, which includes Bimini and Abaco Islands and Grand Bahama. The Supreme Court hears civil and criminal matters throughout the year, beginning on the second Wednesday in January.

New Providence has 15 Magistrates' Courts (including one drug court, one firearms court, one coroner's court, one night civil court and two night traffic courts). Grand Bahama has three Magistrate's Courts (two in Freeport and one in Eight Mile Rock). These courts are presided over by stipendiary and circuit magistrates, including the Chief Magistrate and two senior magistrates, who exercise summary jurisdiction in criminal matters and in civil matters involving amounts not exceeding $5,000. In addition, all Family Island administrators exercise summary jurisdiction in criminal matters of a less serious nature and in civil matters involving amounts not exceeding $400. There are 16 Justices of the Peace (lay magistrates) appointed to hear minor offences in New Providence.

An appeal from a decision of a Family Island administrator acting in his capacity as a magistrate goes to the stipendiary and circuit magistrate, and an appeal from a decision by a stipendiary and circuit magistrate exercising original jurisdiction goes to the Supreme Court. An appeal from a Supreme Court decision lies to The Bahamas Court of Appeal, and an appeal from The Bahamas Court of Appeal lies to the Judicial Committee of the Privy Council in England.

Queen's Counsel

There are currently six members of Her Majesty's Counsel, or Queen's Counsel (QCs), for The Commonwealth of The Bahamas.

These "appointments of silk" are conferred on the most outstanding counsel of the country, and mark the pinnacle of achievement for an attorney-at-law. Eminent lawyers who are senior at the Bar may apply to the Attorney-General, who consults with the Chief Justice, President of the Bar Council and anyone else he sees fit. The Attorney-General recommends appointment to the Prime Minister, who may advise the Governor-General to appoint the applicant a QC. Successful applicants are appointed to the Inner Bar and represent the Crown.

The six members are Sir Orville Turnquest, Governor-General; W E A Callender, retired; Senator Henry Bostwick; Harvey Tynes; Ralph Seligman and Thomas Evans.

JUNKANOO

Junkanoo is the quintessential Bahamian celebration, a parade – or "rush-out" – characterized by colourful costumes, goatskin drums, cowbells, horns and a brass section.

Junkanoo is one of the few examples of uniquely Bahamian culture. The stunning crêpe-paper and cardboard costumes of Caribbean Crayola colours are worked on most of the year. When the celebrations are over, most of them – some of them art masterpieces – are thrown away, although the Junkanoo Expo now preserves the best pieces for exhibit. See **Junkanoo Expo,** following.

Junkanoo, which has been compared to Mardi Gras in New Orleans and Carnival in Rio, is staged in the early hours of Dec 26 and again in the early hours of Jan 1, New Year's Day.

Teamed with hypnotic music conducive to uninhibited dancing, Junkanoo is a never-to-be-forgotten festival of fun and frivolity.

No one knows for certain where it came from or how its name came to be. Some credit it to John Canoe, a legendary West African chieftain. Others say it comes from the French phrase *gens inconnus*, unknown, or masked, people.

Regulars in Junkanoo contests in Nassau include the Valley Boys, Saxons, One Family, Vikings, Music Makers, Most Qualified, Roots, Fancy Dancers, Z-Bandits, Fox Hill Congos, and the PIGS (Progress through Integrity, Guts and Strength).

There is a mini-Junkanoo, or "rush-out," staged somewhere in Nassau and Freeport every week.

Junkanoo Expo

The former Customs warehouse on Prince George Wharf is the site of Junkanoo Expo, showcasing the intricate costumes made with months of handcrafting. Junkanoo Expo is the first sustained effort to display these works of art. The exhibit is open Mon-Sat 9am-5pm, and Sun 3-5pm, admission $2 for adults, 50¢ for children under 12, and 50¢ each for school groups. There is a gift shop and gallery for purchase of Junkanoo books, photographs, souvenirs, paintings, maquettes, T-shirts, CDs and tapes.

LAW FIRMS

Adderley, K Neville, & Co
  Tel 356-6108, fax 356-6109
Adderley, Malcolm E, & Co
  Tel 322-4440/1, fax 322-5848
Adderley, Paul L, The Hon
  Tel 322-2330, fax 356-2138
Albury, Eleanor
  Tel 326-8008, fax 322-5844
Albury, Perry P
  Tel/fax 394-7087
Alexiou, Knowles & Co
  Tel 322-1126,
  fax 328-8395 or 325-0768
Allen, Allen & Co
  Tel 325-4178, fax 326-4452
Bain & Co
  Tel 326-4395, fax 326-4452
Bannister & Co
  Tel 356-4551 or 356-4608;
  fax 356-7236
Barnwell, V C A
  Tel 322-1686, fax 322-6949
Benjamin, Allan J
  Tel 325-4670, fax 322-7333
Bethell, David C, & Co
  Tel/fax 323-7205
* Bostwick & Bostwick
  Tel 322-2038, fax 328-2521
Bowe, Henderson & Co
  Tel 325-8184 or 325-8721;
  fax 325-8217
Butler, Turner, Rose & Co
  Tel 325-1576, fax 325-1578
* Callenders & Co
  Tel 322-2511, fax 326-7666
Campbell, Samuel E, & Co
  Tel 326-5300, fax 322-5554
Campbell-Chase, Elma E
  Tel 326-8916, fax 328-2010
* Cash, Fountain
  Tel 322-2956, fax 322-5453
Cassar, Gavin
  Tel 356-7015, fax 328-4694

Chancery Law Associates
  Tel 356-6108, fax 356-6109
* Christie, Davis & Co
  Tel 322-2715/8, fax 326-7360
Clarke, Clinton O, & Co
  Tel 323-4841, fax 322-3553
Coakley, Wilfred S, & Co
  Tel 325-6666, fax 326-4064
Collie, Sidney S
  Tel 326-3443, fax 326-3586
* Cooke-McIver, Bobbi
  Tel 356-5613, tel/fax 356-5491
Constantakis, Gus
  Tel 323-3523, fax 323-3495
Cooper & Co
  Tel 325-3606, fax 326-4385
Curling, Miriam J
  Tel/fax 322-4288
Deal & Gomez
  Tel 326-3173, fax 356-3960
Dean, Michael A, & Co
  Tel 325-1815, fax 325-3345
Douglas-Sands, E V, & Co
  Tel 328-4192, fax 328-5142
* Dupuch & Turnquest & Co
  Tel 393-3226/9, fax 393-6807
Edwards, Desmond, & Co
  Tel 325-3822, fax 322-4389
Esfakis, Leandra
  Tel 326-5121, fax 356-3156
Evans & Co
  Tel 328-8510 or 322-5178/9;
  fax 322-5942
Ferguson, Lydia S, & Co
  Tel 322-3440, fax 325-0161
Forbes, Arnold A, & Co
  Tel 323-4628/9, fax 323-4622
Gibson & Co
  Tel 362-4645/7, fax 362-4649
Gibson, K M, & Co
  Tel 328-2343/4, fax 328-2345
Gomez, Dennis, & Co
  Tel 328-2959, tel/fax 328-2662
Graham, Thompson & Co
  Tel 322-4130 (to 4), fax 328-1069
Gray, V Alfred, & Co
  Tel 326-8314, fax 322-4617
Green, Terrence Newton
  Tel 356-6240, fax 356-6888
Grimes, Valentine S, & Co
  Tel 356-7791, fax 356-7792
Gwendolyn House
  Tel 356-2038, fax 356-2039

Hall, Rosalie V
  Tel 322-1226, fax 325-8640
Hanna, Arthur D, & Co
  Tel 322-8306, fax 326-5766
Harding-Lee & Co
  Tel 326-4065, fax 326-4067
Harris-Smith, S A Sr, & Co
  Tel/fax 322-7616
Higgs & Johnson
  Tel 322-8571,
  fax 328-7727 or 325-6408
Higgs & Kelly
  Tel 322-7511, fax 325-0724
Hilton, Cecil I, & Co
  Tel 326-8232, tel/fax 326-6766
Hilton, T Langton, & Co
  Tel 322-4080, fax 326-7197
Holowesko, William P
  Tel 322-2315, fax 322-5419
Horton, Michael W
  Tel 325-1877, fax 325-3173
Johnson, Dexter R
  Tel 323-2706, fax 356-9724
Johnson, L B, McDonald & Co
  Tel 328-1815, fax 328-0291
Johnson-Hassan & Co
  Tel 356-3460, fax 356-4747
Kemp, Michael H, & Co
  Tel 325-8730, fax 325-4440
Knowles, McKay & Miller
  Tel 322-3915, fax 326-8434
The Law Chambers
  Tel 356-4551, fax 356-7236
Ledée, Joseph C, & Co
  Tel/fax 325-3738
* Lennox, Paton
  Tel 328-0563, fax 328-0566
Levine, Lionel
  Tel 328-0978, fax 323-8489
Lobosky & Lobosky
  Tel 323-1317, fax 323-1318
Lockhart, Clarita B, & Co
  Tel 356-4500, fax 326-7646
Lockhart, Elliott B, & Co
  Tel 322-1282/4, fax 356-3371
McKay & Moxey
  Tel 322-7474/5, fax 322-2079
* McKinney, Bancroft & Hughes
  Tel 322-4195, fax 328-2520
McKinney, Turner & Co
  Tel 322-8914, fax 328-8326
Mackey, Charles, & Co
  Tel 325-8756, fax 325-8757

Maillis & Maillis
  Tel 322-4292/3, fax 323-2334
Maynard, Peter D, & Co
  Tel 325-5335, fax 325-5411
Minnis, Cartwright & Co
  Tel 323-4845, fax 328-5750
Mortimer & Co
  Tel 356-9777, fax 356-9888
Mosko, Mary C Katina
  Tel 326-5330, fax 326-6639
Moss, Wilbert H, & Co
  Tel 328-1340, fax 325-5565
* Nottage, Miller & Co
  Tel 322-7610, fax 325-2217
Parker, Cedric L
  Tel 322-4954, fax 328-3706
Peet, Vincent A, & Co
  Tel 322-2358, fax 322-8056
* Pinder, Godfrey W, & Co
  Tel/fax 393-5539
Pinder, Marvin L
  Tel 326-2730, fax 328-4707
Pindling & Co
  Tel 325-3443, fax 325-2109
Pyfrom, Jerome E, & Co
  Tel 322-2871, fax 322-2874
Pyfrom & Wells
  Tel 325-4207, fax 356-2593
Quant, Newton & Co
  Tel/fax 326-4002
Regnier, Eliezer, & Co
  Tel 356-5351, fax 364-3521
Richards & Co
  Tel/fax 328-6792
* Roberts, E Dawson, Higgs & Co
  Tel 322-4782/4, fax 322-2048
Roberts, Isaacs & Co
  Tel 322-1751, fax 322-3861
Rolle & Co
  Tel 325-8633/4, fax 325-8658
Russell, Alpin O
  Tel 323-8603, fax 323-3939
Sands, Harry B, & Co
  Tel 322-2670, fax 323-8914
Sears & Co
  Tel 326-3481, fax 326-3483
Serville & Co
  Tel 322-8956, fax 328-8958
Seymour & Co
  Tel 356-0991, fax 356-0993
Sheffields
  Tel 322-7404, fax 322-7168

Simmons & Co
  Tel/fax 323-4810
Smith, Smith & Co
  Tel 326-5886, fax 322-6681
Strachan, Hope, & Co
  Tel 356-4551, fax 356-7236
Tertullien, Mizpah C, & Co
  Tel/fax 322-5206
Thompson, Anthony A, & Co
  Tel 325-1126, fax 322-3919
Thompson, James M
  Tel 322-1490, fax 322-3364
Thompson, Jeanne I
  Tel 322-2605, fax 325-6667
Toothe, E P, & Assoc
  Tel 356-6940, fax 356-6939
Unwala & Co
  Tel 322-7403, fax 356-6663
Virgill & Virgill
  Tel 325-7742, fax 325-3432
Wallace Whitfield, Vincent
  Tel 394-8780, fax 394-8779
* Wallace Whitfield & Co
  Tel 394-8780, fax 394-8779
* Ward, Jan & Co
  Tel 323-1471, fax 325-2377
Watkins, Foulkes & Co
  Tel 322-8970, fax 323-7522
Wells & Wells
  Tel 325-4618, fax 322-4967
Williams, Dudley M, & Co
  Tel 323-8604, fax 323-3939
Williams Law Chambers
  Tel 323-3927, fax 325-8637
Zervos, Nicholas J, & Co
  Tel/fax 325-3902

Freeport office also.

LIBRARIES

Coconut Grove Community Library,
  Acklins St, Coconut Grove:
  Mon-Fri 10am-5:30pm. Tel 323-4310.
College of The Bahamas Library,
  Poinciana Dr:
  Mon-Thur 8am-9pm; Fri 8am-6pm;
  Sat 9am-5pm; Sun 1-5pm
  July-Aug: Mon-Fri 8am-5pm.
  Tel 323-8550 (to 2) ext 4517.
Eastern Public Library, Mackey St:
  Mon-Fri 10am-9pm; Sat 10am-5pm
  July-Sept: Mon-Fri 9am-8pm;
  Sat 10am-4pm. Tel 393-2196.

Fox Hill Public Library, Bernard Rd:
  Mon-Fri 10am-8pm;
  Sat 10am-1pm. Tel 324-1458.
G K Symonette Library, Yellow Elder:
  Mon-Fri 9am-5:30pm. Tel 322-5303.
Kemp Rd Community Library,
  Kemp Rd:
  Mon-Fri 9am-5:30pm. Tel 393-3147.
Learning Resources Library,
  Mackey St:
  Mon-Fri 9am-5:30pm. Tel 393-5379.
Nassau Public Library, Shirley St
  (main library):
  Mon-Thurs 10am-8pm;
  Fri 10am-5pm; Sat 10am-4pm.
  Tel 322-4907.
Southern Public Library, Blue Hill Rd:
  Mon-Fri 10am-9pm; Sat 10am-5pm.
  July-Aug: Mon-Fri 9am-8pm;
  Sat 10am-5pm. Tel 322-1056.

LIQUOR LAWS

The legal drinking age in The Bahamas is 18. Liquor licence applicants must be over 21. It is illegal to sell intoxicating liquor in The Bahamas without a licence. Under the Act Relating to the Sale of Intoxicating Liquors, this includes spirits, wines, ale, beer, porter, stout, cider, perry and other malt liquor, and any fermented or distilled liquor. Exceptions to this rule are:

1. Intoxicating liquor sold by virtue of legal process or law which authorizes the sale.
2. Intoxicating liquor that is pure alcohol and sold in the drug store of a licensed chemist or pharmacist, or is in medicinal form and sold by a qualified medical practitioner or licensed chemist or pharmacist.
3. Intoxicating liquor which forms part of the estate of a deceased person and the Licensing Authority authorizes sale thereof, or where the liquor is sold by a licensed auctioneer under conditions set by the Licensing Authority.
4. Intoxicating liquor sold at premises duly registered as a members' club.
5. Intoxicating liquor sold on board any ship calling at The Bahamas

and lying outside the limits of any port, to be consumed aboard ship.
6. Intoxicating liquor sold to passengers aboard any ship calling at The Bahamas and lying within the limits of any harbour for a period not exceeding 72 hrs, to be consumed aboard ship.

There are six types of liquor licences: general, wholesale, proprietary club, hotel, restaurant and bar and occasional. The occasional licence is granted for the sale of intoxicating liquors for consumption at a stated place and time not exceeding three days at any one time. In New Providence, an occasional licence may be granted by the chairman of the Licensing Authority.

Issuing, cancelling or transferring of a liquor licence is at the discretion of the Licensing Authority. No general licence will be granted in districts where a prohibitive order is in force.

Once a liquor licence has been granted in New Providence or a Family Island, the applicant has three months to pay the fee.

According to the Act, no licensee other than the holder of a hotel, proprietary club or restaurant licence shall sell, expose for sale or dispose of intoxicating liquor on Sun, and before 7am or after 9pm on any weekday, unless otherwise authorized by the Licensing Authority.

Contact the Business Licence and Licensing Authority, Nassau, tel (242) 322-5200, or the Financial Secretary, Ministry of Finance and Planning, PO Box N-3107, Nassau, The Bahamas, tel (242) 327-1530.

See also **Shopping, Cruise ship shopping.**

LOMÉ IV CONVENTION

One of the major advantages of investing in The Bahamas is the privileged access our products have to the world's largest markets.

The Lomé IV Convention is a comprehensive trade agreement between the African-Caribbean-Pacific (ACP) states and the European Union (EU). The Agreement was ratified by The Bahamas government on Dec 15, 1989. The agreement between The Bahamas and the EU for the second financial protocol of Lomé was signed Feb 24, 1997.

Lomé IV embodies a wide package of industrial, financial and trade cooperation principles. Products originating in ACP states may be imported free of Customs duties and import charges or quotas into the EU. The only exceptions are certain products covered by the EU common agricultural policy. While not entitled to free access, they receive preferential treatment.

Although Lomé IV expires in 2000, efforts are being made to ensure its basic principles will be upheld.

Contact the Ministry of Finance and Planning, PO Box N-3017, Nassau, The Bahamas, tel (242) 327-1530 (to 7), fax (242) 327-1618 or 327-1620.

See also **Trade agreements.**

LOTTERIES

Under provisions of The Lotteries and Gaming Act, it is unlawful for any person to be involved in a lottery promoted or proposed to be promoted in The Bahamas. This includes printing of tickets, distribution, advertisements, listing of prize winners and connection with a lottery in any manner. Offenders will be subject to a fine or imprisonment.

However, lotteries (raffles) are permitted when they are incidental to certain entertainment. This includes bazaars, sales of work, dinners, dances and other similar functions, including entertainment by way of bingo, crab-racing and hobby-horse-racing on tables. These functions must be previously approved, in writing, by the Minister with responsibility for gaming.

The following conditions apply:
1. The whole proceeds of the entertainment (including the lottery), after deductions, must be devoted to purposes other than private gain.

2. None of the lottery prizes shall be money.
3. The facilities afforded for participating in lotteries cannot be the only substantial inducement to persons to attend the entertainment.

A private lottery is permitted. This is a lottery in which sale of tickets or chances by the promoters is confined to:
1. Members of one society (clubs, institutions, organizations, etc) established and conducted for purposes not connected with gaming, betting or lotteries.
2. Persons all of whom work on the same premises.
3. Persons all of whom reside on the same premises.

Private lotteries must adhere to several regulations, details of which are available through the Ministry with responsibility for gaming.

Any three or more residents of The Bahamas may organize a lottery for the purpose of fundraising for religious, educational or charitable purposes, promotion of athletic games or cultural activities, or for promotion of the welfare of the community.

Organizers of such lotteries must:
1. Obtain prior approval, in writing, from the Minister with responsibility for gaming.
2. Declare the purposes for which the lottery is being held.
3. Enter into a bond with the Treasurer for payment of 15% of gross receipts of the lottery.
4. Pay this duty within 14 days of the lottery, along with an accountant's statement verifying the amount. The Minister of Finance and Planning may waive or refund duty payable on the lottery.

In New Providence, contact the Ministry with responsibility for gaming, PO Box N-3217, tel 356-6792. In Freeport, contact the senior administrator, Dept of Local Government, PO Box F-40001, tel (242) 352-6332. In the Family Islands, contact the administrator on that island.

MAIL-BOATS
See **Transportation.**

MANUFACTURING

According to latest available figures from the Dept of Statistics, 1994 manufacturing output in The Bahamas totalled $175,979,600. The leading manufactured products are beverages and pharmaceuticals – particularly rum and liqueurs, which have been among leading manufactured items since 1960, when Bacardi shareholders reconstituted their Castro-confiscated Cuban company in The Bahamas. Today, Bacardi & Co Ltd employs 130 persons on a permanent basis, and an additional 40 indirectly. Products include Bacardi Light-Dry, Gold, Dark, Select, 151 and Spice rums, Bacardi 8 and Bacardi 5 Años, Nassau Royale Liqueur, Natasha Vodka and Castillo rums. More than 95% of Bacardi products are exported to Europe and the US. In 1997, the equivalent of 2.2 million nine-litre cases were exported.

Commonwealth Brewery Ltd (CBL), Clifton Pier, represents an investment of over $30 million in The Bahamas. The company has a brewing capacity of 1.7 million cases per annum. The partners comprise international and Bahamian interests: Heineken International and Associated Bahamian Distillers and Brewers (ABDAB). The first two products in CBL's locally produced portfolio were Heineken and Guinness. Then came Vita Malt and the Bahamian beer Kalik – named for the "kalik-kalik" sound of cowbells during Junkanoo – which is the No 1 selling beer in The Bahamas. On July 7, 1992, Kalik was awarded the Monde Selection Gold Medal for the third year in a row by the Intl Institute for Quality Selections (IIQS) in Brussels. For this distinction, CBL has been awarded the Trophy of International High Quality by the IIQS. CBL has launched two product extensions from Kalik, Kalik Gold and Kalik Light. In Aug 1997, CBL began selling Kalik to Royal Caribbean Intl's *Sovereign of the Seas*.

At press time, plans were underway to initiate sales to other cruise lines, including Carnival and Disney. CBL presently exports Kalik to Florida and plans to begin distribution to all states in the US.

At Bahamian trade shows, locally manufactured goods on display include shell crafts, art, wood carvings, ceramics, condiments, beverages, Bahamian cassettes and CDs.

Bahamian factories include Imperial Mattress, Scottdale Bedding and Simmons Manufacturing Co, Ltd, a shoe manufacturer located in the industrial park on Soldier Rd.

Other manufactured goods are Androsia batik fabrics, bleach, soaps, detergents, polystyrene beads, medical devices (stents), pharmaceuticals, soft drinks, beer, handcrafted boats, paint and paper items, bottled water, dolls, gold and shell jewellery, handcrafted furniture and fragrances.

Traditional Bahamian straw goods provide a viable tourist attraction, and yet another way to keep hard currency in the country. Visit such stores as the Plait Lady, Island T'ings, Pyfrom's, The Seagrape, Tropic Traders, Everything's Paradise, Paradise Tees and Big Kahuna for quality, genuine Bahamian-made crafts.

The government has removed many cumbersome manufacturing requirements and introduced incentives to diversify the country's tourism-based economy and encourage a stronger manufacturing sector.

See also **Industry; Trade agreements; Import & export statistics** and **Freeport/Lucaya information, Industry.**

Find out about eco-friendly Bahamas at

bahamasnet
www.bahamasnet.com

ECO-BAHAMAS

PO Box N-7513, Nassau, The Bahamas
Tel (242) 323 5665 Fax (242) 323 5728
email info@bahamasnet.com

MARINAS & CRUISING FACILITIES

Listings for marinas and cruising facilities indicate those which have approx 25 or more slips at their facility. For depth, availability and dockage rate information, contact the facility directly. Most marinas monitor channel 16 and a doctor/nurse or clinic if not on site is usually nearby.
See **Fig 2.0** and **Boating.**

MARINE PARKS & EXHIBITS

Crystal Cay off Arawak Cay, has the world's largest man-made, natural coral reef which can be viewed in an underwater observatory with a 360-degree view. In Sept 1996, the park was acquired by Ruffin Companies, owners of the Nassau Marriott Resort & Crystal Palace Casino. Tel 328-1036.

See also **Marine research; Paradise Island** and **Wildlife preserves.**

MARINE RESEARCH

The reef-rich seas of The Bahamas have inspired national and international research embracing the gamut of marine-oriented subjects – including dolphins and whales, blue holes, lost civilizations, shipwrecks, shoreline ecosystems, plankton, the Bermuda triangle and underwater habitats. Bahamas-based research organizations include:

Atlantic Undersea Testing and Evaluation Centre (AUTEC): See **Bahamas information** heading of the same name.

The Bahamas Marine Mammal Survey: Long-term research programme which documents occurrence, diversity, seasonality and abundance of dolphins and whale species in Bahama waters. Another objective is to determine population estimates and life history parameters of resident species for conservation. The research is funded by a grant from Earthwatch and private contributions. Contact
cont pg 395

FIG 2.0
MARINAS & CRUISING FACILITIES

Location	Slips	Fuel	Electric	Water/ice	Shower/wash/dry	Groc/supply	Rest/bar	Boat/elect repair	Charter/boat rental	Motel/hotel
Abacos										
Boat Harbour Marina, Marsh Harbour (242) 367-2736	180	√	110, 220	√	√	√	√	√	√	√
Conch Inn Marina, Marsh Harbour (242) 367-4000	75	√	110, 220	√	√	√	√	x	√	√
Green Turtle Club & Yacht Club, Green Turtle Cay (242) 365-4271	32	√	110, 220	√	√	√	√	x	x	√
Mangoes Marina, Marsh Harbour (242) 367-4255	30	x	110, 220	√	√	√	√	√	x	x
Marsh Harbour Marina, Marsh Harbour (242) 367-2700	50	√	110, 220	√	√	√	√	√	x	x
Treasure Cay Beach Marina, Great Abaco (242) 365-8250	150	√	110, 220	√	√	√	√	√	√	√
Walker's Cay Marina, (242) 353-1252	72	√	110, 220	√	√	√	√	√	√	√
Berry Islands										
Chub Cay Club Marina (242) 325-1490	92	√	110, 220	√	√	√	√	x	x	√
Great Harbour Cay Marina (242) 367-8005	80	√	110, 220	√	√	√	√	√	√	√
Bimini										
Bimini Big Game Club & Hotel (242) 347-3391	84	√	110, 220	√	√	√	√	x	√	√
Bimini Blue Water Ltd (242) 347-3166	32	√	110, 220	√	√	x	√	√	√	√
Eleuthera, Harbour Island & Spanish Wells										
Harbour Island Club & Marina, Harbour Island (242) 333-2427	30	√	110, 220	√	√	√	√	√	x	√

Location	Slips	Fuel	Electric	Water/ice	Shower/wash/dry	Groc/supply	Rest/bar	Boat/elect repair	Charter/boat rental	Motel/hotel
Spanish Wells Yacht Haven, Spanish Wells (242) 333-4328	32	√	110, 220	√	√	x	√	x	x	√
Valentine's Yacht Club & Marina, Harbour Island (242) 333-2142	36	√	110, 220	√	√	√	√	√	√	√

Exumas

Location	Slips	Fuel	Electric	Water/ice	Shower/wash/dry	Groc/supply	Rest/bar	Boat/elect repair	Charter/boat rental	Motel/hotel
Exuma Docking Service, (242) 336-2578	52	√	110, 220	√	√	√	√	√	√	√
Sampson Cay Colony Ltd George Town (242) 355-2034	40	√	110, 220	√	√	√	√	√	√	√

Grand Bahama

Location	Slips	Fuel	Electric	Water/ice	Shower/wash/dry	Groc/supply	Rest/bar	Boat/elect repair	Charter/boat rental	Motel/hotel
Lucayan Marina, Lucaya (242) 373-8888	150	√	110, 220, 440	√	√	x	√	x	x	√
Port Lucaya Marina, Lucaya (242) 373-9090 (to 2)	125	√	110, 220	√	√	√	√	√	√	√
Running Mon Marina, Freeport (242) 352-6834	66	√	110	√	√	√	√	√	√	√
Xanadu Beach Marina Resort, Freeport (242) 352-6782	77	√	110, 220	√	√	x	√	x	√	√

New Providence

Location	Slips	Fuel	Electric	Water/ice	Shower/wash/dry	Groc/supply	Rest/bar	Boat/elect repair	Charter/boat rental	Motel/hotel
Bayshore Marina, East Bay St (242) 393-8232	150	√	110, 220	√	x	x	x	√	x	x
Brown's Boat Basin, East Bay St (242) 393-3331	70	√	110, 220	√	x	x	x	√	x	x
East Bay Marina, East Bay St (242) 394-1816	25	√	110, 220	√	√	x	√	√	x	x
Lyford Cay Club (private), Lyford Cay (242) 362-4131	74	√	110, 220	√	√	√	√	x	√	√

Location	Slips	Fuel	Electric	Water/ice	Shower/wash/dry	Groc/supply	Rest/bar	Boat/elect repair	Charter/boat rental	Motel/hotel
Nassau Harbour Club, East Bay St (242) 393-0771	65	√	110, 220	√	√	√	√	√	√	√
Nassau Yacht Haven, East Bay St (242) 393-8173	120	√	110, 220	√	√	x	√	x	√	x
Paradise Island Hurricane Hole Marina (242) 363-3600	61	√	110, 220, 440	√	√	√	√	√	√	√

cont from pg 392
Diane Claridge, PO Box AB-20714, Marsh Harbour, Abaco, tel/fax 367-4505.

The **Bimini Biological Field Station:** World-class shark research centre devoted to research, education and conservation of shark species in the wild. Dr Samuel Gruber, professor of marine biology and fisheries at the Univ of Miami's Rosenstiel School of Marine and Atmospheric Science, offers accredited shark awareness and marine biology courses to international high school and college students, and an annual scholarship is also made available to a student in The Bahamas. The station concentrates studies on the reproduction, age, growth and mortality of lemon sharks. Contact Dr Gruber, 9300 SW 99th St, Miami, FL 33176-2050, USA, tel/fax (305) 274-0628, tel 361-4146, e-mail: sgruber@rsmas.miami.edu

The Rob Palmer Blue Holes Foundation: Dedicated to exploration and research of Bahamian blue holes and caverns. Contact Dr Stephanie Schwabe, Blue Holes Foundation, PO Box F-44722, Freeport, Grand Bahama. Tel/fax (242) 373-4483, e-mail: 100432.616@compuserve.com

Caribbean Marine Research Center (CMRC): Lee Stocking Island, Exuma. Internationally recognized for ecology research, natural resource management, coral reef habitats, climatic change, marine geological change, and aquaculture. Of particular concern to The Bahamas is overfishing and reproductive habits of queen conch, spiny lobster and Nassau grouper. CMRC attracts scientists and students from all over the world. Contact island manager, PO Box EX-29001, George Town, Exuma, tel (242) 358-4557, or CMRC, The Perry Foundation, 1501 N Point Parkway, Suite 101, West Palm Beach, FL 33407.

The Dolphin Experience: An educational and research facility at Sanctuary Bay focusing on marine mammal interaction and conservation with dolphins. Daily education programmes. PO Box F-43788, Freeport, Grand Bahama, tel (242) 373-1250, fax (242) 373-3948.

Island Expedition: Non-profit research and educational organization which conducts study excursions throughout The Bahamas and Caribbean. The School at Sea programme involves students from all over the world. PO Box CB-11934, Nassau, tel 325-2573, fax 327-8659.

Much of the marine research carried out in The Bahamas is chronicled in the *Bahamas Journal of Science,* published three times yearly by Media Publications in Nassau.

See also **Bahamas National Trust; Marine parks & exhibits; Nature centres;** and **Wildlife preserves.**

MARRIAGE LICENCES

Marriage licences cost $40 and are obtained in New Providence at the Registrar General's office, R E Bain Bldg, corner of Parliament and Shirley Sts, PO Box N-532, Nassau, The Bahamas. No blood test is required.

Minimum age without parental consent is 18. Minors may be married with both parents' consent if they have reached the age of 15. However, under special circumstances, those between the ages of 13-15 may apply to the Supreme Court for special permission to marry. Consent forms for minors are available at the Registrar General's office.

Applications for marriage licences and consent forms must be filled out in the presence of a marriage officer (including Family Island administrators), the Registrar General, a magistrate, Justice of the Peace, notary public, Registrar of Marriages or other person legally authorized to administer oaths.

Both parties desiring to be married must be in The Bahamas at the time of application and must have resided in The Bahamas at least 15 days immediately prior to the date of application for a marriage licence. The Registrar General may exempt any applicant from this requirement, but a waiver of the 15-day residency requirement will not normally be granted unless both parties have resided in The Bahamas for 24 hours. The waiver from 15 days to 24 hours' residency may be granted by an administrator in the Family Islands and the Registrar General's office in Nassau and Freeport, Grand Bahama.

If either party is a citizen or resident of a country other than the US, a declaration certifying that he or she is not married must be sworn before a notary public or other person authorized to administer oaths in that country.

Applicants from England, Canada or other British Commonwealth countries may provide an affidavit of singlehood from a solicitor or Commissioner for Oaths in their jurisdiction. This declaration must accompany the application. An applicant from any non-Commonwealth country (except Haiti or Jamaica) who has never been married may swear an affidavit of singlehood before a notary public in The Bahamas.

A divorced person is required to provide a certified copy of the final divorce decree, and a person whose former spouse has died must provide a certified copy of the death certificate.

There were 2,806 marriages in The Bahamas in 1997 compared with 2,628 in 1996.

MOTOR VEHICLE INSURANCE

All motor vehicles in The Bahamas must be licensed and insured in accordance with The Bahamas Road Traffic Act.[1] Cost of insurance depends on the make, model, value and use of the vehicle as well as the driver's age and driving record.

Minimum coverage required by law is road "act" coverage.[2] This covers the insured's legal liability for death and bodily injury to a third party other than a passenger in the insured's vehicle. Third party insurance covers legal liability for death, bodily injury (which may include passengers in the insured's vehicle) and property damage. Third party fire & theft coverage is also available and provides the same coverage as third party, but with the addition of fire and theft coverage. Comprehensive coverage encompasses third party liability, fire, theft, windscreen and collision damage. Windstorm, hurricanes, strikes and riots are now covered under some comprehensive policies. If not covered, they can be added for an additional premium. Comprehensive is the most expensive type of coverage.

Normally, only drivers named under the policy are covered to drive. Some

---

[1] A bond is sometimes available in place of insurance.
[2] At press time, plans had been announced to eliminate "act" insurance but legislation was not yet in place.

companies require drivers to fill out proposal forms. Whether or not there is an additional charge depends on the driver's age, experience, and traffic and accident record. In most cases, there is no additional charge for drivers over 25 years old who have had several years' experience, with a clear driving record.

With the exception of act coverage, no-claims discounts are usually allowed for consecutive claim-free years. A no-claims discount entitlement scale is highest under the comprehensive policy.

Example: A 29-year-old owner of a 1998 Nissan Sentra worth approx $20,000, who has never been insured previously yet is a driver in good standing, may be issued a comprehensive policy of approx $2,618 (gross). If the individual has been driving since the age of 17, with insurance in his name since that age with no claims, he could receive a 65% discount for a net premium of $917. This example is based on comprehensive coverage where no-claims discounts build each claim-free year up to a max discount of 60-65%. This max discount is allowed as long as the insured person maintains a claim-free policy. Discounts vary with different insurance companies.

See also **Driver's licence & vehicle information** and **Insurance.**

MUSEUMS
See **Art galleries & museums.**

MUTUAL FUNDS
See **Investing.**

NATIONAL ANTHEM
See **National symbols.**

NATIONAL INSURANCE
The Bahamas National Insurance scheme provides income replacement to qualified insured persons for retirement, invalidity, sickness, maternity and industrial injuries. Upon the death of the insured breadwinner of a family, payments, including funeral and survivors' benefits, are made to surviving dependents. Free unlimited medical care is provided for industrial injury and/or industrial disease.

The Non-Contributory Pension Programme provided under the Old Age Pensions Act, previously administered by the Social Welfare Dept, became the responsibility of the National Insurance Board in 1974. Qualification for assistance is based on need, which is determined by a prescribed test of an applicant's financial resources. These awards, which were increased to $160 per month from Aug 1, 1992, include the Old Age Non-Contributory Pension (OANCP), invalidity, survivors' and sickness assistance.

Registration of workers and collection of contributions from all employed persons over 14 yrs began in 1974. Social security coverage was extended to self-employed persons in 1976.

For the first 10 years, the insurable wage ceiling on which contributions were fixed was $110 per week. This ceiling was raised in July 1984 to $250 per week, or $1,083 per month. The total contribution remained 8.8% of the insurable wage, up to the ceiling of $250 per week/$1,083 per month. Contributions on wages from $60 to $250 are shared at 3.4% from the employee (max weekly portion, $8.50) and 5.4% from the employer (max weekly portion $13.50, for a combined weekly max of $22). Wages under $60 incur contributions of 1.7% from the employee and 7.1% from the employer.

Self-employed persons
Most categories of self-employed persons pay contributions at the rate of 6.8% of their average weekly insurable income up to a max of $250 (max weekly contribution, $17), as they are not eligible to receive industrial benefits. The following categories of self-employed persons pay 8.8% of

their average weekly insurable income up to a max of $250 (max weekly contribution, $22):
1. Drivers owning motor vehicles licensed for hire.
2. Licensed fruit/straw/vegetable vendors.
3. Share-fishermen owning fishing vessels or boats.

Benefits
Under provisions of the National Insurance Act, a previously insured person who is now unemployed may apply to become a voluntarily insured person. Subject to certain prescribed conditions, voluntary contributions count towards retirement, invalidity, survivors' and funeral benefits.

Contributions in this category are 5%, based on the average weekly earnings during the year before the individual ceased to be employed or self-employed.

In the case of civil servants eligible for pensions under the Pension Act, contributions for retirement and invalidity benefits are based on a weekly insurable wage ceiling of $110. For all other benefits, the wage ceiling for this group is $250.

Payment of benefits commenced with sickness benefit in April 1975. Maternity and funeral benefit payments began in Sept 1975.

Employed and voluntarily insured persons became entitled to retirement, survivors' and invalidity benefits in 1977. Self-employed persons became eligible for these benefits in 1979. Previously, retirement benefit was paid to an insured person, 65 years or older, who had retired and paid the required minimum of 150 contributions into the scheme. Under the amended regulations of 1984, insured persons could elect to receive early retirement benefit but at a reduced rate.

For example, individuals electing to retire at age 60 receive 75% of the benefit to which they would have been entitled at age 65. An individual opting to retire at age 61 receives 82%; 62, 88%; 63, 93%; and at age 64 the individual receives 97% of the retirement benefit entitlement.

Individuals retiring at an earlier age will not have their benefit changed when they reach age 65.

The amendments also made it possible for retirees to continue to work as employed persons and earn up to $120 weekly, or $520 monthly, or $6,240 annually, and continue to receive full retirement benefit. Full retirement benefit is $190-$650 per month. The minimum of $165 per month is paid to those who take early retirement at age 60.

Survivors' benefit: Paid to the surviving dependents of a deceased insured person who had paid a minimum of 150 contributions into the scheme. This benefit is paid in order of priority, with the widow/widower being the first priority; unmarried dependent children under 16 yrs, or under 18 yrs if full-time students, the second priority.

Invalidity benefit: Paid to an insured person, 16-65 yrs, who has paid a minimum of 150 contributions and has been diagnosed by the Board's medical referee as being permanently incapable of gainful employment.

The rate of payment for both survivors' (adults) and invalidity benefits is the same as retirement – $190-$650 per month.

Sickness and maternity benefits: These benefits are $43.85-$150 per week for insured persons (60% of the individual's average weekly insurable wage). Minimum contribution requirements apply. Normally, sickness benefit is payable for a max of 156 days for a continuous period of illness, but payment may be extended to 240 days in certain circumstances. Maternity benefit is paid for 13 weeks, commencing within six weeks before the expected week of confinement provided the woman has stopped working. Payment may be extended up to 15 weeks if the confinement is delayed.

As of Oct 1984, all insured women eligible to receive maternity benefit are also entitled to a maternity grant of $250 for each live birth.

Funeral benefit: Paid in the form of a $1,000 grant on the death of an insured person to the individual who has paid, or is liable to pay, the funeral expenses. Minimum contribution requirements apply. Funeral benefit is also paid for funeral expenses of an uninsured deceased spouse, based on contributions of the insured husband or wife.

Industrial benefits: Introduced in 1980 to be paid to, or in respect of, employed persons irrespective of age or contribution status, and to categories of self-employed persons identified above who suffer injury, disability or death as a result of an accident or a prescribed disease arising out of, or in the course of, employment. Minimum contribution requirements apply.

The industrial benefits replaced the provisions of the repealed Workmen's Compensation Act and include injury benefit, paid for a continuous period or in spells, for up to 240 days from the date of the accident, or the date of development of the prescribed disease; disablement benefit, which is paid according to the degree of disablement the person suffers as a result of the accident or prescribed disease; and death benefit, which is paid to the surviving dependents when death results from the accident or prescribed disease.

Injury benefit ranges from $43.85-$167.67 per week (66.66% of the person's insurable wage). Payment of disablement benefit is based on the degree of disablement. If it is more than 1% but less than 25%, the benefit is paid in the form of a cash grant at the rate of $100 for each 1% of disablement.

If the degree of disablement is 25% or greater, benefit is paid both as a grant and a pension. This pension is paid for life or a specified period. Death benefit is paid according to the rate of the injury benefit paid or payable.

In 1986, a provision was introduced in the Act enabling employers to modify the rates of benefits payable under their own pension schemes. It allows employers to integrate their benefits with those provided under the National Insurance Act and to eliminate overlapping benefits.

Employers wishing to change their Occupational Pension Schemes must first submit proposed modification to the Minister responsible for National Insurance, for approval. Employers may modify terms and conditions of the contract of service relating to wage payment during sick, maternity or injury leave, to take into account similar benefits provided under the National Insurance scheme.

Investment

A secondary goal of the National Insurance scheme is to positively impact the socio-economic development of the country. To this end, a significant proportion of the National Insurance Board's (NIB) total investment portfolio, which now well exceeds the three-quarter-billion dollar mark, has been made in areas which would achieve this goal. These areas include government registered stock; long-term loans to quasi-governmental corporations to assist in the development of basic infrastructure, especially in the Family Islands; investment in real property, which includes 17 community health clinics throughout the country, the NIB's income-producing Freeport office complex in Grand Bahama; Alexander House on Robinson Rd; the head office complex on Blue Hill Rd; the Fox Hill complex and the newly established office on Wulff Rd, Nassau.

NIB's investments include a category for social investments, which provides concessional loans through the Bahamas Development Bank (BDB) for entrepreneurial projects in agriculture, fishing and manufacturing.

Administration
The National Insurance scheme is administered by a tripartite board comprising 11 members. Five members are appointed at the discretion of the Minister responsible for National Insurance, three are appointed to represent employers and three represent insured persons. A chairman and deputy chairman are appointed by the Minister.

NIB headquarters are on Blue Hill Rd, New Providence, with a local office on the ground floor and three regional offices: one in the Wulff Road Bldg, one in the Fox Hill complex near the Parade Ground, and one in Alexander House on Robinson Rd. The Board also operates two cashier's windows for payment of contributions in New Providence. These are located on the ground floor of the main post office, East Hill St, and in the post office on Cable Beach.

There are 24 local offices in the major Family Islands, including four offices in Freeport, which provide a full range of services to contributors, claimants and the general public.

The NIB also operates a consumer telephone hotline service Mon-Fri 9am-5:30pm, through which answers to any National Insurance questions may be obtained. Tel 322-1280 or 322-2009.

NATIONAL PARKS & RESERVES, & PROTECTED AREAS
See **Wildlife preserves.**

NATIONAL SYMBOLS
Coat of arms
By royal warrant dated Dec 7, 1971, The Bahamas was granted a new coat of arms, the description of which, in heraldic terms, is as follows:

"Argent a representation of the Santa Maria on a base barry wavy of four Azure on a Chief Azure a demi Sun Or And for the Crest upon a representation of Our Royal Helmet mantled Azure doubled Argent On a Wreath Or and Azure A Conch Shell proper in front of a Panache of Palm Fronds proper And for Supporters On the dexter a Marlin Proper on the sinister a Flamingo proper; And upon a Compartment Per pale Waves of the Sea and Swampland proper together with the motto: FORWARD, UPWARD, ONWARD, TOGETHER."

The new coat of arms was developed from drawings submitted by artist Rev Dr Hervis L Bain, Jr, who also contributed to the design of the Bahamas flag.

Flag
The design of The Bahamas flag is a black equilateral triangle on a background of three equal horizontal stripes of aquamarine, gold and aquamarine. Its design is based on a composite of ideas and suggestions collected from Bahamians in a national competition to design the flag, held two years before independence.

The official symbolism of the flag's colours and design is as follows: Black represents the vigour and force of a united people; the triangle pointing towards the body of the flag represents the enterprise and determination of Bahamians to develop and possess the rich resources of land and sea symbolized by gold and aquamarine respectively; the colours of the flag are symbolic of our bright tropical land of sea and sun.

National anthem
Lift up your head to the rising sun,
   Bahamaland;
March on to glory, your bright banners
   waving high.
See how the world marks the manner
   of your bearing!
Pledge to excel thro' love and unity.
Pressing onward, march together to a
   common loftier goal;
Steady sunward, tho' the weather hide
   the wide and treach'rous shoal.
Lift up your head to the rising sun,
   Bahamaland;

*'Til the road you've trod lead unto
your God,
March on, Bahamaland!*
Timothy Gibson, CBE (1903-1978)

National bird
The national bird is the flamingo, a pink long-legged wader of the genus *phoenicopterus*. The Bahamas is the site of the world's largest breeding colony of flamingoes, in Inagua.

National fish
The blue marlin, sharp-nosed aristocrat of Atlantic game fish, is the national fish.

National flower
The yellow elder *(Tecoma stans or Stenolobium stans)*, a tubular-shaped yellow flower with delicate red stripes on each petal, is the national flower of The Bahamas.

National tree
The lignum vitae, or tree of life *(Guaiacum sanctum)*, is the national tree. It is the heaviest of all woods with clusters of small blue flowers at the branch tips.

NATURE CENTRES
The Bahamas government is committed to enhancing the country's status as a centre for ecotourism. Various projects have been undertaken to reclaim and restore areas of natural beauty and ecological importance. In New Providence, the Adelaide Creek wetlands near Adelaide Village were restored and mangroves and marine life regenerated. Causeways and bridges were built. Since completion of the project, a wide variety of marine wildlife has moved in – including barracuda, shrimp, grey snapper, lobster, bonefish, egrets, ducks and crabs. You may even see an Inagua donkey!

Ardastra Gardens and Conservation Centre is at the forefront of conservation efforts. In 1995, a captive breeding programme was set up to prevent the extinction of the Bahama parrot, which is on the endangered species list. This 5½-acre exotic garden is home to some 300 animals, birds and reptiles, many of them endangered species, and houses a large flock of the West Indian flamingo, The Bahamas' national bird. Marching flamingos perform three times daily. Open daily 9am-5pm. Last admission 4:30pm. Admission fee: adult residents, $5, non-residents, $10; children 4-12, $2.50 residents, $5 non-residents; under four, free. Located off West Bay St, one mile west of city, tel 323-5806.

The **Botanical Gardens** nature centre contains 18 acres of tropical flora. More than 600 species are featured. Contributions from the Republic of China were used for extensive renovations. Open Mon-Fri 8am-4pm Adults, $1; children 12 and under, 50¢. Tel 323-5975.

See also **Bahamas National Trust; Marine parks & exhibits; Tourism,** Ecotourism; and **Wildlife preserves.**

NEWSPAPERS
The Nassau Guardian and *The Tribune* are the two national dailies (Mon-Sat). They are printed in Nassau and widely circulated in Nassau and Freeport with delayed and limited circulation in the Family Islands. Both sell for 50¢.

In Jan 1997, *The Tribune* began printing *The Miami Herald International Satellite Edition*, selling for 50¢. It changed from an afternoon to a morning newspaper in May 1998 and began including the Satellite edition at no extra charge.

Shortly thereafter, *The Nassau Guardian* added an afternoon edition. *The Bahama Journal* is a national daily distributed throughout The Bahamas and selling for 50¢. A British-styled tabloid called *The Punch* is on sale every Mon and Thur for 75¢.

The Freeport News, published daily (Mon-Sat) in Freeport, sells for 50¢.

Caribbean Week, published bi-weekly in Barbados, costs $1. It is distributed in The Bahamas and contains some Bahamian news.

Foreign newspapers usually available include: *The Miami Herald* (Sun edition), *The New York Times, The Wall Street Journal, The Times of London, Financial Times, Barron's* and *USA Today.*

NORTH AMERICAN FREE TRADE AGREEMENT (NAFTA)

The North American Free Trade Agreement (NAFTA) became effective on Jan 1, 1994, as a partnership relaxing – and eventually eliminating – trade barriers between the US, Canada and Mexico. The agreement, which established the world's largest free trade zone, marked the first step in establishment of even broader trade agreements throughout the southern hemisphere.

According to the *1997 Study on the Operation and Effects of the North American Free Trade Agreement,* US two-way trade with NAFTA partners grew 44% since the agreement was signed, compared with 33% for the rest of the world. Exports to Canada and Mexico supported an estimated 2.3 million jobs in 1996, representing an increase of 311,000 jobs since '93, 189,000 supported by exports to Canada and 122,000 by exports to Mexico.

Countries in the Caribbean Basin are seeking inclusion in NAFTA as a result of erosion of trade preferences provided by the Caribbean Basin Initiative (CBI) and increased competition from Mexico in the US market.

At press time, The Bahamas had expressed no interest in becoming part of NAFTA, nor was it qualified to do so.

See also **Free Trade Area of the Americas (FTAA),** and **Trade agreements.**

ORGANIZATION OF AMERICAN STATES (OAS)

The OAS, the world's oldest regional organization, was formed in 1890 as a forum for hemispheric dialogue. The Bahamas became one of its 35 member states in 1982.

The OAS has a long tradition of defending and maintaining peace in the hemisphere. It is the forum for the developing countries of Latin America and the Caribbean to meet with Canada and the US to consider issues facing hemispheric development. These include:
1. Eradication of poverty and unemployment.
2. Defence of social justice.
3. Incentives for investment and economic growth.
4. Expansion and liberalization of external trade.
5. Alleviation of the external debt burden.

The basic purpose of the OAS is to:
1. Strengthen the peace and security of the continent.
2. Promote and consolidate representative democracy, with due respect for the principle of non-intervention.
3. Prevent possible causes of difficulties and ensure the pacific settlement of disputes that may arise among member states.
4. Provide for common action on the part of those states in the event of aggression.
5. Seek the solution of political, juridical and economic problems that may arise among them.
6. Promote, by cooperative action, their economic, social and cultural development.
7. Achieve an effective limitation of conventional weapons so the largest amount of resources can be devoted to the economic and social development of member states.

Contact the Organization of American States (OAS), Queen St, PO Box N-7793, Nassau, The Bahamas, tel 326-7746 or 326-0741; fax 325-0196.

PARADISE ISLAND

This international playground lies across the harbour from Nassau, connected by a toll bridge which costs 50¢ per vehicle, $2 per tour or rental car.

Construction of a second bridge connecting Nassau and Paradise Island was scheduled for completion in Dec 1998. The new three-lane bridge will be approx 2,000 ft long and will cost an estimated $18 million. At press time, plans had been announced to change the bridge toll to $1 for all non-commercial vehicles, once the new bridge is completed. Commercial vehicles would pay more.

At press time, Paradise Island offered 16 hotels with 2,633 rooms, numerous restaurants featuring international cuisine, top-calibre entertainment, one of the world's largest casinos, an 18-hole golf course, medieval Cloister and surrounding gardens, Hurricane Hole Marina, Paradise Island Intl Airport, a heliport and world-famous Paradise Beach.

The Atlantis, Paradise Island development established The Bahamas as the No 1 destination in the Caribbean region. Centrepiece is a 14-acre waterscape encompassing the world's largest open-air aquarium, six exhibit lagoons, over 100 species of fish – including sharks, barracuda and stingrays – waterfalls, underground grottos, a ¼-mile lazy river ride and a 90-ft underwater acrylic viewing tunnel. A $450 million expansion, the Royal Towers at Atlantis, was slated to open in Dec 1998. The expansion includes 1,208 new rooms, a significant increase in casino and convention space and additional water features (including water slides through a shark-infested tank).

Construction began in late 1997 for a new 10-acre 40-berth marina in the lagoon of Paradise Island. With a minimum depth of 11 ft at low tide, the Marina at Atlantis will accommodate yachts up to 200 ft. A new wider channel will link the harbour with the lagoon. An underground tunnel will accommodate vehicles, leaving the channel unencumbered. The Marina at Atlantis was to be completed by the end of 1998.

PASSPORTS

Non-Bahamians

All nationals of foreign countries residing in or visiting The Bahamas must hold valid national passports. Exceptions are for visiting citizens of the US, Canada, the UK and its colonies. US citizens must show proof of citizenship such as a birth certificate or naturalization certificate.

Loss of passport

A national of a foreign country whose passport is lost, damaged or destroyed in The Bahamas should visit the Bahamas-based embassy, consulate or High Commission of their country to receive necessary documentation for repatriation. Contact the Ministry of Foreign Affairs, East Hill St, Nassau. See **Government section, Resident diplomats & honorary consuls.**

If there is no representative embassy, consulate or High Commission, the foreign national should request assistance from the Ministry of Foreign Affairs in procuring a certificate of identity which would enable travel at least to the nearest country in which the relevant embassy, consulate or High Commission is situated.

Bahamian nationals

A Bahamas passport or certificate of identity is required by all Bahamians departing The Bahamas. The categories of passports are: diplomatic, red; official, green; and ordinary, dark blue.

Ordinary passports have 32 pages and are issued for a 10-year period at a cost of $30. All passports issued prior to July 15, 1991, are valid until the dates indicated and are renewable for a further period of five years.

Sub-categories of ordinary passports are for children and frequent travellers.

The former are issued to persons under 11 yrs and are renewable after five years for a total period not exceeding 10 years. The latter are issued to persons who, for whatever reason, travel on a frequent basis (eg, pilots and business persons). Frequent travellers' passports contain 64 pages, and are valid for a 10-year period at a cost of $60.

Certificates of identity are issued for discretionary periods depending on circumstances, although the usual period is one year. Certificates of identity cost $20 and may be renewed for an annual fee of $4.

Possession of a passport or certificate of identity does not exempt the holder from compliance with immigration regulations in force in any territory, or from the necessity of obtaining a visa or permit when required.

Lost, stolen or destroyed passports or certificates of identity should be immediately reported to the Passport Office, then to the local police and if abroad to the nearest Bahamian Mission, Embassy, High Commission or Consulate. See **Government section, Bahamas diplomatic & consular representatives.**

Requirements for a new Bahamas passport or certificate of identity:

1. **Proof of citizenship**
   a. Birth certificate and/or passport. If the birth name is not registered, a baptismal certificate and affidavit signed by two persons who have knowledge of such birth, or such additional evidence as may be requested.
   b. Naturalization certificate.
   c. Registration certificate.
   d. Certificate of citizenship.
   e. In the case of a married woman, a marriage certificate.
   f. Persons claiming Bahamian citizenship by descent should produce a birth certificate, birth certificates of their parents, their parents' marriage certificate or naturalization documents.
   g. Any applicant born in The Bahamas after July 9, 1973, must submit the Bahamian birth certificate of the mother or the Bahamian father's birth certificate together with the parents' marriage certificate, in addition to the documents mentioned in 1(a).

2. **Authentication of application**
   The application must be authenticated and sponsored in Section 5 by a marriage officer, medical practitioner, a counsel and attorney of the Supreme Court, a public officer of or above the rank of senior assistant secretary, a bank officer ranked assistant manager or above, magistrate or Justice of the Peace personally acquainted with the applicant for at least two years. A member of the applicant's immediate family is not an acceptable sponsor.

3. **Photographs**
   Three copies of a recent photograph of the applicant must be included with the application. These must be taken full face without hat or head piece and must not be mounted. The size must not be more than 2½ ins by 2 ins or less than 2 ins by 1½ ins. The person who countersigns the application is also required to endorse the reverse side of one of the photographs with the words: "I certify that this is a true likeness of the applicant (Mr, Mrs, Miss, Ms)" and add his/her signature. All photographs included with an application become the property of The Bahamas government from the time of submission.

4. **Additional information**
   a. A new passport is required by a female who marries and takes her husband's name.
   b. A children's passport is required by anyone under 11 yrs. Application should be made by the father or legal guardian.
   c. All persons under 18 yrs require the father's or legal guardian's

consent for issuance of a passport, except for those under 18 yrs who are married.
d. A police report is required where a previous passport has been lost, stolen or destroyed.

Contact the Passport Office, Thompson Blvd, PO Box N-792, tel 325-2814 (to 7), fax 325-4832. In Freeport, contact the Passport Office, National Insurance Bldg, PO Box F-43536, Freeport, Grand Bahama. Tel (242) 352-5698 or 352-6480; fax (242) 352-5692.

PEOPLE-TO-PEOPLE

This community involvement programme sponsored by The Bahamas Ministry of Tourism is designed to bring visitors and Bahamians together for cultural exchange in New Providence and Paradise Island, Grand Bahama, Abaco, Eleuthera, Exuma, Bimini and San Salvador. Its main objectives are to foster communication and the exchange of ideas and to advance international friendship.

Over 1,000 People-to-People volunteers in Nassau and 400 in Grand Bahama are available as hosts. These volunteers represent a cross-section of the community and are screened by People-to-People executives.

Ministry of Tourism personnel match volunteers and visitors according to age, interests and occupations. Volunteers arrange to meet their guests at an agreed time and location. As most volunteers work, meetings are usually after 5:30pm or on weekends. Visitors do not live with volunteers. The programme is provided free of charge.

A highlight of the programme is the tea party at Government House, held on the last Fri of each month (Jan-Aug). Approx 200 guests attend and are greeted by the wife of the Bahamian Governor-General.

Other programmes include:
1. Home-away-from-home programme. Volunteer hosts act as foster parents to foreign students attending Bahamian colleges.
2. Spouses programme. Activities are planned for spouses while delegates are in conventions.

Preferably, arrangements for participation should be made at least two weeks ahead. Visitors in Nassau may register for People-to-People initiatives at Ministry of Tourism information booths at Nassau Intl Airport, Market Plaza and Rawson Sq, or through social directors or concierges at participating hotels. Overseas, contact Bahamas tourist offices worldwide – see **Tourism, Tourism information,** or contact the Manager, People-to-People, PO Box N-3701, Nassau, The Bahamas, tel (242) 326-5371, 356-0435, 356-0437/8 or 328-7810; fax (242) 356-0434. In Freeport, contact the Coordinator, People-to-People, PO Box F-40251, Grand Bahama, tel (242) 352-8044/5.

In the Family Islands, contact the Nassau office.

PHARMACIES

The Apothecary 328-0722
Betandé Drugs 325-5430
Centreville Pharmacy Ltd 325-4644
Cole-Thompson
   Pharmacies Ltd 322-2062
Doc's Pharmacy 322-3627
Heaven Sent Pharmacy 326-4629
Lowe's Pharmacy 393-4813
McCartney's Pharmacy 325-6068
Palmdale Pharmacy 323-7340
The People's Pharmacy 393-9432
The Prescription Centre
   Pharmacy 356-6434
Prescription Parlour 356-3973
Priceless Drugs 322-1405
Sabre Pharmacy 393-2938
Star Prescription Pharmacy 326-3522
Super Mart Pharmacy 323-1305
Super Saver Pharmacy 393-2393
Tom-Mae's Pharmacy 325-5268
Wilmac's Pharmacies Ltd 322-8888

All these pharmacies fill prescriptions.

POLICE FORCE
See **Royal Bahamas Police Force**.

POPULATION
Population estimate for The Bahamas for 1998 was 293,700. Projected estimate for the year 2000 is 302,800.

The last official census of The Bahamas was taken in May 1990. See **Fig 2.1** for results of that census, as well as the 1980 census.

In 1990, population density (per sq mile) for The Bahamas was 47.4. For New Providence and Grand Bahama, population density was 2,152.5 and 77.2, respectively. The population distribution was 31.61% for people 15 yrs and under, and 4.36% for people 65 yrs and over. For 1996, with an estimated Bahamas population of 284,000, there were 20.7 births per 1,000 people and 5.4 deaths per 1,000 people. In 1997, percentage of population under 15 yrs was estimated at 29.8%; 15-64 yrs, 65.3%; and 65 yrs and over, 4.9%. Average annual estimated population growth in 1997 was 1.65%.

PORTS OF ENTRY
See **Fig 2.2**.

POSTAL INFORMATION
Post office boxes in New Providence are CB for Cable Beach; CR for Carmichael Rd; EE for Elizabeth Estates, FH for Fox Hill; GT for Grant's Town; N for Nassau; SB for South Beach; and SS for Shirley St.

Postage rates may change by 1999.

Air mail
See **Fig 2.3**.

Speed mail
For a fee of $5, in addition to regular postage, items posted for this service will be delivered to the addressee's postal box at the General Post Office within one hour of posting, within three hours to any other post office in New Providence, and within 24 hours to Freeport. International high speed mail is available to most countries of the world. Items must be handed over the stamp counter for processing. Contact the main post office.

Registration fee
The fee for registration of mail inside The Bahamas is 80¢; for all other destinations, $1.20.

Express fee
There is an express (special delivery) fee of $1.20 to all participating countries.

Parcel post (New Providence)
Weight limit is 22 lbs, size limit 3½ ft in length. No parcel post package may exceed 6 ft 7 ins, combined length and girth. Parcels exceeding this size should be sent by air or sea freight.

Incoming parcels from abroad are charged at 80¢ per item and are subject to Customs assessment. Where possible, assessment of duty is included in the notice of arrival sent to the addressee. In other cases, the addressee may be asked to supply invoices or to attend a Customs examination. Parcels are delivered at parcel post after any Customs and/or other charges have been paid.

Parcel post rates

Air	Up to 1 lb	Each extra lb
Canada	$4.15	$2.45
UK	$9.25	$4.15
US	$5.25	$2.45

Surface	Up to 1 lb	Each extra lb
Canada	–	–
UK	$5.05	$2.55
US	$3.50	$2.35

Insurance and compensation
Destination .... all countries
Rate .... 25¢
Insurance .... $50 or part thereof
(max $1,970)
Compensation .... max $1,970
(Goods must be worth value declared).

FIG 2.1
POPULATION OF THE BAHAMAS OFFICIAL CENSUS, 1980 & 1990

Island	1980	1990
Abaco	7,271	10,061
Acklins	618	428
Andros	8,307	8,155
Berry Islands	509	634
Bimini	1,411	1,638
Cat Island	2,215	1,678
Crooked Island (Long Cay included)	553	423
Eleuthera, Harbour Island & Spanish Wells	10,631	10,524
Exumas	3,670	3,539
Grand Bahama	33,102	41,035
Inagua	924	985
Long Island	3,404	3,107
Mayaguana	464	308
New Providence	135,437	171,542
Ragged Island	164	89
Rum Cay & San Salvador	825	539
Total	**209,505**	**254,685**

Small packets (up to 4 lbs)
Overseas countries
4 oz ....50¢
8 oz ....90¢
1 lb $1.60
2 lbs $2.70

NB: All countries participate in the small packet service, but some limit the weight to 1 lb.

Warehouse charge
There is a daily charge of 60¢ on parcels remaining in any post office (including parcel post) in The Bahamas more than 30 days after notice of arrival has been dispatched.

Printed paper rates
(Includes books, newspapers, magazines, Christmas and greeting cards):
Inter-island
1 oz or part thereof..........................15¢

All other countries
1 oz ....20¢
2 oz ....50¢
4 oz ....50¢
8 oz ....90¢

1 lb $1.60
2 lbs $2.70
4 lbs $3.70

Postal collection times & hours of service
See **Fig 2.4**.

Surface (regular) mail letters
Mail posted intra-island – within an island for the same island – is 15¢ per oz.
Inter-island
per 1 oz or fraction thereof............15¢

All other destinations
1 oz ....40¢
4 oz $1.10
8 oz $2.10
1 lb $4.10
2 lbs $7.10
4 lbs $11.50

Post cards
Inter-island ....15¢
All other destinations ....40¢
See also **Courier services, Customs** and **Export entry**.

FIG 2.2
PORTS OF ENTRY

Major ports	Boats	Land planes	Sea planes
Abaco			
Grand Cay	√	√	√
Treasure Cay	x	√	x
Marsh Harbour	√	√	√
Sandy Point (restricted)	√	√	√
Green Turtle Cay	√	x	√
Spanish Cay	√	√	x
Andros			
Congo Town	√	√	√
Fresh Creek	√	√	√
San Andros	√	√	√
Berry Islands			
Chub Cay	√	√	√
Great Harbour Cay	√	√	√
Bimini			
Alice Town	√	x	√
South Bimini	x	√	x
Cat Cay	√	√	√
Cat Island			
Arthur's Town	x	√	x
Bennett's Harbour	√	x	x
New Bight	x	√	x
Smith's Bay	√	x	x
Eleuthera			
Cape Eleuthera (restricted)	√	√	√
Governor's Harbour	√	√	√
Harbour Island	√	x	x
Hatchet Bay	√	x	√
North Eleuthera	x	√	x
Rock Sound	√	√	√
Spanish Wells	√	x	x
Exuma			
Moss Town	√	√	√
Grand Bahama			
Freeport	√	√	√
West End	√	x	√
Inagua			
Matthew Town	√	√	√

Major ports (cont)	Boats	Land planes	Sea planes
Long Island			
Stella Maris	√	√	√
Mayaguana			
Abraham's Bay (restricted)	√	√	x
New Providence			
Nassau	√	√	√
San Salvador			
Cockburn Town	√	√	√
Sufferance wharfs*			
Grand Bahama			
South Riding Point (Burma) (Transshipment facility terminal)	√	x	x
Bell Channel (Freeport)	√	x	x
Jack Tar Marina (West End)	√	x	x
New Providence			
Nassau Yacht Haven	√	x	x
Nassau Harbour Club Marina	√	x	x
East Bay Yacht Basin	√	x	x
Union Dock	√	x	x
Kelly's Dock	√	x	x
John Alfred Dock	√	x	x
Coral Harbour (restricted)	√	x	x
Clifton Pier Bahamas Gas & Fuel Dock (restricted)	√	x	x
Lyford Cay (restricted)	√	x	x
Hurricane Hole, Paradise Island (restricted)	√	x	x
Paradise Island Airport (restricted)	x	√	√
Ocean Cay (restricted)	√	x	x

* Sufferance wharfs are only for use by operators and their guests.

POTTER'S CAY

This tiny cay under the Nassau side of Paradise Island Bridge is a colourful, public marketplace for locally grown produce and fresh seafood. Bahamians buy fresh conch salad spiked with lime juice and fiery-hot finger or goat peppers as well as such locally produced exotic fruit and vegetables as sapodilla, sugar apples, guavas and okra. A police station and public telephones are on site.

Brightly striped canopies give the stalls a cheerful fishing village atmosphere. Most stalls are open every day 6am-8pm, but some close on Sun. Gates at the Cay are closed daily 8pm-5am.

PROPERTY TAX

The statutes provide for a general assessment of real property by the Chief Valuation Officer (CVO) of the Commonwealth of The Bahamas.
Applies to: Bahamians and non-Bahamians owning real property in The Bahamas not exempt from taxation as

FIG 2.3
AIR MAIL POSTAL RATES*

Destination	First class 1 oz	Letters $^1/_2$ oz	Air letter forms	Post cards	2nd class $^1/_2$ oz
Inter-island	25¢	–	–	15¢	–
US (incl Alaska, Hawaii, US Virgin Islands, Puerto Rico), Canada	–	55¢	40¢	40¢	45¢
West Indies	–	55¢	40¢	40¢	45¢
Central & South America, Bermuda, Falkland Islands, UK, all countries in Europe, islands of the Mediterranean ..	–	60¢	40¢	40¢	50¢
Africa, Asia, Australia, Pacific & Indian Oceans	–	70¢	40¢	40¢	60¢

Consult the post office about mailing small packets abroad via second class.
* Contact the East Hill Post Office at 322-3344 to inquire about new rates.

indicated in *Remarks* in this section. A Bahamian is defined as a citizen of The Bahamas or as a company registered under The Companies Act in which at least 60% of the shares are owned beneficially by Bahamians.

Return due: On or before Dec 31 each year.

Filed with: The Chief Valuation Officer, PO Box N-13, Nassau, The Bahamas.

Forms: Owners are required to file a declaration of real property. The return must be signed by the owner and witnessed by an authorized person, defined as a magistrate, attorney, registered medical practitioner, bank officer, minister of religion, Justice of the Peace or notary public within The Bahamas or similar person outside the Commonwealth. Forms may be obtained from the CVO.

Assessment date: Property is assessed annually before Oct 15. If property subject to assessment has not been assessed, the CVO may assess such property retroactively to a max 10 years at the amount required.

Notice of assessment: The CVO is required to publish before Oct 15, once in *The Gazette* and once in a daily newspaper published and circulated in The Bahamas, a notice stating:

1. Copies of the assessment lists are available to the public at the Treasury and office of the CVO.
2. Assessment notices for each owner of property liable to tax are available at places specified in the notice.
3. Five days after the notice's publication, a notice of assessment is deemed served on every owner of property subject to tax.
4. A notice of assessment may be sent by mail to any owner of property by the CVO after publication in *The Gazette*.
5. Any other matters which the CVO, with the Minister's approval, deems necessary.

A notice of assessment is deemed to have been served on every owner of property subject to the tax, five days after publication of the notice in *The Gazette*. Objections to a notice of assessment must be made in writing to the CVO within 30 days of service of the notice, stating grounds upon which the objection is made. The CVO may request that the tax levied be paid in whole or in part at the time of objection.

Taxes due: Within 60 days of the date on which the assessment notice is deemed to have been served. An owner may choose to pay the tax in quarterly instalments. In this case, payment of one or more quarterly instalments must be made within 60 days of the date on which notice of assessment is deemed to have been served.

To whom paid: Taxes due on real property in The Bahamas are paid to

FIG 2.4
POSTAL COLLECTION TIMES & HOURS OF SERVICE

Postal collection (from Nassau General Post Office)

	Days	Hours
Foreign air mail		
US, Central and South America, Asia, Australia and Africa	Mon-Sat	10am & 3pm
Canada, Bermuda, Jamaica, Europe, Haiti and Turks & Caicos	Check with post office for new schedules	
Foreign surface mail		
Via the US	Mon & Wed	10am
Via the UK	Fri	10am

Hours of service (Nassau)

	Days	Hours
General Post Office	Mon-Fri	8:30am-5:30pm
	Sat	8:30am-12:30pm
Parcel post	Mon-Fri	9am-5pm
Postal Savings Bank	Mon-Fri	9am-5:30pm
Cable Beach branch	Mon-Fri	9am-5:30pm
Carmichael Rd branch	Mon-Fri	9am-5:30pm
Elizabeth Estates branch	Mon-Fri	9am-5:30pm
Fox Hill branch	Mon-Fri	9am-5:30pm
Grant's Town branch	Mon-Fri	9am-5:30pm
Shirley St branch	Mon-Fri	9am-5:30pm
South Beach branch	Mon-Fri	9am-5:30pm

---

the Public Treasury directly or via the CVO. Remittance should be in Bahamian or US dollars, as a bank draft or international postal order drawn on a bank in the US or The Bahamas. Personal cheques are not acceptable.

Rate of tax
1. **Owner-occupied property (residential)**
   a. First $100,000 of market value* .... exempt
   b. Over $100,000 and not exceeding $500,000 of market value 1%
   c. Over $500,000 of market value 1½%
2. **Vacant land owned by non-Bahamians**
   a. First $3,000 of market value $30
   b. Over $3,000 and not exceeding $100,000 of market value 1%
   c. Over $100,000 of market value 1½%
3. **All other properties/commercial**
   a. First $500,000 of market value 1%
   b. Over $500,000 of market value 2%

* Market value is defined as the amount the property would realize if sold in the open market without any encumbrances or restrictions.

Penalties: If the return is not filed, the owner is guilty of an offence and liable for fines of up to $3,000 upon conviction. Persons knowingly making false statements may be liable upon conviction to a fine of up to $3,000 or six months' imprisonment, or both. If the tax is not paid on or before the last day due, a 10% surcharge is added.

Extension of time: The CVO may postpone the date on which the tax is due in particular cases, by notice in writing.

Remarks: Property owned by Bahamians and located outside of New Providence is exempt from property tax. Property approved as commercial farmland by the Minister of Agriculture and Fisheries and Minister of Finance and Planning is eligible for property tax exemptions, along with the following:

1. Unimproved property owned by Bahamians, ie, without physical additions or alterations, or any works benefiting the land which have not increased the market value thereof by $5,000 or more.
2. Places of religious worship; school buildings, their gardens and playing areas.
3. Property owned by foreign governments; property owned by foreign nations used for consular offices or residences of consular officials and employees.
4. Property used exclusively for charitable or public service from which no profit is derived. Property of the Bahamas National Trust (BNT).

PROPERTY TRANSACTIONS

In New Providence, real estate agents charge a 10% commission on undeveloped property. The commission for developed property, whether residential or commercial, is 6%. Agents charge a 10% commission for Family Island property, whether land, home or commercial properties. See also **Freeport/Lucaya information, Property transactions.**

The government stamp duty on property conveyances or realty transfers is graded as follows:

From	Up to & including	Stamp duty
$0	$20,000	2%
$20,000.01	$50,000	4%
$50,000.01	$100,000	6%
Over $100,000		8%

In the case of property sales to non-Bahamians, the vendor and purchaser each pay half of the stamp duty. The fee charged by the lawyer who prepares the conveyance is normally 2.5% of the sale price.

Generally, payment of commission, stamp duty and legal fees falls upon the seller. Sometimes property owners list a net sales figure, in which case the agent adds those charges to the price quoted to prospective buyers.

NB: All fees quoted are subject to change.

International Persons Landholding Act, 1993

The Intl Persons Landholding Act has made it easier for non-Bahamians and companies under their control to own property.

1. A non-Bahamian or permanent resident who purchases or acquires an interest in a condominium or property vacant or otherwise to be used by him as a single family dwelling, or for construction of such a dwelling, must apply to the Secretary to the Investments Board to register the purchase. Application for Registration Form I must be filed with the Office of the Prime Minister, PO Box CB-10980, Nassau, along with proof of ownership and payment of stamp duty and real property tax, and a bankers draft/postal money order for $25 made payable to the Public Treasury.
2. Upon receipt of the above, the purchase/acquisition is registered and a certificate of registration issued.
3. A permit to purchase/acquire property is required if the property is undeveloped land and the purchaser would become the owner of five or more contiguous acres. A permit is also required if the non-Bahamian intends to acquire land or an interest therein by way of freehold or leasehold, when the acquisition is not in accordance with (1).
4. Non-Bahamians who own homes in The Bahamas may apply to the

Director of Immigration for an annual home owner's residence card. This card entitles the owner, spouse and any dependent children to enter and remain in The Bahamas for the duration of the validity of the card. This card is intended to facilitate entry into The Bahamas – it does not confer resident status in The Bahamas.

All applications for permits, along with bankers drafts or postal money orders for $25 made payable to the Public Treasury, should be submitted to the Office of the Prime Minister for consideration by the Investments Board. If approved, the permit will be issued by the Secretary to the Board. The schedule of fees for the certificate of registration and permit are:

Fee schedule
Application for registration $25
Application for permit $25
Upon issue of certificate of registration or issue of permit where:
1. The value* of the property is $50,000 and under..................$50
2. The value of the property is over $50,000 but under $101,000 ....$75
3. The value of the property is $101,000 and over $100
Annual home owner's residence card..........................$500

* *Value in relation to a lease is the annual rent reserved times the number of years.*

Certificate of registration or permit (with acquisition documents) must be recorded in the Registrar General's Dept, PO Box N-532, Nassau, tel (242) 322-3316. Permanent residence may be granted if certain conditions are met. See **Immigration, Permanent residence.**
See also **Exchange Control; Immigration; Property tax;** and **Freeport/ Lucaya information, Property transactions.**

PUBLIC FINANCE
See **Fig 2.5.**

PUBLIC HEALTH

The Bahamas Ministry of Health's National Health and Nutrition Survey* provides a comprehensive assessment of the health of the Bahamian community. Indiscriminate eating, lack of exercise and excessive alcohol consumption – problem areas in The Bahamas – have been cited as main contributory causes of diseases such as hypertension and diabetes.

Smoking is less of a concern. According to the World Health Organization (WHO), The Bahamas is the most smoke-free nation in the world – just 19% of men and 3% of women smoke.

One out of every four adults (over 15 yrs) in The Bahamas can be classified as obese. The prevalence of high blood pressure is dramatic, with 13% of 15-64 yr olds and 38% of the elderly suffering from elevated levels. The Ministry's chief priority in preventing and reducing these conditions is promotion of good nutritional habits and regular exercise.

The main health problems afflicting adult Bahamians (15-64 yrs) are HIV and AIDS, accidental injuries, substance abuse, hypertension (due to obesity and poor nutrition), diabetes (due to high blood glucose levels), heart attacks and strokes (due to undesirable cholesterol levels and high density lipoproteins) and cancer.

The number of Bahamians dying of AIDS steadily increased between initial reporting of the disease in 1985 and the end of '96. A slight decrease in the number of new HIV infections reported has been noted since then. By the end of 1997, 6,967 persons were known to be infected with the virus. See **AIDS/HIV.**

Trends in the incidence of sexually transmitted diseases (other than AIDS) – including gonococcal infections and syphilis – have shown a decrease since the reporting of AIDS first began. The

* *In collaboration with the Caribbean Food and Nutrition Inst, Pan-American Health Organization and World Health Organization (WHO).*

FIG 2.5
PUBLIC FINANCE

Total revenue & expenditure 1996-99

Year	Revenue (B$)	Expenditure (B$)
1996/97 July-June	873,170,289 (actual)	777,814,390 (actual)
1997/98 July-June	973,401,593 (estimated)	846,360,900 (estimated)
1998/99 July-June	990,484,723 (estimated)	868,484,723 (estimated)

Revenue of The Bahamas 1996-99

Tax Revenue	Provisional actual revenue 1996/97 B$	Original estimated revenue 1997/98 B$	Estimated revenue 1998/99 B$
Import & export duties	335,552,452	368,600,000	403,925,400
Property tax	25,356,388	31,500,000	32,000,000
Motor vehicle tax	16,382,616	19,300,000	24,900,000
Gaming tax	16,883,244	21,300,000	20,000,000
Tourism tax	58,837,690	70,700,000	70,200,000
Stamp tax	132,331,831	138,887,000	152,000,000
Other taxes	24,171,931	32,326,140	40,720,000
Tax revenue sub-total	**609,516,152**	**682,613,140**	**743,745,400**
% of total revenue	69.80	70.13	75.09

Non-tax revenue

Fees & service charges	56,778,941	60,770,431	71,050,000
Revenue from government property	12,998,788	14,166,750	14,180,600
Interest & dividends	9,662,534	5,705,500	8,036,000
Reimbursement & loan repayment	207,753	750,000	750,000
Services of commercial nature	8,956,585	14,517,500	14,238,000
Non-tax rev sub-total	**88,604,601**	**95,910,181**	**108,254,600**
% of total revenue	10.15	9.85	10.93
Total tax & non-tax rev	**698,120,753**	**778,523,321**	**852,000,000**

Capital revenue

Capital revenue	555,210	0	0
Grants	500,000	5,000,000	5,000,000
Proceeds from borrowings	173,994,326	189,878,272	133,484,723
Capital rev sub-total	**175,049,536**	**194,878,272**	**138,484,723**
% of total revenue	20.05	20.02	13.98
Total capital revenue	**175,049,536**	**194,878,272**	**138,484,723**
GRAND TOTAL all revenue	**873,170,289**	**973,401,593**	**990,484,723**

Expenditure of The Bahamas Government 1996-99

Ministry/dept	Provisional actual expenditure 1996/97 $	Approved estimate 1997/98 $	Proposed estimate 1998/99 $
Governor-General & staff	768,399	868,472	897,357
The Senate	173,120	242,340	265,880
House of Assembly	1,758,152	1,884,892	1,833,686
Dept of the Auditor General	1,455,971	1,630,415	1,602,235
Dept of Public Service	34,332,595	32,492,829	38,820,266
Cabinet Office..........................	2,071,587	1,883,882	2,365,185
Attorney-General's Office & Ministry of Justice	4,406,079	4,600,192	4,865,989
Judicial Dept	3,828,592	4,235,955	4,481,901
Court of Appeal	732,526	923,697	954,022
Registrar General's Dept	1,573,818	1,835,236	1,725,429
Prisons Dept	9,135,964	10,136,518	10,615,789
Parliamentary Registration Dept	3,027,831	1,183,412	1,009,912
Ministry of Foreign Affairs	9,467,176	10,777,028	10,641,709
Office of the Prime Minister......	2,111,405	2,631,764	2,735,090
Office of the Deputy PM	564,277	848,121	846,366
Bahamas Information Services...................................	460,938	623,025	551,990
Government Printing Dept........	1,780,600	1,834,412	1,726,623
Dept of Local Government........	19,952,428	20,322,367	17,879,327
Dept of Physical Planning..........	374,906	445,535	504,570
Dept of Lands & Surveys	1,447,608	1,689,604	1,559,423
Ministry of Finance & Planning..	20,243,429	13,045,034	12,171,839
Treasury Dept	7,399,076	6,174,183	5,634,232
Customs Dept	14,503,262	14,607,249	15,403,477
Dept of Statistics	1,820,739	2,071,228	2,076,854
Magistrates' Courts	2,678,196	3,256,778	3,195,322
Public Debt Servicing – Interest	91,806,008	99,631,716	106,566,423
Public Debt Servicing – Redemption	83,500,730	81,895,211	85,042,197
Ministry of Economic Development.........................	0	2,854,308	3,004,707
Ministry of National Security	872,934	619,750	500,493
Dept of Immigration	7,894,875	8,669,073	8,657,217
Royal Bahamas Police Force	56,090,891	61,178,481	60,357,876
Royal Bahamas Defence Force ..	20,831,514	23,015,111	23,185,698
Ministry of Public Works	5,375,005	6,506,536	5,844,031
Dept of Public Works................	17,149,598	13,376,367	14,259,843
Dept of Education	0	110,766,632	111,583,747
Bahamas Technical & Vocational Inst..................	3,083,616	6,562,587	4,441,970
Dept of Archives	896,986	972,334	1,257,731
Ministry of Education................	111,550,165	20,202,864	19,882,419
College of The Bahamas	12,825,930	12,825,940	13,825,940
Ministry of Youth, Sports & Culture	7,537,032	7,556,373	8,445,537
Boys' Industrial School..............	514,057	646,686	675,534

Expenditure of The Bahamas Government 1996-99 (cont)

Ministry/dept	Provisional actual expenditure 1996/97 $	Approved estimate 1997/98 $	Proposed estimate 1998/99 $
Girls' Industrial School	372,340	402,965	510,728
Ministry of Housing & Social Development	1,028,366	1,921,620	1,981,449
Social Services Dept	15,070,433	19,355,189	19,728,196
Dept of Housing	721,422	793,382	752,265
Ministry of Labour, Immigration & Training	0	2,780,597	3,452,873
Labour Dept	1,535,401	1,677,897	1,769,847
Ministry of Consumer Welfare & Aviation	0	1,385,029	1,213,125
Ministry of Transport	3,994,049	4,297,580	4,008,166
Post Office Dept	5,358,945	5,945,362	5,913,014
Dept of Civil Aviation	10,586,135	11,746,105	12,094,723
Port Dept	3,044,809	3,782,278	3,608,684
Road Traffic Dept	2,606,467	2,748,910	2,889,890
Dept of Meteorology	1,437,571	1,540,326	1,511,939
Ministry of Agriculture & Fisheries	4,546,649	5,065,820	4,701,821
Dept of Agriculture	4,408,032	5,728,640	5,614,723
Dept of Fisheries	986,506	1,168,293	1,165,819
Ministry of Health	16,042,885	17,438,759	19,939,898
Princess Margaret Hospital	43,859,748	47,237,776	48,563,800
Rand Memorial Hospital	9,632,079	11,390,203	11,817,662
Sandilands Rehab Centre	14,700,079	17,068,273	16,370,935
Dept of Environmental Health Services	8,203,971	16,379,334	16,535,665
Dept of Public Health	10,432,609	12,637,438	12,580,437
Ministry of Tourism	51,008,140	53,981,591	57,277,890
The Gaming Board	2,239,739	2,363,385	2,585,338
TOTALS	**777,814,390**	**846,360,900**	**868,484,723**

Totals have been rounded off.

number of new cases of reported infectious diseases has steadily decreased (except for AIDS and Hepatitis B), while tuberculosis, which had been declining, is on the increase. A large percentage of these cases is associated with AIDS.

The Bahamas is not a malarious area, but because of the large number of immigrants from countries where malaria is endemic, there is always a possibility of the disease being re-introduced. Sixteen cases were reported between 1990 and '95. No new cases were reported in 1996.

The annual number of reported cases of gastroenteritis in children under five continues at high levels.

Accidents and acts of violence rate high on the list of causes of untimely death in the overall population. This is most significant among men, particularly those in the 15-44 age group. In 1995, about 10% of all deaths were due to accidents or acts of violence.

Alcoholism and cocaine addiction are chronic problems. The number of new cases of cocaine abusers at community mental health clinics was

102 in 1994. In 1995 new cases were down to 52. There were 114 new cases of cocaine abuse in 1996 and 139 in '97.

On a more positive note, life expectancy is increasing in The Bahamas, from 60 in the early 1950s to approx 73 in the early '90s. Current gender-specific estimates indicate the average female born in The Bahamas lives to approx 76 yrs, while males have a life expectancy of 69 yrs.

The general fertility rate in The Bahamas was estimated at 2.27 in 1996. That is to say, each woman living to the end of her childbearing years will have two children, on average.

Although the rate of teenage pregnancy is declining, it continues to be a concern in the country, with social and health care needs of mothers and babies having to be met at considerable cost to the government.

Public health services
Public health services are administered by the Ministry of Health and health care is delivered through community health clinics in New Providence and the Family Islands. Other services are offered through community-based programmes such as home and district nursing and disease surveillance.

The Ministry operates Princess Margaret Hospital (PMH) and Sandilands Rehabilitation Centre (SRC) in Nassau, and Rand Memorial Hospital in Grand Bahama.

Environmental concerns are managed by the Dept of Environmental Health Services, which oversees management, control and conservation of the environment. Its functions are conducted through the health inspectorate division, the environmental monitoring and risk assessment division and the solid waste collection and disposal division.

See also **AIDS/HIV; Doctors; Hospitals & clinics;** and **Social services.**

RADIO STATIONS
See **Broadcasting.**

REAL ESTATE COMPANIES & DEVELOPMENTS
Following is a sampling of companies and developments based in Nassau. Contact the Bahamas Real Estate Assoc, tel 325-4942, fax 322-4649, for information on licensed real estate agents.

Bahamas Realty
    Tel 393-8618, fax 393-0326
BAYROC
    Tel 327-0112, fax 327-0114
C A Christie & Co Ltd
    Tel 325-7960, fax 326-5684
C Investments Realtors
    Tel 328-7557, fax 328-7994
Cartwright's Real Estate
    Tel/fax 394-3919
Caves Dev Ltd
    Tel 327-1575, fax 327-1569
Damianos Realty
    Tel 322-2305, fax 322-2033
Dupuch Real Estate
    Tel 393-1811, fax 393-8914
Durrant-Harding Real Estate Co Ltd
    Tel 326-2461, fax 326-4509
Gibson, Levi, & Assoc Real Estate
    Tel 322-4654, fax 322-8730
Gold Circle Co Ltd
    Tel 393-8477, fax 393-4508
Graham Real Estate
    Tel 356-5030, fax 326-5005
H G Christie Ltd Real Estate
    Tel 322-1041, fax 326-5642
Hanna, Sterling, Real Estate
    Tel/fax 323-6188
International Management & Investment Services Ltd
    Tel 322-2504, fax 322-6949
Isaacs, Jack, Real Estate Co
    Tel 322-1069, fax 323-8427
Knowles Realty
    Tel/fax 327-5237
Lightbourne, Mike, Real Estate
    Tel 325-1950, fax 325-2765
Lowes, W T, & Assoc Ltd
    Tel 322-1741, fax 322-7600

Lyford Cay Co Ltd (Real Estate Div)
  Tel 362-4280, fax 362-4730
Lyford Cay Real Estate Co Ltd
  Tel 362-4703/4, fax 362-4513
Moir & Ricketts Real Estate
  Tel 362-4895, fax 362-4586
Morley Realty Ltd
  Tel 394-7070, fax 394-7069
Oceania Properties
  Tel 356-4880, fax 356-4628
Palms of Love Beach
  Tel 327-2043, fax 327-2530
Portside Condominiums
  Tel 363-3600, fax 363-3604
Powell's Marketing &
  Management Services
  Tel 328-7238, fax 326-2491
Real Estate Sales & Rentals
  Tel 322-2680, fax 325-6353
Re/Max Nassau Realty
  Tel 394-7777, fax 394-8045
Ritchie, Paul, Real Estate
  Tel/fax 364-3710
Royal Caribbean Estates
  Tel 393-7326, fax 328-4642
Symonett, Oris E, Real Estate
  Tel 325-8280, fax 325-1739
Treasure Cay Ltd, Real Estate Division
  Tel 327-5066, fax 327-5059
Treasure Cove
  Tel 364-6691, fax 364-6694
World Developers Ltd
  Tel/fax 327-8949
See also **Freeport/Lucaya information, Real estate companies.**

RELIGION

Denominations include Anglican, Assembly of God, Ba'hai Faith, Baptist, Brethren, Christian & Missionary Alliance, Christian Science, Church of God of Prophecy, Greek Orthodox, Jehovah's Witnesses, Jewish, Latter Day Saints (Mormon), Lutheran, Methodist, Muslim/Islamic, Pentecostal, Presbyterian, Roman Catholic, The Salvation Army, Seventh-Day Adventist, and other smaller denominations. In New Providence, the three largest denominations are Baptist, Anglican and Roman Catholic, respectively.

ROYAL BAHAMAS DEFENCE FORCE

The Royal Bahamas Defence Force became official in 1980 with the passing of the Defence Act, 1979. Prior to that, since 1976, the Defence Force had worked in cooperation with the now disbanded Marine Division of the Royal Bahamas Police Force, many of whose officers transferred to the Defence Force.

The Defence Force, which comes under the Ministry of National Security, is tasked primarily with defending The Bahamas and maritime law enforcement, but is expanding its mandate to include disaster mitigation, environmental response, search and rescue, peacekeeping, harbour patrol and port security.

Hardware consists of six maritime coastal defence vessels, one auxiliary vessel, and two Dauntless search and rescue craft for harbour and shallow water operations. Two cabin-class fixed wing aircraft, a Cessna Golden Eagle 421C and a Cessna Titan 404, constitute the air wing and are used chiefly for reconnaissance, maritime patrol, search and rescue and passenger transport.

The main base is HMBS Coral Harbour, at the southwestern tip of New Providence. A sub-base was opened in Matthew Town, Inagua, in 1996.

The Defence Force consists of 877 personnel, including 63 officers and 97 women. Personnel train at some of the finest naval establishments in the world, including Britannia Royal Naval College, England; the US Naval War College, RI, and the US Coast Guard Officer Candidate School, Yorktown, VA.

Expansion over the next year calls for enlistment of an additional 123 officers and marines, upgrading of hardware and base facilities, modernization of the fleet, and acquisition of two ocean-going patrol vessels.

Contact Royal Bahamas Defence Force Headquarters, PO Box N-3733, Nassau, tel 322-1994 or 323-3691; fax 328-8912; or the Ministry of National Security, Churchill Bldg, Bay St, PO Box N-3217, Nassau, tel 356-6792, fax 356-6087.

ROYAL BAHAMAS POLICE FORCE

The Bahamas Police Force was formed with 16 men on Mar 1, 1840, under the command of Inspector General John Pinder. This semi-military organization, now led by Commissioner B K Bonamy, comprises 2,023 officers and 220 civilian support staff.

The prefix "Royal" was conferred in 1966 by Her Majesty Queen Elizabeth II during an official visit.

The world-famous Royal Bahamas Police Force Band began with 12 officers in 1893. Women were allowed to join the Force in 1964. During the same year, a canine section was established with six dogs.

In 1980, the Marine Division was taken over by the Royal Bahamas Defence Force. Other significant changes after The Bahamas gained independence in 1973 included the establishment of the Drug Enforcement Unit (DEU), a forensic science laboratory and a community policing section. A computerized records system was introduced in 1990. A fully integrated IBM AS/400 computer enables the Force to link a wide range of incidents and produce data for investigation purposes.

SCHOOLS
See **Education**.

SHIP REGISTRATION

Since the passing of the Merchant Shipping Act, 1976, The Bahamas has become one of the world's fastest growing ship registry centres. More than 1,400 vessels, including cargo and cruise ships, freighters, tankers and tugboats, are registered here.

The Bahamas actively encourages ship owners of all nationalities to register their ships under the Bahamian flag. Luxury vessels registered include Norwegian Cruise Lines ships, *Crystal Harmony* and *M/V Freewinds,* and Disney Cruise Line's *Disney Magic*.

In an effort to register more small cruise ships, luxury yachts and charter boat operators, The Bahamas government has reduced the tariffs and fees for these vessels.

Ships engaged in foreign trade under 12 yrs and weighing over 1,600 net tons are eligible for Bahamian registration. Special permission may be obtained from the Minister of Transport for ships under 1,600 net tons or over 12 yrs under certain conditions.

Several factors make The Bahamas a prime maritime centre:
1. It is a gateway to North and South America and a major destination for cruise ships.
2. It has one of the largest oil storage, blending and transshipment facilities in the western hemisphere and is capable of handling the largest ships in the world.
3. It has modern, state-of-the-art facilities at Nassau and Freeport Harbours.
4. It has offshore banks and trust companies that understand the needs of offshore business such as ship registration.
5. It is a member of the Intl Maritime Organization (IMO), and adheres to its principal safety conventions.

Contact the Bahamas Maritime Authority, PO Box N-4679, Nassau, The Bahamas, tel 323-3130, fax 325-1920.

See also **Ports of entry**.

SHIPPING
Cargo Shipping

Nearly all shipments of cargo coming to The Bahamas from Europe, parts of the Orient and the West Indies are transshipped through ports in Florida, mainly by container storage. An exception is the importation of cars shipped directly from Japan. Nassau has direct cargo connections with the US. Shipments between New Providence and the Family Islands may be sent by mail-boat. See **Transportation**.

Shipping Agencies
Some shipping agencies which serve Nassau are:
Betty K Agencies, Ltd 322-2142
Crowley American Transport....323-8804
Container Terminals Ltd 322-1012
Inter Island Freight 326-2493/4
Leutheran Shipping Lines 322-4443
Pioneer Shipping 325-7889
Seabord Marine.........................356-7624
Seahorse Carriers Ltd 323-2046
Tropical Shipping Co Ltd 322-1012

Cruise Ships
Passenger ships calling twice weekly to Nassau
Disney Magic: to and from Port Canaveral
Fantasy: to and from Miami
Melody: to and from Port Canaveral
Nordic Empress: to and from Miami
Oceanic: to and from Port Canaveral

Passenger ships calling weekly to Nassau
Ecstasy: to and from Miami
Royal Majesty: to and from Miami
Sea Breeze: from Miami to Puerto Rico
Westerdam: from St Thomas to Port Canaveral

Passenger and cruise ships which also call at Nassau
Amazing Grace, Costa Allegra, Costa Classica, Costa Romantica, Crown Jewel, Crown Odyssey, Crown Princess, Dawn Princess, DreamWard, Maasdam, Majesty of the Seas, Meridian, Noordam, Nordic Prince, Regent Sea, Royal Princess, Ryndam, SeaWard, Sensation, Sky Princess, Sovereign of the Seas, Star Odyssey, Stellar Solaris, Statendam, Sun Viking, Universe and *Zenith.*
See also **Ports of entry.**

SHOPPING
Duty-free shopping
Although some are subject to a stamp duty, the following items are 100% Customs duty free: china, crystal, fine jewellery, leather bags, linens and tablecloths, wine and liquor, perfume, cologne and toilet water, cameras and accessories, cashmere sweaters and watches.

Unlike most duty-free ports, The Bahamas does not require proof of foreign residency. Purchases may be carried from the shop or shipped rather than being collected at departure.

The removal of Customs duties refers to those items being imported into The Bahamas. Visitors may still be required to pay duty on goods being brought into their home country after allowed exemptions. See **Customs** for Customs exemptions and restrictions and regulations of the US, Canada and the UK.

Sunday shopping
An amendment to the Public Holidays Act in Oct 1995 allowed many shops to open for the first time on Sun.
A list of these shops follows:
1. Shops which sell:
   a. Ice, ice cream and other dairy products.
   b. Bread, fresh and frozen marine products, fresh fruit, fresh vegetables, butcher's meat.
   c. Any article required for burial of a dead body, or for illness of any person or animal, or for any other emergency.
   d. Fresh water.
   e. Bahamian straw work, art and handicrafts.
   f. Cooking gas.
   g. Shoes.
   h. Clothes.
2. Any retail shop located in a hotel.
3. Beauty salon or barber shop.
4. Coin operated laundry.
5. Photographic studio.
6. Convenience store or petty shop.
7. Service station.
8. Fast food restaurant.
9. Pharmacy.
10. Any other shop in the city of Nassau or Port Area may open for business on Sun when a cruise ship is scheduled to be in the port of Nassau or in the port of Freeport. However, these shops are not

allowed to be open on Good Friday, Easter Sunday, Labour Day, Independence Day or Christmas Day.

The following shops are prohibited from opening after 10am on Sun, Good Friday, Easter Sunday, Labour Day, Independence Day or Christmas Day:
1. Supermarkets.
2. Wholesale or membership clubs.
3. Shops which sell building supplies, construction materials, electrical fixtures or plumbing fixtures.

Cruise-ship shopping
In 1995, the Cruise Ships (Overnighting Incentives) Act was enacted by Parliament allowing cruise ships to operate shops and sell liquor 7pm-3am once the ship is docked at one of the designated ports in Nassau, Great Harbour Cay or Rock Sound.

To operate its shops, the ship must be docked for at least 18 hours and make no less than 20 voyages each year from a port in a country other than The Bahamas to a port in The Bahamas.

Twelve cruise lines are licensed to operate shops and sell liquor when docked at Bahamian designated ports: Carnival, Celebrity Cruises, Costa, Cunard Line/Seabourn, Disney, Dolphin/Majesty, Holland America, Norwegian, Premier, Princess Cruises, Royal Caribbean and Royal.

See also **Customs; Potter's Cay;** and **Straw markets.**

SOCIAL SERVICES

The Dept of Social Services is a government agency within the Ministry of Housing and Social Development. The Dept's mission is to provide timely, effective and compassionate social service and affordable housing to the people of The Bahamas.

The Dept provides structured programmes for those experiencing problems through nine divisions: child welfare, family services, senior citizens, community support, Family Island, school welfare, health social services, disability affairs unit and research/planning/training/community relations.

The Dept of Welfare, which later became the Dept of Social Services, was officially established in 1964 with one full-time child care officer. Today, the Dept employs 263 persons.

The main office is located on Thompson Blvd in the Boulevard Bldg with four outreach centres throughout New Providence – Horseshoe Dr, East St at Odle Corner and in Natl Insurance Bldgs on Fox Hill Rd and Wulff Rd. There are also offices and outreach centres in Abaco, Andros, Crooked Island, Grand Bahama, Eleuthera, Exuma and Long Island. A travelling officer from the New Providence headquarters services the other Family Islands.

Child welfare services
The child welfare section seeks to ensure all children in The Bahamas have a physically safe environment with emotional support and security necessary for healthy growth and development.

Some of its mandates are to investigate reported cases of child neglect, abandonment or abuse; counsel parents and children; remove children from home when necessary and provide alternative care, as well as providing court reports. The Dept also provides services to the Elizabeth Estates Children's Home, Children's Emergency Hostel, The Bilney Lane Children's Home and the Early Childhood Development Centre.

Family services division
This division investigates cases of domestic conflicts, counsels individuals experiencing difficulties in family and social relationships, provides support services to the domestic court and prepares court reports on domestic and family-related matters.

Senior citizens division
This division seeks to ensure the safety and well-being of senior citizens in The

Bahamas by assisting with housing and other miscellaneous services.

Twenty-four hour care is available for senior citizens who are unable to function independently, at the Soldier Rd Senior Citizens Group Home and Tynes House, Fox Hill Rd.

Contact the Dept of Social Services, PO Box N-1545, tel 326-0526.

Non-governmental organizations (NGOs)

The Social Services Dept is assisted in various areas by non-profit NGOs. These include:

Abilities Unlimited: Employment of the physically challenged (paraplegics), mentally challenged, and hearing and speech impaired in areas of ceramic manufacturing, furniture and upholstery repair and souvenir production. Tel 325-2150.

Al-Anon (Families and friends of alcoholics): Not-for-profit organization dedicated to the well-being of those with an alcoholic in their life. Tel 325-2954.

Alcoholics Anonymous: Support through regular meetings for persons with alcohol abuse problems, providing help for recovery and relapse prevention. Tel 322-1685.

Bahamas Assoc for Social Health (BASH): Drug rehab education and prevention facility committed to the alleviation of alcoholism, drug abuse and the illicit drug trade. Tel 323-6117, 356-0566, 356-0536, 356-BASH (2274); fax 356-5252.

Bahamas Council on Alcoholism: Sidearm of Alcoholics Anonymous which studies aspects of alcoholism in The Bahamas to help reduce the problem. Also provides supervised shelter, food and recreation for persons with alcohol abuse problems. Tel 322-1685.

Bahamas Red Cross Centre for the Deaf: Provides, programmes and services for the Bahamian hearing impaired and their families. Tel 323-6767.

The Crisis Centre: Responds to the needs of victims of sexual, physical and psychological abuse. Tel 328-0922, fax 328-7824.

Drug Action Service (Drug/Aids hotline): Provides services and programmes empowering communities to improve quality of life and restore traditional values. Tel 322-2308/9, fax 326-7688.

Narcotics Anonymous: Society of men and women who meet regularly to help each other remain drug-free. Tel 328-2294 or 322-2308/9.

Persis Rodgers Home for the Aged: Bahamian home where elderly people who are not sick can look after themselves with pride and live in peace and dignity. Tel 325-5092.

Ranfurly Homes for Children: Provides a home-like atmosphere for children who are alone because of death, sickness or other misfortune until they can support themselves or are adopted/fostered. Tel 393-3115.

Salvation Army Erin Harrison Gilmour School for the Blind & Visually Handicapped Children and May & Stanley Smith Resource Centre: Co-ed school for blind and partially sighted students. Tel 394-3197 or 393-2745.

Teen Challenge: Housing and outreach programmes for troubled people who have life-controlling problems such as drug or alcohol abuse. Tel 325-2149.

Young Women's Christian Assoc (YWCA): Aims to develop the body, mind and spirit of young Bahamians through summer camps, sports, educational programmes and housing. Tel 323-5526.

SPORTS

Sporting activities play a major role in everyday life and culture in The Bahamas. Competitive and leisure sports, plus individual and team sports at the amateur and professional level, are enjoyed by Bahamians and visitors at a variety of venues. See **Fig 2.6**.

Bahamian athletes excel in international competition. In May 1998,

Bahamian, Mark Knowles and doubles partner Daniel Nestor of Canada defeated the Australian tennis team in French Open semi finals. In July 1998, The Bahamas' women's relay team placed second in the 4 x 400m relay at the Goodwill Games in New York.

Sports venues
Most of The Bahamas' large sports facilities are located at the government-owned Queen Elizabeth II Sports Centre in Nassau's Oakes Field area. These include the Thomas A Robinson Track and Field Stadium, Andre Rodgers Baseball Diamond, Churchill Tener-Knowles National Softball Stadium and Little League and Pony League Baseball Diamonds. Recent additions are the $2.4 million Kendal G L Isaacs Gymnasium and the privately financed and managed National Tennis Centre. Additional facilities in various stages of planning and construction are a 50m swimming pool complex, a four-court beach volleyball complex and a sports heroes memorial park. Other government-owned sports facilities include Haynes Oval (cricket matches), Southern Recreation Grounds, Blue Hills Complex, D W Davis Gymnasium, A F Adderley Gymnasium, C I Gibson Gymnasium, Fort Charlotte (all sports from walking and jogging to soccer), Eastern Parade and Windsor Park (soccer and football), in addition to 54 neighbourhood parks with volleyball/basketball facilities. Other privately owned indoor and outdoor facilities exist in New Providence, as well as three championship golf courses in New Providence – at Cable Beach, South Ocean and Lyford Cay (private) – and one on Paradise Island.

Sports organizations
New Providence organizations registered with the Ministry of Youth, Sports and Culture:
Amateur Boxing Assoc of The Bahamas
Anglican Diocese Softball Committee
Bahamas Amateur Athletic Assoc
Bahamas Amateur Bowlers Federation
Bahamas Amateur Cycling Assoc
Bahamas Assoc of Independent Secondary Schools
Bahamas Assoc for the Physically Disabled
Bahamas Baseball Assoc
Bahamas Basketball Federation
Bahamas Boat Owners Sailing Assoc
Bahamas Bodybuilding Weightlifting & Powerlifting Federation
Bahamas Bridge Assoc
Bahamas Cycling Federation
Bahamas Checkers Assoc
Bahamas Chess Federation
Bahamas Cricket Assoc
Bahamas Domino Federation
Bahamas Football Assoc
Bahamas Golf Federation
Bahamas Government Departmental Basketball Assoc
Bahamas Government Departmental Softball Assoc
Bahamas Hockey Assoc
Bahamas Hot Rod Sports Car Assoc
Bahamas Judo Academy Budo Kan
Bahamas Karate Federation
Bahamas Lawn Tennis Assoc
Bahamas Martial Arts Federation
The Bahamas National Council for Disability
Bahamas National Equestrian Federation
Bahamas Netball Assoc
Bahamas Netball Federation
Bahamas Olympic Assoc
Bahamas Pool Assoc
Bahamas Professional Golf Assoc
Bahamas Rugby Football Union
Bahamas Softball Federation
Bahamas Squash Racquets Assoc
Bahamas Swimming Federation
Bahamas Table Tennis Federation
Bahamas Taekwondo Federation
Bahamas Volleyball Federation
Banker Sports Assoc
Baptist Sports Council
Commonwealth American Football League
Commonwealth Bahamas Darts Assoc
Nassau Domino Assoc
Nassau Go-Kart Assoc
Nassau Nastics Gymnastics Club

cont on pg 428

FIG 2.6
SPORTS INFORMATION

Cruising & Snorkelling	Boat charters	Pleasure cruises
New Providence		
Born Free Charters, 363-2003	$350 half day $700 full day	$500 half day $1,000 full day, equipment available
Brown's Charters, 324-2061	$350-600 half day, snorkelling gear inc	
Chubasco Charters, 322-8148	$350-500 half day $700-$1,000 full day, snorkelling gear inc	
Flying Cloud Catamaran Cruises, 393-1957	$300 hour for a min three hours	$35 half day all day Sun, $50, snorkelling gear inc sunset cruise, $30
Powerboat Adventures, 327-5385	–	$159 adults $99 children (2-12 yrs), full-day trip to Exuma Cays, equipment, lunch

Diving	Gear rental	Intro scuba	Certification course	Snorkelling
New Providence				
Bahama Divers, 393-5644	√	√	√	√
Custom Aquatics, 362-1492	√	√	√	√
Dive Dive Dive Ltd, 362-1401	√	√	√	√
Dive Nassau Ltd, 356-5170	√	√	√	√
Diver's Haven, 393-0869	√	√	√	√
Nassau Scuba Centre Ltd, 362-1964	√	√	√	√
Stuart Cove Dive South Ocean, 362-4171	√	√	√	√
Sun Divers Ltd, 325-8927	√	√	√	√
Sunskiff Divers Ltd, 362-1979	√	√	√	√
Freeport/Lucaya				
Caribbean Divers, 373-9111/2	√	√	√	√
Sunn Odyssey Divers, 373-4014	√	√	√	√
Underwater Explorers Society (UNEXSO), 373-1244	√	√	√	√
Xanadu Undersea Adventures, 352-5856	√	√	√	√
Abaco				
Brendal's Dive Shop Intl Ltd, 365-4411	√	√	√	√
Andros				
Small Hope Bay Lodge, 368-2014	√	√	√	√

Diving (cont)	Gear rental	Intro scuba	Certification course	Snorkelling
Bimini				
Bimini Undersea, 347-3089 or 347-3079	√	√	√	√
Cat Island				
Greenwood Beach Resort & Dive Centre, 342-3053	√	√	√	√
Eleuthera				
Valentine's Dive Centre, 333-2309	√	√	√	√
Long Island				
Stella Maris Marina Inn, 338-2050	√	√	√	√

Golf	Par	Holes	Length (yds) fr blue tees	Designer
New Providence				
Cable Beach Golf Club, 327-6000 or 327-8617	72	18	7,040	Devereux Emmet
Lyford Cay – private, 362-4271	72	18	6,610	Dick Wilson
Paradise Island Golf Club, 363-3925	72	18	6,780	Dick Wilson
South Ocean Golf, Dive & Beach Resort, 362-4391	72	18	6,707	Joe Lee
Freeport/Lucaya				
Bahamas Princess Resort & Casino, 352-6721				
Emerald Golf Course	72	18	6,679	Dick Wilson
Ruby Golf Course	72	18	6,750	Joe Lee
Fortune Hills Golf & Country Club, 373-4500	36 men 37 wmn	9	3,458	Joe Lee
Lucayan Country Club, 373-1066	72	18	6,824	Dick Wilson
Abaco				
Treasure Cay Golf Club, 365-8045	72 men 73 wmn	18	6,985	Dick Wilson
Eleuthera				
Cotton Bay Beach & Golf Club, 334-6156	72 men 73 wmn	18	7,068	R Trent Jones

Horseback riding

New Providence

Happy Trails, 362-1820 — Trail rides, $60 per ride, including transportation to and from stable. Accommodates 2-10 people 9 yrs and older, max weight 200 lbs. Experienced guides. Reservations required

Horseback riding (cont)
Freeport/Lucaya

Pinetree Stables, 373-3600 — Beach rides $45 per 1½ hrs. Horses to suit all levels. Experienced guides, certified coach. Reservations required

Squash & racquetball

	Courts	Fee/hr (non-gsts)	Lessons/hr (non-gsts)	Racquet rental
New Providence				
Radisson Cable Beach Golf Resort, 327-6000	3 squash 3 rktbl	$10 day pass	call for rate	$5
The Village Club with sauna & swimming pool, 393-1580	3 squash intl	$12	$30	$2
Freeport/Lucaya				
Grand Bahama Squash & Tennis Club, 373-4567	Call for information			

Tennis

	Courts	Fee/hr (non-gsts)	Lessons/hr (non-gsts)	Racquet rental
New Providence				
British Colonial Beach Resort, 322-3301	Under renovation at press time			
Nassau Beach Hotel, 327-7711, ext 6273 or 327-8410	6 hard	$5	$40-$45 group lessons at reduced rates	$6
Nassau Marriott Resort & Crystal Palace Casino, 327-6200	See Radisson Cable Beach			
National Tennis Centre, Queen Elizabeth Sports Centre, 323-3933	9 hard	$6-$10	$25-$75	$5
Radisson Cable Beach Golf Resort, 327-6000	5 clay 5 asph	Free	$20 day pass	$5
Sandals Royal Bahamian, 327-6400	Non-guest couples may purchase a $220 day pass or $198 night pass, which gives access to all facilities			
South Ocean Golf, Dive & Beach Resort, 362-4391	Not operational at press time			
SuperClubs Breezes, 327-5356	Non-guests may purchase a $50 day pass or $60 night pass, which gives access to all facilities			

Tennis (cont)	Courts	Fee/hr (non-gsts)	Lessons/hr (non-gsts)	Racquet rental
Paradise Island				
Atlantis, Paradise Island Resort & Casino	9	$20	$50	$5
Coral Towers/Beach Tower, 363-3000	See Ocean Club			
Ocean Club, 363-2501	9 clay	Members & guests only	See pro	–
Club Med, 363-2640	Non-guests may purchase a day or night pass $36/person or $65/couple (Fri night $40/person or $75/couple). Call about access to tennis facilities			
Radisson Grand Resort, 363-2011	4 asph	$15	–	$5
Freeport/Lucaya				
Grand Bahama Squash & Tennis Club, 373-4567	Call for information			
Princess Country Club, 352-6721	6 hard 2 lit	$10	$40	$7
Princess Tower, 352-9661	3 hard	$10 day $12 night	–	–
Silver Sands Hotel, 373-5700	2 hard	$10	–	$20 deposit
Xanadu Beach Hotel, 352-6782	3 hard 1 lit	$25	$25	$5
Abaco				
Bluff House, 365-4247	1 hard	Free	Free	$5
Great Abaco Beach Hotel, 367-2158	2 cmnt	Free	–	–
Berry Islands, Chub Cay				
Chub Cay Club, 322-5599	2 asph	Free	–	–
Bimini				
Bimini Big Game Club & Hotel, 347-3391/3	1 hard	Free	–	–
Eleuthera, Rock Sound				
Cotton Bay Club, 334-6101/3	Closed at press time			
Harbour Island				
Coral Sands Hote,l 333-2350 or 333-2320	1 fbrglss plexi-pave	Free	Free	Free
Dunmore Beach Club, 333-2200	1 plexi-pave	Free	–	–

Tennis (cont)	Courts	Fee/hr (non-gsts)	Lessons/hr (non-gsts)	Racquet rental
Harbour Island cont				
Pink Sands, 333-2061	3 hard 1 lit	$20	–	–
Romora Bay Club, 333-2325	1 hard	$10	–	–
Valentine's Yacht Club, 333-2142	1 hard	$5	–	–
Long Island				
Stella Maris Marina Inn, 338-2050	Under renovation at press time			

cont from pg 423

Nassau Sailing Assoc
Nassau Wholesalers Softball League
New Providence Amateur Basketball Assoc
New Providence Assoc of Umpires & Scorers
New Providence Old Timers Softball Assoc
New Providence Public Primary School Sports Assoc
New Providence Public Secondary Sports Assoc
New Providence Softball Assoc
New Providence Valley 8-Ball Assoc
New Providence Volleyball Assoc
Contact the Sports & Recreation Division, Ministry of Youth, Sports and Culture, East Bay St, Gold Circle House Office Complex, PO Box N-10114, Nassau, tel 394-0445/6, fax 394-5920, 394-7483 or 326-4516.
See also **Hotels.**

STATISTICS

The Dept of Statistics falls within the portfolio of the Ministry of Finance and Planning. Its responsibility is to collect, collate and analyze information from all sectors of the country – economic and social, government and private. Collated information is made available to all government depts to facilitate their planning as well as to the private sector. The Dept protects the confidentiality of specific information from individual and corporate sources.

The two main areas are:
1. Economic statistics relating to imports, exports, prices, income, balance of payments, etc.
2. Social statistics, including population census, migration and vital statistics.

Located in the Clarence A Bain Bldg on Thompson Blvd, the Dept produces a number of publications available at the Dept's library and at Government Publications, the Old Lighthouse Bldg, Bay St. These include:

All Bahamas Survey of Industry 1989-1992 ....$6
Annual Foreign Trade Statistics $12
Annual Reports Subscription $5
Annual Review of Prices $5
Annual Statistical Abstract..............$10
The Bahamas in Figures ....annually, $3
Building, Construction Statistics........................annually, $3
Census of Establishment: The Phase Two Experience $1
Census of Insurance Report ....annually, $5
The Census Report 1970 ....$10
The Census Report 1980:
  Vol 1, Demographic and Social Characteristics............................$16
  Vol 2, Economic Activity & Income $20
  Vol 3, Migration $20
  Vol 4, Fertility & Union Status $10
  Vol 5, Education $16
The Census Report 1990:
  Preliminary Results $2

*Government and
    Sectoral Accounts* $3
*Hotels, Motels and Guest Houses
    in New Providence and
    Paradise Island* ....annually, $3
*Labour Force and Household
    Income Report* ....annually, $7
Life Table Report $2
*The Meaning of
    Inflation* ....occasionally, $1
National Accounts of The Bahamas $3
*Population Projection For The
    Bahamas to the Year 2015* $3
*Quarterly Statistical
    Summary* ....quarterly, $5
*Quarterly Summary of Foreign
    Trade Statistics* ....quarterly, $4
*Retail Price Index: New Providence;
    Grand Bahama* ....monthly, 50¢
*Selected Economic and Social
    Indicators* ....annually, $5
Social Statistics Report $5
Vital Statistics Report ....annually, $5
*Wholesale and Retail
    Trade Statistics* ....annually, $5
*Work and Residence Permit
    Holders Report* ....annually, $3

STOCK MARKET
See **Investing**.

STRAW MARKETS
The hub of Nassau's native shopping experience is the colourful straw market downtown on Bay St, next to the Ministry of Tourism. Shoppers can banter with lively vendors for an armful of bargains in straw bags, hats, mats and novelty gifts, as well as T-shirts, wood carvings, jewellery and other souvenirs. Two smaller straw markets are located on West Bay St, Cable Beach. A 150-space straw market is planned as part of the new development at Atlantis, Paradise Island, scheduled to open at the end of 1998. Straw markets may also be found in the Family Islands and at Freeport/Lucaya, Grand Bahama. See **Freeport/Lucaya information, International Bazaar** and **Port Lucaya Marketplace**.

Quality straw work, artefacts and curios made in The Bahamas from Bahamian materials are available at stores throughout the island – including the Plait Lady, Island T'ings, Pyfrom's, Big Kahuna, The Seagrape, Tropic Traders, Everything's Paradise and Paradise Tees.

TAX BENEFITS FOR CANADIANS
by H Heward Stikeman, OC, QC, LLD, BCL, DS, and Paul J Setlakwe, M Fisc, BCL, BA

Despite restrictions imposed by Canadian income tax law on the use of tax havens, there are many circumstances in which The Bahamas retains its attractiveness for Canadians. The islands continue to prove a sound and durable base from which to invest in Canada or the outside world, or from which to conduct offshore operations for the benefit of Canadians.

In fact, increased investment outside of Canada, exports by Canadian firms and the growing number of multinational families have increased the scope for The Bahamas as a locus for international activity.

The Bahamas, by reason of not imposing income or estate taxes, has no tax treaties with any country. At first blush, it might appear that the consequences of residence in The Bahamas vis à vis Canadian investment could become a handicap when compared with residence in jurisdictions which do have tax treaties with Canada. To some extent this is true, unless appropriate legal steps are taken to account for the situation.

The fact that in Canada, residence remains the foundation of direct taxation for individuals is of assistance to Canadians wishing to take advantage of The Bahamas, especially as compared to the US, which taxes on a citizenship basis.

Under the Canadian federal income tax system, individuals resident in

Canada are taxed on their world income whereas non-resident individuals are taxed only with respect to income from employment in Canada, a business carried on in Canada and from gains realized on the disposition of taxable Canadian property (discussed later). They are not taxed with any reference to the fact that they are or are not Canadian citizens. A corporation not resident in Canada is subject to Canadian federal or provincial tax only on income derived from its business carried on in Canada and from gains realized on the disposition of taxable Canadian property. Like individuals, resident corporations are taxed on their worldwide income.

Canadian companies incorporated after April 26, 1965, are automatically deemed residents of Canada unless they are continued under the laws of another jurisdiction. Corporate continuance is treated as re-incorporation for tax purposes. Consequently, a company's residence for Canadian income tax purposes may be affected by a change in its corporate status.

The Canadian government has enacted an incentive to lure international shipping companies to Canada. If a company deriving all or substantially all (ie, 90%) of its revenue from an international shipping business is incorporated outside of Canada, it can establish its place of central management and control in Canada and yet be deemed a non-resident of Canada. In this way, it avoids Canadian tax on its income.

Canadian withholding tax

The basic Canadian withholding tax on investment income, certain pensions, dividends, interest (save on certain long-term obligations, Canadian or provincial government bonds or certain deposits made with a financial institution which carries on an international banking centre business, see following), rent, certain types of royalties, income from a trust and certain other forms of revenue paid by Canadian residents to persons abroad, is 25%. This tax must be withheld from the gross payment by the payer unless the recipient of the income resides in a country with which Canada has a tax treaty. In that event, the withholding tax may be reduced to 15% or less, depending on the terms of the treaty. As noted above, The Bahamas and Canada do not have a tax treaty.

Old age security payments under the Canada or Quebec Pension Plans made after 1995 are subject to withholding tax. Non-residents of Canada who are recipients of interest on bonds of the federal or a provincial government or a municipality or which are guaranteed by the federal government will remain immune to this tax – there being no tax of any kind withheld from such income.

Special exemption from withholding tax

One of the more significant relieving measures is that which exempts from Canadian withholding tax interest paid by a Canadian resident corporation to arm's length non-resident creditors on certain corporate securities. The exemption will be granted regardless of the currency in which the borrowing is made or the interest is paid. The interest must not be contingent upon the use of, or production from, property in Canada.

Also, interest computed in whole or in part by reference to revenue, profit, cash flow or other similar criteria, or by reference to dividends paid or payable on shares of a corporation, does not qualify for the exemption. Interestingly enough, there is no restriction preventing the guarantee of the debt by a non-resident person who is not at arm's length with the borrower. Thus, Bahamians may lend to Canadians against the security of a guarantee by someone outside of Canada not at arm's length with the borrower, upon terms which may exempt the interest paid from Canadian withholding tax.

The exemption is limited to debts of which the borrower is not obliged to repay more than 25% of the principal amount within five years of the date of issue except in the event of a failure or default, or if terms of the obligation become unlawful or are changed by virtue of legislation or by a court. This will not disqualify a security which gives to the borrower a *bona fide* right of prepayment even if it is exercised before the five-year period ends.

Thin capitalization provisions
The "thin capitalization" provisions contained in subsections 18(4) and following of the Income Tax Act relate to the deductibility of interest paid on money borrowed from abroad by Canadian resident corporations.

Interest payments made to non-residents who hold a substantial interest (ie, 25% of the voting or equity shares) in a Canadian company or which do not deal at arm's length with such a shareholder, are not always entirely deductible in computing income in Canada. They will be disallowed to the extent that the ratio of the company's equity capital as defined to the debt due to such non-resident shareholders or non-arm's length persons is less than one to three.

Bahamas benefits
Despite the restrictive and wide-ranging nature of the Canadian fiscal law, The Bahamas continues to play an important part in Canadian tax planning. In particular, the utilization of testamentary trusts and certain *inter vivos* trusts can yield rewards. Nevertheless, there is today less emphasis on a search for an absolute tax haven, in which no income tax whatever is imposed. Taxpayers are increasingly searching for jurisdictions which offer low rates of tax and appropriate international tax treaties. Treaties may also be used, on expert advice, by Bahamian residents by setting up suitable trusts or corporations in appropriate treaty jurisdictions.

Of the few remaining absolute tax havens, there are not many that offer benefits comparable to The Bahamas in terms of flexibility of corporate structure, top quality accounting and legal services, readily available first class financial and banking services, proximity to major world markets and good docking and harbourage facilities.

The modernization and liberalization of the Bahamian company law now provides a flexibility hitherto unavailable in The Bahamas. The Bahamas can offer a variety of corporate and settlement structures and procedures that are equal to those in any other jurisdiction. A number of Canadian individuals look to The Bahamas as a place from which to conduct some of their business activities. Some achieve this by becoming non-residents of Canada and setting up their homes in The Bahamas. Once they do this, they suffer no income tax in Canada, save the appropriate one on the profits from business done there or the 25% withholding tax on certain kinds of income derived from residents of Canada.

Capital gains tax on non-residents
Non-resident individuals pay income tax to Canada at applicable personal rates on 75% of the capital gains realized by them on the disposition of certain specific kinds of property known as "taxable Canadian property." The top marginal rate on capital gains exceeds 37.5% in most provinces.

"Taxable Canadian property" is defined in paragraph 115(1)(b) of the Income Tax Act and includes Canadian real estate, shares in a Canadian private corporation, and shares in a Canadian public corporation if certain threshold ownership requirements are met. Certain other types of property are also considered taxable Canadian property. In particular, proposed changes to the definition of taxable Canadian property would extend the definition to include shares of corporations and interests in trusts not resident in Canada which derive their value principally from Canadian real estate or resource properties.

If enacted, this measure will subject non-residents to Canadian tax on gains in respect of shares of non-resident corporations or interests in non-resident trusts, even where the gain is not attributable to Canadian assets. Liability to Canadian tax could even be triggered by the death of an individual who happens to own shares of a non-resident corporation with Canadian assets. Broadening the tax base in this way is unprecedented and it is hoped the Dept of Finance will not proceed with its proposals; in the meantime, it is advisable to examine the manner in which Canadian investments are held to determine the possible impact of this measure.

All non-residents must report dispositions of taxable Canadian property to the Canadian fisc, indicate the name of the person to whom the property is sold and pay an amount on account of Canadian tax or furnish acceptable security.

Upon payment of a tax instalment, a "certificate" will be issued to the non-resident which will protect a purchaser of the asset from having to pay some of the tax that might not have been paid by the non-resident.

Becoming a non-resident of Canada

In order to become a non-resident of Canada, an individual must give up his home and most attachments within Canada such as employment, provincial medicare coverage, clubs, bank accounts, credit cards and the like, and acquire a residence in another jurisdiction by purchasing a home or renting an apartment in which he lives as his central family headquarters.

Nevertheless once a former Canadian resident has become a non-resident, he may return to Canada each year for temporary visits without being taxed, provided he does not sojourn in Canada for periods which in the aggregate exceed 182 days in any calendar year.

Thus, because The Bahamas imposes no income tax of any kind, a non-resident Canadian citizen may reside there and remain outside Canada for at least six months in the year, without losing his contacts with his home country and with the advantage of paying to Canada only 25% on certain kinds of investment income derived from Canadian sources and no withholding tax on certain kinds of interest. The same individual, if he wishes to continue his business activities in Canada, may do so as a non-resident and pay tax at the appropriate personal graduated rates in Canada on the profit derived from the business there carried on by him.

The exit tax

A problem which faces Canadians who consider taking up residence in The Bahamas is the exit tax imposed by Canada upon capital gains deemed to arise from the notional realization of certain capital property at the time they give up Canadian residence.

Until recently, an individual giving up Canadian residence was not required to pay capital gains tax on any property that would fall within the category of "taxable Canadian property" listed previously. This is because, after leaving Canada and becoming a non-resident, he would remain taxable in respect of any capital gain on that property as already stated. The departing individual could, however, elect to realize part or all of any capital gain accrued in respect of these properties upon emigration.

The foregoing exception to the exit tax was eliminated for certain types of property by an amendment to the Income Tax Act first announced in Oct 1996. This amendment, like the extension to the definition of taxable Canadian property discussed previously, is unprecedented in the international context and makes Canada less attractive as a place for wealthy individuals to reside.

Corporations leaving Canada are also subject to exit rules. In particular, a corporation is treated as having disposed of all of its property which is not taxable Canadian property for deemed proceeds equal to fair market value and, if it was incorporated or continued into Canada, thereafter to have notionally distributed its net equity thus determined. This fictitious distribution is assimilated to a liquidating dividend and subjected to a special tax in lieu of withholding tax.

Succession duty and estate tax advantages

There are no estate and gift taxes in Canada. However, individuals are deemed to dispose of their property at fair market value at the time of their death. Thus, a non-resident individual may be liable to tax on capital gains at the time of his death if he holds taxable Canadian property directly.

Corporate uses of The Bahamas by Canadians

Under Canadian tax law, a company is resident where its seat of management and control is found (subject to restrictions on companies incorporated or continued into Canada set out previously). This is usually held to be the place where the directors meet or from which the day to day management instructions emanate or are carried out.

In order to prevent a company from being legally resident in Canada and thereby paying tax at corporate rates ranging from 25-50%, management and control must be exercised, *bona fide* and in fact, outside Canada.

A non-resident company may perform useful functions of an extraterritorial nature such as world advertising, worldwide selling, the financing and organizing of sales abroad, the management and servicing of the facilities needed to maintain the products sold abroad and the operation of ships or certain group insurance activities. In each case, it is important to determine whether the income of the Bahamian subsidiary is foreign accrual property income (commonly referred to as FAPI). The FAPI of a "controlled foreign affiliate" of a Canadian resident is attributed to and taxed in the hands of its Canadian resident shareholder on an annual basis.

There have also been cases before the Canadian courts in which attacks made by Revenue Canada on offshore subsidiaries of Canadian corporations have been tested. The income of the subsidiaries has been added, sometimes, to the income of the Canadian parent on the footing that the subsidiary was itself a sham and served no business purpose. Transfer pricing is another line of attack increasingly favoured by Revenue Canada. These cases stand on their own facts and need not pose a threat to normal activities carried on *bona fide* in The Bahamas provided management and control of the Bahamian corporation are not in Canada.

Foreign affiliates

The foreign affiliate rules affect any foreign corporation in which a Canadian resident has a significant interest. A foreign affiliate is defined to include any non-resident corporation in which a Canadian resident holds at least 10% of the shares of any class. A non-resident corporation will also be considered a foreign affiliate of a Canadian resident who holds 1% of the shares of any class where the equity interest of the Canadian resident together with related persons is over 10%.

When a foreign corporation qualifies as a foreign affiliate, the dividends which pass upstream to a Canadian corporate shareholder are tax free when paid out of "exempt surplus." Exempt surplus is income derived by a company resident and carrying on business in a country with which Canada has a treaty.

However, dividends paid by a foreign affiliate from active business profits earned in a non-treaty country are included in full in the income of a

Canadian corporate shareholder, subject to the deduction from that income of an amount in respect of taxes paid to the jurisdiction where the profits were earned.

Passive income is treated quite differently from active business income. The concept of FAPI is meant to tax the passive earnings of foreign affiliates controlled by Canadian taxpayers. In many ways it is not unlike its American counterpart, "Subpart F" of the Internal Revenue Code. Foreign accrual property income is essentially income from property or from a business other than an active business. Each year an appropriate share of the FAPI of a controlled foreign affiliate (and certain trusts), if it exceeds $5,000 in amount, is included in the income of Canadian taxpayers controlling the foreign affiliate in the taxation year in which the foreign affiliate's taxation year has terminated.

FAPI does not include interaffiliate dividends, active business income, and certain amounts received from other affiliates. It similarly does not include capital gains from the disposition of "excluded property" (property used principally in an active business and shares of foreign affiliates carrying on an active business).

Non-resident trusts
A non-resident of Canada who, during his lifetime, has been a Canadian resident for five years or less, can establish by will or gift, a Bahamian resident trust for the benefit of Canadian resident family members, which will escape the application of the income attribution rules which have been enacted to govern most offshore trusts and investment funds. A similar exemption from accrual taxation is available if the settlor has not resided in Canada during the 18-month period preceding the end of the trust's taxation year in question, or in the case of a testamentary trust, during the 18 months preceding death.

The residence of these trusts is important and must be outside Canada, since Canadian-resident trusts are liable to tax on their world income. This requires that the majority of, if not all, trustees having legal and actual control of the trust assets be non-residents of Canada. Expert professional advice in this area is essential, but utilization of Bahamian trusts can pay substantial dividends.

International banking centres
Canadian income tax law provides reasonably generous treatment toward the income of certain financial institutions from an international banking centre business. Essentially, provided certain conditions are met, these rules exempt from Canadian tax the income of a qualifying financial institution from a business, carried on by it through a branch or office located in Montreal or Vancouver, which consists substantially of accepting deposits from, and making loans to or deposits with, arm's length non-residents and other qualifying institutions.

Qualifying institutions include the Bank of Canada, Canadian banks and subsidiaries of foreign banks that are governed by the Canadian Bank Act, certain other financial institutions and, generally, any entity that accepts deposits transferable by order to a third party which satisfies certain deposit insurance and other conditions.

Not only is the income from an international banking centre business of such a qualifying institution exempt from Canadian tax but, as already noted, amounts on account of interest on deposits made with such an institution paid or credited to an arm's length non-resident person or partnership are exempt from Canadian withholding tax. Moreover, the amount of interest payable on such deposits may be contingent or dependent upon the use of or production from property in Canada or be computed by reference to the revenue, profit or cash flow of any person, the price of a commodity or any similar criterion or by reference to dividends paid or payable by any corporation.

Accordingly, a Bahamian resident may take advantage of the above rules to earn interest income which is exempt from Canadian tax on a wide variety of financial products and derivative instruments, subject to the availability thereof at qualifying Canadian financial institutions. Moreover, provided certain conditions are satisfied, a Canadian subsidiary of a Bahamian bank (or other foreign bank) may qualify to carry on an international banking centre business from a branch or office in Montreal or Vancouver and, thereby, earn income which will be exempt from Canadian tax. Withholding tax may, however, apply if and when such earnings are repatriated, for example, in the form of dividends paid by the Canadian subsidiary to its non-resident shareholders.

Current attitudes towards tax planning

The Canadian law contains a number of technical provisions which narrows the field of manoeuvre for the taxpayer. Moreover, Section 245 contains a general anti-avoidance rule (GAAR). The GAAR tests come into play whenever a taxpayer engages in a transaction or series of transactions which results directly or indirectly in a "tax benefit," as broadly defined in that provision. Thus, the uses made by Canadians of Bahamian corporations must be limited to commercially defensible activities and should not be employed merely to hide or artificially minimize truly Canadian income. In this whole field, the area of manoeuvre is narrowing and a conservative and realistic approach should be taken.

H Heward Stikeman,
OC, QC, LLD, BCL, DS, a senior partner in the international law firm, Stikeman, Elliott, has practised law as a tax counsel in Montreal since 1946. Stikeman is a director of Fednav Ltd and Victor Delta Holdings Ltd. He is also editor-in-chief of *Canada Tax Service*, *Canada Tax Letter*, *Doing Business in Canada* and *Canada Tax Cases*, and edits several Canadian tax manuals. Stikeman was born in Montreal and educated at Chestnut Hill Academy, Philadelphia, PA; Trinity College School, Port Hope, Ontario; McGill Univ, Montreal; and the Univ of Dijon, France.

Paul J Setlakwe,
M Fisc, BCL, BA, who collaborated on this article, is a member of the Bars of Quebec and Ontario, and a senior partner in the international practice of Stikeman, Elliott. Setlakwe has lectured in international tax at McGill Univ and Sherbrooke Univ, and has been a frequent speaker at conferences organized by the Canadian Tax Foundation and others. He obtained his law degree from Laval Univ, Quebec City, and a Masters Degree in tax from Sherbrooke Univ.

TAX BENEFITS FOR EUROPEANS
by Howard M Liebman

It has become increasingly difficult for Europeans to utilize offshore investment centres, although opportunities still exist for legitimate tax planning in tax havens such as The Bahamas.

Despite the lifting of European exchange controls, which allowed funds to move more easily out of various European countries, impediments facing Europeans who want to utilize offshore centres include the tendency to look for substance over form and business purpose, the increasing level of information exchanges and tougher penalties for tax evasion.

Trusts and asset protection
Perhaps the most interesting offshore tool for tax- or estate-planning is the common law trust, which can take a number of different forms.

In the past decade or so, asset protection trusts (APTs) have gained in popularity, mostly as a result of the increase in large damages awards in the US against doctors, lawyers, financial planners and other advisors. Even though this type of litigation has not impacted Europe to the same extent, the use of trusts to conserve assets against lawsuits is becoming more common. See **Investing, Asset Protection Trusts (APT).** When seeking to utilize a trust for asset protection purposes, the key is to ensure that the maximum level of control over assets is placed out of the settlor's hands, and thus out of the jurisdiction of the settlor's country of residence.

This is where the conundrum lies, because many Europeans are concerned about their inability to control assets in such circumstances. From thence derives the true nature of the trust: one must have "trust," or faith, in both the trust structure and the chosen trustees. However, certain methods have been devised to provide settlors with a degree of influence. These include using a protector – usually an attorney or other trusted individual who stands between the trustees and the settlor – or appointing the settlor to a committee of advisors or board of directors of a company which is owned by the trust and which holds all the assets. The latter is perhaps somewhat riskier, but still arguably maintains the position that the assets are no longer in the hands of the settlor, even if the latter acts in the capacity of a corporate officer in determining their use or investment.

Certain trust issues are treated differently from country to country. For example, in Belgium, no tax is due on a *don manuel*, or gift of cash. In France, by contrast, a transfer of legal title in property may be regarded as a gift, raising the issue of the level of gift tax to be paid. This, in turn, depends on whether the gift tax is deemed to be due upon transfer to an entirely third party (ie, the trustees) or to closely related parties (such as the beneficiaries). If the trust is revocable, it may be argued that no gift tax is due. In the case of transfers of appreciated property, a capital gains tax may have to be paid, such as in the UK.

If the settlor retains significant powers over the trust, it may be treated as a grantor trust, in which case many jurisdictions will seek to tax the settlor (as the grantor) on the trust's income. Even if the trust passes this test and no tax is due from the grantor/settlor, it is still possible that the beneficiaries will be taxed on any income earned by the trust. In the case of a fully discretionary trust in which the beneficiaries do not receive any income, it may be argued they cannot be taxed until they receive a taxable economic benefit.

Careful planning on a jurisdiction-by-jurisdiction basis is required to minimize the chance of falling into a tax trap.

Fraudulent conveyance laws in various jurisdictions must also be carefully considered, as if an individual is already being sued or is under threat of a suit, transferring assets to an APT may be viewed as an attempt to defraud creditors – even if the suit commences within a certain period of time after the transfer has taken place.

This is one of the first questions a legal advisor is apt to pose when an individual seeks to establish an APT in The Bahamas or elsewhere. No reputable advisor will these days assist anyone in defrauding creditors, since such assistance may, in and of itself, be viewed as aiding and abetting fraud.

Assuming this is not the case, and no fraud is intended, there should be no problem in setting up an APT in The Bahamas – as long as the trust is carefully structured and such home country tax issues as gift tax, income tax and inheritance tax are carefully thought through and understood.

Other uses of trusts

Bahamian trusts are also being utilized by multinational corporations – especially as part of employee stock ownership plans, which are growing in popularity. They are used as an anti-takeover defence, placing shares of publicly-traded companies in "friendly" hands – such as those of employees – under the control of handpicked trustees. They are also a means of giving employees a vested interest in the future of the company.

There are tax and non-tax reasons for utilizing these trusts. Employees may avoid taxation in their home jurisdiction if shares are placed in a trust and are therefore not at their immediate disposal. This, however, depends on the precise terms of the stock ownership plan as well as on the tax laws in the home country.

Even if tax is due, using the vehicle of a trust may still be important for non-tax reasons.

Companies usually retain the shares under their control until a vesting period has passed to stop shares from passing directly into the hands of employees who may leave the company shortly thereafter. Also, if an employee dies, the shares can more readily be sold – and not transferred to the spouse or family members. A trust may also help on the administrative side, by allowing employee-held stock to be aggregated and more easily dealt with in terms of dividends, voting, notices, etc.

A second popular use of trusts is as part of a failsafe device in the event of expropriation. These so-called Phillips trusts were devised around the time of World War II as a means for the shares of a company to be held by trustees for the benefit of the shareholders. In the case of Phillips NV, of the Netherlands, the goal was to allow foreign affiliates to continue operating even when the head office was under German control.

Otherwise, US law (in particular) would have frozen enemy-controlled assets.

Usually, such trusts hold offshore assets only to shelter them from expropriation in the event of the home country seeking to nationalize the shares of stock of the head office itself. This technique has notably been used with regard to the offshore assets of companies located in Latin America.

A third use of offshore trusts relates to in-substance defeasances. This is a technique used by a number of major multinationals to clean up their balance sheets. Basically, it involves transferring liabilities to a trust, along with certain assets or income streams sufficient to pay off such liabilities over a period of time. The trust is established as a non-grantor trust, in which liabilities are removed from the balance sheet of the transferor in order to improve its financial position. Peugeot is one European company to use this technique.

Offshore holding and trading companies

Given The Bahamas' status as a tax haven, a number of different opportunities present themselves to European companies and individuals – assuming they are appropriate and the laws in the country of residence are taken into account.

An important investment tool is the offshore holding company, which serves both tax and non-tax purposes. Its most obvious use is to shelter income from taxation – a benefit which may be limited by home country legislation.

A Bahamas-based holding company would not be able to take advantage of double taxation conventions to reduce withholding taxes, however, since The Bahamas does not benefit from any such conventions. On the non-tax side, using a holding company allows for centralization of shareholdings, leading to some administrative ease and potential cost savings.

A second commonly-used entity in international structuring is the trading company. This can be structured as a commission agent, receiving commissions for assistance in effecting sales of goods or services; or as a buy-sell company which takes title to goods and sells them in its own name as a distributor. Again, anti-abuse provisions in various European and other jurisdictions should be taken into account, most notably the controlled foreign company type of legislation which continues to spread in Europe, as well as transfer pricing rules.

Although The Bahamas is well-suited for the formation of offshore trading companies, it should be noted that in any international tax structuring of this sort, true substance is more and more a *sine qua non*.

The mere establishment of a shell company is unlikely to serve its intended purpose, as it may easily be pierced by tax authorities of one or another country looking at the entity and/or transactions it conducts. Substance requires more than just abiding by corporate formalities. In one sense the old adage, "You get what you pay for," applies. Setting up an inexpensive entity as a screen will be seen as a sham. So if one wishes to take maximum advantage of The Bahamas, a real company must be formed and the expense must be borne to place substance, business activities and business purpose into that entity.

International tax structuring often entails the use of special purpose vehicles, many of which could be located in The Bahamas. These include captive insurance companies, financing vehicles, licensing companies, and service entities such as headquarter operations. The Bahamas can serve any of these functions tax-efficiently.

Home country legislation
As noted, individuals and multinationals seeking to use The Bahamas for tax-planning reasons should take into account the impact of anti-abuse legislation throughout Europe. Such legislation may be broken down into four categories:

1. **Controlled foreign company rules,** which treat certain types of "tainted" income (earned by a foreign company and controlled by domestic taxpayers) as a deemed dividend automatically taxable to those taxpayers or shareholders. It usually includes such "passive" income as dividends, interest and royalties as well as related-party sales or services income.
2. **Transfer pricing rules,** which effectively preclude the shifting of profits from a high-tax to a low-tax jurisdiction such as The Bahamas. If a Bahamian entity has substance and can justify earning a certain level of profit commensurate with the functions it performs, it will usually be in a position to rebut any challenge of intercompany pricing.
3. **Rules tailored to dealings with tax havens.** In certain countries, such as Belgium or Italy, these are effected by means of a formal or informal blacklist, whereas in other countries, they are based on whether tax rates in the offshore jurisdiction are significantly below those of the home country on equivalent income. These anti-tax haven rules often preclude deductions for payments made to a tax-haven entity or the applicability of special provisions such as withholding tax exemptions.
4. **Exchange controls,** which although mostly dismantled in Europe, may still be imposed in the event of currency emergencies, or in cases dealing with tax havens. In some instances, they technically remain on the statute books. Even if funds can be freely transferred out of a country, they may still have to be reported as having been transferred. Although some European countries still impose a form of exit tax, such as Denmark, most Europeans can transfer their residence to The Bahamas, if done properly. The

English, in particular, are fond of taking up Bahamian residence and thereby avoiding or minimizing their tax liability in the UK.

Summary

Traditionally, Europeans have tended to utilize European financial jurisdictions such as Switzerland, Luxembourg, Liechtenstein, Gibraltar, the Channel Islands and the Isle of Man – although The Bahamas effectively offers a viable alternative when used as part of a proper and viable structure with substance, and after taking into account home country tax constraints.

The Bahamas is not too distant from Europe and benefits from excellent communications and transportation links. It has a common law system as in Gibraltar and the Isle of Man, but is close to the US. Indeed, for Europeans looking to deal extensively with either North or South America, The Bahamas may be a useful gateway to, or even a turntable of sorts between, those two continents.

For the individual seeking a change of residence, The Bahamas certainly offers a more attractive climate than most European centres, and benefits from a stable investment climate as well as a stable legal and tax regime, both being prime elements for any jurisdiction seeking to establish itself as a favourable tax-planning location.

Howard M Liebman

is the managing partner of the Brussels office of Morgan, Lewis & Bockius, a US-based law firm of more than 900 attorneys in 14 offices in the US, Europe and Asia. Liebman specializes in international tax and corporate structuring, as well as transborder mergers and acquisitions. In this capacity, he has undertaken the structuring and restructuring of major multinationals and joint ventures, and has led significant cross-disciplinary teams handling all the legal as well as tax aspects of a number of larger European-wide acquisitions. Liebman is a prolific author and speaker, and serves as the EU tax correspondent for *European Taxation* in Amsterdam and the Belgian correspondent for the *Tax Management International Forum* in London. He received his undergraduate degree in International Relations and Economics *summa cum laude* from Colgate Univ and earned a Masters Degree in International Relations with honours there also. He graduated *cum laude* from Harvard Law School and is a member of the District of Columbia and Brussels ("B" list) Bars.

TAX BENEFITS FOR US CITIZENS & COMPANIES

by P Bruce Wright and Arthur J Lynch

A US individual or company can, in some instances, start international operations with relatively small amounts of capital and then expand with tax-free or low-taxed accumulations of earnings instead of net-tax dollars earned in the US. Thus, expansion abroad can be more rapidly accomplished with 100 cent tax-free dollars, instead of 65 cent dollars (which is net after approx 35% US tax).

The tax advantages, or tax deferrals, are available by reason of the foreign taxation provisions of the Internal Revenue Code (IRC) which set forth conditions under which the US will exempt or defer foreign income from US taxation.

To become eligible for US tax advantages, Bahamian business ventures should be operated by a company which, even though controlled by US persons, is granted certain tax advantages and concessions under US tax laws not available to US individuals or partnerships comprised of US individuals. If a Bahamian or other foreign company (except a passive foreign investment company) is not engaged in a US trade or business, and at least 50% of the voting power and value is owned by non-US persons, US tax laws generally do not apply to its foreign income, and only in rare instances will there be any US income tax.

If US persons own 50% or less of the voting power and value of a Bahamian company, none of its foreign income will generally be subject to US taxation unless and until dividends are paid to US shareholders, or they sell their shares, or the assets of the company are distributed.

If a Bahamian or other foreign company is more than 50% controlled or more than 50% of its value is owned (directly or indirectly) by US persons who each own at least 10% of the voting power, it is known under US tax laws as a controlled foreign corporation (CFC). US shareholders who own (directly or indirectly) at least 10% of the voting control of a CFC (US 10% shareholders) are taxable each year on their proportionate share of certain kinds of income of the corporation. The kinds of income currently taxable are, generally:

1. Income from the insurance or reinsurance of risks not located in The Bahamas.
2. Passive income such as dividends, rents, interest, gains from the sale of property which itself produced passive income, capital gains from the sale of stocks and securities, gains on commodities and foreign currency transactions, royalties, etc.
3. Sales income where the goods are either purchased from or sold to a related person.
4. Income from services if rendered to a related person.
5. Increases in investments in US property.
6. Aircraft and shipping income (including income from ocean and space activities).
7. Income attributable to international boycotts.
8. Income attributable to the bribery of foreign government officials.
9. Income which is foreign oil or gas related.

Even so, there are many exceptions and exclusions to the above. In addition, if such income comprises less than 5% of a Bahamian company's adjusted gross income (and less than $1,000,000), none of the company's income will be taxable by the US.

In most cases, however, every other kind of foreign income is free of US taxation. In other words, even if the Bahamian company is US controlled, its US 10% shareholders are not required to include such foreign earnings in their annual taxable income.

A Bahamian company engaged in a US trade or business will be subject to US corporate taxes on income effectively connected with such trade or business. The Tax Reform Act, 1986, added "branch profits tax" to the IRC. Generally, this is a 30% tax imposed on earnings of a US branch of a foreign company that are deemed repatriated to the foreign parent company. Therefore, careful planning is required to minimize the effect of this tax.

The types of US CFCs particularly suitable for operations in The Bahamas and having these US tax advantages include, among others, the following:

1. Manufacturing production.
Income from the sale of products or goods manufactured or produced in The Bahamas is not subject to US taxation even though purchases and sales involve the parent corporation or other related persons.

The same applies to rental income where such products or goods are leased instead of sold, provided certain "active business" tests are met and, in the case of a lease to a related party, the products or goods are used in The Bahamas. Likewise, income from certain incidental services rendered before a sale or in connection with an effort to sell such products or goods is not currently taxable.

2. Sales of products and goods. If the parent corporation or other related person is not involved in the purchase of products or goods, then income from such sales is not subject to current US taxation, no matter where or by whom the products or goods were manufactured, where the sales are made or where such products or goods are used or consumed.

Even if a related person is involved, the sales income is free of current tax if the products or goods are manufactured, produced, grown or extracted in The Bahamas, or if they are for use, consumption or disposition in The Bahamas.

3. Insurance. A Bahamian insurance company is considered a CFC if more than 25% of the voting power or value of its stock is owned by US 10% shareholders. Income earned by a Bahamian insurance or reinsurance company which is a CFC is taxable only to a US 10% shareholder.

In addition, unless certain exceptions are met, if a Bahamas insurance company is at least 25% US-owned, all US shareholders (even if such shareholders own less than 10%) must include in income their *pro rata* share of the company's related person insurance income (premium or investment income on insurance policies where the person insured, directly or indirectly, is a US shareholder or related person). Related person insurance income also includes income from reinsurance if the ceding company or its insured is a US shareholder in the Bahamian insurer.

From 1988, a Bahamian insurance company that is a CFC can elect to be treated as a US corporation for all US tax purposes. If this election is made, US shareholders will not be taxed on the company's income until distributed as dividends. The charge for electing is 0.75% of capital and surplus as of Dec 31, 1987, up to a max charge of $1,500,000.

The Bahamas government provides advantages and incentives for insurance companies insuring and reinsuring non-Bahamian risks.

4. Banks and finance companies. After the Tax Reform Act, 1986, dividends, interest and capital gains of a Bahamian bank that is a CFC became subject to current US taxation. However, interest earned by a Bahamian bank which is a CFC in connection with export financing for related US persons, with certain exceptions, is not subject to US tax.

5. Service companies. This is a broad category and includes any Bahamian corporation rendering services which are technical, managerial, engineering, architectural, scientific, skilled, industrial, commercial or the like.

Many types of companies in The Bahamas fall into this category. A partial list would include engineering, sales promotion, sales engineering, merchandising, consulting, etc. With reference to such companies, income from such services, rendered outside the US and performed for persons who are not related without substantial assistance of related US persons, is exempt from current US taxation.

Income from services rendered within The Bahamas is also exempt even though such services are rendered for, or on behalf of, a related person. Income from services rendered by a foreign company in The Bahamas before a sale or in connection with an effort to sell products or goods manufactured, produced, grown or extracted by it are also exempt from current US tax even though such income is received from a related person.

6. Leasing and royalties. Rents derived in the active conduct of a trade or business in The Bahamas and received from persons not related are not subject to current US taxation.

Rents are also so exempt even when received from a related person if such rents are for use of property located in The Bahamas, unless the CFC is also a "foreign personal holding company" (FPHC). An FPHC is a foreign corporation that derives at least 60%

of its gross income from certain types of passive income, such as rents, royalties, dividends and interest, and more than 50% of the voting power or value of which is owned by, or for, not more than five US citizens or residents.

Royalties, for example, payments in connection with patents, copyrights, inventions, models, designs, secret formulas or processes, are currently exempt from US taxation when derived in the active conduct of a trade or business in The Bahamas and received from persons who are not related, unless the company is an FPHC.

Royalties are also so exempt, even when received from a related person, if such royalties are for the use of property or property rights within The Bahamas, unless the company is an FPHC.

7. Ships and aircraft. Income of a Bahamian company that is a CFC is subject to current US tax when received for the use or hiring or leasing or for services related to the use of any vessel or aircraft in foreign commerce.

Income from transportation, including income from leasing any container used in connection with a vessel or aircraft that begins and ends in the US, is treated as US source income and may be subject to tax. Income from transportation that either begins or ends in the US (but not both) is treated as 50% US source income.

Shipping income will be exempt if the foreign country of incorporation of the ship owner grants an equivalent exemption to US persons.

8. Certain investment income. Dividend and interest income received from a related foreign corporation generally is exempt from current tax if both payer and payee are incorporated in The Bahamas and the payer has a substantial part of its assets used in the business in The Bahamas.

Even if the foreign company is a CFC, the current taxation CFC provisions of the IRC do not apply to US shareholders who own less than 10% of the voting power. However, if more than 50% of total voting power or total value of the shares is owned (directly or indirectly) by five or fewer US persons, and more than 60% of the gross income of the company is interest, dividends and certain other types of passive income, all US shareholders will be taxable on their share of all of the corporation's earnings under the FPHC rules.

Unless the company is more than 50% owned in vote and value by foreign persons, if it is primarily involved in trading in stocks, securities or commodities, the gain recognized on a liquidation or sale of shares will be treated as ordinary income to the extent of the shareholder's *pro rata* share of the earnings of the company.

Passive foreign investment company

The Tax Reform Act, 1986, includes rules governing passive foreign investment companies (PFIC). A Bahamian company is a PFIC if 75% or more of its gross income is "passive" income (dividends, interest, etc), or 50% or more of its assets are held to produce passive income. Thus, a mutual fund, and even a manufacturing company with large retained earnings invested in securities, could be a PFIC.

US shareholders in a Bahamian PFIC may be subject to additional taxes (plus interest) on certain PFIC distributions or on a sale of PFIC stock. A US shareholder of a PFIC may avoid this result by making one of the following two elections. First, a PFIC shareholder can elect to be taxed currently on his *pro rata* share of PFIC ordinary income and capital gains, which then can be distributed tax free. If a shareholder makes this election, he also can elect to defer the current tax but must pay interest on the deferred taxes. Second, a US shareholder of a PFIC may elect to mark-to-market his stock on an annual basis if such stock is marketable (eg, regularly traded on a national securities exchange registered with the SEC).

Coordination rules prevent the same income being taxed twice in cases where a PFIC also qualifies as a CFC.

An important exception is that PFIC rules generally will not apply to *bona fide* insurance companies predominantly engaged in an insurance business, certain banks and certain securities dealers.

Employment of US citizens abroad
Tax benefits are available to US citizens employed abroad who establish a tax home in a foreign country (ie, the foreign country is the taxpayer's principal place of business) and who meet certain other tests prescribed by the IRC (either a "physical presence" or residency test with respect to the foreign country). Although a US citizen generally is subject to US income tax on his worldwide income, a US citizen employed abroad who satisfies the IRC tests described above may exclude from gross income for any taxable year foreign-source earned income (ie, wages or salary for services performed outside the US) up to $72,000. This amount will be increased in $2,000 increments to $80,000 for taxable years 1999 through 2002 and adjusted for inflation for taxable years beginning after 2007. In addition, such individual may either:
1. Exclude from gross income a portion of the housing expenses paid for by his employer, or
2. In the event such expenses are not paid for by his employer, deduct such expenses (subject to certain limitations).

P Bruce Wright, a partner in the firm LeBoeuf, Lamb, Greene & MacRae, LLP, of 125 West 55th St, New York, was employed by the office of the Chief Counsel, Internal Revenue Service, after graduating from law school. During this time he obtained a Master of Law in taxes from Georgetown Univ Law Center. Wright was awarded the designation Chartered Property Casualty Underwriter in 1984. He has written articles in a number of areas involving US tax laws which have appeared in publications such as *The Business Lawyer, Real Estate Review, Risk Management and Cash Flow*.

Arthur J Lynch is also a partner at LeBoeuf, Lamb, Greene & MacRae, LLP, and has been with the firm since graduating from law school. He obtained a Master of Law in Taxation from New York Univ School of Law.

TELECOMMUNICATIONS

Telecommunications services and facilities in The Bahamas are on par with the US and Canada. A 100% digital switching system allows direct distance dialling to more than 100 countries. Fax machines are found in most offices, and hotel switchboards can link visitors with family and business contacts worldwide.

The Bahamas Telecommunications Corp (BaTelCo) is a quasi-public corporation owned by the government but operating without subsidy from it. BaTelCo has authority over a wide range of services, including telephone, fax, telex, cellular and radio phone networks, private line services, packet switching, satellite leasing and radio licensing.

Telephone application, installation and rental
Applicants for a telephone line must complete an application form in person or by telephone.

A deposit is required to cover damage to rental equipment or outstanding bills. The amount is variable, eg, the deposit for a property owner may be as low as $50. Deposits for rental property start at $150. An additional $50 deposit is required if there is no post office box to which bills may be forwarded.

Installation cost for a basic residential telephone is $50 for the first telephone, $60 for a telephone with special features and $25 for each additional telephone. Rental costs start at $10.75 per month.

The basic business telephone system installation cost starts at $331 (one line with two extensions). Rental costs start at $21.25 per month for the line and $2.25 per month for an extension.

Telephone rates
See **Fig 2.6** for long-distance charges within The Bahamas and overseas.

Ships at sea
Rates for radio telephone service to ships at sea via Nassau:
Ocean-going vessels ......$4.92 minimum for 3 mins, $1.64 each additional min
Private yachts ....$1.26 minimum for 3 mins, 42¢ each additional min

Rates for cellular telephones
Monthly access charge $45
Air-time (per min)
    local (7am-7pm) ....45¢
    local (7pm-7am) ....30¢
Roaming rates $3/day
Air time roamer.............99¢/min all day

A roamer is a person from outside The Bahamas who rents temporary use of a line for a cellular telephone.

For a roamer to receive calls, the calling party outside The Bahamas must dial (242) 359-7626 and then the roamer's number (all 10 digits).

Within The Bahamas, the roamer is accessed by dialling 359-7626 and then the 10 digits of the roamer's number.

Roamers need a contract with a carrier outside The Bahamas to receive service.

Fax services
A fax bureau is located at BaTelCo offices on East St, Blue Hill Rd, Golden Gates II, Fox Hill and Shirley St. Canon fax machines may be rented from BaTelCo. The model recommended for office or home is the Fax 270S. The portable Fax 8 is recommended for personal use.

Rental charges

Equipment	Installation charges	Monthly rental
Canon Fax 120	$145.00	$ 65.00
Canon Fax 270S	$185.00	$110.00
Canon Fax 730	$178.00	$138.00

Should the subscriber opt to purchase a fax machine elsewhere, BaTelCo is not responsible for machine installation or maintenance. It will, however, provide a modular block if necessary.

As fax machines are connected to a direct line, charges include monthly rental for the line plus toll charges for overseas transmissions. Toll charges are the same as those for regular long distance calls. There is no charge for local transmissions.

Other
Systems Resource Group offers international fax services through the Internet to the business community, at reduced international toll charges. Features of these services include detailed toll billing, call accounting, store and forward, and client configurable broadcast fax.

Telex services
A fully automated telex switch allows connection from Nassau to most parts of the world without operator assistance. A public telex service is available at BaTelCo offices on East St, Nassau Intl Airport, Jumbey Village, Shirley St, Fox Hill and Freeport.

Rates – one min minimum*   B$
The Bahamas: Inter-island................ .50
    Nassau...................................... .25
Canada..3.50
France..4.00
Germany..4.00
Hong Kong......................................4.00
Mexico...4.00
UK..4.00
US: Miami.......................................2.33
    Other..2.50

* Each additional min or part thereof is charged at the one min rate.

FIG 2.6
LONG DISTANCE TELEPHONE RATES

Islands of The Bahamas	DDD[2] 1 min minimum Day / Night[3]	Operator assisted[1] (station-to-station) 3 min minimum Day / Night
Abaco, Andros, Bimini, Cat Island, Crooked Island, Eleuthera, Exuma, Grand Bahama, Inagua, Long Island, Mayaguana, San Salvador	.40 .30	1.80 1.80

North American continent (except Alaska)	DDD 1 min minimum Std[4] / Dis[5] / SS[6]	Operator assisted (station-to-station) 3 min minimum Std / Dis / SS
Zone 1 (0-500 miles) Alabama, Florida, Georgia, South Carolina	.99 .90 .70	1.50 1.50 1.50
Zone 2 (501-1000 miles) Delaware, District of Columbia, Kentucky, Maryland, Mississippi, North Carolina, Tennessee, Virginia, West Virginia	.99 .90 .70	2.00 2.00 2.00
Zone 3 (1001-2000 miles) Arkansas, Colorado, Connecticut, Illinois, Indiana, Iowa, Kansas, Louisiana, Missouri, Ohio, Maine, Massachusetts, Michigan, Minnesota, Nebraska, New Hampshire, New Jersey, New Mexico, New York, North Dakota, Oklahoma, Pennsylvania, Rhode Island, South Dakota, Texas, Vermont, Wisconsin	.99 .90 .70	2.50 2.50 2.50
Zone 4 (2001-3000 miles) Arizona, California, Idaho, Montana, Nevada, Oregon, Utah, Washington, Wyoming	.99 .90 .70	2.75 2.75 2.75
Canada		
Alberta, Saskatchewan	1.25 1.15 1.15	3.00 3.00 3.00
British Columbia	1.25 1.15 1.15	3.75 3.75 2.50
Manitoba	1.25 1.15 1.15	2.50 2.50 2.50
NWT, New Brunswick, Newfoundland, Nova Scotia, Ontario, Prince Edward Island, Quebec	1.25 1.15 1.15	3.00 3.00 2.00
Yukon	1.25 1.15 1.15	4.00 4.00 3.00

Selected other countries[7]	DDD 1 min minimum 1st min / Add min	Operator assisted (person-to-person) 3 min minimum
Australia	4.00 4.00	5.00
Barbados	2.25 2.00	3.00
Bermuda & West Indies (except Jamaica)	2.25 2.00	3.00

Selected other countries[7] (cont)	DDD 1 min minimum 1st min	Add min	Operator assisted (person-to-person) 3 min minimum
Dominican Republic	2.25	2.00	3.00
France	2.75	2.75	5.00
Germany	2.75	2.75	5.00
Greece	4.00	4.00	5.00
Hawaii	4.00	4.00	5.00
Italy	2.75	2.75	5.00
Jamaica	2.25	2.00	3.00
Mexico	2.75	2.50	3.50
Philippines	4.00	4.00	4.00
Switzerland	2.75	2.75	5.00
Trinidad/Tobago	2.25	2.00	3.00
UK	2.75	2.50	5.00

[1] *For operator assisted calls, each additional min is charged at one third of the 3-min rate. For the US (excluding Hawaii and Alaska) DDD rates for additional mins are 80¢ standard hours (Std); 75¢ discount hours (Dis); and 65¢ supersaver hours (SS). For Canada, DDD rates for additional mins are $1.15 Std and $1.10 for Dis and SS hours.*
[2] *Direct distance dialling.* [3] *Night rate hours are 8pm-6am.* [4] *Std = Standard hours, Mon-Fri 7am-6pm.*
[5] *Dis = Discount hours, Mon-Fri 6-11pm and Sat & Sun 7am-11pm.*
[6] *SS = Supersaver hours, Sat and Sun 11pm-7am.* [7] *No discounts – all hours charged at same rate. Rates subject to change.*

Telegrams
Rates per word:

	Full	Urgent	Night letter[1]
Inter-island (Bahamas)	3½¢	7¢	–
British Commonwealth	26¢	52¢	13¢
UK	42¢	84¢	–
US	24¢	[2]	12¢

[1] *Night letter rates are for 22 words max.*
[2] *Urgent telegrams to the US mainland, known as rush telegrams, pay full rate with an extra word charge for the word "rush."*

See also **Internet**.

TELEVISION
ZNS TV transmitter power is 50,000 watts ERP on Channel 13, which can be viewed 130 miles from Nassau. Channel 13 operates 10 hours per day Mon-Fri, 17 hours on Sat and 16 hours on Sun.

ZNS TV began test transmission on July 4, 1977, and its official programming commenced July 10. HM Queen Elizabeth II officially opened the station on Oct 20 of that year. In 1983, a facility was installed to receive satellite transmission for re-broadcast.

Channel 13 is autonomous of any external television network, and its programming is chosen by the Broadcasting Corp of The Bahamas to serve the national interest.

See also **Broadcasting; Cable television** and **Freeport/Lucaya information, Television**.

THEATRE & PERFORMING ARTS
Performing arts groups established in the 1990s include the government-funded Bahamas National Youth Choir, National Dance Company of The Bahamas, National Children's Choir and National Youth Orchestra. The National Youth Choir has produced six compact discs (two more to come), performed in the US, UK, Canada, Russia and the Caribbean, and appeared on local and international television. Choir founder and director Cleophas Adderley, an attorney, has been the government's Director of Culture since 1994.

Other performing arts groups in The Bahamas include The Bahamas Concert Orchestra, Nassau Operatic Society, Nassau Renaissance Singers, Dundas

Repertory Company, the Diocesan Chorale and James Catalyn and Friends.

The Dundas Centre for the Performing Arts showcases Bahamian talent in locally written plays, revues, musicals and dance, as well as staging non-Bahamian works and hosting international performers. Performance charges at the 334-seat theatre on Mackey St are usually $12 for adults, $7 for children. The season is Jan-May, although performances are staged throughout the year. Tel 393-3728.

See also **Awards**.

TIME

The Bahamas operates on Eastern Time, which is five hours behind Greenwich Mean Time. This puts our archipelago in the same time zone as the major commercial centres of the eastern US and Canada, such as Miami, Washington, DC; New York, Toronto, and Montreal.

When it is noon in The Bahamas, it is 9am in San Francisco and Vancouver; 5pm in London; 6pm in Rome, and 2am in Tokyo. The Bahama Islands are on daylight saving time from the first Sun in April to the last Sun in Oct.

TIME-SHARING

Time-sharing, also known as interval ownership or vacation club membership, is a method of acquiring a holiday home for specific periods during the year, for a specific number of years. It is a popular alternative to regular hotels for vacationers who wish to spend repeat holidays in a familiar place. Some time-sharing projects also offer the option of switching location from year to year.

The Time-sharing Act, 1984, provides guidelines for the creation and management of time-sharing projects. The Act sets out terms and conditions for licences necessary to construct, manage, improve, market and sell timeshare properties in The Bahamas.

Timeshare facilities must be inspected according to standards outlined in The Act, and must comprise at least 25 units in New Providence, or at least 10 units in the Family Islands. Timeshare units may be purchased for a specific period not exceeding six months per year, for a maximum period of 40 years, or as specified by the Foreign Investment Board. Each unit may be sold up to a maximum of 50 weeks per year.

Timeshare projects in New Providence include Club Land'or, Paradise Harbour Club and Marina, Sunrise Beach Villas, Guanahani, Westwind I, Westwind II Club, Royal Holiday Club and Sandyport Beaches Resort. Some timeshare projects operate as part of hotels or residential developments.

TOURISM

In 1997 there were 3,439,466 foreign arrivals in The Bahamas. Of those, 1,617,595 were stop-over visitors, 1,743,736 were cruise visitors and 78,135 were day visitors or in transit. This represents an increase of 0.7% over the 1996 figure of 3,414,823. Total visitor spending in 1997 was estimated at $1.416 billion, an increase of 1.3% on the $1.398 billion spending in 1996. Hotel room occupancies in Nassau/Paradise Island jumped from 71.2% in 1996 to 74.8% in '97, and average room rates rose 8.8% from $103.51 to $112.57. See **Fig 2.7** for visitor arrivals to The Bahamas.

See also **Accommodations; Cruise ship incentives; Gambling;** and **Shopping**.

Tourism promotion boards

Three tourism promotion boards promote maximum interest in Nassau, Paradise Island, Grand Bahama and the Family Islands as separate and ideal vacation destinations. The Nassau/Paradise Island/Cable Beach Promotion Board, tel 322-8384; Bahama Out Islands Promotion Board, tel US toll free (800) 688-4752 or (954) 359-8099; and Grand Bahama

FIG 2.7
MINISTRY OF TOURISM VISITOR ARRIVALS

Year	Nassau	Grand Bahama & Family Islands	Total
1993	1,739,685	1,942,195	3,681,880
1994	1,871,337	1,572,440	3,443,777
1995	1,742,808	1,495,447	3,238,255
1996	1,843,685	1,571,138	3,414,823
1997	1,918,073	1,521,393	3,439,466

Island Tourism Board, tel (242) 352-8044/5 or 352-8356 or US toll free (800) 448-3386; work closely with travel partners and vacationers to provide efficient destination-specific information. Travel partners include tour operators, airlines, travel agents, advertising and public relations agencies, cruise lines, hotels and travel media.

Bahamas Tourism Centres
The Bahamas Ministry of Tourism maintains 10 overseas sales offices abroad which provide information about The Bahamas: five in the US, four in Europe, one in Canada. They are:

UNITED STATES
Chicago:
 8600 W Bryn Mawr Ave, Suite 820,
 Chicago, IL 60631.
 Tel (773) 693-1500,
 fax (773) 693-1114.
Dallas:
 World Trade Center,
 2050 Stemmons St, Suite 116,
 PO Box 420068,
 Dallas, TX 75343-0068.
 Tel (214) 742-1886,
 fax (214) 741-4118.
Los Angeles:
 3450 Wilshire Blvd, Suite 1204,
 Los Angeles, CA 90010.
 Tel (213) 385-0033,
 fax (213) 383-2966.
 Bahamas Film and Television Commission, Darlene Davis,
 Film Commissioner.
 3450 Wilshire Blvd, Suite 1204,
 Los Angeles, CA 90010.
 Tel (213) 385-0033 or (800) 439-6993.

Miami:
 1 Turnberry Pl, Suite 809,
 19495 Biscayne Blvd,
 Aventura, FL 33180-2321.
 Tel (305) 932-0051,
 fax (305) 682-8758.
New York:
 150 East 52nd St, 28th Floor North,
 New York, NY 10022.
 Tel (212) 758-2777,
 fax (212) 753-6531.
CANADA, Toronto:
 121 Bloor St East, Suite 1101,
 Toronto, Ont M4W 3M5.
 Tel (416) 968-2999,
 fax (416) 968-0724.
ENGLAND, Guilford:
 3 The Billings, Walnut Tree Close,
 Guilford, Surrey GU1 4UL.
 Tel (011) 44-14-834-48900,
 fax (011) 44-14-834-489-90.
FRANCE, Paris:
 60 Rue St Lazare, 75009 Paris.
 Tel (011) 33-45-26-62-62,
 fax (011) 33-48-74-06-05.
GERMANY, Frankfurt:
 Leipziger Strasse 67d,
 60487 Frankfurt/Main.
 Tel (011) 49-69-970-8340,
 fax (011) 49-69-970-83434.
ITALY, Milan:
 Via Cusani, No 7,
 20121 Milan.
 Tel (011) 392-720-23003,
 fax (011) 392-720-23123.

Ecotourism
The Bahamas, the largest oceanic-archipelagic nation in the tropical Atlantic Ocean, has one of the world's most extensive ocean hole and limestone cave systems as well as the

world's largest breeding colony of West Indian flamingos.

The Bahamas offers a wealth of ecotourism options in its 700-plus islands and 2,000-plus cays, and boasts no less than 12 eco-rich, state-supported national parks in addition to privately owned sanctuaries.

The nerve centre for studying ecology and promoting enjoyment of the natural environment is the Bahamas National Trust (BNT). See **Bahamas National Trust (BNT).** BNT has implemented a number of initiatives to protect endangered indigenous species such as the Bahama parrot, hutia and white-crowned pigeon.

Eco-tours and adventures offered by a variety of eco-oriented organizations include kayaking, birdwatching, blue hole diving, dolphin watching, bush safaris and nature treks.

Eco-conscious organizations
Abaco Wild Horse Fund
   Milanne Rehor, 2809 Bird Ave,
   #170, Miami, FL 33133.
   e-mail: arkwild@shadow.net
The Adventure Learning Centre
   Randy & Kimberley Grebe,
   tel 361-2120 or 324-3166 (h)
Animals Require Kindness (ARK)
   Debbie Krukowski/Carol Brogden,
   tel 394-3757 or 362-1142
Bahamas Environmental Science & Technology Commission (BEST)
   HE Lynn Holowesko, tel 327-4691
   e-mail: lholowesko@batelnet.bs
The Bahamas Field Station
   Dr Daniel Suchy, tel (242) 331-2520
Bahamas Reef Environmental Educational Foundation (BREEF)
   Sir Nicholas Nuttall, tel 326-7938
   e-mail: breef@bahamas.net.bs
BNT Native Flora Group
   Malcolm Rae, tel 324-3416
BNT Ornithology Group
   Carolyn Wardle, tel 362-1574
Oceanwatch Bahamas
   Stuart Cove/Sally Varani,
   tel 327-8554
   e-mail: oceanwatch@batelnet.bs

Re-Earth
   Sam Duncombe,
   tel 322-3128 or 393-7604

For Bimini Biological Field Station, Rob Palmer Blue Holes Foundation, Bahamas Marine Mammal Survey and Caribbean Marine Research Centre (CMRC), see **Marine research.**

See also **Bahamas Humane Society; Flora & fauna; Marine parks & exhibits; Nature centres;** and **Wildlife preserves.**

TRADE AGREEMENTS
See **Caribbean Basin Initiative (CBI); Caribbean Community & Common Market (CARICOM); CARIBCAN; Free Trade Area of the Americas (FTAA); Lomé IV Convention; North American Free Trade Agreement (NAFTA);** and **World Trade Organization (WTO).**

TRADE UNIONS
New Providence
Airport, Airline & Allied Workers Union,
   PO Box N-3364.
Bahamaland Construction Workers
   Union, PO BOX N-1505
Bahamas Air Traffic Controllers Union,
   PO Box N-3120.
Bahamas Brewery Distillers Workers
   Union, PO Box N-299.
Bahamas Bus Drivers & Transport
   Union, PO Box N-6844.
Bahamas Commercial, Stores, Supermarkets & Warehouse Workers
   Union, PO Box GT-2514.
Bahamas Communication and Public
   Officers Union, PO Box N-3190.
Bahamas Doctors Union,
   PO Box CB-13651.
Bahamas Electrical Contractors Assoc,
   PO Box GT-2176.
Bahamas Electrical Utility Managerial
   Assoc, PO Box GT-2647.
Bahamas Electrical Workers Union,
   PO Box GT-2535.
Bahamas Employers Confederation,
   PO Box N-166.

Bahamas Guild of Artists,
PO Box N-3334
Bahamas Hotel Catering and Allied
Workers Union, PO Box GT-2514.
Bahamas Hotel Employers Assoc,
PO Box N-7799.
Bahamas Hotel Managerial Assoc,
PO Box N-3399.
Bahamas Maritime Port & Allied
Workers Union, PO Box SS-6501.
Bahamas Motor Dealers Assoc,
PO Box N-4824.
Bahamas Musicians & Entertainers
Union, PO Box N-880.
Bahamas Petroleum Retailer Assoc,
PO Box N-7783.
Bahamas Professional Pilots Union,
PO Box CB-13138.
Bahamas Public Managers Union,
PO Box N-9936.
Bahamas Public Services Union,
PO Box N-4692.
Bahamas Taxi-Cab Union,
PO Box N-1077.
Bahamas Telecommunications
Management Union,
PO Box N-9124.
Bahamas Union of Teachers,
PO Box N-3482.
Bahamas Utilities Services & Allied
Workers Union, PO Box GT-2515.
Bahamian Contractors Assoc,
PO Box N-8049.
Commonwealth of The Bahamas Trade
Union Congress, PO Box CB-10992.
Eastside Stevedores Union,
PO Box GT-2167.
National Congress of Trade Unions,
PO Box GT-2514.
New Providence Restaurant Service
& Allied Employees Union,
PO Box N-7799
Public Service Drivers Union,
PO Box N-4071.
Union of Tertiary Educators of The
Bahamas, PO Box CB-13472.
United Brotherhood of Longshoremen's
Union, PO Box N-7311.
Water & Sewerage Management
Union, PO Box N-3905.
See also **Industrial relations** and
**Freeport/Lucaya information,
Trade unions.**

TRANSPORTATION

Taxi rates are government controlled. All taxis are required to have meters in good working condition.

The first quarter-mile is $2.20 for one or two passengers; each additional quarter-mile is 30¢. Additional passengers after the first two pay $3 per person. Accompanied children under three ride free.

Zone rates, applied to most standard routes on request, are set by government. Taxi waiting charge (except when hired by the hour) is 30¢ per minute. Tour cars may be hired for sightseeing at $50 per hour or $13 per person with a two-hour minimum.

Car rental prices are competitive with Hertz, Avis, Budget and Dollar represented at airport and downtown offices. Pick up from a hotel anywhere in New Providence (including Paradise Island) is free of charge. Prices range from $47 per day ($408 per week) for a standard Suzuki Swift to $134.95 per day ($809.70 per week) for a large sedan and include unlimited mileage. Off season rates are slightly less. Insurance and gas are extra.

Visitors may use their home driver's licences here for three months. Traffic moves on the left side of the road.

Motor scooters are $50 per day, 8am-5pm, including gas. Insurance is $5, and a deposit is required (a credit card can be used as deposit). Hourly rentals are available. It is wise for a novice to practise scooter skills in light traffic before attempting downtown streets. There is a law requiring drivers and riders of motor scooters and motor bikes to wear crash helmets. These helmets are available at no extra charge from the rental companies.

The jitney (bus) provides inexpensive touring and a close view of local life. Fare is 75¢, which can take you the length of the island. Service is from 6:30am-8pm. Bus stops are marked. However, time schedules may be unpredictable.

A complimentary bus shuttle operates between Atlantis, Paradise Island hotels at approx 30-min intervals from 7am-12 midnight. A ferry service operates from the Nassau Cruises Dock, Paradise Island, across the harbour to Rawson Sq and back at $2 per person one way. This is a daytime service, 8:30am-7pm (summer), 6pm (winter) with departures from both sides of the harbour about every 20 mins.

A horse-drawn surrey ride costs approx $10 per person for a 25-min tour of Nassau's downtown area. Rates for extended trips should be negotiated with the driver beforehand. The surrey ranks are at Woodes Rogers Walk downtown. Horses are rested 1-3pm, May-Oct; 1-2pm Nov-April.

Mail-boats
An inexpensive and rewarding way to see the Family Islands is by mail-boats which tie up at Potter's Cay under Paradise Island Bridge. The boats, subsidized by the government as mail carriers, take on freight and passengers as well as the priority mailbags. Costs range from around $40 round trip to Eleuthera to $140 round trip to faraway Inagua. Some mail-boats include food with their inter-island transportation service. Check with the dockmaster at Potter's Cay for latest schedules and costs, tel (242) 394-1237 (to 9).

See **Air service; Car rental companies; Driver's licence & vehicle information** and **Motor vehicle insurance.**

TRUSTS
See **Investing.**

VACCINATION REQUIREMENTS
Most visitors to The Bahamas do not need special vaccinations before entering the country. However, travellers over one yr must provide a yellow fever vaccination certificate if they are coming from infected areas.

Bahamians and Bahamas residents travelling abroad should familiarize themselves with vaccination requirements of their destination. According to *International Travel and Health**, a publication of the World Health Organization (WHO), Geneva, no country requires a certificate of vaccination against smallpox and cholera. Bahamians and Bahamas residents travelling to yellow fever or malaria infected countries should consult the Public Health Dept, Ministry of Health, or a doctor regarding vaccinations and other precautionary measures. No vaccinations are required for Bahamians going to the US or Canada.

According to WHO, travellers should be immunized against a certain number of diseases. The organization stresses the distinction between vaccinations required by countries for entry, those recommended for general protection against certain diseases and others which may be advisable in certain circumstances. Travellers are advised to establish a vaccination plan, taking into account their current immune status, destination, duration (especially in malaria infected areas), type of travel and overall state of health.

* *Vaccination requirements and health advice reproduced by permission of* International Travel and Health, World Health Organization, 1998.

VETERINARIANS
New Providence
Dr Patrick Balfe,
  Eastern Veterinary Clinic ..393-3818
Dr Gary Cash, Palmdale
  Veterinary Clinic 325-1354
Dr Basil Sands,
  Central Animal Hospital 325-1288
Dr Dawn Wilson,
  Animal Clinic 328-5635
Bahamas Humane Society
  & Veterinary Clinic............323-5138
   See also **Bahamas Humane Society.**

VISAS FOR BAHAMIANS

Bahamian passport holders can travel virtually anywhere in the world without fear of detainment. As The Bahamas enjoys diplomatic relations with many countries, visitor entry visas are not necessary on all trips abroad. However, relevant authorities must be contacted to obtain necessary entry permits if one is entering a country to do business or as a student. These would include trips to Canada, the UK and the US. For the US, a visa is required if the possessor of the Bahamian passport is in transit or embarking on a cruise.

Bahamians do not require visas for travel to:

Antigua and Barbuda, Anegada,[3] Anguilla,[4] Aruba,[1] Austria, Barbados, Belize, Bermuda, Bonaire,[1] Botswana, Brazil, Canada, Cayman Islands,[4] Chile, Cook Islands, Costa Rica, Curacao,[1] Cyprus, Dominica, Dominican Republic, Ecuador, Fiji, Finland, Galapagos Islands, Gibraltar, Greenland, Grenada, Guyana, Hong Kong (at press time), Holy See (Vatican City), Iceland, Ireland, Israel, Jamaica, Japan, Jost Van Dyke,[3] Kenya, Kiribati (Gilbert Islands), South Korea, Lesotho, Liechtenstein, Macedonia, Malawi, Malaysia, Maldives, Malta, Mauritius, Federated States of Micronesia, Montserrat,[4] Nive, Norway, Palau, Peru, St Eustatius,[1] St Kitts & Nevis, St Lucia, St Maarten,[1] St Vincent & the Grenadines, Saba,[1] San Marino, Seychelles, Singapore, Solomon Islands, Swaziland, Sweden, Switzerland, Tanzania, Tonga, Trinidad & Tobago, Tuvalu, UK (England, Northern Ireland, Wales, Scotland), US, Vanuatu, Virgin Gorda, Yugoslavia,[2] Zambia, Zimbabwe.

Visas are required for visits to:

Afghanistan, Albania, Algeria, Andorra, Angola, Argentina, Armenia, Australia, Azores, Azerbaijan, Bahrain, Bangladesh, Belarus, Belgium, Benin, Bolivia, Bosnia, Brunei, Bulgaria, Burkina Faso, Burundi, Cambodia, Cameroon, Cape Verde, Central African Republic, Chad, China (but not Hong Kong at press time), Colombia, Congo, Federal & Islamic Republic of Comoros, Cote d'Ivoire, Croatia, Cuba, Czechoslovakia, Denmark, Désirade,[6] Djibouti, Egypt, El Salvador, Estonia, Ethiopia, France, French Austral,[5] French Guiana, French Southern & Antarctic Lands (Crozet & Kerguelen), Gabon, The Gambia, Gambier,[5] Republic of Georgia, Germany, Ghana, Gibraltar, Greece, Guadeloupe,[6] Guatemala, Guinea, Guinea-Bissau, Haiti, Herzegovina, Honduras, Hungary, India, Indonesia, Iraq, Isle des Saintes,[6] Italy, Jordan, Kazakhstan, Kuwait, Lao People's Democratic Republic, Latvia, Lebanon, Liberia, Lithuania, Luxembourg, Macao, Madagascar, Mali, Marie Galante,[6] Marquesas,[5] Marshall Islands, Martinique,[6] Mauritania, Mayotte Islands, Mexico, Miquelon Islands, Moldova, Monaco, Mongolia, Morocco, Mozambique, Myanmar (formerly Burma), Namibia, Nepal, Netherlands, New Caledonia,[5] New Zealand, Nicaragua, Niger, Nigeria, Norfolk Island, Oman, Pakistan, Panama, Papua New Guinea, Paraguay, Philippines, Poland, Portugal, Qatar, Reunion, Romania, Russia, Rwanda, St Barthelemy,[6] St Martin,[6] St Pierre, Saudi Arabia, Senegal, Sierra Leone, Slovakia, Society Islands,[5] Somalia, South Africa, Spain, Sri Lanka, Sudan, Suriname, Syrian Arabic Republic, Tahiti,[5] Taiwan, Thailand, Togo, Tortola,[3] Tuamotu,[5] Tunisia, Turkey, Turkmenistan, Turks & Caicos,[4] Uganda, Ukraine, United Arab Emirates, Uruguay, Venezuela, Vietnam, US Virgin Islands, Wallis & Futuna Islands,[5] Western Samoa, Yemen Arab Republic, Zaire.

[1] *Netherlands Antilles.* [2] *Exceptions apply.*
[3] *British Virgin Islands.* [4] *British West Indies.*
[5] *French Polynesia.* [6] *French West Indies.*

Contact the Bahamas-based Honorary Consul of the country in question, or the Ministry of Foreign Affairs, East Hill St, PO Box N-3746, tel 322-7624/5.

See also **Government section, Resident diplomats & consular representatives.**

VOTING

To register in The Bahamas, a prospective voter must:
1. Be a citizen of The Bahamas, either by birth or naturalization, and 18 yrs or older, validated by a birth certificate or passport before first-time voting
2. Be subject to no legal incapacity (eg, incarcerated in prison or a mental institution)
3. Have been a resident of a constituency for three months previous to registration.

To register, application should be made to the Parliamentary Commissioner's Office, former National Insurance Bldg, Farrington Rd, Nassau, or to a revising officer, or to an administrator in the Family Islands.

A prospective voter must be duly registered and must have been ordinarily resident in his constituency for some period during the six months immediately preceding the day of election. If the voter has moved to a new constituency and has lived there for less than six months, he is entitled to vote in his old constituency if he was registered there.

There are now 24 constituencies in New Providence, and 16 in the Family Islands for a total of 40 parliamentary constituencies. The last general election in The Bahamas was held Mar 14, 1997.

In accordance with the Constitution, the next general election is set for 2002. (The Constitution provides for earlier election if the Governor-General, on advice of the Prime Minister, dissolves Parliament and calls for a general election.) In the Family Islands, local government elections are held every three years.

See also **Constitution**.

WAGES

Following is a cross-section of jobs and wage averages per week, provided by the Dept of Labour and Employment Exchange. Wage scales are for a 40-hour week in Nassau, mid-1998:

Job title	B$
Bricklayer (mason)	300
Carpenter (semi-skilled)	187
Carpenter	315
Caretaker (live-in)	130
Certified public accountant	800
Civil engineer	1,083
Computer programmer	577
Cook (short-order)	300
Electrician	231
Executive secretary	550
Farm labourer	125
Financial controller	1,250
Financial intermediator/manager	1,040
Forklift operator	450
Gardener	185
Head chef	769
Heavy equipment mechanic	450
Housemaid/housekeeper	150
Janitor	150
Labourer/handyman	150
Manager (hotel & restaurant)	1,192
Nanny	300
Primary school teacher	446
Portfolio manager	1,250
Project engineer	833
Registered nurse	400
Sales representative	462
Scuba diving instructor	375
Seaman	280
Seamstress	250
Secretary (junior)	300
Senior architect	673
Ship engineer	400
Show girl	408
Sponge worker	250
Stenographer/secretary	400
Systems analyst	769
Truck driver	300
Vehicle mechanic	300
Waitress	100

In 1996, a minimum wage of $4.12 per hour, based on a weekly wage, was introduced for government workers.

See also **Cost of living**.

WATER RATES

Current New Providence water charges (Imperial gallons, 277.274 cu in) are based on the following quarterly rates:
- A minimum charge (including the first 3,000 gals or part thereof) per meter, per quarter in accordance with **Fig 2.8**.
- For every 1,000 gals (or part thereof) in excess of 3,000 gals but not exceeding 13,000 gals per meter, per quarter, $10.60 per 1,000 gals ($11.20 non-residential).
- For every 1,000 gals (or part thereof) in excess of 13,000 gals per meter, per quarter, $17.60 per 1,000 gals ($19.20 non-residential).
- For every 1,000 gals (or part thereof) in excess of 100,000 gals per meter per quarter, $14.26 per 1,000 gals.

In each case, bills are calculated proportionately for periods other than 13 weeks. (See **Fig 2.8**.)

A charge of $8 is made for special meter readings or readings requested by the owner. Reconnection charge after disconnection due to non-payment is $21 when balance due is less than $210, and 10% when balance due is more than $210.

A deposit of $55 is required for dwelling-houses with one water closet or bathroom and $115 for those with two or more. For commercial establishments the deposit is based on estimated water usage per quarter.

Notice of customer's discontinuance of the service should be sent to the General Manager, Water & Sewerage Corp, PO Box N-3905, Nassau, at least seven clear days before discontinuance.

Family islands* water rates (Imperial gallons) are as follows:
- A minimum charge of $15 per quarter (incl the first 2,000 gals or part thereof) per meter per quarter.
- For every 1,000 gals (or part thereof) in excess of 2,000 gals but not exceeding 13,000 gals per meter per quarter, $2.30 per 1,000 gals.
- For every 1,000 gals (or part thereof) in excess of 13,000 gals, but not exceeding 26,000 gals per meter per quarter, $2.90 per 1,000 gals.
- For every 1,000 gals (or part thereof) in excess of 26,000 gals per meter per quarter, $4.00 per 1,000 gals.

*Does not include Grand Bahama.

See also **Freeport/Lucaya information, Water rates & supply**.

WATER SKIING
See **Boating**.

WEATHER
See **Climate** and **Hurricanes**.

WEIGHTS & MEASURES

The Bahamas follows the US in using linear, dry and liquid measure. Twelve inches equal a foot; four quarts in a gallon. The US gallon is 231 cu in; the Imperial gallon is 277.274 cu in. Gas at the pump in The Bahamas is by US gallon.

The Bahamas government appointed a National Committee for Metrication to compile a report determining local programmes, projects, costs and other requirements needed to implement aspects of metrication already taken by US agencies. (All US consumer goods labels printed after Feb 1994 have metric measurements.)

At press time, draft legislation, including a Standards Bill and Regulations and a Weights and Measures Bill and Regulations, had been finalized by the office of the Attorney-General and was expected to be presented to Parliament.

FIG 2.8
WATER RATES
Minimum charge schedule per quarter

Meter size (in inches)	Residential consumer B$	Non-residential consumer B$
1/2	30.00	40.00
3/4	38.50	47.50
1	59.50	73.00
1 1/4	82.00	99.50
1 1/2	104.00	127.50
2	–	191.00
3	–	318.00
4	–	636.00
6	–	1,112.50
8	–	1,590.00

WILDLIFE PRESERVES
Following is a complete list of national parks, national reserves and protected areas maintained by the Bahamas National Trust (BNT):

The Abacos
Abaco National Park, between Cherokee Sound and Hole in the Wall.
Bahama Parrot Preserve, 12th and newest park.
Black Sound Cay National Reserve, a small mangrove island in Black Sound, just off Green Turtle Cay.
Pelican Cays Land and Sea Park, Abaco sister of Exuma Cays Land and Sea Park.
Tilloo Cay National Protected Area, between Marsh Harbour and Pelican Cay.

Conception Island
Conception Island Land and Sea Park, one of several Bahama islands visited by Christopher Columbus in 1492 and a station for many migrating birds and nesting sea turtles.

Exuma
Exuma Cays Land and Sea Park, approx 40 nautical miles from Nassau in a 176 sq mile area notable for yachting, skin-diving, hiking and unique Bahama flora and fauna.

Grand Bahama
Lucayan National Park, the site of one of the world's longest charted cave systems.
Peterson Cay National Park, only cay off Grand Bahama's leeward side.
Rand Nature Centre, 100-acre site two miles from downtown Freeport, Grand Bahama headquarters for The Bahamas National Trust.

Great Inagua
Inagua National Park, site of the world's largest breeding colony of West Indian flamingos.
Union Creek National Reserve, seven sq miles of enclosed tidal creek.

New Providence
The Retreat, 11 acres in residential Nassau with one of the world's largest private collections of palms. Administrative BNT headquarters.

By-laws passed in 1986 govern all land and sea parks and reserves, and include the following stipulations:
1. Land and sea parks are designated marine replenishment areas for The Bahamas. Hunting, trapping, netting, capture or removal of any fish, turtle, crawfish, conch or whelk is prohibited.
2. Destruction, injury or removal of any living or dead plant life, beach

sand, corals, sea fans or gorgonias is prohibited.
3. Molestation, injury or destruction of any land animal or bird life or the eggs of any animal or bird are prohibited. Use of nets or snares also is prohibited.
4. Permission may be granted for the capture or removal of a designated number of land or sea animals or plants required for valid scientific research.
5. Dumping of any wastes, oil or rubbish on land or sea is prohibited.
6. No person shall injure, deface or remove any building, structure, sign, ruins or other artefacts.
7. Posting of any sign, placard, advertisement or notice is prohibited.
8. No person shall display, use, fire, or discharge any explosive, firearm or harpoon gun within the parks.
9. Any person charged with an offence against any of these by-laws is liable on summary conviction to a penalty not exceeding $500. Any boat, vessel or aircraft and all equipment, stores, provisions or other effects used for committing an offence may be confiscated.
See also **Marine parks & exhibits**.

WORLD TRADE ORGANIZATION (WTO)

The General Agreement on Trade and Tariffs (GATT) formed the World Trade Organization (WTO) in early 1995 after the Uruguay Round accomplished dramatic dismantling of trade barriers to increase the volume of world trade.

The Bahamas government is presently reviewing its options regarding the WTO. In the meantime, it has proposed that The Bahamas seek "observer" status, with the view to obtaining full membership in due course.

See also **Trade agreements**.

YACHTS
See **Boating** and **Marinas & cruising facilities**.

YWCA
See **Social Services, Non-governmental organizations**.

ZNS
ZNS, the call letters for Radio Bahamas, were assigned in 1936 when the fledgling radio station was recognized and accredited by the American Federal Communications Commission.

The letter Z was assigned to all British stations in the Caribbean and Atlantic islands. The words attached to the call letters are Zephyr (balmy breeze) Nassau Sunshine.

See also **Broadcasting**.

ZOO
See **Nature centres**.

BANK ON THE BAHAMAS

OFFSHORE BANKING & FINANCIAL INFO

bahamasnet

www.bahamasnet.com

PO Box N-7513, Nassau, The Bahamas
Tel (242) 323 5665 Fax (242) 323 5728
email info@bahamasnet.com

Freeport/Lucaya

Freeport, Gra

Symbol of welcome: International Bazaar's Torii Gate at Freeport/Lucaya

"There is a storehouse of opportunity in Freeport,"

The Bahamas' Prime Minister,
Rt Hon Hubert A Ingraham.

BOOMING
ENTERS T

Unique tax freedoms ar
Tel 242-352-6

nd Bahama

"We're enormously pleased with recent large-scale investments by international companies of the highest calibre,"

E G P St. George,
Grand Bahama Port Authority
Group of Companies chairman.

centives ... Invest now
242-352-4568

FIRST ATLANTIC REALTY LTD

We offer investors information and advice on real estate and business investment opportunities.

Hotels, marinas, condominiums, businesses, beachfront properties, office buildings, luxurious residences, private estates, etc...

Developers and agents for Freeport's luxurious waterfront development, "Queens Cove"

First Atlantic Realty Bldg • John Maxwell St & Queens Hwy
PO Box F-42596 • Freeport, Grand Bahama, The Bahamas
Tel (242) 352-7071 • Fax (242) 351-2505 • Toll free 1-800-232-2965

Waters Edge

Luxurious waterfront

Individual one- and two-storey family homes

Secure gated community

Protective harbour and docking facilities

Beautifully maintained landscaping

Leases from $2,350-$5,000/month. Sales from $295,000-$545,000. Financing available.

Contact Wendy Johnson, Property Manager, Waters Edge Developments Ltd
Tel (242) 352-7511, fax (242) 352-3748.

Innotec
Industrial/Commercial Park

Office/manufacturing/medical and storage facilities for lease. Units from 25 sq ft-17,000 sq ft; 60,000 sq ft total.

Peel St, Freeport
Tel (242) 352-7511, fax (242) 352-3748.

Grand Bahama Island

Builders Depot
Everything for your construction, renovation and repair needs.

In our 70,000 sq ft showroom
- Best price - Wide selection
- Quality products - Fast delivery

Peel St, Freeport
Tel (242) 352-7511, fax (242) 352-3748.

RE/MAX

FREEPORT NORTHERN BAHAMAS

[Formerly Churchill & Jones Real Estate Limited]
Established 1964

FULL SERVICE BROKERS SPECIALIZING IN

- **Real estate sales** • **Property management**
  • **Appraisals** – accurate, affordable
  and based on our market experience

We welcome referrals and
Retirees • Developers • Investors • Businessmen

Qualify for a Bahamas Certificate of Permanent Residence! How?
- Invest $500,000 minimum in a Freeport home
- With excellent financial and character references

In the tax free Bahamas there is
- No income tax • No capital gains tax
- No corporate tax • No inheritance tax

Freeport /Lucaya has superb
infrastructure and great community facilities
No real property tax

FREEPORT IS ON A ROLL !
New container port • Growing industrial base
Mega yacht repairs • Lucayan Strip 1600 rooms
Come and see for yourself!

Hilary V E Jones – Broker Owner
David P L Hunter – Broker Owner

#1 Queens Highway
PO Box F-42480
Freeport, Grand Bahama, The Bahamas
tel (242) 352-7305 • fax (242) 352-3560

E-mail: remaxfpo@concentric.net
Visit our websites: www.bahamasnet.com/bn/realestate
www.caribpro.com/cj • www.interknowledge.com

BAHAMAS OIL REFINING COMPANY INTERNATIONAL LIMITED (BORCO)

Bahamas Oil Refining Company International Limited operates marine terminal storage facilities at Freeport, Grand Bahama. We provide a wide range of services.

- **STORING/TRANSHIPPING AND BLENDING CRUDE, FUEL OIL AND CLEAN PRODUCTS**
- **ON- & OFFSHORE BUNKERING BY BARGE OR PIPELINE**
- **AGENCY AND OTHER MARINE SERVICES**
- **OIL SPILL RESPONSE**

BAHAMAS OIL REFINING CO INTL LTD (BORCO)
TEL (242) 352-9811

Fax (242) 352-3537 or 352-4029 • Cable: Marbrok
Telex 385-30-021, 385-30-055 or 385-30-006
PO Box F-42435 • Freeport, Grand Bahama, The Bahamas

BORCO AGENCY SERVICES
Tel (242) 352-9744
or 352-9811
Fax (242) 352-3537
Telex 297-30-013

LUCAYA SHIPPING & TRADING CO
(Sub-agency)
Tel (242) 352-3581/2
Fax (242) 352-2246
Telex 30711 CAYTRADE BS

BORCO TOWING CO
Tel (242) 352-8864
or 352-9811
Fax (242) 352-4029
Telex 297-30-006
or 297-30-021

Oceanfront Residential Community With A European Flair

Luxury furnished and unfurnished 2-bedroom suites and 3-bedroom townhouse condominiums with a full range of amenities including private beach with panoramic view of the Atlantic Ocean; pool with clubhouse; tennis court and a 25-slip marina.

BELL CHANNEL
CLUB & MARINA

PO Box F-44053, Jolly Roger Dr, Freeport, Grand Bahama
Tel (242) 373-2673 • Fax (242) 373-3802
Viewing by appointment

Shipping, hotels real estate ...

BY SUZANNE TWISTON-DAVIES

It seems there is growth in nearly every sector of Grand Bahama's economy. Find out what's happening in our review of 1998-99 developments.

"For our investment purposes, there are four countries in the English-speaking world that are well-managed: New Zealand, Hong Kong, Singapore and The Bahamas."

This impressive commendation came from West End Resort's chairman Sash Spencer at the ground-breaking for the Old Bahama Bay Hotel (see *The West End's big comeback, page 476*.)

Nine months earlier, Prime Minister Rt Hon Hubert Ingraham had stated, "I confidently expect the Freeport container terminal, international airport and industrial park will assist in catapulting Freeport and The Bahamas to levels of employment growth and business opportunities unseen at any time since Columbus first landed on our shores."

These are perhaps the two most confident speeches made on Grand Bahama since Freeport took off, gold-rush style, in the mid-1960s. The confidence is justified by growth in nearly every sector of Freeport's economy.

Spearheading this growth was the opening of Freeport Container Port in 1997, one of 17 worldwide ports operated by the Hutchison Port Holdings Group (HPH), which handles about 10 per cent of

Freeport Container Port cargo and Concem Ltd cement silos dominate the seascape at this end of Freeport Harbour.

global container traffic. Phase II is set for completion by the end of 1999, giving the port a total of three berths totalling 3,000 ft, seven super post panamax quay cranes, a fleet of 22 straddle-carriers, and the capacity to handle 950,000 TEUs (20 ft containers) per annum. The port area will be expanded from 56 to 88 acres, and at least 60 more Bahamian workers will be hired along with additional staff employed by support companies. Customers include major shipping lines Maersk and Sealand, Mediterranean Shipping, CMA, Cagema, Navieras/TNX and Tropical Shipping.

At the same time, Freeport Harbour Company is undergoing a $10.6 million cruise development project encompassing two new passenger terminals with centralized check-in facilities, and a 20,000 sq ft landscaped retail village to include a traditional Bahamian straw market and more efficient transportation layout for buses and taxis. Each terminal will have the capacity to handle a medium-sized cruise liner and ferry simultaneously. Together, the two terminals could handle a 3,000-passenger homeported cruise vessel. The project was expected to be fully operational by mid-1999.

One of the most recent companies to move into the Freeport Harbour area was Bradford Grand Bahama Ltd, which continues to increase its business in yacht and boat repair. Bradford's staff now consists of four expatriates and 36 Bahamians, most of whom were sent to the Fort Lauderdale-based parent company, Bradford Marine

Yachts and other boats can now be repaired at Bradford Grand Bahama Ltd's harbour facility.

Inc, for training. The company has a five-year programme that includes dock assembly, boat-houses/yacht homes, and a 500-ton floating dry-dock. Its 150-ton travel-lift can hoist 125 ft aluminum and 100 ft steel boats for dry-docking. At press time, Bradford had already accommodated a 316 ft and 200 ft yacht for wet-docking.

The contractor for the yacht-repairing facility is Quality Services, which also offers a refitting service for cruise ships. Vessels repaired by the company include Premier Cruise Line's 748 ft *Rembrandt*, which was wet-docked from October-December 1997, and the new SeaEscape's 600 ft *Arcadia*.

There are major plans afoot at Freeport International Airport for redevelopment of passenger areas and a complete redesign of operations and structure. The 11,000 ft runway can already handle the world's largest aircraft, and the airport is within easy reach of all major United States and European destinations.

The fact that HPH and the Grand Bahama Development Company (GBDevCo) jointly own both the airport and container port is the result of inspired planning. The 786-acre site between the two facilities, to be known as the Grand Bahama Sea/Air Business Centre (SABC), will provide offices, a variety of warehouses, and factory units tailor-built to the specific requirements of potential users. This will enable factories to have raw materials shipped/flown in, processed and shipped/flown out as finished goods, all within the

Baroness Symons

bonded free trade area. Businesses setting up in the SABC will have direct access to the adjacent container port and airport, and the opportunity to capitalize on The Bahamas' preferential trade agreements – including the Caribbean Basin Initiative (CBI), CARIBCAN and the Lomé Convention. See **Bahamas information.**

These agreements were the subject of intense discussion by members of the British Foreign Office and representatives from most of the former British colonies in the Caribbean when the first annual Carib Forum was held in Nassau in February 1998. The focal point was the Lomé Convention, an agreement about aid from the European Union (EU) to less-developed countries in the African, Caribbean and Pacific States (ACP). As the United Kingdom was temporarily president of the EU at the time, the Caribbean countries wanted the UK to ensure Lomé's successor would have sufficient resources to benefit their economies.

Baroness Symons, Under-Secretary to the British Foreign Minister, visited Freeport after the Forum ended to inspect its new projects. Duly impressed, she promised to give a favourable report about Freeport's potential marketing possibilities to Britain's business sector.

Hotels

The $250 million, world-class resort to be called The Lucayan will come onstream in stages during 1999. Encompassing the Lucayan Beach Hotel and the Grand Bahama Beach Hotel, both being

Freeport Container Port

PHASE II EXPANSION

Phase I Comprises
- 2 Berths/1800 ft. (548m)
- 4 Container Cranes
- 10 Straddle Carriers
- 23 Hectares (56 Acres)
- Capacity 560,000 TEU per annum

Phase II Comprises
- 1 Berth/1200 ft. (366m)
- 3 Container Cranes
- 12 Straddle Carriers
- 32 Acres
- Capacity 390,000 TEU per annum

Combined this gives
- 3 Berths/3,000 ft. (914m)
- 7 Container Cranes
- 22 Straddle Carriers
- 37 Hectares (88 Acres)
- Capacity 950,000 TEU per annum

A member of the
Hutchison Port Holdings Group

extensively renovated and refurbished, as well as a new 800-room hotel replacing the imploded Atlantic Beach Hotel, The Lucayan was expected to put the island's name, Grand, back on course.

Situated on 7.5 acres of prime beach front, The Lucayan when completed will have three totally distinct hotel wings, a centralized Manor House for guest check-in, two 18-hole championship golf courses, 20 restaurants, bars and lounges, a casino and a Village

Completed in stages, The Lucayan will be fully operational at the start of the new millennium.

Market with a 10,000 sq ft retail promenade for shops and dining facilities. All renovations, new facilities and amenities will have been phased in place in time for the new millennium.

Construction manager is Fort Lauderdale's Centex Rooney, which was also responsible for Phase I of Atlantis, Paradise Island resort.

The 16-storey Atlantic Beach Hotel was the tallest hotel to be imploded in the Caribbean. Crowds gathered to watch from a nearby beach, roads and from 100 boats anchored offshore as the Prime Minister detonated the implosion on July 16, 1998.

There has been activity in the smaller hotels too. The former Sun Club, now the Royal Palm Resort, accepted its first guests in October 1998. The 144-room Silver Sands Hotel is under renovation, building of a five-star hotel on Fortune Beach was scheduled to start before the end of 1998, and a contract has been signed by an American developer to buy the Arawak Hotel –

Prime Minister Hubert A Ingraham detonated implosion of the 16-storey Atlantic Beach Hotel to make way for a new hotel, part of The Lucayan resort complex.

excluding the Shannon Golf Course, which used to be part of that property. At press time, a buyer was still being sought for this 18-hole championship course.

Real estate and construction

Builders have not been so busy since the boom of the mid-1960s, and in 1997, 383 construction permits valued at over $50 million were issued.

Emerald Bay condominium is being constructed beside a waterway in Bahamia. The apartments with ocean access range from one bedroom, one bathroom to three bedrooms, $3^1/_2$ baths, priced from $150,000 upwards. Owners are offered membership of Princess Resort and free golf at either of the Princess courses.

> **Builders have not been so busy since the boom of the mid-1960s.**

Construction on the attractive canalside condominium Puerto Alegre has been completed on Midshipman Rd. The development comprises two-bedroom, two-bath and five-bedroom, 4½-bath town houses, all comprising a terrace, balcony, garage and dock.

A Builders Depot has been opened in the Peel St area as part of Innotec, which rents warehouses and manufacturing units to small businesses. The facility is run by entrepreneur David Willard, developer of the Waters Edge residential community.

At Regency Park, Bahama Bay Company is building 170 medium-priced homes. With areas of 1,094 to 1,706 sq ft, two-, three-, four- and five-bedroom houses are under construction in attractive landscaping at prices from $70,000 to $140,000. They should be finished by 2001.

Imperial Life Financial opened its 8,400 sq ft building on East Mall Dr during the summer of 1998 and at press time, expected to increase its staff.

GBDevCo is building a major 264,000 sq ft office park and financial centre on East Mall Dr comprising eight two- and three-storey office buildings.

Commerce and manufacturing

Accountants Price Waterhouse have re-opened a Freeport office, this time in the Regent Centre, in response to the upswing in Freeport's economy. At the same time, the company worldwide has gone into partnership with Coopers & Lybrand, and the partnership is now called PricewaterhouseCoopers.

The Chamber of Commerce's construction of a multi-purpose headquarters near the Rand Memorial Hospital was at press time expected to be completed by the end of 1998.

Builders Depot provides the nuts and bolts of life for Freeporters.

Tanja Enterprises Co Ltd

- General Ship Agents
- Custom Brokers
- Ship Chandlers
- Ship Repairs
- Stevedoring
- Warehousing

2nd Floor Tanja Maritime Center,
Freeport Harbour Area, PO Box F-43259
Freeport, Grand Bahama, Bahamas

Tel (242) 352-2328
Fax (242) 352-2329

E-mail: tanja@batelnet.bs

Bahamian flags fly over the Imperial Life facility on East Mall Dr.

Kelly's (Freeport) Ltd, once a lumber and hardware store but now also selling gifts, kitchen, dining and electrical goods, has completed Phase III of its expansion programme. Phase IV is still to come. "We see tremendous opportunity for growth in Grand Bahama, and we want to be ready for it," said president Basil Kelly.

Polymers International Ltd, Pharmaceuticals Fine Chemicals SA and Uniroyal Chemical Company, Freeport's biggest factories, continue to prosper. Pharmaceuticals Fine Chemicals SA – the world's second largest producer of naproxen – is being acquired by AlliedSignal Inc, a speciality chemicals business. The new purchasers have agreed to retain the existing Freeport staff.

> **We see tremendous opportunity for growth in Grand Bahama, and we want to be ready for it.**

Concem Ltd has commenced exporting to ports in the US following upgrading of its facilities to handle some 360,000 metric tons of cement for export. It also exports to islands such as Haiti, Dominican Republic, Cayman and Bermuda, as well as supplying the Bahama islands with 90 per cent of their cement types one and two, white cement and masonry. Extensive renovations are ongoing to make the terminal a world-class plant.

Bhi-Cam Ltd, the Italian company which supplied the container port cranes, has completed a new plant in the port area for fabrication of heavy steel structures such as oil storage tanks and crane girders.

Bahama Rock is building another crushing/screening plant, as well as implementing a $30 million dollar expansion of its existing shiploading facility adjacent to the harbour.

Agriculture/Aquaculture

Minister of Agriculture Hon Dr Earl Deveaux has forecast that Grand Bahama's population will grow rapidly, and the need for fishermen and farmers will increase. Early in 1998, he toured all relevant outlets and announced the introduction of a Small Business Loan Guarantee Act to encourage fishing and farming activities. He also proposed the forming of a Livestock Association and suggested the need for a livestock processing facility.

"The Bahamas is likely to start negotiations soon to enter the World Trade Organization as the first step towards qualifying for

UNITED SHIPPING COMPANY LIMITED

USCL

"Freeport's oldest shipping agent."

Ships' agents • Customs brokerage • Land transportation • Work boat hire • Transhipment

Freeport Harbour Building, Harbour Dr, Freeport
Tel (242) 352-2752
Fax (242) 352-2754 or 352-4034
Telex 297 30048, Cable UNITESHIP
e-mail: united@batelnet.bs

"Serving the Global Maritime Industry for over 30 years"

Minister of Agriculture Hon Dr Earl Deveaux discusses an observation hive with Permanent Secretary Rodella Tynes and Rev Dr Simeon Hall as GloryBee Apiaries' representative Mary Godet listens.

participation in the Free Trade Area of the Americas. That means we have to meet certain requirements with our trade partners," Dr Deveaux said. He cited Lightbourne's Sea Food in Freeport as having put its staff through extensive training to meet both US and EU import requirements for seafood.

There are already some 30 farms in Grand Bahama, ranging from five acres to several hundred acres, and producing vegetables, citrus fruit, apples, bananas, guavas, eggs, chickens and bees. A few breed sheep, goats, pigs and cattle, and there is room for more farmers. Agro-industries, food-processing and mariculture come within investment areas targeted by the government for overseas investors.

American Bill Parker, of Aquatic Farms, is capitalizing on this area of investment. With six employees, he has entered into various mariculture and aquaculture projects in cooperation with the Department of Fisheries. "The Bahamas has an excellent, knowledgeable Minister who encourages research," he said. Parker, who rents the old Film Studios in Lucaya Estates, also grows various herbs and landscaping plants for sale in Grand Bahama and New Providence.

A marine shrimp farm operated by Lucayan Aquaculture – the first of its kind in the Caribbean – is well under way, growing Pacific white shrimp from post-larvae to market size in above-ground ponds. The farm is on 100 acres near the northeast side of Queen's

Cove. Marketing of the grown shrimp will start in Grand Bahama, eventually being extended throughout the Bahama chain.

Communications

COOL 96, Grand Bahama's only privately-owned radio station, launched the BBC World Service in The Bahamas in January 1998, becoming the first station in The Bahamas to re-broadcast top quality world and Caribbean news.

Obtainable on FM 96.1 and offering a mixed programme of Bahamian and classical music, the arts, sport, and public forums on current affairs, the station was an immediate success when launched in 1995 by the late Cay Gottlieb. It has continued to prosper under the leadership of Gottlieb's widow, Andrea, and 11 employees. Listeners can now hear the World News Update at 7am; Caribbean Sports at 7:05am; the World News Update at 9am; the BBC Caribbean Report at 1pm; and the World Service at 6pm.

The Bahamas Telecommunications Corporation (BaTelCo) is installing 2,400 new telephone lines on the island at a cost of $1.2 million. It is also constructing a multi-million dollar four-storey building on East Mall Dr, to be completed by the end of 1999.

REEF Construction Limited

GENERAL CONTRACTORS
RESIDENTIAL • COMMERCIAL • INDUSTRIAL

COMPLETE PROFESSIONAL STAFF FOR NOTED PROJECTS

- SUPREME & MAGISTRATES' COURTS
- CUSTOM LUXURY HOMES
- CHANCERY HOUSE
- REGENT CENTRES
- PORT LUCAYA MARKETPLACE
- CLUB FORTUNA BEACH HOTEL
- CORAL REEF ESTATES I, II & III
- BAHAMA REEF CONDOMINIUMS
- PORT LUCAYA RESORT & YACHT CLUB
- BATELCO OFFICE COMPLEX

Pineridge Road
PO Box F-40053
Freeport, The Bahamas

Tel (242) 352-6387
Fax (242) 352-8086
e-mail: reef@batelnet.bs

Andrea Gottlieb, shown with Hubert Gibson, operates Cool 96, Grand Bahama's only privately owned radio station.

Tourism

Weddings are such big business in Grand Bahama the Ministry of Tourism has appointed its own clergyman. Favourite wedding venues are the Xanadu Beach Hotel, the lawn of the Princess Country Club, and Parrot Jungle's Garden of the Groves.

> **The Bahamas is the only country in the world where the rare Kirtland's warbler takes refuge from Michigan winters.**

The 12-acre Garden of the Groves is a favourite for visitors even if they aren't getting married. At press time, manager Candy Evans was hoping to import primates and alligators to add to attractions which include a petting zoo with pygmy goats and pot-bellied pigs, breathtaking waterfalls, parrots and ducks. There is a café for light refreshments and a straw market outside the gates.

Grand Bahama's various eco-adventure tours were praised by several leading US publications during 1998, including the *New York Post*, *Miami Herald* and *Boston Globe*. Freeport Power Company and Southern Company are cooperating with the Bahamas National Trust (BNT) in its efforts to maintain places of beauty. Apart from relocating power poles and helping clear nature trails, they have also adopted the Flamingo Pond at the Rand Nature Centre and contributed a substantial sum towards erecting a three-level observation deck beside the pond.

The Bahamas is the only country in the world where the elusive Kirtland's warbler takes refuge from Michigan winters. The Michigan Department of Natural Resources, US Forest Service and US Fish and Wildlife Service have joined forces to help the Bahamas Ornithology Group survey the habitat of the grey/yellow/black bird. Representatives visited Grand Bahama for several days of surveying early in 1998, and were rewarded by three definite, and two possible, sightings.

Erika Moultrie, who runs an eco-adventure kayaking trip up the canal between Gold Rock Creek and the Lucayan National Park, has introduced two new tours. One is a birdwatch of species seen nowhere else in the world through different parks and botanical gardens, and the other is a biking nature tour 10 miles along the island's south shore, culminating in a visit to Lucayan Caverns and a swim on a beautiful secluded beach.

BRADFORD GRAND BAHAMA

IN-HOUSE SERVICES:
150 Ton Travel Lift • Prop Shop • Machine Shop • Hydraulic Shop
Fiberglass Shop • Paint Shop • Carpentry Shop • Weld/Fab Shop

Queens Hwy, Freeport Harbour • PO Box F-44867 • Freeport, Grand Bahama • Bahamas
Tel (242) 352-7711 • Fax (242) 352-7695

Restaurants

The Back Home Native Hut on Sergeant Major Dr has reopened under new ownership after $200,000 worth of renovations. Owner "Candy" Rahming was trained not only at Nassau's prestigious Lyford Cay Club, but also on what was once the world's largest cruise ship, the *SS Norway*.

Port Lucaya now has the island's first Irish restaurant, Shenanigan's, selling Irish beer and food from stew to bangers and mash.

McDonald's gave up its franchise and closed down in 1997. It has now been reopened as The Native Eye by restaurateur and Royal Palm Resort owner Mario Donato.

Schools

In January 1998 Pioneer's Loop Secondary School was renamed Jack Hayward High School and opened in the presence of the Prime Minister and various government ministers. The school – comprising four special technical and vocational buildings – was renamed after one of the co-chairmen of the GBPA, which had donated 20 acres of prime land for exclusive use by the school and

Pioneer's Loop Secondary School was renamed Jack Hayward High School, honouring longtime Freeport pioneer, promoter and benefactor Sir Jack Hayward.

contributed $7 million towards construction of Freeport's two newest high schools. The Prime Minister, in thanking Sir Jack for being a great benefactor to Freeport, called him "a decent, plain-speaking honourable man."

On the following day, Goombayland Secondary School became St Georges' High School, named after another GBPA co-chairman,

Goombayland Secondary School was renamed St Georges' High School in recognition of educational contributions made by Edward St George and his wife, Lady Henrietta.

Edward St George, and his wife Lady Henrietta, who have made significant contributions toward education in Grand Bahama – including $250,000 towards building Beacon School (formerly the Catherine Basie School for Exceptional Children).

A primary school and high school were scheduled for 1999 openings.

Sports

The location of the state-of-the-art sports complex being developed by the Grand Bahama Sports Council has been moved from the 88-acre tract near the YMCA to land north of the junction of Settler's Way and Coral Rd. The complex will house baseball and softball stadiums; tennis, volleyball and badminton courts; cricket and soccer pitches; a running track; and a basketball gymnasium. The cost of construction will be covered by the GBPA, Freeport City Council and Grand Bahama Sports Council.

The long-closed 18-hole, 152-acre Bahama Reef Golf Course is being re-designed by Robert Trent Jones Jr for Harbour Plaza Hotels and Resorts. Part of The Lucayan resort complex, this world-class, $5 million project was scheduled for opening in 1999.

GOLF: Veteran golf pro Gary Slatter has been appointed head of all golf operations at The Lucayan, which includes the Lucayan Country Club. Slatter's last appointment was as director of golf at Sun International's Atlantis, Paradise Island.

In January 1998, 200 golfers from The Bahamas, US and Canada competed for over $100,000 worth of prizes in the Annual Princess Crystal Pro Am Tournament at the Ruby and Emerald Golf Courses. The Bahamas' team came third.

Devin Mullings

Efforts are progressing to make cricket a school sport.

TENNIS: Seven Grand Bahama juniors played in recent tournaments at Delray Beach in Florida and Freeport. Devin Mullings, rated the Caribbean's top male player by the International Tennis Federation, won five out of six Under 12 tournaments in Florida, the only Bahamian to achieve this feat. He also won the BORCO, FINCO and ESSO Under 12 tournaments in Freeport.

BAHAMAS GAMES: Grand Bahama won the July 1998 Games, edging out New Providence after two recounts of points.

CRICKET: Lucaya Cricket Club held its 14th Annual International Festival in March 1998, attracting teams from Barbados, Jamaica and Miami. Some Bahamians feel cricket should return to being the national sport. It is being taught in some Nassau schools and efforts are being made to introduce it to Freeport schools. Constitutionally, it is the only sport in which players are allowed time off to play.

BONEFISHING: Bahamian bonefishing is increasingly popular. A prominent fishing magazine names five bonefishing spots in The Bahamas as being in "the top ten anywhere" – two of which are in the waters of Grand Bahama.

VOLLEYBALL: Fifty teams from the US competed in the three-day professional Beach Volleyball tournament on Lucaya Beach in April 1998.

RUGBY: The Freeport Rugby Club started the season badly by losing the prestigious Bahamas Cup for the first time in a decade to

Nassau in November 1997. At Easter 1998, the 18th Annual International Festival attracted players from the US (including Harvard and the President's XV), Hong Kong and Europe.

General

Bahamian Albert Miller, co-chairman and president of the GBPA (see *They spotted a winner in Miller, page 508*), has set the record straight about the benefits of international investment in Freeport. Responding to claims that the average Bahamian would not benefit, he told Freeport Rotary Club, "These investors pay immigration fees, tips, hotel and restaurant bills, apartment rentals, purchases at local stores and other spendings that benefit the average Bahamian directly." He pointed out that larger companies were training Bahamians for permanent and key positions. Southern Company had contributed $180,000 to the GBPA Scholarship Programme since 1995, an addition to the $250,000 contributed annually by the GBPA. "And our new partners, Freeport Harbour Company and Freeport Container Port, have indicated they will now join the programme as well," he added.

"Ladies and gentlemen," he ended, "the future is bright!"

General Contractors

ISLAND CONSTRUCTION CO LTD
and FREEPORT AGGREGATE LTD

Supply and delivery of rock and sand throughout The Bahamas

- **Ready Mix concrete**
- **Concrete blocks**
- **Sand & rock for home & commercial use**
- **Equipment rental**
- **Marine piling**
- **Sea wall installation**

- Engineering consultants
- Excavation
- Land clearing
- Road building
- Heavy equipment
- Drilling & blasting
- Water wells

Give us a call for more information
MIKE HAMILTON
TEL **(242) 352-7435**
OR (242) 352-6363
FAX **(242) 352-7437**
e-mail: lslcons@batelnet.bs
PO BOX F-40035, FREEPORT, GRAND BAHAMA

Aerial view shows Jack Tar Hotel and Marina with middle distance buildings from the Butlin era.

Sir Billy Butlin

The West End's big comeback

BY SUZANNE TWISTON-DAVIES

After 800 years of ups and downs, the westernmost settlement of Grand Bahama hopes the good times are here to stay.

It was a significant day for the sometimes thriving, often impoverished settlement of West End, Grand Bahama. For on February 27, 1998, ground was broken on a $20 million resort and residential development that has restored hope, confidence and the promise of prosperity to an area noted for containing one of the most important archaeological sites in the entire Lucayan archipelago.

Over the past 800-or-so years, West End has witnessed the entry and exit of Lucayan Indians; the possible landing of explorer Juan Ponce de León; Spanish invasions for slave labour; and the get-rich-quick industries of gun-running, ship-wrecking, sponging and bootlegging – all disappearing as quickly as they came.

Sir Billy Butlin made West End the site of Butlin's Vacation Village in 1948, but it failed and closed just two years later. In 1959, Charles Sammons of the Jack Tar Hotel chain acquired the site and built a swimming pool, marina, gardens, golf course and airport. According to West Ender and former Jack Tar employee Vincent Russell, "It had a good run for more than 30 years. But then tourism temporarily took a knock and the unions made unreasonable demands. Even though the pay, pensions and bonuses had been very

William T Criswell   Sash Spencer

good, they just got greedy. Sammons had died, and his heirs weren't prepared to do battle. When it closed in 1990, there was devastation. Hundreds of people were out of work."

The phoenix rises ...
Now, on this February day in 1998, West End Resort Ltd announced the birth of a new era arising from the 2,218-acre ruins of the Jack Tar Village. Company president and CEO Bill Criswell outlined a two-phased 10-year plan for a five-star tourism and residential complex, Old Bahama Bay. The first phase on 150 acres comprises a 47-room, cottage-style resort, 92 residential lots bordering the canal, a completely new state-of-the-art marina with 150 slips for yachts up to 175 ft, waterfront promenades, freshwater swimming pool, fitness facilities, shower and laundry

> **Developers hope West End's location as the nearest port of call from Palm Beach will make it a top US vacation destination.**

FREEPORT TRANSFER LIMITED
COMPLETE CUSTOMS BROKERAGE AND TRUCKING SERVICES

- Storage and warehousing
- Transshipment
- Import and export services
- Air freight agents
- Household goods removals and shipping
- Consolidated containerized freight service: West Palm Beach/Freeport & UK/Freeport
- Forklift rentals

AGENTS FOR ALL MAJOR VAN LINES AND CARRIERS WORLDWIDE

FOREST AVE & PEACH TREE ST • PO BOX F-42520, FREEPORT, GB
TEL (242) 352-7821 • FAX (242) 352-5263
CABLE: FREETRAN

EASTERN FREIGHT FORWARDERS

- COMPLETE SHIPPING
- BONDED TRUCKING
- CONSOLIDATION
- WAREHOUSING
- RAIL SERVICE
- CRATING
- NVOCC TO THE BAHAMAS
- LICENCED CUSTOMS BROKERS

LICENCED BY
IATA
ICC and FMC

We are computerized, facsimilized and personalized

100 WEST MIDDLE RD, RIVIERA BEACH, FL 33404
WEST PALM BEACH • TEL (561) 848-3738 • FAX (561) 848-3772
MIAMI • TEL (305) 949-8331

facilities, tennis and volleyball court, and a convenience store. A 13 ft deep entrance channel to the marina will have lighted markers and range lights – giving boaters the opportunity to navigate at night.

"Careful architectural guidelines are to be followed," Criswell said. "And the community will encompass the people of West End, with a minimum of 200 jobs being provided on construction alone."

Phase two, part of the company's second option on an additional 2,000 acres, may see construction of a five-star, 500-room hotel on the beach, an oceanfront golf course and additional marina facilities.

Along with investors – Sammons Corporation, previous owners of the Jack Tar; Graham Groves, son of Freeport founder Wallace Groves; and the Bahamian company Cavalier Construction – the developers hope West End's convenient location as the nearest port of call from Palm Beach will make it a top US vacation destination, as well as attracting some of the 80 million American baby boomers for second home ownership. Other lures are excellent big-game fishing on the edge of the Gulf Stream and bottom and flats fishing on Little Bahama Bank.

Juan Ponce de León may have visited Grand Bahama.

FREEPORT OIL COMPANY
LIMITED

Look to Focol for the *BEST* in fuels and lubricants, for all automotive, marine and commercial use.

The leading marketer of motor gasoline, diesel and the finest quality lubricants in Freeport and all of Grand Bahama.

Queen's Hwy, Harbour Area, Freeport, Grand Bahama,
The Bahamas, PO Box F-42458
Tel (242) 352-8131
or (242) 352-4379
Fax (242) 352-2986
Cable: FOCOL

THE FINEST QUALITY LUBRICANTS

―――― Available Exclusively at: ――――
Hawksbill Service Station • Tel (242) 352-2045
Allied Service Station • Tel (242) 352-5010
East Mall Service Station • Tel (242) 352-5301
Airport Service Station • Tel (242) 351-3104
Queen's Hwy Service Station • Tel (242) 351-6799

It had long been known the Lucayans were The Bahamas' first inhabitants, but it wasn't until 1973 that anyone believed they had reached Grand Bahama.

Prosperity and stagnation

The history of West End is punctuated by periods of prosperity followed by periods of stagnation. This continuous rise-and-fall cycle started with West End's first inhabitants, the Lucayans, who settled there after migrating from the Andes, only to be forcibly removed by Spaniards seeking slave labour for the gold mines of Hispaniola.

It had long been known the Lucayans were The Bahamas' first inhabitants, but it wasn't until 1973 that anyone believed they had reached Grand Bahama. This was despite the legend that Ponce de León had stumbled across an old Indian woman – possibly the last living Lucayan in The Bahamas – in 1513 while seeking the Fountain of Youth. He claimed to have seen her on a small island off

Walking along this beach, Mr and Mrs Heinz Fischbacher found an artefact that led to discovery of one of the most important sites in the Lucayan archipelago.

the Little Bahama Bank, near West End, which he subsequently named La Vieja (old woman).

In 1973, diver Dr Warren Duncan was exploring the newly-discovered underwater Lucayan Caverns in what is now Lucayan National Park, when he spotted a human shin bone in six ft of water. Further exploration unearthed a skull 12 ft down which the Smithsonian Institution confirmed was Lucayan because of its flat shape. It is known the Lucayans bound their children's heads to a board, but the reason is not clear. Some think it was a beautification process; others think the ritual was meant to toughen youngsters' heads against club blows from cannibalistic Caribs. Later, eight more skeletons were discovered in a ritual burial mound.

The area of the caverns provided a source of fresh water on arable land near the sea, enabling the Lucayans to net turtles, spear or hook fish, catch iguanas and hutia (small rodents), snare pigeons and parrots, and grow maize for making beer, cassava for bread, sweet potatoes, yams and cotton.

It was the Lucayans who invented the hammock, or *hamaca*, and the idea spread to Europe, where sailors adapted them for sleeping on ships. Before wiping the Indians out, the Spaniards adopted some

Concem Ltd

SPECIALIZING IN
- BAG PRODUCTS
- BULK PRODUCTS
- ALL MASONRY CEMENT NEEDS

EXPORT & IMPORT CEMENT FROM GRAND BAHAMA

Tel (242) 352-7606, Fax (242) 351-4221
#1 Fishing Hole Road, PO Box F-42572
Freeport, Grand Bahama, Bahamas

Bahama Cement

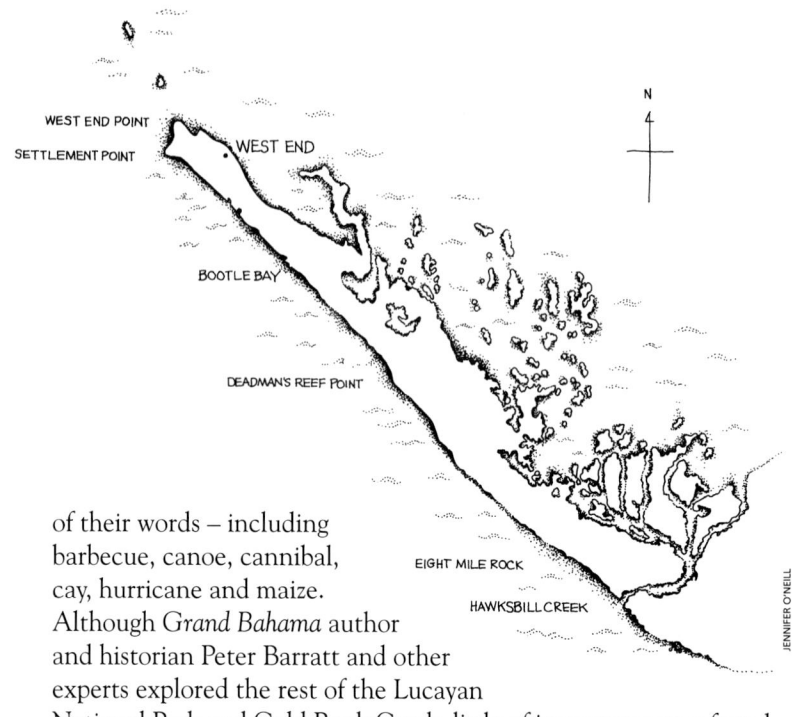

of their words – including barbecue, canoe, cannibal, cay, hurricane and maize. Although *Grand Bahama* author and historian Peter Barratt and other experts explored the rest of the Lucayan National Park and Gold Rock Creek, little of importance was found.

That was, until 1997 when Heinz Fischbacher, Swiss owner of *The Buccaneer* restaurant built by bootlegger Paul Mack, discovered an artefact while walking along the beach with his wife. They notified the Bahamas National Trust (BNT), and within weeks a world-class excavation was under way at the site described by historian Dr Julian Granberry as "one of the most important in the Lucayan archipelago."

Two residents helping out on the dig are Erika Moultrie and Jim Bryce. Moultrie explained, "We divide ourselves into diggers and sifters. Some prefer probing around, while others sieve layers of sediment to find small things such as fish bones, hutia teeth, ceramic pieces, shells which had been honed to a sharp point for digging, carving pottery or spearing fish, and often sizeable shards of red Abaco ware.

"Every 10cm layer is put in plastic bags. We have to be vigilant about washing our hands as germs can linger for centuries. Some pieces of pottery were found around a hearth, as though someone had the intention of returning to eat from them. We wondered what had caused the Lucayans to leave – a hurricane, or an inter-island rumour of invading Spaniards." (See *New views on the Bahamian past*, page 112.)

Pirates, fishermen and tourists

After the Indians were wiped out, West End was uninhabited for centuries, although reef fishermen would call there because of its shallow waters and sources of fresh water.

One of the first European travellers wrote:

> *The Hawksbill turtle is often catcht which has the fine shell so much us'd in England.*

The now protected turtles were probably netted by crews of visiting ships. There is also mention historically of pirates using Grand Bahama as a base, with West End being a strategic position for the pillaging of galleons sailing down the Florida Channel.

The district of West End (as opposed to the settlement) begins at Hawksbill Creek, where there is now a causeway joining it to the rest of Grand Bahama. In 1836 just 370 people lived there, but by the outbreak of the American Civil War in 1861 they numbered nearly 1,500.

During this period, West Enders were heavily involved in gun-running for the Confederate South. Union ships policed the Florida Channel between the mainland and Grand Bahama in an effort to stop guns and food being smuggled via Florida. The Confederates were so short of supplies that anyone with a shallow-draft ship could make up to $300,000 for one delivery. West End's easy access, and

One-third of the Bahamian labour force earned a living from sponging until a blight destroyed sponge beds in 1938.

the fact that it had fresh water, made it a strategic base for stocking up and dodging the blockade.

Wrecking, or "wrack'n," as they say in The Bahamas, provided another good source of income in the 19th century. Many a ship foundered off the coast of West End because of its shallow waters, including the Spanish treasure ship *Nuestra Señora de las Maravillas*, which sank off the Little Bahama Bank in January 1656.

The pickings were good

The purposeful sinking of ships was a profitable way of life for Bahamians, who were widely notorious for it. Maritime law dictated the first people to throw a line to a sinking ship were entitled to salvage rights for that vessel. So locals would put out false beacons to lure boats to the reefs.

The extent of wrecking was such that the government granted wrecking licences and demanded one-tenth of the dividends. According to Barratt, two-fifths of all Bahamian imports in the mid-nineteenth century consisted of goods salvaged from wrecks.

In 1858, there were 302 licensed wreckers in The Bahamas employing 2,679 men as crew. After the hurricane of 1866, 29 of 63 wrecks were declared "mysterious." This finally convinced the

---

CATES & CO.
CHARTERED ACCOUNTANTS

OFFERING A COMPLETE RANGE OF ADVISORY AND ACCOUNTING SERVICES FOR OFFSHORE OPERATIONS AND STRUCTURES:

Accounting, auditing, management and consulting services.

Incorporation and administration of business, investment and shipping companies in The Bahamas and other jurisdictions

Provision of directors, officers and registered offices

Full range of corporate, secretarial, invoicing and portfolio administration.

Suite C, Regent Centre, Explorers Way
PO Box F-42643, Freeport, The Bahamas
Tel 242-351-4025 • Fax 242-351-4050

Imperial Lighthouse Service to erect legitimate beacons and lighthouses throughout the Bahama chain, and the Admiralty produced more accurate charts. Thus, another disreputable *modus vivendi* came to an end.

Fortunately, a more honest way of living had presented itself during the 1840s in the form of the lowly sea sponge, found in huge amounts on the Little Bahama Bank. Demand was high in Europe and the US, and the trained eyes of Bahamian fishermen were soon scanning the multi-coloured waters of shallow sea beds. It was cheap and easy to do, although each sponging trip lasted five to eight weeks. The crew plied from the schooner to sponge beds in small boats, and the harvest was put in a salt-water pen to soak for several weeks before being tapped clean with a wooden bat. The schooner then carried its load to the Sponge Exchange in Nassau.

One-third of the Bahamian labour force earned a living from sponging, and many West Enders remember the last days of the period well. As was the fate of West End, a blight killed off all The Bahamas' sponge beds in 1938, effectively ending a lucrative career. Although the sponges have now grown back, demand considerably decreased in the interim.

Get rich quick

In the meantime, an alternate form of employment had been found as a result of the 1919 Prohibition – the get-rich-quick profession of bootlegging. As kegs went dry in the US, they overflowed along the

Patrol boats like the *MV Perry* plied Gulf Stream waters from 1928-32 for bootleg liquor.

Capt Steve Hollingsworth

main street of West End. Again, its strategic location near the coast of Florida and numerous coves and inlets virtually unnavigable by US Coast Guards made it a popular bootlegging base.

Vessels of all shapes and sizes were commandeered to carry liquor cases by the thousand to larger boats at sea. Some towed cigar-shaped steel tubes of some 400 cases that could be severed should one of the 390 Coast Guard patrol boats appear. They would then be recovered once the coast was clear.

> **As kegs went dry in the US, they overflowed along the main street of West End.**

Capt Steve Hollingsworth, now master of the vessel *Island Bay*, was born and raised in West End. "I was about 16 when I started hanging about with the bootleggers. And I did some work for the Ashley gang. At that age, it didn't occur to me that I was working for murderers." It turned out the American gang had been on the run from US police for a considerable amount of crimes. Hollingsworth continued, "I had the best time, and became West End's first black man to fly an airplane. I was training to do maintenance on post-war biplanes, and learned to fly at the same

Port Lucaya Resort & Yacht Club

Experience a secluded oasis, set in the midst of a multi-million dollar marina. Featuring luxurious over-sized rooms and suites with enchanting views. Delectable taste sensations are offered in the Tradewinds Cafe or poolside, and within walking distance are hot casino action, pristine beaches, and the fabulous Port Lucaya Market Place with over 80 shops, restaurants and entertainment. A wide variety of watersports including diving, sport fishing and the Dolphin Experience are also available across the marina.

Call now for reservations and additional information.
Tel: 1-800-Lucaya-1 or 242-373-6618 ▪ Fax: 242-373-6652
Port Lucaya Resort & Yacht Club
Bell Channel Bay Road ▪ P.O. Box F-42452 ▪ Freeport, The Bahamas

Come to the Port Lucaya Resort & Yacht Club, where land and water meet, and vitality is a way of life.

Keep in touch while on the go ...
WITH A BATELCO CELLULAR

Now more than ever keeping in touch, while on the go is easy with a Batelco cellular telephone. Roaming features allow you to make and receive calls throughout 10 of the major islands of The Bahamas.

Batelco cellular locations:
Abaco • Andros • Berry Islands
Bimini • Cat Island • Long Island
Eleuthera • Exuma
Grand Bahama • New Providence

"Keeping you in touch while on the go."
**For further information call:
Grand Bahama (242) 352-4028
Nassau (242) 394-2355**

Get The Message
NASSAU • FREEPORT • ABACO • ELEUTHERA

BATELpage

EVERYONE NEEDS A PAGER!

A BatelPage Flex Pager can add real flexibility to your life. You can live life to the fullest and know you are still in touch.

For BatelPage support and information please contact:
Grand Bahama (242) 352-PAGE
New Providence (242) 394-7243
Marsh Harbour, Abaco (242) 367-3701
Governor's Harbour, Eleuthera (242) 332-2712

PRINCESS ISLE

THE ESTATES OF PRINCESS ISLE

Just 53 estate-sized home sites on a spectacular 60-acre peninsula with unparalleled water views.

Access to this prestigious enclave is via a manned entry gatehouse.

Each beachfront estate is approximately an acre with 150' water frontage. The canal sites offer superb boat dockage.

The estates of Princess Isle are, quite simply, a unique residential community.

Estate sites from $390,000-$2,700,000.
Homes from $1.5 million.

PRINCESS REALTY LTD
PO Box F-40684
Freeport, Grand Bahama
Tel (242) 352-7411 • Fax (242) 352-7966
Broker participation is invited.

Ralph "Bottles" Capone, Al's brother.

time. You had to do some pretty smart flying to get the liquor in and out from West End's tiny air-strip."

The grass strip was located in the area now encompassing Old Bahama Bay. "Sometimes the pilots landed at Bootle Bay as well," Hollingsworth added. "You came in and bounced down behind the mangroves. Pity if you missed, specially with several cases of Scotch on board! Once I was flying with a drunken pilot. He estimated the distance too low and hit some high tension wires. The plane shuddered like crazy and smashed straight into the ground. The ambulance came and somehow we survived. My mother was all chewed up about it. She offered to buy me a store or restaurant, anything to get me on the straight and narrow. She had become rich by opening *Bootlegging Quarters*, as she called it, to cater for all the people coming in to smuggle or make money in some way.

"Al Capone's brother, Ralph, brought the gang over to look for his speedboat that'd been stolen. I met him shooting pool. People said Al came too, but I never did see him. When I went over to Miami with John Ashley, we took 58 cases of liquor. Boy! Those men were dangerous! Your life was like a shadow. Once I spent two weeks in Georgia with them hiding from police. You heard shots all day and night. 'If you're wise, you'll keep your mouth shut.' That's what Ashley told me. So I did.

"All that booze was comin' out from Canada and Europe, because there wasn't nothing illegal about it until you got to the States. Ricardo DeGregory was a partner in the Kenneth F Butler Company. He ran the Grand Bahama operation and was said to have brought in a million cases of Scotch over the years. People like Gussy Hepburn put up big warehouses all along Bay Shore. The Ashleys were there to steal from the bootleggers – either their money or their liquor, which they would then smuggle to the States themselves. Well, first time in 1925, the gang came over about midday and looked around West End, then they struck Gussy's place about 10pm and tied him up. They took about $8,000 from him and two other warehouses, I think Mr Claridge, and Jody Smith; then they got to DeGregory, and he said they' too late, he already close' down. They missed getting much cash, for $250,000 had been sent on the express mail-boat to Nassau that morning."

The other mail-boat to Nassau got in trouble with the Commissioner for making "slow and irregular" deliveries. The vessel had also been commandeered for the cause, transporting liquor by the case-load to West End.

All the liquor warehouses were destroyed in the great hurricane of 1947. The Seaman's Club which was used to store liquor still stands; an Esso station replaced the Butler warehouse; and the Church of God of Prophecy now sits on the site of one of the biggest warehouses of the era that was owned – ironically enough – by a man named Gusty Heaven.

Back to sleep

The end of Prohibition in 1933 sent West End back to sleep, most of the new millionaires dispersing. Residents went back to fishing and a little farming. The lifestyle was languid, as poet Susan Wallace (née Bethel) noted in *The Place Where I Was Born*, in her book *Bahamian Scene*:

> *Few were the people there,*
> *Lengthy their leisure time,*
> *Lazing on the beaches of the place where I was born.*
> *No dance or movie show,*
> *Nowhere at all to go,*
> *Nothing but to sit and sigh in the land where I was born.*

Poet Susan Wallace

Wallace, who now lives in Freeport, went to West End's one school along with Vincent Russell, who recalled, "Money was short; but then World War II started and the Swedish gentleman who'd bought Paradise Island, Axel Wenner-Gren, built a fish-canning factory, then called Grand Bahama Packing Company. It stood on Bay Shore Rd, then a hard sand path which someone occasionally weeded. Because there was no real road, when there was a funeral, coffins had to be put in a dinghy and pulled along in the water. The mourners walked alongside on the path.

"The factory had generators, for there was no power in West End until 1960. About 200 people were employed there." In those days, two fishermen could catch up to 900 crawfish tails a day, although it was "poor man's food," fetching only $2^1/2$¢ per lb. A high point for the factory workers was when the Duke of Windsor paid a visit in his capacity as Bahamas Governor.

But the factory closed with the end of the war in 1945, and West Enders found themselves out of work once again. The reprieve – although short-lived – came just three years later with the building of Butlin's Vacation Village. Hollingsworth, who was employed at the fish factory and then at Butlin's, recalled, "I was dismayed when the hotel failed in just two years. The problem was it was ahead of its time – it came 20 years too soon."

That brings us back to the Jack Tar and Old Bahama Bay. West Enders feel the future has never looked brighter, and hopes are high that maybe now their star is on a permanent rise.

> **Because there was no real road, coffins had to be put in a dinghy and pulled along in the water. The mourners walked alongside on the path.**

Eileen and Walter Rose surrounded by their children, clockwise, Phyllis, Roland, Anne, David on his mother's lap, Ben, Peter with hand on chin, Colin and Robert kneeling.

A big bunch of Roses

BY SUZANNE TWISTON-DAVIES

The prolific English family that made its mark on Freeport.

Walter Rose's death on April 18, 1997, two days before his 89th birthday, ended a remarkable journey that took him from Britain to Italy and back again before venturing across the Atlantic to Nassau and finally Freeport.

It also ended 65 years of marriage to a woman who bore him nine children – in order of birth, Anne, Winifred, Roland, Phyllis, Ben, Colin, Peter, Robert and the last, David, born in 1953. The various achievements of this big bunch of Roses include winning world fishing titles, major golf trophies and a coveted national photography award, paving the way for an important speleological discovery and changing the face of Freeport forever by planting thousands of trees.

Walter started his career as a gardener's boy on the Birmingham estate of Dame Elizabeth Cadbury, who recognized his talent and enrolled him at an agricultural college. He went on to train at the famous Kew Gardens where he specialized in tropical gardening.

In 1932 Walter received further training in Italy, and at the end of his studies married Eileen Winter. They had met in Chiswick High St, London, when her shoe caught in a tram rail. Walter politely suggested she remove her foot from the shoe, and went on his way. They soon met again on the same street, and this time they went on their way together.

Eileen's father was a major in the Royal Flying Corps. Her mother died soon after her birth, and in 1917 she acquired a kindly French stepmother and was raised in France. When she first met Walter, Eileen was bilingual and working for a French financial newspaper on London's Fleet St.

After Anne was born, Walter took a job in 1934 as head of four gardeners in Italy at the home of millionaire Col Claude Beddington. The second and third Rose children arrived, but then so did World War II, and the Roses were transferred to the Colonel's main residence in Kent.

The patriotic Beddington and his large private yacht were commissioned by the Admiralty. In 1940 he was killed on deck in an attack by two German fighter planes during pullback operations off the beaches of Dunkirk. The Army requisitioned Beddington's mansion and dug holes for gun emplacements on Walter's manicured lawns. "He was incensed both by this and by the German planes which 'hedge-hopped' over us *en route* from fighting in the Battle of Britain. The ultimate insult was when baby Phyllis' nappies were machine-gunned on the clothesline. Walter would take pot-shots at the planes with his sporting gun," recalls Eileen.

Beddington's death put Walter out of work, but eventually the family secured seasonal work picking in the Kent hop-fields, pausing only to fling themselves under vines as Nazi aircraft used them for target practice. Unaware of the danger, Anne was only concerned about the prickly hop-vines. At a time when it seemed things couldn't get worse, Winifred died of diphtheria.

Shell-shocked

Walter tried to enlist, but was told the British military had designated him for a secret wartime job because of his fluency in Italian. While waiting for the job to come up, the Roses moved to Walter's parents' tiny home in Birmingham, and he temporarily joined the Auxiliary Fire Service. While he was away on night duty, a bomb fell in the garden and part of the house toppled on top of Anne, Roland and baby Phyllis. Eileen and her mother-in-law rushed to dig the children out from under the rubble. The girls were screaming. They were brought out unhurt, but Roland was temporarily shell-shocked.

WAUGH CONSTRUCTION (BAHAMAS) LTD

Proud builders of the Treasure Cay Airport

Helping to build a better Bahamas from Walker's Cay in the North West to Mayaguana in the South East.

- Engineering Consultants
- Subdivision Infrastructure
- Road & Airport Construction
- Hot Mixed Asphalt Paving
- Well Drilling & Drainage Wells
- Water & Sewer Pipe Line Construction
- All Underground Utilities
- Member AWWA

For more information contact:
Harold "Sonny" Waugh–*President*
Brian Waugh–*Vice President*
Godfrey Waugh–*Vice President*

Tel (242) 352-9378
Fax (242) 352-2902
Shelley Street, PO Box F-40003
Freeport, Grand Bahama

Walter tried to enlist, but was told the British military had designated him for a secret wartime job.

The family was re-housed locally, and Roland almost succeeded where the Germans had failed by running in front of a double-decker bus. He was saved but his foot was later run over by another bus. Fortunately he was wearing sturdy clogs.

When Ben was born in 1941, he caught pneumonia and started life in an oxygen tent. By then, Eileen had put the smaller children in a day-nursery and was working in a factory testing bombs. Ben created his own excitement by climbing up to a high shelf and swigging battery acid from a bottle. Having his oesophagus stretched every six months because of the burns probably kept him grounded for a while, but he did at least teach Phyllis to talk.

No one had realized she was deaf due to the bomb blast which had

Mrs I Walton Killam dines with Jean Raymond.

buried her, and it was only when she heard Ben talk at her ear level that she understood what speech was all about. Eventually she was fitted with a new ear drum.

In 1943, the authorities produced Walter's long-awaited job. He was put in charge of Italian prisoners-of-war who were working the land in Warwickshire. The Roses soon had a house in Southam and a car. Walter grew vegetables and kept a goat for milk, plus hens and ducks to supplement food rations. A sixth child, Colin, was born in 1944. Peter followed in 1946.

Fate or just plain luck
When the POWs were repatriated in 1947 after the war ended, Walter found himself jobless again.

Call it fate or just plain luck, the Roses' lives were to take a 180-degree turn when Walter was thumbing through a copy of *The Gardener's Chronicle* and spotted a help-wanted advertisement. Mr and Mrs I Walton Killam were looking for a gardener to work in The Bahamas.

> **Call it fate or just plain luck, the Roses' lives were to take a 180-degree turn.**

Killam, a Canadian millionaire in partnership with Lord Beaverbrook, owned a beautiful 18th century great house in Nassau called *Graycliff* – now the Caribbean's only five-star restaurant – built by retired buccaneer Capt John Graysmith. Killam also owned a luxurious home on Hog Island, the future Paradise Island, known as *Grayleath* and now part of Club Med. Walter was interviewed in London and hired as *Grayleath's* head gardener.

The family sailed to New York on the *Queen Elizabeth* and encountered the tail end of a hurricane two days out of Southampton. Everyone was sick except Peter. Roland never left his bunk for the entire voyage. Then he was train-sick on the journey from New York to Miami, airsick on the Pan American flight to Nassau, and seasick on the boat-ride to Hog Island.

Once the Roses settled in, they realized the generous salary which had lured them from Britain did not go far in Nassau, and it was hard to make ends meet. Eileen stocked up each week with fruit and vegetables from J P Sands, and the boys, soon expert fishermen, supplied fish that the family would steam, fry, souse, curry or boil.

Wallace Groves, shown walking with his wife, Georgette, engaged Walter Rose to beautify Freeport.

Once the Roses settled in, they realized the generous salary which had lured them from Britain did not go far in Nassau. Because there was no bridge from Nassau to Hog Island at that time, the children would ride in a boat to Rawson Sq and walk to Queen's College (QC), which was then on Charlotte St. Anne became head girl, Roland head boy.

Ben would "absent-mindedly" read his book and fall off the dock so he wouldn't have to go to school, but his parents soon got wise to it. The eighth child, Robert, was born in 1950, and David in 1953.

Upside down again

Killam's death two years later turned the Roses' life upside down again. No longer needed at *Grayleath*, Walter was once more out of work. But his gardening skills had caught the attention of Sir Stafford Sands, otherwise known as the father of Bahamas tourism, who put Walter in touch with American financier Wallace Groves. Along with Charles Hayward (later knighted) of Great Britain's Firth-Cleveland Group and other visionaries, Groves was breaking ground for a Bahamas "dream city" of industry, leisurely living and elegant resorts. One of the start-up problems, however, was Freeport's flat and dull terrain.

Eileen recalls, "Planes could only land at West End; it was bush everywhere, and you took a plank with you in case your car got stuck in the sand. There was no power, telephone, roads or canals."

Walter was asked to embark on a beautification programme to enhance the subtropical ambience. This led to his building the original shade house at Lucayan Nursery and importing 10,000 golden coconut trees from St Lucia.

Colin, Peter, Bobby and David went to Freeport's little All-Age School. "There was no insulation and we had to be let out if it got

Investing in a strange country can be confusing unless you seek the services of an experienced professional. For over 30 years Harry Dann & Co has negotiated the sale and purchase of large properties in the millions to smaller transactions in the thousands. We offer private and corporate investors information and advice on real estate, certificates of permanent residency and business opportunities in the Freeport area. Additionally, we are now part of the world's largest real estate franchise, Century 21.

Century 21
Harry Dann & Co Ltd
est 1964

Real Estate Brokers & Developers
Suites 21-22, The International Bldg • PO Box F-42431, Freeport, Bahamas
Tel (242) 352-7492 (days, eves & w/ends) • Fax (242) 352-7493
e-mail: century21@harrydann.com • http://www.century21harrydann.com. Licenced in Florida.

The Roses in later years.

too hot. If the rain beat on the roof, we couldn't hear the teacher," Peter remembers.

In 1961, Walter went to look after the gardens at the Colonial Research Institute (now the Immuno Research Centre) for James Rand. Later, the couple became managers of Harbour House Towers, "but with seven directors who couldn't agree we moved on to manage the Palm Club, where we had many happy years until we retired to Queen's Cove," Eileen says.

Shaping their careers

Meanwhile, the Rose youngsters were busy shaping their careers. In Nassau, Anne had become a ticket agent at Pan Am's flying-boat dock on the harbour. She went on to Peterborough Civic Hospital in Canada, rising from student nurse to night supervisor before marrying engineer Eric Graham. She eventually wrote the history of the hospital. She now works voluntarily for the St John Ambulance Brigade and is Commander of the Order of St John of Jerusalem.

Roland started using Anne's box camera then "swapped his harmonica with a kid at primary school for an Ansco Clipper." He was a photographer with the Bahamas Development Board's News

Bureau in Nassau for 31 years and became a freelance photographer in 1982. In 1996, he won the Ministry of Tourism's first Bahamas Cacique award for excellence in photography.

He has not had many adult catastrophes, but nearly caused one when filming entertainment for overseas travel agents at the former Montagu Beach Hotel. The lighting was inadequate for shooting synchronized swimming in a glass-sided swimming pool and he placed hot floodlights too close to the plate glass.

"Suddenly there was a loud crack and a line ran up the window. There were 400 people in the room, and I could envisage those mermaids being swept through the broken glass and water thundering all over the spectators. I had nightmares for a long time afterwards," Roland recalls.

Phyllis took dancing classes and became proficient. She taught ballet for a time in Freeport. Now she makes hand-painted glitter T-shirts, various embroidered or appliquéd garments, and little ming-type trees from beads. Her most unusual products are flower earrings made entirely from fish-scales. "I use hogfish, bonefish, barracuda and this one," she points out proudly, "came from a 264 lb jewfish!"

She had a daughter, conservationist Gail Woon, from her first marriage, and later married Paul Gibson of Gibson's Custom

UNIROYAL CHEMICAL COMPANY, LTD

Manufacturer of Speciality Chemical Additives used by the Worldwide Plastics and Lubricants Industries

ISO 9002-94 Certified and a Responsible Care® Company

Responsible Care®
A Public Commitment

Uniroyal Chemical Company, Ltd
West Sunrise Highway, Freeport, Grand Bahama
PO Box F-42564, Freeport, Bahamas
Tel (242) 352-7861/2 • Fax (242) 352-3136

WE SUPPORT TOTAL ASSOCIATE INVOLVEMENT IN ALL OUR ACTIVITIES

Peter Rose displays his world record 1997 catch, a 46 lb 11 oz dolphin.

Welding. Welding ornamental gates was added to her artistic accomplishments.

Ben also has artistic talent, and paints intricate, colourful sealife pictures. On moving to Freeport, he worked with his father in the gardening business. He then set up his own gardening business until Gulfstream Landscaping bought him out. In 1966 he joined the Underwater Explorers' Society (UNEXSO) as trainee dive guide. He remained for 30 years as guide, scuba instructor, supervisor and finally environmental manager.

Totally fearless

Ben is a gentle man, said to resemble his Rose grandfather who, from the age of nine, worked as a brass foundryman in Birmingham. Also at the age of nine, Ben, totally fearless, defied a shark. "I had a fish on a spear which the shark wanted. It was *my* fish, so I held the spear above my head, whereupon it leaped up and its teeth gripped round my diving mask, leaving four big gashes," he remembers.

Colin Rose holds his 1996 world record 21 lb 9 oz skipjack tuna.

He was diving again the next day, and one of his last innovations at UNEXSO was to introduce shark-feeding demonstrations for scuba-divers. The British *Sunday Express* photographed Ben sitting on the sea-bed circled by 16 sharks. "One flashes at him, then gently lays its head in his lap. He strokes its head and then its belly," the *Express* article revealed.

In the late 1960s Ben heard of a mysterious forest cave where a smallhold farmer used to obtain water for his pigeon-peas. Ben swam inside and discovered a labyrinth of caverns. This led to the discovery by others of one of the world's longest underwater caverns. It contained not only a burial mound of Lucayan Indians, but also the most primitive living crustacean, *Speleonectes lucayensis*. These discoveries led to the founding of Lucayan National Park. In honour of the man who made the discovery, the cavern was named "Ben's Cave." These days, Ben and his wife, Judy, run the exclusive North Riding Point Club where fly-fishermen pursue bonefish in peaceful surroundings that Ben has landscaped.

On leaving school, Peter worked briefly for Rentokil exterminators and then spent two years repairing boats with Colin. But fishing was his real love and he and David set up together as commercial fishermen. With four boats, they caught some three million conchs over eight years. "Eventually I had to stop, as I had sort of a 'diving stroke.' Now I fish for wahoo, tuna and dolphin in my 39 ft *Key West*, sometimes with my wife Linda, occasionally alone. I may catch 1,500 lbs in five days, going up to 200 miles. I love it!"

His particular disaster, aged 20, was to have his jaw badly broken in a car smash. "By coincidence, Dr Albert Antoni, a maxilla-facial surgeon, arrived on the island that same day and did a wonderful repair job," said Peter.

Ben Rose discovered caves later learned to be part of one of the world's longest underwater caverns. Ben's Cave was named after him.

Athlete of the Year

Peter competes in fishing tournaments with Colin in Bermuda, Key West and here in Port Lucaya, with considerable success. Colin has

THE REAL ESTATE EXCHANGE

FULL SERVICE BROKER

Tel (242) 351-4731 • Fax (242) 351-4736
PO Box F-43593 • Freeport, The Bahamas
e-mail: realestatex@batelnet.bs

MEMBER OF BAHAMAS REAL ESTATE ASSOCIATION

WATERFRONT PROPERTY - HOMES
CONDOS - HOTELS
ISLANDS - MARINAS

Business opportunities
Investment services
Property management
Estate management
Property sales
Appraisals

always enjoyed sports, playing tennis and now snow-skiing in New England. Pre-Freeport, he went to Nassau's Queen's College and was Junior Boy Athlete of the Year. He also won painting competitions.

When Colin left school, Sir Jack Hayward offered him a five-year apprenticeship with Freeport Bunkering (now BORCO), where he became a qualified marine journeyman engineer. After two years with Bahamas Tractors, he started his own company, Outboard Services Ltd, "primarily because, to stretch my pay, I spent every spare moment repairing or painting boats and cars, and the Port Authority invited me to get a licence to do so."

Colin still repairs, paints and sells power-boats up to 30 ft long; he also takes advantage of the Small Businesses Manufacturing Act and employs three men to manufacture Freeport skiffs 14-19 ft long. Now every spare moment is spent fishing.

Colin achieved three world records off Grand Bahama in 1996 with a 21.9 lb skipjack tuna, 9.8 lb horse-eye jack, and 6.8 lb horse-eye jack. Peter won the International Light Tackle Tournament in Bermuda in 1987, and together they won the same tournament in Key West in 1995. Peter set a world record in 1997 with a 46.11 lb dolphin.

Colin has been on the board of Bahamas Air Sea Rescue (BASRA) for many years, and organized rescue operations even before its inception. Ben and Peter have assisted their brother. In early Freeport days, Colin and Ben were part of the Volunteer Fire Service.

Bobby was mostly educated at Freeport High where he was an excellent athlete, playing rugby, football and racing track. "I was said to be the fastest white boy in The Bahamas, but then I got a collapsed lung, probably a relic of childhood whooping-cough, so I had to stop," he says.

Bobby's self-inflicted disaster was to jump off a jetty at the moment Roland was speeding in on water-skis. A ski hit Bobby on the head,

DESIGN · HOSTING · DEVELOPMENT
Catch the Wave

bahamasnet

www.bahamasnet.com

PO Box N-7513, Nassau, The Bahamas
Tel (242) 323 5665 Fax (242) 323 5728
email info@bahamasnet.com

Eileen Rose says she was happily married for 65 years.

fracturing his skull. But six months on his back didn't stop him from becoming a champion golfer. He was the "pro" variously at the Bahama Reef, Shannon and Jack Tar Hotel golf courses, winning PGA tournaments in 1976 and 1980 before moving to West Palm Beach.

"I didn't like Florida after The Bahamas," said Bobby, "so I returned, stopped being a pro, and won the Bahamas Amateur Championship in 1993." Now he manages an apartment block.

Lived for fishing

David attended Freeport High after leaving the All-Age School, but he lived for fishing. He says, "When I took a year off in 10th grade to fish with Peter, we bought a boat and a car from our earnings, and then I paid for my last year's education myself. I worked for Rentokil briefly, then went to the California Diving School to study underwater welding. I worked for Burmah Oil for two years, and when Hurricane David tore up a 36-inch diameter pipeline which passed oil from tanker to shore, I was on the team which repaired it."

Since then, it has been non-stop fishing for lobster and conch, first with Peter and now with partner Alfred Sweeting. He plans to start a conch farm one day as an ecotourism project, perhaps at West End, to ensure these gastropods are not fished out and to teach visitors about the conch's life cycle. Like Peter, he also was involved in a car crash, at 23. His arm was so badly broken the surgeon, Dr Charles Clinton-Thomas, implanted a steel plate from wrist to elbow, plus an 11-inch steel pin.

Despite the medley of illnesses and accidents, Eileen has remained a serene lady. "We have had some really wonderful times too, and I was happily married for 65 years," she smiles.

It is said that Eileen once remarked wryly, "If the pill had been around earlier, most of this family wouldn't have been!"

But what a talented lot The Bahamas would have missed. Luckily, the Rose roots have flourished and produced a bountiful garden of ten grandchildren and seven great-grandchildren.

Lustre Kraft SIGNS

Specializing in all types of painted signs

- Desk signs • Silkscreen • Engraving
- Plexiglas • Truck lettering
- Rubber stamps • Specialty printing

Bonded Warehouse #3, Queen's Hwy,
PO Box F-40985
Freeport, Grand Bahama

Tel (242) 352-5412/3 • Fax (242) 352-8722

Grand Bahama Port Authority co-chairman Albert J Miller was voted Bahamas Chamber of Commerce businessman of the year

They spotted a winner in Miller

BY SUZANNE TWISTON-DAVIES

Twice decorated, highly commended, Bahamian Albert Miller is one of the Port Authority's key players.

He's the man the Governor-General of The Bahamas described as "the most straightforward person I know." In February 1998, Sir Jack Hayward and Edward St George asked him to join them in one of the top three positions at the Grand Bahama Port Authority (GBPA); also in 1998 he was voted Bahamas Chamber of Commerce Businessman of the Year.

The man is GBPA co-chairman Albert Joel Miller, former deputy commissioner of the Royal Bahamas Police Force – twice decorated by the Queen – and one of the first black Bahamians to rise above the rank of police sergeant.

Sir Jack and St George are just two Bahamas dignitaries who feel Miller is capable of anything he turns his mind to. As former Governor-General Sir Gerald Cash, GCMG, GCVO, OBE, put it, "He is loyal, dedicated and trustworthy, both as one of my best friends and as a businessman. In every endeavour he undertakes he gives his all – and he is always a success."

Miller was born February 23, 1926 – the youngest of seven brothers and three sisters – in Miller's, Long Island, a settlement named for an 18th century Loyalist who moved there after the

Albert Miller joins the police force.

He receives the MBE from the Queen's Bahamas representative, Royal Governor Sir Robert Stapledon. From left: Chief Justice, Sir Robert, Miller, Wenzel Granger, George Lavelle.

American War of Independence.

Miller's father, a Baptist minister, had a smallholding and modest store. Shoes were a luxury worn only at Sunday School. "Albert told me he virtually invented the flip-flop," Sir Jack said. "He would flatten a piece of rubber from a motor car tyre and fasten a piece of string like a thong round the big toe to make a sandal. It certainly helped with the four-mile walk to school and back."

Grand Bahama Port Authority

The Grand Bahama Port Authority has run the 233 sq miles of Freeport since the Hawksbill Creek Agreement was signed in 1955. Its responsibilities include owning and operating water, utilities, oil, improvement, licensing approved businesses in the Port area and jointly running the harbour and airport companies along with divisions of the Hutchison Whampoa Group of Companies.

As a result of its partnership with Hutchison, a mega-container port and Sea/Air Business Centre have been created, and plans are under way for airport development, ship repair and homeporting. Hutchison is building a new hotel and renovating two others as part of The Lucayan resort, as well as refurbishing Bahama Reef golf course.

A miracle he survived

"It's a miracle Albert survived his infancy," his cousin and friend, Conrad Knowles, exclaimed. "When he was four months old, his mother went to Nassau by sailboat. A hurricane wrecked them in the Exuma Cays. His mother had to stand on a rock in the water for so long that she dropped Albert in the sea, and a crewman named McPhee scooped him up and wrapped him in his coat. My aunt – who never recovered from the exposure – died three years later, and Albert was brought up by his sister, Florrie.

"We were inseparable. We went to school together, even though I was older, and defied the rules by going swimming at lunch time. After school we'd do our homework at my house. Then I went to Nassau and joined the police."

Conrad Knowles says it's a wonder Miller survived infancy.

After his father died when Miller was just 14, he went to live with another sister in Nassau. Sharing his friend's ambition to join the police, Miller brought his education to the required level by studying in the evenings with two priests at St Augustine's College. When his education was complete, he put in his application. "Academically, I was of the right standard," he said, "but I wasn't tall enough. Luckily, Commissioner R A Erskine-Lindop thought I had the talent and allowed me to join anyway. I exercised very hard so that I would grow."

Off duty one day, Miller met the woman who was to be his wife. Laurie (née Gibbs) recalled, "I was walking along the street when this young man got off his bicycle and asked my name. Then he asked for a date and wouldn't take no for an answer. We've never looked back! We were married on his birthday at St Mary the Virgin Church in Nassau. He was earning £2.11½d a week." The Millers were to have three children – Debbie, who owns a flower shop; Mark Anthony, who owns Photo Magic in Freeport; and Russell, assistant manager of Paradise Island's Ocean Club.

It's never easy being a policeman's wife, and Laurie has had her share of sleepless nights. "In the early days, there weren't too many criminals around. But as the years went by, and crimes got more violent, I would worry more and more," she explained.

Her husband added, "Only once, when I was investigating the theft of lumber in Eleuthera, was I fired at. I wasn't too happy about it as I couldn't even see where the shots were coming from."

Dramatic rise

Miller's rise through the police was dramatic. By 1953 he had been promoted to detective sergeant, and he continued to be promoted every two years.

In 1969, in the rank of deputy commissioner, Miller was sent to Grand Bahama to establish intelligence and security methods and modernize the police establishment, which then consisted of a sergeant, constable and auxiliary police force. He was approached by a representative of the GBPA and offered a top position with Bahamas Amusements Ltd, the company which controlled Freeport's casino operation. Miller declined. His ambition was to become commissioner of police for The Bahamas.

> **When the news reached flamboyant real estate broker Aileen Matheson ... she exclaimed, "I think they've spotted a winner in Miller."**

The GBPA refused to give up, however, and the offer was made twice more. Miller finally accepted – but only after weeks of thought and soul-searching. In November 1971, he was appointed vice-president of Bahamas Amusements.

When the news reached flamboyant real estate broker Aileen Matheson, known as *Madame Fifi de la Hat* because of her exotic headgear, she exclaimed, "I think they've spotted a winner in Miller!"

She was proved right. On July 1, 1976, he was appointed president of the GBPA.

This came as no surprise to Sir Gerald, Miller's lifelong friend. "When he asked my advice on whether to take the position in

Supreme Court Justice Emmanuel Osadebay met Miller in Nassau. Both live in Freeport now.

T Baswell Donaldson, former Bahamas Ambassador in Washington, DC, has known Miller since the 1940s.

Freeport, we had long, frank discussions and decided it was in his best interests to accept. Albert has lived up to my best expectations and made me very proud," he said.

"It couldn't have happened to a better man," added Judge Emmanuel Osadebay of Freeport's Supreme Court. "We met professionally when he was commanding a police district in New Providence and I was a magistrate, but became friendly in and out of the job too. You could rely on Albert like a brother! Everything he does he makes it a point to succeed in.

"I know he was torn about taking the Freeport job because he was committed to the police force, but then he took it as a challenge. And now ... well, it would be difficult to find a businessman with more zeal." Besides his directorships within the GBPA, Miller is also chairman of the Grand Bahama Island Tourism Board, the Bahamas Telecommunications Corporation (BaTelCo) and Freeport Oil Co Ltd; a director of Solomon Brothers Ltd and Pepsi-Cola (Bahamas) Ltd; and president of IAT (Bahamas) Ltd.

Professional acumen

Bahamas Governor-General Sir Orville Turnquest, GCMG, QC, has high praise for Miller's personal qualities and professional acumen. He said, "I met him soon after he joined the police. We went to the same church, then got to know each other professionally and developed a friendship. When I was an attorney and he was in the CID, we often worked against each other on a case; but if Albert knew the truth, he would never hold anything back to make points. His reputation was that you took his word always, for anything."

> **If Albert knew the truth, he would never hold anything back ... His reputation was that you took his word always, for anything.**

"He's easy to work with, so long as you're honest and play the game straight," Gerald Stevenson, recently retired president of the Grand Bahama Development Company (GBDevCo) explained. "He gives you your head, and will stand behind you if you're working in the best interests of the company. When he became president, he asked me to come work with him as treasurer. I later found that, in true CID manner, he'd had me investigated first! When the casino eventually changed hands, I went with him to the next job, and we always had a good relationship. When my wife died recently, he could not have been more kind and helpful."

Queen's honours

During his career with the Royal Bahamas Police Force, Miller was made a Member of the Most Excellent Order of the British Empire (MBE) in 1963 and awarded the Colonial Police Medal in 1965. "Not for specific deeds – just for good police work, I suppose," he said, modestly.

Two more awards came Miller's way. The first was the Queen's Police Medal in 1970. The second came as a complete surprise. After the Queen had opened the Freeport Law Courts in March 1994, Miller and his wife were invited to dine on the Royal Yacht in Nassau. After dinner, a secretary announced the Queen wanted to see him.

"The Queen came over and talked to me for 10 minutes about the GBPA. She had so much grace and charm," Miller explained. "Then she said, 'I have something for you,' and to my astonishment, she invested me with the Lieutenant of the Royal Victorian Order (LVO). I had absolutely no idea."

Michael Power and Miller don hard hats at the container port site.

Pride and joy

Miller and his wife are devout churchgoers, giving much support to Christ the King Church in Freeport. Another of Miller's passions outside the office is game-fishing, and the 42 ft Bertram game-fishing boat *Modalena* docked outside his Freeport home is his pride and joy. He also enjoys walking, listening to music, playing pool, and reading the works of John Grisham, Tom Clancy, James Clavell and John Le Carré.

"I have known Albert since the '40s, when he went to St John's Baptist Church where my father was minister," said Timothy Baswell Donaldson, former Bahamian Ambassador in Washington, DC. "I left to go to University, and then when I was in the Ministry of Finance our careers went upwards on parallel lines. He had a wonderful reputation for administrative skill, and was also a competitive tennis player."

Top left: Former Governor-General Sir Gerald Cash helped Miller decide to take the Freeport position. Top right: Sir Jack Hayward says, "We think the world of Albert." Bottom: Albert and Laurie Miller attend the Silver Jubilee gala ball held in Freeport/Lucaya in August 1998.

Luis Reynoso, a Freeport friend of 20 years ago, confirmed, "Albert is a very good tennis player, but so unorthodox – it's more like he's playing ping-pong!

"We used to go bottom-fishing together, and I remember once my little 20 ft boat got engine trouble 30 miles from nowhere. We had to wait 24 hours to be rescued in the middle of a tropical storm, but Albert's sense of humour didn't desert him. He can be very funny. When he came on a conference with me to my home town of Vigo, Spain, his wit would come out at the wrong moment. But he made many friends there. He really has a lot of spice."

Life at the Port Authority gives Miller many a chance to smile. "I get some laughs with Sir Jack Hayward," he said. "He's a great actor. When the Freeport Players' Guild put on *My Fair Lady*, Jack was playing Alfred Doolittle. One day, he was dancing around in his office above my head practising *I'm Getting Married in the Morning*, and I had to call his secretary to tell him to stop before he crashed through the floor. I went up to find him leaping about – typical millionaire – with a large hole in his shoe."

The bond between Miller and Sir Jack is apparent in anecdotes such as these. "We think the world of Albert," Sir Jack is fond of saying. "We trust him and the great thing is that he's apolitical, and just gets on with the work. He can do anything."

FREEPORT/LUCAYA CLASSIFIED DIRECTORY

*See also **Bahamas Classified Directory**, pgs 255-264*

ACCOUNTANTS/ACCOUNTING FIRMS
Cates & Co Chartered Accountants 486
KPMG 182
PricewaterhouseCoopers 181

AIRCRAFT COMMUNICATION SYSTEMS/RADAR EQUIPMENT
Bahamas Electronic Lab Co 230

AIR FREIGHT AGENTS/SHIPPING AGENTS
DHL Worldwide Express 202
Eastern Freight Forwarders 479
Freeport Transfer Ltd 479
Lucaya Shipping
 & Trading Co Ltd .... bet 456-457
United Shipping Co Ltd 467
Wide World Airfreight 519
Wide World Forwarding 519

ART SUPPLIES
Lustre Kraft Signs Ltd 507

AUDIT & RELATED SERVICES
See **Accountants/Accounting Firms.**

AUTOMOBILE ACCESSORIES, PARTS & REPAIRS
Automotive and Industrial
 Distributors Ltd (AID) 154

BATTERIES – AUTOMOTIVE/HEAVY EQUIPMENT/MARINE
Automotive and Industrial
 Distributors Ltd (AID) 154

BEEPERS/PAGERS
Bahamas Electronic Lab Co 230
BaTelCo .... bet 488-489

BROADCASTING
See **Communications & Broadcasting.**

BUILDING CONTRACTORS
Freeport Aggregate Ltd 475
Island Construction Co Ltd 475
Reef Construction Ltd 469
Waugh Construction (Bahamas) Ltd 495

BUSINESS SYSTEMS CONSULTING, MANAGEMENT, TROUBLESHOOTING
IBM Bahamas Ltd 177
KPMG 182

CAR RENTALS
Avis 323

CHEMICAL PRODUCTS
Bahama Rock Ltd 517
Uniroyal Chemical Co Ltd 501

CELLULAR SERVICES
BaTelCo .... bet 488-489

CLAIMS SETTLING
McKinney, Bancroft & Hughes 172
Nassau Survey Agency Ltd 119

COMPUTER SERVICES
IBM Bahamas Ltd 177

COMMUNICATIONS & BROADCASTING
Bahamas Electronic Lab Co 230
BaTelCo .... bet 488-489
Broadcasting Corp
 of The Bahamas, The .... bet 216-217
ZNS Network .... bet 216-217

CONSTRUCTION SUPPLIES
Bahama Cement 483
Bahama Rock Ltd 517
Builders Depot .... bet 456-457
Concem Ltd 483
Freeport Aggregate Ltd 475
Island Construction Co Ltd 475

CONTAINER PORT
Freeport Container Port 461

CORPORATE FINANCE, MANAGEMENT & ADVISORY SERVICES
Cates & Co Chartered Accountants 486
KPMG 182
PricewaterhouseCoopers 181

COURIER SERVICE
DHL Worldwide Express 202
Federal Express (FedEx) 233

CUSTOMS BROKERS
Eastern Freight Forwarders 479
Freeport Transfer Ltd 479
Lucaya Shipping
 & Trading Co Ltd .... bet 456-457
Tanja Enterprises Co Ltd 465
United Shipping Co Ltd 467
Wide World Forwarding 519

ELECTRONIC EQUIPMENT – SUPPLIES & REPAIRS
Bahamas Electronic Lab Co 230

ENGINEERING CONSULTANTS
Freeport Aggregate Ltd 475
Island Construction Co Ltd 475
Waugh Construction (Bahamas) Ltd 495

ENGRAVING
Lustre Kraft Signs Ltd 507

EXCAVATION & LAND CLEARING
Freeport Aggregate Ltd 475
Island Construction Co Ltd 475
Waugh Construction (Bahamas) Ltd 495

GROCERS – RETAIL
Winn Dixie Food Stores 161

HARDWARE & HOME IMPROVEMENT
Automotive and Industrial
   Distributors Ltd (AID) 154
Builders Depot ....bet 456-457

HEAVY EQUIPMENT (RENTALS)
Freeport Aggregate Ltd 475
Island Construction Co Ltd 475

HOTELS
Old Bahama Bay 54
Port Lucaya Resort & Yacht Club .... opp 488

IMPORT & EXPORT SERVICES
DHL Worldwide Express 202
Freeport Transfer 479
Lucaya Shipping
   & Trading Co Ltd .... bet 456-457
Wide World Forwarding 519

INCORPORATION SERVICES
Cates & Co Chartered Accountants 486
PricewaterhouseCoopers 181
See also **Law Firms.**

INDUSTRIAL/COMMERCIAL PARK
Innotec .... bet 456-457

INFORMATION TECHNOLOGY SERVICES
IBM Bahamas Ltd 177
KPMG 182

INSURANCE
Bahamas First
   General Insurance Co Ltd 119
Nassau Underwriters Agency Ltd 119
Royal & Sun Alliance .... opp 185

INVESTMENT ADVISORY/ASSET MANAGEMENT SERVICES
Cates & Co Chartered Accountants 486
KPMG 182
PricewaterhouseCoopers 181

INVESTMENT OPPORTUNITIES
Grand Bahama Port Authority .. bet 456-457
See also **Real Estate.**

LAW FIRMS
Christie, Davis & Co 191
Dupuch & Turnquest & Co 190
McKinney, Bancroft & Hughes 172
Pindling & Co 174

LIMESTONE SUPPLIER
Bahama Rock Ltd 517

MANAGEMENT CONSULTING
Cates & Co Chartered Accountants 486
KPMG 182
PricewaterhouseCoopers 181

MARINAS/MARINE SERVICES
Bell Channel Club & Marina .... opp 457
Bradford Grand Bahama 471
Lucayan Marina Village 52
Old Bahama Bay 54

Wide World Forwarding
Freeport and Nassau

Ships agents, customs brokers, freight forwarders, truckers, packers

And to better serve you...

Wide World Airfreight
Offering reliable cargo service Freeport/Miami and Nassau/Miami with connections to and from worldwide destinations.

Wide World Travel

Get your business or shopping trip off to a great start with **the experienced travel professionals.**
Tel (242) 352-6253. PO Box F-40576

IN FREEPORT tel (242) 352-3636. PO Box F-43869
IN NASSAU tel (242) 377-5605. PO Box N-560
In Miami tel (305) 513-0496. 2600 NW 75th Ave, Miami, FL 33152

Port Lucaya Resort & Yacht Club ...... opp 488
Tanja Enterprises Co Ltd 465

MEDIA
See **Communications & Broadcasting, Newspaper** and **Radio/Television Station**.

MOVERS
Freeport Transfer Ltd 479
Wide World Forwarding 519

NEWSPAPER
The Freeport News 111

OIL COMPANIES/PETROLEUM PRODUCTS
Bahamas Oil Refining Co
   International Ltd (BORCO) .. bet 456-457
Chevron Supreme Lubricants
   (FOCOL exclusive) 481
Freeport Oil Co Ltd (FOCOL) 481

PRINTING
The Freeport News 111

PROPERTY DEVELOPMENT/MANAGEMENT
Century 21 499
Churchill & Jones
   Real Estate Ltd .... bet 456-457
First Atlantic Realty Ltd .... bet 456-457
Harry Dann & Co Ltd 499
Real Estate Exchange, The 504
Re/Max Freeport
   Northern Bahamas .... bet 456-457

RADIO/TELEVISION STATION
Broadcasting Corp
   of The Bahamas, The .... bet 216-217
ZNS Network .... bet 216-217

READY MIX CONCRETE & CONCRETE BLOCKS
Freeport Aggregate Ltd 475
Island Construction Co Ltd 475

REAL ESTATE
Bell Channel Club & Marina .... opp 457
Century 21 499
Churchill & Jones
   Real Estate Ltd .... bet 456-457
First Atlantic Realty Ltd .... bet 456-457
Harry Dann & Co Ltd 499
Innotec .... bet 456-457
Lucayan Marina Village 52
Old Bahama Bay 54
Princess Isle .... opp 489
Princess Realty Ltd .... opp 489
Real Estate Exchange, The 504
Re/Max Freeport
   Northern Bahamas .... bet 456-457
Waters Edge .... bet 456-457

RESTAURANT
Port Lucaya Resort & Yacht Club ....opp 488

ROAD & SURFACE CONSTRUCTION
Freeport Aggregate Ltd 475
Island Construction Co Ltd 475

Waugh Construction (Bahamas) Ltd 495

RUBBER STAMPS
Lustre Kraft Signs Ltd 507

SCHOOLS – TECHNICAL & VOCATIONAL
The Bahamas Technical
   and Vocational Institute 158

SHIP'S AGENTS
Lucaya Shipping
   & Trading Co Ltd .... bet 456-457
Tanja Enterprises Co Ltd 465
United Shipping Co Ltd 467
Wide World Forwarding 519

SHIPPING COMPANIES
DHL Worldwide Express 202
Eastern Freight Forwarders 479
Federal Express (FedEx) 233
Freeport Transfer Ltd 479
Tanja Enterprises Co Ltd 465
United Shipping Co Ltd 467
Wide World Forwarding 519

SHIP SERVICES/CHANDLERS
Borco Agency Services .... bet 456-457
Borco Towing Company .... bet 456-457
Bradford Grand Bahama 471
Freeport Container Port 461
Lucaya Shipping
   & Trading Co Ltd .... bet 456-457
Tanja Enterprises Co Ltd 465
United Shipping Co Ltd 467

SIGNS – ALL TYPES
Lustre Kraft Signs Ltd 507

STORAGE
Eastern Freight Forwarders 479
Freeport Transfer Ltd 479
Innotec .... bet 456-457

TRUCKING
Eastern Freight Forwarders 479
Freeport Transfer Ltd 479
Tanja Enterprises Co Ltd 465
United Shipping Co Ltd 467

UNDERGROUND UTILITIES/SUBDIVISION INFRASTRUCTURE
Waugh Construction (Bahamas) Ltd 495

WELL DRILLING & DRAINAGE WELLS
Freeport Aggregate Ltd 475
Island Construction Co 475
Waugh Construction (Bahamas) Ltd 495

WORK BOAT HIRE
United Shipping Co Ltd 467

---

bahamasnet
www.bahamasnet.com
PO Box N-7512, Nassau, The Bahamas
Tel (242) 323 5665 Fax (242) 323 5728
email info@bahamasnet.com

Freeport/Lucaya Information

Blue page index, this section

Accommodations
Accounting firms
Agriculture
Air service
Ambulance/air ambulance services
Animals
Architectural firms
Bahamas National Trust
Banking
Birds
Boating
Building contractors & engineers
Building costs & permits
Business licence fee
Cable television
Camping
Car rental companies
Casinos
Chamber of Commerce
Churches
Cinemas
Clinics
Climate
Community organizations
Cost of living
Courier services
Cruising
Cultural activities
Customs
Defence Force
Dentists
Departure tax
Diving & snorkelling
Divorce
Doctors
Driver's licence & vehicle information
Education
Electricity
Emergency numbers
Employers' organizations
Encouragement acts
Engineers
Entertainment
Exchange Control
Export entry
Fire brigade
Fishing
Freight services
Gambling
Geography
Golf courses
Government offices
Grand Bahama Humane Society
Gun permits
Harbour control
Hawksbill Creek Agreement
Health/medical services
History
Hospitals & clinics
Hotels
Housing
Immigration
Import entry
Industry
International Bazaar
Judicial system
Junkanoo
Law firms
Libraries
Licensing
Marinas & cruising facilities
Marriage licences
Museums
National Insurance
Nature centres
Newspapers
Passports
People-to-People
Police certificates
Population
Port Lucaya Marketplace
Postal information
Property transactions
Radio stations
Real estate companies
Religion
Schools
Service clubs
Shipping
Shopping
Snorkelling
Sports venues
Straw markets
Supermarkets
Tax incentives
Telecommunications
Television
Theatre & dramatic arts
Tourism
Trade unions
Transportation
Veterinarians
Wages
Water supply & rates
Weather

The central port and tourism area of Freeport/Lucaya is governed by terms of the Hawksbill Creek Agreement between The Bahamas government and businesses licensed by the Grand Bahama Port Authority (GBPA). For this reason, certain headings are specific to Freeport/Lucaya only. As the rest of Grand Bahama is governed on the same terms as New Providence and other Bahama islands, see **Bahamas information** for general information not specific to Freeport/Lucaya or Grand Bahama.

ACCOMMODATIONS

Accommodations for visitors range from luxury beachfront properties to apartment complexes booked through local real estate agencies. Apartments usually include television hook-up, maid service, coin-operated washers/driers, swimming pools and beach access.

Small hotel rates are about $75 per day in summer, double or single occupancy, and $95 in winter, with an added tax of 8%. Daily maid service is approx $3.50 per person per day.

Larger hotel rates start at approx $98-$108 per day in summer, double occupancy, and $125-$135 in winter, plus 8% tax. Maid service is usually included in the price, or at an extra cost of $4.00 per person per day.

All hotels have swimming pools, tennis courts, access to golf courses and live entertainment, and some offer scuba diving, weekly beach barbecues and moonlight cruises.

See also **Bahamas information, Hotels,** and, this section, **Cost of living.**

ACCOUNTING FIRMS

Cates & Co	351-4025
Deloitte & Touche	373-3015
Hepburn, Michael & Co	352-7354
KPMG	352-9384
Pannell Kerr Forster	352-2912
PricewaterhouseCoopers	352-8471

AGRICULTURE

Agricultural development in Grand Bahama is a priority concern of the Ministry of Agriculture and Fisheries. There is an established Dept of Agriculture with professionally trained resident extension officers responsible for issuing permits for importation of all fresh fruit and vegetables, plants and propagative materials, as well as domestic animals. The Freeport-based dept, with the cooperation of the USDA, is participating in the ongoing survey of Grand Bahama with emphasis on ports of entry and the farm area for exotic insects.

The Dept of Agriculture is not only involved in issuing permits for fruit, vegetables, plants and animals, but is responsible in Freeport for:

1. Inspection of imported produce and plants to ensure they are insect and disease free.
2. Receiving and interviewing applicants for agricultural crown land.
3. Regular visits and assistance to livestock and crop farms.
4. Management of the fruit and vegetable vendors' market.

Bahamas Poultry Group of Companies, 11,070 acres, including three companies on four sites: Bahamas Poultry Ltd, Sunshine GB Ltd and GB Food Co Ltd. Major producers of fruit, vegetables, poultry and eggs. Chief crops: bananas, plantain, mixed citrus, cabbage, lettuce and tomatoes.

Bahamas Poultry Ltd, largest poultry producer in The Bahamas, 18 broiler chicken houses with approx 25,000 chickens in each.

Sunshine GB Ltd, three divisions: Sunshine Egg Farms, 200 acres, processes 215 cases of eggs daily. Sunshine Citrus and Sunshine Banana divisions, 1,907 acres, 1,000 acres still to be cleared, avocados, Persian limes, grapefruit, oranges, plantain, bananas and lemons.

Grand Bahama Food Ltd, farm division: 500 acres under cyclic cultivation from mid-Sept to mid-June. A joint venture with a group of Florida farmers to develop the technology and equipment for viable large-scale farming in Grand Bahama proved successful, and large marketable crops of lettuce, celery, onions, tomatoes, potatoes, cabbage, thyme, cauliflower, squash, zucchini, parsley, broccoli and cucumber have been harvested.

Buds and Blooms, five acres, ornamental plants.

Oscar Campbell, 10 acres, exotic fruit, guava, peaches, mangoes, apples.

Coopers Farm, owned by GB Food Ltd, 200 acres, bananas, with two other plantations at Sunshine Farms and GB Food. Mainly young suckers and immature trees after Hurricane Andrew and two recent winter storms decimated the plantations.

Freeport Citrus, 140 acres with 10,000 mature trees producing mainly limes, also oranges, grapefruit and mangoes. Average citrus yield during the season, 800 cases a week.

Daniel Curry, 10 acres, pigs, fruit and vegetables.

Freeport Farms, 36 acres, 30 acres of sweet potatoes, 6 acres of mixed vegetables.

Gina Farms, 15 acres, ornamental plants and fruit.

Bill Grant, 10 acres, mangoes, coconuts, citrus, bananas, avocados, sugar apples.

Joan Green-Bowe, 30 acres, 10 acres cleared, organic fruit and vegetables.

Havard Cooper, 100 acres (60 acres cleared, 45 planted), Persian limes and mixed vegetables.

Hydroflora Enterprises, five acres, ornamental plants.

Lucaya Nursery & Landscaping, ornamental plants.

Marine Shrimp Farm, operated by Lucayan Aquaculture Ltd on 100 acres near the airport. The shrimps are farmed from post-larvae to market size in four above-ground tanks. This is the first operation of its kind in the Caribbean.

Morganic Farms, 45 acres on three sites, citrus, bananas, Persian limes, guava, mangoes, sugar apples, grapefruit, lettuce, tomatoes, cabbage, sweet peppers and papaya.

Oral Poitier, 10 acres, hot and sweet peppers, cabbages and pork production.

Pineyard Farms, 20 acres, Persian limes and bananas on five acres, remaining acreage used to fatten more than 300 pigs.

Polly's Farm, 90 acres, livestock (sheep, goats, pigs, cattle), plus papaya, Persian limes, bananas.

Hastin Russell, 10 acres, mangoes, coconuts, citrus, bananas, avocados, sugar apples.

Sawyers Farms, 100 acres (20 acres cleared, 12 planted), bananas, plantain, mixed citrus, cabbage and tomatoes.

James Taylor, beekeeper, bottles honey for local sale and supplies hives to farms.

Tartar Farms, 25 acres, root crops, bananas, plantain, papaya and citrus.

Wallace Whitfield Farms, 400 acres (22 acres under cultivation), major producers of guava, also mangoes, grapefruit and oranges.

Other farmers cultivating five to 10 acres of fruit and vegetables include Baby Johnson, Jetta Baptiste and Tony Scott.

Most of the above farmers have more land to be cleared and planted.

See also **Bahamas information, Agriculture.**

AIR SERVICE

Freeport Intl Airport, the largest privately owned airport in the world, has a runway 11,000 ft long and 150 ft wide with taxiways 75 ft wide. The six storey control tower was built by the Grand Bahama Port Authority (GBPA) Group of

Companies at a cost of $2 million. It is equipped with direction-finding equipment, weather radar, weather satellite-receiving equipment and a lighted beacon. Airport terminal space includes a 6,000 sq ft in transit lounge with snack bar and telephones.

The airport has US Customs and Immigration pre-clearance facilities.

Scheduled airlines serving Grand Bahama include:

American Eagle
Seven times daily to **Miami** on 34-seater Saab 340 aircraft.

Bahamasair
Regular flights to **Nassau,** the **Family Islands** and **Miami** several times daily on Dash-8 aircraft.

Continental Connection (formerly Gulfstream Intl)
Three flights daily to **Miami** and six to **Ft Lauderdale.** Some flights continue on to St Petersburg, Orlando, Naples, Key West, Gainesville and Marathon. Also serving **West Palm Beach** daily.

LB Ltd (formerly Laker Airways)
Twice daily to **Ft Lauderdale,** three times on Sun; once daily, and three times on Sat to **West Palm Beach** in 727 aircraft. Also flights to **Richmond, Chicago, Baltimore, Hartford, Cleveland, Raleigh-Durham** and **Cincinnati. Hartford, CT** and **Cleveland, OH** only in winter, **Memphis, TN, Greenville, SC** and **Allentown, PA** during summer. Three-, four- and seven-night packages are available through Princess Casino Vacations, (242) 352-3050 for golfing or gambling.

Major's Air Services
Daily flights to **Bimini, Walker's Cay, Marsh Harbour, Treasure Cay** and many other **Family Islands,** on six planes varying from five- to 15-seaters.

Taino Air
Serves many **Family Islands** including **Abaco, Eleuthera** and **Andros.** Charters available on three nine-seater planes.

See also **Bahamas information, Air service** and **Airports.**

AMBULANCE/AIR AMBULANCE SERVICES
Air ambulances
AA Amelia
  Airways Inc 1-800-546-4648
Advance Air
  Ambulance (AAA)....1-800-633-3590
Air Ambulance Professionals Inc
  (Ft Lauderdale).........1-800-752-4195
        or call collect (954) 491-0555
Global Med-Tec
  Ambulance ......351-3333 (Freeport)
Major's Air Services
  (Freeport to Nassau) 352-5778
Medical Air Services
  Assoc Intl (for members) 351-5122
  (Bahamas to any US city)
Ground ambulance
  Rand Memorial Hosp 352-2689
        or 352-6735

See also **Bahamas information, Ambulance/air ambulance services,** and, this section, **Emergency numbers** and **Hospitals & clinics.**

ANIMALS
See **Bahamas information, Animals,** and, this section, **Grand Bahama Humane Society** and **Nature centres.**

ARCHITECTURAL FIRMS
Architects & Engineers 373-6938
Architects Inc.........................352-4835
Architectural Group 352-3558
L V Evans Master
  Architects ....351-5644 or 352-3558
Grant, Carver & Co 352-4333
Griffiths & Assoc 352-2101
Moss, Charles J & Assoc 352-5204

BAHAMAS NATIONAL TRUST (BNT)
The Bahamas National Trust (BNT) administers three national parks in

Grand Bahama – the BNT Rand Nature Centre, Lucayan National Park and Peterson Cay National Park.

See also **Bahamas information, Bahamas National Trust,** and, this section, **Nature Centres.**

BANKING

There are seven clearing banks in Freeport/Lucaya: the Bank of The Bahamas Ltd; Barclays Bank plc; CIBC Bahamas Ltd; Citibank; Commonwealth Bank Ltd; Bank of Nova Scotia; and Royal Bank of Canada. Barclays, CIBC, the Bank of Nova Scotia and Royal Bank of Canada offer 24-hour banking with automated teller machines.

Other banks that offer commercial banking services are: Finance Corp of The Bahamas Ltd (FINCO) and the British American Bank (with Western Union).

The Bahamas Development Bank (BDB) assists in the establishment and financing of local business.

Commercial banks (authorized dealers) may issue and approve certain foreign currency payments without Exchange Control permission.

Commercial banking hours are Mon-Thurs 9:30am-3pm and Fri 9:30am-5pm. Commonwealth Bank opens at 8:30am.

See also **Bahamas information, Bahamas Development Bank; Banking; Banks; Exchange Control;** and **Import entry.**

BIRDS

There has been an influx of Red-winged blackbirds on Grand Bahama Island. Colourful painted buntings and indigo buntings, rarely seen before, now visit occasionally. One of the rarest birds in the world, the yellow and black Kirtland's warbler, was sighted in Nov 1995 by an ornithological group visiting the Lucayan National Park, and two more were later seen in the same area. These birds winter only in The Bahamas. Purple gallinules and olive-capped warblers, which visit only a few of our islands, have also been spotted.

See also **Nature centres.**

BOATING

Marinas, boat dealers and repairers, charter agencies and fishing guides exist throughout Freeport/Lucaya and at West End to serve boating and fishing enthusiasts.

Volunteers from the Bahamas Air Sea Rescue Assoc (BASRA) keep a 24-hour watch for boaters in Bahamian waters in collaboration with the US Coast Guard.

Bell Channel was re-dredged to give greater facility to large yachts entering Port Lucaya. The Grand Lucayan Waterway was dredged to 6½ ft at Mean Low Water (MLW) at North Shore. Boaters from West End seeking a direct route to Abaco or Walker's Cay must clear the 26 ft Casuarina Bridge.

See also **Harbour Control** and **Marinas & cruising facilities.**

BUILDING CONTRACTORS & ENGINEERS

A & A Construction & Maintenance Co
Albacore Construction
Arawak Construction & Truss Co Ltd
B & H Construction Co Ltd
Broncestone Construction Co Ltd
Cavalier Construction Co
Coibesa Bahamas Ltd
Diesel Engineers Ltd
FES Construction
Freeport Construction Co Ltd
Glenerik Intl Ltd
Gibson Construction
Grand Bahama Construction Co Ltd
Grant, W Carver (consulting engineers)
H & S Construction
Industrial/Mechanical Engineering Ltd
Island Construction Ltd
Island Electric Ltd
Island Projects Ltd
Knowles Construction Co Ltd
Mechanical Engineering
 & Construction Co Ltd
Outten's Trucking and Ditching
Qualfast Construction Co

Reef Construction Ltd
Roberts, Terry V
Russell Construction Co Ltd
SRA Construction
Virmar Construction
Waugh Construction (Bah) Ltd
W G & S Construction Ltd

BUILDING COSTS & PERMITS

All major building work needs prior approval of the Ministry of Public Works. Permit fees vary according to type of building and inspections are made at prescribed stages. Regulations on building within the Port Authority area are similar to those in Nassau.

Building permit applications are available at the building dept, GBPA, East Atlantic Dr, tel 352-6611, ext 2053. Guidance pamphlets are at the same address or from full service real estate companies.

BUSINESS LICENCE FEE

Businesses in the Freeport area must be licensed by the Licensing Dept at the Grand Bahama Port Authority (GBPA), PO Box F-42666, tel 352-6711.

Outside the GBPA area, see **Bahamas information, Business licence fee.**

CABLE TELEVISION

See **Bahamas information, Cable Television,** and, this section, **Television.**

CAMPING

Camping is not illegal in The Bahamas, but it is not recommended. Before pitching a tent in Grand Bahama, it is advisable to contact the Grand Bahama Island Tourism Board, tel 352-8044. Before lighting a fire, obtain permission from the Fire Brigade at non-emergency number 352-8441.

If camping in a remote area, inform someone of your intended whereabouts.

CAR RENTAL COMPANIES

Car rentals vary from $55 daily for a sub-compact to $114 for a luxury car. The weekly rental rate is $380-$689. Most companies give unlimited mileage. Collision damage waiver is optional, at approx $15.95 daily or $111.65 weekly.

Avis ....352-7666 (airport)
　　　　　　　　　　　　　　or 373-1102
Bahama Buggies 352-8750
Courtesy Rentals....352-5212/3 (airport)
　　　　　　　　　　　　　　or 352-7054
Dollar...................................352-9325
Hertz ....352-9250 (airport)
Star ....352-5953 (Old Airport Rd)
Thrifty 352-9308

CASINOS

See **Entertainment** and **Gambling.**

CHAMBER OF COMMERCE

The Grand Bahama Chamber of Commerce, affiliated with the Bahamas Chamber of Commerce in Nassau, has 220 members. President is Constance McDonald. Contact the Chamber of Commerce, Pioneers Way, PO Box F-40808, tel 352-8329.

CHURCHES

See **Religion.**

CINEMAS

The Columbus Twin Theatre,
　on The Mall 352-7478
An on-site movie theatre is planned as part of The Lucayan resort, scheduled to open before the new millennium.

At press time, construction was to begin by the end of 1998 on a five-screen RND cinema on East Mall Dr. Anticipated completion date was Oct 1999.

CLINICS

See **Hospitals & clinics.**

CLIMATE
Because of its northerly location, Grand Bahama has winter temperatures slightly below those of New Providence, although the weather tends to be similar throughout the rest of the year.

Grand Bahama temperatures traditionally are at their lowest in Feb, with a daily max temperature of about 76°F. In the summer, April-Nov, the daily max temperature is in the 80s.

Humidity can be high, although tempered by prevailing breezes. Wind speeds are below 10 knots most of the year but can reach 25 knots in winter.

Grand Bahama has a May-Oct rainy season and rainfall is especially heavy in Sept. The Bahamas can be affected by hurricanes or tropical storms June-Nov, the greatest risk being in Aug, Sept and Oct.

See also **Bahamas information, Climate.**

COMMUNITY ORGANIZATIONS & SERVICE CLUBS
American Women's Club
   of Grand Bahama 352-3245
Bahamas Air Sea Rescue Assoc
   (BASRA) ......352-2628 or 352-2880
Bahamas National Trust 352-5438
Bahamian Women's Club 352-7222
   or 373-3454
Business & Professional Women's Assoc
   of Grand Bahama Island 373-8188
Canadian Men's Club............352-5105
Canadian Women's Club 373-9457
Chamber of Commerce 352-8329
Freeport Grand Bahama
   Chamber of Commerce 352-8329
Freeport Garden Club 340-4016
Freeport Jaycees....................373-2706
   or 352-3589
Freeport Lions Club 352-8171
   (ext 4337)
Freeport Toastmasters 352-7367
Freeport Toastmistresses
   2406 ITC 352-7256
GB Red Cross Centre 352-7163
Grand Bahama
   Children's Home 352-7852
Human Rights Assoc 373-4331
Kiwanis Club of
   Eight Mile Rock 352-3410
Kiwanis Club of Freeport 352-7031
Kiwanis Club of Lucaya 352-9191
Narcotics Anonymous 351-3413
Northern Bahamas Council
   for the Disabled 352-7720
Operation Hope
   (Drug Abuse Hot Line) 352-3002
Operation Outreach
   Teen Centre 352-2092
Pilot Club of Freeport............352-7483
Rotary Club of Freeport 352-7421
Rotary Club of Lucaya 352-2286
Sunrise Rotary Club 352-6611
YMCA 352-7074
Zonta Club Freeport/Lucaya 352-4934

COST OF LIVING
Food costs in Freeport are generally slightly higher than in Nassau because of its lower population. As Grand Bahama imports 90% of all consumer goods from the US, its cost of living is directly tied to the US Consumer Price Index.

Most rented homes and apartments are furnished and have refrigerators, stoves and facilities for washers and driers. Most apartment blocks have pools; duplexes generally do not.

Rents vary widely depending on amenities. There are two different rental scales in Freeport: employees of port licensees can rent "bonded" (no duty paid) apartments at the lower end of the scale. Visitors must rent duty-paid apartments, which sometimes include maid service, linen and cutlery, etc, at the higher end of the scale.

Efficiencies generally rent from $350-$440 per month; one bedroom, $350-$850; two bedrooms, $550-$1,650; three bedrooms, $750-$2,000 or more for bonded accommodation. A good three-bedroom house with garage and pool rents for $2,000 upwards, depending on location and amenities.

Building costs vary according to location and finish. A house with above-average finishes costs at least

$75 per sq ft to build. Office and industrial construction costs from $68 per sq ft, and steel-framed warehouses from $30-$38 per sq ft to build.

Rental prices have risen by about 10% in the past two years as a result of a housing shortage caused by an influx of investors and personnel attached to new companies setting up in Freeport.

See also **Housing.**

COURIER SERVICES
There are several courier services based in Freeport, including UPS (GWS), tel 352-3434; DHL, tel 352-6415; and Federal Express, tel 352-3402. It costs $10 to send a package weighing up to 1 lb to Nassau, $18 to Miami, and $18 to New York.

See also **Postal information.**

CRUISING
See **Bahamas information, Marinas & cruising facilities,** and this section, **Boating** and **Marinas & cruising facilities.**

CULTURAL ACTIVITIES
The Freeport Players' Guild (Kay Hardy, tel 373-8400) and the Grand Bahama Players (Delores Kellman, tel 373-3821) stage several plays throughout the year at the 450-seat Regency Theatre.

CUSTOMS
All persons entering Freeport/Lucaya, except Grand Bahama Port Authority Licensees, must adhere to Customs regulations as set in **Bahamas information, Customs.**

Licensees, however, have been granted certain duty exemptions on import and export of goods until the year 2054 under the Hawksbill Creek Agreement, which allows certain "supplies and manufacturing supplies" to be imported or purchased without payment of duty.

1. Supplies are defined as: all materials, supplies and things of every kind and description, equipment, building materials and supplies, factory plant and apparatus, replacement parts, spare parts, machine and hand tools, contractor's plant, vehicles to be used for the business purposes of a licensee only, vessels, petroleum products and nuclear fission products other than consumable stores.
2. Manufacturing supplies are defined as: all materials, supplies and things, whether raw, partly processed or processed, or any combination thereof of every kind and description, other than consumable stores, imported for the purpose of any manufacturing, industrial or other business, undertaking or enterprise within the Freeport area.
3. Consumable stores are defined as: any article imported for personal use or made available after its importation for personal use either by sale or gift. Also, any article imported into the Freeport area and subsequently exported from the Port Area to any other part of the Commonwealth, and any article assembled, processed or manufactured within the Freeport area and subsequently exported to any other part of The Bahamas, except pine lumber products or pine timber processed within the Freeport area.

The provisions of the Hawksbill Creek Agreement also permit licensees to erect or purchase one private residence, duty free, for the personal use and occupation of:

1. A licensee and his family.
2. A bona fide employee of a licensee and that employee's family.

Duty-free contents of the residence include: cooking range or stove, dishwasher, refrigerator, vacuum cleaner, washing machine and drier, non-portable TV sets, non-portable radios and record players, all permanent fixtures in the house, curtains, lamps and lampshades, carpets and pictures.

Conditions for obtaining Customs exemptions

The Hawksbill Creek Agreement places full responsibility upon each licensee to ensure duty-free materials are used only for the prescribed purposes within the Freeport area, since it is the use of goods exclusively in the licensee's business that generates the duty exemptions conferred by the Agreement. Consequently, the licensee must either own the goods himself or be in such a close relationship with the true owner (eg as hirer or fully responsible agent for an absent owner) as to be able to exercise full and effective control of the subsequent use of the goods.

The Agreement says there are only three incidences when a licensee may claim duty-free privileges for his goods:
1. When the goods are imported into the Freeport area.
2. When the goods are taken out of a Customs-bonded warehouse in The Bahamas.
3. When the goods are purchased in The Bahamas, duty having been paid and the licensee is claiming a refund of such duty.

When a licensee wishes to claim Customs duty exemption on any goods at these points, he must first enter the goods on a Conditionally Free Entry form. On this form, the licensee declares that the goods are intended to be used solely as supplies or manufacturing supplies within the Freeport area. It is a criminal offence to make a false declaration.

In addition to this declaration, the value of the imported goods and the rates of duty to which they would be liable must be declared. Where applicable, evidence of freight and insurance should be attached. Original invoices, copy bills of lading and packing lists should be submitted with the entry. To facilitate the calculation of varying rates of duty and to ensure importers obtain any refund to which they are entitled, original invoices must in all cases show unit prices.

Licensee's bond

Licensees are required to enter a legally binding bond to pay double duty to the government on any goods admitted duty free which are subsequently used or applied to any purpose other than those permitted under the Hawksbill Creek Agreement.

Customs authorities may require licensees to provide a surety for the bond. Although the bond is a continuing obligation, the licensee is released from it on specific goods when satisfactory evidence can be produced that:
1. He has paid the proper duty.
2. The goods no longer exist (he must produce a destruction certificate).
3. The goods have been exported to foreign parts from The Bahamas either in their original state or in a different state resulting from manufacturing, processing or assembly in the Freeport area.
4. The goods have been transferred to the bond of another licensee.

Further information on Freeport Customs regulations can be found in the *Guide to Customs Duties Exemptions and Procedures in Freeport, Grand Bahama Island, under the Hawksbill Creek Agreement*, published jointly by the Ministry of Finance and the Grand Bahama Port Authority (GBPA).

See also **Hawksbill Creek Agreement.**

DEFENCE FORCE
See **Bahamas information, Royal Bahamas Defence Force.**

DENTISTS

Dr Catherine Adderley-Stanley,
Eight Mile Rock Clinic 348-2227/8
Dr Kenneth Alleyne,
Regent Centre 352-4191
Dr Larry Bain, Insurance
Management Bldg 352-8492
Dr Edward L Colson,
Sunrise Medical Centre 373-3333
Jeanette Gardiner-Green (dental
hygienist, c/o Dr Bain) 352-8492
Dr Sonia Guerrero,
Hawksbill Clinic 352-7722
Dr Kendal Major (periodontist c/o
Dr Larry Bain), first Fri and Sat
of the month 352-8492
Dr Leatendore Percentie,
Sunrise Medical Centre 373-3333
(emergency 352-7469)
Dr Hayward E Romer, Bloneva Bldg,
The Mall 352-4082
Dr Barry Russell (orthodontist, monthly,
c/o Dr Larry Bain), every fourth Fri
and Sat 352-8492
Dr Erskine Smith (periodontist c/o
Dr Percentie) Wed and
Thur..................................373-3333
Dr Woodley Thompson (orthodontist
c/o Dr Romer) one day every
two weeks 352-4082

Freeport Dental Centre (an affiliate of Dent-Plan Ltd). This centre uses the Health Maintenance Organization (HMO) concept as a means of providing Bahamians with affordable dental care.

Contributions are received by salary deduction. The centre has the only Panarex scanner in The Bahamas. Two dentists and a dental hygienist are available. Pioneer's Professional Bldg, Pioneer's Way. Tel 352-4552.

DEPARTURE TAX
Air
A $15 tax must be paid in cash by every traveller six years and over upon leaving The Bahamas. It is collected at check-in counters. There is an additional $3 security fee for non-Bahamian passengers.

Sea
Departure tax for ship passengers is built into the fare. The fee is $15 per passenger on ships remaining in The Bahamas for more than a day. For one-day excursion passengers, it is $13. Children under six years are exempt.

There is also a $7 ticket tax on the price of each airline or cruise ship ticket purchased in The Bahamas. This is included in the price of the ticket and should not be confused with the departure tax.

DIVING & SNORKELLING
Grand Bahama is renowned as a first-class diving and snorkelling destination with thriving, healthy reefs, blue holes, wrecks, caves, walls and drop-offs.

The world-famous Underwater Explorers Society (UNEXSO) at Port Lucaya Marketplace offers dive training with highly-qualified instructors, night dives, shark dives, a dolphin encounter programme and more. It also has a photo/video facility.

A number of full service diving operations throughout Freeport/Lucaya offer instruction at all levels; guided tours (shark, wreck, reef and night dives); underwater videos and diving equipment sales, rental and repair. All staff are professionally trained.

Dive and snorkelling companies
Caribbean Divers 373-9111
Grand Bahama Scuba 373-4661
Paradise Watersports 352-2887
Pat & Diane Snorkelling 373-8681
Sunn Odyssey Divers' Club 373-4014
Underwater Explorers Society
(UNEXSO) 373-1244
Xanadu Undersea
Adventures 352-3811
See also **Bahamas information, Sports.**

DIVORCE
See **Bahamas information, Divorce.**

DOCTORS
Medical officers
Eight Mile Rock,
  Dr M Kavala 348-2227/8
Freeport, see **Hospitals & clinics.**
Hawksbill, Dr J Ebarle 352-7722
High Rock, Dr K Gutam 353-5600
West End, Dr R Fernandez 346-6464

DRIVER'S LICENCE & VEHICLE INFORMATION
Driver's and motor vehicle licences can be obtained from the Road Traffic Dept, National Insurance Bldg, Freeport. Cars must be inspected for roadworthiness at Workers House, Settler's Way.

EDUCATION
PRESCHOOL & KINDERGARTEN
Central Church of God, Coral Rd. Two qualified teachers, 49 children 2-5 yrs. 9am-2pm. $20 per week plus $5 for collecting and returning children. After school programme 2-6 yrs, $10 per week. Principal, Mrs Russell. PO Box F-41519, tel 373-5355.
Freeport Nursery School and Play Group (Calvary Academy), Kinglake Lane. Three terms, Sept through June. Four qualified teachers, 102 children. Day care, six weeks to 1½ yrs, 7:30am-6pm. Nursery, 2½-3½yrs, $335 per term. Children's group, 3½-6 yrs, $350 per term, 7 yrs, $375 per term. 8:45am-2:30pm. After-school care, $50 per term, 2:30-5:30pm. Operated by Calvary Temple. Apply to Principal, Rev Sobig Kemp, PO Box F-41576, tel 352-5490.
St John's Kindergarten, Ponce de Leon & Coral Rd. Five Christian-trained teachers, up to 100 children 2-5 yrs. $80 per month, transport $20 per month. Principal, Mrs Cooper. PO Box F-40176, tel 352-2276.

PRIMARY
Discovery Primary School, Beach Way Dr. Anglican prep school (with kindergarten), for Freeport High School. 19 teachers, one aide, 280 pupils. Three terms, $660 per term, plus $75 for text books. Principal, Marlene Smith, PO Box F-40667, tel 373-4391.
Hugh Campbell Primary School, Mahogany St. Govt operated. 843 pupils 4-12 yrs, also preschool for 4-yr-olds. 32 teachers. 27 classrooms, plus computer and science lab, arts and crafts rooms. Tuition free. Principal, Mrs McCartney, PO Box F-44129, tel 351-6990.
Mary Star of the Sea School, Sunrise Hwy. Roman Catholic. Kindergarten to 6th grade, 582 pupils, one Franciscan sister, 35 lay teachers, 5 aides. Three terms, $500 per term plus $60 per year registration. Headmistress, Beatrice Ferguson, PO Box F-42418, tel 373-3456.
St Vincent de Paul, Hunter's. Roman Catholic. Kindergarten to 6th grade, 179 pupils, 12 teachers. Registration $20, tuition $412 per term, books $40, insurance $15. 8:25am-2:55pm. Uniforms. Headmistress, Dorothy Lewis, PO Box F-42517, tel 353-7727.
Walter Parker Primary School, Beachway Dr. Govt operated. 31 teachers, 969 pupils 5-11+ yrs. Music, PE rooms and library. Tuition free. Principal, Ross Smith. PO Box F-42542, tel 373-5129.

PRIMARY & SECONDARY
St Paul's Methodist College, Clive Ave. Administered by the board of the Methodist Church in the Caribbean and the Americas (MCCA) board of trustees. 405 pupils 3-16 yrs, 30 teachers. Infant dept, reception, Kindergarten, $500 per term; Junior dept, grades 1-6, $560 per term; Junior and senior high, grades 7-12, $635 per term; 10% discount for children other than oldest in school from one family. Registration, $20. Uniforms same as Queen's College, Nassau. SAT, Advance Placement and BGCSE. Principal, Mrs Glinton, PO Box F-40897, tel 352-6225.
Sunland Lutheran School, Gambier Dr. 600 pupils from nursery to grade 12. 36 teachers. Nursery (3 yrs) and

Kindergarten (4 yrs), $650; grades 1-12, $700. Registration, $100. Includes textbooks up to and including grade 9. Headmistress, Myrton King; vice-principal, Della Thomas. PO Box F-42469, tel 373-3700/1.
Tabernacle Baptist Christian Academy, 7 Settlers Way. Pre-school through grade 12. 500 pupils, 30 teachers. Fees per term: kindergarten, $335; grades 1-6, $365; grades 7-9, $390; grades 10-12, $420. Principal Norris Bain, PO Box F-42705, tel 352-9556.

SECONDARY
Freeport High School, East Sunrise Hwy. Administered by the Anglican Diocese of The Bahamas. 480 pupils 11-19 yrs, 36 teachers. Registration, $50 per year, tuition $715 per term, 5% deduction per term for second child. Non-refundable seat fee of $50. Books cost an additional $200-$300. BGCSE, Pitman and American College Board exams. Uniforms. Principal, Marlene Smith, PO Box F-40667, tel 373-3579.
Grand Bahama Catholic High School, East Settler's Way. Roman Catholic. 400 pupils, grades 7-12, 26 teachers. Two semesters. BJC, BGCSE, PSAT, Pitman, RSA, SAT, ACT exams. $640 per term. Uniforms. Principal, Daisy McPhee, PO Box F-42635, tel 352-2544.
St Georges' High School (formerly Goombay Land High School), Alcester Rd. Govt operated. 1,322 pupils 11-16 yrs in 30 classes, 85 teachers. BJC, BGCSE, Pitman, RSA plus technical and vocational courses. Tuition free. Uniforms. Principal, Mary Cooper, PO Box F-40787, tel 352-7373.
Jack Hayward High School (formerly Pioneers Loop High School), Pioneers Rd. Govt operated. 1,250 pupils 11-18 yrs, 90 teachers. BJC, BGCSE, Pitman. Uniforms. Tuition free. Principal, Hezekiah Dean, PO Box F-41314, tel 373-8750.

TERTIARY EDUCATION
Bahamas Hotel Training College, Grand Bahama Trade School Bldg. Diploma in hospitality operations, apprentice chef, culinary skills, front office, housekeeping, management certificate, industry training and adult education programmes. Full-time and part-time courses. Eight full-time and 5 part-time instructors. Chief Training Officer, Ellen Romer. PO Box F-41679, tel 352-2896. E-mail: bhtc@batelnet.bs
Bahamas Technical and Vocational Institute (formerly ITC), GB Trade School Bldg, West Settler's Way. One-year programmes from Sept-July. Evening classes in carpentry, electrical installation, electronics, office technology, plumbing and welding, auto mechanics, hair dressing, cosmetology, computer operations and a/c and refrigeration. Day classes in cosmetology and office technology. There are 9 full-time programmes. Registration fee, $75, books and tools not included. Tuition free. Short general interest courses on demand, fee $150, subject to change. Coordinator Samuel Rigby, PO Box F-40477, tel 352-2190.
College of The Bahamas, GB Trade School Bldg, West Settler's Way. Eight full-time lecturers and 14 part-time teachers. Fees $50 per credit, 3 credits per course. Associate degrees in banking and finance, accounting, management and economics and computer data processing. There is a part-time course for a Bachelor's Degree in accounting and management. Qualified teachers may work toward the Diploma in Education. Evening classes include fashion design, electrical, plumbing, vehicle maintenance, conversational Spanish, French and Creole. Two-hour lectures throughout the day, 8am-12 noon and 4-6pm. Evening classes, 6-10pm. Provost, Sylvia Darling, PO Box F-42766, tel 352-9761.
First Providence Community College and Seminary, Settler's Way. Day and evening classes in secretarial, business and accounting, computers, finance,

psychology and communications.
Fees $150 per subject per term.
PO Box F-44127, tel 351-6764.

SPECIAL EDUCATION
Beacon School for Special Education (formerly Catherine Basie School for Exceptional Children). Dedicated to the memory of Diana, Princess of Wales, this school has been rebuilt with equal funding from Lady Henrietta St George and the government. 80 students, non-residential. Principal, Miriam Sweeting. PO Box F-40032, tel 352-8445.

Grand Bahama Centre for the Deaf and **Unit for the Blind,** Jobson Ave. Six teachers, 20 students. Govt operated, non-residential. Principal, Cheryl Woods. PO Box F-42595, tel 352-2107.

ELECTRICITY

Electricity is generated by Freeport Power Co Ltd at the Peel St generating plant. Freeport Power is jointly owned by the Grand Bahama Port Authority and Southern Electric Inc. Facilities consist of an 18,000 kilowatt diesel plant, two gas turbines totalling 35,000 kilowatts and a 75,000 kilowatt steam plant. Total installed generating capacity is 128,000 kilowatts.

Total net MWh generated by Freeport Power Co
1993 260,784
1994 279,552
1995 284,499
1996 309,861
1997 299,247

Total average active meters
1993 14,108
1994 14,479
1995 14,434
1996 14,832
1997 15,135

Supply voltage and frequency
3 phase, 4 wire, 208/120 volts, 60 cycles
3 phase, 4 wire, 240/120 volts, 60 cycles
1 phase, 3 wire, 240/120 volts, 60 cycles
1 phase, 3 wire, 208/120 volts, 60 cycles
3 phase, 4 wire, 480/277 volts, 60 cycles
All the above depend on location.

Tariffs
Principal rates are:
  1. **Residential (monthly)**
  First 350 kWh, 12.5¢/kWh
  Next 450 kWh, 14.54¢/kWh
  Additional kWh, 17¢/kWh
  Min charge, $10/month
  2. **Temporary service (TS)**
  All kWh, 17¢/kWh
  Min charge, $10/month
  Meter rental, $10/month
  3. **Commercial service (CS)**
  All kWh, 14¢/kWh
  First 5 kVA (kilovolt ampere) or less, $30
  Additional kVA, $6/kVA/month
  Min charge, same as demand charge
  4. **General service (GS)**
  First 100,000 kWh, 12.8¢/kWh
  Additional kWh, 12¢/kWh
  First 30 kVA or less, $180/month
  Additional kVA, $6/kVA/month
  Min charge, same as demand charge.
  5. **GS Large (GSL)**
  First 100,000 kWh, 11.04¢/kWh
  Next 400,000 kWh, 10.8¢/kWh
  Additional kWh, 10¢/kWh
  First 1,000 kVA or less, $46/month
  Additional kVA, $6/kVA/month
  Min charge, same as demand charge
  6. **Reconnection for non-payment** $25

Freeport Power provides electricity services to the entire Grand Bahama community from West End in the west to McLean's Town in the east, and to the offshore communities of Deep Water Cay and Sweeting's Cay.

Freeport Power has a substation on Fishing Hole Rd. Equipped with state-of-the-art components, this station serves the Freeport Container Port, Bahama Rock Ltd and CONCEM.

EMERGENCY NUMBERS
Ambulance 352-2689

Bahamas Air Sea Rescue Assoc
 (BASRA) ...... 352-2628 or 352-2880
Fire brigade .... 352-8888 or 919
Police 919
Rand Memorial Hospital 352-6735
Water company 352-6300
Grand Bahama Island
 Tourism Board 352-8044/5
Embassies (All in Nassau)
British High
 Commission .... (242) 325-7471 (to 3)
Canadian Consulate .... (242) 393-2123/4
US Embassy .... (242) 322-1183
Credit card companies
American Express
 Cards 1-800-327-1267
 Travellers Cheques 1-800-221-7282
Citibank Visa/MasterCard
 (call collect) .... (605) 335-2222
Royal Bank Visa 1-800-847-3911
 See also **Ambulance/air ambulance services.**

EMPLOYERS' ORGANIZATIONS
Employers' interests are generally looked after by the Grand Bahama Chamber of Commerce, although there is also a Grand Bahama Hotel Assoc and Freeport Hotel Restaurant Employers' Assoc.
 See also **Chamber of Commerce.**

ENCOURAGEMENT ACTS
As well as absence of taxes, other enticements for investors to do business in The Bahamas include the Caribbean Basin Initiative (CBI), Industries Encouragement Act, Hotels Encouragement Act, Lomé Convention and the Agricultural Manufacturers Act (see **Bahamas information, Agriculture**). For information on initiatives, see relevant headings in **Bahamas information.**
 Licensees of the 230 sq mile Grand Bahama Port Authority (GBPA) area gain an extra bonus over the rest of The Bahamas: until Aug 2054 at the earliest, they do not pay excise or import duties on materials or equipment used by their businesses. Nor, until Aug 2015, will businesses under the Liquor Licences Act, the Shop Licences Act or the Road Traffic Act pay a business licence fee. Also until Aug 2015, non-Bahamian owners of Freeport/Lucaya property are exempt from paying real property tax.
 See also **Customs** and **Hawksbill Creek Agreement.**

ENGINEERS
See **Building Contractors & Engineers.**

ENTERTAINMENT
The Princess Casino is one of the largest casinos in the western hemisphere. Slot machines are open from 9am and gaming tables from 12 noon until the early hours. There is a floor show twice nightly and two first-class restaurants.
 A new 30,000 sq ft casino is planned as part of The Lucayan resort, scheduled to open before the new millennium.
 There are several nightclubs and discos on the island, including Club 69 and Jokers Wild Supper & Show Club on Midshipman Rd. Other night spots include Captain Kenny's in the Intl Bazaar, Port Lucaya Yacht Club, Count Basie Square in Port Lucaya, the Bahama Mama Lounge in Port Lucaya, Islander's Roost near Ranfurly Circus and Yellow Bird Club in the Intl Bazaar.
 See also **Gambling.**

EXCHANGE CONTROL
Regulations apply as in Nassau. The Central Bank's Exchange Control office is on the first floor of the Regent Centre West. PO Box F-41666, tel 352-5963.
 See **Bahamas information, Exchange Control.**

EXPORT ENTRY

An Export entry form is required for all goods exported by ship or air freight. It is advisable to export goods through a freight service that will supply forms and deal with Customs.

Ordinary parcels such as clothing and gifts sent through the post office at Explorer's Way do not pay the $10 stamp tax and do not require an export entry form, but must have a post office-issued label giving weight and value of contents.

Customs brokers

Darvikson Bahamas Ltd 352-7821
Expert Customs Brokers 352-7494
Freeport Transfer 352-7821
General Shipping, Trading
   & Storage 352-3311
Hunt's Import/Export 352-8301
Lucaya Shipping &
   Trading Co Ltd 352-3581
Swann's Shipping..................352-7705
Tanja Enterprises Co Ltd 352-2328
Taylor & Taylor Ltd 352-7250
United Shipping Co Ltd 352-9315
Wide World Forwarding........352-3636

See also **Bahamas information, Export entry** and **Customs.**

FIRE BRIGADE

Stationed just outside city limits, the Grand Bahama Fire Brigade has four large fire trucks and is manned by 30 firefighters. To report a fire, call 919. For permission to start a controlled bonfire, tel 352-8441.

FISHING

Gamefish found in Grand Bahama waters include sailfish, blue marlin, dolphin, kingfish and wahoo. Records locally include a 122 lb wahoo caught on 80 lb test line by Peter Rose. A 25½ lb cobia (rarely seen here) has been caught on 16 lb test line, and Ralph Eickelbeck caught a yellowfin tuna weighing 47 lbs on 8 lb test line. Bunny Louis took a 56 lb yellowfin tuna on 12 lb test line. Mary-Ellen Spiker holds the record for wahoo, 89.2 lbs on 30 lb test line.

In 1985, Margaret Hall set a world record by catching a 61 lb wahoo on 16 lb test line, but this record was broken in another country in '96. Lydia Blaser holds the local record for kingfish (72 lbs), and sailfish (71 lbs) on 30 lb test line. The unconfirmed 1932 record for barracuda (103 lbs 4 oz) caught off West End by C E Benet still stands.

Three world records were achieved by Colin Rose in 1996. On April 14 he caught a skipjack tuna of 21.9 lbs on 4 lb test line. On July 17 he took a 9.8 lb horse-eye jack on 2 lb test line, and on Nov 20 he caught a 6 lb 8 oz horse-eye jack on a 6 lb tippet.

In 1997, his brother Peter Rose made a new world record by catching a 46 lb 11 oz dophin on an 8 lb tippet.

A blue marlin was caught on 30 lb test line with an international reel in 1990.

Commercial fishing

In 1997, commercial fishermen in Grand Bahama caught 1,817,310 lbs of fish, with a total value of $8,773,227. The largest catches were crawfish tails, 599,791 lbs; conch, 290,716 lbs; Nassau grouper, 319,149 lbs; and snapper, 283,037 lbs.

For fishing regulations, see **Bahamas information, Fishing.**

FREIGHT SERVICES

Freight may be shipped to and from Freeport/Lucaya by sea or air. Scheduled airlines provide regular freight service and Convair cargo service, which flies Tues-Fri, is operated by Wide World Forwarding.

From Miami to Nassau to Freeport, there is a minimum charge of $45 per 100 lbs or less. However, in order to encourage the Grand Bahama export market, Wide World Forwarding charges $30 for the same weight, adding 36¢ per lb up to 1,000 lbs and 34¢ per lb over 1,000 lbs. From Miami to Freeport the minimum charge is $45 up to 1,000 lbs and 34¢ per lb for 1,001 lbs and over. Ocean freight rate for a 20 ft container is $900 plus insurance and for a 40 ft container, $1,400 plus insurance.

Five shipping lines provide freight service between Freeport and Florida. Crowley American and Savoy Shipping sail three times a week from Port Everglades; Seaboard Marine sails four times a week from Miami to Freeport; and Tropical Shipping, four times a week from Riviera Beach. Bahmar arrives twice a week via Nassau. Major container companies serving Grand Bahama are Maersk/Sealand, CMA, Navieras/NPR, Cagema and Mediterranean Shipping Co. A container service to England takes two to three weeks to deliver. Cost of shipping depends on the commodity and weight.

Now that Freeport Harbour's entrance channel has been widened to 500 ft and dredged to a depth of 47 ft, it can accommodate the largest container ships in the world.

Persons moving to The Bahamas are advised to contact a reputable international van line which can offer complete door-to-door service from point-of-origin to island residence. There is paperwork involved and Customs procedures that must be followed. Van lines and their agents in Freeport provide this service. Original copies of all invoices and other documents must accompany goods or be sent on ahead. Clearance and delivery take at least 24-36 hours.

Household and personal belongings coming to Freeport must be inspected by Customs. This could take one to two days. Freeport agents ship door-to-door anywhere in the world.

See also **Shipping agents.**

GAMBLING
Casino gambling is legal in The Bahamas for non-residents 18 yrs and older. There is presently one casino in Freeport, the Princess Casino operated by Princess Casinos Ltd, a subsidiary of Princess Properties Intl. It offers a full service Las Vegas-style Sports Book. Patrons wager on sporting games or events including football, basketball, hockey, golf, tennis and boxing. Wagering options include straight bets, parlays, teasers, moneylines, runlines, round robins and propositions.

The Lucayan Beach Resort and Casino was bought in mid-1997 by a subsidiary of the Hong Kong conglomerate, Hutchison Whampoa Ltd. At press time, the casino was closed, but was to be reconstructed as part of The Lucayan resort.

See also **Entertainment.**

GEOGRAPHY
Grand Bahama covers an area of 530 sq miles. The highest point is 68ft.

See also **Bahamas information, Geography.**

GOLF COURSES
There are three 18-hole championship golf courses operating in Freeport/ Lucaya: Emerald and Ruby golf courses at the Bahamas Princess Resort & Casino, and Lucayan Country Club. Bahama Reef, another 18-hole course, was to be redesigned by Robert Trent Jones Jr over 1998 and '99 and reopened as The Reef as part of The Lucayan resort development.

Fortune Hills Golf & Country Club operates a nine-hole course. At West End, a 27-hole course is temporarily closed. Numerous local, inter-island and international tournaments are held at the various courses throughout the year.

See **Bahamas information, Sports,** and, this section, **Sports venues.**

GOVERNMENT OFFICES
Following is a list of government offices in Grand Bahama:

Ministry of Agriculture & Fisheries
Produce Exchange, West Mall
PO Box F-40006
Tel 352-2144, fax 352-4935

Office of the Attorney-General
Garnet Levarity Justice Centre
PO Box F-42218
Tel 351-5785, fax 352-7896

Dept of the Auditor General
National Insurance Bldg
PO Box F-40182
Tel 352-2355, fax 351-6159

Bahamas Information Services
Caraway Bldg, W Atlantic Dr
PO Box F-40001
Tel 352-9424, fax 352-8520

Bahamas Investment Authority
Caraway Bldg, W Atlantic Dr
PO Box F-40001
Tel 352-8525, fax 352-8520

Bahamas Mortgage Corp
Intl Bldg, Suite 4
PO Box F-42605
Tel 352-7513/4, fax 352-6478

Bahamas Telecommunications Corp
(BaTelCo)
Kipling Bldg, 2C
PO Box F-42483
Tel 352-9352 or 352-6731, fax 352-4708

Central Bank of The Bahamas
Exchange Control Dept
Regent Centre West, Suites B & C
PO Box F-42521
Tel 352-5963, fax 352-5397

College of The Bahamas
West Settler's Way
PO Box F-42766
Tel 352-9761, tel/fax 352-9671

Commissioner's Office
Caraway Bldg, W Atlantic Dr
PO Box F-40001
Tel 352-6332, fax 352-9027

Customs Dept
Administrative Office
National Insurance Bldg
PO Box F-42484
Tel 352-7361, fax 351-4339

Ministry of Education
Kipling Bldg, Suite 30C
PO Box F-42595
Tel 352-9688, fax 351-4028

Ministry of Finance & Planning
Bain Bldg, W Atlantic Dr
PO Box F-42521
Tel 352-5963, fax 352-5397

Gaming Board
Intl Bldg, 3rd floor
PO Box F-42313
Tel 352-9007, fax 352-6507

Ministry of Health
Kipling Bldg, 5D
PO Box F-40680
Tel 352-5074, fax 352-4358

Dept of Immigration
Churchill Bldg
PO Box F-40062
Tel 352-9338, fax 352-5275

Dept of Labour
Churchill Bldg
PO Box F-40589
Tel 352-7865/6, fax 352-9869

Dept of Local Govt
Caraway Bldg, W Atlantic Dr
PO Box F-40001
Tel 352-6332, fax 352-9027

Minister of State for the Public Service
Churchill Bldg
PO Box F-40001
Tel 352-7529, fax 352-9716

National Insurance Board
National Insurance Bldg
PO Box F-42618
Tel 352-7222/3, fax 352-6143

Passport Office
National Insurance Bldg
PO Box F-43536
Tel 352-5698, fax 352-5672

Police Dept
Intl Bldg
PO Box F-40082
Tel 352-8352

Port Dept
(Registration of motor boats, tugs, etc)
National Insurance Bldg
PO Box F-42044
Tel 352-9163, fax 351-4538

Post Office Dept
Explorer's Way
PO Box F-40000
Tel 352-9371, fax 352-6170

Office of The Prime Minister
Caraway Bldg, W Atlantic Dr
PO Box F-40001
Tel 352-8525, fax 352-8520

Ministry of Public Works
National Insurance Bldg
PO Box F-40530
Tel 352-2478, fax 352-9160

Registrar General's Dept
Regent Centre, 16/17
PO Box F-42602
Tel 352-4934, fax 352-4060

Probation Division
Dept of Rehabilitative Welfare Services
National Insurance Bldg
PO Box F-41599
Tel 351-7357, fax 351-6216

Dept of Housing
Ministry of Social Development
National Insurance Bldg
PO Box F-40997
Tel 352-3630, fax 352-9244

Dept of Statistics
National Insurance Bldg
PO Box F-40680
Tel 352-7196, fax 352-2930

Supreme & Magistrates Courts
Garnet Levarity Justice Centre
PO Box F-40174
Tel 352-6806, fax 352-2984

Ministry of Tourism
Intl Bazaar (above China Temple)
PO Box F-40251
Tel 352-8044, fax 352-2714 or 352-7840

Ministry of Transport
Road Traffic Dept
National Insurance Bldg
PO Box F-40338
Tel 352-7204/5, fax 352-4874

Treasury Dept
National Insurance Bldg
PO Box F-42485
Tel 352-2351, fax 352-2145

Ministry of Youth, Sports & Culture
National Insurance Bldg
PO Box F-41599
Tel 352-7335, fax 352-8464

See also **Government.**

GRAND BAHAMA HUMANE SOCIETY

Just off Queen's Hwy on Cedar St, this organization is operated by two full-time and seven part-time volunteers, a kennel-man and a dog-catcher. Strays are given necessary medication and housed in kennels – 16 for dogs and 10 for cats. If unclaimed, the animals are put up for adoption. Tel 352-2477.

See also **Bahamas information, Animals** and **Bahamas Humane Society.**

GUN PERMITS

Applications for gun licences should be made to CID, Peel St, tel 352-9774. A shotgun licence costs $50, and a rifle licence is $100. A separate application must be made for each gun. Presentation of the gun licence and payment of duty, if an import, will bring the gun into possession.

See also **Bahamas information, Gun permits.**

HARBOUR CONTROL

Freeport Harbour Control gives clearance to all ships leaving and entering Freeport Harbour. Permission must be obtained from Harbour Control (open 24 hours) for movement from one berth to another within the harbour. Operators of small fishing boats and small pleasure craft should contact Harbour Control before departing the harbour so their whereabouts can be ascertained if overdue. Tel 352-9651.

Harbour Control's VHF radio frequency is Channel 16 (156.80 Mc s), after which further directions as to frequency are given from a choice of 12, 14, 20, 65, 66, 68, 73, 74, 79. AM radio ship-to-ship frequencies are 2182, 2638 and 2670 kHz.

The international emergency frequency, 2182 kHz, is controlled by Bahamas Telecommunications Corp (BaTelCo). For commercial traffic, AM frequency 2198 kHz should be used. Single sideband frequencies are 3300.0, 4139.5, 5057.0, 8100.0.

MARISAT (the Marine Satellite System) enables the placing of overseas telephone and telex calls to ships at sea throughout the world via Atlantic or Pacific satellites. Dial "0" for the marine operator, who will book calls via a Marisat operator. No collect or credit card charges are accepted for this service. Freeport residents may use an improved VHF-FM radio telephone service to ships at sea through the Eight Mile Rock marine operator.

The entrance to Freeport Harbour is through a straight channel 1,800 ft long. The channel has been widened to 500 ft and dredged to a depth of 47 ft (51 ft alongside) to accommodate the world's largest container ships. The average range of tide in Freeport is 3 ft.

See also **Boating** and **Marinas & cruising facilities.**

HAWKSBILL CREEK AGREEMENT

The Hawksbill Creek Agreement, essentially a contract between The Bahamas government and Freeport businesses licensed by the Grand Bahama Port Authority (GBPA), was the foundation stone of Freeport/Lucaya. Under the Agreement signed in 1955, the government granted the GBPA 50,000 acres of unused Crown Land to be developed as an international port. Later, the Port Authority obtained additional land from the Crown and from private sources, for a total holding of 149,000 acres, or 233 sq mi.

To encourage business development on this land, the government granted further concessions to the Port Authority and its licensees to apply only to the Freeport area. Principal concessions were:

1. Freedom from taxation – there was a contractual guarantee that at least until 1990, there would be no personal income taxes, no corporate profit taxes, no capital gains taxes or levies on capital appreciation and no personal or real property or inventory taxes. A two-year extension was granted, then a one-year extension. From Aug 4, 1993, the exemptions – which include real property tax on non-Bahamian owners of Freeport/Lucaya property – were extended 22 yrs to 2015 "notwithstanding anything to the contrary in any other law." See also **Bahamas information, Property tax.** Persons or companies carrying on business in the Port Area under the Road Traffic Act, Liquor Licences Act or Shop Licences Act are exempt from the Bahamian business licence fee until Aug 4, 2015.

2. Freedom from Customs duties – at least until Aug 2054, no excise or import duties will be levied on equipment or materials used by licensees. Only goods for personal use or consumption are dutiable.

Persons interested in starting a business in Freeport/Lucaya should acquaint themselves with the Hawksbill Creek Agreement and other encouragement acts. See also **Encouragement acts.**

The port area covers about one-third of the island, and should be checked with a map by drivers of bonded cars which cannot be driven outside the area without incurring penalties, eg, Eight Mile Rock is outside the area.
See also **Customs** and **History.**

HEALTH/MEDICAL SERVICES
See **Ambulance/air ambulance services; Dentists; Doctors;** and **Hospitals & clinics.**

HISTORY
Remains and artefacts found in Grand Bahama provide evidence that Lucayan tribes lived here until the time of the Spanish conquerors. The island was probably deserted for some time thereafter.

During the late 18th century, a few settlements grew up as people drifted over from other islands. West End had spurts of activity (due to its proximity to the Florida coast) as a haven for gun-runners during the American Revolution and rum-runners during Prohibition.

Three big finds of treasure from sunken galleons have been made off the Grand Bahama coast since 1964, including the salvaging of the *Nuestra Señora de las Maravillas.*

It is only in the last quarter-century that the island has been fully developed. With a population of about 4,000 in the 1950s, it has risen to over 41,000 in the '90s, due entirely to the advent of American-born Wallace Groves and his Abaco Lumber Co. While cutting the island's crop of Caribbean pine, Groves devised a plan for making a huge free port and industrial centre in the midst of the scrub and swamp around Hawksbill Creek.

Groves started the Grand Bahama Port Authority (GBPA) with a grant of 50,000 acres of land, which was eventually increased to 149,000 acres from the Bahamian government. In return, the GBPA built houses, churches, schools and roads under the terms of the Hawksbill Creek Agreement. A deepwater harbour was dredged for oil tankers and an oil refinery was erected. An airport, hotels and casinos were also added. By 1966, there were 214 miles of paved roads, hundreds of buildings and areas set apart for shops and light and heavy industry. Hotels, golf courses, beaches and marinas were soon to make it a tourist haven.

In 1993, Southern Electric Intl, from Georgia, became a 50/50 partner with the Freeport Power Co, resulting in the provision of electric power to the outlying parts of the island. In 1995, the largest container company in the world, Hutchison Port Holdings Ltd, became an equal partner with the GBPA. A contract was signed to build a massive container transshipment port, which opened up enormous potential for Freeport. In 1998 another subsidiary, Hutchison Lucaya Ltd, embarked on construction of a giant hotel complex in Lucaya. See also **Bahamas information, History,** and, this section, **Hawksbill Creek Agreement.**

HOSPITALS & CLINICS
Rand Memorial Hospital, East Atlantic Dr. Govt owned, 82-bed community-type hospital. Departments: medical, surgical, gynaecology and obstetrics, paediatrics, accident and emergency, psychiatry, pathology, clinical laboratories, physiotherapy, general practice clinics and radiology. Staff: 34 doctors. Associates include four district medical officers, two dentists and a school health officer. Admission deposit $50. Administrator: Catherine Weech. Tel 352-6735.
Sunrise Medical Centre, East Sunrise

Hwy, is the oldest medical facility on the island. Team of physicians, dentist and other allied healthcare professionals offering medical, surgical, pediatrics, obstetric and gynaecology services in a six bed in-patient facility, as well as a walk-in clinic. The centre is presently being upgraded with state-of-the-art equipment such as MRI and Cat-Scan, plus a cardiology and ICU unit. The second and third phases of development will take the centre to full hospital status and will include an ambulatory centre. The centre operates a walk-in clinic weekdays 6-10:30pm, Sat 1-10:30 pm, Sun 8:30am-10:30pm. Administrative dept tel 373-3333 (to 6), fax 373-3342.

Lucayan Medical Centre West, Adventurers Way. Multispeciality ambulatory care clinic including diagnostic and ambulatory surgery facilities. 22 physicians provide care in family medicine, internal medicine, obstetrics and gynaecology, kidney diseases, ophthalmology, paediatric, psychiatry, podiatry, general surgery, orthopaedic surgery, ENT surgery, urology, dentistry and oral surgery, and the only renal dialysis unit on the island. Audiology and speech therapy specialists. Diagnostic facilities include x-ray and ultrasonography, laboratory and electrocardiography. Full service pharmacy 8:30am-5:30pm. Administrator, Dr Pamela Etuk. Tel 352-7288.

Lucayan Medical Centre East, East Sunrise Hwy. Multispeciality ambulatory care clinic with four physicians providing care in general/family medicine, internal medicine, psychiatry, obstetrics and gynaecology. Gynaecologist/obstetrician Dr Havard Cooper has an emergency number 352-6222 PIN 1133. Dental unit offers care in dentistry and oral-maxillo facial surgery. Walk-in clinic in evening hours daily 5:30-7pm except Sun. Full service pharmacy, x-ray and laboratory services. Administrator, Dr Pamela Etuk. Tel 373-7400.

Government clinics
Hawksbill, tel 352-7722; Eight Mile Rock, tel 348-2227; West End, tel 346-6463; McLean's Town, tel 353-7030; High Rock, tel 353-5600; and Sweeting's Cay, tel 353-2178. Govt clinics are served by doctors and nurses who provide medical services at minimal fees. There are three government dentists in Grand Bahama and a visiting dental surgeon.

Private care
ABC Holistic Health-World Clinic, Pioneers Way. Dr R Roop is a holistic physician. Tel 352-2222.
Acupuncture Health Centre, 4B Kipling Bldg. Allen Lok, acupuncturist. Specializing in spinal cord physiotherapy, nerve and muscle pain, nasal diseases, liver/kidney illness, asthma and insomnia. Thur and Sun, 7:45am-2pm. Tel 351-6112.
Immunology Research Centre (IAT) Bahamas, East Atlantic Dr. Cancer patients treated on out-patient basis. Three medical doctors. Tel 352-7455.
Nursing Agency, five private nurses for midwifery, special care and general nursing, also available for overseas travel. Contact Mrs McKay at 373-5497 or Mrs Iseard at 352-2940.

HOTELS
See **Bahamas information, Hotels,** and, this section, **Accommodations.**

HOUSING
At present, there is a shortage of rental accommodation on Grand Bahama, due to the influx of expatriate workers and executives, as well as Bahamians from other islands, relocating to set up new businesses. The Bahamas government promotes the development of low-cost housing in Freeport through a guaranteed mortgage financing programme granting purchasers long-term

financing (up to 30 years) at below-market interest rates to encourage low-income families to purchase homes. Finance Corp (FINCO), British American Bank, Bahamas Mortgage Corp and Commonwealth Bank participate in this programme. East Coral Estates has been developed and a second area is under development in Eight Mile Rock. Independent developers have built low-cost housing in other subdivisions, utilizing the government's guaranteed mortgage financing programme. Other areas include the Hawksbill City area, Arden Forest, Yeoman Wood and Grasmere. Middle-cost housing is available in Hudson Estate, Columbus Estate and the East and West sections.

Some of the more exciting upscale real estate developments are Oceanview Condominium on Lucaya Beach, Lucayan Marina Village, overlooking the marina or Bell Channel, The Village at Water's Edge, Puerto Alegre, Bell Channel Club and Marina, and Club Nautica Resort. The Princess Isle development offers half-acre to four-acre building lots on the ocean, or the canal.

See also **Cost of living.**

IMMIGRATION

To apply for immigration status specifically in Freeport/Lucaya, contact the Dept of Immigration, Churchill Bldg, PO Box F-40062, tel 352-9338. Inquiries may also be made at the Grand Bahama Port Authority (GBPA), tel 352-6611, PO Box F-42666, or any reliable real estate company, about the possibilities of permanent residency for serious investors. The procedure for applying for a work permit is the same as in Nassau. Freeport applications are dealt with regularly when the Immigration Board meets in Freeport.

See **Bahamas information, Immigration.**

IMPORT ENTRY

Regulations apply as in Nassau. The Central Bank's Exchange Control Office in Freeport is on the first floor of Regent Centre West, PO Box F-42521, Freeport, Grand Bahama, tel 352-5963.

See **Bahamas information, Import entry.**

INDUSTRY

Several large industries have been established in Freeport, attracted by tax advantages, a first-class infrastructure and availability of certain natural resources.

The first industry was established in 1958, a bunkering terminal that was absorbed in the late '60s by the **Bahamas Oil Refining Co (BORCO).** The huge oil refinery ceased processing crude oil in 1985 as a result of deteriorating refining economics in the Caribbean. BORCO concentrates presently on continuing terminal operations – transshipping, storing and blending of oil and bunkering of ships. Total oil imports for 1997 were 7,394,132 barrels of oil; exports were 4,840,234 barrels. BORCO has 107 employees.

Bradford Grand Bahama Inc is constructing a luxury yacht repair facility, which will provide a full range of services to all types of commercial and private vessels up to 250 ft. At press time, it was anticipated that the office, docks, boat houses and service stores would be in place by mid-1999.

South Riding Point Holding Ltd. An $80 million transshipment terminal, with a 1,470 ft offshore terminal capable of handling vessels up to 450,000 DWT. The company has a contract with the Norwegian government to store 42 million barrels of oil per year, which represents 70% of capacity and expects to book additional business to utilize the remaining 30% of storage.

WMS Marine Services (Bah) Ltd, a subsidiary of Wijsmuller Intl Towage of Holland, provides towage service to all of Grand Bahama, particularly South Riding Point and the Freeport Harbour Co. It also offers towage, salvage, ship management and brokerage to The Bahamas and the Caribbean, and employs 28 Bahamians.

Bahama Rock quarries and crushes limestone for export to the US, Caribbean, and (in small quantities) various Bahamian islands. It also processes material used in stack emission control for power plants, and lime used in chemical, industrial and agricultural applications.

Pharmaceuticals Fine Chemicals (PFC) SA, purchased Syntex Pharmaceutical Intl Ltd Freeport plant in 1996, with the aim of continuing the production of naproxen sodium. PFC is currently expanding and upgrading its naproxen production facilities to manufacture naproxen for the generic industry. Output from the Freeport plant is destined primarily for the North American market. PFC also produces other bulk active fine chemicals, including topical steroids, anti-fungal agents and veterinary drugs. PFC was purchased by AlliedSignal Inc in 1998.

Uniroyal Chemical Co Ltd, a subsidiary of Crompton & Knowles Corp, is another member of the chemical manufacturing sector on Grand Bahama. Uniroyal Chemical manufactures high performance antioxidants (known as HPAOs), a key additive used by plastic manufacturers to prevent degradation of their products by heat and oxygen. Also made at the site are performance additives used by the lubricants market.

Polymers Intl Ltd. This facility produces expandable polystyrene, a plastic resin used in the manufacture of disposable food service containers and packaging. The plant was commissioned in Sept 1997 with initial shipments of product destined for customers in Canada, Mexico, England and the US.

Picmelco, a new company, has recently introduced a 35 proof ready-mixed Margarita to add to the spirits collection of the local stores.

Grand Bahama Food Ltd Wholesale Division serves a customer base throughout Grand Bahama, as well as several large wholesalers and hotels in Nassau. It presently maintains an on-hand inventory of some 3,000 different product lines, including fresh produce, paper and plastic products, chemicals and cleaning supplies, fresh and frozen meats, fish, and seafood.

Fashion and perfume play a role in the Freeport industrial scene. **Fragrance of The Bahamas** at the Intl Bazaar affords visitors the opportunity to see first hand how perfumes are made, packaged and prepared for the Bahamian market. **Androsia,** a batik fabric featuring Bahamian designs and colours, was introduced by Rosi Birch in 1973. Androsia products are sold in the Port Lucaya Marketplace and in the Intl Bazaar.

See also **Agriculture.**

INTERNATIONAL BAZAAR

One of Freeport's attractions is the International Bazaar, a $3.5 million shopping complex featuring more than 80 businesses and offering the merchandise and cuisine of three dozen countries.

Completed in 1967, the 10-acre Bazaar was designed by a motion picture special effects expert. Visitors are greeted at the entrance of the Bazaar by a Torii gate, the Japanese symbol of welcome. Also represented in the Bazaar are Spain, South America, the Caribbean, Scandinavia, France, Denmark, Norway, Sweden, England and the Middle East. There are restaurants, cafés and snack parlours, as well as colourful street entertainment and an extensive straw market.

The Bazaar is open Mon-Sat, 10am-6pm, except Tue and Thur, when it opens at 9:30am. Also open Sun 10am-5pm. Some stores open earlier than the standard time.

JUDICIAL SYSTEM

Freeport has two Supreme Courts and three Magistrates' Courts. A fourth

Magistrate's Court is located at Eight Mile Rock. There are two permanent judges.
See also **Bahamas information, Judicial system.**

JUNKANOO
A Junkanoo parade is held on New Year's Day from 5-11pm at the Intl Bazaar. This event is staged by the Grand Bahama Junkanoo Committee. Groups compete for prizes of $5,500 for first place, $4,500 second place, $3,500 third place. First place winner for best group costume receives $1,500, second place $1,000, third place $500. Best individual costume receives $750, with $500 for second place and $250 for third place. Awards are also presented for best banner and best music.
See also **Bahamas information, Junkanoo.**

LAW FIRMS
Bain & Co
  Tel 352-5971, fax 352-6075
Bridgewater & Co
  Tel 351-5101, fax 351-8007
Brown, Simeon, & Co
  Tel 352-2316, fax 352-5605
Cafferata & Co
  Tel 351-4086, fax 351-3506
Carroll, Norris R, & Co
  Tel 352-8635, fax 352-3162
Chancery Law Associates
  Tel/fax 351-6373
Darville & Co
  Tel 352-3008, fax 352-2524
Glinton, Maurice O, & Co
  Tel 352-4484, fax 352-4256
Gray, V Alfred, & Co
  (incorporating Hall, Moses, & Co)
  Tel 352-7043, fax 352-4010
Lundy & Co
  Tel 352-3534, fax 352-3856
McDonald & Co
  Tel 352-4545, fax 352-7649
Maynard, Rawle
  Tel 352-4222, fax 352-4232
Thompson, Fayne, & Co
  Tel/fax 352-7668

Thompson, James Roosevelt
  Tel 352-7451, fax 352-7453
Tynes & Tynes
  Tel 352-4761, fax 352-6209
Wells-Carmona, Gottlieb & Co
  Tel 352-7291, fax 351-4524
Wilchcombe, Stephen, & Co
  Tel 352-7696, fax 352-3437

Fourteen Nassau law firms also maintain Freeport offices.
See also **Bahamas information, Law firms.**

LIBRARIES
The Sir Charles Hayward Library in the grounds of the Rand Memorial Hospital was opened by James Henry Rand in 1962. The lending library is operated by an all-volunteer group under a permanent librarian.

Subscription fees are $15 per year, with subscribers entitled to check out three books for two weeks. Library hours: Mon, Wed and Fri 10am-5pm; Sat 10am-2pm (closed on holidays). Librarian: Elaine Talma. Tel 352-7048.

The **Sir Charles Hayward Children's Library** was established in 1994. Subscription fees are $5 per year. Two books may be checked out for two weeks. Librarian: Josephine Zonicle. Tel 352-3524.

The **Grand Bahama Public Youth Library** is in the Syntex Teen Centre. Tel 352-2092.

LICENSING
All businesses operating in the Freeport area must be licensed by the Grand Bahama Port Authority Ltd (GBPA).

Licensees, whether individual, limited company or other corporate entity, are eligible for all tax benefits granted under the Hawksbill Creek Agreement as part of Bahamian law.

Customs concessions continue until 2054. The GBPA levies an annual licence fee for businesses operating in the port area. This fee varies according to size and type of business, with the lower limit being $10 for a non-profit organization.

A non-refundable deposit of $250 is charged as a processing fee in respect of all GBPA business licence applications. The fee is spent not only on maintaining the area around the licensee's business, but contributes to the annual GBPA Group of Companies' spending on landscaping, road repairs, garbage collection, etc.
To apply for a licence:
1. A detailed description of the nature of business, including facilities, equipment and staff, must be submitted to the GBPA on a licence proposal form.
2. From information on the form, together with a detailed reference check, financial affidavit and business competence report, the project is analyzed by the GBPA.
3. Upon approval by the licensing committee of the GBPA and subsequent notation by the government of The Bahamas, a letter of intent is issued to the licensee outlining terms and conditions of the business and indicating duration of the licence and initial fee payable to the GBPA.
4. Upon acceptance of these terms by the licensee, the formal licence agreement dictating finalized terms and location of the business is drawn up. Any subsequent changes or additions require an amendment to the licence.

See also **Customs** and **Hawksbill Creek Agreement.**

MARINAS & CRUISING FACILITIES

Year-round boating weather and excellent full-service marinas make Freeport/Lucaya a popular venue with the yachting crowd. Marinas include:
Bell Channel Club and Marina. Slips are primarily for condominium owners, but are available to the public when not in use. There are enough slips to accommodate up to 18 vessels, including 10 boats up to 30 ft, two up to 40 ft and six for 50 ft boats.
Lucayan Marina Village. State-of-the-art facilities and trained staff. Slips for 125 vessels of varying size up to 200 ft include 35-40 slips for boats up to 65 ft, 25-30 slips for boats up to 80 ft, 15-20 up to 90 ft, and 3-4 slips for boats up to 120 ft. Telephone and television hook-up available. Pool complex with waterside bar. Water shuttle to Port Lucaya Marketplace. Fuelling dock open 24 hrs.
Port Lucaya Marina & Yacht Club. Slips accommodating up to 100 vessels of varying sizes, including 18 up to 100 ft and three or four up to 160 ft. Telephone and cable TV hook-ups available at minimum charges. The marina specializes in yacht services; every facility is provided including boat-cleaning inside and out, caretaking in owner's absence and a shopping service. A full-scale refuelling operation is open 7am-3am. There is also a separate yacht club with a piano, films and a bar/restaurant.
Running Mon Marina and Resort. 66 slips – including 18 for boats up to 54 ft. Short term dockage rates from $1 per sq ft per day. Long-term dockage rates by arrangement. Diesel fuel and gas are available on site as are laundry facilities, showers and a boat repair facility with lifting ability. There is also a restaurant/bar, hotel/motel with deluxe guest rooms and swimming pool. Fishing charters available. A marina store provides bait, tackle and snacks.

See also **Bahamas information, Boating,** and, this section, **Boating; Harbour Control;** and **Telecommunications.**

MARRIAGE LICENCES

Marriage licences may be obtained from the Registrar General's Office, 16/17 Regent Centre, Freeport at a cost of $40. Tel 352-4934.

See also **Bahamas information, Marriage licences.**

MUSEUMS

Ye olde Pirate Bottle House, Port

Lucaya Marketplace, exhibits antique European and Colonial bottles and has an audio presentation.

NATIONAL INSURANCE

There are four local National Insurance offices in Grand Bahama – one in Freeport on The Mall, PO Box F-42618, tel 352-7222; one at Eight Mile Rock, one at West End and one at High Rock.

See also **Bahamas information, National Insurance.**

NATURE CENTRES

The **Bahamas National Trust (BNT) Rand Nature Centre,** East Settler's Way, a 100-acre pineland preserve. Wide variety of bird species, including a captive native Bahama parrot, and reptiles such as the Bahama boa. A flock of West Indian flamingos frequents the wildlife garden and pond. There is a replica Lucayan village. Guided tours through the pine forest trails highlight native plants and their medicinal and cultural uses. Guided bird walks first Sat of every month, 8am, and wildflower walks last Sat, 8am. Group tours by appointment. Open Mon-Fri 9am-4pm, Sat 9am-1pm. Admission $5, children 5-12 yrs $3. Tel 352-5438.

The **Lucayan National Park,** 42 acres, is managed by BNT through a volunteer committee. Nature trails and boardwalks lead to a variety of ecosystems, including pinelands, hardwood hammocks and coppices, mangrove swamps and sand dunes. Two large caves, part of one of the longest underwater cavern systems in the world, Ben's Cave and Burial Mound Cave, are habitats for rare underwater crustaceans and migratory bats in summer. Swimming is prohibited and diving requires a special permit. There is a beach, creek, orchids in spring, rare Ming trees and an array of birds such as herons, least grebes, ducks and songbirds. The park is open 9am-4pm daily. Tel 352-5438.

Peterson Cay National Park, also managed by BNT, is a small island one mile off the south coast of Grand Bahama. For those with access to a boat, active coral reefs surrounding the cay are excellent for snorkelling and/or diving, and there is a multitude of gulls and crabs. Fishing is prohibited. Tel 352-5438. See also **Birds.**

The **Hydroflora Gardens,** East Beach Dr and East Sunrise Hwy, gives an interesting percept of Grand Bahama's flora and hydroponics. Open Mon-Sat. Admission $3 unguided, $5 for guided tour, call ahead. Group rates available. Tel 373-5668.

Parrot Jungle's Garden of the Groves, Midshipman Rd and Magellan Dr. A tropical theme park featuring 12 acres of waterfalls, lakes, indigenous plantlife, macaws, ducks, cockatoos, iguanas and a petting zoo with pygmy goats and Vietnamese potbellied pigs. Scenic trails and well-manicured lawns. There is a snack bar and mini-straw market. Open daily 9am-4pm, Sun 10am-4pm. Admission $7.95 adults, $4.95 children. Tel 373-5668.

See also **Bahamas information, Bahamas National Trust** and **Marine parks & exhibits.**

NEWSPAPERS

One daily newspaper, *The Freeport News,* is published in Freeport and printed every morning, Mon-Sat, except holidays, 50¢. Also available are the two Nassau newspapers, *The Tribune,* a morning newspaper, and *The Nassau Guardian,* which has morning and afternoon editions. Both *The Tribune* and *Nassau Guardian* sell for 50¢.

Some New York and Miami papers are available the same day of publication and some a day later at increased cost due to air freight charges. Magazines from abroad also cost more for the same reason.

PASSPORTS

Bahamian residents of Grand Bahama may obtain or renew passports at the National Insurance Bldg in Freeport.

Persons seeking US visas or first time Bahamian passports may make use of GWS Worldwide Express at the Air Freight Bldg, Cargo Bay E, which will deliver their application to Nassau. Foreign nationals may contact GWS worldwide express for information on transporting passports for renewal. Tel 352-3434.

See also **Bahamas information, Passports.**

PEOPLE-TO-PEOPLE
Visitors who would like to spend time with Bahamians and learn more about their host country should complete an application form from their local tourism office, or write directly to the Coordinator, People-to-People, PO Box F-40251, Freeport, Grand Bahama, tel (242) 352-8044.

See also **Bahamas information, People-to-People.**

POLICE CERTIFICATES
Police certificates documenting an individual's past police record are often required in The Bahamas, eg, by prospective employers and in applications for immigration status.

The certificates may be obtained from CID, Peel St, at a cost of $2.50. Waiting period is 48 hours. Office hours: 9am-1pm and 2-3:30pm Tel 352-9774/5.

POPULATION
According to the official 1990 census, Grand Bahama's population was 41,035. In 1980, it was 33,102. The entire population of The Bahamas is 254,685 (1990 census). There will be a new census in 2000.

See also **Bahamas information, Population.**

PORT LUCAYA MARKETPLACE
This gaily painted 7½-acre waterside village is popular with visitors as well as Bahamian shoppers. There are some 62 varied stores, 30 restaurants and bars and a large straw market stocked with gift items, souvenirs, T-shirts and all manner of straw hats, bags and baskets. There are also steel bands, strolling guitarists and firework displays at various times.

See also **Museums** and **Shopping.**

POSTAL INFORMATION
The main post office, Explorers Way, provides the same service as the Nassau post office. Branch offices are located in West End, Eight Mile Rock, Smith's Point, High Rock, McLean's Town and Sweeting's Cay. Postal rates are the same as Nassau's.

See also **Courier services** and **Bahamas information, Postal information.**

PROPERTY TRANSACTIONS
The government of The Bahamas charges a stamp duty (equivalent to a transfer tax) on all property conveyances, leases and agreements, and on mortgages.

The government stamp duty on property conveyances or realty transfers is graded as follows:

From	Up to & including	Stamp duty
$0	$20,000	2%
$20,000.01	$50,000	4%
$50,000.01	$100,000	6%
Over $100,000		8%

Duty on mortgages is payable by the borrower at a rate of $1 for every $100 (or fraction thereof) borrowed. The Bahamas Bar Assoc recommends a scale of minimum fees which act as guidelines. A separate scale is established for leases, agreements, wills and other recorded documents. Each party retains and pays his own attorney. On small transactions, minimum fee is $500 for various services performed by an attorney. The minimum recommended fee for a conveyance is 2.5% of the sale price.

Commissions charged by real estate agents vary according to the type of property and should be agreed in writing between the seller, who normally pays the commission, and his agent.

In Freeport, much of the vacant land is owned by international investors, and unlike Nassau, the majority of transactions still involve foreigners, either as buyers or sellers, or both. This inevitably increases overheads. When there is a glut of undeveloped land on the market, many sellers offer high incentive commissions for quick cash sales. As a guideline, the following commission scales* apply:

Sale of undeveloped land	10%
(but not less than $500)	
House	10%
Condominium/apartment bldg	10%
Commercial property	10%

* Scales are under continual review.

See also **Bahamas information, Property transactions.**

RADIO STATIONS

ZNS-3, Radio Bahamas' Northern service, is one of three stations operated by the Broadcasting Corp of The Bahamas. Headquartered in Freeport, ZNS-3 covers Grand Bahama, Abaco and the Biminis, with local programming and advertising as well as national programming originating in the Nassau studio.

100 JAMZ, the first private radio station in The Bahamas, transmits on a frequency of 100.3 FM with 5,000 watts. Its programme of island and urban music is also received in Grand Bahama.

Cool 96, Grand Bahama's first private radio station, started in 1995, broadcasts on FM 96. Format is Bahamian, popular and classical music, and local advertising. The BBC WORLD News is broadcast at 9am and 6pm.

See also **Bahamas information, Broadcasting.**

REAL ESTATE COMPANIES

Following is a list of full-service companies that service Grand Bahama:

Century 21 Harry Dann & Co Ltd	352-7492
First Atlantic Realty	352-7071
Levi Gibson & Assoc	352-9727
Robert Hall & Assoc	351-6609
J Stuart Robertson	352-7201
Real Estate Exchange	351-4731
Re/Max Freeport Northern Bahamas	352-7302
Tennant & Cooper Ltd	352-7841
Thompson Real Estate Ltd	373-9050

RELIGION

Many denominations are established in Freeport/Lucaya:

Anglican/Episcopal: Christ the King, tel 352-5225; Church of the Ascension, tel 352-6245; Church of the Good Shepherd, tel 353-7661.

Assembly of Brethren: Freeport Gospel Chapel, tel 373-5600.

Assembly of God: Calvary Temple, tel 373-1986.

Baptist: First Baptist, tel 352-9224; Emmanuel Missionary Baptist, tel 352-6461; Upper Zion Baptist, tel 353-7771; St John's Native Baptist, tel 352-2276; and Fellowship Union Baptist, tel 373-4011.

Calvary Bible Church: (Independent), tel 373-4975.

Christian Science Society: tel 373-2044.

Church of God of Prophecy: tel 373-3464.

Freeport Hebrew Congregation: Luis De Torres Synagogue, tel 373-2008.

Jehovah's Witnesses: Kingdom Halls – Freeport West, tel 351-6711; Freeport East, tel 373-6821; and Freeport/Lucaya, tel 352-8505.

Lutheran: Our Saviour Lutheran Church, tel 373-3500.

Methodist: St Paul's, tel 373-5752.

Presbyterian: Lucaya Presbyterian Kirk, tel 373-2568.

Roman Catholic: Mary Star of The Sea, tel 373-3300; St Vincent de Paul Catholic Church, tel 353-7986.

Salvation Army:
tel 352-4863.
Seventh Day Adventist:
tel 373-3349.

SCHOOLS
See **Education**.

SERVICE CLUBS
See **Community organizations & service clubs**.

SHIPPING
Cruise Ships
Many cruise ships call regularly at Freeport Harbour, some of them several times a week. Most frequent callers are *Discovery Sun*, the new *SeaEscape*, Contessa Cruises' *Casino*, Palm Beach Cruises' *Palm Beach Princess*, Carnival Cruise Line's *Fantasy*, Majestic Cruises' *Freewinds*, Windjammer Barefoot Cruises' *Amazing Grace*, and Tropicana Cruises' *Starship Oceanic*.

Other cruise ships come into port frequently, as do the Royal Navy, US Navy, Royal Canadian Navy and Coast Guard ships. Large cruise ships and giant container ships dock in Freeport's deep-water harbour. Four vessels were wet-docked in 1997, and at press time three more had been wet-docked in 1998. A feasibility study is underway for the provision of dry-docking at Freeport Harbour.

Shipping Agents
Bahmar Agencies Ltd 352-5092
                         or 352-9413
BORCO Agency Services........352-9744
Freeport Transfer Ltd 352-7821
General Shipping
   Trading & Storage 352-3311
Global Agencies.....................352-2752
   (agents for Savoy Shipping)
Lucaya Shipping &
   Trading Co 352-3581/2
Professional Customs Brokers....351-3839
SeaEscape Agencies Ltd 352-3333
Swann's Shipping..................352-8024

Tanja Enterprises Ltd 352-2328
United Shipping Co Ltd 352-9315
Wide World Forwarding........352-3636

SHOPPING
Main shopping areas for clothes, leather goods, jewellery and perfume are the Port Lucaya Marketplace, Lucaya, and the Intl Bazaar. In downtown Freeport are Churchill Square, the West Mall Shopping Centre, Seventeen Shopping Mall and Regent Centre.

See also **International Bazaar** and **Port Lucaya Marketplace**.

SNORKELLING
See **Diving & snorkelling**.

SPORTS VENUES
Bahamas Princess Resort & Casino
   Emerald & Ruby
   Golf Courses ....352-6721, ext 4600
Lucayan Country Club 373-1066
Fortune Hills Golf
   & Country Club 373-4500
Freeport Rugby Club 373-2952
Grand Bahama Tennis
   & Squash Club..................373-4567
Hawksbill Yacht Club 373-1144
League of Basketball
   (YMCA) 352-7074
Lucayan Cricket Club 373-1460
Pinetree Stables 373-3600
YMCA 352-7074
Most hotels have tennis courts.
See **Bahamas information, Sports**, and, this section, **Diving & snorkelling**.

STRAW MARKETS
See **International Bazaar** and **Port Lucaya Marketplace**.

SUPERMARKETS
Winn Dixie and Grand Union, downtown Freeport, Mon-Sat 7am-6pm; Sun 8-10am.

Winn Dixie, Seahorse Plaza, Mon-Sat 7am-6pm; Sun 8-10am.
Food World, Coral Rd, Lucaya, Mon-Sat 7am-6pm; Sun 8-10am.
Solomon's Wholesale Club, Cedar St, Mon-Sat 8am-8pm.

TAX INCENTIVES
The Bahamas is a world-class tax haven, and Freeport in particular has further advantages to offer.
 See **Encouragement acts** and **Bahamas information, Tax benefits for Canadians, Tax benefits for Europeans, Tax benefits for US citizens and companies** and **Trade agreements.**

TELECOMMUNICATIONS
All long distance telephone service facilities are provided by Bahamas Telecommunications Corp (BaTelCo), with direct distance dialling available to most countries.
 Freeport residents can use an improved VHF-FM radio telephone service to ships at sea, through the Eight Mile Rock marine operator reached by dialling "0." Contact BaTelCo, PO Box F-42483, Freeport, Grand Bahama, tel 352-7778.
 See also **Bahamas information, Telecommunications.**

TELEVISION
Cable Television has been available in Grand Bahama for more than 20 years, initially supplied by Grand Bahama CATV Ltd.
 The Broadcasting Corp introduced local programmes to the CATV Cable System in Freeport, Grand Bahama in 1990. The Bahamian channel ZNS is received on Channel 13, and operates Mon-Fri 6:30-11pm.
 In 1995 Cable Bahamas, owned by Canadian-based Cable 2000 Inc and Bahamian interests, acquired Grand Bahama CATV Ltd and rebuilt the system to supply approx 40 channels of basic television and up to 60 channels of premium television.
 See also **Bahamas information, Television** and **ZNS.**

THEATRE & DRAMATIC ARTS
See **Cultural activities.**

TOURISM
See **Fig 1.0** for Grand Bahama tourism figures.
 The Grand Bahama Island Tourism Board (GBITB) is located above the China Temple in the Intl Bazaar, PO Box F-40251, tel 352-8044/5.
 The office provides visitors with information, coordinates Junkanoo and People-to-People events, monitors standards in hotels and restaurants and subsidizes the Hotel Training College.

TRADE UNIONS
Bahamas Communications &
  Public Officers' Union
  Tel 352-5077
Bahamas Hotel &
  Allied Workers' Union
  Tel 352-9804/5
Bahamas Public Service Union
  Tel 352-7810
Bahamas Union of Teachers
  Tel 352-8854
Commonwealth Transport Distributors
  & Allied Workers' Union
  Tel 352-9361
Commonwealth Union of Hotel
  Service and Allied Workers
  Tel 352-9361
Grand Bahama Construction Refinery
  Maintenance & Allied Workers' Union
  Tel 352-2476
Grand Bahama Taxi Union
  Tel 352-7101 or 352-7858

TRANSPORTATION
Taxi rates are set by government and are the same as Nassau; metered $2.20 for the first quarter mile and 30¢ for

FIG 1.0

MINISTRY OF TOURISM VISITOR ARRIVALS, GRAND BAHAMA

Year	Air arrivals	Sea arrivals	Total
1993	433,552	952,787	1,386,339
1994	348,261	551,313	899,574
1995	317,350	601,093	918,443
1996	295,675	898,013	1,193,688
1997	277,059	583,521	860,580

each additional quarter mile. For two passengers, approx fare from the airport to Lucaya is $11; to Bahamas Princess and the downtown area, $6. From the harbour area to Bahamas Princess, $12; to Lucaya, $15, and to the airport, $10. For more than two passengers, there is an additional charge of $3 per person.

Adult bus fare is 75¢. Bicycles rent for $20 per day with a $50 deposit. Motor scooters are $40, with a $100 deposit for a two-seater. Half a tank of gasoline is supplied by the agency and there is no mileage charge. Insurance is included. A valid driver's licence is required. By law, drivers and passengers must wear helmets, supplied free by the agency.

Fishing boats and yachts are available for charter.

See also **Ambulance/air ambulance services; Air service;** and **Car rental companies.**

VETERINARIANS

Dr Alan Bater
 & Dr Lee Bennett 352-6521
Dr Valentino Grant,
 Dr Brian Weekes
 & Dr Robert Allen....351-3647 (dogs)
  or 351-2287 (cats)

WAGES

Uniforms and meals for housemaids are at the employer's discretion. Gardeners are generally paid $30 a day or more, 9am-4pm. Cocktail waitresses earn about $100 per week basic pay and bartenders about $163, plus tips. Uniforms and meals are usually supplied by the employer.

Average weekly wage

Top executive secretary $650
Stenographer/secretary $300-320
Large hotel/restaurant
 manager.......................$920-1,350
Head cook or chef........................$330
Short-order cook..........................$244
Receptionist $270
Executive housekeeper..........$500-570
Janitor..$240
Security guard.............................$259
Farm helper.................................$130
Housemaid (40-hr week)..............$140
Truck driver $297
Fork lift operator ....$350-$450

The slight difference in wages between Freeport and Nassau is due to the higher cost of living in Freeport, according to the Nassau Labour Dept.

See also **Bahamas information, Wages.**

WATER SUPPLY & RATES

The Grand Bahama Utility Co supplies water to Freeport and several other communities in Grand Bahama. Total developed well field capacity is nine million gallons per day from six well fields. Average daily water consumption is about 6.4 million gallons.

Monthly water rate for residential, commercial and industrial consumers in Freeport is $3.10 per thousand for the first 10,000 US gallons; $3.70 per thousand for the next 10,000 gallons; and $4.40 per thousand for usage in excess of 20,000 gallons.

See also **Bahamas information, Water rates.**

WEATHER
See **Climate.**

Government

SILVER JUBILEE ANNIVERSARY HONOURS

On July 10, 1998, 100 Bahamians and institutions received specially minted $250 gold coins and certificates honouring their contribution to The Bahamas' growth and development over the last 25 years. Presented at Government House grounds, the awards were bestowed by Governor-General Sir Orville Turnquest, Prime Minister the Rt Hon Hubert A Ingraham and Opposition Leader Perry Christie. Following is the list of awardees.

CONSTITUTIONAL DEVELOPMENT, GOVERNMENT & POLITICS
The Rt Hon Sir Lynden O Pindling, KCMG
Sir Gerald Cash, GCMG, GCVO, OBE, JP
Sir Clifford Darling, GCVO, JP
The Hon Janet G Bostwick, MP
Sen The Hon J Henry Bostwick, QC
HE Sir Arlington Butler, KCMG, JP
HE Arthur A Foulkes
The Hon Paul L Adderley
The Hon Arthur D Hanna
HE Geoffrey A D Johnstone, CMG
The Hon Sir Clement Maynard
HE Maurice E Moore
Norman S Solomon
Sir Leonard Knowles, CBE

EDUCATION
Sen The Hon Dame Dr Ivy Dumont, DCMG
The Diocese of Nassau and The Bahamas including the Turks and Caicos Islands (Anglican)
The Bahamas Union of Teachers
The Bahamas Baptist Missionary and Educational Convention
The Bahamas Conference of the Methodist Church
The Roman Catholic Diocese of Nassau
The Salvation Army
The Bahamas Conference of Seventh Day Adventists
Dr Keva Bethel, CMG
Patrick Bethel
Juanita M Butler
Lillian Coakley, BEM
Marjorie W T Davis, OBE
Dr John Knowles

Jacqueline Malcolm
Canon D John Pugh, MBE
Lady Henrietta St George

MEDICINE
Dr Cecil W M Bethel, MBE
Dr I Earl Farrington, MBE

NURSING
The Bahamas Nurses Association
Hilda V Bowen, MBE

TOURISM
Dr Baltron B Bethel, CMG
George E R Myers

FAMILY ISLAND DEVELOPMENT
Warren J Levarity
Capt Leonard Thompson
Carter Williams

BANKING
The Hon William C Allen, MP
Anthony C Allen
T Baswell Donaldson, CBE

BUSINESS
Garet O Finlayson
William "Billy" Lowe
Andrew K McKinney
Albert J Miller, LVO, MBE, QPM, CPM
Judy V C Munroe
Franklyn Pinder
Rupert W Roberts, Jr

TRADE UNIONS & LABOUR
The Bahamas Public Services Union
The Bahamas Hotel Catering and Allied Workers Union
The Bahamas Taxi-Cab Union
Sir Randol Fawkes

RELIGION
Rt Rev Michael H Eldon, CMG, OM
Msgr Preston A Moss
Rev Dr Charles W Saunders, CBE

AGRICULTURE
Niven R Nutt, Jr
Claude A M Smith

FISHERIES
Roosevelt F Curry
Vendal Pinder

COOPERATIVES
Juliette J Barnwell, LVO

MANUFACTURING
Ralph C Barnett
Jefferson W Pinder

Jacqueline Malcolm of Freeport receives her award for contribution in the field of Education. From left: Perry Christie, Rt Hon Hubert A Ingraham, Malcolm and the Governor-General, Sir Orville A Turnquest.

ENVIRONMENT
The Bahamas National Trust

CULTURE
Kayla C Lockhart-Edwards
Edmund S Moxey
Winston V Saunders

LITERATURE AND HISTORY
Dr D Gail Saunders
Susan J Wallace

ART
Amos I Ferguson, MBE
R Brent Malone, MBE

MUSIC
The National Youth Choir
Lou G Adams, MBE
Ronnie Butler
John "Chippie" Chipman, MBE
"King" Eric Gibson
Errol Strachan, MBE
J Berkley "Peanuts" Taylor, MBE

JUNKANOO
Winston "Gus" R Cooper, MBE
Percival "Vola" Francis, MBE
Paul A C Knowles

BROADCASTING
H R "Rusty" Bethel
E Charles Carter
Wendell K Jones

PRINT MEDIA
The Nassau Guardian
The Tribune

SPORTS
Deacon Leviticus "Lou" Adderley, OBE, OM
Elizabeth "Betty" M Cole, MBE
Capt Rolly B Grey, BEM
Sir Durward Knowles, OBE, OM
Leonard "Boston Blackie" Miller
Thomas "Tommy" A Robinson, MBE

CHARITABLE ORGANIZATIONS
The Bahamas Red Cross Society
The Star of The Bahamas Charity Guide

PUBLIC SERVICE
Peter I Bethel, CMG
Livingstone B Johnson, CBE
E George Moss
Leon L Smith, OBE
Salathiel H Thompson, CMG, LVO, QPM, CPM

PETER RAMSAY

Rt Hon Hubert A Ingraham presents a gold coin to Amos I Ferguson for Art.

GOVERNOR-GENERAL

HE Sir Orville Alton Turnquest, GCMG, QC, JP, LLB
Governor-General, Government House, Duke St, Nassau

Governor-General since Jan 1995. Former Deputy Prime Minister, Attorney General, Minister of Foreign Affairs. Barrister-at-law, Dupuch & Turnquest & Co (inactive senior partner). Born July 19, 1929, Nassau. Son of the late Robert and Gwendolyn (née Wake) Turnquest. Educated: Government High School, Nassau. Articled law student to Hon A F Adderley, and called to The Bahamas Bar in June 1953. Univ of London (LLB Hons) and Lincoln's Inn, England; called to the English Bar in 1960. Married to Lady Turnquest (née Edith Thompson) of Nassau. Three children. Religion: Anglican. Chancellor of the Anglican Diocese in Nassau and The Bahamas; member of the Board of Governors of St John's College and St Anne's High School. Hobbies: tennis, swimming, music, reading.
PO Box N-8301, Nassau.

Governor-Generals From Independence-July 10, 1973

1973 Sir John Warburton Paul, GCMG, OBE, MC; appointed July 10, 1973; retired July 31, 1973.
1973 Sir Milo Butler, from Aug 1, 1973.
1976 Sir Gerald Cash, GCMG, GCVO, OBE, JP; Acting Governor-General, Sept 2, 1976 – Sept 23, 1979.
1979 Sir Gerald Cash, GCMG, GCVO, OBE, JP; appointed Governor-General, Sept 24, 1979; retired June 25, 1988.
1988 Sir Henry Milton Taylor, Kt, JP; Acting Governor-General, June 26, 1988 – Feb 28, 1991.
1991 Sir Henry Milton Taylor, Kt, JP; appointed Governor-General, Mar 1, 1991; Retired Jan 1, 1992.
1992 Sir Clifford Darling, Kt, JP; Appointed Jan 2, 1992; retired Jan 2, 1995.
1995 Sir Orville A Turnquest, GCMG, QC, JP; appointed Jan 3, 1995; still in office.

Cabinet Ministers & Portfolios

The Rt Hon Hubert Alexander Ingraham, PC, MP
Prime Minister, Sir Cecil V Wallace Whitfield Centre, West Bay St, Nassau

The Cabinet Office
Coordination of ministries and government business; coordination of parliamentary business; disaster preparedness; charities; Official Gazette; Hansard. Tel (242) 322-2805, fax (242) 328-8294.

Office of The Prime Minister
Economic policy planning; Bahamas Investment Authority (BIA); relations with the Hotel Corp of The Bahamas; relations with The Bahamas Mortgage Corp; radio and television broadcast; relations with the Broadcasting Corp; cable television; Environment, Science and Technology Commission (BEST); urban renewal and improvement; relations with National Insurance Board; relations with Grand Bahama Port Authority. Tel (242) 327-5826, fax (242) 327-5806.

Bahamas Information Services
Bahamas Information Services.

Government Printing Dept
Government publications; printing and stationery.

Dept of Lands and Surveys
Lands and surveys; acquisition of lands.

Dept of Physical Planning
Physical planning and land use; town planning.

Dept of Public Service
Public service; public service unions; pensions and gratuities; office accommodation; organization and methods.

(See also **House of Assembly – North Abaco, Abaco**)

CABINET MINISTERS & PORTFOLIOS

Watson *Bostwick* *Smith*

THE HON
FRANK H WATSON, MP
Deputy Prime Minister and Minister of National Security
Churchill Bldg, Bay St, Nassau

Office of the Deputy Prime Minister
Tel (242) 356-6792, fax (242) 356-6087.
Public Enterprises
Relations with the public corporations, viz Bahamas Electricity Corp (BEC), Bahamas Telecommunications Corp (BaTelCo), Bahamas Water and Sewerage Corp (WSC), Bahamasair.
The Gaming Board
Relations with the Gaming Board; lotteries and gaming.
Ministry of National Security
Public safety; flags and coats of arms; cinemas and films.
Royal Bahamas Police Force
Police.
Royal Bahamas Defence Force
Defence.
Prisons Dept
Prisons; prisoners; prerogative of mercy.
(See also **House of Assembly – Adelaide, New Providence**)

THE HON
JANET G BOSTWICK, MP
Minister of Foreign Affairs, East Hill St, Nassau

Ministry of Foreign Affairs
Foreign affairs; foreign missions; protocol matters; political refugees; extradition; treaty succession; coordination of applications for technical assistance; law of the sea; CARICOM affairs; notaries public.
Tel (242) 322-7624, fax (242) 328-8212.
Passport Office
Passports; visas.
Parliamentary Registration Dept
Parliamentary registration; elections.
Bureau of Women's Affairs
Women's Affairs.
(See also **House of Assembly – Yamacraw, New Providence**)

THE HON
CORNELIUS A SMITH, MP
Minister of Tourism, Market Plaza, Bay St, Nassau

Ministry of Tourism
Promotion and development of tourism; tourism product improvement; relations with Nassau Tourism and Development Assoc; relations with promotion boards; timesharing and vacation clubs; tourism publicity and advertisement; straw markets; Nassau Flight Services. Tel (242) 322-7500, fax (242) 322-4041.
(See also **House of Assembly – Pineridge, Grand Bahama**)

Cabinet Ministers & Portfolios

Dumont

SEN THE HON DAME DR IVY L DUMONT
Minister of Education, Ministry of Education, Shirley St, Nassau
Minister of Youth, Sports and Culture, Gold Circle House, East Bay St, Nassau

Ministry of Education
Education; scholarships; relations with College of The Bahamas; relations with Univ of the West Indies; relations with church operated and other private schools; relations with School Boards. Tel (242) 322-5495, fax (242) 322-6327.

Dept of Education
Pre-schools; primary, secondary and tertiary education; public libraries and reading centres.

Dept of Archives
Archives, old public records and antiquities; museums; historical sites including forts.

Ministry of Youth & Culture
Youth development; community development.

Dept of Sports
Sports; recreation; development of playgrounds, community pools and sporting complexes.

Dept of Culture
Development of artistic and cultural expression; Junkanoo.
Tel (242) 322-3140, fax (242) 322-6347.

Allen

THE HON WILLIAM C ALLEN, MP
Minister of Finance and Planning, and Minister of Economic Development, Sir Cecil V Wallace Whitfield Centre, West Bay St, Nassau

Ministry of Finance and Planning
Government finance and borrowing; Central Bank of The Bahamas; banks and trust companies; The Bank of The Bahamas; spirits and beers; auctions; treasure trove. Tel (242) 327-1530, fax (242) 327-1618.

Securities Exchange
Mutual funds and securities.

Customs Dept
Revenue.

Treasury Dept
Budgetary control.

Ministry of Economic Development
International trade; Lomé convention; NAFTA; Bahamas Development Bank; licensing of shops and businesses; hotel licensing; insurance (excluding National Insurance).

Dept of Statistics
Statistics; retail price index.

Registrar General's Dept
Registration of documents; companies; business names; registration of commission merchants; copyrights; patents and trademarks.
(See also **House of Assembly – Montagu, New Providence**)

CABINET MINISTERS & PORTFOLIOS

Wells

Moxey-Ingraham

Allen

THE HON TENNYSON R G WELLS, LLB, MP
Attorney General and Minister of Justice, Post Office Bldg, East Hill St, Nassau

Attorney General
Tel (242) 322-1141, fax (242) 322-2255.
Dept of Legal Affairs
Legal advisor to the Government; mutual legal assistance; law reform and revision; legal education; coroners.
Dept of Public Prosecutions
Criminal proceedings.
Public Defender's Office
Public defence; legal aid.
Judicial Dept
Administration of justice; law courts; law reports; enquiries; Justices of the Peace.
(See also **House of Assembly – Bamboo Town, New Providence**)

THE HON THERESA M MOXEY-INGRAHAM, MP
Minister of Labour, Immigration and Training, Post Office Bldg, East Hill St, Nassau

Ministry of Labour, Immigration and Training
Bahamas Hotel Training College; Bahamas Technical and Vocational Institute; apprenticeship and training including public service training; industrial arts and crafts training; Technical Cadet Corps.
Tel (242) 322-6250, fax (242) 322-6546.

Dept of Labour
Employment; employment agencies; trade unions; industrial relations; industry and manufacturing; relations with Bahamas Industrial and Agricultural Corp; inspection and safety; workman's compensation.
Dept of Immigration
Immigration; emigration; nationality; citizenship.
(See also **House of Assembly – Golden Gates, New Providence**)

THE HON ALGERNON S P B ALLEN, LLB (Hons), MP
Minister of Housing and Social Development, Frederick House, Frederick St, Nassau

Ministry of Housing and Social Development
Tel (242) 356-0765/6, fax (242) 323-3883.
Dept of Housing
Housing.
Dept of Social Services
Social services; old age pensions; child protection; school welfare; public assistance; indigent and aged persons; care facilities; disabled persons.
Dept of Rehabilitative Services
Rehabilitative services; industrial schools.
(See also **House of Assembly – Marathon, New Providence**)

Cabinet Ministers & Portfolios

Dupuch  *Turnquest*  *Knowles*

THE HON PIERRE V L DUPUCH, MP
Minister of Consumer Welfare and Aviation, Commission of Inquiry Bldg, Thompson Blvd, Oakes Field, Nassau

Ministry of Consumer Welfare and Aviation
Consumer welfare; consumer protection; consumer education; weights and measures; hire purchase; minimum standards; consumer credit.
Tel (242) 326-4550, fax (242) 328-1160.
Dept of Environmental Health Services
Environmental control; poisons; solid waste; collection and disposal; vector control; beautification of roads; beautification and maintenance of parks, verges, beaches and cemeteries.
Dept of Civil Aviation
Aviation; air transport licensing.
Dept of Meteorology
Meteorology.
(See also **House of Assembly – Shirlea, New Providence**)

THE HON ORVILLE ALTON THOMPSON (TOMMY) TURNQUEST, MP
Minister of Public Works, Ministry of Public Works, John F Kennedy Dr, Nassau

Ministry of Public Works
Tel (242) 323-7240, fax (242) 326-7344.
Dept of Public Works
Public works; roads, bridges and cemeteries; maintenance of public buildings, roads and bridges; explosives and volatile substances; private roads and subdivisions; Paradise Island Bridge Authority; local improvement assocs; Down Home Fish Fry; Montagu Beach and foreshore; The Caves; Saunders Beach; Goodman's Bay.
Dept of Local Government
Family Island affairs; relations with local Family Island authorities.
Tel (242) 325-4560, fax (242) 326-5561.
(See also **House of Assembly – Mount Moriah, New Providence**)

THE HON JAMES F KNOWLES, MP
Minister of Transport, Post Office Bldg, East Hill St, Nassau

Ministry of Transport
Tel (242) 323-7814, fax (242) 325-2016.
Dept of Road Traffic
Ground transportation; road traffic; motor vehicles; drays and surreys.
Post Office Dept
Postal service; Post Office Savings Bank.
Port Dept
Maritime affairs; merchant ship registration; inter-island passenger, freight and mail services; lighthouses; wrecks; ports and harbours; abutments; boat registration; shipping and navigation; Prince George Dock.
Bahamas Maritime Authority
The Bahamas' ship register; maritime affairs and training; casualty

CABINET MINISTERS & PORTFOLIOS

Deveaux

investigation; ship inspection and survey; port state control.
(See also **House of Assembly – Long Island and Ragged Island**)

THE HON DR EARL D DEVEAUX, MP
Minister of Agriculture and Fisheries, Levy Bldg, East Bay St, Nassau

Ministry of Agriculture and Fisheries
Natural history specimens; reefs and blue holes; Potters Cay.
Tel (242) 325-7502, fax (242) 322-1767.
Dept of Agriculture
Agriculture; protection of wild animals and birds; protection of plants; veterinary services and animal diseases; public markets; slaughter houses; agricultural land; quality control – testing and cost for food processing and preservation of food and beverages.
Dept of Fisheries
Fisheries.
Dept of Cooperatives
Cooperatives.
(See also **House of Assembly – North Andros and Berry Islands**)

Knowles

SENATOR THE HON DR RONALD KNOWLES
Minister of Health, Royal Victoria Gardens, Shirley St, Nassau

Ministry of Health
Tel (242) 322-7425, fax (242) 322-7788.
Dept of Public Health
Public health; vaccination; quarantine; port health; dangerous drugs; medical, nursing and health services; pharmacies; regulation of manufacturing of drugs and pharmaceuticals; Public Analyst Labs.

MINISTERS OF STATE

See Cabinet Ministers and Portfolios, pages 558-563 for more information.

THE HON DAVID C THOMPSON, MP
Minister of State for the Public Service, Office of the Prime Minister, Clarence Bain Bldg, Thompson Blvd, Nassau
(See also **House of Assembly – Marco City, Grand Bahama**)

THE HON CARL W BETHEL, MP
Minister of State for Economic Development, Clarence Bain Bldg, Thompson Blvd, Nassau
(See also **House of Assembly – Holy Cross, New Providence**)

THE HON ANTHONY C ROLLE, MP
Minister of State for Public Enterprises, Churchill Bldg, Bay St, Nassau
(See also **House of Assembly – Carmichael, New Providence**)

THE HON VERNON SYMONETTE, MP
Minister of State for Family Island Affairs, Ministry of Public Works, John F Kennedy Dr, Nassau
(See also **House of Assembly – MICAL**)

THE HON DION A FOULKES, MP
Minister of State for Education, Ministry of Education, Shirley St, Nassau
(See also **House of Assembly – Blue Hills, New Providence**)

THE HON ZHIVARGO S LAING, MP
Minister of State for Youth, Sports and Culture, Gold Circle House, East Bay St, Nassau
(See also **House of Assembly – Fort Charlotte, New Providence**)

SENATORS

GOVERNMENT

SEN THE HON JOHN HENRY BOSTWICK, QC, LLB. President of the Senate. Barrister-at-law, Gray's Inn, Bostwick & Bostwick (partner). President of The Bahamas Bar Assoc, 1991-1995. Born May 3, 1939. Educated: Univ of Exeter, Devonshire, England. Married to The Hon Janet (née Musgrove) Bostwick.

SEN THE HON GENEVA ELIZABETH MAJOR-RUTHERFORD. Vice-president of the Senate. Director of Training, Grand Bahama Port Authority. Educator. Born April 4, 1948, Mortimer's, Long Island, to Clifton and Doris Major. Educated: Mortimer's All Age School, Long Island; Aquinas College, Nassau; St Benedict's High School, St Joseph, MN; College of St Benedict, St Joseph, MN (BA History); teacher certification, Minnesota Dept of Education; Univ of Miami, FL, (Master's Education). A teacher since 1970 and principal at the Catholic Board of Education's Mary Star of the Sea School in Freeport, Grand Bahama, 1979-97. Active in educational associations and conferences and in civic committees, including Women in Action and FNM Women's Assoc. Married to Willard Rutherford. One stepson. Denomination: Roman Catholic.

SEN THE HON DAME DR IVY LEONA (née Turnquest) DUMONT, DCMG, DPA. Minister of Education and Minister of Youth, Sports and Culture. Government Leader in the Senate. Born Oct 2, 1930, Rose's, Long Island. Daughter of Alphonzo Turnquest and Elizabeth (née Darville) Turnquest. Educated: Nova Univ and Univ of Miami, FL. Former Minister of Health and Environment (1992-94). Married to Reginald Deane Dumont. Two children. Denomination: Brethren. Hobbies: dressmaking, public speaking and horticulture. Member: Assemblies of Brethren in The Bahamas; past president (founding member) Women's Aglow International (Bahamas); past vice-president Bahamas Humane Society; and past secretary (founding member) Bahamas Union of Teachers.

SEN THE HON DR RONALD KNOWLES. Minister of Health. Born May 12, 1947, Nassau. Son of Mr and Mrs Conrad Knowles. Educated: St Augustine's College, Government High School, Nassau; Univ of West Indies (MB BS 1970); Princess Margaret Hospital internship; Wayne State Univ, Detroit, MI; Univ of Miami School of Medicine, Miami, FL. Member Medical Assoc of The Bahamas; American Society of Nephrology; International Society of Nephrology; and National

Kidney Foundation. Former head consultant, Dept of Medicine at Princess Margaret Hospital. Appointed to the Senate Mar 20, 1997. Married to the former Gwendolyn Madison. One child. Denomination: Anglican. Hobbies: squash, walking.

SEN THE HON CALVIN JAMES JOHNSON, BSc. Parliamentary Secretary, Ministry of Tourism. FNM MP for Fort Fincastle, 1992-97. Banker. Former Parliamentary Secretary, Office of the Deputy Prime Minister and Ministry of Health and Environment. Deputy chairman, Bahamas Mortgage Corp, 1992-1993. Born Aug 7, 1953, West End, Grand Bahama. Son of Merlene Deal. Educated: Wayne State Univ (BSc in Business Admin), Detroit, MI. Married to the former Linda Joyce Smith. Two children. Denomination: Roman Catholic. Hobbies: reading, jogging. Member: Alpha Phi Alpha Fraternity.

SEN THE HON DAPHNE ANNETTE DUNCOMBE COOPER, JP. Counsel and attorney-at-law, notary public. Born Nov 26, 1960, New Providence. Parliamentary Secretary, Ministry of Finance and Planning; former vice-president, Torchbearers Assoc; called to The Bahamas Bar, Aug 1991. Appointed to the Senate, April 1997. Former Deputy Comptroller, Inland Revenue. Chairman, New Providence Port Authority. Educated: Queen's College, Nassau; Benedict College, Columbia, SC (BSc, Economics); *Juris doctor* (candidate), LaSalle Univ, Philadelphia, PA. Married to Rev Dr Reuben Edward Cooper Jr. Member: FNM Central Council. Denomination: Baptist. Hobbies: travelling, cultural exploration, reading, sewing, listening to classical music.

SEN THE HON DESMOND F L EDWARDS, JP. Attorney-at-law. Senior partner, Desmond Edwards & Co Law Chambers. Chairman, Bahamas Plays and Films Control Board; deputy chairman, Television Regulatory Authority; president, Bahamas Guild of Artists; first vice-chairman, FNM. Former acting stipendiary and circuit magistrate. Born Nov 22, 1946, Nassau, son of the late Rev Cebert F and Amiee (née Foulkes) Edwards. Educated: West Indies College, Mandeville, Jamaica (AS); Atlantic Union College, South Lancaster, MA (BSc & BA); Institute of Bankers (AIB); Licentiate of Royal Schools of Music (LRSM); articled law clerk; called to Bahamas Bar in 1981. Married to Kayla Lockhart-Edwards, deputy Director of Culture. Two children. Denomination: Worldwide Church of God. Hobbies: Bahamian folk music, classical music, keyboard accompaniment and arrangement, sports car restoration, computers, reading.

SEN THE HON ROSTON H MILLER. Architect, Roston Miller & Assoc. Born July 13, 1934, Mangrove Cay, Andros. Son of the late Rosald "Roy" Miller and Emma Elizabeth (née Adderley) Miller. Educated: Nassau public schools; Northwestern Senior High School, Miami, FL; Howard Univ, Washington, DC (BA, Architecture, 1963). Worked as an architect in Washington/Maryland area until returning to Nassau in 1970. Member: American Institute of Architects, Royal

Institute of British Architects. Founder and president of the Institute of Bahamian Architects. Listed in *Who's Who in the World* in art and architecture and *Dictionary of Intl Biography* for distinguished achievements in architecture. Secretary general of FNM. Charter member and past secretary, Nassau chapter of Sigma Pi Phi fraternity, the oldest Greek-lettered fraternity for professional black men. Past president of Rotary Club of West Nassau and Paul Harris fellow. Married to the former Janice McCants of Wilmington, DE. Four daughters. Denomination: Anglican. Hobbies: music, jogging, reading.

SEN THE HON MICHAEL A BETHEL. Master mariner and businessman. Born Aug 21, 1961, Cherokee Sound, Abaco. Son of the late Capt Archie Bethel and the former Sharon Hodgkins. Educated: Cherokee All Age School. Captain of the vessel *Duke of Topsail,* United Abaco Shipping. Deputy chairman of FNM, South Abaco. Past deputy chairman of Island council, South Abaco. Past chairman of Cherokee Sound, Casuarina Pt town committee. Married to the former Maria McCollum. Three children. Denomination: Methodist. Hobbies: watersports.

SEN THE HON DARRON B CASH, MBA, CPA, BSc. Certified public accountant, Ernst & Young. Born Nov 14, 1966, Nassau. Son of Cleo Cash. Educated: St Augustine's College and College of The Bahamas, Nassau; Manhattan College, Riverdale, NY (BSc, Accounting, 1989); Rutgers State Univ, NJ (MBA Finance, 1995). Fulbright scholar. Member and past president, College of The Bahamas Alumni Assoc; former chairman, The Bahamian Interest Forum; former secretary, National Assoc of Black Accountants Inc, New York chapter. Appointed to the Senate, April 1997. Hobbies: music, international affairs.

SEN THE HON LONNIE EMMELINE DIXON ROLLE, JP. Waitress, Club Mediterranean Resort. Born Aug 1, 1954. Daughter of the late Frank Anthony Dixon and Sybil Joy Smith-March. Educated: St Francis School, Our Lady's School, Oakes Field Secondary School and Nassau Academy of Business, Nassau. Served as chairman for Hatchet Bay/Gregory Town local govt, 1992-96. Elected member Hatchet Bay town committee. Assistant secretary general for the FNM. Appointed to the Senate June 1997. Appointed a trustee to the Bahamas State Association of Elks in May 1997. Elected daughter ruler for freedom temple #1367 of the Improved Benevolent Protective Order of Elks of the World. Married to Cedric Alexander Rolle of Hatchet Bay. One child. Denomination: Roman Catholic.

SEN THE HON PAULINE VIOLA COOPER-NAIRN. Computer Operations Supervisor, Grand Bahama Port Authority (GBPA). Born Aug 16, 1962, Pinder's Point, Grand Bahama. Daughter of Prescola Louise (née Pinder) Hepburn and Loften Harrison Cooper, both deceased. Educated: Lewis Yard Primary School; Freeport High School; Indian River Community College, Fort Pierce, FL

(AA, Business Administration, 1980), Mississippi State Univ, Starkville, MS (BA, Business Administration, 1982). Elected to local govt in July 1996, and served as deputy chairman for Pinder's Point Township. Serves as first vice president, Business & Professional Women's Club of Grand Bahama. Married to Archie Nairn. One child. Denomination: Baptist. Hobbies: geneaology.

OPPOSITION

SEN THE HON DR MARCUS C BETHEL. Opposition leader in the Senate. Physician. Born July 7, 1947, Nassau. Son of Jane Bethel and the late Marcus Bethel. Educated: Government High School, Nassau; McGill Univ, Montreal (BSc and MD); internship, Toronto General Hospital, Toronto; residency, Internal Medicine, Mayo Clinic, Rochester, MN. Medical director/administrator/consultant internist, Lucayan Medical Centre, Freeport. Member: Grand Bahama Medical Assoc, Medical Assoc of The Bahamas, American College of Physicians. Married to the former Chantal Victor. Three sons. Denomination: Anglican. Hobbies: travelling, reading, boating.

SEN THE HON FREDERICK A MITCHELL, JR, MPA, LLB, BA. Counsel & attorney-at-law. Former chairman of the Senate Select Committee on Culture. Public Relations consultant for Al Dillette & Assoc. Opposition spokesman on foreign affairs, labour and immigration. Born Oct 5, 1953, Nassau. Son of Mr and Mrs Frederick A Mitchell. Educated: St Augustine's College, Nassau; Antioch Univ, OH and John F Kennedy School of Government, Harvard Univ, MA. Univ of Buckingham, England. Founding member of The Bahamas Committee on Southern Africa. Member: New Providence Human Rights Assoc. Denomination: Anglican.

SEN THE HON OBIE WILCHCOMBE. Journalist. Chairman of the Progressive Liberal Party. Born November 4, 1958, Freeport, Grand Bahama to the late Jackson and Mary Wilchcombe. Educated: Univ of the West Indies, Kingston, Jamaica. President, Commonwealth American Football League and president, Grand Bahama Basketball Assoc.

SEN THE HON DAMIAN ANSELM LEROY GOMEZ. Barrister-at-law. Born Aug 17, 1962, Nassau. Son of Rt Rev Drexel W Gomez and Carol Gomez. Educated: St John's Preparatory School, Nassau; Harrison College, Barbados; Univ of the West Indies, Barbados; Holborn Law Tutors, England; Univ of Bristol, England; called to the Bar of England and Wales, 1988; called to Bahamas Bar, 1989. Married to Creselle Lavern. Two children.

House Of Assembly

SPEAKER: Rome Italia Johnson (see pg 571)
DEPUTY SPEAKER: Michael (Mike) Smith (see pg 574)
NOTE: There are 40 seats in the House of Assembly. 35 are held by the Free National Movement (FNM), 5 by the Progressive Liberal Party (PLP), the Official Opposition. Cabinet Ministers devote full time to Government. Occupations for Cabinet Ministers are for background information only.

NEW PROVIDENCE

ADELAIDE

THE HON FRANK HOWARD WATSON, MP (FNM). Deputy Prime Minister. Minister of National Security with responsibility for the Public Service and Public Utilities. Born Mar 24, 1940, Gordon's, Long Island. Son of William C and Olga (née Major) Watson. Educated: Government High School, Nassau; Univ of the West Indies. Two children. Denomination: Anglican. Hobbies: tennis, fishing. Residence: Cunningham Acres, PO Box N-4066, Nassau.

BAIN TOWN

GREGORY JAMES WILLIAMS, MBA, MP (FNM). Parliamentary Secretary, Ministry of Works. Businessman. Born Oct 1, 1954, Nassau. Son of the late John Williams and Rhoda Williams. Educated: St Augustine's College, Nassau; Freed-Hardeman College, Henderson, TN; Winthrop College, Rock Hill, SC. Married to the former Jennifer Fawkes of Inagua. Six children. Denomination: Church of Christ. Hobbies: tennis, chess. Residence: Rupert Dean Ln, PO Box GT-2113, Nassau.

BAMBOO TOWN

THE HON TENNYSON ROSCOE WELLS, LLB, MP (FNM). Attorney General and Minister of Justice. Barrister-at-law, Wells & Wells (inactive partner), businessman. Born Dec 30, 1946, Deadman's Cay, Long Island. Son of Cleveland and Emma (née Cartwright) Wells. Educated: St John's College, Nassau; St Mary's Univ, Halifax, NS, Canada; Univ of London, England. Married to the former Stephanie Ann Thompson of Nassau. Three children. Hobbies: reading, swimming. Denomination: Anglican. Residence: Blue Hill Estates, PO Box N-9665, Nassau.

BLUE HILLS

THE HON DION ALEXANDER FOULKES, BA, MP (FNM). Minister of State for Education. Attorney-at-law. Born Oct 9, 1956, Nassau. Son of Arthur and Naomi Foulkes. Educated: R M Bailey High School, Nassau; École des Roche, Switzerland; Indiana Univ (BA), Indiana Univ Graduate School of Business, IN. Became articled law student in 1986. Called to the Bar Oct 1990. Married to the former Emma Jane Thompson of Abaco. Four children. Denomination: Roman Catholic. Hobbies: reading, stamp collecting. Member: The Bahamas Bar Assoc, The Bahamas Law Guild. Residence. West Bay St, PO Box CB-12125, Nassau.

CARMICHAEL

THE HON ANTHONY CHARLES ROLLE, MP (FNM). Minister of State for Public Enterprises, Office of the Deputy Prime Minister. Born June 29, 1945, Nassau. Son of Charles (Boozie) and Amanda Rolle. Educated: Portsmouth College of Advanced Technology, Hampshire, England. Married to the former Elva Russell. Three children. Denomination: Baptist. Hobbies: chess, whist, softball, squash. Member: Kiwanis Club of Fort Montagu, St Anne's Scottish Masonic Lodge. Residence: Highland Park, PO Box N-3406, Nassau.

CENTREVILLE

PERRY GLADSTONE CHRISTIE, LLB, MP (PLP). Leader of The Opposition. Barrister-at-law, Christie, Davis & Co (partner). Senator, 1974-77; Minister of Health and National Insurance, 1977-82; Minister of Tourism, 1982-84; Minister of Agriculture, Trade and Industry, 1990-92. Co-deputy leader of the Progressive Liberal Party, 1992-97. Born Aug 21, 1943, Nassau. Son of Gladstone and Naomi (née Allen) Christie. Educated: Eastern Senior School, Nassau; Univ Tutorial College, London, England; Honours, Birmingham Univ and Inner Temple, England. Founding member of the Valley Boys Junkanoo Group and the Pioneers' Sporting Club. Married to the former Bernadette Joan Hanna, an attorney and chartered accountant of Nassau. Three children. Denomination: Anglican. Residence: Cable Beach, PO Box N-7940, Nassau.

DELAPORTE

FLOYD CLINTON WATKINS, BA (Hons, Law), MP (FNM). Barrister-at-law, Watkins, Foulkes & Co (partner). Born June 24, 1949, Staniard Creek, Andros. Son of Carl and Rebecca Watkins. Educated: Queen's College, Nassau; Ealing College and Lincoln's Inn, London, England. Married to the former Vera Astwood of New Providence. Three children. Denomination: Methodist. Hobby: reading. Residence: Marlin Dr, Highland Park, PO Box GT-2503, Nassau.

ENGLERSTON

PHILIP C GALANIS, MP (PLP). Managing Director, Bahamas Venture Capital Fund Ltd. Born Aug 23, 1954, Nassau. Son of Clifford and Zoe Galanis. Educated: St Joseph's Catholic School, St Augustine's College, Nassau; St John's Univ, Collegeville, MN; Rutgers Univ, NJ. Former president, Bahamas Institute of Chartered Accountants (1988-92) and Institute of Chartered Accountants of the Caribbean. Appointed to the Senate, Sept 1992. Elected to Parliament, Mar 1997. Married to the former Tonya Bastian. One child. Denomination: Roman Catholic. Hobbies: golf, reading. Residence: Delaporte Point, PO Box CB-11323, Nassau.

FORT CHARLOTTE

THE HON ZHIVARGO LAING, MP (FNM). Minister of State for Youth, Sports and Culture. Born Sept 7, 1967, Nassau. Son of Cedric Tyronne Laing and the former Senator Naomi Seymour. Educated: Lewis Yard Primary and

Hawksbill High School, Grand Bahama; College of The Bahamas, Nassau; Univ of Western Ontario, London, Ont, Canada; George Washington Univ, Washington, DC. Worked as a business administrator and an investment analyst with the Bahamas Investment Authority. Married to the former Zsa Zsa LaRoda. Two children. Denomination: Assemblies of God. Hobbies: basketball, computers, reading. Residence: Perpall Tract, PO Box CB-11907, Nassau.

FOX HILL

JAUNIANNE RAHMING DORSETT, BSc, MP (FNM). Chairman, Hotel Licensing Board. Manager of two family businesses. Vice-chairperson of Free National Movement (1994-96). Vice-chairperson, New Providence Licencing Authority (1992-94). Formerly a marketing manager at British American Bank and administrative assistant at the World Bank in Washington, DC. Born Oct 18, 1947 to John and Alfreda Rahming. Educated: Univ of Maryland, MD. Hobbies: writing, sewing and photography. Married to Bernard Dorsett. Three children. Residence: Hampshire St, Westward Villas, PO Box CB-11478, Nassau.

GARDEN HILLS

THE HON ROME ITALIA JOHNSON, BSc, BA, MP (FNM). Speaker of the House. Insurance director, Bahamas Insurance Brokers and Agents Ltd. Born Aug 1, 1954, Nassau. Daughter of Oscar and Sylvia Johnson. Educated: St Anne's Primary & High Schools and Queen's College, Nassau; Miami Dade Community College and Univ of Miami, Miami, FL; Georgetown Univ, Washington, DC. Denomination: Baptist. Hobbies: reading, writing, business concepts, travelling. Member: Transfiguration Baptist Church – Children's Church; FNM's Women's Assoc; The Bahamas Economic Forum. Residence: Swans Court, West Bay St, PO Box N-1505, Nassau.

GOLDEN GATES

THE HON THERESA MARIA MOXEY-INGRAHAM, MP (FNM). Minister of Labour, Immigration and Training. Born Oct 15, 1953, Nassau. Daughter of Helen Hutcherson. Educated: St Anne's High School, Government High School, Nassau; McMaster Univ, Hamilton, Ont, Canada; Univ of Miami, FL. One child. Married to Kirk S Ingraham. Denomination: Anglican. Hobbies: reading, doll making, collecting poetry. Member: Business & Professional Women's Assoc; Improved, Benevolent & Protected Order of Elks; Caribbean Women for Democracy. Residence: Yamacraw Hill Rd, PO Box N-1806, Nassau.

GRANT'S TOWN

BRADLEY BERNARD ROBERTS, MP (PLP). Businessman. Director, Sunshine Holdings Ltd; Burns House Ltd; Commonwealth Brewery Ltd; Freeport Oil Ltd; Arawak Homes Ltd; House of Music Ltd; Associated Bahamian Distillers; Autos Breweries (1979) Ltd; Eleuthera Properties Ltd. Managing director and chief executive of Bethell Robertson & Co; president, Inflight Kitchens Ltd; former chairman, Bahamas Electricity Corp; former chairman, Port Authority, Nassau; former chairman, Housing Commission; former chairman, Bahamas Gaming Board; former director, Development Corp, now BAIC. Born Dec 25, 1943, Nassau. Second son of the late RA Cyril (Tony) and Merle (née Albury)

Roberts. Educated: St Francis Xavier's, St Augustine's College, Government High School Evening Inst, Nassau. Married to the former Hartlyn M Mackey of Eleuthera. Three children, one grandchild. Denomination: Roman Catholic. Hobbies: music, travelling. Member: past president and member Rotary Club of West Nassau; Royal Eagle Lodge. Residence: Skyline Heights, PO Box N-8208, Nassau.

HOLY CROSS

THE HON CARL WILSHIRE BETHEL, LLB, MP (FNM). Minister of State for Economic Development. Barrister-at-law. Born July 1, 1961, Nassau. Son of Wilshire Z and Yvette V Bethel. Educated: St Andrew's School and Queen's College, Nassau; Yateley Manor, UK; Lester B Pearson College of The Pacific (United World College), Canada; Univ of London, London School of Economics, Holborn Law Tutors, London, England. Called to English and Bahamas Bars, 1985. Married to the former Lisa Marie Foulkes of Nassau. Four children. Denomination: Anglican. Hobbies: chess, Japanese chess, reading, walking, debating. Past president of the Torchbearers Youth Assoc of FNM; past vice-chairman of FNM; past president of Kiwanis Club of Fort Montagu. Member: Free Masons. Residence: Vista Marina, PO Box N-4303, Nassau.

KENNEDY

BERNARD J NOTTAGE, MB, ChB, FRCOG, FAMS, JP, MP (PLP). Obstetrician/gynaecologist. Born Oct 23, 1945, Nassau. Son of the late Bernard J and Olivia (née Johnson) Nottage. Educated: Government High School, Nassau; Univ of Aberdeen, Scotland. Deputy leader of the PLP, 1993-97. Parliamentary leader of the Opposition, 1993-97. Minister of Education, 1990-92. Minister of Consumer Affairs, 1989-90. Chairman, Water & Sewerage Corp, 1989-90. Chairman, National Insurance Board, 1987-89. President, Central American and Caribbean Athletic Confederation, 1982-90. Member: Medical Assoc of The Bahamas. Past president, Bahamas Amateur Athletic Assoc; Bahamas Doctors' Union; Bahamas Planned Parenthood Assoc; Medical Assoc of The Bahamas. Vice-president, North American, Central American & Caribbean Area Assoc (IAAF); Pan American Athletic Commission. Married to the former Portia Butterfield. One son. Denomination: Anglican. Hobbies: jogging, reading. Residence: Buttonwood Hills, PO Box N-446, Nassau.

MALCOLM CREEK

LESTER M TURNQUEST, BSc, MP (FNM). Parliamentary Secretary, Ministry of Health. Private banker. Born June 8, 1957, Nassau. Son of the late Lester and Valderine Turnquest. Educated: Government High School and College of The Bahamas, Nassau; Georgia Institute of Technology, GA. One daughter. Denomination: Anglican. Hobbies: fishing, reading. Former chairman, Bahamasair Holding Ltd; chairman, Nassau Flight Services Ltd. Residence: Brooklyn Rd, PO Box N-469, Nassau.

MARATHON

THE HON ALGERNON S P B ALLEN, LLB (Hons), MP (FNM). Minister of Housing and Social Development. Barrister-at-law. First elected to Parliament in 1987. Born April, 16, 1950, Nassau.

Son of the late Harry R Allen and Jestina (née Johnson) Allen. Educated: Government High School, Nassau; Kings College of London Univ and Middle Temple, England. Married to Anita (née Bethel) Allen, Supreme Court Justice. Six children. Denomination: Roman Catholic/Ecumenical. Hobbies: reading, writing. Residence: Nassau East, PO Box N-10114, Nassau.

MONTAGU

THE HON WILLIAM CLIFFORD ALLEN, BSc, MBA, MP (FNM). Minister of Finance and Planning and Minister of Economic Development. Former Minister of Planning and the Public Service; former member of the Senate; former governor of the Central Bank of The Bahamas; former chairman of the board of directors of Bahamasair; former deputy chairman of The Bahamas Mortgage Corp; former president of the Scout Assoc of The Bahamas; former deputy president and executive committee member of The Bahamas National Trust. Born Mar 15, 1937, Nassau. Educated: St Augustine's College, Nassau; Rhodes School, School of Commerce, New York Univ; Baruch College of City Univ of New York, NY. Married to the former Aloma Delores Munnings. Four children. Denomination: Methodist. Hobbies: golfing, fishing. Residence: Prospect Ridge, PO Box CB-10993, Nassau.

MOUNT MORIAH

THE HON O A T (TOMMY) TURNQUEST, MP (FNM). Minister of Public Works. Born Nov 16, 1959, Nassau. Son of HE Sir Orville A Turnquest, GCMG, QC, LLB, Governor-General, and Lady Turnquest (née Edith Thompson).

Educated: St Anne's High School, Nassau; Malvern College, England; Univ of Western Ontario (BA, Hons), London, Ont, Canada; Fellow Institute of Canadian Bankers. Married to the former Shawn Carey of Nassau. Three children. Denomination: Anglican. Hobbies: tennis, boating. Residence: Harrold Rd, PO Box N-682, Nassau.

ST CECILIA

DR CYNTHIA PRATT, MP (PLP). Opposition Whip. Retired nurse, educator and coach. Born Nov 5, 1947, Nassau to the late Herman and Rose Moxey of Andros and Eleuthera, respectively. Educated: Woodcock Primary School, Western Junior and Western Senior Schools, Princess Margaret School of Nursing, A F Adderley, C C Sweeting and Aquinas College evening institutions, Nassau; St Augustine's College, Raleigh, NC (BSc). Honorary Doctor of Humane Letters, St Augustine's, Raleigh, NC. Part-time lecturer and Asst Director of student activities at College of The Bahamas. An all-round athlete and coach, "Mother" Pratt has represented The Bahamas internationally in softball, basketball and volleyball. Married to Joseph Pratt. Six children. Hobbies: working with underprivileged people, coordinating sports events, coaching, meeting people. Residence: Coconut Grove, PO Box N-1572, Nassau.

ST MARGARET

SYLVIA EUJENETH SCRIVEN, MP (FNM). Government Whip. Former chairman, Bahamas Mortgage Corp. Accountant/sales representative, H G Christie Ltd. Born Jan 23, 1939,

Nassau. Daughter of Obediah and Lillian (née Wells) Smith of Long Island. Educated: Eastern Senior School, Nassau; Gordon Arlene College, London, England. Chairman, Road Traffic Dept; former chairman, Housing Corp; past-president, FNM's Women's Assoc; former vice-chairman, FNM; treasurer, Caribbean Women for Democracy (Bahamas) Division; chairman, Division 22 of the EC & C of Kiwanis International; president, Kiwanis Club of Fort Montagu; hon secretary of The Bahamas Real Estate Assoc; chairman, St Barnabas Usher Board. Three children. Denomination: Anglican. Hobbies: cooking, entertaining, music, theatre. Residence: Westward Villas, PO Box CB-12684, Nassau.

SHIRLEA

THE HON PIERRE VALIANT LAUNCELOT DUPUCH, BA, BSc, MP (FNM). Minister of Consumer Welfare and Aviation. Former Minister of Agriculture and Fisheries. Printing executive. Born April 23, 1938, Nassau. Son of the late Sir Etienne Dupuch and Lady Dupuch (née Marie Plouse). Educated: St Augustine's College, Nassau; De La Salle High School, Canada; St John's Univ, MN, and Carnegie Mellon Univ, PA. Married to the former Susan Thompson of Kent, England. Five children. Denomination: Roman Catholic. Hobbies: horses, fishing, boating. Residence: Camperdown Heights, PO Box N-4555, Nassau.

SOUTH BEACH

MICHAEL DOUGLAS SMITH, BSc, JP, MP (FNM). Deputy Speaker of the House. Executive chairman, Broadcasting Corp of The Bahamas. Born Nov 30, 1948, Nassau. Son of the late Samuel A and Cynthia K (née Hudson) Smith. Educated: Government High School, Nassau; Mankato State Univ, MN; Ryerson Polytechnical Institute, Toronto, Ont, Canada. Married to the former Suzanne Joaquin of Bermuda. Two children. Denomination: Non-denominational. Member: advisory committee for the Salvation Army. Hobbies: gardening, reading, creative writing. Trustee for the Endowment for the Performing Arts of The Bahamas. Residence: Westward Villas, PO Box CB-12668, Nassau.

YAMACRAW

THE HON JANET GWENNETT BOSTWICK, MP (FNM). Minister of Foreign Affairs. First woman elected to Parliament and first elected female to serve as a minister in Cabinet. Attorney-at-law, Bostwick & Bostwick (inactive partner). Born Oct 30, 1939, Nassau. Daughter of Nick and Lois (née Bethel) Musgrove. Educated: Government High School, Commercial Studies, Nassau. Articled law student to Gerald Corlett, former Attorney-General. Called to The Bahamas Bar April 1971. Crown counsel, 1971-74. Crown prosecutor, 1972-74. Attorney-General and Minister of Foreign Affairs 1994-97. Minister of Justice and Immigration, 1993-94. Minister of Housing and National Insurance, 1992-93. Past president Bahamas Bar Assoc; past president, FNM's Women's Assoc; president, Caribbean Women for Democracy. Member: executive committee, Girls' Brigade; executive committee, Bahamas Girl Guides Assoc. Past secretary general Bahamas Public Services Union. Past patron, Hope House (Home for Unwed Mothers). Married to Senator the Hon J Henry Bostwick, QC (FNM). Four children, four grandchildren. Denomination: Anglican. Hobbies:

fishing, reading, animal farming. Residence: Lookout Hill, Winton, PO Box N-1605, Nassau.

THE FAMILY ISLANDS

ABACO

NORTH ABACO

THE RT HON HUBERT A INGRAHAM, PC, MP (FNM). Prime Minister. Attorney-at-law. Elected to the House in 1977, as an Independent candidate '87. Leader of the FNM since May 1990. Prime Minister since Aug 1992. Minister of Housing and National Insurance, 1982-84. Former chairman, Bahamas Mortgage Corp. Born Aug 4, 1947, Pine Ridge, Grand Bahama. Son of Jerome Ingraham and the late Isabella (née Cornish) Laroda. Educated: Cooper's Town Public School, Abaco; Southern Senior School and Government High School Evening Institute, Nassau. Married to the former Delores Velma Miller of Miller's, Long Island. Six children. Denomination: Baptist. Hobbies: reading, swimming. Residence: Croton Ave, PO Box CB-10976, Nassau.

SOUTH ABACO

ROBERT PERCIVAL SWEETING JR, MP (FNM). Businessman. Owner, Rich's Boat Rentals. Born Feb 4, 1945, Nassau. Son of Robert Percival and Venie Sweeting. Educated: Man-O-War All Age School, Abaco. Married to the former Margaret Russell of Hope Town, Abaco. Three children. Denomination: Brethren. Hobbies: softball, sailing. Member: Abaco Concerned Citizens Committee; Abaco Chamber of Commerce. Residence: Marsh Harbour. PO Box AB-20012, Abaco.

ANDROS

NORTH ANDROS & BERRY ISLANDS

THE HON DR EARL D DEVEAUX, MP (FNM). Minister of Agriculture and Fisheries. Born Mar 31, 1949, Staniard Creek, Andros. Son of the late Clarence "Cap" and Alice (née Saunders) Deveaux. Educated: Queen's College, Nassau; Univ of Miami (Economics), Miami, FL; Penn State Univ, Erie, PA (MA, agricultural economics); Honorary Doctorate, Lycoming College, Williamsport, PA. Former member, American Society of Agricultural Consultants; government planning officer; research and credit officer, World Banking Corp; manager, Bahamas Agricultural Research Training and Development Project, Andros, 1974-78; Asst Director of Agriculture, 1979-83; commercial farmer, 1983-87; consultant to The Bahamas Agricultural and Industrial Corp and Ministry of Agriculture, 1987-93; Director of Agriculture, 1993-96. Married to the former Barbara Clancy. Two daughters. Denomination: Methodist. Hobbies: fishing, reading, writing, farming. Residence: Danottage Estates, PO Box N-688, Nassau.

SOUTH ANDROS & MANGROVE CAY

RONALD ANTHONY BOSFIELD, MP (FNM). Teacher and businessman. Born July 14, 1954, Mangrove Cay, Andros. Educated: Mangrove Cay Public School; Bahamas Teachers' College; South Andros Evening Institute; Queen's Univ, Kingston, Ont, Canada (BA); Univ of Miami (MBA). Principal of High Rock Primary School, South Andros, 1976-82; taught business at

A F Adderley Senior High School, Nassau, 1984-87. Managing director, Horizontal Printing and Busy Business Centre, Nassau. Married to the former Sharon Lightbourne. Denomination: Brethren. Two children. Residence: Seabreeze, PO Box CB-11082, Nassau.

CAT ISLAND, SAN SALVADOR AND RUM CAY

JAMES H MILLER, MP (FNM). Former teacher. Operator with BORCO and Syntex, Grand Bahama, and currently chairman, Air Transport Advisory Board. Born Jan 18, 1953, Miller's, Long Island. Son of the former Eliza Butler and the late Bishop John Miller. Educated: Miller's All Age School, San Salvador Teachers Training College; Univ of Miami, Miami, FL. Member: Cat Island United General Council, Cat Island Sailing Club. Married to the former Delma Dean. Three children. Denomination: Calvary Temple Assemblies of God. Hobbies: community work, sailing. Residence: #1 Fortune Bay Dr, PO Box F-44494, Freeport.

ELEUTHERA

NORTH ELEUTHERA

ALVIN A SMITH, MP (FNM). Teacher. Executive Chairman, Bahamas Agricultural and Industrial Corp. Born Sept 23, 1951, Hatchet Bay, Eleuthera to the late Alfred Smith and the former Bernice Johnson. Educated: Hatchet Bay All Age School (now P A Gibson); San Salvador Teacher's Training College; Univ of Miami, Miami, FL (BSc). Taught approx 24 years in the government school system. Former trustee, Bahamas Union of Teachers. Former chairman of Government Schools Sports Coaches' Committee. Member: National Sports Advisory Council, 1991-92. Vice-president, Bahamas Senate, 1992-95. Chairman, Air Transport Advisory Board, 1995-97. Parliamentary Secretary, Ministry of Education, 1995-97. Married to the former Arnette Pinder. Two children. Denomination: Methodist. Hobbies: fishing, flying, softball, reading. Residence: South Beach, PO Box FH-14610, Nassau.

SOUTH ELEUTHERA

ANTHONY C MILLER, BSc, MP (FNM). Government Deputy Whip. Offshore banker. Executive chairman, Bahamasair (national flag carrier). Former chairman Town Planning Committee. Born Mar 17, 1955, Green Castle, Eleuthera. Son of Mable Miller. Educated: Windermere High School, Savannah Sound, Eleuthera; Cheyney Univ, Cheyney, PA. Married to the former Bernell Pinder of Deep Creek, Eleuthera. Three children. Denomination: Protestant. Hobbies: golf, tennis, reading. Member: Green Castle, Eleuthera Development Assoc. Residence: Winton Meadows, PO Box EE-17020, Nassau. E-mail tonym@batelnet.bs

EXUMA

ELLIOTT B LOCKHART, MP (FNM). Counsel & attorney-at-law. Elliott B Lockhart & Co. Born Mar 30, 1955, Duncan Town, Ragged Island. Son of the late Vernon E Lockhart and Olga P Lockhart. Chairman, Bahamas Gaming Board, 1992-95. Elected chairman of the FNM in 1990. Married to the former Clarita Taylor. Five children. Denomination: Anglican. Hobbies: boating, fishing, carpentry, mechanics. Residence: Seabreeze Estates, PO Box N-8615, Nassau.

GRAND BAHAMA

EIGHT MILE ROCK

LINDY H RUSSELL, MP (FNM). Parliamentary Secretary in the Office of the Prime Minister. Born Jan 4, 1954, Eight Mile Rock, Grand Bahama. Son of Harris Russell Sr and Gennive (née Smith) Russell, both deceased. Educated: Eight Mile Rock All Age School, Freeport Anglican High School. Former airline agent with Delta, and manager with Air Florida and Gull Air. Elected to local govt, Eight Mile Rock east township chairman, July 1996. Elected to House of Assembly Mar 1997. Active in local church and sports organizations. Married to the former Nell Lavern Wildgoose of Eight Mile Rock. Two children. Denomination: Baptist. Hobbies: baseball, water skiing, basketball. Residence: Russell Town, PO Box F-40557, Eight Mile Rock.

HIGH ROCK

KENNETH RUSSELL, JP, MP (FNM). Drawing office supervisor and maintenance planning coordinator, BORCO. Registered, licensed architectural technician. Born Oct 22, 1953, Bailey Town, Bimini. Son of Olsworth Russell and the former Eunice Lightbourne. Educated: Hawksbill High School; CR Walker Technical College; Bahamas Teachers College; Nova Southeastern Univ, Fort Lauderdale, FL. Member: Housing Commission for Grand Bahama 1992-present. Elected to House of Assembly March 1996 and appointed chairman of town planning for New Providence April '96. Local govt council for Freeport June 1996-Jan '97. Married to the former Georgina Bridgewater. Four children. Denomination: Church of God. Hobbies: politics, designing houses, car and motorcycle racing. Residence: #7 Harlow Rd, PO Box F-42950, Lucaya.

LUCAYA

NEKO C GRANT, I, JP, MP (FNM). Business executive, Burns House Ltd (senior vice-president). Born Mar 1, 1950, West End, Grand Bahama. Son of Reva L Grant. Educated: West End All Age School, Grand Bahama; St John's College, Nassau; La Salle Extension Univ, (Business Management), Chicago, IL. Member: Diamond Distinguished past president of Kiwanis International; past and honorary president The Bahamas Softball Federation, past president West End Offshore Power Boat Assoc, past president Kiwanis Club of Lucaya. Inducted into the Intl Softball Hall of Fame Aug 1997. Married to the former Barbara Evans of George Town, Exuma. Two children. Denomination: Baptist. Hobbies: softball, fishing. Constituency Office: East Sunrise Shopping Centre, PO Box F-44200, Freeport.

MARCO CITY

THE HON DAVID C THOMPSON, MP (FNM). Minister of State for the Public Service in the Office of the Prime Minister. Former Minister of State, Office of the Prime Minister with responsibility for Grand Bahama and Family Island Affairs including the Dept of Local Government. Former Minister of State for the Public Service and Labour, Ministry of Finance and Planning. Attorney-at-law. Born Jan 5, 1950, Duncan Town, Ragged Island. Son of the late Charles David and Earlene (née Lockhart) Thompson. Educated: Western Junior & Senior Schools, Government High School, Nassau. Articled law clerk 1971. Called to The Bahamas Bar in Aug 1976.

Former chairman, Bahamas Mortgage Corp. Former chairman, Road Traffic Authority. Director and past chairman, YMCA of Grand Bahama. Life member of Kiwanis International and past president of Kiwanis Club of Freeport. Former Synod representative and people's warden of the Church of the Ascension Anglican Church, Lucaya. Married to the former Agatha Robinson of Nassau. Three children. Denomination: Anglican. Hobbies: tennis and reading. Residence: Lagnappie Circle, Fortune Bay, PO Box F-40001, Freeport.

PINERIDGE

THE HON CORNELIUS A SMITH, MP (FNM). Minister of Tourism. Business executive. Born April 7, 1937, North End, Long Island. Son of Sylvanus and Susan Smith. Educated: Glinton Public School, Long Island; Bahamas Teachers College, Nassau; Univ of Miami (MBA), FL. Married to the former Clara Knowles of Tarpum Bay, Eleuthera. Three children. Denomination: Anglican. Hobby: fishing. Member: Jaycees; Kiwanis; Freeport Chamber of Commerce; Bahamas Assoc for Manpower Training & Development. Residence: 9 Seahorse Ln, PO Box F-43879, Freeport and PO Box N-4891, Nassau.

WEST END AND BIMINI

DAVID G WALLACE, MP (FNM). Life insurance agent. Born May 26, 1959, Holmes Rock, Grand Bahama to the late David Genise Wallace and Zytha (née Gray) Wallace. Educated: Holmes Rock All Age School, Martin Town Primary, Freeport Anglican High School. Member of Million Dollar Round Table, Crown Life President's Circle, Crown Life Royal Club. Chairman Grand Bahama Housing Commission. Married to the former Charmaine Moxey of Ragged Island. Four children. Denomination: Baptist. Hobbies: bowling, reading, music. Residence: 110 Fern Court, PO Box F-42622, Freeport.

LONG ISLAND AND RAGGED ISLAND

THE HON JAMES FRANKLIN KNOWLES, MP (FNM). Minister of Transport. Attorney-at-law. Born Dec 25, 1942, Fox Hill. Son of the late Alexander Knowles and Agnes (née Pinder) Knowles. Educated: Sandilands All Age School, Queen's College, Nassau. Married to the former Amarylis Rosien Treco. Three children. Denomination: Anglican. Hobbies: gardening, boating. Residence: Yamacraw Hill Rd, PO Box N-7088, Nassau.

MICAL (MAYAGUANA, INAGUA, CROOKED ISLAND, ACKLINS & LONG CAY)

THE HON VERNON JOSEPH SYMONETTE, JP, MP (FNM). Minister of State for Family Island Affairs. Speaker of the House 1992-97. Accountant. Born Nov 8, 1937, Matthew Town, Inagua. Son of W A Geoffrey Symonette and Ira G Glover, both deceased. Educated: Inagua Public School and Inagua Evening Institute. Charter president, Kiwanis Club of Inagua; charter member L L Dean Lodge, Modern, Free and Accepted Masons; past treasurer, Zion Baptist Church, Inagua; past president, Inagua Union (Burial) Society. Married to the former Phyllis Estelle Hanna of Matthew Town, Inagua. Four children. Denomination: Baptist. Hobbies: reading, fishing, shooting. Residence: Victoria St, Inagua.

Parliamentarians' Salaries

	Salary	Duty Allowance
Prime Minister	$86,000	$25,000
Deputy Prime Minister	$76,000	$15,000
Attorney General	$60,000	$5,000
Cabinet Ministers with portfolio	$66,000	$5,000
Minister of State	$60,000	$5,000
Speaker of the House	$62,000	$3,000
Deputy Speaker	$32,000	–
Parliamentary Secretaries	$45,000	$3,000
Leader of the Opposition	$50,000	–
Members of Parliament (House of Assembly)	$28,000	–
Government Whip	–	$11,550
Government Deputy Whip	–	$6,000
Opposition Whip	–	$11,250
President of the Senate	$17,500	–
Vice-President of the Senate	$15,000	–
Leader of the Senate	$15,000	–
Senators	$12,500	–

Cabinet Ministers hold full-time positions. Senators and House members meet regularly but not on a full-time basis, and customarily hold positions in a profession or business.

Members of Parliament (MP) who hold other positions in Government are paid these salaries in addition to the MP salary. In the case of MPs holding more than one Cabinet position, only one Cabinet salary is received in addition to the MP salary.

A Subsistence Allowance for international travel is based on official destination, length of stay, etc. A claim is submitted afterwards. Family Island representatives receive a Constituency Allowance for travel to and from their constituencies.

Parliamentary Secretaries

LINDY HARRIS RUSSELL, MP
  Office of the Prime Minister, West Bay St, Nassau
SENATOR THE HON CALVIN JOHNSON
  Ministry of Tourism, Market Plaza, Bay St, Nassau
SENATOR THE HON DAPHNE DUNCOMBE COOPER
  Ministry of Finance and Planning, West Bay St, Nassau
GREGORY JAMES WILLIAMS, MP
  Ministry of Public Works, John F Kennedy Dr, Nassau
LESTER TURNQUEST, MP
  Ministry of Health, Shirley St, Nassau

Permanent Secretaries

The Cabinet
  Basil O'Brien, CMG
  Secretary to the Cabinet
Office of the Prime Minister
  M Teresa Butler
  Wendell Major, Dept of
    Public Service
**Office of the Deputy Prime Minister
  & Ministry of
  National Security**
  Harcourt Turnquest, Natl Security
  Deanza Cunningham, Public
    Enterprises
**Office of the Attorney General &
  Ministry of Justice**
  Leila Greene
Government House
  Vernita Johnson, LVO,
  Secretary to the Governor-General
Ministry of Agriculture & Fisheries
  Rodella Tynes
**Ministry of Consumer Welfare
  & Aviation**
  Roosevelt Butler
Ministry of Education
  Willamae Salkey
Ministry of Finance and Planning
  Ruth Millar, CMG, Financial Secretary
  Wilfred Horton, Economic Div
Ministry of Foreign Affairs
  Luther Smith
Ministry of Health
  Joshua Sears
**Ministry of Housing & Social
  Development**
  Creswell Sturrup
**Ministry of Labour, Immigration
  & Training**
  Thelma Ferguson-Beneby
**Ministry of Public Works &
  Local Government**
  Ronald Thompson
Ministry of Tourism
  Dr Patricia Rodgers
Ministry of Transport
  Archie Nairn
Ministry of Youth, Sports & Culture
  Anita Bernard

Commission Chairpersons

Public Service Commission ....Harold Munnings, OBE
Legal and Judicial Service Commission ....The Hon Dame Joan Sawyer
Police Service Commission ....Rev Dr Charles W Saunders, CBE
Public Disclosure Commission ....Oswald Isaacs

PUBLIC SERVICE OFFICIALS

DEPT OF AGRICULTURE
Carl Smith, Director
Simeon Pinder, Acting Deputy Director
Valarie Outten, Acting Deputy Director
(Freeport)

AUDIT DEPT
Roger Forbes, Acting Auditor General
Carolyn Patton, Senior Asst Auditor
(Freeport)

DEPT OF ARCHIVES
Dr D Gail Saunders, Director

BAHAMAS AGRICULTURAL & INDUSTRIAL CORP
Alvin Smith, MP, Chairman

BAHAMAS DEVELOPMENT BANK
Larry Gibson, Chairman of the Board
Paul D Major, Managing Director
Anthony Woodside, Deputy Managing Director
George Miller, Operations Manager
Justin A Sturrup, Manager
(Freeport operation)

BAHAMAS ELECTRICITY CORP (BEC)
Freeman Duncanson, General Manager

BAHAMAS GAMING BOARD
Alonzo M Butler, Acting Secretary

BAHAMAS HOTEL CORP
Berkley S Evans, Chief Executive Officer

BAHAMAS INFORMATION SERVICES
Christopher Symmonett, Acting Director

BAHAMAS MORTGAGE CORP
Paul King, Managing Director
Dennis Lightbourne, Manager and Senior Loan Officer (Freeport)

BAHAMAS TELECOMMUNICATIONS CORP (BATELCO)
Michael Symonette, General Manager

BAHAMASAIR
Glen Pickard,
General Manager

BOYS' INDUSTRIAL SCHOOL
Holland Dean, Acting Asst Superintendent

BROADCASTING CORP OF THE BAHAMAS
Edwin Lightbourn, General Manager

CENTRAL BANK OF THE BAHAMAS
Julian Francis, Governor

CIVIL AVIATION DEPT
Ciano Strachan, Director

COLLEGE OF THE BAHAMAS
Dr Leon Higgs, President

DEPT OF COOPERATIVES
Nathaniel Adderley, Director

CUSTOMS DEPT
John Rolle, Comptroller

ROYAL BAHAMAS DEFENCE FORCE
Commodore Davey Rolle, Commander

DEPT OF ENVIRONMENTAL HEALTH SERVICES
Dr Donald Cooper, Director

FIRE DEPT
Hosea Douglas, Director

DEPT OF FISHERIES
Michael Braynen, Acting Director

GIRLS' INDUSTRIAL SCHOOL
Darnell Miller, Superintendent

GOVERNMENT HOUSE
Locksley Knowles, Comptroller

GOVERNMENT PRINTING DEPT
John Burrows, Chief Superintendent

GOVERNOR-GENERAL'S OFFICE
Vesta Williams, Personal Assistant
Vernita Johnson, LVO,
  Secretary to the Governor-General

HOUSE OF ASSEMBLY
Edward Ellis, Hansard
Maurice Tynes, Chief Clerk

DEPT OF HOUSING
Lorraine Symonette-Armbrister,
  Chief Housing Officer
Melvern Johnson, Office Manager
  (Freeport)

IMMIGRATION DEPT
Melvin Seymour, Director

INDUSTRIAL RELATIONS BOARD
Patrenda Russell, Secretary

JUDICIAL DEPT
Dame Joan Sawyer, Chief Justice
Nathaniel Dean, Registrar of the
  Supreme Court
Supreme Court Justices:
  Joseph Alfred; Anita Allen; Hartman
  Longley; Ricardo Marques;
  Emmanuel Osadebay;
  Joseph Strachan
Stipendiary and Circuit Magistrates:
  Jon Isaacs (chief magistrate), Cheryl
  Albury, Carolita Bethel, Jethlyn
  Burrows (Freeport), Joan Ferguson,
  Roger Gomez, Petra Hanna-Weeks
  (Freeport), Rengin Johnson, Gladys
  Manuel, Marilyn Meeres, Winston
  Saunders (Coroner), Vera Watkins,
  Sharon Wilson

LABOUR DEPT
Donald Symonette, Director
Harcourt Brown, Asst Director of
  Labour (Freeport)

DEPT OF LANDS & SURVEYS
Tex Turnquest, Deputy Director

LEGAL AFFAIRS DEPT
Michael Hamilton, Director

DEPT OF LOCAL GOVERNMENT
Brenville Hanna, Consultant

MARITIME AFFAIRS
J W Dempster, Director (London)
Judith Francis, Senior Deputy Director
  (London)

METEOROLOGICAL DEPT
Kenneth Lightbourne, Director

MINISTRY OF EDUCATION
Iris Pinder, Acting Director

MINISTRY OF FINANCE
Ruth Millar, Financial Secretary
George Sherman, Director of Budget
Ehurd Cunningham, Secretary
  for Revenue
C G Sands, Under Secretary

MINISTRY OF FOREIGN AFFAIRS
George P Stewart, Director General
Jacqueline Bethel, Chief of Protocol

MINISTRY OF HEALTH
Dr M Dahl-Regis, Chief Medical Officer
Mary Johnson, Director of Nursing
Michaela Storr, Chief Hospital
  Administrator, Ministry of Health
Herbert Brown, Hospital Administrator,
  Sandilands Hospital
Andil Laroda, Hospital Administrator,
  Princess Margaret Hospital
Catherine Weech, Hospital
  Administrator, Rand Memorial
  Hospital (Freeport)

MINISTRY OF PUBLIC WORKS
Anthony Butler, Director
Melanie Roach, Deputy Director
Roland Bevans, Engineering Asst
  (Freeport)

MINISTRY OF TOURISM
Vincent Vanderpool-Wallace,
  Director General

**MINISTRY OF YOUTH, SPORTS
AND CULTURE**
Winston Cooper, Director of Sports,
Cleophas Adderley, Director of Culture
Charles Beneby, Director of Youth
Patricia Francis, Director of
  Community Affairs

NATIONAL INSURANCE BOARD
Lennox McCartney, Director

**PARLIAMENTARY
REGISTRATION DEPT**
Errol Bethel, Parliamentary Commissioner

PASSPORT OFFICE
Lillian Rolle,
   Acting Chief Passport Officer

DEPT OF PHYSICAL PLANNING
Michael Major, Director

ROYAL BAHAMAS POLICE FORCE
Bernard K Bonamy, LLB, LVO,
   Commissioner

PORT DEPT
Capt Anthony J Allens,
   Port Controller
Glenward Bain, Deputy Controller
Pamela Gomez, Senior Clerk (Freeport)

POST OFFICE
John Saunders, Postmaster General

PRISONS DEPT
Philip Turner, Superintendent

REGISTRAR GENERAL'S DEPT
Sterling Quant, Registrar General
Stephana Saunders, Asst Registrar
   (Freeport)

**DEPT OF REHABILITATIVE
& WELFARE SERVICES**
Mellany Zonicle, Director

ROAD TRAFFIC DEPT
Brensil Rolle, Acting Controller

SOCIAL SERVICES DEPT
Blanche Deveaux, Director
Lillian Quant-Forbes, Chief Welfare
   Officer (Freeport)

STATISTICS DEPT
Charles Stuart, Director
Clara Lowe, Officer in Charge (Freeport)

TREASURY DEPT
Franklyn Kemp, Treasurer

WATER & SEWERAGE CORP (WSC)
E George Moss, General Manager
Lester DeGregory,
   Graduate Engineer I (Freeport)

MOST COMPLETE, INTERESTING, ACCURATE, UP-TO-DATE

bahamasnet

http://www.bahamasnet.com
PO BOX N-7513, NASSAU, THE BAHAMAS
TEL 242-323-5665 • FAX 242-323-5728 • E-MAIL:dupuch@bahamasnet.com

GOVERNMENT OFFICES

1. **CHURCHILL BUILDING** – Cabinet Office, Treasury
2. **TOURIST INFORMATION CENTRE**
3. **HOUSE OF ASSEMBLY**
4. **SENATE**
5. **PARLIAMENT SQUARE BUILDING** – Registrar of Insurance
6. **CENTRAL POLICE STATION**
7. **SUPREME COURT**
8. **POST OFFICE BUILDING** – General Post Office, Attorney-General's Office, Ministry of Justice, Ministry of Labour, Immigration and Training, Ministry of Transport
9. **CENTRAL BANK OF THE BAHAMAS** – Central Bank, Exchange Control
10. **GOVERNMENT HOUSE** – Office and residence of Governor-General
11. **PRINCE GEORGE DOCK** – Port and Marine Dept
12. **MARKET PLAZA** – Ministry of Tourism
13. **VEHICLE INSPECTION CENTRE** – Vehicle licensing and inspection
14. **POLICE AND FIRE BRIGADE HEADQUARTERS**
15. **PRINCESS MARGARET HOSPITAL**
16. **MINISTRY OF EDUCATION**
17. **BROADCASTING CORP OF THE BAHAMAS** – Radio Bahamas, ZNS-TV
18. **MOSKO BUILDING** – Dept of Immigration
19. **DEPT OF FISHERIES**
20. **DEPT OF LANDS AND SURVEYS**
21. **POLICE TRAFFIC DIVISION**
22. **PRODUCE EXCHANGE**
23. **DEPT OF ARCHIVES**
24. **MINISTRY OF FOREIGN AFFAIRS**
25. **NASSAU COURT** – Environmental Health, Environmental Sanitation (Health Inspectorate Dept), Environmental Monitoring & Risk Assessments Division/Public Analyst Lab (PAL)
26. **LEVY BUILDING** – Dept of Cooperatives, Ministry of Agriculture and Fisheries, Bahamas Agriculture & Industrial Corp (BAIC)
27. **RODNEY E BAIN BUILDING** – Registrar General's Office, Dept of the Registrar General, Dept of the Auditor General, Coroner's Court
28. **FREDERICK HOUSE** – Business Licensing and Valuation Dept, Ministry of Housing and Social Development
29. **HOTEL CORP OF THE BAHAMAS**
30. **THE OLD LIGHTHOUSE BUILDING** – Government Publications Office, Police Marine (Harbour Control), Public Disclosure Office
31. **ROYAL VICTORIA GARDENS** – Ministry of Health, Nursing Council of The Bahamas
32. **GOLD CIRCLE HOUSE** – Ministry of Youth, Sports and Culture (south of 19 on map)

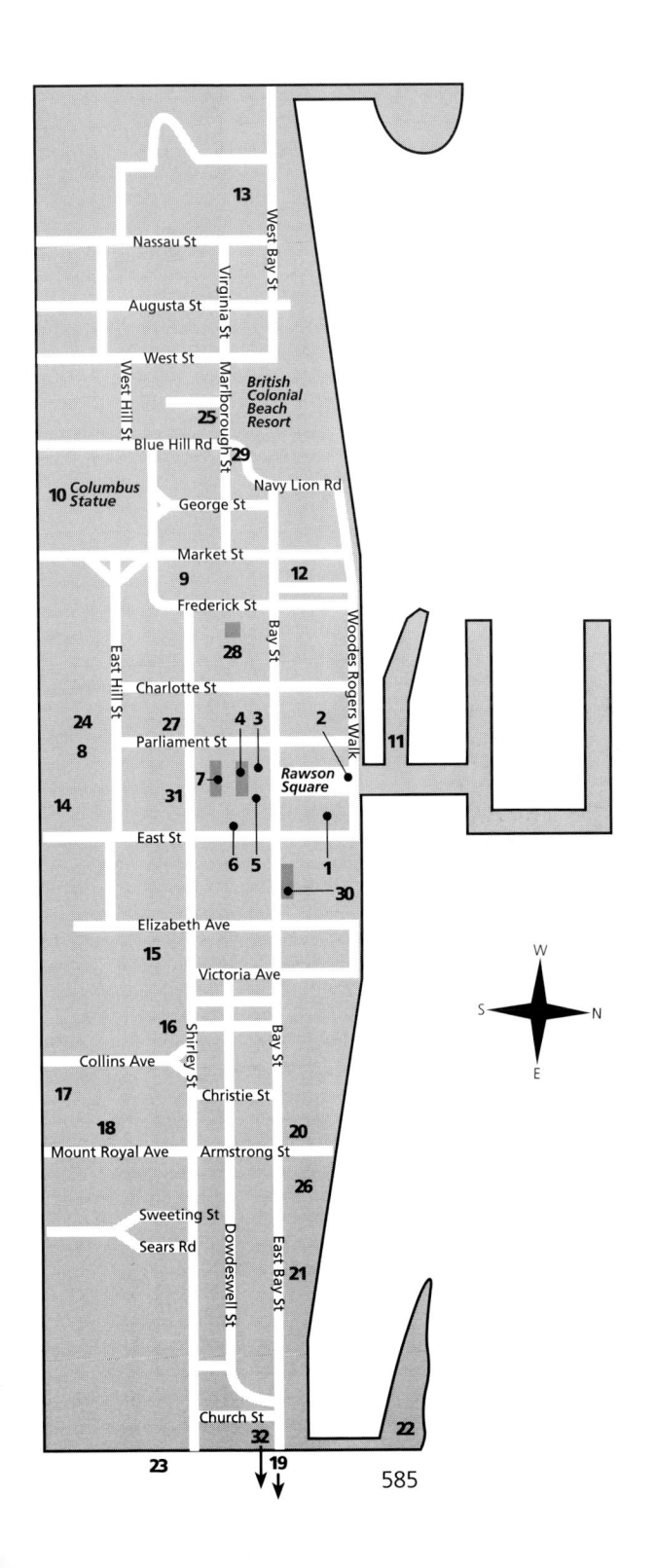

Nassau

Nassau St	
Augusta St	
West St	
	British Colonial Beach Resort
Blue Hill Rd	25
	29
	Navy Lion Rd
10 Columbus Statue	
	George St
	Market St
	9 12
	Frederick St
	28
	Charlotte St
24 27	4 3 2
8	Parliament St
	7 Rawson Square
14	31
	East St
	6 5 1
	30
	Elizabeth Ave
	15
	Victoria Ave
	16
	Collins Ave
17	Christie St
	18 20
	Mount Royal Ave Armstrong St
	26
	Sweeting St
	Sears Rd
	21
	Church St
23	32 19 22

585

GOVERNMENT OFFICES

1. **Boulevard Bldg, Thompson Blvd:**
   Criminal Investigation Dept, Dept of Housing & Social Services, Passport Office
2. **Bahamas Mortgage Corp, Russel Rd**
3. **Clarence Bain Bldg, Thompson Blvd:**
   Ministry of Labour, Dept of Public Service, Dept of Economic Development, Dept of Statistics, Post Office, Public Service Commission, Road Traffic Dept, Vehicle Inspection Centre
4. **Monument Shopping Centre, Oakes Field:**
   Public Service Centre for Human Resource Development, Ministry of Consumer Welfare and Aviation (Commission of Inquiry Bldg), Industrial Tribunal
5. **Customs House:**
   Thompson Blvd, Oakes Field
6. **National Insurance Board, Blue Hill Rd**
7. **Bahamas Telecommunications Corp, John F Kennedy Dr**
8. **Ministry of Public Works Bldg, John F Kennedy Dr:**
   Town Planning, Ministry of Public Works, Water and Sewerage Corp
9. **Nassau Intl Airport:**
   Dept of Civil Aviation, Dept of Meteorology
10. **Sir Cecil V Wallace Whitfield Centre, Cable Beach:**
    Prime Minister's Office, Bahamas Investment Authority (BIA), Bahamas Investment & Trade, Ministry of Finance and Planning, Bahamas Environment, Science & Technology Commission (BEST)
11. **Bahamas Development Bank, Cable Beach**
12. **Former National Insurance Board Bldg, Farrington Rd:**
    Parliamentary Commissioner's Office
13. **Police Training College, Thompson Blvd**
14. **Ministry of Education Testing and Evaluation Unit, Thompson Blvd**
15. **Criminal Records Office, Thompson Blvd**
    Gun Licensing Dept, Fingerprinting Dept
16. **Bahamas Tourism Training Centre, Thompson Blvd:**
    Bahamas Hotel Training College, Univ of the West Indies, Industry Training Dept (Bahamahost)
17. **Water & Sewerage Corp**
    #87 Thompson Blvd
18. **Admin Offices – Roads, Parks & Grounds Beautification, Farrington Rd**
19. **Gaming Board**
    Bahamas Information Services, Gaming Board of The Bahamas

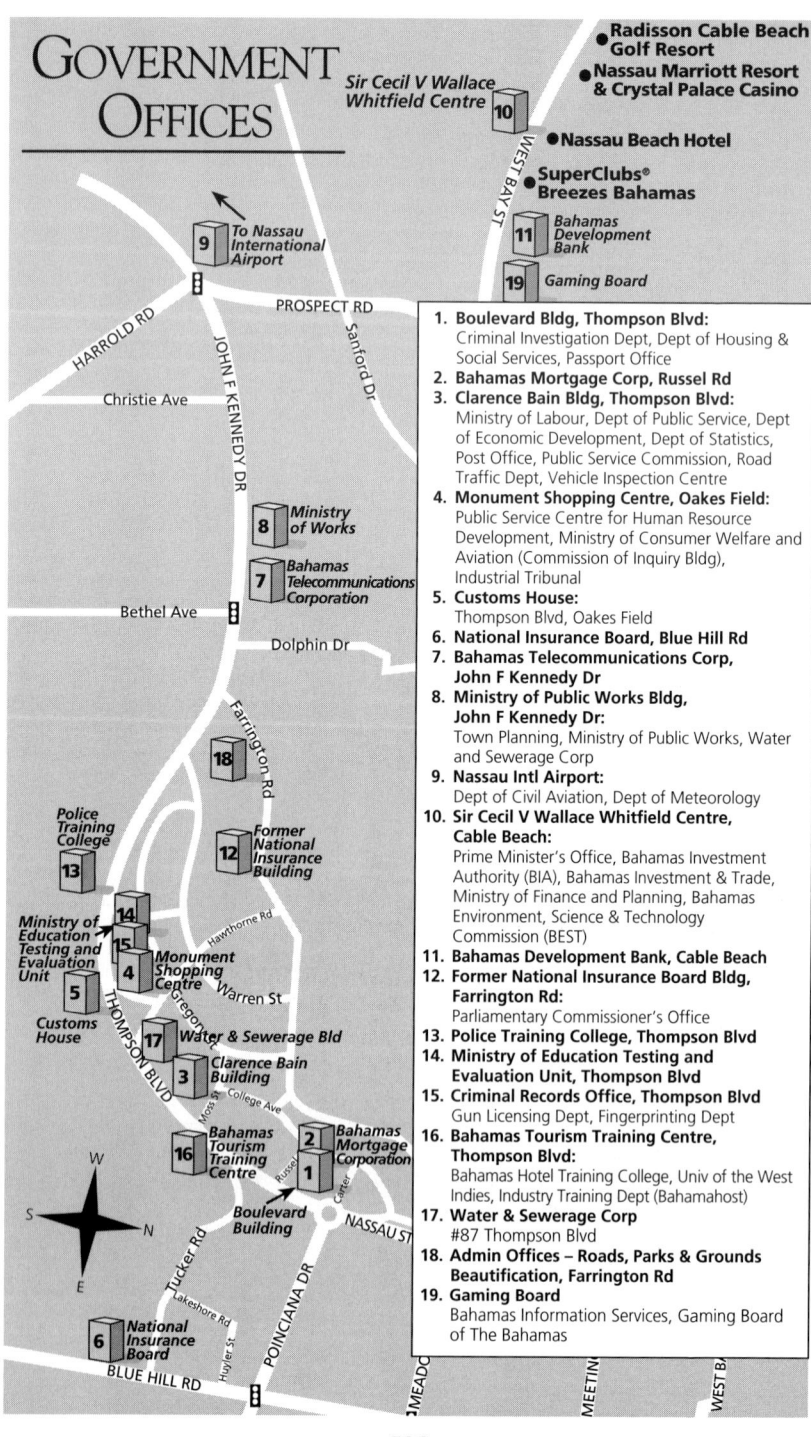

BAHAMAS DIPLOMATIC & CONSULAR REPRESENTATIVES

ANTIGUA AND BARBUDA 
His Excellency (HE) A Leonard Archer
High Commissioner (non-resident)
Address: The High Commission for the Commonwealth of The Bahamas to Antigua, c/o The Ministry of Foreign Affairs, PO Box N-3746, Nassau, The Bahamas. Tel (242) 322-7624/5.

REPUBLIC OF ARGENTINA 
HE Geoffrey Johnstone, CMG
Ambassador (non-resident)
Address: The Embassy of the Commonwealth of The Bahamas to the Republic of Argentina, c/o The Ministry of Foreign Affairs, PO Box N-3746, Nassau, The Bahamas. Tel (242) 322-7624/5.

BARBADOS
HE A Leonard Archer
High Commissioner (non-resident)
See Antigua and Barbuda

BELGIUM
HE Arthur A Foulkes
Ambassador (non-resident)
See United Kingdom

BELIZE
HE A Leonard Archer
High Commissioner (non-resident)
See Antigua and Barbuda

FEDERATIVE REPUBLIC OF BRAZIL
HE Geoffrey Johnstone, CMG
Ambassador (non-resident)
See Argentina

CANADA 
HE A Missouri Sherman-Peter
High Commissioner
Address: The High Commission for the Commonwealth of The Bahamas, Metropolitan Life Centre, 50 O'Connor St, Ottawa, Canada K1P 6L2. Tel (613) 232-1724.
Diplomatic Staff: Julie Campbell, Second Secretary; Viana Bain, Attaché (investment & trade)

REPUBLIC OF CHILE
HE Geoffrey Johnstone, CMG
Ambassador (non-resident)
See Argentina

REPUBLIC OF COLOMBIA
HE Sir Arlington Butler, KCMG
Ambassador Designate (non-resident)
See United States

REPUBLIC OF COSTA RICA
HE Peter Galanos
Ambassador Designate (non-resident)
See Panama

REPUBLIC OF CUBA 
HE Dr Davidson L Hepburn
Ambassador (non-resident)
Address: The Embassy of the Commonwealth of The Bahamas to the Republic of Cuba, c/o The Ministry of Foreign Affairs, PO Box N-3746, Nassau, The Bahamas. Tel (242) 322-7624/5.

DOMINICA
HE A Leonard Archer
High Commissioner (non-resident)
See Antigua and Barbuda

COMMISSION TO THE EUROPEAN UNION
HE Arthur A Foulkes
Ambassador
Address: c/o The High Commission for the Commonwealth of The Bahamas, 10 Chesterfield St, London, England W1X 8AH. Tel (0171) 408-4488.
Diplomatic Staff: Donna Knowles-Lowe, First Secretary and Consul; Melvin Van Claridge, Second Secretary; Frank Davis, Second Secretary

FRANCE
HE Arthur A Foulkes
Ambassador (non-resident)
See United Kingdom

FEDERAL REPUBLIC OF GERMANY
HE Arthur A Foulkes
Ambassador (non-resident)
See United Kingdom

GRENADA
HE A Leonard Archer
High Commissioner (non-resident)
See Antigua and Barbuda

REPUBLIC OF GUATEMALA
HE Peter Galanos
Ambassador Designate (non-resident)
See Panama

THE COOPERATIVE REPUBLIC OF GUYANA
HE A Leonard Archer
High Commissioner (non-resident)
See Antigua and Barbuda

THE REPUBLIC OF HAITI
HE Dr Davidson L Hepburn
Ambassador (non-resident)
Address: The Embassy of the Commonwealth of The Bahamas to the Republic of Haiti, c/o The Ministry of Foreign Affairs, PO Box N-3746, Nassau, The Bahamas. Tel (242) 322-7624/5.
Diplomatic Staff: Sally E Moss, Chargé d'Affaires; Craig Powell, Third Secretary and Vice Consul; Nedley Martinborough, Attaché (defence)

REPUBLIC OF HONDURAS
HE Peter Galanos
Ambassador Designate (non-resident)
See Panama

ITALY
HE Arthur A Foulkes
Ambassador (non-resident)
See United Kingdom

JAMAICA
HE A Leonard Archer
High Commissioner (non-resident)
See Antigua and Barbuda

JAPAN
HE Sir Sidney Poitier, KBE
Ambassador
Address: The Embassy of the Commonwealth of The Bahamas to Japan, c/o The Ministry of Foreign Affairs, PO Box N-3746, Nassau, The Bahamas. Tel (242) 322-7624/5.

MEXICO
HE Sir Arlington Butler, KCMG
Ambassador (non-resident)
See United States

REPUBLIC OF NICARAGUA
HE Peter Galanos
Ambassador Designate (non-resident)
See Panama

ORGANIZATION OF AMERICAN STATES (OAS)
HE Sir Arlington Butler, KCMG
Permanent Representative
Address: c/o The Embassy of the Commonwealth of The Bahamas, 2220 Massachusetts Ave, NW, Washington, DC 20008. Tel (202) 319-2660.
Alternate representatives: Sheila Carey, Edda Dumont-Adolph, Rhoda Jackson, Eugene Torchon-Newry

REPUBLIC OF PANAMA
HE Peter Galanos
Ambassador (non-resident)
Address: The Embassy of the Commonwealth of The Bahamas to the Republic of Panama, c/o The Ministry of Foreign Affairs, PO Box N-3746, Nassau, The Bahamas. Tel (242) 322-7624/5.

ST KITTS AND NEVIS
HE A Leonard Archer
High Commissioner (non-resident)
See Antigua and Barbuda

ST VINCENT AND THE GRENADINES
HE A Leonard Archer
High Commissioner (non-resident)
See Antigua and Barbuda

SURINAME
HE A Leonard Archer
High Commissioner (non-resident)
See Antigua and Barbuda

THE REPUBLIC OF TRINIDAD AND TOBAGO
HE A Leonard Archer
High Commissioner (non-resident)
See Antigua and Barbuda

UNITED KINGDOM
HE Arthur A Foulkes
High Commissioner
Address: The High Commission for the Commonwealth of The Bahamas, 10 Chesterfield St, London, England W1X 8AH. Tel (0171) 408-4488, fax (0171) 499-9937.
Diplomatic Staff: Donna Knowles-Lowe, First Secretary; Melvin Van Claridge, Second Secretary; Frank Davis, Second Secretary; Judith Francis, Attaché (Maritime)

INTERNATIONAL MARITIME ORGANIZATION
HE Arthur A Foulkes
Permanent Representative
Alternate Representatives: J W Dempster, Director; Judith Francis, Senior Deputy Director
Address: c/o The High Commission for the Commonwealth of The Bahamas, 10 Chesterfield St, London, England W1X 8AH. Tel (0171) 290-1500, fax (0171) 290-1540.

UNITED STATES
HE Sir Arlington Butler, KCMG
Ambassador
Address: The Embassy of the Commonwealth of The Bahamas, 2220 Massachusetts Ave, NW, Washington, DC 20008. Tel (202) 319-2660, fax (202) 319-2668.
Diplomatic Staff: Sheila Carey, Minister Counsellor/Consul; Edda Dumont-Adolph, First Secretary/Legal; Rhoda Jackson, First Secretary; Eugene Torchon-Newry, Second Secretary

UNITED NATIONS
HE Maurice Moore
Ambassador
Address: The Permanent Mission of the Commonwealth of The Bahamas to the United Nations, 231 East 46th St, New York, NY 10017. Tel (212) 421-6925/6.
Diplomatic Staff: Sharon Brennen-Haylock, Counsellor; Allison Christie, Second Secretary

THE ORIENTAL REPUBLIC OF URUGUAY
HE Geoffrey Johnstone, CMG
Ambassador (non-resident)
See Argentina

MIAMI

Franklyn Rolle
Consul General
Address: The Consulate General of the Commonwealth of The Bahamas, Suite 818, Ingraham Building, 25 SE 2nd Ave, Miami, FL 33131. Tel (305) 373-6295.
Consular Staff: Jacqueline Simmons, Third Secretary and Vice Consul; Dorothea LaFleur, Third Secretary and Vice Consul

NEW YORK

Dr Doswell Coakley
Consul General
Address: The Consulate General of the Commonwealth of The Bahamas, 231 East 46th St, New York, NY 10017. Tel (212) 421-6420, fax (212) 688-5926.
Consular Staff: Monique Major, Third Secretary; Peter Goulandris, Consul (Maritime Affairs)

BAHAMAS ENVIRONMENT, SCIENCE & TECHNOLOGY COMMISSION (BEST)

HE Lynn P Holowesko
Ambassador
Address: Bahamas Environment, Science & Technology Commission, Office of the Prime Minister, PO Box CB-10980, Nassau, The Bahamas, tel (242) 327-4691/4, fax (242) 327-4626.

BAHAMAS INVESTMENT & TRADE

HE James Smith
Ambassador
Address: Bahamas Investment & Trade, Office of the Prime Minister, PO Box CB-10980, Nassau, The Bahamas, tel (242) 327-5970, fax (242) 327-5907.

DECORATIONS, DEGREES, HONOURS

AS	Associate in Science	KCMG	Knight Commander of the Order of St Michael and St George
BA	Bachelor of Arts		
BD	Bachelor of Divinity		
BEd	Bachelor of Education	Kt	Knight
BSc	Bachelor of Science	LVO	Lieutenant of Royal Victorian Order
CBE	Commander of the Order of the British Empire		
		LLB	Bachelor of Laws
CCFP	Certificate of the Canadian Family Physician	LLD	Doctor of Laws
		MBA	Master of Business Administration
CMG	Companion of the Order of St Michael and St George		
		MD	Doctor of Medicine
CPA	Chartered Public Accountant	MP	Member of Parliament
ChB	Bachelor of Surgery	MPA	Master of Public Administration
DCMG	Dame Commander of the Order of St Michael and St George		
		MSW	Master of Social Work
		MSc	Master of Science
DHL	Doctor of Humane Letters	MB BS	Bachelor of Medicine and Bachelor of Surgery
FRCOG	Fellow of the Royal College of Obstetricians and Gynaecologists		
		MB ChB	Bachelor of Medicine and Bachelor of Surgery
GCMG	Knight or Dame Grand Cross of the Order of St Michael and St George	OBE	Officer of the Order of the British Empire
		PC	Privy Council
JP	Justice of the Peace	PhD	Doctor of Philosophy
KBE	Knight Commander of the Order or the British Empire	QC	Queen's Counsel

Resident Diplomatic & Consular Representatives
In the Commonwealth of The Bahamas

BRITISH HIGH COMMISSION
Ansbacher House (3rd Floor),
East St, PO Box N-7516, Nassau.
Tel (242) 325-7471 (to 3),
fax (242) 323-3871.
HE Peter Young, OBE,
   High Commissioner
Phil Culligan,
   Deputy High Commissioner
Col Anthony Lindsay Moorby,
   Defence Adviser (Resident in Kingston, Jamaica)
Jane Lloyd,
   Commercial/Information Officer

EMBASSY OF THE UNITED STATES OF AMERICA
Mosmar Building, Queen St,
PO Box N-8197, Nassau.
Tel (242) 322-1181
HE Arthur L Schechter, Ambassador
Pamela Bridgewater,
   Deputy Chief of Mission
Tracy A Jacobson, First Secretary and Consul (Administration)
Vincent A Principe, Consul General, Head of Consular Division
Elizabeth Martinez, First Secretary (Political/Economic)
Mark Libby,
   Economic Commercial Officer
Carlos Garcia,
   Second Secretary, Narcotics Affairs
Elise Patterson, Consul, Chief of Visa
Peter S Hargraves, Attaché (Regional Security)
Toni Teresi, Attaché (Narcotics)
Comdr Leonard Jones,
   Naval Liaison Officer
Lt Comdr Robert Thomas,
   Coast Guard Liaison Officer
Arthur Flores, Officer-in-Charge (Agriculture/Nassau)
Erick Babilonia, Officer-in-Charge (Agriculture/Freeport)
Francis Mullin, Officer-in-Charge (Customs/Nassau)
Timothy O'Connor, Officer-in-Charge (Customs/Freeport)
Thomas Smiley, Officer-in-Charge (Immigration/Nassau)
David W Blosvern and Maria Desoto, Inspector (Immigration/Freeport)

EMBASSY OF THE REPUBLIC OF HAITI
Sears House, Shirley St,
PO Box N-666, Nassau.
Tel (242) 326-0325,
fax (242) 322-7712
Joseph J Etienne, Consul General, Chargé d'Affaires, ai
Jean-Pierre Celestin, Consul
Delan Joseph, Vice-Consul

THE CONSULATE GENERAL OF THE GAMBIA
Lyford Cay, PO Box N-7776, Nassau.
Tel (242) 362-5611,
fax (242) 362-5424
Irving Gould, Consul General

EMBASSY OF THE PEOPLE'S REPUBLIC OF CHINA
Sandyport,
PO Box CB-13500, Nassau.
Tel (242) 327-5206,
fax (242) 327-3620
HE Ma Shuxue, Ambassador
Zhang Haihe, Third Secretary
Fu Changhua, Attaché

INTERNATIONAL ORGANIZATIONS' REPRESENTATIVES
IN THE COMMONWEALTH OF THE BAHAMAS

ORGANIZATION OF AMERICAN STATES
Office of the General Secretariat, 42 Queen St, PO Box N-7793, Nassau.
  Tel (242) 326-7746, fax (242) 325-0196.
Wesley Kirton, Director

EUROPEAN UNION
Delegation of the European Commission – Office in The Bahamas, Frederick House
  (2nd Floor), Frederick St, PO Box N-3246, Nassau. Tel (242) 325-5850
HE James Moran, Ambassador, Head of Delegation resident in Jamaica
Nicola Cole, Administrative Officer

PAN-AMERICAN HEALTH ORGANIZATION (PAHO)/
WORLD HEALTH ORGANIZATION (WHO)
Royal Victoria Gardens, PO Box N-9411, Nassau. Tel (242) 326-7390
Dr Claudette Harry, Representative

INTER-AMERICAN DEVELOPMENT BANK
IDB House, East Bay St, PO Box N-3743, Nassau. Tel (242) 393-7159
Hugo E Souza, Representative

HONORARY CONSULS & REPRESENTATIVES
IN THE COMMONWEALTH OF THE BAHAMAS

HONORARY CONSULS UNLESS INDICATED OTHERWISE.

S Anders Wiberg, Dean of Honorary
  Consul Corps (see Sweden)
Ralph Seligman, QC, Vice-Dean of
  Honorary Consul Corps (see Israel)
Jonathan C B Ramsay, Secretary to
  Honorary Consul Corps (see Belgium)

AUSTRIA
Heinz R Kloihofer, PO Box SS-6519,
Nassau. Tel (242) 363-2929 (wk) or
363-1323 (hm); fax (242) 363-2308.

BARBADOS
Carlton I Jones, PO Box N-8759,
Nassau. Tel (242) 325-5591 (wk) or
327-5697 (hm); fax (242) 322-6353.

BELGIUM
Jonathan C B Ramsay (Secretary to
Honorary Consul Corps), PO Box
N-52, Nassau. Tel/fax (242) 323-7421
(wk) or 324-2525 (hm).

BRAZIL
Pedro G Wassitsch, PO Box N-4893,
Nassau. Tel (242) 394-8150,
394-8143 (wk) or 323-4749 (hm);
fax (242) 394-8326.

CANADA
Robert Nihon,
Monique Brooks, Vice Consul,
PO Box SS-6371, Nassau.
Tel (242) 393-2123/4,
fax (242) 393-1305.

Ian Burchette, Trade Commercial Representative, PO Box 1500, Kingston, 10, Jamaica. Tel (876) 926-1500 (to 4), fax (876) 960-3861.

CHILE
Carmen Massoni, PO Box N-4949, Nassau. Tel (242) 325-1950 (wk) or 327-5592 (hm); fax (242) 325-2765.

COSTA RICA
Robert S Jagger, Honorary Consul General, PO Box CB-11297, Nassau. Tel (242) 327-3796 (wk) or 327-6246 (hm); fax (242) 327-3416.

CYPRUS
Themis Themistocleous, Honorary Vice Consul, PO Box N-7140, Nassau. Tel (242) 322-7450 (wk) or 362-4786 (hm); fax (242) 323-3467.

DENMARK
Berlin W Key, PO Box N-4005, Nassau. Tel (242) 322-1340 (wk) or 324-2727 (hm); fax (242) 323-8779.

FRANCE
Baroness Irene von Hoyningen-Huene, PO Box CB-13557, Nassau. Tel (242) 326-5061, fax (242) 326-1351.

GERMANY
Ernst Brokmeier, PO Box N-3035, Nassau. Tel (242) 322-8032/3 (wk) or 324-3780 (hm); fax (242) 325-5731.

GREECE
Gus Constantakis, PO Box N-7682, Nassau. Tel (242) 323-3523 (wk) or 362-5065 (hm); fax (242) 323-3523.

GRENADA
Viktor Kozeny (Designate), PO Box N-7776, Nassau. Tel (242) 362-5888, fax (242) 362-5887.

ISRAEL
Ralph Seligman, QC, Honorary Consul General (Vice-Dean of Honorary Consul Corps), PO Box N-7776, Nassau. Tel (242) 322-2670, fax (242) 323-8914.

ITALY
Vacant at press time.

JAMAICA
Patrick Hanlan, PO Box N-3451, Nassau. Tel (242) 356-8500 (wk) or 324-3897 (hm); fax (242) 322-6575.

JAPAN
Basil L Sands, PO Box N-4665, Nassau. Tel (242) 322-8560/1 (wk) or 393-0391 (hm); fax (242) 326-7524.

REPUBLIC OF KOREA
Maxwell E Gibson, PO Box N-623, Nassau. Tel (242) 326-4745 (wk) or 327-8408 (hm); fax (242) 328-4211.

MEXICO
Manuel J Cutillas, PO Box N-838, Nassau. Tel (242) 362-1412 (wk) or 362-4214 (hm); fax (242) 362-1859.

MONACO
Eric J Crowch, PO Box N-3618, Nassau. Tel (242) 325-1166 (wk) or 327-8221 (hm); fax (242) 326-6414.

THE NETHERLANDS
Peter Newton Andrews, PO Box N-44, Nassau. Tel/fax (242) 356-3336, Marion Beatty, tel (242) 356-3336.

NICARAGUA
Dr K J A Rodgers, PO Box N-386, Nassau. Tel (242) 323-7997 (wk) or 363-2585 (hm); fax (242) 325-1647.

NORWAY
Berlin W Key, PO Box N-4005, Nassau. Tel (242) 322-1340 (wk) or 363-2727 (hm); fax (242) 323-8779.

PANAMA
David McGrath, Honorary Consul General, PO Box N-7776, Nassau. Tel (242) 362-4429 (wk) or 362-4429 (hm); fax (242) 362-4886.

PERU
Rosa Sweeting, (Representative), PO Box N-3211. Tel (242) 328-8916 (wk) or 327-7447 (hm); fax (242) 328-8917.

PORTUGAL
Robert Arnold, PO Box N-7776, Nassau. Tel (242) 362-4449, fax (242) 362-5140.
Manuela Camacho-Major, Honorary Vice Consul, PO Box SS-19407, Nassau. Tel (242) 324-6150, fax (242) 364-5427.

SPAIN
Francisco Carrera-Justiz, PO Box N-838, Nassau. Tel (242) 362-1271 or 362-1412; fax (242) 362-1918.

SWEDEN
S Anders Wiberg, Honorary Consul General (Dean of Honorary Consul Corps), PO Box CB-11000, Nassau. Tel (242) 327-7944, fax (242) 327-7782.

SWITZERLAND
Beat Wernli, PO Box SS-6312, Nassau. Tel (242) 325-1531 (wk) or 393-2675 (hm); fax (242) 323-8561.

UGANDA
John Thompson Dorance III, PO Box N-7776, Nassau. Tel (242) 362-4887, fax (242) 362-5013.

URUGUAY
Analia Whitehead, PO Box SS-6208, Nassau. Tel (242) 328-5165 (wk) or 324-3347 (hm); fax (242) 325-9127.

BAHAMAS HONORARY CONSULS ABROAD

CHILE
Johann Schmaelzle, Casilla 65, Correo 30, Santiago, Chile. Tel 562-231-7986, fax 562-232-3494.

DOMINICAN REPUBLIC
Dr Hernando Perez Montas, Yuma No 1, NACO – Santo Domingo, Dominican Republic. Tel (809) 566-1451 or 688-3787; fax (809) 682-0237.

FRANCE
Claude Le Gris, 5 Rue de Beaune, Paris, France 75007. Tel 4286-0400.

HONG KONG
John Meredith, 19th Fl, Hutchison House, 10 Harcourt Rd, Central Hong Kong. Tel 852-2521-3121 (852-8121-3121 from outside HK) fax 852-2521-0781 (852-8121-0781 from outside HK)

ISRAEL
Talia Glantz, 44 Veidat Katouit St, Tel-Aviv 62300, Israel. Tel 03-45-8902, fax 03-44-9687.

ITALY
Michaelangela Vismara, Via Cusani, 10, 20121 Milan. Tel 011-392-7202-3003, fax 011-392-7202-3123.

MONACO
Niccolo Caissotti Chiusano, Eni International Bank Ltd, 74 Boulevard d'Italie, MC 98000 Monaco. Tel 377-9315-5454, fax 377-9315-5496.

SWITZERLAND
Katherine Helena Klainguti, Weinbergstrasse 41, 8802 Kilchberg, Switzerland. Tel 01-715-5227, fax 01-715-5229.

The year in review

Bahamas diary, September 1997-August 1998

Changes, events, issues and trends over the year September 1997-August 1998 have left indelible marks on The Bahamas. Construction of large foreign-financed resort complexes continued with major projects like Atlantis, Paradise Island nearing completion and The Lucayan on Grand Bahama taking shape. Cruise lines acquired more private islands as tropical stopovers and sparked controversy with gay and lesbian travel cruises. Bahamian athletes excelled in international competition in track, tennis, boxing and weightlifting, and visual and performing artists took Bahamian culture international.

Land development and acquisition spawned resentment as public access to Bahamian beaches was eroded. Rising crime and increased drug trafficking and transshipment were concerns.

Plans for privatization of government-owned entities including the Bahamas Telecommunications Corporation (BaTelCo), Bahamas Electricity Corporation (BEC) and Bahamasair generated speculation, as did the prospect of the Bahamas Securities Exchange. Meanwhile several companies went public and shares offered in most cases were oversubscribed.

Among notable happenings were:

September 1997
- **1** Bahamians mourn the death of Princess Diana. Books of condolence open at Government House and British High Commission.
- **4** BaTelCo breaks ground on $8 million, 40,000 sq ft administrative building on East Mall Dr, Freeport.
- **5** FNM's Ronald Bosfield wins by-election for vacant South Andros seat formerly held by retiring PLP leader Sir Lynden Pindling.
- **10** Approx $72 million earmarked for "significant expansion" of Defence Force base at Coral Harbour, Deputy Prime Minister Frank Watson announces.
- **14** Prime Minister Hubert Ingraham leads investment mission of government ministers and business professionals to Hong Kong and mainland China.
- **20** Freeman Barr becomes the second Bahamian boxer to win a world title when he outpoints American Larry Brown to win the IBO middleweight crown. Elisha Obed is a former WBC junior middleweight champion.
- **22** A 24-hour a day hotline is set up by the Ministry of Housing and Social Development in its fight against child abuse. • Drug Enforcement Agency (DEA) agent warns International Asset Forfeiture and Money Laundering Seminar of shift back to Bahamas as drug transshipment route.
- **24** CIBC Bahamas Ltd goes public, offering five million shares of common stock.
- **25** Deputy PM Watson announces plans for establishment of a Bahamas law school.
- **27** American Matt Alcone repeats as winner of the Atlantis Bahamas Super Boat Challenge race around Paradise Island. Bahamian Alan Wardle finishes second in production class.
- **29** Michael Dingman donates $2 million for a Centre for Entrepreneurship at the College of the Bahamas.

October
- **1** PM Ingraham returns from China with commitment from Hutchison Whampoa to add 250 rooms and a 600-room five-star hotel to its Freeport development, as well as a Technical Assistance Agreement for a $3.6 million Chinese government grant to fund a national convention centre. • MPs' $1,500 monthly allowance to maintain constituency offices becomes effective.
- **6** Abaco Markets Ltd becomes first Family Island business to go public, offering 1.1 million shares (40% ownership).
- **7** Barclays Bank officially opens its first Bahamas Offshore Banking Centre on Bay St, celebrating 50 years of banking in The Bahamas.
- **9** Templeton Global Advisors Ltd opens $5 million office building at Lyford Cay to house investment management offices of Franklin/Templeton Group. • The Centre for Entrepreneurship opens at COB, funded partly by $2 million from entrepreneur Michael D Dingman, who pledges $2 million more.
  • Government awards $20 million contract to Dutch firm, Interbeton BV, to design and build new Paradise Island bridge.

From left: Prime Minister the Rt Hon Hubert A Ingraham and Mrs Michael Dingman smile at remarks by Dingman, who donated $2 million and later pledged another $2 million to the College of The Bahamas.

17 Royal Caribbean's *Enchantment of the Seas* makes inaugural voyage to Nassau, with capacity to transport an extra 1,950-2,446 passengers a week.

November
10 Fidelity Bank & Trust Intl Ltd launches FINDEX, a local barometer of the performance of impending Bahamian stock market. • *The Tribune's* photograph of "sleeping" MP in House of Assembly causes Speaker R Italia Johnson to tighten rules for photographers.
11 Bahamian weightlifter Kevin Woodside wins silver medal at World Powerlifting Championships in Prague.
20 The first Ambassador from the People's Republic of China presents his credentials to Governor-General Sir Orville Turnquest.
22 *Adventures with the Duchess* airs on ABC-TV, featuring Duchess of York Sarah Ferguson in a shark dive with Jean-Michel Cousteau and divers from Nassau Scuba Centre at Shark Wall off Clifton Pier.

December
7 Lady Sassoon, the former Evelyn Barnes of Tennessee, renowned Nassau hostess and founder of the Sir Victor Sassoon Heart Foundation in memory of her husband, dies in Nassau at 77.
8 Deputy PM and Minister of National Security Watson notes increased drug trafficking through The Bahamas over the past six months, following seizure of a boat with $17 million worth of cocaine speeding to South Florida from The Bahamas.

12 Holland America Cruise Line officially opens its private $22 million cruise destination, Half Moon Cay (Little San Salvador).
29 Dr Granville Bain, orthopaedic surgeon and founding member of the FNM, dies at 57.
30 Orlando "El Duque" Hernandez, one of Cuba's top ballplayers and half-brother of Marlins' pitcher Livan Hernandez, is detained in Nassau pending ruling on his political asylum bid for the United States. He later leaves for Costa Rica and a $6.6 million New York Yankees contract.

January 1998
19 James "Jimmy" Nixon of Inagua, 82-year-old father of 11, wins 1998 Cacique Lifetime Achievement Award for 45 years dedicated to preservation of the flamingo, The Bahamas' national bird.
26 Unmasked gunman robs Public Treasury of $500,000 in $50 notes.
28 Count Alfred de Marigny, 89, acquitted in the 1943 Nassau murder of his father-in-law, Sir Harry Oakes, dies in Texas.
30 New Customs House on Thompson Blvd officially opens. • Bahamian Freeman Barr defends his IBO middleweight title with a jaw-breaking 7th round TKO over American Tommy Small.

February
3 Sun International scraps $50 million entertainment and shopping complex at Paradise Island because of local opposition to the project.
4 BaTelCo workers demonstrate against privatization plans.
5 Impending visit of cruise ship carrying gays stirs controversy and anti-gay demonstrations led by Bahamas Christian Council. Prayers and "Divine intervention" bring bad weather which prevents the ship from mooring in the Berry Islands.
13 British Secretary of State Robin Cook announces $800,000 fight against Caribbean drug-running at Nassau's UK-Caribbean Forum.
17 Bahamasair directors announce purchase of two Boeing 737-200 series advanced aircraft to prepare for increase in hotel rooms.
20 The Water & Sewerage Corp signs $12.8 million deal to relocate and refurbish 27.5 miles of distribution pipes on New Providence. • New Bahamas Humane Society headquarters opens.
23 Caribbean region's largest and most modern seawater reverse osmosis plant, Waterfields, joint venture of Bacardi and DeSalco, opens on New Providence.
25 Trustee Act, 1998, is passed in Parliament, replacing Trustee Act, 1893, and other trust legislation.
27 Construction starts on $20 million Old Bahama Bay resort and residential complex in Grand Bahama's West End.

March
1 Bobby Symonette, former Speaker of the House of Assembly, international sailor and astute businessman, dies at 73.
5 Bahamas is chosen as a site for HIV/AIDS prevention vaccine tests.

Bobby Symonette

Dr Granville Bain

- **6** Minister of Health Dr Ronald Knowles confirms closing of Oncology Associates Ltd radiation treatment facility.
- **7** Phoenix Aviation, a fixed base operation (FBO) opened at Nassau International Airport in March 1997, becomes Million Air Nassau, the 27th franchise of the company Million Air Interlink Inc, the first in The Bahamas and Caribbean.
- **15** Bahamian sprinter Debbie Ferguson, representing the University of Georgia, wins silver medals in 200- and 55-metre NCAA Indoor Championships in Indianapolis.
- **16** Self-proclaimed millionaire and philanthropist Derek Rolle closes shop at the Towne Hotel after promising to pay off bills for thousands, for a $60 legal fee. Police say beware of "financial angel."
- **18** Construction starts on Atlantis, Paradise Island's 10-acre, 63-slip marina.
  - PM says privatization of BaTelCo will mean job losses.
- **22** Crooner Tony Bennett and Prince Philip are among celebrities attending gala dinner and reception for Governor-General's Youth Awards (formerly Duke of Edinburgh Awards) at Atlantis.

April

- **1** Dr John Lunn, president of Oncology Associates Ltd, begins pre-retirement leave amid controversy initiated by American College of Radiology report of substandard radiation treatment at OAL and "excessive and unnecessary morbidity and mortality to patients have been documented." • American John MacCausland wins 1998 Star Class Spring Championships of the Western Hemisphere at Nassau Yacht Club with 20 boats from five countries competing.
- **13** Bahamas track team finishes 5th in Carifta Games in Trinidad, with 15 medals (2G, 3S, 10B). • More than 300 demonstrators sneer and shout at "gay chartered" cruise ship at Prince George Dock. Ministry of Tourism apologizes to travel agency that initiated the cruise.

15 Sun International starts interviews for 2,000 jobs. More than 7,000 apply.
16 The Bahamas becomes 30th nation in the 34-member Organization of American States to sign a hemispheric treaty banning illegal guns.
18 With only 22 swimmers, Bahamas finishes 3rd in Carifta swim meet in Guadeloupe with 46 medals including 19 golds. • PM attends Second Summit of the Americas in Santiago, Chile. • Dr Jay Buckey, 41, son of Bahamian Jean Buckey, is among astronauts aboard Columbia space shuttle "Neurolab" in 16-day mission from Cape Canaveral.
21 Sixteen hundred Bahamas Hotel Catering and Allied Workers vote to strike.
24 RHK Hotels Inc of Toronto buys South Ocean Golf and Beach Resort for a reported $18 million. The same firm bought the British Colonial Hotel in 1996.
28 Bahamas Chamber of Commerce names Grand Bahama Port Authority president, Albert Miller, 1998 Business Person of the Year.

May

3 Rats, roaches are evicted as downtown straw market gets cleanup.
5 Michael and Philip Herman Bethel, sons of former Transport Minister Philip Bethel, are found guilty in 100-kilo cocaine deal.
6 Director Cleophas Adderley leads 48-member Bahamas National Youth Choir on visit to two Russian cities.
11 Coren Jones, 30, is sentenced to 16 months in prison after pleading guilty in January to possession of 11 pounds of cocaine stashed in her wheelchair. • Savatheda Fynes and Chandra Stirrup finish second and third to US star Marion Jones in China in a 100-metre race billed as "contest of the world's fastest."
14 Ground breaking takes place for $50 million commercial and residential Bayside development at Orange Hill, to include Pictet and Oceanic Banks.
21 Wendy's on Bay St closes temporarily as rats from straw market cleanup relocate. • Sixty-one Cuban rafters are deported. • Coroner's Court rules April 1997 drowning of Valencia Woods during "demon exorcism" by two Baptist ministers manslaughter by negligence.
22 Bahamian tennis pro Mark Knowles and doubles partner Daniel Nestor of Canada defeat Australian "Woodies," Todd Woodbridge and Mark Woodforde, 6-4, 6-2 in French Open semi-finals.
23 Col Gordon Cooper, one of the original US Mercury 7 and Gemini astronauts, opens six-day goodwill and educational visit to Nassau.
29 Supermodel Cindy Crawford, 32, and nightclub entrepreneur Rande Gerber, 36, marry at sunset in a $300,000 barefoot ceremony at the Ocean Club on Paradise Island.
30 *The Tribune,* traditionally an evening newspaper, switches to morning field.
31 Traffic pattern in downtown Nassau reverses, with Bay St now one-way east, and Shirley St one-way west, among other changes.

Supermodel Cindy Crawford married Rande Gerber in a sunset ceremony on Paradise Island.

June

1 Bahamian artist and internationally renowned sculptress Janine Antoni of Freeport and New York, is awarded a $225,000 MacArthur Foundation Fellowship.

2 Bahamas Olympic Committee president, Sir Arlington Butler, becomes first English speaking recipient of the prestigious Merit Award of the Association of National Olympic Committees at Seville, Spain.

6 Bahamian and University of Georgia sprinter, Debbie Ferguson, wins both 100- and 200-metre titles at the NCAA Championships in Buffalo, NY.

10 Unemployment dipped to an all-time low of 9.8 per cent in 1997, says Minister of Housing and Social Development Algernon Allen.

15 Bahamas participation in the proposed Free Trade Area of the Americas (FTAA) is yet to be negotiated, says the PM, and at best, could not come about before 2005.

17 Ministry of Tourism official tells Caribbean Hotel Industry Conference (CHIC) the world backs Bahamas welcoming gay cruise ship.

18 Bahamasair marks 25 years of service.

22 Mark Knowles loses to Britain's Chris Wilkinson, 7-5, 6-0, 6-1 at Wimbledon after recurrence of a back injury.

23 Former Prime Minister Sir Lynden Pindling calls for abolition of the monarchy in The Bahamas, replacing the Queen with a president, and redesigning the Bahamian flag.

30 Drug traffickers are back in The Bahamas according to both the DEA and Bahamas National Security Minister and Deputy PM Watson. Agents seized more cocaine in first three months of 1998 than in three previous years.

July

1 Bahamas Financial Services Board launches joint private sector and government agency to promote Bahamas' financial services abroad.
6 The morning newspaper, *The Nassau Guardian,* begins publishing an afternoon edition as well.
10 As the country celebrates the 25th birthday of Independence with re-enactment of the historic July 10, 1973 flag-raising, Deputy PM Watson collapses and is hospitalized. He is later fitted with a pacemaker.
14 Philip Herman Bethel is sentenced to four years in prison on cocaine conspiracy conviction.
16 The Atlantic Beach Hotel in Freeport is imploded to make way for redevelopment of the Lucayan hotel strip into "The Lucayan" resort complex.
19 Veteran tennis star Roger Smith retires from tour competition after 12 years and after competing in Guadalahara as The Bahamas beats Mexico 3-2 in Zone 1 Davis Cup action.
20 Fire aboard the Carnival cruise ship *Ecstasy* cancels at least two cruises to The Bahamas costing some $330,000 from loss of port fees, departure tax and visitor spending.
22 Bahamian 4 x 100-metre ladies' relay team wins silver medal at Goodwill Games in Uniondale, NY.

August

1 Veteran educator Dr Leon Higgs replaces COB president Dr Keva Bethel, who is retiring after 23 years of academic and administrative leadership at the college. • *Disney Magic* arrives in Nassau on its maiden voyage before sailing to Disney Cruise Lines' private island, Castaway Cay (Gorda Cay) in Abaco.
7 Twenty-two of an eventual 102 cases of a mysterious viral illness plagues guests and staff at the all-inclusive Venta Club at Winding Bay, Eleuthera.
10 Two people are injured when a 30-ft section of the domestic departure lounge roof at Nassau International Airport collapses.
11 Land clearing of a 35-acre site begins at Freeport Container Port to start $71 million phase two expansion of the transshipment terminal.
22 Bodies of two female tourists are found near the golf course on Paradise Island. An American, Lori Fogleman, had been missing since July 20. Joanne Clarke, 24, of Oxfordshire, England, disappeared Aug 20.
25 Government offers $200,000 reward for information leading to arrest and conviction in Paradise Island murders. Scotland Yard and FBI are asked to assist.
27 UK government issues travel advisory for British tourists, citing serious crime in Nassau and Freeport. • Minister of State for Economic Development Carl Bethel opens two-day seminar on Free Trade Area of the Americas in Freeport.
30 A newly-arrived Scotland Yard detective, here to help investigate murders of two female tourists found at Paradise Island, is robbed of $500 at gunpoint at Fort Fincastle. • International Law Conference of the Organization of Commonwealth Caribbean Bar Associations opens in Nassau.
31 COB and UWI sign agreement for four-year degree course in hospitality and tourism.

Advertisers In This Book

Also see CLASSIFIED DIRECTORIES, *pgs 255-264; pgs 518-520*

NEW PROVIDENCE

AMEE International 195
Alan E H Bates & Co 258
Ansbacher (Bahamas) Ltd .... bet 184-185
Asa H Pritchard Ltd 129
Atlantic Accounting .... opp 248
Atlantic Financial Network .... opp 248
Atlantic First Insurance Co .... opp 248
Automotive & Industrial
  Distributors Ltd (AID) 154
Avis 323
AXXESS International Ltd 26
Bahamas Financial
  Services Board .... bet 120-121
Bahamas First General
  Insurance Co Ltd 119, 205
Bahamas Incorporation Services Ltd 209
Bahamas Institute of
  Chartered Accountants 210
Bahamas Investment Authority Financial
  Services Secretariat (BIA) .... opp 153
Bahamas Marine Construction ..... opp 249
Bahamas Ministry of Tourism 24
Bahamas Realty 231
Bahamas Technical &
  Vocational Institute (BTVI) 158
Bahamas Telecommunications Corp
  (BaTelCo) 132-133
Bahamas Waste Management
  Systems Ltd 251
Bahamasair 115
Bahamasnet .... 228, bet 248-249, 263, 505
Banco Santander Trust & Banking
  Corp (Bahamas) Ltd 214
Bank of Nova Scotia Trust Co
  (Bahamas) Ltd, The 211
Banque Privée Edmond
  de Rothschild Ltd 33
Banque SCS Alliance (Nassau) Ltd 22
Barclays Bank PLC 169
Bay Properties Ltd .... bet 248-249
BAYROC Exclusive Beach Residences 38
BDO Mann Judd 225
BEL Communications Ltd 230
Best Funds Distributors Inc 183
Britannia Consulting Group, The 196
Broadcasting Corp
  of The Bahamas, The .... bet 216-217
Budget 141
C A Christie Real Estate 247
C Investments Realtors (Century 21) 190
Cardinal International
  Group, The 203
Central Bank
  of The Bahamas, The .... bet 120-121

Charleston Private Management Ltd 215
Chase Manhattan Private Bank
  & Trust Co (Bahamas) Ltd, The 199
Christie, Davis & Co 191
City Markets Food Stores 161
Commonwealth Brewery Ltd 44
Commonwealth Building
  Supplies Ltd 253
Damianos Realty Co Ltd .... opp 217
Darier Hentsch
  Private Bank & Trust Ltd 175
Deltec Panamerica Trust Co Ltd 173
DHL Worldwide Express 202
Doctors Hospital (1986) Ltd 131
Dominion Investments Ltd 206
Dupuch & Turnquest & Co 190
Durrant-Harding Real Estate Co Ltd 227
Esso Standard Oil SA Ltd .... bet 216-217
Executive Printers
  of The Bahamas Ltd 254
Exponential Electrical Industry, The 247
Federal Express (FedEx) 233
Ferrier Lullin Bank & Trust
  (Bahamas) Ltd 19
Fidelity Bank & Trust
  International Ltd .... opp 216
Foster & Dunhill (Bahamas) Ltd 48
Frank Hanna Cleaning Co Ltd 237
Gold Circle Co Ltd 240
Gomez & Nairn 199
Graham Real Estate 223
Guta Bank & Trust Ltd .... bet 152-153
H G Christie Ltd Real Estate 221
Handelsfinanz-CCF Bank
  International Ltd .... bet 184-185
Harbourside Marine 102
Holowesko & Co 243
Hurricane Hole Marina 30
IBM Bahamas Ltd 177
Insurance Governors .... opp 248
InterDesign 242
International Portfolio Analytics Ltd 188
International Trade & Investments Ltd .. 189
Investment Masters .... opp 248
Island Business Centre 193
Island Seafoods Ltd 262
Islandwide Airconditioning Co Ltd 258
JBR Building Supplies Ltd 238
Jeanne I Thompson 229
Jerome E Pyfrom & Co 225
KPMG 182
Kairos Development &
  Construction Co Ltd 236
Land Design of Nassau Ltd 239
Lennox Paton 207

LifeFlight 136
Lignum Technologies (Bahamas) Ltd 222
Lyford Cay Real Estate Co Ltd 228
McKinney, Bancroft & Hughes 172
MeesPierson Trust .... bet 152-153
Miami Children's Hospital 136
Ministry of Tourism 24
Montaque Securities International 211
Morgan & Morgan Group 213
Morley Realty Ltd 245
Morymor Trust Corp Ltd 213
Mosko's Group
    of Building Cos .... opp 249
Mosko's Furniture .... opp 249
Mosko's United Construction .... opp 249
Mount Sinai Medical Center 136
Nassau Bicycle Co Ltd 257
Nassau Guardian, The 111
Nassau Survey Agency Ltd 119
Nassau Underwriters Agency Ltd 119
New Oriental Cleaners 259
NP Building Supplies .... opp 249
Nordfinanz Bank Zurich .... opp 184
Norshield International 36
Oceanic Bank & Trust Ltd 178
Oceania Properties Ltd .... bet 248-249
Orbitex Group of Funds .... opp 120
Paul H Carey & Assoc (Century 21) 190
Pictet Bank & Trust Ltd 200
Pindling & Co 174
Portside Condominiums 31
Powell's Marketing &
    Management Services 242
PricewaterhouseCoopers 181
Private Trust Corp Ltd, The 213
RBC Dominion Securities
    (Global) Ltd .... Back cover
Real Estate Sales & Rentals
    (Bahamas) Ltd 237
Re/Max Nassau Realty 226
Royal & Sun Alliance .... opp 185
Royal Bank of Canada .... Back cover
Royal Bank of Scotland
    International, The .... opp 121
Royal Caribbean Estates .... opp 248
Satellite Bahamas 157
Scotiatrust 211
Securities Commission
    of The Bahamas .... opp 152
Small Treasures 21
    Bay View Village, Club Land'or, Compass Point Beach Club, Dillet's Guest House, Graycliff, Orange Hill Beach Inn, Paradise Harbour Club & Marina, Red Carpet Inn, Sunrise Beach Club & Villas, The Villas on Crystal Cay
Surety Bank & Trust Co Ltd 180
Systems Resource Group, The 113
Taylor Industries Ltd 261

Templeton Global Advisors Ltd 17
Tops Hardware
    & Plumbing Supplies 238
Tropical Brokerage Services Ltd 155
UBS (Bahamas) Ltd.................................171
United European
    Bank & Trust (Nassau) Ltd 191
Vaughn L Culmer & Assocs 194
Western Electric 262
Wide World Airfreight 519
Wide World Forwarding 519
Wide World Travel 519
ZNS Network .... bet 216-217

GRAND BAHAMA & FREEPORT
Automotive & Industrial
    Distributors Ltd (AID) 154
Avis 323
Bahama Cement 483
Bahama Rock Ltd 517
Bahamas First
    General Insurance Co Ltd 119
Bahamas Electronic Lab Co 230
Bahamas Oil Refining Co International
    Ltd (BORCO) .... bet 456-457
Bahamas Technical & Vocational Institute
    (BTVI) 158
Bahamasair 115
BaTelCo .... bet 488-489
Bell Channel Club & Marina .... opp 457
Borco Agency Services .... bet 456-457
Borco Towing Company .... bet 456-457
Bradford Grand Bahama 471
Broadcasting Corp
    of The Bahamas, The .... bet 216-217
Builders Depot .... bet 456-457
Cates & Co Chartered Accountants 486
Century 21 499
Chevron Supreme Lubricants
    (FOCOL exclusive) 481
Christie, Davis & Co 191
Churchill & Jones
    Real Estate Ltd .... bet 456-457
Concem Ltd 483
DHL Worldwide Express 202
Dupuch & Turnquest & Co 190
Eastern Freight Forwarders
    (Freeport Transfer Ltd) 479
Federal Express (FedEx) 233
First Atlantic Realty Ltd .... bet 456-457
Freeport Aggregate Ltd 475
Freeport Container Port 461
Freeport News, The 111
Freeport Oil Co Ltd (FOCOL) 481
Freeport Transfer Ltd 479
Grand Bahama Port Authority .... bet 456-457
Harry Dann & Co Ltd 499
IBM Bahamas Ltd 177
Innotec .... bet 456-457

604

Island Construction Co Ltd 475
KPMG 182
Lucaya Shipping & Trading
    Co Ltd .... bet 456-457
Lucayan Marina Village 52
Lustre Kraft Signs Ltd 507
McKinney, Bancroft & Hughes 172
Nassau Survey Agency Ltd 119
Nassau Underwriters Agency Ltd 119
Old Bahama Bay 54
Pindling & Co 174
Port Lucaya Resort
    & Yacht Club .... opp 488
PricewaterhouseCoopers 181
Princess Isle .... opp 489
Princess Realty Ltd .... opp 489
Real Estate Exchange, The 504
Reef Construction Ltd 469
Re/Max Freeport
    Northern Bahamas .... bet 456-457
Royal & Sun Alliance .... opp 185
Tanja Enterprises Co Ltd 465
Uniroyal Chemical Co Ltd 501
United Shipping Co Ltd 467
Waters Edge .... bet 456-457
Waugh Construction
    (Bahamas) Ltd 495
Wide World Airfreight 519
Wide World Forwarding 519
Wide World Travel 519
Winn Dixie Food Stores 161
ZNS Network .... bet 216-217

Bay Properties Ltd .... bet 248-249
Broadcasting Corp
    of The Bahamas, The .... bet 216-217
Oceania Properties Ltd .... bet 248-249

ABACO
Automotive & Industrial Distributors
    Ltd (AID) 154
Bahamas Realty 231
Bahamasair 115
Broadcasting Corp
    of The Bahamas, The .... bet 216-217
H G Christie Ltd Real Estate 221
Treasure Cay Hotel Resort & Marina 42

ANDROS
Automotive & Industrial
    Distributors Ltd (AID) 154
Bahamasair 115

ELEUTHERA
Automotive & Industrial
    Distributors Ltd (AID) 154
Bahamasair 115
H G Christie Ltd Real Estate 221

EXUMA
Automotive & Industrial
    Distributors Ltd (AID) 154
Bahamasair 115

Index

A
Abaco(s), 15, 128-129, 131, 139, 140, 144, 164, 235, 239, 248-249, 269, 274, 292, 298, 344, 357, 405, 455, 602
Abaco Markets, 197, 596
Accommodations, 268, 523
Accounting firms, 268, 523
Acklins & Crooked Island, 131, 274, 357
Adderley, Augustus, 66
Adderley, Cleophas, 56, 446, 582, 600
Adderley, Harold, 69
Adderley, Nathaniel, 581
Agricultural Manufactories Act, 269
Agriculture, 268, 523, **see also Farms**
AIDS/HIV, 270, 413, 598
AIDS Foundation, 270, 304
AIDS Secretariat, 271
Air service, 271, 524, **see also Flights**
Airport(s), 273, 274-275
Albury, Cheryl, 582
Alcone, Matt, 596
Alfred, Joseph, 582
Allen, Hon Algernon SPB, 27, 561, 572, 601
Allen, Anita, 582
Allen, Hon William C, 187, 560, 573
Allens, Capt Anthony J, 583
AlliedSignal Inc, 466
Ambulance/air ambulance services, 273, 525
Andrews, Peter Newton, 593
Andros, 94, 99, 157, 235, 269, 274, 292, 357
Androsia, 159, 392, 544
Animals, 273, 283, 525, 539
Antoni, Dr Albert, 504
Antoni, Janine, 601
Aquaculture, 468
Aranha, Keith, 114
Arawak Cay, 276
Arawak Hotel, 462
Archaeology(ists), 99, 125-136
Archer, HE A Leonard, 587, 588, 589
Architectural firms, 276, 525
Archives, Dept of, 125, 126, 130, 131, 145, 277-278, 415, 560, 581, 584, 585
Ardastra Gardens, 49
Armbrister, GW, 69
Arnold, Robert, 594
Art galleries & museums, 278
Ashley gang, 488, 489, 490
Asset Protection Trusts (APTs), 380
Atlantic Beach Hotel, 76, 462, 463
Atlantic Undersea Testing & Evaluation Centre (AUTEC), 279
Atlantis, lost continent, 76, 80-102
Atlantis Bahamas Super Boat Challenge, 596
Atlantis, Paradise Island, 219, 222, 337, 403, 462, 473, 595, 599
Attorney-General, 287, 309, 386, 415, 538, 561, 569, 579, 580
Awards, 159, 162, 279-280, 351, 501, 514, 598, 599, 601

B
Babilonia, Erick, 591
Bacardi (Rum), 391
Bahama Rock Ltd, 467
Bahamahost, 280
Bahamas Steamship Co Ltd, 60
Bahamas Agricultural & Industrial Corp (BAIC), 281, 376
Bahamasair, 595, 598, 601
Bahamas Air Sea Rescue Assoc (BASRA), 281, 304, 505
Bahamas Amusements Ltd, 512
Bahamas Christian Council, 598
Bahamas Classified Directory, 255-263
Bahamas Development Bank (BDB), 76, 281-282, 385, 399, 526
Bahamas diplomatic and consular reps, 587-590
Bahamas Environment, Science & Technology Commission (BEST), 449, 590
Bahamas Electricity Corp (BEC), 183, 297, 334, 595
Bahamas Family Planning Assoc, 282, 304
Bahamas Financial Services Board, 166, 178, 282-283, 602
Bahamas Historical Society, 125, 126, 283
Bahamas Hotel Training College, 331
Bahamas Humane Society, 283, 598
Bahamas information, 265-456
Bahamas Investment Authority (BIA), 216, 217, 283-284, 380, 384, 385, 538, 558
Bahamas Maritime Authority, 167, 419
Bahamas Multi Media Ltd, 380
Bahamas National Trust (BNT), 107, 125, 155, 284, 292, 345, 449, 470, 484, 525-526
Bahamas Oil Refining Co, 474, 543, 550
Bahamas On-Line, 379
Bahamas Plays and Films Control Board, 300
Bahamas Real Estate Assoc, 417
Bahamas Red Cross Society, 285
Bahamas Road Traffic Act, 396
Bahamas Securities Exchange/Stock Market, 165, 186-198, 383, 595
Bahamas Shipowners Assoc, 167
Bahamas Telecommunications Corp (BaTelCo), 183, 297, 352, 443, 469, 513, 595, 596, 598, 599
Bahamasnet, 380
Bain, Glenward, 583
Bain, Dr Granville, 598, 599
Balance of payments, 286
Banking, 285, 526
Banks, 39, 288-291
Banks & Trust Cos Regulation Act, 1965, 306
Barbados, 61, 299
Barclays Bank plc, 288, 289, 526
Barr, Freeman, 596, 598
Barratt, Peter, 484, 486
BaTelNet, 379, 380
Bay View Village, 160
BAYROC, 224

Bayside Development, 228
Beaverbrook, Lord, 109, 110, 497
Beddington, Col Claude, 494
Bell Channel Club & Marina, 546
Bell's Column, 98
Belongers, 372
Beneby, Charles, 582
Benedictines, 116, 117
Ben's Cave, 503
Bennett, Tony, 599
Berman, Dr Mary Jane, 128
Bermuda, 61, 299
Bernard, Anita, 580
Berry Islands, 274, 292, 298, 303, 357
Bethel, Alonzo A, 65
Bethel, Hon Carl W, 564, 572, 602
Bethel, Carolita, 582
Bethel, Errol, 583
Bethel, Jacqueline, 582
Bethel, Dr Keva, 602
Bethel, Sen Hon Dr Marcus C, 568
Bethel, Sen Hon Michael A, 567
Bethel, Michael, 600
Bethel, Owen, 192
Bethel, Philip Herman, 600, 602
Bethel, Hon Philip M, 600
Bethlehem Steel Corp, 120
Bevans, Roland, 582
Bhi-Cam Ltd, 467
Bimini, 81-102, 236, 272, 274, 298, 303, 357, 405
Bimini Bay Hotel, 236
Bimini Biological Field Station, 395
Bimini Road, 81-102
Bird(s), 153, 291, 344, 471, 526
Blackwell, Chris, 20
Blackwell, Edison "Moose," 159
Blockade runners, 105, 108
Blosvern, David W, 591
Boating, 293, 526
Boer War, 60, 70
Bonamy, Bernard K, 583
Bonefishing, 474
Bosfield, George, 60
Bosfield, Ronald A, 575, 596
Boston Globe, 470
Bostwick, Hon Janet G, 559, 574
Bostwick, Sen Hon John Henry, 565
Bouvier, Lee, 110
Bradford Grand Bahama, 458, 459, 543
Braynen, Michael, 581
Bridgewater, Pamela, 591
British Colonial Hotel, 76, 222, 229, 600,
  see also Hotel Colonial
British Guiana, 61-62
Broadcasting, 77, 294
Brokmeier, Ernst, 593
Brooks, Monique, 592
Brown, Harcourt, 582
Brown, Herbert, 582
Bryce, Jim, 484
Buckey, Dr Jay, 600
Buckey, Jean, 600
Builders Depot, 464
Building contractors (& engineers), 295, 526
Building costs & permits, 295, 310, 527
Burchette, Ian, 593

Burns, Robert, 69
Burnside, Jackson III, 106-107
Burrows, Jethlyn, 582
Burrows, John, 581
Business Licence Act, 296
Business licence fee(s), 296, 527
Business name registration, 297, 306
Butler, Alonzo M, 581
Butler, Anthony, 582
Butler, HE Sir Arlington G, 587, 588, 589, 601
Butler, Ida, 70, 71
Butler, Kenneth F Co, 490
Butler, M Teresa, 580
Butler, Sir Milo B, 78
Butler, Roosevelt, 580
Butlin, Sir Billy, 476, 477
Butlin's Vacation Village, 491

C

Cabinet ministers & portfolios, 309, 558-563
Cable Beach, 76, 222, 224, 241
Cable television, 297-298, 527
Cacique, 134
Cacique awards, 159
Cadbury, Dame Elizabeth, 493
Camping, 298, 527
Canada, 273, 275, 287, 299, 300, 312, 315, 317, 337, 368, 374, 375, 377, 396, 402, 403, 406, 410, 411, 423, 429-435, 443, 446, 447, 448, 451, 452, 490, 587, 592
Caonabo, 134
Capone, Al, 108
Capone, Ralph, 489
Captive insurance, 166, 379
Cars, 322, 396
Car rental (cos), 298, 527
Carib(s), 483
Carib Forum, 460
Caribbean, 93, 110, 134, 150, 151, 176, 178, 184, 185, 197, 291, 298, 337, 446, 460, 462, 468, 509, 599
Caribbean Basin Initiative (CBI), 298, 460
Caribbean Community & Common Market (CARICOM), 299
Caribbean Hotel Assoc, 162
Caribbean Hotel Industry Conf (CHIC), 601
Caribbean Marine Research Centre (CMRC), 395
CARIBCAN, 299, 460
Carifta Games, 599, 600
Carnival Cruises, 167, 421, 602
Carrera-Justiz, Francisco, 594
Carstairs, Marion "Joe," 70, 71
Carter, Gov GT, 66, 70, 71
Cash, Sen Hon Darron B, 567
Cash, Sir Gerald C, 509, 512-513, 516
Casino(s), 337, 348, 527
Castaway Cay, 15, 29, 139, 140, 164, 168, 239, 602, **see also Gorda Cay**
Cat Island, 131, 239, 269, 274, 358
Cavalier Construction, 480
Caves Point, 226, 229, 241
Cayce, Edgar, 81, 99
Cayman(s), 197, 291, 299, 452, 466
CEDEL, 192
Celebrity Cruises, 421

607

Celestin, Jean-Pierre, 591
Censorship (films, plays & printed material), 300
Centex Rooney, 462
Central Bank (of The Bahamas), 166, 188, 219, 278, 285, 287, 288, 307, 326, 337, 338, 339, 373, 381, 382, 383
Central Securities Depository, 197
Chamber of Commerce, 301, 464, 509, 527, 600
Chamberlain, Joseph, 66
Chamberlain, Neville, 66
Changhua, Fu, 591
Cherokee Sound, 157
Chevron, 167
Chief Valuation Officer, 409, 410
China (People's Republic of), 368, 452, 591, 596, 600
China (ROC), Republic of, 401, **see also Taiwan**
Chipman, Reece, 192
Chiusano, Niccolo Caissotti, 594
Christie, HC, 64
Christie, HG, Real Estate Co, 417
Christie, Sir Harold G, 117, 118
Christie, Perry G, 570
Churches, 34, **see also Religion**
Cigars, 62, 112
Cinemas, 301, 527
Citizenship, 301
Civil Aviation, 273, 274
Civil War, American, 108, 485
Clarke, Joanne, 602
Clarke, Rosemary, 138, 139, 142
Cleare, Angela, 153, 160
Clifton Cay, 229
Clifton Pier, 45
Climate, 303, 528
Clinics, 356, 541, **see also Hospitals & clinics**
Clinton-Thomas, Dr Charles, 507
Club Fortuna, 239
Club Med, 348, 497
Club Peace and Plenty, 160
Coakley, Dr Doswell, 590
Coakley, JC, 62
Coakley, Livingstone, 168, 172
Coat of Arms, 400
Cole, Nicola, 592
College of The Bahamas (COB), 77, 126, 328, 332, 533, 596, 597, 602
Columbus, Christopher, 116, 129, 134, 353, 457
Comfort Suites, 159, 160, 162
Commission chairpersons, 580
Commissions, **see Embassies**
Commonwealth Brewery Ltd, 391
Community orgs (& service clubs), 304, 528
Companies Act, 1992, 202, 204, 206, 305, 306, 307, 308
Companies (holding & trading), 437
Companies, regular, 201, 204-208
Company formation, 305
Compass Point, 20
Concem Ltd, 458, 466
Connery, Sean, 13
Constantakis, Gus, 593

Constitution, 301, 302, 308
Construction, 79, 219, 232, 235, 310, 403
Consulates, **see Embassies**
Consumer protection, 309
Cook, Robin, 598
Cooper, Dr Donald, 581
Cooper, Col Gordon, 600
Cooper-Nairn, Sen Hon Pauline V, 567
Cooper, Winston, 582
Copyright laws, 310
Corner House, 123
Corrigan, Archbishop Michael, 116, 117, 121
Cost of living, 310, 528
Costa Cruises, 421
Cottell, Eric and Betty, 120
Courier services, 311, 529
Court(s), 309, 319, 340, 385, 404, 421, 539, 561, 584
Cousteau, Jean-Michel, 597
Crawford, Cindy, 600, 601
Crime, 311, 602, **see also Drugs**
Criswell, Bill, 237
Crooked Island, 128, 274
Crowch, Eric J, 593
Cruise ship gaming, 349
Cruise ship incentives, 312, 421
Cuba, 60, 127, 129, 130, 135, 176, 183, 184, 185, 291, 367, 391, 587
Culligan, Phil, 591
Culture & cultural activities, 312, 529
Cunard Line, 421
Cunningham, Deanza, 580
Cunningham, Ehurd, 582
Currency, 312
Customs, 232, 293, 313-318, 324, 529
Cutillas, Manuel, 593

D

Dahl-Regis, Dr M, 582
Davis Cup, 602
Dawkins, Opal, 146
Deadman's Reef, 128, 131, 135
DeGregory, Lester, 583
Dean, Holland, 581
Dean, Nathaniel, 582
Defence Force, Royal Bahamas, **see Royal Bahamas Defence Force**
Dempster, John W, 582
Dentists, 318, 531
Departure tax, 318, 531
Deveaux, Blanche, 583
Deveaux, Dr Earl D, 567, 575
Different of Abaco, 155, 156
Dillet's Guest House, 160
Diplomatic & consular reps abroad, 587-590
Disney Cruise Line, 15, 29, 167, 168, 239, 421, 602
Diving & snorkelling, 531
Divorce, 319
Dockendale House & Manx Corp Centre, 224
Dockendale Shipping, 167
Doctors, 319-321
Doctors Hospital, 228, 310, 356
Dolphins, 37, 395
Donaldson, T Baswell, 187, 513, 515

Donato, Mario, 472
Donato, William, 83, 93, 100, 101, 102
Dorrance, John Thompson III, 594
Dorsett, Hon Jaunianne Rahming, 571
Douglas, Hosea, 581
Douglas, Robert, 34, 112
Doyle, Sir William, 112, 114
Driver's licence & vehicle information, 322, 532
Drugs, 287, 325, 596, 597, 598, 601
Dudley, Lord & Lady, 104, 108, 110
Duho(s), 127, 130
Duke of Edinburgh, 71, 599
Duke & Duchess of Kent, 110
Duke & Duchess of Windsor, 109, 110
Duke of Windsor, 491
Dumont, Sen Hon Dame Dr Ivy L, 560, 565
Duncan, Dr Warren, 483
Duncanson, Freeman, 581
Duncombe Cooper, Sen Hon Daphne A, 566, 579
Dupuch, Sir Etienne, 78
Dupuch, Etienne Jr Publications, 380
Dupuch, Hon Eugene AP, 78
Dupuch, Mrs Leon EH, 64
Dupuch, Hon Pierre VL, 562, 574
Duty free, **see Customs; Industries encouragement; Shopping**

E

East Hill St, 105, 106
Eco-resorts, 18, 149-162
Ecotourism, 448
Economy, 326
Education, 327-334, 532-534, 538
Edwards, Sen Hon Desmond FL, 566
Electricity, 78, 334, 534
Eleuthera, 89, 123, 239, 249, 269, 274, 292, 298, 303, 358, 405, 512, 602
Elizabeth Harbour, 151
Ellis, Edward, 582
Ellis, Richard, 82, 92
Embassies, 587, 591
Emerald Bay Resort, 237
Emerald Palms Resort, 235
Emergency nos, 336, 535
Emiliani, Dr Cesare, 93
Employers' orgs, 336, 535
Encouragement Acts, 535
Endangered species, 276, 345
Engineering cos, 336, **see also Building contractors & engineers**
Entertainment, 337, 535
Environmental Protection Agency, 151
Erskine-Lindop, Commissioner RA, 511
Etienne, Joseph J, 591
EUROCLEAR, 192
European Economic Community (EEC), 76
European Union (EU), 460, 592
Evans, Berkley, 581
Evans, Candy, 470
Exchange Control, 206, 207, 288, 296, 308, 337, 438, 535
Exempted limited partnerships, 201, 208-210, 308
Export entry, 339, 536, **see also Import & export entry**

Export Manufacturing Industries Act, 215
Extinct species, 345
Extradition, 340
Exuma(s), 27, 64, 153, 237, 238, 249-250, 269, 274, 292, 344, 358, 405, 455, 511
Exxon Intl, 167

F

Fair, Ian, 177, 179, 180
Family planning, 282, 304
Farm(s), 268-270, 467-468
February Point, 238
Ferguson, Amos I, 556
Ferguson, Debbie, 599, 601
Ferguson, Joan, 582
Ferguson, Sarah, Duchess of York, 597
Ferguson-Beneby, Thelma, 580
Fidelity Bank & Trust, 198
Fields, Donnie, 83, 97
Films/movies, 300, 354, 527
FINDEX, 198
Fire Brigade, 70, 536
Fire Services, 340
Fischbacher, Mr & Mrs Heinz, 482, 484
Fisher, Rector J Hartman, 68
Fishing, 77, 341, 480, 505, 536
Fitness, 343
Flag, 73, 400, 601
Flagler, Henry M, 60, 61
Flagler, Mary Lily, 61
Flamingo(s), 292, 401, 455
Flamingo Bay, 238
Fletcher, Peter G, 201, 217
Flights, 271, 524-525
Flora & fauna, 32, 344
Flores, Arthur, 591
Florida Museum of Natural History, 130
Fogleman, Lori, 602
Fold, The, 123
Forbes, Roger, 581
Fort(s), 347
Foulkes, HE Arthur A, 587, 588, 589
Foulkes, Hon Dion A, 564
Fox, Rick, 77
Fragrance of The Bahamas, 544
Francis, Judith, 582
Francis, Julian, 188, 190, 581
Francis, Patricia, 582
Frank, Joseph, 83
Franklin, Glenn, 152, 160
Fraser, Charles, 65
Frasier, Harrington "Skeebo," 159
Fraudulent Dispositions Act, 380
Free National Movement (FNM), 75, 78, 170, 172, 179, 355
Free trade, 184
Free Trade Area of the Americas (FTAA), 177, 347, 468, 601, 602
Freeport, 250-251
Freeport Container Port, 51, 75, 180, 181, 220, 355, 457-458, 475, 602
Freeport Harbour, 220, 458
Freeport Harbour Co, 458, 475
Freeport Intl Airport, 457, 459
Freeport/Lucaya Classified Directory, 518
Freeport/Lucaya hotels & resorts, 460-463, 523, **see also Hotels**

609

Freeport/Lucaya information, 521-552
Freeport/Lucaya real estate/construction, 463, **see also Real Estate**
Freeport/Lucaya restaurants, 472
Freeport News, 401
Freeport Oil Co, 513
Freeport Players' Guild, 529
Freeport Power Co, 470
Freight services, 348, 536
French, Mrs Nathaniel, 107
French's Hotel, 108
Fynes, Savatheda, 600

G

Galanis, Sen Hon Philip C, 570
Galanos, HE Peter, 587, 588
Gambling/gaming, 337, 348, 349, 390, 537
Gaming Board, 416, 538, 559, 581
Garcia, Carlos, 591
Garden of the Groves, Parrot Jungle's, 470
Garzaroli, Enrico, 108, 110
Geography, 349, 537
Geology(ists), 84, 85, 88, 93, 94, 95, 96, 97
George Town, 151
Gerber, Rande, 600, 601
Gibson, Larry, 186-187, 198, 581
Gibson, Maxwell E, 593
Gibson, Paul, 501
Glantz, Talia, 594
Gnivecki, Dr Perry, 128
Godet, Mary, 468
Gold Circle House, 232
Gold Rock Creek, 471, 484
Gold's Gym, 343, 344
Golf, 425, 473, 537
Gomez, Sen Hon Damian A, 568
Gomez, Pamela, 583
Gomez, Roger, 582
Goodman's Bay Corp Centre, 224
Gorda Cay, 139, 140, 164, 168, 239, **see also Castaway Cay**
Gotstick, Rev FW, 65
Gottlieb, Andrea, 470
Gottlieb, Cay, 469
Gould, Irving, 591
Government House, 70, 71, 105, 106, 107, 109, 120, 405, 596
Government offices, 537, 584-586
Governor(s)-General, 74, 78, 301, 309, 557
Governors, 349-351
Graham, Eric, 500
Grand Bahama, 179, 182, 190, 219, 220, 235, 250-252, 275, 292
Grand Bahama Beach Hotel, 76, 460
Grand Bahama Development Co (GBDevCo), 459, 464, 514
Grand Bahama Humane Society, 539
Grand Bahama Island Tourism Board, 513
Grand Bahama Players, 529
Grand Bahama Port Authority (GBPA), 75, 110, 475, 508, 509, 510, 512, 513, 543
Grand Bahama SeaAir Business Centre (SABC), 459-460, 510
Granberry, Dr Julian, 125, 136, 484
Granger, Wenzel, 510
Grant, Elizabeth, 282
Grant, Neko C, 577

Graycliff, 104, 107, 108, 110, 123, 497
Graycliff Cigar Factory, 112
Grayleath, 497, 499
Graysmith, Capt John Howard, 107, 497
Greene, Leila, 580
Grey, Sir Ralph, 120
Grody, Allan D, 198
Gross Domestic Product (GDP), 75, 170, 287, 326, 376
Gross National Product, 327
Groves, Graham, 480
Groves, Wallace, 78, 480, 498, 499
Gruber, Dr Samuel, 395
Guaranty Trust Bank, 229
Gun permits, 351, 539
Guta Bank and Trust, 232

H

Haihe, Zhang, 591
Haiti, 588
Half Moon Cay, 29, 168, 239, 598, **see also Little San Salvador**
Hall, Rev Dr Simeon, 468
Hamilton, Michael, 582
Hanlan, Patrick, 593
Hanley, Dr Joan, 101
Hanna, Brenville, 582
Hanna-Weeks, Petra, 582
Harbour Control, 352, 540
Harbour Island, 303
Hard Bargain, 145
Hargraves, Peter S, 591
Harry, Dr Claudette, 592
Hartford, Huntington II, 47
Hawksbill Creek Agreement, 354, 510, 540
Hayward, Sir Charles, 499
Hayward, Sir Jack, 472, 505, 509, 510, 516, 517
Hazlewood, Fred A, 184
Healing Hole, 99
Health/medical services, 353
Hearty, Dr Paul J, 82, 92
Heaven, Gusty, 490
Heliports, 273
Hepburn, HE Dr Davidson L, 587, 588
Hepburn, Gussy, 490
Hernandez, Livian, 598
Hernandez, Orlando "El Duque," 598
Higgs, Dr Leon, 581, 602
Higgins, Carol, 150, 151, 152
Higgins, David, 150, 151, 153, 154
Higgins Landing, 149, 150, 151, 154
Hispaniola, 126, 128, 129, 134, 135, 482
Historical Nassau Renovation Committee, 107
Historical Society, Bahamas, 283, 305
History, 82, 91, 103-136, 353, 541
Hog Island, 46, 65
Holidays, 356
Holistic medicine, 542
Holland America Cruise Lines, 29, 167, 421, 598
Hollingsworth, Capt Steve, 488, 491
Holowesko, HE Lynn P, 590
Home owner's residence card, 369, 413
Hong Kong, 327, 368, 444, 452, 457, 475, 537, 594

Honorary consuls & reps (in The Bahamas), 592-594
Honorary consuls abroad, Bahamas, 594
Honours & decorations (incl degrees), 514
Horton, Wilfred, 580
Hospital(s & clinics), 356, 541
Hotel(s), 357-366, **see also Freeport/Lucaya hotels & resorts**
Hotel Colonial, 60, 64, 65, 69
Hotel Corp, 235
Hotel Training College, Bahamas, 331
Hotels Encouragement (Act), 215, 358
House of Assembly, 67, 309
Housing, 542, **see also Accommodations**
Humane Society, Bahamas, 283, 305, 539,
Humidor, The, 112
Hunter, Christina, 74
Hunter, Rachel Rogers 74
Hunting, 292, **see also Birds**
Hurricane(s), 63, 75, 153, 303, 366
Hutchison Lucaya Ltd, 541
Hutchison Port Holdings (HPH), 75, 327, 457, 459, 541
Hutchison Whampoa Group of Cos, 51, 180, 510, 537, 596
Hutia, 483, 484

I
Iguana(s), 344
Immigration, 367-373, 543, **see also Citizenship**
Immunology Research Centre, 500, 542
Imperial Life Financial, 464, 466
Imperial Lighthouse Service, 118, 487
Import & export entry, 314, 373, 543, **see also Export entry**
Import & export statistics, 373, 374
Inagua, 89, 275, 292, 298, 344, 345, 358, 455
Independence, 73, 78, 367
Industrial relations, 373
Industrial Tribunal, 375
Industries Encouragement (Act), 215, 375
Industry, 376, 543
Inflation, **see Economy**
Ingraham, Rt Hon Hubert A (Prime Minister), 74, 75, 347, 558, 575
Innotec, 464
Insurance, 377-379, 441, 443
Insurance Act, 306, 377, 378
Inter-American Development Bank, 170, 592
Intl Bazaar, 544
Intl Business Co (IBC), 166, 167, 201-204, 307
Intl Org of Securities Commission, 192
Intl orgs' reps, 592
Intl Persons Landholding Act, 412
Internet, 379
Investing, 380-385
Investments Board, 338
Investment incentives, 383
Investment Policy, **see National Investment Policy**
Isaacs, Jon, 582
Isaacs, Sir Kendal, 78
Isaacs, Oswald, 580
Island Expedition, 395

Island Heritage, 34
Islands of Old Fort, 228
Issa, John, 182, 184

J
Jack Tar Resort & Marina, 236, 476, 477, 478, 480, 491
Jacobson, Tracy, 591
Jagger, Robert S, 593
Jamaica, 61, 197, 299, 300, 333, 377, 396, 411, 445, 446, 452, 474, 588
Japan, 588
John Bull, 176, 184
Johnson, Sen Hon Calvin J, 566, 579
Johnson, Dame Doris, 78
Johnson, Sir George & Lady, 118
Johnson, Mary, 582
Johnson, Melvern, 582
Johnson, Rengin, 582
Johnson, Hon Rome Italia, 571, 597
Johnson, Vernita, 580, 582
Johnstone, HE Geoffrey, 587, 589
Jones, Carlton I, 592
Jones Communications Ltd, 77
Jones, Comdr Leonard, 591
Jones, Robert Trent Jr, 473
Joseph, Delan, 591
Judicial and Legal Service Commission, 309
Judicial system, 385, 544
Junkanoo, 232, 278, 386, 391, 545

K
Keefe, Bill, 85, 98
Keegan, William F, 128, 130
Kelly, Basil, 466
Kelly, David, 183
Kelly, Nancy, 183, 184, 185
Kemp, Franklyn, 583
Kennedy, Jacqueline, 110
Key, Berlin W, 593
Key West, 70
Killam, Mr I Walton, 108, 497, 499
Killam, Mrs I Walton, 496, 497
King, Paul, 581
Kirton, Wesley, 592
Klainguti, Katherine Helena, 594
Kloihofer, Heinz, 592
Knowles, Conrad, 511
Knowles, Hon James F, 562, 578
Knowles, Locksley, 581
Knowles, Mark, 77, 423, 600, 601
Knowles, Sen Hon Dr Ronald, 563, 565, 599
Knowles, Sandra, 187, 190, 192, 194
Kozeny, Viktor, 593
Kruger, Stephanus Johannes Paulus, 71

L
Laing, Hon Zhivargo, 564, 570
Laroda, Andil, 582
Lavelle, George, 510
Law firms, 387-389, 545
Leach, Polly, 108
Leader of the Opposition, 570
Le Gris, Claude, 594
Leigh, Raymond Jr, 99
Liebman, Howard M, 435, 439
Libby, Mark, 591

Libraries, 389, 545
Licensing, 545
Liechtenstein, 201
Lightbourn, Edwin, 581
Lightbourne, Dennis, 581
Lightbourne, Kenneth, 582
Limited Duration Company, 308
Liquor laws, 389
Little San Salvador, 168, 239, 292, **see also Half Moon Cay**
Literacy, 328
Lloyd, Jane, 591
Lockhart, Elliott B, 576
Lofthouse, THC, 62
Long Island, 127, 130, 134, 269, 275, 298, 358, 509
Longley, Hartman, 582
LOME IV Convention, 390
Lotteries, 390
Lowe, Clara, 583
Lowndes, Rev William, 118
Lucayan Beach Hotel, 76, 220, 460
Lucayan(s), 124-136, 139, 353, 482, 483
Lucayan, The (resort), 76, 220, 236, 355, 460, 462, 473, 510, 595, 602
Lucayan Aquaculture, 468
Lucayan Caverns, 125, 131, 471, 483
Lucayan Marina Village, 251, 546
Lucayan National Park, 131, 471, 483, 484, 503
Lunn, Dr John, 599
Lyford Cay, 228, 229, 242, 243, 310, 472, 596
Lyford Cay Hospital/Heart Inst, 310, 357
Lynch, Arthur J, 439, 443

M

MacCausland, John, 599
Mack, Paul, 484
MacVean, Jeremy, 160, 162
Maersk Line, 167, 458
Maguana Kingdom, 134
Mail-boats, 451
Maillis, Pericles, 155
Major, Michael, 583
Major, Paul, 581
Major, Wendell G, 580
Major-Rutherford, Sen Hon Geneva E, 565
Malcolm, Barry, 166, 168, 283
Malcolm, Jacqueline, 555
Manuel, Gladys, 582
Manufacturing, 391
Manx Ltd, 167, 224
Marinas (& cruising facilities), 392, 393-395, 480, 546, 599
Marine parks & exhibits, 392
Marine research, 392
Marriage licences, 396, 546
Marques, Ricardo, 582
Martinez, Elizabeth, 591
Massoni, Carmen, 593
Matheson, Aileen, 512
Mayaguana, 275, 358
Maynard, Sir Clement T & Lady, 55
Maynard, Julian, 117
Mayol, Jacques, 37
McAlpine, Sir Robert, 110

McBride, Eustace, 144-145
McCartney, Lennox, 583
McGrath, David, 593
McLean's Town, 143
Meadows, Sean, 146
Medical centres, 356, 541, **see also Hospitals & Clinics**
Mediterranean Shipping, 458
Meeres, Marilyn, 582
Meeres, Paul, 121
MeesPierson (Bahamas) Ltd, 177
Members of Parliament, 569-578
Mercantile Petroleum, 123
Meredith, John, 594
Miami Herald, 268, 401, 470
Millar, Ruth, 580, 582
Millar's Pond, 230
Miller, Albert J, 475, 508-517, 600
Miller, Anthony C, 576
Miller, Darnell, 581
Miller, Debbie, 511
Miller, George, 581
Miller, James H, 576
Miller, Laurie, 511, 516
Miller, Mark Anthony, 511
Miller, Sen Hon Roston H, 566
Miller, Russell, 511
Million Air Nassau, 599
Ministers of State, 564
Ministry of Agriculture & Fisheries, 269, 563, 580, 584
Ministry of Agriculture (Incorporation) Act, 269
Ministry of Consumer Welfare, 309
Ministry of Education, 327
Ministry of Finance & Planning, 314, 358, 376, 379, 390
Ministry of Foreign Affairs, 452
Ministry of Health, 271, 357, 413, 417, 451
Ministry of Housing & Social Development, 561, 596
Ministry of Labour, Immigration & Training, 373
Ministry of National Security, 418
Ministry of Public Works, 295, 298, 358
Ministry of Tourism, 153, 160, 280, 314, 380, 405, 470, 501, 599, 601
Ministry of Youth, Sports & Culture, 428
Mitchell, Sen Hon Frederick A Jr, 568
Mitchell, Stephen, 130
Money laundering, 287, 596
Montagu Beach Hotel, 76, 232, 501
Montague Sterling Centre, 232
Montas, Dr Hernando Perez, 594
Moorby, Col Anthony Lindsay, 591
Moore, HE Maurice E, 589
Moore, Sir Walter K, 114
Moore's Island, 139, 140, 143, 144
Moran, HE James, 592
Moss, E George, 583
Motor vehicle insurance, 396, **see also Insurance**
Moultrie, Erika, 128, 471, 484
Mountbatten, Countess, 123
Mountbatten, Lord, 105, 110, 122, 123
Mountbatten House, 123
Moxey-Ingraham, Hon Theresa M, 561, 571

Mullin, Francis, 591
Mullings, Devin, 474
Munnings, Harold, 580
Munson, Mrs Cora, 118
Munson Shipping Lines, 118
Museum(s), 397, 546, **see also Art galleries & museums**
Mutual fund(s), 166, 381, 397, **see also Investments**

N

Nairn, Archie, 580
NASDAQ, 197
Nassau Beach Hotel, 224
Nassau Guardian, The, 59, 60, 66, 107, 116, 401, 602
Nassau Harbour, 15, 106, 120, 167, 222, 352
Nassau Intl Airport, 168, 272, 314, 599, 602
Nassau Yacht Club, 599
Nassau Yacht Haven, 232
National anthem, 397, 400
National Art Gallery, 112, 114
National bird, 401
National Economic Council, 284, 384
National fish, 401
National flower, 401
National Insurance, 77, 397, 547
National Investment Policy, 212-217, 383
National parks, 455
National symbols, 400
National tree, 401
National Youth Choir, 56, 446
Nature centres, 401, 471, 547, **see also Parks**
Nestor, Daniel, 423, 600
New Providence, 275, 405
New York Post, 470
New York Times, 311
Newspapers, 401, 547
Nightclubs, 337
Nihon, Robert, 592
Nixon, Jimmy, 598
North American Free Trade Agreement (NAFTA), 177, 402
North Riding Point Club, 503
Norwegian Cruise Line, 421
Nottage, Bernard J, 572
Nuestra Señora de las Maravillas, 353

O

Oakes, Sir Harry, 598
Obed, Elisha, 77, 596
O'Brien, Basil, 580
O'Connor, Timothy, 591
O'Donnell, Columbus, 121, 122
O'Donnell House, 117, 121, 123
O'Donnell-Clark, Sibilla, 121, 122, 123
O'Keeffe, Rev Cornelius George, 116, 117
Oceania Heights Development, 238, 250
Oceanic Bank & Trust, 228, 600
Offshore insurance, 378
Old Age Pensions Act, 397
Old Bahama Bay, 236, 251, 457, 478, 489, 491, 598, **see also West End**
Old Fort Bay, 228, 244
Orange Hill Beach Inn, 160

Organization of American States (OAS), 76, 402, 588, 592, 600
Osadebay, Emmanuel, 513, 582
Outten, Valarie, 581

P

Palmer, Rob, 353, 395
Pan American Airlines, 76
Pan-American Health Org, 592
Pantin, David, 220
Paradise Island, 16, 46, 65, 76, 126, 127, 128, 159, 219, 244-246, 272, 298, 403, 405, 491, 596, 600, 601
Paradise Island Bridge, 222, 232, 273, 596
Parker, Bill, 468
Parks (national), **see Nature centres**
Parliamentarians' salaries, 579
Parliamentary Secretaries, 579
Passport(s), 368, 403, 547
Patterson, Elise, 591
Patton, Carolyn, 581
Paul, Sir John, 74
People-to-People, 405, 548
Permanent residence, 371
Permanent Secretaries, 580
Petroleum, 377
Pharmaceutical Fine Chemicals, 466, 544
Pharmacies, 405
Phoenix Aviation, 599
Pickard, Glen, 581
Pictet Bank, 228, 600
Pillars of Hercules, 81, 82
Pinder, Iris, 582
Pinder, Simeon, 581
Pindling, Sir Lynden O, 73, 74, 596, 601
Plato, 81, 85, 86, 93
Poisonous species, 344
Poitier, HE Sir Sidney, 588
Police certificates, 548
Police Force, **see Royal Bahamas Police Force**
Police Service Commission, 309
Polymers Intl Ltd, 466, 544
Ponce de León, Juan, 480, 482
Population, 406, 407, 548
Port Atlantic Shores, 235
Port Lucaya Marina Yacht Club, 546
Port Lucaya Marketplace, 548
Port New Providence, 232
Ports of entry, 408-409
Poseidia, 96, 97
Post Office, 232
Postal information, 406, 407, 410, 411, 548
Postern Gate, 110, 112
Potter's Cay, 269, 409
Power, Michael, 180, 515
Pratt, Dr Cynthia, 573
Premier Cruises, 421, 459
PricewaterhouseCoopers, 464
Prime Minister (incl Office of the Prime Minister), 74, 75, 212, 216, 283, 309, 347, 358, 375, 377, 384, 385, 457, 462, 463, 596, 597, 600, **see also Ingraham, Rt Hon Hubert A**
Prince Charles, 73, 74
Prince George Dock (Wharf), 170, 232, 278, 386, 599

613

Prince Philip, 599
Princess Alice, 109, 110
Princess Cruises, 421
Princess Hotels/Resort, 463, 470
Princess Isle, 252
Princess Margaret Hospital, 310, 328, 356
Principe, Vincent A, 591
Private banking, 287
Privy Council, 309
Progressive Liberal Party (PLP), 75, 170
Prohibition, 490
Property tax, 409
Property transactions, 412, 548
Public finance, 414-416
Public health, 413
Public Service Board of Appeal, 309
Public Service Commission, 309
Public Service officials, 581
Public Works, 239
Pyfrom, Jerome, 69
Pyfrom, Jerome E, & Co, 201
Pyfrom, William Robert, 114

Q

Quant, Sterling, 583
Quant-Forbes, Lillian, 583
Queen Elizabeth II, 446
Queen Elizabeth Sports Centre, 423
Queen Victoria, 69, 71
Queen's Counsel, 386

R

Radio station(s), 77, 294, 469, 470, 549, **see also Broadcasting and Harbour Control**
Radziwill, Prince Stanislaus, 110
Ragged Island, 275
Rahming, Candy, 472
Rahming, Charles, 138, 139, 142, 143, 146, 147
Rahming, Doris, 138, 139, 140, 143, 144, 147
Rahming, Yvonne, 145
Ramsay, Jonathan CB, 592
Rand, James, 500
Rand Memorial Hospital, 142, 464
Rand Nature Centre, 471
Ranora House, 118, 120
Rawson Square, 70
Raymond, Jean, 496
Real estate (homes, condominiums), 241-252, **see also Freeport/Lucaya real estate**
Real estate cos (& developments), 417, 549
Real property tax, **see Property tax**
Rebikoff's Pier, 94
Red Cross Soc, Bahamas, 285
Reefs and marine life, 344
Registrar General, 306, 307, 396, 413
Regular companies, 201
Religion, 105, 418, 549, **see also Churches**
Rents, **see Accommodations, Cost of living**
Reptiles, 344
Resident diplomatic & consular reps (in The Bahamas), 591
Reynoso, Luis, 516

RHK Group, 76
Richards, Dr Douglas, 98
Richardson, Jim, 98
Roach, Melanie, 582
Roberts, Bradley B, 571
Roberts, Larry, 235
Rodgers, Dr KJA, 593
Rodgers, Dr Patricia E, 580
Rogers, Capt Woodes, 74
Rolle, Hon Anthony C, 564, 570
Rolle, Brensil, 583
Rolle, Sister Clare, 270
Rolle, Cdre Davey, 581
Rolle, Derek, 599
Rolle, Franklyn, 590
Rolle, John, 581
Rolle, Lillian, 583
Rolle, Sen Hon Lonnie ED, 567
Rose, Walter & Eileen (family), 492-507
Royal Bahamas Defence Force, 77, 318, 418
Royal Bahamas Police Force, 77, 311, 406, 419, 514
Royal Caribbean Cruise Line, 168, 391, 421, 597
Royal Palm Resort, 462, 472
Royal Towers, 222
Royal Victoria Hotel, 60, 61, 62, 76, 105
Royall Beach Estates, 230
Rum Cay, 275
Rum runners, 105
Running Mon Marina, 546
Russell, Lindy H, 577, 579
Russell, Kenneth, 577
Russell, Patrenda, 582
Russell, Vincent, 477, 491
Ryan, Rev JA, 117

S

St Andrew's Presbyterian Church, 34
St Francis Xavier Cathedral, 105, 114, 116, 117
St Francis Xavier Church, 116, 117, 120-121
St Francis Xavier College, 121
St George, Edward, 110, 473, 509
St Mary the Virgin Anglican Church, 118, 511
St Mary's Villa, 118
Salazar, Francisco, 93
Salkey, Willamae, 580
Samaritan Ministry, 270
Sammons, Charles, 477, 478
Sampras, Pete, 77
San Salvador, 71, 90, 126, 128, 131, 275, 405
Sandals Royal Bahamian Hotel, 76, 224, 229, 230
Sands, Basil L, 593
Sands, CG, 582
Sands, Reginald, 197
Sands, Sir Stafford L, 499
Sandilands Rehabilitation Centre, 71, 356
Sandyport, 224, 246, 344
Sassoon, Lady, 597
Saunders, Rev Dr Charles W, 580
Saunders, Dr Gail, 581
Saunders Group, Henry E, 77
Saunders, John, 583

Saunders, Stephana, 583
Saunders, Winston, 582
Sawyer, Chief Justice Joan, 580, 582
Schechter, HE Arthur, 591
Schmaelzle, Johann, 594
School(s) 78, 327, 472-473, **see also Education**
Schreiner, Fr Chrysostom, 66, 67
Schwabe, Dr, Stephanie, 395
Scriven, Sylvia E, 573
SeaEscape, 459
Seaman's Club, 490
Sears, Joshua, 580
Securities Board, 186
Securities Commission, 186, 187, 190, 192, 198, 383
Securities Industry Act, 192, 194
Securities Task Force, 187
Seligman, Ralph, 592, 593
Senate, 40
Senators, 565-568
Service clubs, **see Community orgs**
Setlakwe, Paul J, 429, 435
Seymour, Melvin, 582
Shannon Golf Course, 463
Sherman, George, 582
Sherman-Peter, Angela Missouri, 587
Shipping, 75, 167, 419, 550
Ship registration, 419
Shopping, 420, 550
Shuxue, HE Ma, 591
Silver Jubilee, honours, 280, 554
Silver Sands Hotel, 462
Simms, Kerstella, 146
Singer Sewing Machine Co, 62
Sisters of Charity, 116, 117, 120, 121
Slatter, Gary, 473
Small Business Loan Guarantee Act, 467
Small Hope Bay Lodge, 157, 159
Smiley, Thomas, 591
Smith, Alvin A, 576, 581
Smith, Carl, 581
Smith, Hon Cornelius A, 559, 578
Smith, HE James H, 174, 176, 590
Smith, Luther, 580
Smith, Michael D, 574
Smith, Roger, 77, 602
Smithsonian Institution, 483
Social Services, 421
Soldwedel, Frederic, 118
Solomon, Norman, 170
Solomon Bros, 513
South Ocean Beach Hotel, 229, 600
Southern Company, 470, 475
Souza, Hugo E, 592
Spanish Wells, 303
Speaker (of the House), 569, 571
Spencer, Sash, 457, 478
Sponges/sponging, 59, 62, 485, 487
Sports, 422-428, 473-474
Sports betting, 348
Sports orgs, 423
Sports venues, 423, 550
Stamp duty, 313, **see also Property transactions**
Standard Oil, 71
Stapledon, Sir Robert, 510

Star Class Spring Championships, 599
Statistics, 428
Stevenson, Gerald, 514
Stewart, George P, 582
Stikeman, H Heward, 429, 435
Stirrup, Chandra, 600
Stock market/exchange, **see Bahamas Securities Exchange**
Stocking Island, 149, 150, 151
Storr, Michaela, 582
Strachan, Ciano, 581
Strachan, Joseph, 582
Straw markets, 429
Stuart, Charles, 583
Stuart, Doris, **see Rahming, Doris**
Stuart, Hubert, 147
Stuart, Loretta, 139, 140
Stuart, Neville, 139, 140, 143, 144
Sturrup, Cresswell, 580
Sturrup, Justin, 581
Sun Intl Hotels Ltd, 76, 598, 600
Sunday Express, 503
Sunningridge, 117
SuperClubs® Breezes, 76, 160, 182, 224
Supermarkets, 186, 550
Supreme Court, 309, 404
Sweeting, Robert P Jr, 236, 575
Sweeting, Rosa, 593
Switzerland, 201
Symonett, Christopher, 581
Symonette, Donald, 582
Symonette, Michael, 581
Symonette, Netica, 156, 157
Symonette, Robert H (Bobby), 598
Symonette, Sir Roland T, 78
Symonette, Hon Vernon, 564, 578
Symonette-Armbrister, Lorraine, 582
Symons, Baroness, 460

T

Taino, 134,135
Taiwan, 401, **see also China, Republic of**
Tariff Act, 313, 376, 384
Tax benefits for Canadians, 429
Tax benefits for Europeans, 435
Tax benefits for US cos, 439
Tax haven(s), 167
Tax incentives, 551
Taylor, Coral, 147
Teekay Shipping, 167
Telecommunications, 443, 551
Telephone rates/charges, 444-446
Television, 446, 551
Templeton Global Advisors Ltd, 596
Teresi, Toni, 591
Theatre & performing/dramatic arts, 446
Themistocleous, Themis, 593
Thomas, Lt Comdr Robert, 591
Thompson, Hon David C, 564, 577
Thompson, Ronald, 580
Three Dog (excavation), 128, 131
Time, 447
Timeshare, 447
Todd, Richard, 112
Tongue of the Ocean, 93, 279, 349
Tourism, 75, 79, 184, 405, 447, 551
Trade agreements, 449

Trade unions, 449, 551
Traffic, 23, 600
Transportation, 450, 551
Treasure Cay, 249
Treasure Cove, 230
Trees, 345, 401
Tribune, The, 77, 78, 401, 600
Tribune Radio Ltd/100 JAMZ, 379
Trinity Methodist Church, 114
Tropical Shipping, 458
Trust(s), 381, 436, **see also Asset Protection Trusts (APTs)**
Trust cos, 285, 288-291, 327
Trustees Act, 1998, 382, 598
Trusts (Choice of Governing Law) Act, 381
Turks and Caicos, 62, 128, 129, 131
Turner, Philip, 583
Turnquest, HE Harcourt L, 580
Turnquest, Lester M, 572, 579
Turnquest, Governor-General Sir Orville Alton, 514, 557, 597
Turnquest, Hon Orville Alton Thompson (Tommy), 562, 573
Turnquest, Tex, 582
Tynes, Maurice, 582
Tynes, Rodella, 580

U

Underwater Explorers Society (UNEXSO), 37, 502
Uniroyal Chemical Co, 466, 544
United Kingdom (UK), 220, 273, 275, 285, 287, 301, 302, 308, 315, 316, 317, 318, 328, 340, 354, 368, 374, 375, 403, 406, 410, 411, 420, 439, 444, 446, 452
United Nations, 76
United States (US), 273, 285, 291, 337, 340, 354, 368, 374, 377, 396, 402, 403, 411
Univ of the West Indies, 333

V

Vaccination requirements, 451
Valentin, Marc, 93, 102
Valentine, Dr J Manson, 81
Vanderpool-Wallace, Vincent, 582
Vehicle information, 79, **see also Driver's licence & vehicle information; Motor vehicle insurance**
Venice Bay, 230
Veterinarians, 451, 552
Victoria House, 107-108
Villa Doyle, 112, 114
Visas for Bahamians, 452
Visas for visitors, 368, **see also Immigration**
Vismara, Michaelangela, 594
von Hoyningen-Huene, Baroness Irene, 593
von Hoyningen-Huene, Baroness Nancy Oakes, 114
Voting, 453

W

Wages, 453, 552
Wallace, David G, 578
Wallace, Susan, 490, 491
Walker's Cay, 272
Wallace Whitfield, Sir Cecil, 78

Wardle, Alan, 596
Wassitsch, Pedro, 592
Water rates, 454, 552
Water skiing, 293
Water supply, 168, 552
Water & Sewerage Corp, 168, 598
Waterfields, 164, 168, 598
Waterous, Jeffrey, 117, 123
Water's Edge, 252
Watkins, Floyd C, 570
Watkins, Vera, 582
Watling's Island, 71
Watson, Hon Frank H, 559, 569, 596, 601, 602
Weather, 303, **see also Climate**
Web site(s), 379
Webb, Hon Jacob, 121
Weech, Catherine, 582
Weights & measures, 454
Wells, Hon Tennyson RG, 561, 569
Wenner-Gren, Axel, 46, 117, 118, 491
Wernli, Beat, 594
West End, 236, 476-491, 598
West End Resort Ltd, 478
West Hill House, 110
West Hill St, 105-123
West India Regiment, 108
Whale Cay, 70, 71
Whitehead, Analia, 594
Wiberg, S Anders, 592, 594
Wilchcombe, Sen Hon Obie H, 568
Wild Birds Protection Act, 292
Wildlife preserves, 49, 455, **see also Nature centres**
Wilkinson, Chris, 601
Willard, David, 464
Williams, Gregory J, 569, 579
Williams, Lavern, 145
Williams, Vesta, 582
Wilson, Sharon, 582
Windermere Island, 123, 249
Winding Bay, 249, 602
Woodbridge, Todd, 600
Woodforde, Mark, 600
Woods, Valencia, 600
Woodside, Anthony, 581
Woodside, Kevin, 597
Woon, Gail, 501
Work permits, 369
World Health Org (WHO), 451, 592
World Trade Org (WTO), 153, 177, 456, 467
Wrecking, 486
Wright, P Bruce, 439, 443

XYZ

Xanadu Beach Resort, 142, 470
Yachts, **see Boating and Marinas**
Yoga retreat, 344
Young, HE Peter, 591
Yuchi Indians, 83, 99
Zig Zag Airlines, 144
Zink, Dr David, 96, 102
Zonicle, Mellany, 583
ZNS, 294, 456
Zoo, 470, **see also Nature centres**

TO ORDER DIRECT FROM THE BAHAMAS

Please rush me the
**NEW
2000
edition of
BAHAMAS
handbook**

SOFTBACK EDITION	
	US$
USA	45.00
CANADA	43.90
UK	55.80

(Price includes $28.95 book and airparcel/handling).
Contact Publisher for other mail rates.

as soon as it is available

Name _____

Street _____ (Please Print) _____

City _____ State or Province ____

Country _____ Signed _____

Payment in US$ must be enclosed
Bahamas Handbook, PO Box N-7513, Nassau, The Bahamas

1.

TO ORDER DIRECT FROM THE BAHAMAS

Please rush me the
**NEW
2000
edition of
BAHAMAS
handbook**

SOFTBACK EDITION	
	US$
USA	45.00
CANADA	43.90
UK	55.80

(Price includes $28.95 book and airparcel/handling).
Contact Publisher for other mail rates.

as soon as it is available

Name _____

Street _____ (Please Print) _____

City _____ State or Province ____

Country _____ Signed _____

Payment in US$ must be enclosed
Bahamas Handbook, PO Box N-7513, Nassau, The Bahamas

2.

WORLDWIDE CREDIT CARD ORDERS
For book price, shipping and handling, contact:

Taylor & Francis
47 Runway Rd
Suite G
Levittown, PA 19057-4700
USA

Phone toll free 1-800-821-8312
Tel 215-269-0400
Fax 215-269-0363
or e-mail: bkorders@tandfpa.com

Please reference code: BH 00

**BAHAMAS
handbook
2000
edition**

Etienne Dupuch Jr Publications • Tel (242) 323-5665 • Fax (242) 323-5728